C0-AQI-518

Beihefte zur Zeitschrift für die alttestamentliche Wissenschaft

Edited by
John Barton, Reinhard G. Kratz, Nathan MacDonald,
Sara Milstein and Markus Witte

Volume 547

The Scribe in the Biblical World

A Bridge Between Scripts, Languages and Cultures

Edited by
Esther Eshel and Michael Langlois

GRADUATE THEOLOGICAL UNION LIBRARY 1962

DE GRUYTER

BS
1110
Z37
v. 547
6tJ

ISBN 978-3-11-099668-5
e-ISBN (PDF) 978-3-11-098429-3
e-ISBN (EPUB) 978-3-11-098449-1
ISSN 0934-2575

Library of Congress Control Number: 2022948048

Bibliographic information published by the Deutsche Nationalbibliothek
The Deutsche Nationalbibliothek lists this publication in the Deutsche Nationalbibliografie;
detailed bibliographic data are available on the internet at http://dnb.dnb.de.

© 2023 Walter de Gruyter GmbH, Berlin/Boston
Printing and binding: CPI books GmbH, Leck

www.degruyter.com

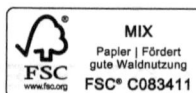

MIX
Papier | Fördert
gute Waldnutzung
FSC
www.fsc.org
FSC® C083411

b19345446

Table of Contents

Esther Eshel and Michael Langlois

Introduction

During our joint work on the project *The Alphabet: History and Development in the First Millennium BCE Southern Levant*, we asked ourselves, "what is the role of the individual scribe in the writing process?" Much research has been devoted to the characteristics of scripts in ancient times and to their development. A fresh look at the status of the scribe in each society, his training, practices, and work in the biblical world, was still needed.

As part of our research, the idea of having a conference on the question of the scribe during the biblical period developed gradually. Focusing on the eastern Mediterranean region, we invited scholars from various fields to ask questions such as: What was the scribe's role in these societies? Were there rival scribal schools? What was their role in daily life? How many scripts and languages did they grasp? Did they master political and religious rhetoric? Did they travel or share foreign traditions, cultures, and beliefs? Were scribes redactors, or simply copyists? What was their influence on the redaction of the Bible? How did they relate to the political and religious powers of their day? Did they possess any authority themselves? Though we may have been unable to fully answer all these questions, these theoretical concerns were central to the preparation of this volume.

The conference was held at the University of Strasbourg on June 17–19, 2019, with the participation of scholars from Europe, Israel, and the United States, as well as an audience of students and interested laypersons. The conference served as the basis for this publication.

This book includes fifteen articles dealing with the various questions mentioned above and covering a wide geographical and chronological range, from Late Bronze Age royal scribes (André Lemaire) to refugees in Masada at the end of the Second Temple period (Guy Stiebel). The heart of the conference was the Hebrew Bible and the people who wrote it; accordingly, the first article, written by Emanuel Tov, outlines the varying—and even individual—approaches of scribes to the biblical text.

To better define what a scribe is or can be, Tania Notarius and Paul Mandel each focus on the word ספר itself: Tania Notarius looks at origins and parallels in other Semitic languages, while Paul Mandel studies the evolution of סֹפֵר and סְפַר in later periods.

Moving out of Canaan and focusing on the influence of other cultures, Aren Wilson-Wright looks at Egyptian influence on West Semitic and Israelite scribal practice. Stefan Jakob Wimmer also shows the influence of Egypt on Hebrew scribes through the use of hieratic numerals on Iron Age tax bullae.

Besides Egypt, one may also consider Mesopotamian influence. Sara Milstein searches for the origins of biblical law from the perspective of scribal training in Mesopotamia. Aaron Demsky follows scribal traditions from Babylonia to Canaan and back, focusing on the practice of cursing an authority. Jeffrey Stackert presents evidence for, and implications of, scribal fatigue in revisionary composition from the Gilgamesh epic to the Pentateuch. William M. Schniedewind looks at letter writing in West Semitic literature and the Hebrew Bible.

Scribal training is also reflected in the use of various scripts and their evolution throughout time and space. Anat Mendel-Geberovich presents an updated survey of Judean Glyptic finds which has implications for ancient Hebrew paleography. Jan Dušek looks at the Aramaic script and attempts to identify nests of scribal cultures in the Levant from the 9th through 7th centuries BCE. Esther Eshel focuses on the combination of different types of scripts in Aramaic Lapidary inscriptions. Michael Langlois examines the practice of writing theonyms in paleo-Hebrew in Dead Sea Scrolls that otherwise use the Jewish Aramaic script.

The conference was supported by a Maimonides grant from the Israeli Ministry of Science and Technology, the Israeli Ministry of Foreign Affairs and International Development, and the French Ministry of Higher Education and Research. It was also supported by Bar Ilan University, the University of Strasbourg, the Jeselsohn Epigraphic Center for Jewish History, the Helsinki Collegium for Advanced Studies and the French Research Center in Jerusalem. We want to thank these institutions and the wonderful people who run them. We also thank all of our colleagues who joined us for this project, as well as Thibault Foulon, who helped us organize the conference.

Emanuel Tov

Approaches of Scribes to the Biblical Text in Ancient Israel

1 Introduction

I've always philosophized about the existence of two basic scribal approaches to the text, a free or popularizing approach and a conservative approach with several intervening shades. A free approach could come to light in the insertion of many small changes (additions, omissions, content changes), in freedom in matters of orthography and language, and in scribal procedures. A careful or conservative approach usually disallows changes in content, language, and orthography, and is also observed in scribal precision. These two basic attitudes are also visible in ancient translations. Some translators tried to stay close to their Hebrew parent text without inserting exegetical elements, while other translators allowed for translational freedom. This time I turn to the ancient scribes, wishing to examine whether the attitudes that are observable in some groups of texts can also be identified in individual scrolls. I want to investigate the little that is known about the approaches of individual scribes to the biblical text. Maybe I want to do the impossible when attempting to enter the mind of a scribe in order to examine what he considered was his task in copying the Scripture text. We could *not* do the same with regard to the Masoretic Text of the Middle Ages, because that text is not the product of an individual but the collective product of generations of anonymous scribes. Likewise, we can't know the minds of the scribes of the Samaritan Pentateuch and those of the *Vorlage* of the Septuagint, because they too could be collective products. We can try to identify individuality only in creations by individuals, but possibly even that is a hazardous enterprise, because what was the background of that individual? I realize the difficulties in assessing the scribes' intentions.

I am focusing on scribes who were copyists.[1] Yet other scribes were author-scribes; many authors copied their own words and therefore should also be considered scribes. For example, David was named a *sopher* in 11QPs[a] XXVII 2 as that

---

[1] The so-called Sopherim that transmitted the Masoretic Text with great care are a group of such scribes, but only one group of them, and we should not be misled by assuming that all scribes were similar to them.

text refers to his many psalmic compositions.[2] Copyist-scribes gave further shape to the books in transmitting the finished compositions while also inserting occasional changes. Early scribes were thus far removed from the medieval copyists and the sopherim of the Masoretic Text, because these scribes were mere copyists who did not intervene in the text at all.[3] Our analysis starts with scribes who are known to us from the scrolls or manuscripts they left in caves or libraries, and in the case of Scripture we can go back no further than the earliest Qumran evidence dating to around 250 BCE. In a way, this is a relatively late group of scribes.

All the *technical* aspects of the copying have been studied in great detail by myself in my monograph *Scribal Practices* of 2004[4] and by several other scholars. These aspects have been studied more than the approaches of scribes to the texts. It is much easier to examine technicalities than approaches; scholars have usually refrained from doing the latter, and when they did, their statements were often based on unproven suppositions. Indeed, there are objective problems in the description of scribal intentions because of lack of information. An approach of a scribe can be described best when we know the text from which he copied; in that case, the scribe's changes or lack of changes can be evaluated most easily. However, such ideal conditions are not encountered in our area. Only rarely do we recognize that the text of a scribe A is exclusively close to source B, but even in such cases there is no certainty that one depended on the other, since there could have been intermediate stages between A and B. For example, it has been suggested that 1QIsaᵃ was the base for quotes from the book of Isaiah in 4QTanḥumim, but I believe that there must have been an intermediate stage between the two sources.[5] A few additional examples of quotations from this scroll

---

etc. ויהי דויד בן ישי חכם ואור כאור השמש וסופר ונבון... ויכתוב תהלים שלושת אלפים ושש מאות **2**

3 On the other hand, Alan R. Millard, "In Praise of Ancient Scribes," *BA* (1982): 143–53 opined that scribes in the ancient Near East meticulously represented their *Vorlagen*, allowing only for minor orthographic variations. However, that description does not address the whole spectrum of the reality in antiquity.

4 Emanuel Tov, Scribal Practices and Approaches Reflected in the Texts Found in the Judean Desert, STDJ 54 (Leiden: Brill, 2004).

5 However, Flint assumes a direct connection, especially in frgs. 8–11: Peter W. Flint, "The Interpretation of Scriptural Isaiah in the Qumran Scrolls: Quotations, Citations, Allusions, and the Form of the Scriptural Source Text," in *A Teacher for All Generations: Essays in Honor of James C. VanderKam, Vols. 1–2*, ed. Eric F. Mason et al.; JSJSup 153/1 (Leiden: Brill, 2012), 1:388–406 (403). According to my count, the two agree four times in small details, and ten times in spelling: According to Flint, 4Q176 agrees in eight of its fourteen "alternative" readings with 1QIsaᵃ. My tabulations are different, but indeed among the variants of this scroll four remarkable readings stand out. In line 8 the two agree in a plus of the Tetragrammaton against MT 54:6, in line 10 they agree in the reading ובחסדי against MT 54:8 ובחסד, in line 11 they agree in a plus of עד

have been suggested as well.[6] Likewise, the third section in 4QTestimonia quotes from a scroll very close to 4QDeut[h], but not from that scroll itself, since there are a few differences. 4QTestimonia also quotes from 4QPsJosh, or vice versa.[7] In all these cases of a close relationship between texts, the exact relation between them is unclear, and in no case can direct parentage be established. Possibly the best candidate for direct parentage is 4QDan[b] that may have been copied from 4QDan[a], as suggested by Eugene Ulrich, although Ulrich leaves room for the possibility that there was an intermediate stage. The two scrolls agree closely with each other in an overlapping section, and they have the same layout of the text (in the "eight lines where the two Qumran manuscripts overlap in the Dan 8:1–5 passage, five lines actually end with exactly the same word").[8] Further, 4QDan[a] and 4QDan[b] stand in the same text tradition in contrast to MT, and 4QDan[b] is later than 4QDan[a] regarding paleography and orthography.

When a scribe's source is unknown, many aspects of his approach towards the *Vorlage* are also undetermined, but the combined evidence nevertheless allows us to make *some* assumptions. As a result, we allow ourselves some statements about the attitudes of individual scribes, but more so about groups of scribes.

Scribes of Scripture texts not only devised or followed systems for copying and correcting the text, but they also had ideas, sometimes philosophies, about the way they should represent their source text. However, since we don't know the scribes' *Vorlagen*, it is very hard to separate the views of the known scribes from those of previous generations. The common perception among scholars is

---

(1QIsa[a] עוד), and in line 12 they resemble each other in the form תתמוטטנה (1QIsa[a]: תתמוטינה) against MT 54:10 תמוטנה. See further Herrmann Lichtenberger in James H. Charlesworth, *The Dead Sea Scrolls, Hebrew, Aramaic, and Greek Texts with English Translations, Vol. 6B, Pesharim, Other Commentaries, and Related Documents* (Tübingen: Mohr Siebeck, 2002), 332 (Isa 49:13, 16); 338–340 (Isa 54:6, 8, 9). However, the two also disagree, according to my counting ten times in small details and six times in spelling. Therefore, I do not think that the large Isaiah scroll was the direct *Vorlage* of 4Q176, but a scroll like it, as the two share some readings and a free approach to Scripture as well as the same orthographic and morphological system.

6 For example, Isa 6:10 השמן MT LXX] 1QIsa[a] השמ (sic) = 1QH[a] XV 6, XXI 6 (השם); 57:15 להחיות MT] 1QIsa[a] לחיות = 1QH[a] XVI 37; 66:2 ונבה MT] 1QIsa[a] ונכאי = 1QH[a] XXIII 16 and 1QM XI 10. See Armin Lange, *Handbuch der Textfunde vom Toten Meer, I: Die Handschriften biblischer Bücher von Qumran und den anderen Fundorten* (Tübingen: Mohr Siebeck, 2009), 288.

7 4QTest lines 21–30. Most scholars believe that 4QTest quoted from 4QPsJosh, but Hanan Eshel, "The Historical Background of the Pesher Interpreting Joshua's Curse on the Rebuilder of Jericho, *RevQ* 15 (1992): 409–20 believes that the quoting went in the opposite direction.

8 Eugene Ulrich, *The Dead Sea Scrolls and the Origins of the Bible* (Grand Rapids: Eerdmans; Leiden: Brill, 1999), 148–62 (162, n. 27).

that all details of a scroll are the product of the scribe's thinking. I don't know whether scholars have given much thought to this issue, but the impression is created from the scholarly literature that the scribes themselves were responsible for all the details that appear to us to be differences from MT. Possibly these details also differed from the scribe's *Vorlage*. However, usually the issue of the scribe's source is not mentioned at all in scholarly discussions. For example, in the following references, scholars assume that the scribes themselves inserted certain changes in the scrolls and exclude the possibility that these details were copied from the scribe's *Vorlage*. I include a quote from my own writings, as I too sometimes indulged in this practice.

Table 1: References to the Intentions of Scribes in the Scholarly Literature

Deut 5:15] "4QDeut[n] has added the reason for the sabbath observance from the Exodus version of the fourth commandment." (Sidnie White Crawford, *DJD* XIV, 126)

1 Sam 1:22 כאשר גמלתו] "...and 4QSam[a] would seem to have omitted it here also..." (Frank Moore Cross, *DJD* XVII, 35);

1 Sam 2:9 כי לוא בכח יגבר איש] "Probably this colon has attracted the long plus which found its way into 4QSam[a] G" (ibidem, 37);

1 Sam 2:16 הכוהן כיום] "The plus of 4QSam[a] is secondary (an explicating plus)." (ibidem, 41).

1 Sam 2:16	MT	קַטֵּר יַקְטִירוּן כַּיּוֹם הַחֵלֶב (= LXX S V)
		Let them < the sons of Eli> first burn the fat.
	4QSam[a]	יקטר הכוהן כיום הֹ[חלב]
		Let the *priest* first burn the [fat].

In MT, the owner of the sacrifice makes a general statement about the burning of the fat by the sons of Eli, while 4QSam[a] ascribes this action to the priest. This change is probably made in accordance with Lev 7:31.[9]

Now, ascribing these actions to the scribes of these scrolls is problematic, since we don't know whether they were carried out by the scribes of 4QDeut[n] and 4QSam[a] or by a previous generation of scribes. I do not suggest that I can solve this problem, but with an awareness of the issues and with some improved knowledge about individual scribes we may get closer to a solution in some instances.

---

9 Emanuel Tov, *Textual Criticism of the Hebrew Bible*, 3rd ed., rev. and enl. (Minneapolis: Fortress, 2012), 253.

2 Scribal Approaches Visible through Intervention in the Completed Text

The problem at stake is that it is almost impossible to disentangle scribes from the scribal traditions that were part of their cultural heritage. We need to identify the individuality of scribes in other details that are not related to matters of exegesis. If we want to understand a scribe's attitude to the text, possibly there's something to be learned from his approach to scribal activity. In this corner, we see the scribe in action as a copyist, and not as an exegete. If he displays freedom or strictness as a copyist, he may also be free or strict in his general approach to the biblical text. For this purpose, I suggest examining the scribe's intervention in the completed written text and the scribe's contextual and harmonizing changes in the running text. The carefulness of the transmission may be judged by examining the amount of scribal intervention in the completed text, that is, the frequency of linear or supralinear corrections as visible in deletions, erasures, and reshaping of letters. After the writing had been completed, a careful and scrupulous scribe would change a minimum of details in the text or make no changes at all. In texts written on leather, all such changes are easily visible because it is hard to erase letters, and even when they are erased, the inscribed letters are still visible. The great majority of scribal interventions pertain to mistakes made by the first scribe, as can be shown by the internal logic of the correction and the script. The amount of scribal intervention can be measured by dividing the number of preserved lines by the number of instances of scribal intervention.[10] The second parameter to be examined is the addition of harmonizations and exegetical changes in the running text itself and not between the lines. These features are not found in all texts, since not all texts lend themselves to harmonizing and exegetical additions. I submit that there often is a correlation between a scribe's intervention in the text and the existence of harmonizing and exegetical changes in the running text. When the text does not lend itself to harmonizing, it may also display other exponents of freedom. This experiment is meant to distinguish between the individuality of the scribe and the scribal traditions transmitted to him.

---

10 For details, see Tov, *Scribal Practices*, Appendix 1, col. 8 for the nonbiblical scrolls and Appendix 8, col. 11 for the biblical scrolls, occasionally corrected by the data in Table 2 in this study.

In this way, a high level of scribal intervention (an average of one correction in every four lines) is visible in 1QIsaᵃ.[11] This scroll is also known for its many harmonizing and exegetical pluses (see below, Tables 5 and 6).

I admit that the measurements are only approximate because I do not distinguish between complete and fragmentary lines. Usually the scribal intervention was executed by the first scribe, but at times it is unclear whether a second scribe was involved. Despite these uncertainties, a few conclusions emerge about the individuality of scribes as opposed to the traditions that had been handed down to them.

The individuality of scribes comes to light in the best way possible in the differences between two groups of tefillin. It should be remembered that the tefillin contain Scripture like all other Scripture texts, displaying the same textual profiles such as MT, pre-Samaritan texts, LXX, and independent (nonaligned) texts. Many tefillin from Qumran are written in the ultra-plene orthography style. Now, we find evidence of different groups of tefillin distinguished by their textual character and content. Some groups reflecting the text of the MT family contain the four required passages of the rabbis and are found mainly outside Qumran. At Qumran, we find mainly the so-called "Qumran tefillin" that contain several passages in addition to the required passages of the rabbis, or only such additional passages; these tefillin do not reflect the text of MT. I will not go into detail regarding the five groups of tefillin but will emphasize the differences between two groups.

One group of tefillin (MurPhyl, 34SePhyl, 8QPhyl I, XHevSe Phyl) contain only the required texts of the rabbis.[12] They reflect the text of MT with no exegetical additions and *no scribal intervention*.[13] These tefillin are also identical internally: XQPhyl 1 and MurPhyl reflect the same text of Exod 13:1–10.[14]

Another group of tefillin, written in the Qumran Scribal Practice (QSP), contain combinations of required and nonrequired texts (4QPhyl A, B, G-H-I, L-N, O, P, Q), while 4QPhyl J-K contains only nonrequired texts. These documents do not reflect the text of MT, *they display scribal intervention* (see Table 2, first part) and

---

[11] See Table 2 below.

[12] 34SePhyl was republished in *DSD* 24 (2017): 112–37. The first three texts agree exactly with codex L. The last text includes a few negligent mistakes as well as a few unique readings, but it does not reflect any exegetical readings.

[13] I don't include XHev/Se 5 (XHev/SePhyl) since that was written by a negligent scribe.

[14] MurPhyl is fully identical with the medieval text, while XQPhyl 1 has 5 plene spellings.

we observe a clear tendency towards harmonization[15] (see the light gray elements in Table 3).

The differences between the two types of scribes are thus visible in the scribal intervention in the Qumran tefillin (Table 2, first part) and the lack of such intervention in the rabbinic tefillin (Table 2, second part). Remarkably, a special prescription in rabbinic law forbids such insertions (supralinear letters) in tefillin, supporting the connection between rabbinic-type tefillin and rabbinic law: תולים במזוזות ולא בתפילין לא תולין אין ,בספרים, "One may <hang the letters above the line> in scrolls, but one may not hang <the letters above the line> in tefillin or mezuzot" (y. Meg. 1.71c). The difference between the two types is clearly visible in Table 2. The typical Qumran tefillin in the first part of Table 2 contain combinations of required and nonrequired texts while 4QPhyl J-K contain only nonrequired texts. They are written in the QSP style, and there is harmonization. The rabbinic tefillin in the second part of Table 2 reflect only the required rabbinic texts and there is no harmonization or intervention in the text.

Table 2: Scribal Intervention in Tefillin

	One scribal intervention in an average number of X lines	Number of scribal interventions
"Qumran tefillin"		
4QPhyl G-H-I (QSP)	11	6
4QPhyl Q (QSP)	11 (short document)	0
4QPhyl B (QSP)	14	2
4QPhyl J-K (QSP)	14	7
4QPhyl P (QSP)	14 (short document)	0
4QPhyl A (QSP)	15	4
4QPhyl O (QSP)	24 (short document)	0
4QPhyl C (LXX-SP-ind)	29	0
4QPhyl L-N (QSP)	31	2
"Rabbinic tefillin, MT"		
XHevSe Phyl (proto-MT)	21 (short document)[16]	0
34SePhyl (proto-MT)	22 (short document)	0
8QPhyl I (proto-MT)	37	0
MurPhyl (proto-MT)	130	0

---

15 4QPhyl B has harmonizing pluses in the Decalogue based on Exodus. 4QPhyl G-H-I provides the text of Deut 5:1–21, with occasional harmonizing pluses from other passages in Deut like the plus in 5:1 היום מצוכה אנכי deriving from Deut 6:5. Especially frequent are the harmonizing changes and pluses in G 5:1–26 in the segment of the Decalogue.

16 In these cases, the figures indicate the number of lines in the documents.

5/6HevPs (proto-MT)　　　　142　　　　　0

Table 2 establishes the existence of two types of scribes. The scribes in the first part of the table reflect freedom, while the scribes in the second part are loyal to the transmitted text. These are ceremonial texts, but they are matched by the approaches of scribes of other Scripture texts, and therefore their character is not determined by their being tefillin. Thus, for example, there is a similar opposition between the free style of 1QIsaᵃ in orthography and harmonization and the more reserved style of 1QIsaᵇ.

Returning to the tefillin, the opposition between the two types of scribes in individual documents is clearly visible in the inclusion or non-inclusion of harmonizing details in the text of Exod 13:1–10. This biblical text has been preserved in tefillin of two different types: in two proto-MT tefillin, MurPhyl and XQPhyl 1 (left column), and in the "Qumran tefillin," 4QPhyl A, L (right column). The proto-MT tefillin contain no harmonizing elements, while such elements frequently have been inserted in the Qumran tefillin (indicated in light gray).[17] The harmonized elements adapt the text of Exodus 13 to other texts in Exodus and Deuteronomy.

Table 3: Exegetical Elements, Especially Harmonizations, in a Group of "Qumran Tefillin"

	XQPhyl 1, MurPhyl (= MT)		4QPhyl A, L
Exod 13:3	ממצרים	4QPhyl A	מאר[ץ] מצרים[18]
13:5	הכנעני והחתי והאמרי והחוי והיבוסי	4QPhyl A	האמו[רי הפרזי]החוי היבוסי הגרג[שי][19]
13:3	ממצרים	4QPhyl L	בוה מארץ] מצרים[20]
13:5	יהוה	4QPhyl L	יהוה אלוהיכה[21]
13:5	והחתי והאמרי והחוי והיבוסי	4QPhyl L	הח[תי האמו[ר]י הפרזי והחוי היבוסי הגרגשי[22]

---

17 They are named so because they contain segments that are not required by the rabbis: Phyl A: *Deut 5:1–6:3*, *Deut 10:12–11:12*, Deut 11:13–21, *Exod 12:43–51*, Exod 13:1–10; B: *Deut 5:1–6:3*, Deut 6:4–9, Exod 13:1–10; L: *Deut 5:1–6:3*, *Exod 12:43–51*, Deut 6:4–9. The italicized passages have not been prescribed by the rabbis.

18 Cf. Exod 12:50 preceding this passage.

19 The longer list as in LXX SP and Phyl L. The inclusion of the גרגשי and פרזי harmonizes to Deut 7:1; Josh 3:10, 24:11.

20 Thus Phyl I SP LXX: grammatical simplification after יצאתמה.

21 Cf. Deut 7:1 also referenced in n. 19. Idem Phyl R and SP LXX.

22 Cf. n. 19.

13:5	אשר	4QPhyl L	כ‍אשר‍[23]
13:6	שבעת	4QPhyl L	ש[שת‍[24]
13:6	תאכל	4QPhyl L	תואכל‍[25]
13:8	עשה יהוה לי	4QPhyl L	עשה לי יהוה

The picture is clear. In the rabbinic tefillin texts, there was no scribal intervention or harmonization, while in the Qumran tefillin texts we observe scribal intervention and harmonization. In both cases, the scribes probably copied from master copies,[26] and in any event we have here a rare opportunity to observe the individuality of some scribes who copied the same types of documents.

It is more difficult to discern this individuality in other cases in which we often need to content ourselves with the views of groups of scribes rather than individuals. In several instances, we observe clear tendencies. At the top of the list in Table 4 are texts that display a high level of scribal intervention. These are mainly scrolls that I name textually independent or nonaligned (indicated in dark gray), that is, scrolls that are not close to MT, LXX, or SP. For example, 4QCant[b] reflects much scribal intervention (average of one intervention in every seventeen lines) and not necessarily harmonization, but a very free approach to the text in other details. In this scroll, we observe major shortening, Aramaic influence, and many mistakes. In addition, there are six scribal signs in the margin of the text.[27] Among these fragments, are many texts written in the Qumran Scribal Practice such as 1QIsa[a] with one intervention in every four lines and 11QPs[a] (average of one intervention in every nine lines); these scrolls also insert many harmonizations and contextual changes, exemplified in Tables 5 (11QPs[a])

---

23 Cf. v. 10.

24 Thus Phyl I, R and SP LXX; cf. Exod 12:15; Deut 16:8.

25 Cf. Exod 12:15.

26 See Emanuel Tov, "The Qumran Tefillin and Their Possible Master Copies," in *On Wings of Prayer. Sources of Jewish Worship; Essays in Honor of Professor Stefan C. Reif on the Occasion of his Seventy-fifth Birthday*, ed. Nuria Calduch-Benages, Michael W. Duggan, and Dalia Marx, Deuterocanonical and Cognate Literature Studies 44 (Berlin: de Gruyter, 2019), 135–49. I suggest that a few scrolls that were previously described as liturgical scrolls are master copies from which several Qumran tefillin were copied, especially 4QDeut[j].

27 Much has been written on this scroll. Torleif Elgvin believes that the omissions did not result from abbreviation but point to a variant edition of Canticles: Torleif Elgvin, *The Literary Growth of the Song of Songs during the Hasmonean and Early-Herodian Periods*, Contributions to Biblical Exegesis and Theology 89 (Leuven: Peeters, 2018). Mathias Hopf believes that the scribal signs point to a dramatic re-enactment of the songs: Matthias Hopf, *Liebesszenen, Eine literaturwissenschaftliche Studie zum Hohelied als einem dramatisch-performativen Text*, AThANT 108 (Zurich: Theologischer Verlag, 2016).

and 6 (1QIsaᵃ).[28] Scrolls with very little or no scribal intervention are indicated in light gray. Special attention must be given to the starred texts.

Table 4: Scribal Intervention in Select Judean Desert Scripture Scrolls

	One scribal intervention in an *average number* of X lines	*Number* of scribal interventions
1QIsaᵃ (QSP) (independent)	4	398
5QDeut (independent)	4	4
4QJerᵃ (MT-like)*	4	32
4QSamᶜ (QSP) (ind)	5	15
4QQohᵃ (QSP) (ind)	5	7
4QIsaᵃ (ind)	7	10
4QDeutᵐ (QSP) (ind)	8 (short document)	2
4QJudgᵇ (ind)	8 (short document)	3
4QXIIᶜ (QSP) (ind)	8	13
4QXIIᵉ (QSP) (ind)	8	8
4QJoshᵇ (ind)	9 (short document)	3
11QPsᵃ (QSP)	9	56
4QRPᵃ (4Q158) (SP?)*	10	9
4QPhyl G-H-I (QSP)	11	6
4QDeutᵏ¹ (QSP) (ind)	12 (short document)	2
4QPsᵉ (ind)	12	6
4QGenᵍ (MT-like)	13 (short document)	2
4QGenᵏ (ind)	13 (short document)	1
4QIsaᵇ (MT-like)*	13	17
4QDeutᵇ (ind)	14 (short document)	2
4QPhyl B (QSP)	14	2
4QPhyl J-K (QSP)	14	7
4QPhyl A (QSP)	15	4
4QDeutʰ (ind)	16	3
4QExodᶜ (ind)	17	8
4QIsaᵈ (MT-like)*	17	6
4QCantᵇ (ind)	17	3
4QDanᶜ (ind?)	20	2
XHevSe Phyl (proto-MT)	21 (short document)	0
4QDanᵃ (ind)	22	5
4QDanᵈ (ind)	22	2
34SePhyl (proto-MT)	22 (short document)	0
4QPhyl O (QSP)	24 (short document)	0
4QJerᶜ (MT-like)*	25	7
4QDeutᶜ (ind)	27	6

---

28 See further 4QDeutᵏ¹ 11:8 (3x); 4QDeutᵐ 3:20; 4QIsaᶜ 26:1, 51:11; 4QXIIᶜ Hos 4:3 (cf. v 1); Joel 2:19; 4QQohᵃ 7:2 (cf. v. 4).

4QJosh^a (ind)	28	2
4QIsa^c (QSP) (ind)	28	8
4QGen-Exod^a (MT-like)	**30**	**2**
4QDeut^j (ind)	30	3
MasLev^b (proto-MT)	**30**	**3**
4QLev^d (SP?)	**31 (short document)**	**0**
4QLam (QSP) (ind)	33	1
4QDeut^n (ind)	33	2
4Q[Gen-]Exod^b (ind)	35	2
11QPs^b (QSP) (ind)	36	0
2QRuth^a (MT-like)	**37**	**1**
8QPhyl I (proto-MT)	**37**	**0**
4QNum^b (QSP) (SP) (LXX)	38	10
4QXII^g (ind) (QSP?)	38	9
4QDan^b (ind?)	39	2
4QPs^d (ind)	41	1
4QDeut^g (MT-like) (SP)	43	1
4QPs^b (ind)*	43	4
4QDeut^{k2} (QSP) (ind)*	45	1
4QXII^a (ind)*	46	2
4QGen^e (MT-like)	49	0
4QSam^b (LXX)*	50	1
4QPs^c (MT-like)	52	2
4QRP^b (4Q364) (SP?)*	53	6
1QIsa^b (MT-like)	55	8
11QPs^c (ind) (QSP?)*	56	0
4QExod-Lev^f (SP) (ind)*	57	1
4QIsa^e (MT-like)	58	1
2QJer (QSP) (ind)*	60	0
4QPs^f (ind)*	61	2
4QGen^b (proto-MT)	62	1
11QPs^d (ind) (QSP?)	64	2
11QpaleoLev^a (ind)*	66	2
MasPs^a (proto-MT)	74	0
MurXII (proto-MT)	75	8
4QPs^a (ind)*	87	1
4QIsa^f (MT-like)	92	1
4QpaleoGen-Exod^l (MT-like)	105	2
4QSam^a (ind) (LXX)*	110	8
4QpaleoDeut^r (ind)*	114	0
MurPhyl (proto-MT)	130	0
4QLev^b (MT-like)	136	0
5/6HevPs (proto-MT)	142	0
4QpaleoExod^m (SP)	197	3

The texts at the top of the list in Table 4 (indicated in dark gray) that feature much scribal intervention are also characterized by harmonization, if the text allows for that possibility, or by other exponents of freedom. Harmonization was exemplified in Table 3 for 4QPhyl A, L, and is exemplified in Table 5 for 11QPs[a]. The harmonizing changes or pluses (light gray) conform to other psalms or other verses in the same psalm.

Table 5: Harmonization in 11QPs[a]

Ps 105:37	MT	ויוציאם
	11QPs[a]	ויוצא עמו cf. v. 43 ויוצא א[ת עמו
Ps 121:1	MT	שיר למעלות
	11QPs[a]	שיר המעלות cf. Ps 123:1, etc. שיר המעלות
Ps 130:6	MT	נפשי לאדני
	11QPs[a]	הוחלתי cf. v. 5 הוחילי [נפשי לאדני and Ps 42:6, 12
Ps 119:16	MT	בחקתיך
	11QPs[a]	חקיך cf. v. 12 בחקיך
Ps 119:70	MT	שעשעתי
	11QPs[a]	שע[ש]עי cf. vv. 24, 77, 92, 143 שעש[ו]עי[ו]עי

Contextual changes (light gray) in these texts are exemplified by 1QIsa[a] in which we find much scribal intervention. In this scroll, seemingly irregular forms are often adapted to the context.

Table 6: Contextual Changes in 1QIsa[a]

Isa 1:23	MT	(שריך סוררים וחברי גנבים) כלו אהב שחד ורדף ...
	1QIsa[a]	כולם אוהבי שוחד רודפי ... (cf. G T S V)
Isa 14:30	MT G T	(והמתי ברעב שרשך ושאריתך) יהרג
		(I will kill your stock by famine) and *it* shall slay (the very last of you).
	1QIsa[a]	אהרוג *I* shall slay (cf. V)
Isa 46:11	MT	(דברתי אף אביאנה) יצרתי אף אעשנה
		(I have spoken, so I will bring it to pass;) I have designed <it>, so I will complete it.
	1QIsa[a]	יצרתיה אף אעשנה
		I have designed *it*, so I will complete it.
Isa 51:19	MT	מי אנחמך
	1QIsa[a]	מי ינחמך (cf. G)

The scrolls with very little or no scribal intervention, found mainly at the bottom of the list in Table 4 (indicated in light gray), are mainly proto-MT texts (e.g., 4QpaleoGen-Exod[l] with one intervention in every 105 lines). It is a remarkable phenomenon that they occur in the proto-MT texts.

Equally remarkable, the same lack of scribal intervention is found in the pre-Samaritan scrolls such as 4QpaleoExod[m], 4QExod-Lev[f], 4QNum[b], 4QRP[b] (4Q364), 4QLev[d] (but not 4QRP[a] [4Q158]).[29] There is little or no scribal intervention in these scrolls, but they do contain small harmonizing changes. Apparently, the pre-Samaritan scrolls were transmitted with the same care as the MT family, even though their prototype was of a harmonizing nature. This feature goes to show that in this case the harmonizing, a sign of textual freedom, was followed up by cautious scribal transmission. The pre-Samaritan scrolls were initially Jewish scrolls that had been transmitted carefully just like the Masoretic scrolls.

Table 4 presents merely a sample of texts and obviously not all scribes behaved in the same way. It is clear that some scribes behaved differently from the expected pattern. Thus, 4QJer[a] (MT-like; average of one intervention in every four lines) differs from the pattern of the other Masoretic scrolls. This scroll displays much scribal intervention, while it stays close to MT and does not reflect much contextual exegesis. Further, textually independent or nonaligned texts often show much scribal intervention, but 4QSam[a] shows that this independent text, close to the LXX, was written with great care and with little scribal intervention (one intervention in every 110 lines).

In sum, the tefillin were used as the main example showing that scribes of identical texts show their individuality by their scribal intervention in the text or lack of it and by their possible adding of exegetical elements. These features may also be expressed as scribal precision or imprecision or a careful or free approach toward the biblical text. The same contrast was found between 1QIsa[a] and 1QIsa[b], while similar features were found in groups of texts but without a clear contrast. The proto-MT texts and pre-SP texts display a careful approach to the text, while the ultraplene and independent (nonaligned) texts display a free approach, but these are very general classifications. I see a basic contrast between two groups of texts, but they are not black and white as there are many intervening shades.

So far, I have not spoken about content exegesis, to which I turn next.

---

29 See Emanuel Tov, "Textual Harmonization in the Five Books of the Torah: A Summary," in *The Bible, Qumran, and the Samaritans,* ed. Magnar Kartveit and Gary N. Knoppers, SJ 104, Studia Samaritana 10 (Berlin: de Gruyter, 2018), 31–56.

3 Content Exegesis

The scrolls contain many elements of content exegesis that are significant for our discussion of scribal approaches, but at the same time they are difficult to evaluate. I illustrate this aspect by referring to 4QSamᵃ, a scroll that reflects much content exegesis.[30] However, we are interested mainly in the exegesis that was inserted by the scribe himself, and not in the exegetical elements that were passed on to him by others. When trying to identify this scribe's exegesis, we thus need to disregard several types of elements:

a. Elements that this scribe shares with *other texts*. Thus, exegetical readings that 4QSamᵃ shares with the LXX are not indicative of the scribe's approach. For example, the well-known reading אך יקם יהו[ה היוצא מפיך in 1 Sam 1:23 is remarkable in the light of MT אַךְ יָקֵם יְהוָה אֶת־דְּבָרוֹ, but it is irrelevant as a source for establishing the scribe's intentions since this reading is also reflected in the LXX. The readings that the scroll shared with the LXX were not invented by our scribe.

b. Presumed *original* elements of the scroll that differ from the other sources, since they cannot be original and exegetical at the same time. Thus the well-known reading בקר משלש [בן בפר], "[along with (a)] *three-year-old* [*bull* from] the herd" in 1 Sam 1:24 for MT בְּפָרִים שְׁלֹשָׁה, "along with three bulls" is irrelevant for determining exegesis because the scroll probably reflects the original reading.[31]

c. Presumed exegetical traditions, such as those shared with Josephus in the case of this scroll.[32]

When these elements are disregarded, numerous exegetical readings remain, among them theological readings of various types, such as nomistic and midrashic elements.[33] A well-known example of an exegetical reading is the plus in 1

---

30 See Jason Driesbach, *4QSamuelᵃ and the Text of Samuel*, VTSup 171 (Leiden: Brill, 2016), 183–209 and passim.

31 See Tov, Textual Criticism of the Hebrew Bible, 236.

32 See Eugene Charles Ulrich, *The Qumran Text of Samuel and Josephus*, HSM 19 (Missoula, MT: Scholars, 1978), 165–91.

33 See the summary of Jason Driesbach, *4QSamuelᵃ and the Text of Samuel*, VTSup 171 (Leiden: Brill, 2016), 297–302 .

Sam 1:22 describing Samuel as a Nazirite[34] ([חייו] כול ימי [וֹנת[תֿיהו נזיר עד עולם.[35]
Within the present context, we need to ask ourselves whether we possess the
tools in order to determine whether content exegesis of this type was initiated by
the scribe or by a previous generation. As mentioned in the beginning of this paper, scholars tend to ascribe all exegetical elements to the scribe. However,
there's a difference between small contextual changes and content exegesis. In
the first case, it is probably true that it was the scribe of 4QSamᵃ who changed the
irregular קֶשֶׁת גִּבֹּרִים חַתִּים in 1 Sam 2:4 to קשת גברים חתה. But I am not certain in
the case of the naming of Samuel a Nazirite. Would a careful scribe have done
this? The only piece of evidence in our possession is that 4QSamᵃ was copied with
great care. I note merely one scribal correction in an average of 110 lines.[36] I therefore suggest cautiously that this scribe did not initiate this exegesis, but I hesi-
tate.[37] The same problem obtains regarding other scrolls that contain much content exegesis such as 4QJoshᵃ, 4QRPᵈ (4Q366), and 4QRPᵉ (4Q367). Until I find
evidence to the contrary, I will not favor the opinion that these scribes initiated
this exegesis. However, I do admit that exegesis started somewhere with some
scribe, but not necessarily with the scribes that are known to us.

---

34 From v. 11 it is clear that Samuel was to be a *nazir* (thus also Ben Sira 46:13 and m. Nazir 9.5),
and even more so from a plus in LXX in that verse ("and wine and strong drink he shall not
drink"), yet the actual term *nazir* is not used in the MT and LXX *ad loc.* In the textual tradition of
Samuel, the term thus occurs only in 4QSamᵃ as part of a long plus.

35 Some scholars therefore systematically downplayed the importance of this scroll for text-crit-
ical analysis: Stephen Pisano, S.J., *Additions or Omissions in the Books of Samuel: The Significant
Pluses and Minuses in the Massoretic, LXX and Qumran Texts*, OBO 57 (Freiburg/Göttingen: University Press, 1984). According to Alexander Rofé, "Midrashic Traits in 4Q51 (So-called
4QSamᵃ)," in *Archaeology of the Books of Samuel: The Entangling of the Textual and Literary History*, ed. Philippe Hugo and Adrian Schenker, VTSup 132 (Leiden: Brill, 2010), 75–88, several
additional readings in this scroll are midrashic (such as 2 Sam 24:16–17; a large addition before
1 Sam 11:1) causing him to rename this scroll as 4QMidrash Samuel. Thus also idem, "4QMidrash
Samuel?: Observations Concerning the Character of 4QSamᵃ," *Textus* 19 (1998): 63–74 and idem,
"A Scroll of Samuel or Midrash Samuel? The Transfer of the Ark to Jerusalem according to 4Q51,"
Meghillot V–VI (2007): 237–43 (Heb.).

36 This manuscript, ascribed to 50–25 BCE, is a luxury scroll written in large columns with large
top and bottom margins.

37 Neither Pisano, *Additions*, 283–85 nor Driesbach, *4QSamuelᵃ*, 297–302 refer to this dilemma.
However, the latter occasionally makes the point that the scribe of this manuscript rather than
a tradition behind him may be the source of a reading: pp. 70 (1 Sam 2:25), 105 (2:22, linguistic
change). Cross or Ulrich do not remark on this issue.

4 Comparison with Nonbiblical Texts

The scribes who copied the biblical Dead Sea Scrolls did not work in isolation from those that copied the nonbiblical scrolls. On the contrary, some scribes copied scrolls of both types.

The most prominent example of a scribe who copied both biblical and non-biblical scrolls is the one who copied the nonbiblical texts 1QS, 1QSa, 1QSb, 4QTest (4Q175),[38] and the biblical text 4QSam[c], and whose hand is also visible in several corrections in 1QIsa[a].[39] Indeed, AMS analysis yielded similar dates for 4QSam[c] and 1QS, usually ascribed to 100–75 BCE.[40] The earmarks of this scribe are his special orthography and morphology and the use of the four dots (tetra-puncta)[41] for the tetragrammaton.[42] Within the present framework, it is relevant to remark that this scribe intervened equally frequently in the biblical and non-biblical texts, as shown by Table 7.[43] This scribe thus approached the biblical and nonbiblical texts in a similar way.

Table 7: Scribal Intervention in Biblical and Nonbiblical Scrolls Written by One Scribe

Composition	One scribal intervention in an *average number* of X lines	Number of scribal interventions
4QSam[c] (ind)	5	15

---

38 According to Eric Larson and Lawrence H. Schiffman, "4Q481b. 4QNarrative G" in George Brooke et al., in consultation with James C. VanderKam, *Qumran Cave 4.XVII: Parabiblical Texts, Part 3*, DJD XXII (Oxford: Clarendon, 1996), 311–12 was copied by the scribe of 1QS, while Malachi Martin, *The Scribal Character of the Dead Sea Scrolls*, I–II, Bibliothèque du Muséon 44, 45 (Louvain 1958), II.710 tentatively identified the final hand of 1QS with hand B of 1QpHab.
39 Eugene Ulrich, "4QSam[c]: A Fragmentary Manuscript of 2 Samuel 14–15 from the Scribe of the *Serek Hayyaḥad* (1QS)," *BASOR* 235 (1979): 1–25" and Eibert J. C. Tigchelaar, "In Search of the Scribe of 1QS," in *Emanuel: Studies in Hebrew Bible, Septuagint, and Dead Sea Scrolls in Honor of Emanuel Tov*, ed. Shalom M. Paul, Robert A. Kraft, Lawrence H. Schiffman, and Weston W. Fields, VTSup 94 (Leiden: Brill, 2003), 439–52. In addition, 1QS (to the right of V 1, VII bottom margin, and IX 3) and 1QIsa[a] (VI 22 in the margin to the right of Isa 7:8) share three unusual marginal signs that were probably inserted by this scribe, although they could also have been inserted by a reader.
40 See Frank Moore Cross, in Scrolls from Qumran Cave I. The Great Isaiah Scroll, The Order of the Community, The Pesher to Habakkuk from Photographs by John C. Trever (Jerusalem: The Albright Institute of Archaeological Research and the Shrine of the Book, 1972). 4.
41 Tov, Scribal Practices, 218.
42 For a detailed study of the idiosyncrasies of this scribe, see Tigchelaar, "In Search of the Scribe."
43 For details, see Tov, *Scribal Practices*, Appendix 1b.

1QS	4	67
1QSa	9	6
1QSb	27	3
4Q175	2	13

This scribe corrected his *Vorlage* freely in 1QS. In col. VII, he added words that had been omitted (line 6); he erased and corrected several words in lines 20–23, and even changed the content. In line 8, in the second paragraph, the base text says that if one bears a grudge against his fellow man, the punishment is to be deprived "sixty days" of the privileges of the community, while the correction extends this punishment in a remark above the line, to שנה אחת, "one year" (as in line 2, under different circumstances).

This scribe approached the biblical and nonbiblical texts in the same way, and I note that the area of this research could be expanded to nonbiblical scrolls, at least to those that were considered authoritative such as the Temple Scroll, Jubilees, and possibly all sectarian texts. The question to be asked is: What was the approach of these scribes to their *Vorlagen*? I have not gone into this area but noted one group of texts that are very relevant to the study of the Scripture texts. The scribal care of the proto-MT scrolls is paralleled by a group of texts with a halakhic background that display very little scribal intervention, as shown by Table 8:

Table 8: Scribal Intervention in Nonbiblical Scrolls of a Halakhic Nature

	One scribal intervention in an average number of X lines	Number of interventions
4QHalakha A (4Q251)	80	1
4QMisc Rules (4Q265)	70	0
4QToh A (4Q274)	25	2
4QRit Pur A (4Q414)	90	0
4QpapRitMar (4Q502)	90	5
4QpapRitQuot (4Q503)	50	8

In summary, scribes of Scripture texts not only devised or followed systems for copying and correcting the text, but they also had ideas, sometimes philosophies, about the way the source text should be represented. However, it is very hard to separate the views of the scribes from those of previous generations. We have been able to gather some information about individual scribes, especially those who copied the Bible text included in tefillin and some other texts, but more about groups of scribes. I see a basic difference between two groups of texts, but they are not black and white as there are many intervening shades. I suggest that

scribes who did not intervene in the completed text were those who also disal-
lowed the insertion of contextual and harmonizing elements, especially scribes
of the rabbinic tefillin, and Masoretic texts. The pre-Samaritan texts had a special
status. Other scribes allowed for scribal intervention and for the addition of exegetical elements in the text. Both groups of scribes employed the same systems
for copying scrolls and they did not distinguish between biblical and nonbiblical
scrolls. The scribal approach to the biblical text is paralleled by approaches to
nonbiblical texts, and this topic requires further research.

5 Bibliography

Cross, Frank Moore. Pages 1–5 in *Scrolls from Qumran Cave I. The Great Isaiah Scroll, The Or-
der of the Community, The* Pesher *to Habakkuk from Photographs by John C. Trever.*
Jerusalem: The Albright Institute of Archaeological Research and the Shrine of the
Book, 1972.
Driesbach, Jason. *4QSamuelᵃ and the Text of Samuel.* VTSup 171. Leiden: Brill, 2016.
Elgvin, Torleif. *The Literary Growth of the Song of Songs during the Hasmonean and Early-He-
rodian Periods*, Contributions to Biblical Exegesis and Theology 89. Leuven: Peeters,
2018.
Eshel, Hanan. "The Historical Background of the Pesher Interpreting Joshua's Curse on the Re-
builder of Jericho." *RevQ* 15 (1992): 409–20
Flint, Peter W. "The Interpretation of Scriptural Isaiah in the Qumran Scrolls: Quotations, Citations, Allusions, and the Form of the Scriptural Source Text." Pages 388–406 in *A
Teacher for All Generations: Essays in Honor of James C. VanderKam.* 2 Volumes. Edited by Eric F. Mason et al. JSJSup 153/1. Leiden: Brill, 2012, Vol. 1.
Hopf, Matthias. *Liebesszenen, Eine literaturwissenschaftliche Studie zum Hohelied als einem
dramatisch-performativen Text*, AThANT 108. Zurich: Theologischer Verlag, 2016.
Lange, Armin. *Handbuch der Textfunde vom Toten Meer, I: Die Handschriften biblischer Bücher
von Qumran und den anderen Fundorten* (Tübingen: Mohr Siebeck, 2009).
Larson, Eric and Lawrence H. Schiffman. "4Q481b. 4QNarrative G." Pages 311–12 in *Qumran
Cave 4.XVII: Parabiblical Texts, Part 3.* Edited by George Brooke et al., in consultation
with James C. VanderKam. DJD XXII. Oxford: Clarendon, 1996.
Lichtenberger, Herrmann. Pages 332 and 338–40 in *The Dead Sea Scrolls, Hebrew, Aramaic,
and Greek Texts with English Translations, Vol. 6B, Pesharim, Other Commentaries,
and Related Documents.* Edited by James H. Charlesworth. Tübingen: Mohr Siebeck,
2002.
Martin, Malachi. *The Scribal Character of the Dead Sea Scrolls.* Vols. I–II. Bibliothèque du
Muséon 44, 45. Louvain 1958.
Millard, Alan R. "In Praise of Ancient Scribes." *BA* (1982): 143–53
Pisano, Stephen, S.J. *Additions or Omissions in the Books of Samuel: The Significant Pluses
and Minuses in the Massoretic, LXX and Qumran Texts*, OBO 57. Freiburg/Göttingen:
University Press, 1984.

Rofé, Alexander. "Midrashic Traits in 4Q51 (So-called 4QSamᵃ)." Pages 75–88 in *Archaeology of the Books of Samuel: The Entangling of the Textual and Literary History*. Edited by Philippe Hugo and Adrian Schenker. VTSup 132. Leiden: Brill, 2010.

Rofé, Alexander, "4QMidrash Samuel?: Observations Concerning the Character of 4QSamᵃ." *Textus* 19 (1998): 63–74.

Rofé, Alexander, "A Scroll of Samuel or Midrash Samuel? The Transfer of the Ark to Jerusalem according to 4Q51." *Meghillot* V–VI (2007): 237–43. Heb.

Tigchelaar, Eibert J. C. "In Search of the Scribe of 1QS." Pages 439–52 in *Emanuel: Studies in Hebrew Bible, Septuagint, and Dead Sea Scrolls in Honor of Emanuel Tov*. Edited by Shalom M. Paul, Robert A. Kraft, Lawrence H. Schiffman, and Weston W. Fields. VTSup 94. Leiden: Brill, 2003.

Tov, Emanuel. *Scribal Practices and Approaches Reflected in the Texts Found in the Judean Desert*. STDJ 54. Leiden: Brill, 2004.

Tov, Emanuel. *Textual Criticism of the Hebrew Bible*. 3rd edition, revised and enlarged. Minneapolis: Fortress, 2012.

Tov, Emanuel. "Textual Harmonization in the Five Books of the Torah: A Summary." Pages 31–56 in *The Bible, Qumran, and the Samaritans*. Edited by Magnar Kartveit and Gary N. Knoppers. SJ 104. Studia Samaritana 10. Berlin: de Gruyter, 2018.

Tov, Emanuel. "The Qumran *Tefillin* and Their Possible Master Copies." Pages 135–49 in *On Wings of Prayer. Sources of Jewish Worship; Essays in Honor of Professor Stefan C. Reif on the Occasion of his Seventy-fifth Birthday*. Edited by Nuria Calduch-Benages, Michael W. Duggan, and Dalia Marx. Deuterocanonical and Cognate Literature Studies 44. Berlin: de Gruyter, 2019.

Ulrich, Eugene C. *The Qumran Text of Samuel and Josephus*. HSM 19. Missoula, MT: Scholars, 1978.

Ulrich, Eugene C. "4QSamᶜ: A Fragmentary Manuscript of 2 Samuel 14–15 from the Scribe of the *Serek Hayyaḥad* (1QS)." *BASOR* 235 (1979): 1–25.

Ulrich, Eugene C. Pages 148–62 in idem, *The Dead Sea Scrolls and the Origins of the Bible*. Grand Rapids: Eerdmans; Leiden: Brill, 1999.

André Lemaire
West Semitic Royal Scribes *ca.* 1250–600 BCE

The aim of this paper is to better understand the importance of the West Semitic scribes in the *temps social*, taking into account the Near Eastern context of the late second millennium and the first half of the first millennium BCE. Our main sources will be the contemporaneous West Semitic inscriptions as well as biblical texts connected with this period, but we may occasionally use other documents such as iconography or material archaeology. For such a long period we do not claim to be complete though the documentation itself is very limited since most of the West Semitic texts were written on papyrus or leather that did not reach us. As a result, we can only catch a few glimpses into the role of the royal scribe during this long period.

1 Ugarit (ca. 1250–1180 BCE)

There is, however, an important exception in Ugarit on the northern Syrian coast where nearly 5000 inscribed objects have been found, mainly tablets with cuneiform writing that could break but did not disappear as easily as parchment or papyrus. A study by José-Ángel Zamora López clearly shows that we would not know much about Ugarit had the scribes written on parchment or papyrus.[1] This documentation reveals the work of at least 51 scribes.[2] We are mainly interested here in scribes who used a cuneiform alphabet of 30 letters and produced some 2000 alphabetic texts: they are "the most direct witnesses to the indigenous

---

1 José-Ángel Zamora López, "Les utilisations de l'alphabet lors du IIe millénaire av. J.-C. et le développement de l'épigraphie alphabétique : une approche à travers la documentation ougaritique en dehors des tablettes (I)." Pages 9–47 in *Le royaume d'Ougarit de la Crète à l'Euphrate : Nouveaux axes de recherche. Actes du Congrès international de Sherbrooke 2005.* Edited by Jean-Marc Michaud (Sherbrooke, Québec: GGC Editions, 2007).
2 Wilfred Hugo van Soldt, *Studies in the Akkadian of Ugarit: Dating and Grammar* (AOAT 40. Kevelaer/Neukirchen-Vluyn: Butzon & Becker / Neukirchener Verlag, 1991), 19–25; F. Ernst-Pradal, *Scribes d'Ougarit et paléographie akkadienne : Les textes juridiques signés* (Ras Shamra – Ougarit 27. Leuven: Peeters, 2019), 31–145.

scribal and intellectual traditions of the Levantine coast."[3] The importance of this documentation in order to understand the role of West Semitic royal scribes would deserve a full paper. As it has been much studied during the last ten years by several scholars (cf. *infra*), I shall only emphasize here the main aspects.

It must be stressed that these Ugaritian scribes studied and wrote first in Akkadian, according to the general scribal tradition of the Ancient Near East, albeit with a few particularisms.[4] At that time, Akkadian was the *lingua franca* of the entire Near East, as clearly shown by the El-Amarna letters. This Akkadian tradition, which included some Sumerian, was foreign to the Ugarit kingdom, to the extent that it "had to be learned in school, artificially and often rather superficially."[5] This implied that Mesopotamian style "literary texts" were copied, studied, and archived by ancient Ugaritian scholars as shown by Daniel Arnaud.[6]

During the last ten years, the date and the context of the appearance of the Ugaritian cuneiform alphabetic script became clearer. The appearance of the name of the king 'Ammiṭṭamru (III) written on a seal inscribed in cuneiform alphabet[7] seems to indicate that the new script appeared during his reign and probably under his patronage. That means that this new script appeared or was only

---

3 Robert Hawley, Dennis Pardee, Carole Roche-Hawley, "The Scribal Culture of Ugarit," *Journal of Ancient Near Eastern History* (Berlin/Boston) 2, 2015, 229–267, esp. 230; Carole Roche, "Classification de l'utilisation du cunéiforme mésopotamien dans les textes ougaritiques," in *Proceedings of the 51st Rencontre Assyriologique Internationale*. Edited by Robert D. Biggs, Jennie Meyers and Martha Roth (Studies in Ancient Oriental Civilization 62. Chicago: The Oriental Institute of the University of Chicago, 2008), 155–170; *eadem*, "Language and Script in the Akkadian Economic Texts from Ras Shamra." Pages 107–122 in *Society and Administration in Ancient Ugarit*. Edited by Wilfred van Soldt (PIHANS 114. Leiden, 2010), 107–122; *eadem*, "Procédés d'écriture des noms des divinités ougaritaines en cunéiforme mésopotamien." Pages 149–179 in *Scribes et érudits dans l'orbite de Babylone*. Edited by Carole Roche-Hawley and Robert Hawley (Orient et Méditerranée 9. Paris: De Boccard, 2012).
4 W. Van Soldt, *Studies in the Akkadian of Ugarit*, 1991.
5 R. Hawley, D. Pardee, C. Roche-Hawley, "The Scribal Culture of Ugarit," 2015, 233.
6 Daniel Arnaud, Corpus des textes de bibliothèque de Ras Shamra-Ougarit (1936–2000) en sumérien, babylonien et assyrien (Aula Orientalis – Supplementa 23, Barcelona: Editorial Ausa, 2007), esp. 12–16.
7 Pierre Bordreuil – Dennis Pardee, "Le sceau nominal de 'Ammiḏtamrou, roi d'Ougarit," *Syria* 61, 1984, 11–14; Adnan Bounni, Élisabeth Lagarce, Jacques Lagarce "La tablette RIH 78/12 et le sceau nominal de 'Ammishtamru." Pages 153–158 in *D'Ougarit à Jérusalem. Recueil d'études épigraphiques et archéologiques offert à Pierre Bordreuil*. Edited by Carole Roche (Orient et Méditerranée 2. Paris: De Boccard, 2008).

institutionalized[8] about the mid-13th century BCE. It was used by the local bureaucracy for administrative texts, such as lists and accounts, as well as internal
correspondence, religion, and literature.

Thus, from *ca.* 1250 until *ca.* 1180 BCE, the Akkadian and Ugaritic scripts co-
existed: "the Ugaritic cuneiform alphabet was used primarily for setting down
local religious culture (mythological poetry, ritual and liturgical texts) and recording day-to-day *ephemera* (economic and administrative lists and accounts,
domestic correspondence) while the Mesopotamian logo-syllabic script and, for
the most part, the Babylonian language, were used for what was regarded as Mesopotamian literary culture, for the drafting of domestic legal documents, and for
international communication (diplomatic and epistolary in nature)."[9]

Scribes were the leaders of this dual culture: they "were making use of both
graphic technologies (and of the languages associated with them)."[10] As a matter
of fact, scribes used the same tools (clay tablet and bronze or wood stylus) to
write in both scripts[11]; the cuneiform alphabet was an adaptation of the earlier
linear alphabet for scribes who were used to writing with a stylus on a clay tablet.
It seems that "many of the Ugaritic scribes who used the local cuneiform alphabetic system had also undergone traditional training in the Mesopotamian logo-
syllabic system."[12] For instance, "even though the 'Assyrian' scribe Naḫiš-Šalmu
and his (presumably local) apprentices insisted on using Mesopotamian cuneiform, the actual language in which the documents were written (and read) was
probably partly Ugaritic"[13] and "bi-graphic" school texts are attested.[14] "Schools
formed around individual scribes in a domestic setting,[15] where these very
scribes, often acting at high levels of the royal administration, not only taught
but carried out their duties."[16]

---

8 See, for instance, Robert Hawley, "On the Transmission of Knowledge and Lore in the Alphabetic Tradition of Ugarit." Pages 67–80 in *Devins et Lettrés dans l'orbite de Babylone*. Edited by
Carole Roche-Hawley and Robert Hawley (Orient et Méditerranée, archéologie 16. Paris: De Boccard, 2015).
9 R. Hawley, D. Pardee, C. Roche-Hawley, "The Scribal Culture of Ugarit," 2015, 237.
10 *Ibidem*, 235.
11 John L. Ellison, "The Scribal Art at Ugarit." Pages 157–190 in *Epigraphy, Philology, and the
Hebrew Bible. Methodological Perspectives on Philological Comparative Study of the Hebrew Bible
in Honor of Jo Ann Hackett*. Edited by Jeremy M. Hutton and Aaron D. Rubin (Ancient Near East
Monographs 112, Atlanta: SBL Press, 2015).
12 R. Hawley, D. Pardee, C. Roche-Hawley, "The Scribal Culture of Ugarit," 2015, 237
13 *Ibidem*, 240; see already C. Roche, "Language and Script," 2010.
14 R. Hawley, D. Pardee, C. Roche-Hawley, "The Scribal Culture of Ugarit," 2015, 243.
15 See Carole Roche, "Scribes, Houses and Neighborhoods at Ugarit," *UF* 44, 2013, 413–444.
16 R. Hawley, D. Pardee, C. Roche-Hawley, "The Scribal Culture of Ugarit," 2015, 246.

Besides the "Assyrian scribe" Naḫiš-Šalmu just mentioned,[17] two other scribes have especially been the subject of personal studies: Ṭab'ilu and 'Ilîmilku.

The scribe Ṭab'ilu was only identified after the publication of RS 19.039 in *PRU* V, 1 where the reading *d ṭb'l*, "of Ṭab'ilu," was deemed ambiguous and its interpretation debated.[18] The discussion truly began in 1998 with the discovery of RIH 98/02, a literary tablet found at Ras Ibn Hani, a few kilometers from Tell Ras Shamra, that presented a few original characteristics: Dennis Pardee could compare them to several other tablets written in Hurrite, Akkadian or Ugaritic. The archaeological context of RIH 98/02 points to the mid-13th century BCE and suggests "that Ṭab'ilu was one of a 'school' of scribes—probably a very small one— working at Ras Ibn Hani."[19] The peculiar script of the Ṭab'ilu tablets[20] seems to reveal that the alphabetic cuneiform script was still in an experimental phase with numerous variations. Thus Ṭab'ilu might even have been the inventor of the Ugaritic alphabetic writing. According to Pierre Bordreuil, Robert Hawley and Dennis Pardee: "Il est maintenant nécessaire de réévaluer l'importance du scribe *Ṭab'ilu* ... Dans leur grande majorité, les mythes et légendes peuvent être classées, avec plus ou moins de certitude, soit dans l'œuvre de *'Ilîmilku*, soit dans celle de *Ṭab'ilu* ... deux maîtres des belles-lettres ougaritiques."[21]

The scribe 'Ilîmilku wrote several colophons and was thus quickly identified as the copyist or author of the Baal cycle, Kirta and Aqhatu.[22] His writing with a very small stylus is generally regular and he always identifies himself first as *spr*,

---

17 See also Wilfred van Soldt, "Naḫiš-Šalmu. An Assyrian Scribe Working in the 'Southern Palace' at Ugarit." Pages 429–444 in *Veenhof Anniversary Volume. Studies Presented to Klaas R. Veenhof on the Occasion of His Sixty-Fifth Birthday.* Edited by J. G. Dercksen, N. J. C. Kouwenberg, Th. J. H. Krispijn (Uitgraven van het Nederlands Historisch-Archaeologisch Instituut te Istanbul 89. Leiden: Nederlands Instituut voor het Nabije Oosten, 2001), 429–444.

18 Cf. Dennis Pardee, "Deux tablettes ougaritiques de la main d'un même scribe, trouvées sur deux sites distincts: RS 19.039 et RIH 98/02," *Semitica et Classica* 1, 2008, 9–38, esp. 20–21.

19 R. Hawley, D. Pardee, C. Roche-Hawley, "The Scribal Culture of Ugarit," 2015, 257.

20 See, for instance, Robert Hawley, Caroline Sauvage, Dennis Pardee, "The Scribe Ṭab'ilu as Attested in the Epigraphic Finds from the 5th Season of Excavations at Ras Shamra," *UF* 44, 2013, 383–411.

21 Pierre Bordreuil, Robert Hawley, Dennis Pardee, "Données nouvelles sur le déchiffrement de l'alphabet et sur les scribes d'Ougarit," *CRAI* 2010, 1623–1635, esp. 1634.

22 See, for instance, Anne-Sophie Dalix, *Ilumilku, scribe d'Ougarit au XIIIe siècle avant J.-C.* (Institut Catholique de Paris thesis 1997); Nicolas Wyatt, *Religious Texts from Ugarit. The Words of Ilimilku and His Colleagues* (The Biblical Seminar 53. Sheffield: Sheffield Academic Press, 1998); *idem*, "The Evidence of the Colophon in the Assessment of Ilimilku's Scribal and Authorial Role," *UF* 46, 2015, 399–446.

"scribe." He also presents himself as a "student of Attēnu the diviner (*prln*)" without specifying whether Attēnu taught him alphabetic cuneiform writing or, perhaps more probably, divination. As a matter of fact, he further presents himself as a "*ṭaʿāyu*-official of Niqmaddu [IV], king of Ugarit," that is, "in direct service to the king;"[23] this title indicates that he was officially a kind of exorcist performing *ṭaʿû* sacrifice. Moreover, in a letter sent to Urtenu, 'Ilîmilku appears to be very close to the queen[24] while RS 92.2016 is a mythico-magic text written by Ilîmilku.[25] This last tablet contains a fragmentary colophon where after presenting himself as a "student of Attēnu the diviner" (line 40') he refers to the document and specifies *w 'ind ylmdnn*, "and no one taught it (to him)" (line 42'). This addition seems to mean that this text was "new material of his own creation."[26] "It appears necessary to conclude that the scribe was claiming to be himself a poet"[27] who could be the real author of texts that were not copied from other texts but may have been influenced by some oral tradition.

Thus, in Ugarit, the scribe, generally at least bilingual[28] and bi-script, could be "a person firmly entrenched not only in the royal household but also in the cultic establishment,"[29] as well as "proud of his accomplishments, both as a poet and as an inscriber of signs."[30] The connection between the scribe and the king

---

23 Dennis Pardee, *The Ugaritic Texts and the Origins of West Semitic Composition* (The Schweich Lectures of the British Academy 2007. Oxford: Oxford University Press, 2012), 44.

24 Pierre Bordreuil, Dennis Pardee, Robert Hawley, *Une bibliothèque au sud de la ville. Textes 1994–2002 en cunéiforme alphabétique de la maison d'Ourtenou* (Ras-Shamra-Ougarit 18. Lyon: Publications de la Maison de l'Orient et de la Méditerranée, 2012), 156–162.

25 André Caquot – Anne-Sophie Dalix, "Un texte mythico-magique (n° 53)." Pages 393–405 in *Études ougaritiques I. Travaux 1985–1995*. Edited by Marguerite Yon and Daniel Arnaud (Ras-Shamra-Ougarit 14. Paris: Éditions Recherche sur les Civilisations, 2001).

26 R. Hawley, D. Pardee, C. Roche-Hawley, "The Scribal Culture of Ugarit," 2015, 251.

27 *Ibidem*, 253.

28 See already Anne-Sophie Dalix, "Exemples de bilinguisme à Ougarit: 'Iloumilkou: la double identité d'un scribe." Pages 81–90 in *Mosaïques de langues, mosaïque culturelle. Le bilinguisme dans le Proche-Orient ancien*. Edited by Françoise Briquel-Chatonnet (Antiquités sémitiques 1. Paris: Maisonneuve, 1996). See also Carole Roche, "Les scribes et l'écriture," Pages 127–131 in *"Orient des palais" : le Palais Royal d'Ougarit au Bronze récent*. Edited by Michel Al-Maqdissi – Valérie Matoïan (Damas: Direction Générale des Antiquités et des Musées, 2008); Alice Mouton – Carole Roche-Hawley, "La polyvalence des scribes d'Anatolie hittite et d'Ougarit." Pages 191–204 in *Devins et lettrés dans l'orbite de Babylone*, 2015.

29 D. Pardee, *The Ugaritic Texts*, 2012, 46.

30 Ibidem, 49.

explains that, as well stated by Gregorio del Olmo Lete: "l'ensemble de la littérature ougaritique s'est développée, en grande partie, comme véhicule de l'exaltation du roi et de la dynastie."[31]

2 Lachish (13th–12th c. BCE)

In the Southern Levant, the Shephelah seems to have played an important role in the transmission of the alphabetic linear writing from the Late Bronze Age to the Iron Age.[32] Even though scribal tradition over there is much less clear than in Ugarit, as all inscriptions on leather or papyrus disappeared, a few hints reveal that "by the end of the Late Bronze Age,[33] this town and its outskirts was a center of writing."[34] Orly Goldwasser notes first that the Egyptian scribes used "administrative hieratic that exhibited no specific provincial affinities"[35] and agrees with

---

31 Gregorio del Olmo Lete, "Littérature et pouvoir royal à Ougarit: sens politique de la littérature d'Ougarit." Pages 241–250, esp. 248 in *Études ougaritiques II*. Edited by Valérie Matoïan, Michel Al-Maqdissi, Yves Calvet (Ras Shamra-Ougarit 20. Leuven/Paris/Walpole, MA: Peeters, 2012). See already Nicolas Wyatt, "Ilimilku's ideological programme: Ugaritic royal propaganda and a biblical postscript," *UF* 29, 1997, 775–796. See also Silvia Ferrara, "A 'top-down' re-invention of an old form: Cuneiform alphabets in context." Pp. 15–28 in *Understanding Relations Between Scripts II. Early Alphabets*. Edited by Philip J. Boyes – Philippa M. Steele (Oxford/Philadelphia: Oxbow,2020), esp. at 19: "it seems that the scribal class is piloted, guided and directed to recording all things local that specifically involve royal influence and royal affairs."
32 See already Ryan Byrne, "The Refuge of Scribalism in Iron I Palestine," *BASOR* 345, 2007, 1–31.
33 Yosef Garfinkel ("Lachish Fortifications and State Formation in the Biblical Kingdom of Judah in Light of Radiometric Datings," *Radiocarbon* 2019, 1–18) prefers to call Level VI: "Iron IA" but this question of terminology is minor as, according to him, Level VI represents "the last Canaanite city."
34 Orly Goldwasser, "From the Iconic to the Linear — The Egyptian Scribes of Lachish and the Modifications of the Early Alphabet in the Late Bronze Age." Pages 118–160, esp. 151 in *Alphabets, Texts and Artifacts in the Ancient Near East. Studies presented to Benjamin Sass*. Edited by Israel Finkelstein, Christian Robin, Thomas Römer (Paris: Van Dieren éditeur, 2016), with a reference to Israel Finkelstein – Benjamin Sass, "The West Semitic Alphabetic Inscriptions, Late Bronze II to Iron IIA: Archaeological Context, Distribution and Chronology," *HeBAI* 2, 2013, 149–220, esp. 153, 200.
35 O. Goldwasser, "The Egyptian Scribes of Lachish," 2016, p. 151; cf. Deborah Sweeney, "The Hieratic Inscriptions." Pages 1601–1617 in *The Renewed Archaeological Excavations at Lachish (1973–1994) III*. Edited by David Ussishkin (Tel Aviv: Emery and Claire Yass Publications in Archaeology, 2004), 1601–1617

Koch[36] that there apparently was active contacts between Canaanites and Egyptians. According to her, "Most likely, Egyptian scribes who resided in Canaan and had to deal with such issues were bilingual and possibly even of Canaanite background."[37] Deborah Sweeney already noted: "The scribes who penned these tax receipts may have been Egyptian or Canaanite scribes who had received an Egyptian education (see Redford 1992:198; Feucht 1990:199 for the Egyptian education of vassals' children) after which they might return to Canaan in the service of the Egyptian administration or of vassal princes (Higginbotham 2000:63)."[38] The language and script situation is complicated enough since, besides hieratic and alphabetic inscriptions, Level VI also produced a fragmentary Linear A inscription on a stone bowl probably coming from the vicinity of Lachish.[39] What is clear is that we have on the same site and for the same level (VI) ink hieratic and alphabetic linear inscriptions that seem to have been written with the same tools: pen/brush and ink on bowl, tools which could be used by the same scribe(s). Moreover, the presence of alphabetic linear inscriptions in level VII and VI not only supposes that there was someone in Lachish who could write them, but also that a few inhabitants could read them, indicating that there was a West Semitic alphabetic scribal culture.[40]

A small level VI West Semitic incised inscription on a jar sherd, discovered by the excavations directed by Yosef Garfinkel, could throw new light on this Lachish West Semitic scribal culture. It only contains three lines and could be complete:[41]

1. PKL
2. SPR
3. *YP*'

---

36 Ido Koch, "Goose Keeping. Elite Emulation and Egyptianized Feasting at Late Bronze Lachish," *Tel Aviv* 41, 2014, 161–179.

37 O. Goldwasser, "The Egyptian Scribes of Lachish," 2016, 151.

38 D. Sweeney, "The Hieratic Inscriptions," 2004, 1615.

39 Margalit Finkelberg, Alexander Uchitel, David Ussishkin, "The Linear A Inscription (Lach ZA 1)," *ibidem*, 1629–1638; Yoram Eshel, "Appendix: Micropaleontological Examination of the Bowl bearing the Linear A Inscription," *ibidem*, 1639.

40 Cf. Alice Mendel, "Reading and Writing Remembrance in Canaan," *HeBAI* 7, 2018, 253–284, esp. 266–275; N. Na'aman, "Egyptian Centres and the Distribution of the Alphabet in the Levant," *Tel Aviv* 47, 2020, 29-54.

41 Benjamin Sass, Yosef Garfinkel, Michael G. Hasel, Martin G. Klingbeil, "The Lachish Jar Sherd: An Early Alphabetic Inscription Discovered in 2014," *BASOR* 374, 2015, 233–245; A. Lemaire, "Notes d'épigraphie sémitique 1. Le tesson de jarre inscrit de Lakish : essai d'interprétation," *Semitica* 58, 2016, 237-243.

This short incised inscription can be tentatively translated: "Pikol scribe of *Yapiʿa*." The last name, though uncertain, seems to be the same name as one of the last Canaanite kings of Lachish in Joshua 10:3. This might not be a simple coincidence, but what matters here is the existence of a West Semitic scribe who could well be a "royal" scribe. When added to the argument presented above, this "royal" scribe was probably able to write hieratic as well as West Semitic alphabetic inscriptions.

As is well known, the transition from the Late Bronze Age to the Early Iron Age is a major archaeological and historical problem, for which solutions vary depending on location. Several studies have shown there was not a total disappearance of Levantine Late Bronze civilization[42]; this is especially true for literacy, though the use of the cuneiform alphabet seems to have indeed completely disappeared.[43]

3 Byblos (11th–10th c. BCE)

Monumental inscriptions from 10th-century-BCE Byblos are well known and easily found in epigraphic textbooks. Though their date in the 10th century BCE has been doubted and tentatively lowered by Benjamin Sass,[44] strong paleographical

---

42 Cf. Emmanuel Pfoh, "Cambio y continuidades en el Levante (ca. 1300–900 a. n. e.): Una propuesta de síntesis sociopolitica," *Revista del Instituto de Historia Antigua Oriental (RIAHO)* 20, 2019, 123–140 (https:doi.org/10.34096/riaho.n20.7112).
43 See, for instance, William M. Schniedewind, *How the Bible Became a Book. The Textualization of Ancient Israel* (Cambridge: Cambridge University Press, 2004), 5–63; R. Byrne, "The Refuge of Scribalism in Iron I Palestine," *BASOR* 345, 2007, 1–31; I. Finkelstein – B. Sass, "The West-Semitic Alphabetic Inscriptions, Late Bronze II to Iron IIA ...," *HeBAI* 2, 2013, 149–220; Brent David, "Literacy in Cyprus and the Levant in the Early Iron Age: Continuities from the Bronze Age." Pages 603–611 in *Tell it in Gath. Studies in the History and Archaeology of Israel. Essays in Honor of Aren M. Maeir*. Edited by Itzhaq Shai *et alii* (ÄAT 90. Münster: Zaphon, 2018).
44 See, for instance, Benjamin Sass, "The Emergence of Monumental West Semitic Alphabetic Writing with an Emphasis on Byblos," *Semitica* 59, 2017, 109–141; *idem*, "The Pseudo-Hieroglyphic Inscriptions from Byblos. Their Elusive Dating and Their Affinities with the Early Phoenician Inscriptions." Pages 157–180 in Ina ᵈmarri u qan ṭuppi. *Par la bêche et le stylet ! Cultures et sociétés syro-mésopotamiennes. Mélanges offerts à Olivier Rouault*. Edited by Philippe Abrahami – Laura Battini (Archaeopress Ancient Near Eastern Archaeology 5. Oxford: Archaeopress, 2019).

and historical arguments[45] confirm a 10th century date, among them the reference to a Levantine diplomatic custom attested in a Ugaritic letter. The existence of these monumental inscriptions points to a wider use of writing, and it is possible to speak of a West Semitic Byblian scribal tradition.[46] As a matter of fact, "West Semitic epigraphy of the 11th-10th centuries BCE informs us of at least six, and possibly eight kings, of the small Phoenician kingdom of Byblos"[47]: Zakarbaal and Ozibaal (11th century BCE), Aḥirom (*ca.* 1000 BCE), Ittobaaal/Pilisbaal[48] (*ca.* 990/980), Yeḥimilk (*ca.* 970/960), Abibaal (*ca.* 945), Elibaal (*ca.* 924), Shipitbaal (*ca.* 900).

The Wenamun report, around the early 11th century BCE, seems to confirm and specify the importance of this scribal tradition: the king of Byblos "had the daybook of his forefathers brought and had it read before me"[49]; thus, the king of Byblos apparently had archives that he could consult. Moreover, even though these archives were most probably written in the Byblian local and royal script, the general context of the relations with Egypt and with envoys from Egypt suggests that this written local scribal tradition was also directly connected with Egyptian culture and its script. Zakarbaal had probably at his disposal one or several scribes who knew both Egyptian language and script. Unfortunately, no Byblian archive has preserved the name of a Byblian scribe. We may note, however,

---

45 See for instance, A. Lemaire, "La datation des rois de Byblos Abibaal et Élibaal et les relations entre l'Égypte et le Levant au Xᵉ siècle av. notre ère," *CRAI* 2006, 1697-1716; Christopher Rollston, "The Dating of the Early Royal Byblian Phoenician Inscriptions: A Response to Benjamin Sass," *Maarav* 15, 2008, p. 57–93; Alan Millard, "Scripts and Their Uses in the 12th-10th Centuries BCE." Pages 405–412 in *The Ancient Near East in the 12th-10th Centuries BCE. Culture and History.* Edited by Gershon Galil, Ayelet Gilboa, Aren M. Maeir, and Dan'el Kahn (AOAT 392. Münster: Ugarit-Verlag, 2012).

46 Reinhard G. Lehmann, "Calligraphy and Craftsmanship in the Aḥirōm Inscription. Considerations on Skilled Linear Flat Writing in Early First Millennium Byblos," *Maarav* 15.2, 2008, 119–164.

47 A. Lemaire, "West Semitic Epigraphy and the History of the Levant during the 12th-10th Centuries BCE." Pages 291-307, esp. at 294-295, in *The Ancient Near East in the 12th-10th Centuries BCE, Culture and History.* Edited by Gershon Galil, Aren M. Maeir, and Dan'el Kahn (AOAT 392. Münster: Ugarit-Verlag, 2012).

48 Cf. Reinhard G. Lehmann, "Wer war Aḥirōms Sohn (KAI 1:1)? Eine kalligraphisch-prosopographische Annäherung an eine epigraphisch offene Frage," Pages 119–166 in *Neue Beiträge zur Semitistik. Fünftes Treffen der Arbeitsgemeinschaft Semitistik in der Deutschen Morgenländischen Gesellschaft vom 15.—17. Februar 2012 an der Universität Basel.* Edited by Viktor Golinets, Hanna Jenni, Hans-Peter Mathys, Samuel Sarasin (AOAT 425. Münster: Ugarit-Verlag, 2015).

49 Miriam Lichtheim, "The report of Wenamun." Pages 89–93, esp. 91a in *The Context of Scripture I. Canonical Compositions from the Biblical World.* Edited by William W. Hallo (Leiden: Brill, 2003).

that two small incised inscriptions bearing the reading SPR, "scribe," and probably dated to the 10th c. BCE, were published by Maurice Dunand, who thought that they were used to indicate a scribal shop;[50] his interpretation is very uncertain and those inscriptions could rather refer to royal scribe(s). We may note that Dunand also published an inscribed stone tablet with a list of names, apparently a writing exercise, meaning that there was some teaching of the alphabetic script in Byblos.

4 Jerusalem: the scribe of David[51]

"The first references to a scribe in the Hebrew Bible occur within two lists of officials connected to the reign of David in the Book of Samuel (2 Sam 8:16–18; 2 Sam 20:23–26)"[52] and Daniel D. Pioske has devoted a whole paper to this figure as a royal scribe in the context of the Ancient Near East. I shall not repeat here this analysis but only quote his conclusion: "In light of the paucity of textual and archaeological evidence that attests directly to the life of David's scribe, the portrait developed here of this individual has been rendered through an assemblage of indirect traces and tentative affiliations, in which the question of the historicity of the biblical references surrounding this scribal official has been bracketed in order to attend to a different interpretive method and set of historical concerns."[53] As a matter of fact, the discovery of a 10th-century jar inscription in Jerusalem itself[54] together with our study above indicate that the existence of such royal scribe in Jerusalem is plausible.

---

50 Maurice Dunand, *Fouilles de Byblos I. 1926–1932*, Paris: Maisonneuve, 1939, 95–96, pl. XXXIV; *II. 1933–1938* 368, pl. CXLIV.
51 This is not the place to venture into a detailed critical analysis of early Biblical historiography but, with most epigraphers, we don't accept the *a priori* affirmation that there was no administrative document and Hebrew literature before 800 BCE. See A. Lemaire, "Levantine Literacy ca 1000–750 BCE." Pages 14–46 in *Contextualizing Israel's Sacred Writings*. Edited by Brian B. Schmidt (Ancient Israel and its Literature 22. Atlanta: SBL Press, 2015). See also footnote 65 *infra*. For a critical appreciation of the thesis of David W. Jamieson-Drake, *Scribes and Schools in Monarchic Judah. A Socio-Archaeological Approach* (JSOTS 109. Sheffield: Almond Press, 1991), see A. Lemaire, *JAOS* 112, 1992, 707–708.
52 Daniel D. Pioske, "The Scribe of David: a Portrait of a Life," *Maarav* 20, 2013, 163–188, esp. 163.
53 *Ibidem*, 188.
54 Eilat Mazar, David Ben-Shlomo, Shmuel Aḥituv, "An Inscribed Pithos from the Ophel, Jerusalem," *IEJ* 63, 2013, 39–49; see lately David Hamidović, "L'inscription du pithos de l'Ophel à

The same goes for the two sons of David's scribe, Elihoreph and Ahijah, who are mentioned within the list of Solomon's servants (1 Kings 4:3).

5 Karkamish: Yariri (*ca* 800 BCE)

On a basalt statue base found in Karkamish, in a Luwian inscription, Yariri claims to know twelve languages and to have been trained in at least four different scripts,[55] among them the Phoenician/Aramaic script. It is probably an exceptional example of the polyglot training of royal scribes to be understood in the geographical context of the Neo-Hittite kingdom of Karkamish. Yet, if Yariri boasts of knowing twelve languages and four scripts, it is probably because knowing several languages and practicing two or three scripts was not so exceptional for a contemporary scribe in Upper Mesopotamia.

6 Zencirli: Barrakib and his scribe

Monumental inscriptions from Zencirli in the 9th and 8th centuries BCE are well known. They are written in three languages: Phoenician (Kulamuwa), Sam'alian and official/imperial Aramaic. Among the last group, West Semitic epigraphy textbooks mention a short inscription on a stele: "My lord is Baal Harran. I am Barrakib son of Panamuwa."[56] This is obviously a stele to the glory of the king, who is represented sitting on his throne.[57] Yet it presents another important figure

---

Jérusalem," *Semitica* 56, 2014, 137–149; A. Lemaire, "The Ophel Inscription on Pithos: A Fragmentary West Semitic Writing Exercise," to be published in *Ronny Reich Volume* (Eretz-Israel 36. Jerusalem).

55 See for instance Jonas C. Greenfield, "Of Scribes, Scripts and Languages." Pages 926–938, esp. 932–934 in *'Al Kanfei Yonah: Collected Studies of Jonas C. Greenfield on Semitic Philology 2.* Edited by Shalom M. Paul, Michael E. Stone and Avital Pinnick (Leiden: Brill, 2001); K. Lawson Younger, "The Scripts of North Syria in the Early First Millennium: The Inscription of Yariri (KARKAMIŠ A15b) Once Again." Pages 169–183 in *Bible et Proche-Orient. Mélanges André Lemaire.* Edited by J. Elayi – J.-M. Durand (Transeuphratène 46. Pandé: Gabalda, 2014).

56 See, for instance, Josef Tropper, *Die Inschriften von Zincirli* (ALASP 6. Münster: Ugarit-Verlag, 1993), 145–146.

57 See, for instance, James B. Pritchard ed., *The Ancient Near East. An Anthology of Texts and Pictures* (Princeton: Princeton University Press, 1958), n° 127.

standing in front of the king with all the tools of a scribe and this second person-
age must be a royal scribe who could play a kind of second political role in the
kingdom of Sam'al (Fig. 1).

One should also note that king Barrakib had at least two seals: one in alphabetic Aramaic[58] and another one in neo-Hittite hieroglyphic.[59] Accordingly, his
royal scribe probably knew at least three languages (Sam'alian, Aramaic and
Luwian) and two scripts (West Semitic alphabet and Neo-Hittite hieroglyphs).

This royal scribe may also have been able to use the Neo-Assyrian cuneiform
script. Yet, excavations have uncovered no 8th c. BCE Neo-Assyrian inscription
in Zencirli so far; knowledge of the cuneiform script was perhaps not absolutely
necessary: by the second half of the 8th c. BCE, Aramaic could be used within the
Neo-Assyrian empire (see, for instance a cylinder-seal of a scribe *infra*), especially
with regards to the Levant.

7 Inscribed seals of scribes

A scene similar to that of Barrakib, but generally interpreted as a worshipper
standing in front of a goddess, appears on the second-largest stamp seal bearing
a West Semitic inscription (45×32×27 mm). It reads: LHWDW SPR', "Belonging to
Hodu the scribe" (Fig. 2). In *WSS* 754 it is approximately dated to the 7th century
BCE, but it is probably earlier, from the second half of the 8th century. It is tempt-
ing to see here an allusion to the representation of a royal scribe in front of a king
(see above). Another Aramaic seal, this time a cylinder-seal, with the title SPR',
"the scribe," has just been published by Zoltán Niederreiter and Benjamin Sass.[60]
It is unprovenanced and kept in the Musées royaux d'art et d'histoire in Brussels.
Thanks to its typical Mesopotamian iconography, it can be dated to the second

58 As attested from a bulla: J. Tropper, *Die Inschriften von Zincirli*, 1993, 150; Nahman Avigad –
Benjamin Sass, *Corpus of West Semitic Stamp Seals* (*WSS*) (Jerusalem: Israel Academy/Israel Ex-
ploration Society/Institute of Archaeology, 1997), n° 750
59 Felix von Luschan, *Ausgrabungen in Sendschirli V. Die Kleinfunde* (MOS 15. Berlin, 1943), 73,
Abb 38; Emmanuel Laroche, "Documents hiéroglyphiques hittites provenant du palais d'Uga-
rit." Pages 97–106, esp. 103, fn. 5, in *Ugaritica III*. Edited by Claude F. A. Schaeffer (BAH 64.
Paris: Geuthner, 1956); Johannes Friedrich, "Das bildhethitische Siegel des Br-Rkb von Samal,"
Orientalia 26, 1957, 345–347; Mario Liverani, "Bar-Guši e Bar-Rakib," *RSO* 36, 1961, 185–187.
60 Zoltán Niederreiter – Benjamin Sass, "On a Neo-Assyrian Period Cylinder Seal with a Cult
Scene and an Unusual Aramaic Legend," *Semitica et Classica* 11, 2018, 219–226.

half of the 8th century; it reads: LNBD SPR', "Belonging to Nabudu(?), the scribe."

We have several other 8th-7th c. BCE West Semitic inscribed seals with the title *spr*, "scribe." They are either Hebrew (*WSS* 21, 22, 23, 417), Moabite (*WSS* 1007, 1008, 1009, 1010), Phoenician (*WSS* 720), or Ammonite. Unfortunately, it is impossible to specify the exact function of these scribes: they may somehow be connected to royal administration, but were not all on the same level of responsibility.

One may note that the existence and education of these scribes from the 8th century and later is now obvious from epigraphic discoveries as emphasized by several studies.[61]

8 A Jerusalem Royal Scribe acting in a crisis: Shebna

Without discussing here in detail the role of the official designated *hassofer* "the scribe" in the royal administration of Jerusalem during the First Temple period,[62]

---

61 See Christopher Rollston, "Scribal Education in Ancient Israel: The Old Hebrew Epigraphic Evidence," *BASOR* 344, 2006, 47–74; *idem, Writing and Literacy in the World of Ancient Israel: Epigraphic Evidence from the Iron Age* (ABS 11. Atlanta: Society of Biblical Literature, 2010); *idem*, "Scribal Curriculum during the First Temple Period: Epigraphical Hebrew and Biblical Evidence." Pages 71–101 in *Contextualizing Israel's Sacred Writings: Ancient Literacy, Orality and Literary Production*. Edited by Brian Schmidt (Ancient Israel and its Literature 22. Atlanta: SBL Press, 2015); Erhard Blum, "Die altaramäischen Wandinschriften vom Tell Deir 'Alla und ihr institutioneller Kontext." Pages 21–52 In *Metatexte. Erzählungen von schrifttragenden Artefakten in der alttestamentliche und mittelalterlichen Literatur*. Edited by Friedrich-Emanuel Focken – Michael R. Ott (Materiale Textkulturen 15 / Schriften des Sonderforschungsbereiches 933. Heidelberg: De Gruyter, 2016); Christopher Rollston, "Scripture and Inscriptions: Eighth-Century Israel and Judah in Writing." Pages 457–473 in *Archaeology and History of Eighth-Century Judah*. Edited by Zev I. Farber – Jacob L. Wright (Ancient Near East Monographs 23. Atlanta: SBL, 2018); Erhard Blum, "Institutionelle und kulturelle Voraussetzungen der israelitischen Traditionsliteratur." Pages 3–44 in *Tradition(en) im alten Israel*. Edited by Ruth Ebach – Martin Leuenberger (Forschungen zum Alten Testament 127. Tübingen: Mohr Siebeck, 2019).

62 See, for instance, Roland de Vaux, *Les institutions de l'Ancien Testament I* (Paris : Cerf, ²1961), 201–202; Tryggve N. D. Mettinger, *Solomonic State Officials. A Study of the Civil Government Officials of the Israelite Monarchy* (Coniectanea Biblica. Old Testament Series 5. Lund: CWK Gleerups Förlag, 1971), 25–51; Yitzhak Avishur – Michael Heltzer, *Studies on the Royal Administration in Ancient Israel in the Light of Epigraphic Sources* (Tel Aviv: Archaeological Center Publication, 2000), esp. 54–62; N. Sacher Fox, *In the Service of the King. Officialdom in Ancient Israel and*

I should like to emphasize two aspects that clearly appear in 2 Kings 18:17–19:2 in the context of a well-dated event: the campaign of Sennacherib against Judah in 701 BCE. During the just outside Jerusalem meeting of the three Sennacherib's envoys with the three Hezekiah's envoys, one notes the presence of "Shebna the scribe" (2 Kings 18:18.28.37; 19:2), apparently one of the three Judean officials. This clearly shows the importance of the royal "scribe." Moreover, Shebna himself apparently became later "who is over the house" ('ŠR 'L HBYT) (Is 22:13), the equivalent of "Prime minister," revealing the high position of the royal scribe and the fact that he was an important member of the royal cabinet. In this story, we have another important information about the royal scribe and the other members of the royal cabinet: "Eliakim son of Hilkiah, Shebna, and Joab said to the chief officer: 'Please, speak to us in Aramaic, for we understand it'..." (2 Kings 18:26). This means that these high officials, designated as "scribes" or by another title, were at the very least bilingual, thus confirming the role of Aramaic as an international language toward the end of the 8th century BCE.

9 Phoenician scribes around Cilicia

The owner of the last Phoenician seal mentioned above (*WSS* 720) with the title HSPR "the scribe" is named MWNNŠ "Muwananis," a typical Luwian name. In fact, this seal belongs to a group of seals that probably originates in or around Cilicia.[63] We may compare this name to the name of the scribe mentioned at the end of the Cebelireis Daği Phoenician inscription (*KAI* 287): PHL'Š HSPR (C3); this last name is also typically Luwian and this scribe apparently wrote under the authority of MLK WRYK, "king Urikki" (B8). We are therefore in front of a Luwian royal scribe who knows Phoenician and is apparently bilingual: Luwian and Phoenician. Indeed, the kingdom of Que itself was officially bilingual and bi-

Judah (Cincinnati: Hebrew Union College Press, 2000); Izabela Eph'al-Jaruzelska, "Officialdom and Society in the Book of Kings. The Social Relevance of the State." Pages 467–500 in *The Books of Kings. Sources, Composition, Historiography and Reception*. Edited by Baruch Halpern – André Lemaire (VTS 129. Leiden/Boston: Brill, 2010).

63 A. Lemaire, "Essai sur cinq sceaux phéniciens," *Semitica* 27, 1977, 29–40; *idem*, "L'écriture phénicienne en Cilicie et la diffusion des écritures alphabétiques." Pages 133–146 in *Phoinikeia Grammata. Lire et écrire en Méditerranée*. Edited by Cl. Baurain, C. Bonnet, V. Krings (Studia Phoenicia/Collection d'études classiques 6. Liège/Namur: Société des études classiques, 1991).

script in the 9th-8th centuries BCE[64] as shown by the bilingual Çineköy and Karatepe inscriptions.

The cases presented in this paper are but a few glimpses into the importance of West Semitic royal scribes at the end of the Late Bronze Age and during most of the Iron Age. Though the number of documented royal scribes is small due to the disappearance of leather and papyrus, epigraphic and literary documentation suffices to show that Late Bronze Age and Iron Age Levantine kingdoms possessed royal scribes able to write alphabetic inscriptions in their local language. At the same time, these royal scribes were often at least bilingual and used at least two scripts. Moreover, as exemplified in Ugarit, they were able to write local "literature" as a kind of royal propaganda, which was eventually used in scribal training curriculum.[65]

10 Bibliography

Arnaud, Daniel.
2007   *Corpus des textes de bibliothèque de Ras Shamra-Ougarit (1936–2000) en sumérien, babylonien et assyrien* (Aula Orientalis – Supplementa 23, Barcelona: Editorial Ausa, 2007).
Avigad, Nahman. Sass Benjamin.
1997   *Corpus of West Semitic Stamp Seals (WSS)* (Jerusalem: Israel Academy/Israel Exploration Society/Institute of Archaeology).
Avishur Yitzhak. Heltzer, Michael.
2000   *Studies on the Royal Administration in Ancient Israel in the Light of Epigraphic Sources* (Tel Aviv: Archaeological Center Publication).

---

64 A. Lemaire, "Les langues du royaume de Sam'al aux IXe-VIIIe s. av. J-C. et leurs relations avec le royaume de Qué." Pages 185–193 in *La Cilicie: espaces et pouvoirs locaux (2e millénaire av. J.-C. – 4e siècle ap. J.-C.)* Edited by Eric Jean, Ali M. Dinçol, Serra Durugönül (Varia Anatolica XIII. Paris: De Boccard, 2001).
65 See, for instance, Matthieu Richelle, "Elusive Scrolls: Could Any Hebrew Literature Have Been Written Prior to the Eighth Century BCE?," *VT* 66, 2016, 556–594; Christopher A. Rollston, "Inscriptional Evidence for the Writing of the Earliest Texts of the Bible, Intellectual Infrastructure in Tenth- and Ninth- Century Israel, Judah and the Southern Levant." Pages 15–45 in *The Formation of the Pentateuch. Bridging the Academic Cultures of Europe, Israel and North America.* Edited by Jan C. Gertz *et alii* (FAT 111. Tübingen: Mohr Siebeck, 2016); Erhard Blum, "Institutionelle und kulturelle Voraussetzungen der israelitischen Traditionsliteratur," Pages 3–44 in *Tradition(en) im alten Israel. Construktion, Transmission und Transformation.* Edited by Ruth Ebach – Martin Leuenberger (FAT 127. Tübingen: Mohr Siebeck, 2019).

Blum, Erhard.

2016   "Die altaramäischen Wandinschriften vom Tell Deir 'Alla und ihr institutioneller Kontext." Pages 21–52 In *Metatexte. Erzählungen von schrifttragenden Artefakten in der alttestamentliche und mittelalterlichen Literatur.* Edited by Friedrich-Emanuel Focken and Michael R. Ott (Materiale Textkulturen 15 / Schriften des Sonderforschungsbereiches 933. Heidelberg: De Gruyter).

2019   "Institutionelle und kulturelle Voraussetzungen der israelitischen Traditionsliteratur." Pages 3–44 in *Tradition(en) im alten Israel.* Edited by Ruth Ebach and Martin Leuenberger (Forschungen zum Alten Testament 127. Tübingen: Mohr Siebeck).

Bordreuil, Pierre.

2019   "Ilimilkou le Shoubanite, mythographe d'Ougarit: le scribe, le collaborateur, l'auteur." Pages 95–106 in *Nuit de pleine lune sur Amurru. Mélanges offerts à Leila Badre.* Edited by Françoise Briquel-Chatonnet, Emmanuelle Capet, Éric Gubel & Carole Roche-Hawley (Paris: Geuthner).

Bordreuil, Pierre. Hawley, Robert. Pardee, Dennis.

2010   "Données nouvelles sur le déchiffrement de l'alphabet et sur les scribes d'Ougarit", *Comptes rendus des séances de l'Académie des Inscriptions et Belles-Lettres* 2010, p. 1623–1635.

Bordreuil, Pierre. Pardee, Dennis,

1984   "Le sceau nominal de 'Ammiḍtamrou, roi d'Ougarit", *Syria* 61, p. 11–14.

Bordreuil, Pierre. Pardee, Dennis. Hawley, Robert.

2012   *Une bibliothèque au sud de la ville. Textes 1994–2002 en cunéiforme alphabétique de la maison d'Ourtenou* (Ras-Shamra-Ougarit 18. Lyon: Publications de la Maison de l'Orient et de la Méditerranée).

Bounni, Adnan. Lagarce, Élisabeth. Lagarce, Jacques.

2008   "La tablette RIH 78/12 et le sceau nominal de 'Ammishtamru." Pages 153–158 in *D'Ougarit à Jérusalem. Recueil d'études épigraphiques et archéologiques offert à Pierre Bordreuil.* Edited by Carole Roche (Orient et Méditerranée 2. Paris: De Boccard).

Burlingame, Andrew R.

2019   "Writing and Literacy in the World of Ancient Israel: Recent Developments and Future Directions," *Bibliotheca Orientalis* 76, col. 49–74.

Byrne, Ryan.

2007   "The Refuge of Scribalism in Iron I Palestine," *Bulletin of the American Schools of Oriental Research* 345, p. 1–31.

Caquot, André. Dalix, Anne-Sophie.

2001   "Un texte mythico-magique (n° 53)." Pages 393–405 in *Études ougaritiques I. Travaux 1985–1995.* Edited by Marguerite Yon and Daniel Arnaud (Ras-Shamra-Ougarit 14. Paris: Éditions Recherche sur les Civilisations).

Dalix, Anne-Sophie.

1996   "Exemples de bilinguisme à Ougarit: 'Iloumilkou: la double identité d'un scribe." Pages 81–90 in *Mosaïque de langues, mosaïque culturelle. Le bilinguisme dans le Proche-Orient ancien.* Edited by Françoise Briquel-Chatonnet (Antiquités sémitiques 1. Paris: Maisonneuve).

1997   *Ilumilku, scribe d'Ougarit au XIIIᵉ siècle avant J.-C.* (Institut Catholique de Paris, thesis).

Davis, Brent.
2018   "Literacy in Cyprus and the Levant in the Early Iron Age: Continuities from the Bronze Age." Pages 603–611 in *Tell it in Gath. Studies in the History and Archaeology of Israel. Essays in Honor of Aren M. Maeir.* Edited by Itzhaq Shai *et alii* (ÄAT 90. Münster: Zaphon).

Del Olmo Lette, Gregorio.
2012   "Littérature et pouvoir royal à Ougarit: sens politique de la littérature d'Ougarit." Pages 241–250 in *Études ougaritiques II.* Edited by Valérie Matoïan, Michel Al-Maqdissi, Yves Calvet (Ras Shamra-Ougarit 20. Leuven/Paris/Walpole, MA: Peeters).

De Vaux, Roland.
1961   *Les institutions de l'Ancien Testament I* (2ᵉ édition. Paris: Cerf).

Dunand, Maurice.
1939   *Fouilles de Byblos I. 1926–1932* (Paris: Maisonneuve).

Ellison, John L.
2015   "The Scribal Art at Ugarit." Pages 157–190 in *Epigraphy, Philology, and the Hebrew Bible. Methodological Perspectives on Philological Comparative Study of the Hebrew Bible in Honor of Jo Ann Hackett.* Edited by Jeremy M. Hutton and Aaron D. Rubin (Ancient Near East Monographs 112. Atlanta: SBL Press).

Eph'al-Jaruzelska, Izabela
2010   "Officialdom and Society in the Book of Kings. The Social Relevance of the State." Pages 467–500 in *The Books of Kings. Sources, Composition, Historiography and Reception.* Edited by Baruch Halpern and André Lemaire (VTS 129. Leiden/Boston: Brill).

Ernst-Pradal, Françoise.
2019   *Scribes d'Ougarit et paléographie akkadienne : Les textes juridiques signés* (Ras Shamra – Ougarit 27. Leuven: Peeters).

Eshel, Yoram.
2004   "Appendix: Micropaleontological Examination of the Bowl bearing the Linear A Inscription." Page 1639 in *The Renewed Archaeological Excavations at Lachish (1973–1994) III.* Edited by David Ussishkin (Tel Aviv: Emery and Claire Yass Publications in Archaeology).

Ferrara, Silvia.
2020   "A 'top-down' re-invention of an old form: Cuneiform alphabets in context." Pages 15–28 in *Understanding Relations Between Scripts II. Early Alphabets.* Edited by Philip J. Boyes and Philippa M. Steele (Oxford/Philadelphia: Oxbow).

Finkelberg, Margalit. Uchitel, Alexander. Ussishkin, David.
2004   "The Linear A Inscription (Lach ZA 1)," Pages 1629–1638 in *The Renewed Archaeological Excavations at Lachish (1973–1994) III.* Edited by David Ussishkin (Tel Aviv: Emery and Claire Yass Publications in Archaeology).

Finkelstein, Israel. Sass, Benjamin.
2013   "The West Semitic Alphabetic Inscriptions, Late Bronze II to Iron IIA: Archaeological Context, Distribution and Chronology", *Hebrew Bible and Ancient Israel* 2, p. 149–220.
2020   "The Emergence and Dissimination of Writing in Judah," *Semitica et Classica* 13, p. 269–282.

Fox, N. Sacher.
2000   *In the Service of the King. Officialdom in Ancient Israel and Judah* (Cincinnati: Hebrew Union College Press).
Friedrich, Johannes.
1957   "Das bildhethitische Siegel des Br-Rkb von Samal," *Orientalia* 26, p. 345–347
Garfinkel, Yosef.
2019   "Lachish Fortifications and State Formation in the Biblical Kingdom of Judah in Light of Radiometric Datings," *Radiocarbon* 2019, p. 1–18.
Goldwasser, Orly.
2016   "From the Iconic to the Linear — The Egyptian Scribes of Lachish and the Modifications of the Early Alphabet in the Late Bronze Age." Pages 118–160 in *Alphabets, Texts and Artifacts in the Ancient Near East. Studies presented to Benjamin* Sass. Edited by Israel Finkelstein, Christian Robin and Thomas Römer (Paris: Van Dieren éditeur).
Greenfield, Jonas C.
2001   "Of Scribes, Scripts and Languages." Pages 926–938, in *'Al Kanfei Yonah: Collected Studies of Jonas C. Greenfield on Semitic Philology 2*. Edited by Shalom M. Paul, Michael E. Stone and Avital Pinnick (Leiden: Brill).
Hamidović, David.
2014   "L'inscription du pithos de l'Ophel à Jérusalem," *Semitica* 56, p. 137–149.
Hawley, Robert.
2015   "On the Transmission of Knowledge and Lore in the Alphabetic Tradition of Ugarit." Pages 67–80 in *Devins et lettrés dans l'orbite de Babylone*. Edited by Carole Roche-Hawley and Robert Hawley (Orient et Méditerranée, archéologie 16. Paris: De Boccard).
Hawley, Robert. Pardee, Dennis. Roche-Hawley, Carole.
2015   "The Scribal Culture of Ugarit," *Journal of Ancient Near-Eastern History* (Berlin/Boston) 2, p. 229–267.
Hawley, Robert. Sauvage, Caroline. Pardee, Dennis.
2013   "The Scribe Ṭab'ilu as Attested in the Epigraphic Finds from the 5th Season of Excavations at Ras Shamra," *Ugarit-Forschungen* 44, p. 383–411.
Jamieson-Drake, David W.
1991   *Scribes and Schools in Monarchic Judah. A Socio-Archaeological Approach* (JSOTS 109. Sheffield: Almond Press).
Koch, Ido.
2014   "Goose Keeping. Elite Emulation and Egyptianized Feasting at Late Bronze Lachish," *Tel Aviv* 41, p. 161–179.
Laroche, Emmanuel.
1956   "Documents hiéroglyphiques hittites provenant du palais d'Ugarit." Pages 97–106 in *Ugaritica III*. Edited by Claude F. A. Schaeffer (BAH 64. Paris: Geuthner).
Lehmann, Reinhard G.
2008   "Calligraphy and Craftsmanship in the Aḥīrōm Inscription. Considerations on Skilled Linear Flat Writing in Early First Millennium Byblos," *Maarav* 15/2, p. 119–164.
2015   "Wer war Aḥīrōms Sohn (KAI 1:1)? Eine kalligraphisch-prosopographische Annäherung an eine epigraphisch offene Frage," Pages 119–166 in *Neue Beiträge zur Semitistik. Fünftes Treffen der Arbeitsgemeinschaft Semitistik in der Deutschen Morgenländischen Gesellschaft vom 15.-17. Februar 2012 an der Universität Basel*. Edited by

Viktor Golinets, Hanna Jenni, Hans-Peter Mathys, Samuel Sarasin (AOAT 425. Münster: Ugarit-Verlag).

Lemaire, André.

1977 "Essai sur cinq sceaux phéniciens," *Semitica* 27, p. 29–40.

1991 "L'écriture phénicienne en Cilicie et la diffusion des écritures alphabétiques." Pages 133–146 in *Phoinikeia Grammata. Lire et écrire en Méditerranée.* Edited by Cl. Baurain, C. Bonnet, V. Krings (Studia Phoenicia/Collection d'études classiques 6. Liège/Namur: Société des études classiques).

1992 "Review of D. W. Jamieson-Drake, *Scribes and Schools* ...", *Journal of the American Oriental Society* 112, p. 707–708.

2001 "Les langues du royaume de Sam'al aux IXe-VIIIe s. av. J-C. et leurs relations avec le royaume de Qué." Pages 185–193 in *La Cilicie: espaces et pouvoirs locaux (2e millénaire av. J.-C. – 4e siècle ap. J.-C.)* Edited by Eric Jean, Ali M. Dinçol, Serra Durugönül (Varia Anatolica XIII. Paris: De Boccard).

2006 "La datation des rois de Byblos Abibaal et Élibaal et les relations entre l'Égypte et le Levant au Xe siècle av. notre ère,", *Comptes rendus des séances de l'Académie des Inscriptions et Belles-Lettres* 1697-1716.

2012 "West Semitic Epigraphy and the History of the Levant during the 12th-10th Centuries BCE." Pages 291–307, in *The Ancient Near East in the 12th-10th Centuries BCE, Culture and History.* Edited by Gershon Galil, Aren M. Maeir, and Dan'el Kahn (AOAT 392. Münster: Ugarit-Verlag).

2015 "Levantine Literacy ca 1000–750 BCE." Pages 14–46 in *Contextualizing Israel's Sacred Writings.* Edited by Brian B. Schmidt (Ancient Israel and its Literature 22. Atlanta: SBL Press).

2016 "Notes d'épigraphie sémitique 1. Le tesson de jarre inscrit de Lakish : essai d'interprétation," *Semitica* 58, p. 237–243.

In press "The Ophel Inscription on Pithos: A Fragmentary West Semitic Writing Exercise," in *Ronny Reich Volume* (Eretz-Israel 36. Jerusalem).

Lichtheim, Miriam.

2003 "The report of Wenamun." Pages 89–93 in *The Context of Scripture I. Canonical Compositions from the Biblical World.* Edited by William W. Hallo (Leiden: Brill).

Liverani, Mario.

1961 "Bar-Guši e Bar-Rakib," *Rivista degli studi orientali* 36, p. 185–187.

Mazar, Eilat. Ben-Shlomo, David. Aḥituv, Shmuel.

2013 "An Inscribed Pithos from the Ophel, Jerusalem," *Israel Exploration Journal* 63, p. 39–49.

Mendel, Alice.

2018 "Reading and Writing Remembrance in Canaan," *Hebrew Bible and Ancient Israel* 7, p. 253–284.

Mettinger, Tryggve N. D.

1971 *Solomonic State Officials. A Study of the Civil Government Officials of the Israelite Monarchy* (Coniectanea Biblica. Old Testament Series 5. Lund: CWK Gleerups Förlag, 1971).

Millard, Alan.
2012   "Scripts and Their Uses in the 12th-10th Centuries BCE." Pages 405–412 in *The Ancient Near East in the 12th-10th Centuries BCE. Culture and History*. Edited by Gershon Galil, Ayelet Gilboa, Aren M. Maeir and Dan'el Kahn (AOAT 392. Münster: Ugarit-Verlag).

Mouton, Alice. Roche-Hawley, Carole.
2015   "La polyvalence des scribes d'Anatolie hittite et d'Ougarit." Pages 191–204 in *Devins et lettrés dans l'orbite de Babylone*. Edited by Carole Roche-Hawley and Robert Hawley (Orient et Méditerranée, archéologie 16. Paris: De Boccard).

Na'aman, Nadav.
2020   "Egyptian Centres and the Distribution of the Alphabet in the Levant." *Tel Aviv* 47, p. 29–54.

Niederreiter, Zoltán.
2020   *Catalogue of the Cylinder Seals in the Royal Museums of Art and History I. Neo-Assyrian, and Neo-Babylonian Periods (circa 1000–500 B.C.)* (Antiqua et Orientalia 7: Budapest).

Niederreiter, Zoltán. Sass, Benjamin.
2018   "On a Neo-Assyrian Period Cylinder Seal with a Cult Scene and an Unusual Aramaic Legend," *Semitica et Classica* 11, p. 219–226.

Pardee, Dennis.
2008   "Deux tablettes ougaritiques de la main d'un même scribe, trouvées sur deux sites distincts: RS 19.039 et RIH 98/02," *Semitica et Classica* 1, p. 9–38.
2012   *The Ugaritic Texts and the Origins of West Semitic Composition* (The Schweich Lectures of the British Academy 2007. Oxford: Oxford University Press).

Pfoh, Emmanuel.
2019   "Cambio y continuidades en el Levante (ca. 1300–900 a. n. e.): Una propuesta de síntesis sociopolitica," *Revista del Instituto de Historia Antigua Oriental* 20, p. 123–140 (https:doi.org/10.34096/riaho.n20.7112).

Pioske, Daniel D.
2013   "The Scribe of David: a Portrait of a Life", *Maarav* 20, p. 163–188.

Pritchard, James (ed.)
1958   *The Ancient Near East. An Anthology of Texts and Pictures* (Princeton: Princeton University Press).

Richelle, Matthieu.
2016   "Elusive Scrolls: Could Any Hebrew Literature Have Been Written Prior to the Eighth Century BCE?" *Vetus Testamentum* 66, p. 556–594.

Roche, Carole.
2008   "Les scribes et l'écriture," Pages 127–131 in *"Orient des palais": le Palais Royal d'Ougarit au Bronze récent*. Edited by Michel Al-Maqdissi and Valérie Matoïan (Damas: Direction Générale des Antiquités et des Musées).
2008   "Classification de l'utilisation du cunéiforme mésopotamien dans les textes ougaritiques." Pages 155–170 in *Proceedings of the 51st Rencontre Assyriologique Internationale*. Edited by Robert D. Biggs, Jennie Meyers and Martha Roth (Studies in Ancient Oriental Civilization 62. Chicago: The Oriental Institute of the University of Chicago).

2010   "Language and Script in the Akkadian Economic Texts from Ras Shamra." Pages 107–122 in *Society and Administration in Ancient Ugarit*. Edited by Wilfred van Soldt (PIHANS 114. Leiden).

2012   "Procédés d'écriture des noms des divinités ougaritaines en cunéiforme mésopotamien." Pages 149–179 in *Scribes et érudits dans l'orbite de Babylone*. Edited by Carole Roche-Hawley and Robert Hawley (Orient et Méditerranée 9. Paris: De Boccard).

2013   "Scribes, Houses and Neighborhoods at Ugarit," *Ugarit-Forschungen* 44, p. 413–444.

Rollston, Christopher.

2006   "Scribal Education in Ancient Israel: The Old Hebrew Epigraphic Evidence," *Bulletin of the American Schools of Oriental Research* 344, p. 47–74.

2008   "The Dating of the Early Royal Byblian Phoenician Inscriptions: A Response to Benjamin Sass," *Maarav* 15, p. 57–93.

2015   "Scribal Curriculum during the First Temple Period: Epigraphical Hebrew and Biblical Evidence." Pages 71–101 in *Contextualizing Israel's Sacred Writings: Ancient Literacy, Orality and Literary Production*. Edited by Brian Schmidt (Ancient Israel and its Literature 22. Atlanta: SBL Press).

2016   "Inscriptional Evidence for the Writing of the Earliest Texts of the Bible, Intellectual Infrastructure in Tenth- and Ninth- Century Israel, Judah and the Southern Levant." Pages 15–45 in *The Formation of the Pentateuch. Bridging the Academic Cultures of Europe, Israel and North America*. Edited by Jan C. Gertz *et alii* (FAT 111. Tübingen: Mohr Siebeck).

2018   "Scripture and Inscriptions: Eighth-Century Israel and Judah in Writing." Pages 457–473 in *Archaeology and History of Eighth-Century Judah*. Edited by Zev I. Farber – Jacob L. Wright (Ancient Near East Monographs 23. Atlanta: SBL).

Sass, Benjamin.

2017   "The Emergence of Monumental West Semitic Alphabetic Writing with an Emphasis on Byblos," *Semitica* 59, p. 109–141.

2019   "The Pseudo-Hieroglyphic Inscriptions from Byblos. Their Elusive Dating and Their Affinities with the Early Phoenician Inscriptions." Pages 157–180 in Ina ᵈmarri u qan ṭuppi. *Par la bêche et le stylet ! Cultures et sociétés syro-mésopotamiennes. Mélanges offerts à Olivier Rouault*. Edited by Philippe Abrahami and Laura Battini (Archaeopress Ancient Near Eastern Archaeology 5. Oxford: Archaeopress).

Sass, Benjamin. Garfinkel, Yosef. Hasel, Michael G. Klingbeil, Martin G.

2014   "The Lachish Jar Sherd: An Early Alphabetic Inscription Discovered in 2014," *Bulletin of the American Schools of Oriental Research* 374, p. 233–245.

Schniedewind, William M.

2004   *How the Bible Became a Book. The Textualization of Ancient Israel* (Cambridge: Cambridge University Press).

2019   *The Finger of the Scribes: How Scribes Learned to Write the Bible* (New York: Oxford University Press).

Sweeney, Deborah.

2004   "The Hieratic Inscriptions." Pages 1601–1617 in *The Renewed Archaeological Excavations at Lachish (1973–1994) III*. Edited by David Ussishkin (Tel Aviv: Emery and Claire Yass Publications in Archaeology).

Tropper, Josef.

1993   *Die Inschriften von Zincirli* (ALASP 6. Münster: Ugarit-Verlag).

Van Soldt, Wilfred Hugo.
1991   *Studies in the Akkadian of Ugarit: Dating and Grammar* (AOAT 40. Kevelaer/Neu-
        kirchen-Vluyn: Butzon & Becker / Neukirchener Verlag).
2001   "Naḫiš-Šalmu. An Assyrian Scribe Working in the 'Southern Palace' at Ugarit." Pages
        429–444 in *Veenhof Anniversary Volume. Studies Presented to Klaas R. Veenhof on
        the Occasion of His Sixty-Fifth Birthday*. Edited by J. G. Dercksen, N. J. C. Kouwenberg,
        Th. J. H. Krispijn (Uitgraven van het Nederlands Historisch-Archaeologisch Instituut
        te Istanbul 89. Leiden: Nederlands Instituut voor het Nabije Oosten).
Von Luschan, Felix.
1943   *Ausgrabungen in Sendschirli V. Die Kleinfunde* (MOS 15. Berlin).
Weissbein, Itamar. Garfinkel, Yosef. Hasel, Michael G. Klingbeil Martin G., Brandl Baruch &
        Misgav Hadas.
2019   "The Level VI North-East Temple at Tel Lachish." *Levant* 51, p. 76–104.
Wyatt, Nicolas.
1997   "Ilimilku's Ideological Programme: Ugaritic Royal Propaganda and a Biblical Post-
        script," *Ugarit-Forschungen* 29, p. 775–796.
1998   *Religious Texts from Ugarit. The Words of Ilimilku and His Colleagues* (The Biblical
        Seminar 53. Sheffield: Sheffield Academic Press).
2015   "The Evidence of the Colophon in the Assessment of Ilimilku's Scribal and Authorial
        Role," *Ugarit-Forschungen* 46, p. 399–446.
Younger, K. Lawson.
2014   "The Scripts of North Syria in the Early First Millennium: The Inscription of Yariri
        (KARKAMIŠ A15b) Once Again." Pages 169–183 in *Bible et Proche-Orient. Mélanges
        André Lemaire*. Edited by J. Elayi and J.-M. Durand (Transeuphratène 46. Pandé: Ga-
        balda).
Zamora Lopez, José-Angel.
2007   "Les utilisations de l'alphabet lors du IIe millénaire av. J.-C. et le développement de
        l'épigraphie alphabétique : une approche à travers la documentation ougaritique en
        dehors des tablettes (I)." Pages 9–47 in *Le royaume d'Ougarit de la Crète à l'Euph-
        rate. Nouveaux axes de recherche. Actes du Congrès international de Sherbrooke
        2005*. Edited by Jean-Marc Michaud (Sherbrooke, Québec: GGC Editions).

Figure 1: King Barrakib and his scribe. Courtesy Staatliche Museen zu Berlin.

Figure 2: "Belonging to Hodu the scribe" (WSS 754). Courtesy Benjamin Sass.

Sara Milstein

The Role of Legal Texts in Scribal Education: Implications for Biblical Law

The question of the origins of biblical law has been at the forefront of biblical scholarship for the past half century. Much discussion has centered on the relationships between different law collections, whether the Laws of Hammurabi (LH) and Exodus 20–23, Exodus 20–23 and Deuteronomy 12–26, or the Middle Assyrian Laws A and Deuteronomy 12–26.[1] Taking a different tack, some have contended that the Covenant Code and/or parts of Deuteronomy are rooted in Israelite court proceedings.[2] This argument is in line with the theory in Assyriology that Mesopotamian law—and in particular, LH—is in large part rooted in actual cases that were stripped of their particulars and generalized into law.[3] I would like to approach this question from a different angle by considering it from the perspective of scribal training. While the Israelites' penchant for perishable writing material has left us with only scant evidence of their scribal education, education in Mesopotamia is far better documented, thanks to the Mesopotamians'

* I am grateful to Michael Langlois and Esti Eshel for including me in such an inspiring and thought-provoking colloquium. I also wish to thank Gabriella Spada for her generous help regarding the model contracts and Jeffrey Stackert for his helpful response at the workshop.

1 On the relationship between LH and Exodus 20–23, see David P. Wright, *Inventing God's Law: How the Covenant Code of the Bible Used and Revised the Laws of Hammurabi* (New York: Oxford University Press, 2009); on the relationship between Exodus and Deuteronomy, see Bernard Levinson, *Deuteronomy and the Hermeneutics of Legal Innovation* (New York: Oxford University Press, 1997). The parallel between the overarching Deuteronomic programme and Tablet A of the Middle Assyrian Laws has been most strongly drawn by Eckart Otto, who sees both as evidence of legal reforms (*Das Deuteronomium: Politische Theologie und Rechtsreform in Juda und Assyrien*, BZAW 284 [Berlin: De Gruyter, 1999]).

2 On the Covenant Code, see Eckart Otto, "Town and Rural Countryside in Ancient Israelite Law: Reception and Redaction in Cuneiform and Israelite Law," *JSOT* 57 (1993): 3–22. For Alexander Rofé, Deut 22:13–19 and Deut 25:5–10 in particular "almost read like transcripts of trials later rewritten as laws" (*Deuteronomy: Issues and Interpretation*, OTS [London: T&T Clark, 2002], 184).

3 For discussion, see Jean Bottéro, "The 'Code' of Hammurabi," in *Mesopotamia: Writing, Reasoning, and the Gods*, trans. Zainab Bahrani and Marc van de Mieroop (Chicago: University of Chicago Press, 1992), 156–84, esp. 169–77; and Raymond Westbrook, "Biblical and Cuneiform Codes," in *Law from the Tigris to the Tiber: The Writings of Raymond Westbrook, The Shared Tradition*, vol. 1, ed. Bruce Wells and F. Rachel Magdalene (Winona Lake, IN: Eisenbrauns, 2009), 3–20.

use of the more durable medium of clay.[4] In addition to lexical lists, hymns, proverbs, and other genres, a range of legal texts were used in Mesopotamian pedagogical contexts, including extracts from law collections, legal phrasebooks, sample contracts, and fictional court cases. While this "law school" training cannot be presumed for all Mesopotamian scribes, let alone for all Israelite scribes, the evidence from Mesopotamia nonetheless provides evidence of the *types* of legal texts to which advanced Near Eastern scribes were potentially exposed. I propose that this diverse material has much untapped potential for addressing some of the thorniest questions regarding the origins of biblical law.

1 Setting the Bar High: Legal Education in Mesopotamia

In the past twenty years, there has been a flurry of scholarship on scribal education in Mesopotamia, particularly with respect to the Old Babylonian (OB) period (2000–1600 B.C.E.), for which there are the most data. Most significantly, as Eleanor Robson explicates, scholars have shifted from using the texts *about* school (i.e., the "edubba" texts) to reconstruct scribal education to basing their conclusions on material culture, with attention to actual scribal exercises.[5] This content, together with curricular lists, has enabled scholars to reconstruct sequential phases in early Babylonian scribal education. After learning writing techniques, lexical lists, and mathematical tables, scribes progressed to copying short texts (e.g., proverbs), and finally longer literary compositions.[6] The bulk of this content

---

4 For an exception to the rule, see William Schniedewind's treatment of the Kuntillet ʿAjrud material as pedagogical in nature (*The Finger of the Scribe: How Scribes Learned to Write the Bible* [New York: Oxford University Press, 2019], 23–48).
5 Eleanor Robson, "The Tablet House: A Scribal School in Old Babylonian Nippur," *RA* 95 (2001): 39–66. As Robson points out, the problem with the edubba texts is that they reflect a stylized and likely exaggerated portrait of schools; moreover, they provide no insight into regional variation, chronological change, or the physical environment of schools (39–40).
6 Much rests on the foundational work of Miguel Civil, who analyzed collections of lexical tablets at multiple locations and categorized them into four formats, known as Types I–IV. Type I tablets are large, multi-columned tablets; Type II are large, "teacher-student" copies that are inscribed on one side by the teacher and on the other by the student; Type III are single-column extracts of compositions; and Type IV are round tablets, or "lentils," that consist of 2–4 lines of composition and show signs of inscription by teachers and students ("Old Babylonian Proto-Lu: Types of Sources," in *The Series lú = ša and Related Texts*, ed. Miguel Civil and Erica Reiner, MSL 12 [Rome: Pontificium Institutum Biblicum, 1969], 27–28; *Ea A = nâqu, Aa A = nâqu, with Their*

was in Sumerian, despite the fact that Akkadian had replaced Sumerian as the dominant spoken language and the language of administrative, business, and legal documents.[7] Scholars have enhanced the picture of OB scribal education with full-length studies of some of these texts, including core literary texts, mathematical texts, and practice ("model") letters.[8] Unfortunately, however, when it comes to the position of *legal* texts in Mesopotamian education, there is no single volume to date that brings together all of the evidence. Thus, school exercises such as the "Laws of Rented Oxen" or the "Sumerian Laws Exercise Tablet" are published separately from editions of sample contracts ("model contracts") and fictional court cases ("model cases").[9] It should be added that there is no col-

---

Forerunners and Related Texts, ed. Civil et al., MSL 14 [Rome: Pontificium Institutum Biblicum, 1979], 5–7; and "Ancient Mesopotamian Lexicography," *CANE* 4: 2308). Niek Veldhuis then used this information to reconstruct four phases in the elementary scribal curriculum at Nippur ("Elementary Education at Nippur: The Lists of Trees and Wooden Objects" [PhD diss., Rijksuniversiteit Groningen, 1997], 35–36, 40–63). Veldhuis's work was supplemented by Steve Tinney, who determined that at a more advanced stage, scribes learned two sets of literary texts that he dubbed the "Tetrad" and the "Decad" ("Texts, Tablets, and Teaching: Scribal Education in Nippur and Ur," *Expedition* 40 [1998]: 40–50; "On the Curricular Setting of Sumerian Literature," *Iraq* 61 [1999]: 159–72). Robson provided further confirmation for Tinney's hypothesis in her analysis of tablet finds at House F in Nippur, for the schoolhouse yielded numerous copies of "Decad" texts alongside obvious school exercises ("Tablet House," 51).

7 Laurie E. Pearce, "The Scribes and Scholars of Ancient Mesopotamia," *CANE* 4: 2265–2278, here, 2270; Robson, "Tablet House," 30.

8 On the core curricular texts, see Niek Veldhuis, *History of the Cuneiform Lexical Tradition*, GMTR 6 (Münster: Ugarit Verlag, 2014); and Paul Delnero, *The Textual Criticism of Sumerian Literature*, JCSSS 3 (Boston: ASOR, 2012). On mathematical texts, see Christine Proust, *Tablettes mathématiques de Nippur: Première partie: reconstitution du cursus scolaire. Deuxième partie: édition des tablettes conservées à Istanbul*, Varia Anatolica 18 (Istanbul: Institut Français d'Études Anatoliennes-Georges Dumézil, 2007), idem, *Tablettes mathématiques paléo-babyloniennes de la collection Hilprecht* (Wiesbaden: Harrassowitz, 2008); and Eleanor Robson, *Mathematics in Ancient Iraq: A Social History* (Princeton: Princeton University Press, 2008). On the model letters, see Alexandra Kleinerman, *Education in Early 2nd Millennium BC Babylonia: The Sumerian Epistolary Miscellany*, CM 42 (Leiden: Brill, 2011); and Miguel Civil, "From the Epistolary of the Edubba," in *Wisdom, Gods, and Literature: Studies in Assyriology in Honour of W.G. Lambert*, ed. Andrew George and Irving L. Finkel (Winona Lake, IN: Eisenbrauns, 2000).

9 On the exercises, see Martha Roth, *Law Collections from Mesopotamia and Asia Minor*, 2nd ed., WAW 6 (Atlanta: SBL Press, 1997). On the contracts, see Gabriella Spada, "I modelli di contratto nell'edubba paleo-babilonese: un esempio di contratto di adozione," *Annali dell'Università degli Studi di Napoli "L'Orientale"* 72 (2012): 133–148; idem, "Two Old Babylonian Model Contracts," *Cuneiform Digital Library Journal* 2 (2014): 1–13; idem, *Sumerian Model Contracts from the Old*

lected volume of the model cases, only a handful of articles, mostly on independent texts.[10] Likewise, only a limited number of the hundreds of known model contracts have been edited. Extracts from law collections are cited and used as sources to reconstruct their "parent" law collections in their entirety, but are not typically published as stand-alone documents. Legal phrasebooks are discussed in the context of other lexical lists.[11] As such, it has been difficult for scholars to assess in full the role that legal texts played in Mesopotamian scribal education, and to evaluate their relationship to the world of law beyond the school setting. By extension, this content has not been fully mined by biblical scholars, who otherwise have profiled Mesopotamian pedagogical texts in the context of efforts to reconstruct the contours of Israelite education.[12] A brief review of these texts is thus in order.

1.1 Model Contracts

Although not all ancient legal transactions would have required documentation, thousands of texts from Mesopotamia indicate that scribes from the third millennium B.C.E. on were employed to produce all types of written contracts: marriage and divorce contracts, adoptions, loans, hires, sales, rentals, wills, and so on. It is thus logical that model contracts were a key part of OB scribal education, for

---

Babylonian Period in the Hilprecht Collection Jena, Texte und Materialien der Frau Professor Hilprecht Collection of Babylonian Antiquities in Eigentum der Friedrich-Schiller-Universität Jena XI (Wiesbaden: Harrassowitz, 2018); and Walter Bodine, *How Mesopotamian Scribes Learned to Write Legal Documents: A Study of the Sumerian Model Contracts in the Babylonian Collection at Yale University* (Lewiston, NY: Edwin Mellen Press, 2014).

10 See, e.g., William H. Hallo, "A Model Court Case Concerning Inheritance," in *Riches Hidden in Secret Places: Ancient Near Eastern Studies in Memory of Thorkild Jacobsen,* ed. Tzvi Abusch (Winona Lake, IN: Eisenbrauns, 2002), 141–54; Thorkild Jacobsen, "An Ancient Mesopotamian Trial for Homicide," in *Toward the Image of Tammuz and Other Essays on Mesopotamian History and Culture,* ed. William Moran, HSS 21 (Cambridge: Harvard University Press, 1970), 193–215; Martha T. Roth, "Gender and Law: A Case Study from Ancient Mesopotamia," in *Gender and Law in the Hebrew Bible and the Ancient Near East,* ed. Bernard Levinson, Tikva Frymer-Kensky, and Victor H. Matthews, JSOTSup 262 (Sheffield: Sheffield Academic Press, 1998), 173–84; and Jacob Klein and Tonia M. Sharlach, "A Collection of Model Court Cases from Old Babylonian Nippur (CBS 11324)," *ZA* 97 (2007): 1–25.

11 Veldhuis, History of the Cuneiform Lexical Tradition, 188ff.

12 See, e.g. Karel van der Toorn, *Scribal Culture and the Making of the Hebrew Bible* (Cambridge, MA: Harvard University Press, 2009); and David Carr, *Writing on the Tablet of the Heart: Origins of Scripture and Literature* (New York: Oxford University Press, 2005).

they provided scribes with the skills for drawing up functional contracts.[13] Indeed, in one document, a scribe boasts of his ability to write "contracts for formalizing marriages and for business partnerships; for selling houses, fields, and slaves; for deposits of silver; for leasing cultivation fields or palm-groves; and tablets for contracts of adoption."[14] Model contracts are similar in format and content to actual contracts, but unlike their real-life counterparts, they typically lack witnesses, seals, and dates.[15] In some cases, they exist in duplicates, thus providing additional evidence of their pedagogical *Sitz im Leben*. In other cases, multiple contracts—sometimes as many as twenty—are separated by a double line on the same tablet (a "Sammeltafel"), another indicator of their educational provenance.[16] The existence of tablets with proverbs on one side and model contracts on the other (e.g., N 5863) indicates that these text-types were learned at the same (early) phase of scribal education. While some model contracts betray an unpracticed hand, others suggest the experienced work of a professional, apparently a teacher. A number of model contracts were discovered at House F in Nippur, the southern Babylonian city that accounts for over 80% of all known Sumerian literary texts and appears to have been a center for scribal education.

1.2 Model Court Cases

Model cases are fictional or fictionalized court cases that were also used in OB scribal education, though they are attested in far fewer numbers than the model

---

13 In his article on Nippur, Stephen Lieberman identified two modes of instruction: the "paradigmatic" approach, in which one learned a series of words, phrases and clauses; and "pattern practice," when a student copied a series of sample legal and administrative records ("Nippur: City of Decisions," in *Nippur at the Centennial: Papers Read at the 35e Rencontre Assyriologique Internationale, Philadelphia 1988*, ed. Maria de Jong Ellis, Occasional Publications of the Samuel Noah Kramer Fund (Philadelphia: University Museum, 1992), 127–135.
14 Dominique Charpin, *Hammurabi of Babylon* (London: I.B. Tauris, 2012), 14.
15 Some refer to the omitted witnesses with generic statements ("The witnesses, its month, and its year"), though in other instances, separate witness lists were used in education; and one text features a date but no witnesses (Bodine, *How Mesopotamian Scribes Learned to Write Legal Documents*, 160–162).
16 Spada, *Sumerian Model Contracts*, 44. As Bodine points out, neither of these factors alone is a definitive indicator: functional contracts could also be preserved in duplicate copies; and likewise, copies of functional contracts could be recorded on a single archival tablet. These features are therefore most telling when combined with other indicators, such as anonymity, unusual features, blank spaces, mistakes, and dedication to the patron goddesses of scribes, Nisaba or Haia (*How Mesopotamian Scribes Learned to Write Legal Documents*, 160–179).

contracts. Although scholars have tended to assume that these model cases were rooted in actual cases, there is no hard evidence to support that claim.[17] Like the model contracts, the model cases lack witnesses, seals, and dates, a sign of their educational provenance. In one instance, two model contracts and a model case are preserved on the same tablet.[18] The limited "corpus" includes a homicide case, two cases of adultery, several inheritance disputes, a case regarding the rape of a slave-girl, a dispute over office, and a few others. Several of the model cases are also peppered with colorful features.[19] In one of the adultery cases, for example, the cuckolded husband ties his wife and her lover to the bed and then carries the bed to the assembly.[20] In the homicide case known as the "Nippur Homicide Trial," after the chief priest of Nippur is murdered by three known assailants, the assembly members engage in a heated debate regarding his wife's culpability in the crime.[21] Such features are not found in the contemporaneous trial records, which tend to preserve only laconic snippets of the proceedings.

1.3 Extracts from Law Collections and Related Exercises

When OB scribes were in the process of learning a long literary text, they would divide the composition up into four parts, or "extracts," and copy each section in sequence before producing a copy of the complete work.[22] The extracts are small, one-columned tablets with 10–30 lines of a composition; on some occasions, they include a catch-line to the next section. A similar practice seems to have been

17 Samuel Greengus's statement is paradigmatic of this earlier stance: "[T]he literary legal decisions appear to be records of such real cases from which general principles of adjudication could have been extracted" ("A Textbook Case of Adultery in Ancient Mesopotamia," *HUCA* 40–41 [1969–70]: 33–44, here, 43).
18 Klein and Sharlach, "Collection of Model Court Cases from Old Babylonian Nippur."
19 For Hallo, this was an indicator of their pedagogical function ("Model Court Case," 150–151). For a similar argument, see Piotr Steinkeller's discussion of a model contract pertaining to the loss of a seal text ("Seal Practice in the Ur III Period," *Seals and Sealing in the Ancient Near East*, BibMes 6 (1977), ed. McGuire Gibson and Robert D. Biggs, 41–53, here, 49). As Samuel Greengus points out, however, functional marriage contracts were often drawn up because of abnormal circumstances, so the assumption that unusual features are indicative of school settings may be problematic ("The Old Babylonian Marriage Contract," *JAOS* 89.3 [1969]: 505–532, here, 512–513).
20 Greengus, "Textbook Case of Adultery in Ancient Mesopotamia."
21 See Jacobsen, "Ancient Mesopotamian Trial for Homicide," and Roth, "Gender and Law."
22 On the phenomenon, see Paul Delnero, "Sumerian Extract Tablets and Scribal Education," *JCS* 62 (2010): 53–69.

employed for the law collections, though not necessarily with the same aim of working up to a full manuscript. One extract of the Laws of Eshnunna and dozens of extracts from the Laws of Hammurabi have been discovered. The LH extracts date from the early second through the late first millennium B.C.E. These extracts vary in length, with some including only a handful of laws, in David Wright's estimation.[23] A related phenomenon is represented by two texts that Martha Roth dubbed "A Sumerian Laws Exercise Tablet" (SLEx) and the "Laws about Rented Oxen" (LOx).[24] SLEx has ten preserved laws, though the colophon indicates that this particular tablet originally included 190 lines. Both exercises include topics that appear in the law collections: a brawl-induced miscarriage, negligence regarding boats, failure to fulfill obligations as an adopter or adoptee, assault of an unengaged woman, and liabilities concerning rented oxen. What is legible of the unpublished obverse likewise pertains to legal situations that are elsewhere attested in the collections. It is important to note, however, that neither SLEx nor LOx can be called an "extract," as their contents do not overlap precisely with any attested section of codified law. Rather, they are more like mash-ups of "classic" legal quandaries. These exercises are thus similar in nature to the fragmentary set of seven cuneiform laws that was found at Hazor and dates to the Middle Bronze Age.[25] Like SLEx and LOx, "Hazor 18" includes similar content to that which appears in LH, but it is not a direct replica of any one section of that collection.[26] While the editors of this text propose that the two fragments that comprise Hazor 18 point toward the existence of an independent "Code of Hazor" akin

---

23 See Wright, *Inventing God's Law*, 118–120. These are to be distinguished from tablets that belong to a series, though it is difficult in some cases to determine the difference. The existence of a colophon aids in identifying it as part of a series, but this is not always preserved.
24 Roth, *Law Collections*, 40–45. While SLEx is known only from one copy, LOx is attested in a number of copies. In addition, LOx was copied on a tablet together with model contracts and in the appendix to the lexical series *ana ittišu*.
25 Wayne Horowitz, Takayoshi Oshima, and Filip Vukosavović, "Hazor 18: Fragments of a Cuneiform Law Collection from Hazor," *IEJ* 62 (2012): 158–176.
26 Thus while LH §§196–208 includes a series of laws involving compensation for injury to a free man, commoner, and slave, the laws in Hazor 18 consistently involve three parties: they deal with compensation for injury to a slave who has been hired by a free man from a slave owner. The closest parallel is LH §199, but that law does not reference a slave owner and only makes reference to injuries to an eye and bone. The sequence of body parts in Hazor 18 also differs from those preserved in LH and in the Laws of Eshnunna (Horowitz, Oshima, and Vukosavovic, "Hazor 18," 170–171).

to LH, I suggest instead that the fragments once belonged to a comparable legal exercise.[27]

1.4 Legal Phrasebooks and Collections of Contract Clauses

As Niek Veldhuis points out, two OB legal phrasebooks were standardized and attested after the OB period: the Sippar version and the Nippur version. While the Nippur version is less well attested, the Sippar version was added to the front of the thematic list Ura and was widely copied in scribal centers. Both phrasebooks include common words for loans, family members, types of fields, and other technical terms pertinent to contracts. The Sippar version also includes several model contracts in their entirety. Finds from other sites indicate that these were only two of a number of local versions of such phrasebooks.[28] A similar combination of phrases and model contracts is preserved in a text that Roth calls the Sumerian Laws Handbook of Forms (SLHF). This text features sample contractual clauses, some of which overlap with content in the model contracts, as well as a handful of laws (mostly pertaining to boating accidents) that overlap with laws from the collections.[29]

★ ★ ★

It is evident that this diverse legal-pedagogical content belonged to the same cultural matrix as actual legal documents and codified law. Thus, for example, model contracts and functional contracts from Nippur pertaining to manumission feature the same basic elements in sequence.[30] Clauses prohibiting a man's heirs from raising claims against the man's slave or her children appear in the model contracts and in LH §171. A clause in a slave-hire model contract that promises a reward to anyone who finds the slave if he/she escapes is echoed in the

---

27 Horowitz, Oshima, and Vukosavović dismiss this possibility because the signs are well written and the tablet is structured carefully, features that they interpret as the markings of an experienced scribe. Such features, however, could reflect the hand of an instructor, as is sometimes the case with the model contracts. As they note, a lexical text (Hazor 6) and a mathematical text (Hazor 9) were also found at the site, in addition to a smattering of other texts ("Hazor 18," 173).
28 Veldhuis, History of the Cuneiform Lexical Tradition, 188–190.
29 Roth, *Law Collections*, 46–54.
30 See Spada, *Sumerian Model Contracts*, 19. One difference is that the model contracts include the formula "PN mu-ni-im" ("named PN") while functional contracts do not.

Laws of Ur-Namma (LU) §16 and LH §17.[31] As Aaron Skaist notes, model contracts and functional contracts for barley loans include similar clauses that specify the location where the loan is to be repaid (most frequently, in both, the quay of a town).[32] Interest rates in barley and silver loan model contracts are formulated using similar clauses to those in the functional contracts. The same rates—20% for silver loans, 33% for barley or grain loans—occur in the model contracts, functional contracts, and the law collections.[33] The large number of precepts in LH that deal with the same topics as those of the contracts (e.g., field rentals, loans and interest rates, marriage, inheritance, rentals and hires) and include similar types of conditional clauses seem to suggest that Hammurabi's lawmakers were familiar with the content and format of contracts, whether model or functional.

In addition, as scholars have observed, the OB model cases appear to share parallels with certain laws from the same period. In the Nippur Homicide Trial, for example, the majority contingent claims that the widow, Nin-Dada, was having an affair with one of the assailants and arranged to have her husband killed. This argument is ultimately persuasive, and the judges conclude that she, too, should be executed. As Thorkild Jacobsen notes, a similar situation appears in LH §153: "If a man's wife has her husband killed on account of (her relationship with) another male, they shall impale that woman."[34] Samuel Greengus similarly observes that his "textbook adultery case" parallels LH §§141–143, in that both feature wives committing three crimes of appropriating goods, squandering household possessions, and being wayward.[35] Another model case dealing with adultery resembles LH §129.[36] Finally, the model case concerning the rape of a slave woman corresponds to LE §31, as noted by J. J. Finkelstein.[37] The question

---

31 LU §16 states that "if…a female slave escapes and crosses the township limits, and someone brings her back, the owner of the slave will pay two shekels of silver to the man who brought her back." See discussion in Miguel Civil, "The Law Collection of Ur-Namma," in *Cuneiform Royal Inscriptions and Related Texts in the Schøyen Collection*, ed. Andrew George, CUSAS 17 (Bethesda, MD: CDL Press, 2011), 221–286, here, 241.

32 Aaron Skaist, *The Old Babylonian Loan Contract: Its History and Geography* (Ramat Gan: Bar-Ilan University Press, 1994), 190–191; see also Spada, *Sumerian Model Contracts*, 43.

33 See discussion in Skaist, *Old Babylonian Loan Contract*, 106; and in Spada, *Sumerian Model Contracts*, 46 and 50–51.

34 Jacobsen, "Ancient Mesopotamian Trial for Homicide," 212–213.

35 Greengus, "Textbook Case of Adultery," 37–38.

36 In this text, the husband is said to have caught his wife "in the lap" of her lover; the king then puts both the woman and her lover to the stake (Raymond Westbrook, *Old Babylonian Marriage Law*, AfOB 23 [Horn: Verlag Ferdinand Berger & Söhne, 1988], 133).

37 J. J. Finkelstein, "Sex Offenses in Sumerian Laws," *JAOS* 86.4 (1966): 360.

remains as to how to explain these parallels, given that the content is largely contemporaneous. On the one hand, the notion that the model cases could have spawned these laws, as scholars initially proposed, aligns with the theory that cuneiform laws are rooted in specific cases that were generalized into law. On the other hand, the main criterion that was used to demonstrate that the model cases generated the laws—namely, that the cases referred to people who are known from earlier periods—has since been called into question.[38] In any case, what can be said is that the model cases share parallels in logic with codified law and appear to have played some role in Mesopotamian scribal education.

2 The Origins of Exodus 21–22 and Deuteronomy 19–25

The role of legal texts in Mesopotamian scribal education was thus twofold. There was both a practical side to this training, in that scribes acquired basic skills for drafting legal documents, and yet also an intellectual-cultural side, in that scribes copied selections of "classic" laws. Perhaps not coincidentally, this legal-pedagogical material flourished concurrently with the emergence of extensive law collections, especially LH. I suggest that knowledge of these legal-pedagogical genres and their links to law beyond the school setting is applicable to our reconstruction of the roots of Pentateuchal law.

2.1 The Search for Origins I: Israelite "Model Cases"

Among the miscellany of ethical precepts and cultic rules in Deuteronomy 19–25 is a group of casuistic laws that appear to have operated as a set. These include the two cases of manslaughter in Deut 19:4–13, the man with two wives and two sons in Deut 21:15–17, the rebellious son in Deut 21:18–21, the case and counter-case regarding the slandered bride in Deut 22:13–21, the adulterous couple in Deut 22:22, the assault series in Deut 22:23–29, the two-time divorcee in Deut 24:1–4, and the man who dies without a son (the "levirate law") in Deut 25:5–10.

---

[38] See discussion in Sara Milstein, "Making a Case: The Repurposing of 'Israelite Legal Fictions' as Deuteronomic Law," *Supplementation and the Study of the Hebrew Bible*; ed. Saul Olyan and Jacob Wright, BJS 361 (Providence: Brown Judaic Studies, 2017), 161–81, here, 167–168.

Scholars such as Eckart Otto, Carolyn Pressler, and Alexander Rofé have observed the shared themes and terminology across some of these laws and have suggested that they once belonged to an old collection of "family law."[39]

What is unusual about the biblical laws, however, is that most of them are stand-alone units: Deut 21:15–17, 21:18–21, 22:22, 24:1–4, and 25:5–10. This pattern is thus at odds with the standard format of Near Eastern law collections, i.e., laws are generally organized in clusters whereby a basic scenario is modified by one or more factors, resulting in different outcomes. Moreover, on the few occasions when these laws are presented in a pair or cluster (Deut 19:4–13; 22:13–21; and 22:23–29), one or more of the laws in the set is conspicuously marked by the death penalty for the perpetrators and formulaic language regarding "sweeping away" evil from the land, protocol and language that overlap with the apostasy laws in Deut 13:2–19 and 17:2–7.[40] Elsewhere, I have proposed that the laws featuring this harsh punishment and repetitive language reflect the work of post-Deuteronomic editors who put the traditional Near Eastern mode of lawmaking toward radically new ends.[41] Rather than use this method to cover as much legal ground as possible, they apparently used it to repackage old (private) legal conflicts as major threats to the cultic order. Upon excluding the laws with these themes and overt editorial language (Deut 19:11–13, 21:18–21, 22:20–21, 22:22, 22:23–24, 22:25–27), we are left with six independent or once-independent laws:

---

39 Rofé suggests that Middle Assyrian Laws Tablet A serves as an apt analogy to this "reconstructed [biblical] tractate," a collection that includes the texts cited above along with Exod 22:15–16, the seduction of the unengaged virgin; and Exod 21:22–25, the injury of a pregnant woman during a fight (*Deuteronomy: Issue and Interpretation*, 172). For Otto, the "Familienrechtsammlung" includes Deut 21:15–21aα; 22:13–21a.22a.23.24a.25.27.28f.; 24:1–4a; and 25:5–10 (*Das Deuteronomium*, 217). Along with the usual set, Carolyn Pressler includes the law pertaining to the captive bride in Deut 21:10–14 (*The View of Women Found in the Deuteronomic Family Laws*, BZAW 216 [Berlin: De Gruyter, 1993], 4, 9–10).

40 Specifically, Deut 19:11–13, 22:20–21, and 22:23–27. For discussion of the relationship between these laws and the apostate laws in Deuteronomy 13 and 17, see Milstein, "Making a Case," 172–175. I develop these arguments further in *Making a Case: The Practical Roots of Biblical Law* (New York: Oxford University Press, 2021).

41 See Milstein, "Making a Case," 175–177. This conclusion is somewhat in line with Otto's notion that the Dtr redactor supplemented pre-Dtr laws with reference to social responsibility and the purity of the people (see, e.g., "Soziale Verantwortung und Reinheit des Landes: Zur Redaktion der kasuistischen Rechtssatze in Deuteronomium 19–25," in *Kontinuum und Proprium: Studien zur Sozial- und Rechtsgeschichte des Alten Orients und des Alten Testaments*, OBC 8 [Wiesbaden: Harrassowitz, 1996], 123–138). Otto and I diverge, however, in what we take to be part of this pre-Dtr collection and with its general nature.

Deut 19:4–6*, 21:15–17, 22:13–19, 22:28–29, 24:1–4*, and 25:5–10.[42] It is notable
that these units do not parallel known cuneiform law and instead appear to be
native expressions of the Israelite legal mind. None of them, moreover, features
the death penalty; rather, most pertain to financial penalties or the reinstitution
of rights to vulnerable individuals. Several read more like legal narratives or
cases than "law" per se, with direct speech and literary flourishes, much like the
Sumerian model cases. Four of the texts feature the root ש.נ.א. ("to hate"), a term
that in legal contexts, Z. H. Szubin and Bezalel Porten claim refers to the demotion of someone without grounds.[43] Conversely, these texts focus on protecting
the rights of disenfranchised individuals: the son of the "hated" wife in Deut
21:15–17, for example, is entitled to his birthright; the "hated" bride can never be
divorced; and the widow in Deuteronomy 25 is entitled to produce an heir for her
late husband's property. Rather than take these as remnants of a family law collection, I suggest that this entire group is best understood as deriving from a set
of Israelite model cases that were utilized in scribal education.[44]

---

42 Regarding Deut 19:4–6*, while both cases of manslaughter (vv. 4–6 and 11–13) are now embedded in a discussion of the cities of refuge, the first case can easily be detached from that
context. This is suggested by the doubling of the relative clause in v. 4 (אֲשֶׁר־יָנוּס שָׁמָּה וָחָי וַאֲשֶׁר
יַכֶּה אֶת־רֵעֵהוּ בִּבְלִי־דַעַת), "who escapes there and lives, who strikes his friend unintentionally"
and by the doubling of the apodosis: the first deals with the killer's escape to one of the cities of
refuge, where he is protected from the wrath of the blood avenger, while the second is in the
form of a court ruling: he shall not get the death penalty because he was not this man's enemy
in the past. There is also an evident Wiederaufnahme in v. 7, echoing the language in v. 2. This
unit, moreover, is presented not as a law per se, but rather as a single paradigmatic case that
highlights the factor of intent: "This is the case of the killer who unintentionally slays his friend
. . . ." As noted by Zipora Talshir, the opening clause, וְזֶה דְּבַר הָרֹצֵחַ, is paralleled in five biblical
texts and also in the Shiloah Tunnel Inscription, where the account of the two sets of diggers
finally meeting one another—intriguingly, also with axes—is forever memorialized:
וזה.היה.דבר.הנקבה, "This was the story of the tunnel . . . " ("The Detailing Formula ... וזה
דבר(ה)," *Tarbiz* 51 (1981/2): 23–36 [Hebrew]). I thank Esti Eshel for drawing this article to my
attention. Regarding Deut 24:1–4*, I suggest that the last part of v. 4, with its concerns regarding
bringing "sin upon the land" (אַחֲרֵי אֲשֶׁר הֻטַּמָּאָה כִּי־תוֹעֵבָה הִוא לִפְנֵי יְהוָה וְלֹא תַחֲטִיא אֶת־הָאָרֶץ
אֲשֶׁר יְהוָה אֱלֹהֶיךָ נֹתֵן לְךָ נַחֲלָה:) is secondary.
43 Zvi Henri Szubin and Bezalel Porten, "The Status of a Repudiated Spouse: A New Interpretation of Kraeling 7 (*TAD* B3.8)," *ILR* 35 (2001): 46–78.
44 Indeed, Clemens Locher already recognized the parallels between Deut 22:13–19 and a Sumerian model case regarding a raped slave girl ("Deuteronomium 22, 13–21 vom Prozessprotokoll
zum kasuistichen Gesetz," in *Das Deuteronomium: Entstehung, Gestalt und Botschaft*, ed. Norbert
Lohfink, BETL 68 [Leuven: Leuven University Press, 1985], 298–303); see also idem, *Die Ehre
einer Frau in Israel: Exegetische und rechtsvergleichende Studien zu Deuteronomium 22,13–21,*

2.2 The Search for Origins II: Israelite (Model) Contracts

Although we do not have access to actual Israelite contracts, three biblical laws (Deut 21:15–17, Deut 25:5–10, and Exod 21:7–11) share considerable content, format, and terminology with extant Near Eastern contracts, suggesting that they might have their roots either in analogous practical documents or in lists of standard contract clauses. I shall examine one of these in detail: Deut 25:5–10.[45]

Deuteronomy 25:5–10 states that in the instance that a man dies without an heir, the man's brother should marry and impregnate his brother's widow and produce a child who can inherit his brother's land.[46] What has not been recognized is that the law bears strong resemblances to wills from the 14th–12th century B.C.E. Hittite vassal city of Emar (modern-day Meskene, Syria, on the Euphrates River). Emar is a particularly rich site for legal history, with two-thirds of its 700+ published cuneiform tablets pertaining to legal matters.[47] Among these documents are nearly 50 wills. Legal documents at Emar exhibit two radically distinct formats, what Daniel Arnaud first dubbed "Syrian" and "Syro-Hittite," and what Sophie Démare-Lafont and Daniel Fleming have more recently distinguished as "Conventional Format" and "Free Format."[48] The "Conventional Format" wills open with the formulaic statement that "on this day" (*ištu ūmi annîm*), PN₁, son of PN₂, "while of sound body" (*ina balṭūti/bulṭūtīšu*), "caused his 'brothers' to be seated (*ahhīšu ušēšibma*). He decided the fate of the house (and) of his

PN₁

OBO 70 (Freiburg, Switzerland: Universitätsverlag; Göttingen: Vandenhoeck & Ruprecht, 1986), esp. 93–101.

45 The section that follows is developed in more detail in "Will and (Old) Testament: Reconsidering the Roots of Deuteronomy 25,5–10," in *Writing, Rewriting and Overwriting in the Books of Deuteronomy and the Former Prophets*, ed. Thomas Römer, Ido Koch, and Omer Sergi, BETL 304 (Leuven: Peeters, 2019), 49–63.

46 While the MT features the term "son" (בן), the LXX has the more generic "seed" (σπέρμα).

47 Sophie Démare-Lafont, "Éléments pour une diplomatique juridique des textes d'Émar," in *Trois millénaires de formulaires juridiques*, ed. Sophie Démare-Lafont and André Lemaire, Hautes Études Orientales – Moyen et Proche-Orient 48 (Genève: Librairie Droz S.A., 2010), 43–84, here, 43.

48 Daniel Arnaud, "Catalogue des textes cunéiformes trouvés au cours des trois premières campagnes à Meskéné-Qadimé Ouest," *AAAS* 25 (1975): 87–93; Sophie Démare-Lafont and Daniel Fleming, "Ad Hoc Administration and Archiving at Emar: Free Format and Free Composition in the Diviner's Text Collection," in *AuOr* 36.1 (2018): 29–63 and idem, "Emar Chronology and Scribal Streams: Cosmopolitanism and Legal Diversity," *RA* 109 (2015): 45–77. "Conventional Format" tablets, as the name implies, are more conservative in formulation and display links to older Babylonian practice, while "Free Format" tablets are marked by innovations in script, shape, and layout.

sons. He spoke as follows . . . " (*šīmti bītīšu mārīšu išīm kīam iqbi*).[49] The testator then specifies what he bequeaths to his wife and children, with larger portions typically allotted to the firstborn male. The children are often entreated to support their widowed mother until her death.[50] The wills also commonly include a range of conditional clauses. As much as they offer protection to widows, they also impose restrictions on their legal rights, evidently as a means of keeping the property in the family. In one instance, the testator states, "If my wife Abnu should go after a strange man, she shall place her garment on the stool and go where she pleases."[51] Similar concerns regarding a wife giving goods to "an outsider" (*nakru*) or to a daughter marrying outside the family are elsewhere attested.[52] In RE 23, a man makes alternative arrangements for inheritance, should his son(s) and/or wife die without bearing sons.[53] In *Emar VI* 185, the testator stipulates that if his son becomes a widower, he must remarry and cannot leave the house.[54] In over twenty cases, the man protects his wives and daughters by pronouncing them "mother and father," "male and female," or in one case, "the

---

49 See, e.g., Daniel Arnaud, *Recherches au pays d'Aštata, Emar VI/3: Textes sumériens et accadiens,* OBO 20 (Paris: Éditions Recherche sur les Civilisations, 1985); henceforth *Emar VI*), 176, 180 (p. 193), 183 (p. 196), 188 (p. 202), and 189 (p. 202). The ubiquitous reference to "brothers sitting" is also featured in one Emar marriage contract and a division of property document (Gary Beckman, *Texts from the Vicinity of Emar in the Collection of Jonathan Rosen,* HANE/M II [Padova: Sargon srl, 1996], 80 and 118). My references to texts within these two collections follow their transliterations/translations. As Démare-Lafont notes, the "brothers" refers not to the testator's own brothers but to a collective entity, as indicated by the expression LÚ-MEŠ which precedes it. In Munbāqa (ancient city of Ekalte, north of Emar), the "Brothers" have a seal and intervene in private contexts, as at Emar ("Éléments," 54).
50 Josué Justel, "Women and Family in the Legal Documentation of Emar (with Additional Data from Other Late Bronze Age Syrian Archives)," *KASKAL* 11 (2014): 57–84, here, 65.
51 Beckman, *Texts from the Vicinity of Emar,* 13–15 (RE 8). The "garment clause" is widely attested throughout the wills and other practical legal documents.
52 For the former, see Beckman, *Texts from the Vicinity of Emar,* 27–28; for the latter, see Arnaud, *Emar VI,* 176, 188–189. In addition to *nakru,* the West Semitic term *ṣarrāru* occurs in nine documents at Emar and two at Ekalte. The Northwest Semitic term *sarru* is also attested (Justel, "Women and Family in the Legal Documentation of Emar," 66). The term *za-ra-ri* (as in Beckman, *Texts from the Vicinity of Emar,* 14) or *sa-ar-ra* (as in Arnaud, *Emar VI,* 188) is typically translated as "strange" or "stranger," though some translate "criminal," reading *sarrāru* as opposed to *zâru* (Marten Stol, *Women in the Ancient Near East,* trans. Helen and Mervyn Richardson [Boston/Berlin, Walter de Gruyter, 2016], 289, n. 85). See RE 8 and *Emar VI* 176, where serious repercussions are pledged for the wife who marries "a strange man."
53 Beckman, Texts from the Vicinity of Emar, 39–40.
54 Arnaud, *Emar VI,* 185, 197–198.

male son," legal fictions that granted them full capacity to manage the inheritance.[55] In RE 15, curses are sworn against whoever contests the agreement; other wills prohibit claims against the outlined stipulations.[56]

Like the wills from Emar, Deut 25:5–10 is concerned with the fate of a man's wife and property after her husband has predeceased her. As in the Emarite wills, there are blatant exogamic restrictions: the man's wife is not permitted to marry someone from "outside, a stranger" (לֹא־תִהְיֶה אֵשֶׁת־הַמֵּת הַחוּצָה לְאִישׁ זָר). Both the biblical text and the wills evidently have the same interest: to restrict the wife's legal rights in order to keep the property in the family.[57] At the same time, the very act of restriction implies that the woman has the right to remain on the property. This is further suggested by the woman's designation: she is not a widow (אַלְמָנָה) but rather "the wife of the dead man" (אֵשֶׁת־הַמֵּת), a distinction that appears in other Near Eastern contexts and was apparently used to indicate a woman who still had rights to her dead husband's property.[58] In addition, although the Emarite wills do not prescribe levirate marriage per se, it is notable that in one instance, a man likewise entreats his wife to give her possessions to "whomever supports her among her deceased husband's brothers."[59]

The brother-in-law's refusal to fulfill his obligations and the consequences of this refusal also share parallels with Emarite wills. The inclusion of clauses that stipulate penalties for parties who refuse to fulfill their obligations is a preeminent feature of all sorts of Emarite legal documents, including wills, adoptions, and marriage contracts. As in Deut 25:8, where the man states, "I do not wish to

───────

55 See, e.g., RE 15: "Now my wife Dagan-ni is father and mother of my household . . .. Now I have [in]stalled my two [daughters] Abī-namī and Išarte in female and [male] status" (Beckman, *Texts from the Vicinity of Emar*, 27). See also RE 28 and RE 85 (ibid., 47 and 107–108) and Arnaud, *Emar VI*, 185 (pp. 197–198); for discussion, see Raymond Westbrook, "Social Justice and Creative Jurisprudence in Late Bronze Age Syria," in *Law from the Tigris to the Tiber: The Writings of Raymond Westbrook: Cuneiform and Biblical Sources*, vol. 2, ed. Bruce Wells and F. Rachel Magdalene (Winona Lake, IN, Eisenbrauns, 2009), 101–125, here, 123–124. This type of "gender transformation" is also attested at Nuzi and in Old Assyrian documents (Démare-Lafont, "Éléments," 55).

56 Beckman, Texts from the Vicinity of Emar, 28.

57 The notion of marrying outside the family is also attested in Judg 12:9, where Ibzan of Bethlehem is said to have married off thirty daughters "outside" (הַחוּצָה) and to have brought in thirty women "from the outside" (מִן־הַחוּץ) to marry his sons.

58 See David Owen, "Widows' Rights in Ur III Sumer," *ZA* 70 (1980): 170–184.

59 Beckman, *Texts from the Vicinity of Emar*, RE 15 (p. 28). For Jack Lundbom, ". . . the Babylonians and Assyrians attained the same end (as levirate marriage) by legitimating children of slave-wives and concubines and by adoption; therefore, they had no need of a levirate marriage" (*Deuteronomy: A Commentary* [Grand Rapids, MI: Eerdmans, 2013], 706).

marry her" (לֹא חֲפֵצְתִּי לְקַחְתָּהּ), the refusals in the Emar contracts are stated as oral formulae that presumably would have been uttered before witnesses: "If PN says, 'You are not my father/mother,' 'You are not my son,'[60] 'You are not my brothers,'[61] 'I will not honor you . . ..'" These anticipated rejections, moreover, are followed by penalties: typically, the person's loss of his/her inheritance (or dowry). The penalty for the negligent brother-in-law, who is to be known thereafter as "'The house of the one whose sandal was removed,'" may have had similar financial implications.

2.3 The Search for Origins III: Extracts and Legal Exercises

I close with brief attention to the much-debated origins of the Covenant Code. David Wright has advanced a painstaking argument that all of Exod 20:23–23:19 is directly dependent on LH (with some additional sources).[62] The vast majority of scholars, however, wholly reject the model of direct dependence.[63] How could such extreme positions have developed? To my mind, the reason is that certain laws, such as the goring ox series, are strikingly similar to known cuneiform law. Others, including Exod 21:33–34, 22:5, 22:9–12, have no precise parallel in the cuneiform collections. Moreover, while certain laws in Exodus parallel precepts in LH, others are closer in content to those in other collections, such as the Laws of Eshnunna (LE). This is all in addition to the fact that the apodictic sections in Exod 21:12–17 and 22:18–24 share far less explicit overlap with cuneiform precepts.

Much of this discussion, however, has either assumed or denied the Israelites' knowledge of LH. It is possible, however, that a legal exercise would better account for the contents of Exod 21:18–22:16 in particular. It is first notable that the laws in this core casuistic section cover only two major topics: physical damages to a person or animal (one man strikes another in a fight; a man strikes his slave; men fight and cause a miscarriage; a man injures his slave; an ox gores a person; an ox gores another ox; a thief is beaten to death) and property damages (damage via livestock, fire, and theft; a man borrows an animal and it dies; a man's daughter is violated). These laws overlap most closely with LH §206 (Exod 21:18–19); LH §§207–208/HL §2 (Exod 21:20–21), LH §§209–210, with echoes of

---

60 See, e.g., RE 25 and RE 28 in Beckman, *Texts from the Vicinity of Emar*, 42–43 and 46–47.
61 Arnaud, *Emar VI*, 181.
62 Wright, *Inventing God's Law*.
63 See literature review in Wright, *Inventing God's Law*, 16–24.

§§197–205 (Exod 21:22–25); LH §201 & §199 (Exod 21:26–27); LE §§54–55/LH §§250–252 (Exod 21:28–32); LE §53 (Exod 21:35–36); LH §8 (Exod 21:37); LE §§12–13//LH §22 (Exod 22:1); LH §§57, 53–55 (Exod 22:4); LE §§36–37/LH §§124–126 (Exod 22:6–8); LH §§244–249 (Exod 22:13–14); and LH §130/LE §26/MAL A §55 (Exod 22:15–16). How to explain this non-linear hodgepodge? Rather than presume that the Israelite scribes responsible for this unit had access to all of LH, it seems more plausible that they had access to a "Laws on Damages" exercise that shared content and terminology with known cuneiform law yet also included some variations. In turn, the Israelites would have produced their own version of this legal exercise and then framed it mainly with apodictic laws that were marked by four innovative features: Yahweh's first-person voice/the second-person address to the Israelites, a standard death penalty formula, a concern with ethics, and cultic regulations.[64] It is notable that these four features are also prominent in the editorial additions to the posited "model cases" in Deuteronomy.

3 Conclusion

My aim in showcasing the diverse legal-pedagogical texts that were produced in OB scribal schools is not to suggest that the Israelites had knowledge of this content or that versions of all of these genres were developed by Israelite scribes. There is no evidence, for example, that the Israelites developed legal phrasebooks, and the specific obligation of OB scribes to learn Sumerian was obviously particular to Mesopotamia. At the same time, the Mesopotamian evidence gives us a sense as to the legal-pedagogical content that was actually attested in the ancient Near East. It gives us a starting point, a blueprint, a model for what might have been. The notion that legal texts played some sort of role in Israelite scribal education is indeed plausible, given both the practical need for scribes to draft legal documents and perhaps also the very existence of law in the Bible itself. While it does seem that the Israelites had access to some selection of Mesopotamian law, it is important to note that not all of biblical law was borrowed or adapted. In fact, some of the most detailed and most colorful laws in the Bible—such as the two-time divorcee in Deut 24:1–4, the levirate law in Deut 25:5–10, or

---

64 On the second-person address, see William Morrow, "A Generic Discrepancy in the Covenant Code," *Theory and Method in Biblical and Cuneiform Law: Revision, Interpolation, and Development*, ed. Bernard Levinson, reprint (Sheffield: Sheffield Phoenix Press, 2006), 134–149.

the slandered bride in Deut 22:13–19—have no parallel to cuneiform precepts. Moreover, the Israelites' application of the law collection genre to ethical situations and cultic regulations, as in both Exodus and Deuteronomy, is largely unprecedented in the ancient Near East. The notion of "religious law," something that is now taken as a given, is arguably the most distinctive legacy of the ancient Israelites. Ironically, however, it was this innovation that allowed for the preservation of old legal school texts that otherwise might have remained forever lost.

4 Bibliography

Arnaud, Daniel. "Catalogue des textes cunéiformes trouvés au cours des trois premières campagnes à Meskéné-Qadimé Ouest." *AAAS* 25 (1975): 87–93.

Arnaud, Daniel. *Recherches au pays d'Aštata, Emar VI/3: Textes sumériens et accadiens*. OBO 20. Paris: Éditions Recherche sur les Civilisations, 1986.

Beckman, Gary. *Texts from the Vicinity of Emar in the Collection of Jonathan Rosen*. HANE/M II. Padova: Sargon srl, 1996.

Bodine, Walter. *How Mesopotamian Scribes Learned to Write Legal Documents: A Study of the Sumerian Model Contracts in the Babylonian Collection at Yale University*. Lewiston, NY: Edwin Mellen Press, 2014.

Bottéro, Jean. "The 'Code' of Hammurabi." Pages 156–84 in *Mesopotamia: Writing, Reasoning, and the Gods*. Translated by Zainab Bahrani and Marc van de Mieroop. Chicago: University of Chicago Press, 1992.

Carr, David. *Writing on the Tablet of the Heart: Origins of Scripture and Literature*. New York: Oxford University Press, 2005.

Charpin, Dominique. *Hammurabi of Babylon*. London: I.B. Tauris, 2012.

Civil, Miguel. "Ancient Mesopotamian Lexicography." Pages 2305–14 in *Civilizations of the Ancient Near East*, vol. 4. Edited by Jack Sasson. New York: Charles Scribner's Sons, 1995.

Civil, Miguel. *Ea A = nâqu, Aa A = nâqu, with Their Forerunners and Related Texts*. Edited by Miguel Civil, with the collaboration of Wilfred G. Lambert and Margaret W. Green. MSL 14. Rome: Pontificium Institutum Biblicum, 1979.

Civil, Miguel. "From the Epistolary of the Edubba." Pages 105–18 in *Wisdom, Gods, and Literature: Studies in Assyriology in Honour of W.G. Lambert*. Edited by Andrew R. George and Irving L. Finkel. Winona Lake, IN: Eisenbrauns, 2000.

Civil, Miguel. "The Law Collection of Ur-Namma." Pages 221–86 in *Cuneiform Royal Inscriptions and Related Texts in the Schøyen Collection*. Edited by Andrew R. George. CUSAS 17. Bethesda, MD: CDL Press, 2011.

Civil, Miguel. "Old Babylonian Proto-Lu: Types of Sources." Pages 24–73 in *The Series lú = ša and Related Texts*. Edited by Miguel Civil and Erica Reiner. MSL 12. Rome: Pontificium Institutum Biblicum, 1969.

Delnero, Paul. "Sumerian Extract Tablets and Scribal Education," *JCS* 62 (2010): 53–69.

Delnero, Paul. *The Textual Criticism of Sumerian Literature*. JCSSS 3. Boston: American Schools of Oriental Research, 2012.

Démare-Lafont, Sophie. "Éléments pour une diplomatique juridique des textes d'Émar." Pages 43–84 in *Trois millénaires de formulaires juridiques*. Edited by Sophie Démare-Lafont and André Lemaire. Hautes Etudes Orientales - Moyen et Proche-Orient 48. Geneva: Librairie Droz, 2010.

Démare-Lafont, Sophie, and Daniel Fleming. "Ad Hoc Administration and Archiving at Emar: Free Format and Free Composition in the Diviner's Text Collection." *AuOr* 36.1 (2018): 29–63.

Démare-Lafont, Sophie, and Daniel Fleming. "Emar Chronology and Scribal Streams: Cosmopolitanism and Legal Diversity." *RA* 109 (2015): 45–77.

Finkelstein, J. J. "Sex Offenses in Sumerian Laws." *JAOS* 86.4 (1966): 355–72.

Greengus, Samuel. "The Old Babylonian Marriage Contract." *JAOS* 89.3 (1969): 505–32.

Greengus, Samuel. "A Textbook Case of Adultery in Ancient Mesopotamia." *HUCA* 40–41 (1969–70): 33–44.

Hallo, William H. "A Model Court Case Concerning Inheritance." Pages 141–54 in *Riches Hidden in Secret Places: Ancient Near Eastern Studies in Memory of Thorkild Jacobsen*. Edited by Tzvi Abusch. Winona Lake, IN: Eisenbrauns, 2002.

Horowitz, Wayne, Takayoshi Oshima, and Filip Vukosavović. "Hazor 18: Fragments of a Cuneiform Law Collection from Hazor." *IEJ* 62.2 (2012): 158–176.

Jacobsen, Thorkild. "An Ancient Mesopotamian Trial for Homicide." Pages 193–215 in *Toward the Image of Tammuz and Other Essays on Mesopotamian History and Culture*. Edited by William Moran. HSS 21. Cambridge, MA: Harvard University Press, 2014.

Justel, Josué. "Women and Family in the Legal Documentation of Emar (with Additional Data from Other Late Bronze Age Syrian Archives." *KASKAL* 11 (2014): 57–84.

Klein Jacob, and Tonia M. Sharlach. "A Collection of Model Court Cases from Old Babylonian Nippur (CBS 11324)." *ZA* 97.1 (2007): 1–25.

Kleinerman, Alexandra. *Education in Early 2nd Millennium BC Babylonia: The Sumerian Epistolary Miscellany*. CM 42. Leiden: Brill, 2011.

Levinson, Bernard. *Deuteronomy and the Hermeneutics of Legal Innovation*. New York: Oxford University Press, 1997.

Lieberman, Stephen. "Nippur: City of Decisions." Pages 127–36 in *Nippur at the Centennial: Papers Read at the 35e Rencontre Assyriologique Internationale, Philadelphia 1988*. Edited by Maria de Jong Ellis. Occasional Publications of the Samuel Noah Kramer Fund. Philadelphia: University Museum, 1992.

Locher, Clemens. "Deuteronomium 22, 13–21 vom Prozessprotokol zum kasuistichen Gesetz." Pages 298–303 in *Das Deuteronomium: Entstehung, Gestalt und Botschaft*. Edited by Norbert Lohfink. BETL 68. Leuven: Leuven University Press, 1985.

Locher, Clemens. *Die Ehre einer Frau in Israel: Exegetische und rechtsvergleichende Studien zu Deuteronomium 22,13–21*. OBO 70. Freiburg, Switzerland: Universitätsverlag; Göttingen: Vandenhoeck & Ruprecht, 1986.

Lundbom, Jack. *Deuteronomy: A Commentary*. Grand Rapids, MI: Eerdmans, 2013.

Milstein, Sara. *Making a Case: The Practical Roots of Biblical Law* (New York: Oxford University Press, 2021).

Milstein, Sara. "Making a Case: The Repurposing of 'Israelite Legal Fictions' as Deuteronomic Law." Pages 161–81 in *Supplementation and the Study of the Hebrew Bible*. Edited by Saul Olyan and Jacob Wright. BJS 361. Providence: Brown Judaic Studies, 2017.

Milstein, Sara. "Will and (Old) Testament: Reconsidering the Roots of Deuteronomy 25,5–10." Pages 49–63 in *Writing, Rewriting, and Overwriting in the Books of Deuteronomy and the Former Prophets.* Edited by Thomas Römer, Ido Koch, and Omer Sergi. BETL 304. Leuven: Peeters, 2019.

Morrow, William. "A Generic Discrepancy in the Covenant Code." Pages 134–49 in *Theory and Method in Biblical and Cuneiform Law: Revision, Interpolation, and Development.* Edited by Bernard M. Levinson. Reprint. Sheffield: Sheffield Phoenix Press, 2006.

Otto, Eckart. *Das Deuteronomium: Politische Theologie und Rechtsreform in Juda und Assyrien.* BZAW 284. Berlin: De Gruyter, 1999.

Otto, Eckart. *Kontinuum und Proprium: Studien zur Sozial- und Rechtsgeschichte des Alten Orients und des Alten Testaments.* OBC 8. Wiesbaden: Harrassowitz, 1996.

Otto, Eckart. "Town and Rural Countryside in Ancient Israelite Law: Reception and Redaction in Cuneiform and Israelite Law." *JSOT* 57 (1993): 3–22.

Owen, David. "Widows' Rights in Ur III Sumer." *ZA* 70.2 (1980): 170–84.

Pearce, Laurie E. "The Scribes and Scholars of Ancient Mesopotamia." Pages 2265–78 in *Civilizations of the Ancient Near East*, vol. 4. Edited by Jack Sasson. New York: Charles Scribner's Sons, 1995.

Pressler, Carolyn. *The View of Women Found in the Deuteronomic Family Laws.* BZAW 216. Berlin: De Gruyter, 1993.

Proust, Christine. *Tablettes mathématiques de Nippur: Première partie: reconstitution du cursus scolaire. Deuxième partie: édition des tablettes conservées à Istanbul. Varia Anatolica* 18. Istanbul: Institut Français d'Études Anatoliennes-Georges Dumézil, 2007.

Proust, Christine. *Tablettes mathématiques paléo-babyloniennes de la collection Hilprecht.* Wiesbaden: Harrassowitz, 2008.

Rofé, Alexander. *Deuteronomy: Issues and Interpretation.* OTS. London: T&T Clark, 2002.

Robson, Eleanor. *Mathematics in Ancient Iraq: A Social History.* Princeton: Princeton University Press, 2008.

Robson, Eleanor. "The Tablet House: A Scribal School in Old Babylonian Nippur." *RA* 95.1 (2001): 39–66.

Roth, Martha T. "Gender and Law: A Case Study from Ancient Mesopotamia." Pages 173–84 in *Gender and Law in the Hebrew Bible and the Ancient Near East.* Edited by Bernard Levinson, Tikva Frymer-Kensky, and Victor H. Matthews. JSOTSup 262. Sheffield: Sheffield Academic Press, 1998.

Roth, Martha T. *Law Collections from Mesopotamia and Asia Minor.* 2nd ed. WAW 6. Atlanta: SBL Press, 1997.

Schniedewind, William. *The Finger of the Scribe: How Scribes Learned to Write the Bible.* New York: Oxford University Press, 2019.

Skaist, Aaron. *The Old Babylonian Loan Contract: Its History and Geography.* Bar-Ilan Studies in Near Eastern Languages and Culture. Ramat Gan: Bar-Ilan University Press, 1994.

Spada, Gabriella. "I modelli di contratto nell'edubba paleo-babilonese: un esempio di contratto di adozione." *AION* 72 (2012): 133–148.

Spada, Gabriella. *Sumerian Model Contracts from the Old Babylonian Period in the Hilprecht Collection Jena.* Texte und Materialien der Frau Professor Hilprecht-Collection of Babylonian Antiquities im Eigentum der Friedrich-Schiller-Universität Jena XI. Wiesbaden: Harrassowitz, 2018.

Spada, Gabriella. "Two Old Babylonian Model Contracts." *CDLJ* 2 (2014): 1–13.

Steinkeller, Piotr. "Seal Practice in the Ur III Period." Pages 41–53 in *Seals and Sealing in the Ancient Near East.* Edited by McGuire Gibson and Robert D. Biggs. BibMes 6. Malibu: Undena, 1977.

Stol, Marten. *Women in the Ancient Near East*. Translated by Helen and Mervyn Richardson. Boston/Berlin: Walter de Gruyter, 2016.

Szubin, Zvi Henri, and Bezalel Porten. "The Status of a Repudiated Spouse: A New Interpretation of Kraeling 7 (*TAD* B3.8)." *ILR* 35.1 (2001): 46–78.

Talshir, Zipora. "The Detailing Formula … דבר(ה) וזה," *Tarbiz* 51 (1981–82): 23–36 (Hebrew).

Tinney, Steve. "On the Curricular Setting of Sumerian Literature." *Iraq* 61 (1999): 159–72.

Tinney, Steve. "Texts, Tablets, and Teaching: Scribal Education in Nippur and Ur." *Expedition* 40 (1998): 40–50.

Toorn, Karel van der. *Scribal Culture and the Making of the Hebrew Bible*. Cambridge, MA: Harvard University Press, 2009.

Veldhuis, Niek. "Elementary Education at Nippur: The Lists of Trees and Wooden Objects." PhD diss., Rijksuniversiteit Groningen, 1997.

Veldhuis, Niek. *History of the Cuneiform Lexical Tradition*. GMTR 6. Münster: Ugarit Verlag, 2014.

Westbrook, Raymond. "Biblical and Cuneiform Codes." Pages 3–20 in *Law from the Tigris to the Tiber: The Writings of Raymond Westbrook*, vol. 1, *The Shared Tradition*. Edited by Bruce Wells and F. Rachel Magdalene. Winona Lake, IN: Eisenbrauns, 2009.

Westbrook, Raymond. *Old Babylonian Marriage Law*. AfOB 23. Horn: Verlag Ferdinand Berger & Söhne, 1988.

Westbrook, Raymond. "Social Justice and Creative Jurisprudence in Late Bronze Age Syria." Pages 101–26 in *Law from the Tigris to the Tiber: The Writings of Raymond Westbrook, vol. 2, Cuneiform and Biblical Sources*. Edited by Bruce Wells and F. Rachel Magdalene. Winona Lake, IN, Eisenbrauns, 2009.

Wright, David P. *Inventing God's Law: How the Covenant Code of the Bible Used and Revised the Laws of Hammurabi*. New York: Oxford University Press, 2009.

Aaron Demsky

Cursing an Authority: Scribal Tradition from Babylonia to Canaan and Back

Scribal schools where writing, editing, translating and preserving literary culture flourished, existed in the Ancient Near East during the second millennium BCE. Once Mesopotamian influence on writing waned in the Late Bronze Age, with the decline of the hegemony of the Hittite and Egyptian empires, their Canaanite cultural heirs developed centers of writing, primarily on the Phoenician coast. It is no coincidence that the earliest known royal inscriptions written in linear alphabetic script were discovered in Byblos.[1] Phoenicia suffered less than other areas from incursions by new tribes, like the marauding Sea Peoples. Moreover, Canaanite scribes, as we find in the written artifacts excavated at Hazor, Megiddo, Apheq and other sites, in addition to the el-Amarna archive, were educated in the ancient literary tradition associated with Mesopotamian scribal culture.[2] Thus, with the rapid development of the alphabetic script in the late second millennium, it was only natural that these centers became foci for the fusion of local and foreign literary traditions and genres. In this paper, I would like to illustrate Mesopotamian influence on Canaanite scribes which reflects on formal scribal education and attests to the flexibility of the recipients to transcend languages, writing systems, and literary functions.

A criterion for discerning literary borrowing would be to identify a composition which has undergone "a process of fixation," i.e., a set order of its components. A literary composition of this kind can be identified by the nature of its internal organization, even when it is a translation. Furthermore, if this literary

---

1 There was another enigmatic non-alphabetic script created by local scribes: see Benjamin Sass, "The Pseudo-Hieroglyphic Inscriptions from Byblos, Their Elusive Dating, and Their Affinities with the Early Phoenician Inscriptions," in Philippe Abrahami et Laura Battini (eds), *Ina dmarri u qan ṭuppi. Par la bêche et le stylet ! Cultures et sociétés syro-mésopotamiennes Mélanges offerts à Olivier Rouault* (Summertime, Oxford, 2019), pp. 157–180. While I agree with Sass that there is an overlapping between these two contemporary writing traditions, I still maintain the earlier chronology of the 10th – early 9th centuries for the Byblian alphabetic monumental inscriptions.
2 W. Horowitz, T. Oshima, S. Sanders, *Cuneiform Sources from the Land of Israel in Ancient Times* (Jerusalem, 2006); Yoram Cohen, "Cuneiform Writing in Bronze Age Canaan," A. Yasur-Landau, E. H. Cline and Y. M. Rowan (eds), *The Social Archaeology of the Levant: From Prehistory to Present* (Cambridge, Cambridge University Press, 2019), pp. 245–264. See also Zippora Cochavi-Rainey, *To the King My Lord - Letters from El-Amarna, Kumidi, Taanach and Other Letters from the Fourteenth Century BCE* (Jerusalem, 2005) (Hebrew).

unit would be detached from the broader literary work in which it is embedded, it could be reused and would have greater circulation and influence than the "home" text. The assumption that borrowing has taken place will gain plausibility if textual problems in the translated text could be explained by going back to the original primary text.

Curse formula is a literary genre which can be examined by using this method. In the pagan world, curses were associated with specific gods who might be mentioned by name. Even in a text that does not mention them, curses may be arranged according to the deity's seniority in the pantheon. This order reflects scribal education and knowledge which included learning lists of the gods[3] and knowing their mythology. A fixed series of curses may serve as a model of scribal borrowing in the Ancient Near East, especially since it is not limited to any specific type of text. In fact, such ordered curse formulae are found in monumental display and burial inscriptions, in codices, on boundary stones, and in treaties. Interestingly, this genre generally outlasted the specific document in which it was originally embedded.

1 Ahiram Inscription[4]

The curse formula on the Ahiram inscription illuminates the process of transmission of the scribal tradition and work method.[5] In 1924, the inscription, replete with errors, was discovered chiseled on the side of the lid of the sarcophagus of Ahiram king of Byblos (circa 1000 BCE). According to the dedication, Ahiram was

---

3 For the centrality of lists, specifically in scribal literacy, see Jack Goody, *The Domestication of the Savage Mind* (Cambridge, 1977), pp. 74–111.

4 P. Kyle McCarter, "The Sarcophagus Inscription of 'Ahirom King of Byblos," W.W. Hallo and K. Lawson Younger Jr (eds), *The Context of Scripture* vol 2 (Leiden, Brill, 2000), p.181; Marilyn J. Lundberg, "Editor's Notes: The Ahiram Inscription," *Maarav* 11.1 (2004), pp. 81–93; Cf. www.inscriptifact.com; Reinhard. G. Lehmann *Die Inschrift(en) des Ahirom-Sarkophags und die Schachtinschrift des Grabes V in Jbeil (Byblos)*, (Mainz, Zabern, 2005); idem, "Calligraphy and Craftsmanship in the Ahirom Inscription: Considerations on Skilled Linear Flat Writing in Early First Millennium Byblos," *Maarav* 15.2, (2008), pp.119–164, 217–222.

5 See my earlier studies: "The Cultural Continuum of a Canaanite Curse," *Leshonenu* 34 (1970), pp. 185–186 (Hebrew); "Mesopotamian and Canaanite Literary Traditions in the Ahiram Curse Formula," *Eretz Israel* 14 (H.L. Ginsberg Volume) 1978, pp. 7–11 (Hebrew); English summary, p. 122*.

placed in this impressive sarcophagus by his son Ittoba'al.[6] Art historians deliberated about whether an earlier sarcophagus was reused for Ahiram which implies that the inscription is later than the coffin or whether the sarcophagus and the inscription are contemporary.[7] Because of the lacunae in the stone, especially at the end of the second line on the lid, where the letters were incised cognizant of the chipped surface, I assume that it was a secondary burial. The funerary inscription, with my suggested readings inserted, begins with a dedication providing the historic context of the burial, and then concludes with the curse formula addressing three holders of high office, who are liable to disturb the repose of the deceased. The address formula is followed by a series of four curses:

ואל מלך במלכם וסכן בס<כ>נם ותמא מחנת עלי<על> גבל ויגל ארן זן
תחתסף חטר משפטה
תהתפך כסא מלכה
ונחת תברח על גבל
והא ימח ספרה לפ[ן] <קד<ש> <ג<בל

If there be a king among kings, *or* a governor among go<ver>nors, *or* an army *officer* who rises up <against > Byblos, and who shall uncover this coffin,

Let his judicial staff be broken!
Let his royal throne be turned over!
May peace flee from Byblos!
And for him, may his inscription[8] be erased *before <the holy ones> of Byblos!*[9]

In the nineteen-thirties, H. L. Ginsberg[10] noted that the Phoenician scribe quoted from a longer version of the first two curses, known from the Ugaritic Ba'al myth:

---

6 This reading has been challenged by Lehmann who completes the name as פלסבעל, "Wer war Aḥīrōms Sohn (KAI 1:1)? Eine kalligraphisch-prosopographische Annäherung an eine epigraphisch offene Frage," in V. Golinets, H. Jenni, H.-P. Mathys and S. Sarasin (eds.), *Neue Beiträge zur Semitistik. Fünftes Treffen der Arbeitsgemeinschaft Semitistik in der Deutschen Morgenländischen Gesellschaft vom 15.–17. Februar 2012 an der Universität Basel* (AOAT 425, Münster, Ugarit-Verlag, 2015), pp. 163–180.

7 Henri Frankfort, *The Art and Architecture of the Ancient Orient* (Harmondsworth, 1969), p. 159 (dated the sarcophagus to the 13th century BCE); Edith Porada, "Notes on the Sarcophagus of Ahiram," *JANES* 5 (1973), pp. 355–372 (dated it to ca. 1000 BCE).

8 The word *sfrh* can be translated either referring to the divine book of life (Exod. 32:32), or the mythic *ṭuppi šimati* " tablet of destinies," or preferably it refers to the erasing of "his inscription," which will replace that of Ahiram, i. e., measure for measure.

9 See below for this emendation.

10 H.L. Ginsberg, "The Rebellion and Death of Ba'lu," *Orientalia* 5 (1936), p. 179.

1) lys' alt ṯbtk
2) lyhpk ksa mlkk
3) lyṯbr ḫṭ mtpṭk
Surely, he would pull up the foundations of your seat,
Overturn the throne of your kingship,
Break the staff of your rulership.[11]

This quote seems to indicate that Iron Age Phoenician scribes probably studied these earlier texts in a linear alphabetic version which they may have copied or learned orally. Furthermore, while following a fixed order, as I will argue, the Byblian scribe demonstrates a certain flexibility by adapting a local poetic formula with a significant addition.

Figure 1: Ahiram sarcophagus

---

11 Translation by Dennis Pardee. "The Baʻlu Myth," in William W. Hallo and K. Lawson Younger Jr. (eds), *The Context of Scripture* vol 1 (Leiden, 1997), p. 248.

2 Azitawada Inscription[12]

In 1946, following the discovery and publication of the inscription of Azitawada, the ruler of Azitawadia (Karatepe), an intra-Phoenician parallel to the Ahiram inscription was noted in the slightly different three-fold address:

ואם מלך במלכם ורזן ברזנם ואדם אש אדם שם.[13]

If a king among kings or a prince among princes if a man who is a man of renown....

Noteworthy is the addition of a fourth man of authority, i.e. a man of renown, not listed in Ahiram. Albeit, this parallel indicates a common Canaanite scribal tradition in the dialects of Byblos and Tyre, the latter being that of Azitawada.

Figure 2: Azitawada Inscription

---

12 H. Donner-W. Röllig, *Kanaanäische und Aramäische Inschriften* #26; K. Lawson Younger Jr, "The Azitawada Inscription," William W. Hallo and K. Lawson Younger Jr (eds), *The Context of Scripture* vol 2, (Leiden, 2000), pp.148–150.
13 Note the differences: The Ahiram scribe uses the term *skn* borrowed from Akkadian *šakin//sakin* "regent/governor," while the Azitawada scribe uses the Canaanite equivalent *rzn*, cf. Judg 5,3; Hab 1,10; Psalms 2,2; Prov 8,15;31,4. He also preferred to add the term אדם שם, a cognate of the Hebrew אנשי השם (Gen 6:40) "men of renown." As I will argue below, the Tyrian trained scribe had this formula before him, which his earlier Byblian colleague deleted.

Like the Ahiram inscription, the threefold address formula is followed by the curses that imply expected infringements of the enemy. In Azitawada, the transgression is specifically erasing or damaging this inscription for whatever reason. Needless to say, this echoes and confirms the suggested interpretation of the fourth Ahiram curse: והא ימח ספרה, i.e., "as for him, may his inscription be erased." Furthermore, the continuation, which lists protective deities, expresses that same concern for protecting Azitawada's name:

אש ימח שם אזתוד בשער ז ושת שם
אם אף יחמד את הקרת ז
ויסע השער ז אש פעל אזתוד
ויפעל לשער זר ושת שם עלי
אם בחמדת יסע
אם בשנאת וברע יסע השער ז
ומח בעל שמם ואל קן ארץ ושמש עלם
כל דר בן אלם ...
אית הממלכה הא ואית המלך הא
ואית אדם הא אש אדם שם אפס שם אזתוד
יכן לעלם כם שם שמש וירח

Who shall erase the name of Azitawada from this gate, and shall place (his) name (on it); if indeed he shall covet this city, and shall tear away this gate, which Azitawada has made, or shall make for himself a different gate, and place (his) name on it—if from covetousness he shall tear (it) away—if from hate or from evil he shall tear away this gate—then shall Baʻal Shamem and El, creator of the earth and Shemesh the eternal, and the whole group of the children of the gods erase that kingdom, and that king and that man who is a man of renown.

Only may the name of Azitawada exist forever like the name of the sun and the moon!

There is another point of comparison between Ahiram and Azitawada that should be mentioned: this one regarding the question of dating Ahiram in relation to the other Byblian monarchs who left us monumental building inscriptions. The usually accepted dates for them, that I follow, place Ahiram circa 1000 BCE and the other Byblian kings to the mid-10th to early 9th centuries BCE.[14] The lynchpin is the fact that the inscriptions of Abibaal and Elibaal are engraved on the statues of the contemporary Egyptian kings Sheshonq I (945–924 BCE) and his son

---

14 William F. Albright, "The Phoenician inscriptions of the Tenth Century BC from Byblus," *JAOS* 67 1947–48, pp. 153–160; Benjamin Mazar, "The Phoenician Inscriptions from Byblus," *Leshonenu* 14 (1946), pp.166–181, reprinted in "The Phoenician Inscriptions from Byblus and the development of the Phoenician-Hebrew alphabetic Inscriptions," B. Mazar, *Excavations and Discoveries* (Jerusalem, 1986), pp. 185–204 (Hebrew).

Osorchon I (924–887 BCE), respectively. It is plausible that the choice of this writing surface expressed an act of allegiance to the Egyptian overlords. This chronology has been challenged by Benjamin Sass and Israel Finkelstein[15] who prefer a lower date for Ahiram based on paleographic grounds bringing him closer in time to the 8th century BCE date of Azitawada.

An unrecognized religious aspect that emanates from the curse formula should add support for the earlier date of Ahiram. If, indeed, the Byblian scribe applied a curse formula beginning with one attributed to 'Il, the leading deity of Canaan in the second millennium BCE, it seems that he was still influenced by an earlier Late Bronze scribal tradition, whereas the Tyrian trained scribe, who composed the Azitawada inscription lists the gods in the curse formula in the following order: Baal Shamem, then 'Il Qone 'Aretz, Shamash and the rest of the pantheon. This order reflects the religious change that took place in Canaan by the end of the Late Bronze – Early Iron Age, when Baal, in his manifestation as Ba'al Shamem, assumed the leadership of the Canaanite pantheon.[16]

When comparing the Ahiram and Azitawada inscriptions, it seems to me that the slightly different three-fold address formula found in each document is actually a shortened version of a *fourfold list of* authority figures:

מלך במלכם
סכן בסכנם // רזן ברזנם
תמא מחנת
אדם אש אדם שם.

15 Israel Finkelstein and Benjamin Sass, "The West Semitic Alphabetic Inscriptions, Late Bronze II to Iron IIA: Archaeological context, distribution and chronology," *Hebrew Bible and Ancient Israel 2* (2013), pp. 149–220; but see Christopher Rollston, "The Dating of the Early Royal Byblian Phoenician Inscriptions; A Response to Benjamin Sass," *Maarav* 15. 1 (2008), pp. 57–93; also Alan Millard, "Ancient Hebrew Inscriptions, Their Distributions and Significance," in Israel Finkelstein, Christian Robin, Thomas Römer (eds.), *Alphabets, Texts and Artifacts in the Ancient Near East* (Paris, 2016), pp. 270–278, esp. 274–75.
16 Ba'al Shamem appears already in the Yehimilk building inscription, KAI #4 line 3.

3 Codex Hammurapi

This group of four authority figures is found in the epilogue of the Old Babylonian Codex Hammurapi, col. xxvib, lines 18–80 (CH), which seems to be the model for this type of address:[17]

LU.GAL	*lu šarrum*
EN	*lu bēlum*
ENSÍ	*lu iššiakkum*

Awīlūtum ša šumam nabiat

i.e., **a king, a lord, or a governor, or any person called by name**.[18]

A close reading of that text shows that not only the address but also the similarity of some of the curses, albeit in different languages and scripts, indicate Mesopotamian influence on the Phoenician scribes. To the best of my knowledge, the Ahiram inscription would be the earliest known case to date of a translation of an Akkadian text into Phoenician using a linear alphabetic script.[19] This assumption can explain some of the differences between the two Phoenician inscriptions as well as aid in correcting the errors in the Ahiram inscription.

---

[17] Scholars noted some linguistic similarity between the Ahiram text and the CH, see H. Donner "Zur Formgeschichte der Ahiram-Inschrift," *Wissenschaftliche Zeitschrift der Karl-Marx Universität* (1953–54), pp.283–287.

[18] An interesting parallel is found in the Yahdun-Lim foundation inscription of the Shamash Temple from Mari. In this literary composition, he describes his campaign to the Mediterranean coast, particularly to the cedar and boxwood mountains where he brought back different kinds of choice wood. From the Mari texts we learn of Yahdun-Lim and his son Zimri-Lim's political, economic and marital ties to the trans-Euphrates kingdoms stretching out to the Mediterranean Sea. This foundation inscription dating a generation before Hammurapi employs a curse formula addressing the same four authorities spelled syllabically: lu šar-ru-rum, lu ša-ka-na-ku-um, lu ra-bi-a-nu-um, lu a-wi-lu-tum šum-šu, which A. Leo Oppenheim translated: "be this man a king, or a general, or a mayor, or whoever else," in James B. Pritchard (ed.), *Ancient Near Eastern Texts Relating to the Old Testament with Supplement* (Princeton, 1969), p. 557; Douglas Frayne translates: "that man, whether he be king, viceroy, mayor or common man," in W.W. Hallo and K. Lawson Younger Jr (eds), *The Context of Scripture* vol. 2 (Leiden, 2000), p. 260 lines 132–136. Also Abraham Malamat, "Campaigns to the Mediterranean by Iahdun-Lim and other Early Mesopotamian Rulers," *Anatolian Studies* 16 (1965), pp. 365–372.

[19] On translations from Sumerian and Akkadian to Canaanite (in cuneiform), see Pinhas Artzi, "Glosses in the El Amarna Documents," *Sefer Bar-Ilan* vol.1 (Ramat-Gan, 1963), pp. 24–57 (Hebrew); Anson. F. Rainey, "Two Cuneiform Fragments from Tel-Aphek," *Tel Aviv* 2 (1975), pp. 125–129; idem, "A Tri-Lingual Cuneiform Fragment from Tel-Aphek," *Tel Aviv* 3 (1976), pp.137–140.

For further clarity, I will present the relevant excerpt in Akkadian followed by an English translation.[20]

18–19	šum-ma a-wi-lum šu-ú <a-na> a-wa-ti-ya
20–22	ša i-na NA.RU-ya aš-ṭú-ru la i-qul-ma
23–26	ir-ri-ti-ya i-me-eš-ma ir-ri-it ì-lí la i-dur-ma
27–28	di-in a-di-nu up-ta-as-sí-is
29–32	a-wa-ti-ya uš-te-pi-el ú-ṣú-ra-ti-ya ut-ta-ak-ki-ir
33–34	šu-mi ša-aṭ-ra-am ip-ši-iṭ-ma
35–36	šum-šu iš-ta-ṭár aš-šum ir-re-tim ši-na-ti
37–38	ša-ni-a-am-ma uš-ta-ḫi-iz
39	a-wi-lum šu-ú
40	lu LUGAL
41	lu EN
42	lu ENSÍ
43–44	ù-lu a-wil-lu-tum ša šu-ma-am na-bi-a-at
*45–46	*AN* ra-bu-um *a-bu i-lí*
47	na-bu-ú PAL-ya
48–49	ME.NE šar-ru-tim il-te[4]-ir-su
*50–51	[GIŠ]*PA-šu li-iš-be-ir*
52	ši-ma-ti-šu li-ru-ur
*53–54	[DINGIR]*EN.LIL be-lum mu-ši-im ši-ma-tim*
*55–58	*ša ki-bí-sú la ut-ta-ka-ru*, mu-šar-bu-u šar-ru-ti-ya
59–62	te-ši la šu-ub-bi-im ga-ba-ra-aḫ ḫa-la-qí-šu i-na šu-ub-ti-šu
*63–63	li-ša-ap-pí-ḫa-aš-šum *PAL ta-ne-ḫi-im*
*65–67	u[4]-mi i-ṣú-tim *ša-na-a-at ḫu-ša-aḫ-ḫi-im*
68–69	ik-li-it la na-wa-ri-im
70	mu-ut ni-ṭi-il i-nim
*71–73	*a-na ši-im-tim li-ši-im-šum* ḫa-la-aq URU-šu
74	na-ás-pu-úḫ ni-ši-šu
75	šar-ru-sú šu-pí-lam
76–68	šum-šu ù zi-kir-su i-na ma-tim la šu-ub-ša-a-am
79–80	i-na KA-šu kab-tim li-iq-bi

(But) should that man not heed my pronouncements, which I have inscribed upon my stela, and should he slight my curses and not fear the curses of the gods, and thus, overturn the judgments that I rendered, change my pronouncements, alter my engraved image, erase my inscribed name and inscribe his own name (in its place)—or should he, because of fear of these curses, have someone else do so-that man, whether he is **a king, a lord, or a governor, or any person who is called by name,**[21]

---

20 For the Akkadian text and the English translation, see Martha T. Roth, *Law Collections from Mesopotamia and Asia Minor* (Atlanta: Scholars Press,1995), pp. 136–137.
21 Roth reads: ù-lu a-wil-lu-tum ša šu-ma-am na-bi-a-at "or any person at all."

> May the great god Anu, father of the gods, who has proclaimed my reign, deprive him of the sheen of royalty, **smash his scepter,** and curse his destiny.
>
> May the god Enlil, the lord, who determines destinies, whose utterance cannot be countermanded, who magnifies my kingship, incite against him even in his own residence disorder that cannot be quelled and a rebellion that will result in his obliteration; may he cast as his fate a reign of groaning, of few days, of years of famine, of darkness without illumination, and of sudden death; may he declare with his venerable speech **the obliteration of his city,** the dispersion of his people, the supplanting of his dynasty, and **the blotting out of his name and his memory from the land.**

Already in the second millennium BCE, the Codex, especially the curses against anyone who acts against Hammurapi and desecrates his stele, had become a model text to be copied many times in ancient Mesopotamian scribal circles.[22] For example, R. Borger[23] noted that the same formula appears in abbreviated form in a treaty between Marduk-zakir-shumi I, king of Babylon, and Shamshi-Adad V, king of Assyria (823–810 B.C.). Borger was able to reconstruct the later text from the original, which I indicate above in italics (on the lines with asterisks). We have here clear evidence that the curse formula in the CH Epilogue continued to serve as a model, at least for Akkadian scribes in Babylonia, for over 800 years! On the basis of literary parallels appearing in the same order, such as the fourfold address, I believe that a version of the CH epilogues reached in one form or another the scribal centers on the Phoenician coast.

Cf. G.R. Driver and John C. Miles, *The Babylonian Laws* (Oxford,1955), vol.2, p 101: "or any of mankind that bears a name." I prefer to translate: "any person who is called by name."

22 As Roth writes ibid., p.74: "We have recovered dozens of duplicates and extracts of the Laws, as well as commentaries, references to the composition in a first-millennium catalogue, and a bilingual Sumerian-Akkadian manuscript, from a variety of sites in Mesopotamia. Some of the manuscripts date to Hammurabi's immediate successors in the First Dynasty of Babylon, while others are copies from a thousand years later. This wide and varied evidence attests to the enduring popularity of the Laws of Hammurabi, which was both an influence on and a reflection of contemporary literary, political, as well as legal thought. The numerous manuscripts suggest more than one original exemplar, and what are sometimes viewed as discrepancies and errors in some manuscripts may be the results of different traditions."

23 R. Borger, "Marduk-zakir-šumi I and the Codex Hammurapi," *Orientalia* 34 (1965): pp. 168–169.

Figure 3: Codex Hammurapi

The curses in the CH epilogue are attributed to the following gods listed according to their seniority in the Mesopotamian pantheon: Anum, Enlil, Ninlil, Ea, Shamash, Sin, Adad, Ishtar, Ibaba, Nergal, Nintu, Ninkarrak. Each god is noted with his or her particular curses. Not only is the divine order fixed, but so are curses. In the laconic Ahiram curse formula there is no mention of specific gods. However, three of the four curses in that inscription have parallels in the epilogue; for instance, the first curse attributed by H. L. Ginsberg to Canaanite Il: תחתסף חטר משפטה translates the curse of Anu: ^{GIŠ}PA-*šu li-iš-be-ir* (ll. 50–51). The third and fourth Ahiram curses parallel two of Enlil's curses in the same order. One against his domain[24]: ונחת תברח על גבל parallels *te-ši la šu-ub-bi-im ga-ba-ra-aḫ ḫa-la-qí-šu i-na šu-ub-ti-šu li-ša-ap-pi-ḫa-aš-šum* (ll. 59–63). And the other: הא, ימח ספרה לפף שבל — at least in the opening three words — parallels: *šum-šu ù zi-kir-šu i-na ma-tim la šu-ub-ša-a-am* (ll. 76–78). These last two curses were translated freely by the Phoenician scribe, maintaining the prose form of the Babylonian original. It should be noted that the Phoenician scribe localized the neutral terms *šubtišu* "his dwelling" and *ina mātim* "in the land," so that they conform to the limited geographical area of Ahiram's domain, i.e. the kingdom of Byblos in contrast to the far-flung dominion of Hammurapi.

If the Phoenician scribe followed an older Mesopotamian text, how are we to explain the addition of the second Phoenician curse תתהפך כסא מלכה that is not found in CH? Ginsberg, in his commentary to the Baʿal epic, already observed the poetic nature of the first two curses, expressed in meter and parallelism. It seems that the Phoenician scribe chose to translate the curse of Anu, Father of the Gods: ᴳᴵˢPA-*šu lišbir*, by a similar curse attributed to Il, the supreme deity of the Canaanite pantheon, with which he was familiar, i.e., תחתסף חטר משפטה. He could not resist the parallelism it evoked, and added the second stich, תהתפך כסא מלכה also attributed to Il. This parallelism was apparently deeply rooted in the literary consciousness of Canaanite scribes. The throne and the staff parallelism continued to function as symbols of authority at least from the sixteenth to the sixth century B.C.E.

If indeed we have uncovered the Vorlage of these Phoenician curses, perhaps I can now deal with the last two words in this line לפף שבל that remain a long-standing enigma. There are many strange explanations of these two words, especially by scholars who consider them as completing the fourth curse and not the beginning of a supposed fifth one. On the basis of old photos, Javier Teixidor proposed the most plausible reading: לפן גבל.[25] However, Marilyn Lundberg and Reinhard Lehmann who have examined the inscription in detail, independently rejected this suggestion. Both present a detailed paleographic study, differing

---

24 Roth, pp.136–137: May the god Enlil, the lord, who determines destinies, whose utterance cannot be countermanded, who magnifies my kingship, incite against him even in his own residence disorder that cannot be quelled and a rebellion that will result in his obliteration; may he cast as his fate a reign of groaning, of few days, of years of famine, of darkness without illumination, and of sudden death; may he declare with his venerable speech **the obliteration of his city, the dispersion of his people,** the supplanting of his dynasty, and the **blotting out of his name and his memory from the land.**

25 See Javier Teixidor, "L'inscription d'Aḥiram à nouveau," *Syria*, 64, 1/2 (1987), pp. 137–140.

only on the second-last letter which they read respectively: לפפ שבל or לפפ
שרל.²⁶

While paleographic studies are fundamental in deciphering epigrapha, there
are other factors that should be taken into consideration.²⁷ Foremost, this text is
the work of two individuals: the first was the royal scribe who composed the text
of the inscription and the second was the engraver who had to chisel this text into
the fractured stone surface. As evidenced by the last two letters riding up the edge
of the damaged surface, he had to adjust to the physical conditions of the stone
surface as well as the work area as described by Lehmann: "In the vault, especially at its quite narrow southern side and presumably under bad light conditions for a scribe or engraver, such deviations in letter shape and angle of inclination are really to be expected."²⁸ If so, the carver might have considered abbre-
viating the final clause. As I suggest regarding the third curse, it is quite plausible
that the scribe wanted to localize it applying it to Byblos (*gbl*). However, since the
new photographs clearly indicate a *shin*, either in the enigmatic *unknown* Semitic
terms שבל or שרל, I assume that the engraver actually had before him a suitable
expression which he abbreviated. I suggest that the scribe's text followed local
scribal tradition found in the blessing formula of later Byblian royal inscriptions
of Yeḥimlk:²⁹ לפן אל גבל קדשם and Yeḥawmlk: פן כל אלן גבל.³⁰ Therefore, I propose that the engraver had before him the phrase לפ[ן] ש[קד] [ג]ב[ל] "before [the
Hol]y Ones of [G]bl!

In conclusion, I have attempted to illustrate how literary texts were borrowed,
learned and adapted by ancient Near Eastern scribes writing in different dialects
and scripts. As a case in point, I chose the curse formula in the laconic funeral
inscription of Aḥiram king of Byblos and compared it to the curses in the later
display inscription of Azitawada reflecting a local Phoenician tradition. I then
suggested that these curses actually go back to an Akkadian model found in the
Codex Hammurapi Epilogue. That primary list of curses went through a process
of fixation based on the hierarchy of the Mesopotamian pantheon. This tradition
was adapted by bi-lingual western scribes in Mesopotamian-Canaanite scribal

---

26 Lundberg, "Ahiram," pp. 88–89; plate XXIV (p. 138). Lehmann, following Dussaud, suggests
לפפ שרל, explaining *srl* as a Hittite/Luwian term *sarli* for a kind of libation or offering for the
dead.

27 See Aaron Demsky. "Reading Northwest Semitic Inscriptions," *Near Eastern Archaeology*
70/2, pp. 68–74.

28 Lehmann, op.cit., p. 138.

29 Donner and Rollig, *KAI* 4:7.

30 Ibid, 10:16.

schools, which we assume to have been in various sites, notably in Ugarit and Byblos, during the El-Amarna period. In subsequent years, the received text underwent slight changes in the translation process. In turn, the Aḥiram scribe abbreviated it, due to technical reasons regarding the confined writing surface on the lid of the sarcophagus, and, on the other hand, enhanced it by poetic association. A further adjustment was necessary due to the different size realms of Hammurapi and Aḥiram. I propose then that we see in these documents a "stream of scribal tradition" extending from Babylonia and reaching Phoenicia, reflecting both a fixed order of components as well as a fluidity allowing for creative change.

4 Biblical Echoes

This was not the end of this literary tradition. Since the throne and staff were symbols of royal authority in the Ancient Near East, it is no surprise that we find the pair in the Bible.[31]

See Psalms 45:7:

כִּסְאֲךָ אֱלֹהִים עוֹלָם וָעֶד   שֵׁבֶט מִישֹׁר שֵׁבֶט מַלְכוּתֶךָ.

"Your throne of judgement is everlasting; Your royal scepter is a scepter of righteousness."

Another example is echoed in the prophecy of Haggai 2:21–22 speaking to a lay audience in Jerusalem:

אֱמֹר אֶל-זְרֻבָּבֶל פַּחַת-יְהוּדָה לֵאמֹר   אֲנִי מַרְעִישׁ אֶת-הַשָּׁמַיִם וְאֶת-הָאָרֶץ.
וְהָפַכְתִּי כִּסֵּא מַמְלָכוֹת וְהִשְׁמַדְתִּי חֹזֶק מַמְלְכוֹת הַגּוֹיִם
וְהָפַכְתִּי מֶרְכָּבָה וְרֹכְבֶיהָ וְיָרְדוּ סוּסִים וְרֹכְבֵיהֶם אִישׁ בְּחֶרֶב אָחִיו.

"And I will overturn the thrones of kingdoms and destroy the might[32] of the kingdoms of the nations. I will overturn the chariots and their drivers; horses and their riders shall fall, each by the sword of his fellow."

As I have shown elsewhere,[33] the Writing Prophets were a vehicle for the spread of literacy and bringing "book culture" to a popular audience.

---

31 Zeev Falk, "Two Symbols of Justice," *Vetus Testamentum* 10 (1960), pp 72–74.
32 The word "might" חֹזֶק, beginning with the letter *het*, may preserve an anticipated חטר "staff."
33 *Literacy in Ancient Israel* (Jerusalem: Mossad Bialik, 2012), pp. 253–272; 306–310.

5 Babylonian Talmud, Gitin 35a

This of course opens the discussion of how formal, or scribal culture, reached the masses, if it did. A case in point would be the late story found in the Babylonian Talmud Gitin 35a:

ההיא דאתאי לקמיה דרבה בר רב הונא.

אמר לה: מאי אעביד ליך דרב לא מגבי כתובה לארמלתא,

ואבא מרי לא מגבי כתובה לארמלתא.

אמרה ליה: הב לי מזוני.

אמר לה: מזוני נמי לית ליך, דאמר רב יהודה אמר שמואל: התובעת כתובתה בבית דין אין לה מזונות.

אמרה ליה: **אפכוה לכורסיה,** כבי תרי עבדא לי.

הפכוה לכורסיה ותרצו, ואפילו הכי לא איפרק מחולשא.

> That widow woman who came before Rabbah bar Rav Huna.
>
> He said: What can I do for you, since Rav (of Sura) does not give *ketubah* money to a widow.
>
> She said to him: (In that case,) give me sustenance allowance.
>
> He said to her: Here too you get no sustenance allowance, for Rav Yehudah said in the name of Samuel (of Nehardea)—One who demands her bridal money in court gets no allowance.
>
> She said to him: Turn over his judicial throne! He has judged me according to both opinions.
>
> (Rabbah bar Huna's students) turned over the throne and then set it aright. Even so, it did not save him from illness.

This passage describes a case of an injustice made by a rabbinic court which dealt harshly[34] with a widow who asked for payment of her bridal money (*ketubbah*) and when this was refused, she requested payment for sustenance (*mezonot*). Rabbah bar Rav Huna, the presiding judge, concludes that because of earlier decisions of the usually competing authorities, Rav and Samuel, he could not grant her any financial remunerations.

At this point, out of frustration she cursed the rabbinic court judge saying: "Overturn his chair!," i.e., the seat of his authority.[35]

---

34 See Adin Steinsaltz, Gitin, p. 153 (Hebrew) and the reference to Ein Yaakov who in this context points to Proverbs 20:28: חֶסֶד וֶאֱמֶת יִצְּרוּ-מֶלֶךְ **וְסָעַד בַּחֶסֶד כִּסְאוֹ** "Kindness and truth protect the king, He strengthens his throne with kindness." In other words, the king's throne, i.e. his seat of authority, should be strengthened by mercy and loving kindness.

35 See Rashi: "תשפל גדולתו."

Fearing the efficacy of the curse, the attendants quickly overturned his chair; however, this did not save the rabbi from falling into ill health.

This Talmudic passage illustrates how a literary expression formulated by scribes in a late second millennium BCE Canaanite setting, where it was joined by another curse seemingly taken from Codex Hammurapi from Babylon, found its way over two thousand years later into common oral lore used by a destitute woman in the rabbinic courts in the same vicinity along the Euphrates River.

6 Bibliography

Albright, William F., "The Phoenician Inscriptions of the Tenth Century BC from Byblus," *JAOS* 67 (1947–48), pp. 153–160.

Artzi, Pinhas, "Glosses in the El Amarna Documents," *Sefer Bar-Ilan* vol.1 (Ramat-Gan, 1963), pp. 24–57 (Hebrew).

Borger, R., "Marduk-zakir-šumi I and the Codex Hammurapi," *Orientalia* 34 (1965), pp. 168 - 169.

Cochavi-Rainey, Zippora, *To the King My Lord - Letters from El-Amarna, Kumidi, Taanach and Other Letters from the Fourteenth Century BCE* (Jerusalem, 2005) (Hebrew).

Cohen, Yoram, "Cuneiform Writing in Bronze Age Canaan," A. Yasur-Landau, E. H. Cline and Y. M. Rowan (eds.), *The Social Archaeology of the Levant: From Prehistory to Present* (Cambridge, Cambridge University Press, 2019), pp. 245–264.

Demsky, Aaron, "The Cultural Continuum of a Canaanite Curse," *Leshonenu* 34 (1970), pp. 185–186 (Hebrew).

Demsky, Aaron, "Mesopotamian and Canaanite Literary Traditions in the Ahiram Curse Formula," *Eretz Israel* 14 (H.L. Ginsberg Volume) 1978, pp. 7–11 (Hebrew); English summary, p. 122*.

Demsky, Aaron, "Reading Northwest Semitic Inscriptions," *Near Eastern Archaeology* 70/2 (2007), pp. 68–74.

Demsky, Aaron, *Literacy in Ancient Israel* (Jerusalem, Mossad Bialik, 2012) (Hebrew).

Donner, Herbert, "Zur Formgeschichte der Ahiram-Inschrift," Wissenschaftliche Zeitschrift der Karl-Marx Universität (1953–54), pp.283–287.

Donner, Herbert-Wolfgang Röllig, *Kanaanäische und Aramäische Inschriften* (Wiesbaden, 1964).

Driver, Godfrey R. and John C. Miles, *The Babylonian Laws* (Oxford,1955), 2 vols.

Falk, Zeev, "Two Symbols of Justice," *Vetus Testamentum* 10 (1960), pp 72–74.

Finkelstein, Israel, and Benjamin Sass, "The West Semitic Alphabetic Inscriptions, Late Bronze II to Iron IIA: Archaeological context, distribution and chronology," *Hebrew Bible and Ancient Israel 2* (2013), pp. 149–220.

Frankfort, Henri, *The Art and Architecture of the Ancient Orient* (Harmondsworth, 1969), p. 159.

Frayne, Douglas, "Iahdun-LIM (2.111)", in W.W. Hallo and K. Lawson Younger Jr (eds.), *The Context of Scripture* vol. 2 (Leiden 2000), p. 260.

Ginsberg, Harold L., "The Rebellion and Death of Ba'lu`," *Orientalia* 5 (1936), pp. 161–198.

Goody, Jack, *The Domestication of the Savage Mind* (Cambridge, 1977), pp. 74–111.

Horowitz Wayne, T. Oshima, Seth Sanders, *Cuneiform Sources from the Land of Israel in Ancient Times* (Jerusalem, 2006).

Lehmann, Reinhard. G., *Die Inschrift(en) des Ahirom -Sarkophags und die Schachtinschrift des Grabes V in Jbeil (Byblos)*, (Mainz, Zabern, 2005).

Lehmann, Reinhard. G., "Calligraphy and Craftsmanship in the Ahirom Inscription: Considerations on Skilled Linear Flat Writing in Early First Millennium Byblos," *Maarav* 15.2 (2008), pp. 119–164, 217–222.

Lehmann, Reinhard. G., "Wer war Aḥīrōms Sohn (KAI 1:1)? Eine kalligraphisch-prosopographische Annäherung an eine epigraphisch offene Frage," in V. Golinets, H. Jenni, H.-P. Mathys and S. Sarasin (eds.), *Neue Beiträge zur Semitistik. Fünftes Treffen der Arbeitsgemeinschaft Semitistik in der Deutschen Morgenländischen Gesellschaft vom 15.–17. Februar 2012 an der Universität Basel* (AOAT 425, Münster, Ugarit-Verlag, 2015), pp. 163–180.

Lundberg, Marilyn J., "Editor's Notes: The Ahiram Inscription," *Maarav* 11.1 (2004), pp. 81–93.

Mazar, Benjamin, "The Phoenician Inscriptions from Byblus," *Leshonenu* 14 (1946), pp. 166–181, reprinted in "The Phoenician Inscriptions from Byblus and the Development of the Phoenician-Hebrew Alphabetic Inscriptions," in B. Mazar, *Excavations and Discoveries* (Jerusalem, 1986), pp. 185–204 (Hebrew).

Malamat, Abraham, "Campaigns to the Mediterranean by Iahdun-Lim and other Early Mesopotamian Rulers," *Anatolian Studies* 16 (1965), pp. 365–372.

McCarter, P. Kyle, "The Sarcophagus Inscription of 'Ahirom King of Byblos," in W.W. Hallo and K. Lawson Younger Jr (eds.), *The Context of Scripture* vol 2 (Leiden, Brill, 2000), p. 181.

Millard, Alan R., "Ancient Hebrew Inscriptions: Their Distribution and Significance," in Israel Finkelstein, Christian Robin and Thomas Römer (eds.), *Alphabets, Texts and Artifacts in the Ancient Near East* (Paris, 2016), pp. 270–278.

Oppenheim, A. Leo, in James B. Pritchard (ed.), *Supplements- The Ancient Near East* (Princeton, 1969), p. 557.

Pardee, Dennis, "The Ba'lu Myth," in William W. Hallo and K. Lawson Younger Jr. (eds.), *The Context of Scripture* vol 1 (Leiden, 1997), p. 248.

Porada, Edith, "Notes on the Sarcophagus of Ahiram," *JANES* 5 (1973), pp. 355–372.

Rainey, Anson. F., "Two Cuneiform Fragments from Tel-Aphek," *Tel Aviv* 2 (1975), pp. 125–129.

Rainey, Anson. F., "A Tri-Lingual Cuneiform Fragment from Tel-Aphek," *Tel Aviv* 3 (1976), pp. 137–140.

Rollston, Christopher, "The Dating of the Early Royal Byblian Phoenician Inscriptions; A Response to Benjamin Sass," *Maarav* 15. 1, pp. 57–93.

Roth, Martha T., *Law Collections from Mesopotamia and Asia Minor* (Atlanta, Scholars Press,1995), pp. 136–137.

Sass, Benjamin, "The Pseudo-Hieroglyphic Inscriptions from Byblos, Their Elusive Dating, and Their Affinities with the Early Phoenician Inscriptions," in Philippe Abrahami and Laura Battini (eds.), *Ina dmarri u qan ṭuppi. Par la bêche et le stylet ! Cultures et sociétés syro-mésopotamiennes Mélanges offerts à Olivier Rouault* (Summertime, Oxford, 2019), pp. 157–180.

Steinsaltz (Even Yisrael), Adin, *Talmud Bavli, Masekhet Gitin* (Jerusalem, 1993).

Teixidor, Javier, "L'inscription d'Aḥiram à nouveau," *Syria*, 64, 1/2 (1987), pp. 137–140.

Younger, K. Lawson Jr, "The Azitawada Inscription," in William W. Hallo and K. Lawson Younger Jr (eds), *The Context of Scripture* vol 2, (Leiden, 2000), pp. 148–150.

Jan Dušek

The 'Nests' of the Aramaic Scribal Culture in the Late 9th – Early 7th Centuries BCE Levant: An Attempt at Identification

1 Introduction

Holger Gzella distinguished three varieties of Aramaic in the 9th and 8th centuries BCE:
- the language of the Tell Fekheriye inscription (eastern Syria),
- an Aramaic dialect attested by various inscriptions in central Syria,
- the language of some inscriptions in the Sam'alian dialect from the kingdom of Sam'al/Ya'udi (northwestern Syria).[1]

The central Syrian group, according to Gzella's definition, is the largest one, and he labeled its language as an "Aramaic *koiné.*" This group includes, according to Gzella, the following inscriptions: the inscriptions from Sefire, Bar-Hadad's inscription on the stela for Melqart, the inscription of Zakkur and the small inscribed stela fragment from Tell Afis, the graffiti from Hamath, the inscribed stelae fragments from Tel Dan, the Aramaic inscriptions from Sam'al (*KAI* 216–221), the Deir 'Allā inscription, the inscriptions from Eretria, Samos, and Arslan Tash mentioning Haza'el, and the Aramaic inscription on the stela from Bukān. On the basis of the high degree of orthographic consistency of this group, Gzella concluded that these inscriptions stem from the same scribal tradition, which existed in central Syria. He hypothesized the existence of a single scribal school that

* I would like to thank Aren Wilson-Wright for his valuable and helpful comments on my paper. Of course, I am the only one responsible for all possible errors. This study is a result of the research funded by the Czech Science Foundation as the project GA ČR 20-26324S "Scribal traditions in the Aramaean territories of the Levant in the Iron Age: centers of scribal cultures and their spread."
1 Holger Gzella, *A Cultural History of Aramaic. From the Beginnings to the Advent of Islam*, HdO 111 (Leiden – Boston: Brill, 2015), 62–77.

formed the scribes who produced the inscriptions.[2] The validity of this conclusion, based on the orthography, shall be checked by an examination of aspects
other than orthographic ones. In this paper, I would like to focus on some of the
scribal and engraving practices reflected in the Aramaic inscriptions of the 9th to
early 7th centuries BCE, which might allow us to verify whether the hypothesis of
a single scribal school that educated the scribes of the central Syrian Aramaic
inscriptions (according to Gzella's definition) is valid or not.

My analysis is not focused only on Gzella's central Syrian group, but also includes the inscriptions belonging to the northwest Syrian group. I pay special
attention to the inscriptions carved in stone (stelae, orthostats, statues), because
they provide solid comparative material. Small Aramaic inscriptions on ivories,
seals, or metal objects are also taken into account, but the graphic needs of short
and small inscriptions may be different from those which are carved on the larger
surfaces of stelae or orthostats. The elements allowing us to study the differences
between the Aramaic inscriptions are:

- the separation of the words (dividers are used or not, and if so, which form do
  they have?);
- the use of guidelines (attested only in a few inscriptions);
- the style of engraving (engraving letters in stone or carving in raised relief
  ["champlevé"]);
- the form of the *zayin* (the *zayin* in the form of a Z or in the form of a lying H
  [Fig. 1]).

Z-form of the *zayin*   Lying H-form of the *zayin*

Figure 1: Two variants of the zayin

The inscriptions included by Gzella in the northwest Syrian and central Syrian
groups can be regrouped according to their belonging to one of the three supposed scribal nests: Sam'al/Yaudi, the environs of Aleppo, and the inscriptions
related to Damascus and Hama. I do not deal with the inscriptions from Tell
Fekheriye and Tell Halaf, whose style is different from most of the other Aramaic

---

2 "Perhaps scribes working in different local chancelleries had been trained in the same scribal
school or at least according to the same curriculum; alternatively, the production of these monumental inscriptions was outsourced to shared administrative centres." Gzella, *Cultural History*,
69.

inscriptions. I also leave aside the inscription from Bukān, which was probably not produced in Syria.

2 Sam'al/Ya'udi

2.1. An original style of engraving West-Semitic stone inscriptions was introduced in Sam'al/Ya'udi by Kulamuwa in his Phoenician inscription written in the late 9th century, approximately around 825 BCE.[3] The inscription and the iconographic elements decorating the inscription are carved in a stone orthostat, situated in the entrance to Building J, the palace of Kulamuwa, which stood in the northwestern area in Zincirli.[4] The text and the iconographic representations on the orthostat are a combination of various cultural and scribal elements, which together form a very specific style of the Zincirli inscriptions, more or less faithfully imitated by the successors of Kulamuwa in the 8th century BCE. These elements are Assyrian, West Semitic, and perhaps also Luwian. Actually, Zincirli can be considered a crossroads of these cultural and political influences. The orthostat, probably produced by a local artist, is decorated with an Assyrian-like figure, with details referring to the Assyrian iconography and perhaps also Neo-Hittite elements.[5] In the inscription, Kulamuwa explicitly confirms that he adhered to the Assyrian political power when he states that he had hired the Assyrian king in order to defeat the king of the Danunians.[6] The language of the inscription is Phoenician. The text of the inscription is carved in raised relief ("champlevé"), a style typical of the Hieroglyphic Luwian inscriptions produced in the Neo-Hittite polities, but also used in some West Semitic inscriptions (see section 2.4 below). The lines of the inscription are separated by horizontal ruling lines, also in raised relief. The words are separated by dots.

The tradition introduced by Kulamuwa continued, with some modifications, in Sam'al/Ya'udi for approximately a century. The available epigraphic evidence

---

3 Josef Tropper, *Die Inschriften von Zincirli*, ALASP 6 (Münster: Ugarit-Verlag, 1993), 27.
4 Alessandra Gilibert, *Syro-Hittite Monumental Art and the Archaeology of Performance*, Topoi: Berlin Studies of the Ancient World 2 (Berlin – New York: De Gruyter, 2011), 81, Fig. 44, no. 3.
5 Winfried Orthmann, *Untersuchungen zur späthethitischen Kunst*, Saarbrücker Beiträge zur Altertumskunde 8 (Bonn: Rudolf Habelt Verlag, 1971), 66–67.
6 "Now the king of the Danunians was more powerful than I (or: too powerful for me), but I engaged against him the king of Assyria." *COS* 2.30, 147.

allows us to distinguish two phases in the reception of Kulamuwa's scribal tradition: first, the late 9th and first half of the 8th century, and second, the second half of the 8th century BCE.

2.2. The inscriptions written during the first phase (the late 9th and first half of the 8th century BCE) share the following elements: the *zayin* in the form of a lying H (as in the Kulamuwa inscription) and dividers in the form of dots. None of the inscriptions belonging to the first phase, after Kulamuwa's inscription, were found at Zincirli. The closest imitation of the style of Kulamuwa's inscription was found at Ördekburnu, and the inscription of Panamuwa I was discovered at Gerçin.

The inscription from Ördekburnu, a site situated ca. 18 km south of Zincirli, which was approximately dated between 820 and 760 BCE,[7] seems to be the closest follower of the Kulamuwa inscription. The text, carved in raised relief, is guided by ruling lines, and the words are separated from each other by dots. The scribe used the *zayin* in the form of a lying H, the same as was also used in Kulamuwa's inscription and in the inscription of Panamuwa I on the statue of Hadad.

The inscription of Panamuwa I on the statue of Hadad is dated to the second quarter of the 8th century BCE, approximately between 770 and 760 BCE, and was found at Gerçin, ca. 7 km northeast of Zincirli, a site considered to be the necropolis of the kings of Sam'al/Ya'udi.[8] Its style is more independent of Kulamuwa's tradition (there are no ruling lines, and the inscription is larger than the inscriptions on stelae and orthostats). It is carved in raised relief, with dots as dividers, and with the *zayin* in the form of a lying H.

2.3. The inscriptions written in the second half of the 8th century BCE all contain the *zayin* in the form of a Z; the form of the lying H is abandoned. The form of the dividers alternates between dots and vertical lines. The inscriptions can be hierarchically divided into three groups, with the degree of their adhesion to Kulamuwa's tradition decreasing from the first to the last.

---

[7] André Lemaire and Benjamin Sass, "The Mortuary stele with Sam'alian Inscription from Ördekburnu near Zincirli," *BASOR* 369 (2013): 126.

[8] Tropper, *Inschriften von Zincirli*, 54–97, Abbildungen 9–11.

2.3.1. The Aramaic building inscription of Bar-Rākib (Bar-Rākib 1)[9] was created almost a century after the inscription of Kulamuwa. The inscription was discovered in front of Hilani IV, which was probably part of the new palace built by Bar-Rākib.[10] The inscribed orthostat was probably originally situated at the entrance to Bar-Rākib's palace, the construction of which is reported in the inscription.[11] The style of the inscription is very similar to that of Kulamuwa, which, in the time of Bar-Rākib, probably still decorated the entrance of Kulamuwa's palace, and Bar-Rākib must have known it. The text, the ruling lines, and the word dividers are carved in raised relief and in Phoenician letters, similarly to the Kulamuwa inscription. The words are also separated by dots, as in the text of Kulamuwa. The political adherence to the Assyrian power by the king of Sam'al is also explicitly affirmed: Bar-Rākib is proud to be a vassal of Tiglath-pileser III.[12] The only scribal aspect that differs from the inscription of Kulamuwa is the *zayin* in the form of a Z (Kulamuwa's inscription contains a *zayin* in the form of a lying H). The imitation of Kulamuwa's style by Bar-Rākib's scribe and engraver was very probably conscious, and was not limited only to scribal and engraving practices, but also concerned the architectural disposition of the building, as noted by Alessandra Gilibert.[13] The language of Bar-Rākib 1 is different from the inscription of Kulamuwa; it is written in Aramaic. This fact demonstrates that, in this case, the language was not the main medium of the transmission of an ideology. The main means of Bar-Rākib's expression of his adherence to the tradition of Kulamuwa, with its Assyrian connotations, was the style in which the inscription was carved, not the choice of the language.[14]

2.3.2. Other stone inscriptions of Bar-Rākib from Zincirli also closely follow the style of Kulamuwa's inscription, but the similarity is not as strict as in the

---

9 I use the numeration of Bar-Rākib's inscriptions fixed by Tropper, *Inschriften von Zincirli*. For inscription Bar-Rākib 1, see Tropper, *Inschriften von Zincirli*, 132–39 and 163; *Sendschirli IV*, 379, Abb. 275–76, p. 379.

10 *Sendschirli IV*, 377; Gilibert, *Syro-Hittite Monumental Art*, 87.

11 "They had the house of Kulamuwa; and it was a winter house for them; and it was a summer house (too). But I built this house!" *COS* 2.38, lines 17–20, p. 161.

12 "I am Bar-Rakib, son of Panamuwa, king of Sam'al, the servant of Tiglath-Pileser (III), lord of the four quarters of the earth [...] my lord, Tiglath-Pileser, caused me to reign upon the throne of my father." *COS* 2.38, lines 1–7a, p. 161.

13 "[T]he southern façade and entrance of the 'palace of Barrakib' is a conscious architectural replica of the 'palace of Kilamuwa,' with a larger, three-columns-portico at the west side and a smaller, single-column portico at the east side, each leading into separate functional units." Gilibert, *Syro-Hittite Monumental Art*, 88.

14 The Aramaic of the inscriptions of Bar-Rākib is sometimes explained as a result of Bar-Rākib's political orientation to Assyria.

case of Bar-Rākib 1. The inscriptions Bar-Rākib 2 and 3 were part of the new palace built by Bar-Rākib, as Bar-Rākib 1.[15] The inscriptions Bar-Rākib 2 and 4–6 are also carved in raised relief, with ruling lines,[16] but the dividers used in the inscriptions are different from Kulamuwa's tradition: they consist of short vertical lines.[17] The same practice is also used in the stela of Kutamuwa, dated approximately to the same period as Bar-Rākib's inscriptions and written in a language similar to the Sam'alian dialect.[18] These dividers in the form of vertical lines are also used in some of the small inscriptions of Bar-Rākib, on a seal impression (Bar-Rākib 7) and on two of the three silver ingots bearing Bar-Rākib's name (Bar-Rākib 9–10). It is possible that the dividers in the form of dots in Bar-Rākib 1 were an imitation of the older style of Kulamuwa, whereas the dividers in the form of vertical lines represented the practice currently used by the scribes in Zincirli in the second half of the 8th century BCE.

2.3.3. The inscription of Bar-Rākib for his father Panamuwa II, written approximately in 733/2–727 BCE, was discovered at Tahtalı Pınarı, halfway between Zincirli and Gerçin, but was probably originally placed in the necropolis of the kings of Sam'al/Ya'udi in Gerçin, and only thereafter removed to Tahtalı Pınarı.[19] The style and the language of the inscription are very similar to those of the older inscription of Panamuwa I on the statue of Hadad. Both inscriptions are carved in raised relief, thus adhering to the local engraving practice, and both are carved without ruling lines. Both inscriptions contain dividers in the form of dots, which are used in the inscriptions of Kulamuwa and its later stylistic imitation, the building inscription of Bar-Rākib 1. It is probable that the style of the inscription for Panamuwa II imitated the style of the older inscription of Panamuwa I. The *zayin* in the form of a Z, commonly also used in the Aramaic inscriptions of Bar-Rākib, represents an innovative element in the inscription for Panamuwa II with regard to the *zayin* in the form of a lying H in the inscription of Panamuwa I, and probably reflects the current scribal practice in Sam'al/Ya'udi in the second half of the 8th century BCE.

---

15 The orthostat with inscription Bar-Rākib 2 was probably one of the orthostats that decorated Hilani IV, together with the orthostat with the inscription Bar-Rākib 3. See Gilibert, *Syro-Hittite Monumental Art*, 86–88 (Zincirli 74 bears inscription Bar-Rākib 1; Zincirli 75 is inscribed with Bar-Rākib 2; Zincirli 66 is inscribed with Bar-Rākib 3).
16 The inscription Bar-Rākib 3 consists of only one inscribed line.
17 Tropper, *Inschriften von Zincirli*, 140–49; Abbildungen 16–18, 349–50.
18 Dennis Pardee, "A New Inscription from Zincirli," *BASOR* 356 (2009): 57 (third quarter of the 8th century BCE). Concerning the language, see pp. 66–69.
19 *Sendschirli I*, 55–84; Tropper, *Inschriften von Zincirli*, 98–131.

2.4. I summarize the scribal situation in Sam'al/Ya'udi. The stone inscriptions of Bar-Rākib demonstrate that various styles and languages could have been used at the same time under one ruler. The scribe and engraver of Bar-Rākib 1 (the inscription situated in the vicinity of the Kulamuwa inscription) probably consciously imitated the style of the Kulamuwa inscription (ruling lines, dividers in the form of dots). The other inscriptions of Bar-Rākib from his palace (Bar-Rākib 2 and 3, perhaps also 4–6?), as well as the inscription of Kutamuwa, depart slightly from Kulamuwa's tradition (dividers in the form of vertical lines instead of dots). Bar-Rākib's inscription for Panamuwa II, perhaps originally produced for the site of Gerçin, seems adapted to the style of the older inscription of Panamuwa I from Gerçin (Sam'alian dialect, dividers in the form of dots, no ruling lines). It means that the style, and perhaps also the language of the inscription (in the case of Panamuwa II), could have been influenced by the style of the older inscriptions already present *in situ* (either the royal palace or a cultic site) that the ruler, who commissioned the new inscriptions, wanted also to adopt for the newly produced stone inscriptions.

Concerning the languages in Sam'al/Ya'udi, it is interesting to note that the official inscriptions carved in the context of the royal palaces of the Sam'alian kings (Kulamuwa and Bar-Rākib) are written in Phoenician (late 9th century BCE) and in Aramaic (late 8th century BCE). Other monumental inscriptions that are not part of this royal *topos* in the center of the Sam'alian power in the palace at Zincirli are written in the Sam'alian dialect and were produced for a mortuary/sacrificial context (the stela from Ördekburnu, Panamuwa I on the statue of Hadad, Bar-Rākib for Panamuwa II, the stela of Kutamuwa).

The monumental inscriptions from Zincirli and other related sites are carved in a specific style introduced by Kulamuwa. The scribal practices in later stone inscriptions associated with Sam'al/Ya'udi during the century when these inscriptions were produced (from the late 9th to the late 8th century BCE) reflect a switch from the *zayin* in the form of a lying H (late 9th and first half of the 8th century BCE) to the form of a Z (second half of the 8th century BCE), as well as the switch from dividers in the form of dots to those in the form of vertical lines. Both innovative elements (the Z-form of a *zayin* and the dividers in form of vertical lines), apparently introduced in Sam'al/Ya'udi in the second half of the 8th century BCE, were already used in the vicinity of Aleppo in the late 9th/early 8th century BCE (see below).

One of the factors causing some variants in scribal practices in Sam'al/Ya'udi is the *place* where the new inscription had to be situated (royal palace, etc.), and the degree to which the new inscriptions had to imitate the older inscriptions already present *in situ*. The *purpose* of the inscription could also have played some role, especially in the case of funerary inscriptions (the Sam'alian dialect and its features in the funerary inscriptions).

The stone inscriptions associated with Sam'al/Ya'udi allow us to distinguish clearly between the work of the *scribes* who probably traced the inscription, and the work of the *engravers* who executed the inscription in the stone. The scribes probably traced the letter forms on the stone and determined their shape and the disposition of the text. We can observe variations and a development in their work between the inscription of Kulamuwa and those of Bar-Rākib. It is also possible to observe affinities of their work with other Levantine scribes, associated with other scribal nests.

Concerning the work of the engravers, they proved to be extremely conservative during ca. hundred years of production of the stone inscriptions at Sam'al/Ya'udi. They carved the inscriptions in stone in a very consistent manner: in raised relief. The engraving practice in raised relief was common to all of the stone inscriptions, and was probably defined by one central power – the kings of Sam'al/Ya'udi. This engraving practice, typical of Hieroglyphic Luwian inscriptions, is also attested in two fragments of Iron Age West Semitic inscriptions. One of them, published by Pierre Bordreuil, is unprovenanced and it was presumably found near ʿAqaybe, ca. 10 km south of Byblos.[20] Bordreuil dated the inscription on palaeographical grounds approximately to the third quarter of the tenth century BCE. Benjamin Sass proposed to date it to the second half of the 9th century BCE at earliest,[21] it means approximately to the same period of time when the Kulamuwa inscription for the entrance of Building J in Zincirli was engraved. Nevertheless, the authenticity of the ʿAqaybe inscription is uncertain,[22] and so it is difficult to use it as evidence. The second Iron Age fragment is an Aramaic inscription in the National Museum of Aleppo mentioning Rešef and Kubaba,

---

20 Pierre Bordreuil, "Une inscription phénicienne champlevée des environs de Byblos," *Semitica* 27 (1977): 23–27.

21 Benjamin Sass, *The Alphabet at the Turn of the Millennium. The West Semitic Alphabet ca. 1150–850 BCE. The Antiquity of the Arabian, Greek and Phrygian Alphabets*, Tel Aviv, Journal of the Institute of Archaeology of Tel Aviv University, Occasional Publications 4 (Tel Aviv: Tel Aviv University Press, 2005), 32–33, and 30, Fig. 10.

22 André Lemaire, "West Semitic Epigraphy and the History of the Levant during the 12th–10th Centuries BCE," in *The Ancient Near East in the 12th–10th Centuries BCE: Culture and History. Proceedings of the International Conference held at the University of Haifa, 2 – 5 May, 2010*, ed. Gershon Galil, Ayelet Gilboa, Aren M. Maeir, and Dan'el Kahn (AOAT 392, Münster: Ugarit-Verlag, 2012), 291–307, especially 295, note 27.

which is said to have been discovered at Tell Sifr,[23] a site that I am unable to locate in the Aleppo region.[24] Aramaic stone inscriptions engraved in raised relief were also produced in later periods in northwestern Arabia, in Tayma. Two or three such Persian period inscriptions are known,[25] and also a later Nabataean inscription, equally found in Tayma.[26]

Among the inscriptions analyzed in this article, ruling lines guide the text only in some of the inscriptions associated with Sam'al/Ya'udi, in the Phoenician inscription of Kulamuwa, and in the inscriptions that more or less faithfully imitate its style, the inscription on the stela from Ördekburnu, on the stela of Kutamuwa, and in the Aramaic inscriptions Bar-Rākib 1, Bar-Rākib 2 and Bar-Rākib 4–6, as well as the small inscription on the seal Bar-Rākib 7.

---

23 Franco Michelini Tocci, "Un frammento di stele aramaica da Tell Sifr," *OrAnt* 1 (1962): 21–22. I am grateful to André Lemaire for this reference.
24 The character of the inscription and the fact that it is stored in the National Museum of Aleppo make it unlikely that the site can be identified with Tell Sifr in Mesopotamia (perhaps ancient Kutalla, 14 km far from Larsa; see Trevor Bryce, *The Routledge Handbook of the Peoples and Places of Ancient Western Asia. From the Early Bronze Age to the Fall of the Persian Empire* [London – New York: Routledge, 2009], 400). The identification of Tell Sifr with Tell Sefire in the vicinity of Aleppo does not seem to be likely: the name of the site is not identical, and the practice of engraving in raised relief is completely different from what is attested in the Sefire inscriptions. Can Tell Sifr be the Syrian site Tell Sfeir, ca. 72 km northeast of Tell Rifʿat, near the Syrian-Turkish border? For the location, see John Matthers (ed.), *The River Qoueiq, Northern Syria, and its Catchment. Studies arising from the Tell Rifa'at Survey 1977–79*, Part i (BAR International Series 98 [i], Oxford: B.A.R, 1981), 17 (no. 69), Fig. 35a, and the map on p. 21, Fig. 6.
25 It is the stela from Tayma in Musée du Louvre, inv. no. 1505, discovered in 1880 (published e.g. in *CIS* II 1 113; *KAI* 228). The second stela was discovered in Tayma in 1979 and published by Alasdair Livingstone et al., "Taimā': Recent Soundings and New Inscribed Material," *Atlal* 7, Part III (1983): 102–18, especially 108–11. A sandstone slab from Tayma inscribed with an Aramaic funerary inscription of "*'In* daughter of *Šb'n*" in raised relief is also on display in the Musée du Louvre, inv. no. AO 5074. The label in the museum dates the inscription to the 5th century BCE.
26 It is the fragment of a Nabataean inscription from Tayma in Musée du Louvre, Paris, inv. no. AO 26599 (*CIS* II 1 336).

3 The environs of Aleppo

3.1. Aleppo is an ancient site, with a long tradition already attested in the 3rd millennium BCE.[27] The site yielded Luwian inscriptions;[28] nevertheless, thus far, no Aramaic inscriptions have been reported as coming from the ancient city of Aleppo. In the 9th and 8th centuries BCE, Aleppo was surrounded by the Aramaean population, whose Aramaic inscriptions were found within a radius of ca. 50 km around the ancient city.[29] The Aramaic inscriptions were found at Tell Afis (ca. 45 km southwest of the ancient Aleppo), Sefire (ca. 23 km southeast of the ancient Aleppo), Nērab (ca. 7 km southeast of the ancient Aleppo), and Brēdj (ca. 7 km north of Aleppo).

The inscriptions were produced in three different political contexts. The inscriptions from Tell Afis (the stela of Zakkur and a fragment of another stela) may be dated to the end of the 9th/beginning of the 8th century BCE and are associated with the reign of Zakkur, king of Hamath and Luʿaš. The votive inscription of Bar-Hadad on the stela of Melqart from Brēdj is dated approximately to the same period as the inscriptions from Tell Afis, around 800 BCE or to the early 8th century BCE, and is attributed to the kingdom of Arpad/Bīt-Agūsi.[30] The inscriptions from Sefire were produced in the kingdom of Arpad/Bīt-Agūsi, probably in or around 755–754 BCE. Finally, the inscriptions on the two mortuary stelae from Nērab can be dated to the early 7th century BCE, when the region already belonged to one of the Assyrian provinces established in the second half of the 8th century BCE.

The Aramaic inscriptions found in the proximity of Aleppo can be divided into two chronologically successive groups. First, the inscriptions of the late

---

27 See Horst Klengel, "Die historische Rolle der Stadt Aleppo im vorantiken Syrien," in *Die Orientalische Stadt: Kontinuität, Wandel, Bruch*, ed. Gernot Wilhelm (Colloquien der Deutschen Orient-Gesellschaft [CDOG] 1, Berlin: Deutsche Orient-Gesellschaft, in Kommission bei SDV Saarbrücker Druckerei und Verlag, Saarbrücken, 1997), 359–74.

28 John David Hawkins, "The inscriptions of the Aleppo temple," *Anatolian Studies* 61 (2011): 35–54.

29 On the presence of the kingdom of Hamath at Aleppo, see Zsolt Simon, "Aramaean Borders: the Hieroglyphic Luwian Evidence," in *Aramaean Borders. Defining Aramaean Territories in the 10th–8th Centuries B.C.E.*, ed. Jan Dušek and Jana Mynářová (CHANE 101, Leiden – Boston: Brill, 2019), 127–48, especially pp. 140–41; and Matthieu Richelle, "The Fluctuating Borders of Hamath (10th–8th Centuries B.C.E.)," in *Aramaean Borders. Defining Aramaean Territories in the 10th–8th Centuries B.C.E.*, ed. Jan Dušek and Jana Mynářová (CHANE 101, Leiden – Boston: Brill, 2019), 203–28, especially 211–28.

30 Wayne T. Pitard, "The Identity of the Bir-Hadad of the Melqart Stela," *BASOR* 272 (1988): 3–21; Émile Puech, "La stèle de Bar-Hadad à Melqart et les rois d'Arpad," *RB* 99 (1992): 311–34.

9th/early 8th century BCE (Tell Afis and Brēdj); and second, the inscriptions from the mid-8th to the early 7th centuries BCE (Sefire and Nērab).

3.2. Three Aramaic inscriptions belong to the group of the late 9th/early 8th century BCE:
- the inscription on the stela of Zakkur, king of Hamath and Lu'aš, probably written in the early 8th century, and found at Tell Afis;[31]
- a stela fragment from Tell Afis, inscribed in the late 9th or early 8th century BCE;[32]
- the Aramaic inscription of Bar-Hadad on the stela of Melqart, probably inscribed around 800 or in the early 8th century BCE.[33]

Even if the inscriptions were commissioned by kings of various polities,[34] their style is very similar. The scribes in the three inscriptions used the *zayin* in the form of a Z (but the Melqart stela, line 1, also contains a *zayin* in the form of a lying H). All three inscriptions contain dividers in the form of vertical lines; they have the same size as the letters in the inscription on the Melqart stela, and they have the form of short strokes on the stela of Zakkur. Among the Phoenician inscriptions of the Iron Age, this type of divider is attested in Byblos, for example in the inscriptions of Ahiram (*KAI* 1, ca. 1000 BCE), Yeḥimilk (*KAI* 4, ca. mid-10th century BCE) and Eliba'al (*KAI* 6, ca. 915 BCE).[35] Because of the lack of evidence we do not know how the scribal culture of Byblos could have influenced the Aramaic scribes of the late 9th century BCE and later, but a connection with the Byblian scribal culture is likely.[36]

---

31 Among the numerous editions, see for example *KAI* 202; Frederick Mario Fales and Giulia Francesca Grassi, *L'aramaico antico. Storia, grammatica, testi commentati* (Udine: Forum, 2016), 123–31.
32 Maria Giulia Amadasi Guzzo, "Un fragment de stèle araméenne de Tell Afis," *Or* 78 (2009): 336–47. She dated the stela approximately to 807–803 BCE, the end of the reign of Haza'el of Damascus and the beginning of the reign of Zakkur.
33 Pitard, "The Identity"; Puech, "La stèle de Bar-Hadad." This date around 800 BCE or in the early 8th century is the most likely one for this inscription.
34 The stela of Zakkur, and probably also the inscribed stela fragment from Tell Afis, were commissioned by the king of Hamath and Lu'aš. The stela of Bar-Hadad for Melqart was commissioned by a son of Attarsumki of Arpad.
35 The form of the *zayin* is nevertheless different from that of the Aramaic inscriptions: it has the form of a lying H.
36 Concerning the origin of dividers in the form of vertical strokes in Byblos, see June Ashton, "The Persistence, Diffusion and Interchangeability of Scribal Habits in the Ancient Near East before the Codex" (PhD diss. The University of Sydney, 1999), 123 and 130.

Other hints pointing to a Phoenician cultural or scribal context are present in the inscriptions of Zakkur and on the Melqart stela. Zakkur erected his inscribed stela before Iluwer, probably at Tell Afis. But his personal divinity was different. The god who is said to have delivered Zakkur from the siege of the enemy armies was Baʿal-šamayin, a god with a name referring to a Phoenician rather than an Aramaean context. In the case of the Melqart stela, the Phoenician context is even more evident: Melqart on the stela, wearing a Phoenician garment, was the god of the Phoenician city of Tyre. Moreover, the style of the Phoenician dedicatory inscriptions was recognized in the Aramaic inscription, which could be a translation or an imitation of a Phoenician original.[37]

All these elements allow us to hypothesize that the scribes who carved these inscriptions were somehow attached to the Phoenician scribal world, more particularly perhaps the scribal tradition of the city of Byblos (because of the style of the inscriptions).

3.3. The inscriptions produced in the vicinity of Aleppo in the later phase (mid-8th to early 7th century BCE) reflect a scribal style different from that of the inscriptions written in the late 9th/early 8th centuries BCE. Two sets of Aramaic inscriptions belong to this group: the inscriptions from Sefire (mid-8th century BCE) and the inscribed funerary stelae from Nērab (early 7th century BCE). Both sets have one particular feature: no dividers are used.

The Sefire inscriptions may all be dated to around the mid-8th century.[38] Sefire I and II are inscribed on basalt stelae of a very similar form, and their content also seems to have been very similar; both contain an *adê*-treaty concluded between Matiʾel of Arpad and Bar-Gaʾyah of KTK. Sefire III is inscribed on an orthostat and also contains an *adê*-treaty concluded between two kings whose names are missing, but one of them was probably Matiʾel of Arpad. All the Sefire inscriptions are carved in *scriptio continua*, using no dividers or other means of separation between words. The *zayin* has the form of a lying H. These elements make it clear that the scribe who carved the inscriptions was educated in a school whose style was different from the Aramaic inscriptions produced in the vicinity of Aleppo

---

37 Giorgio Levi Della Vida and William F. Albright, "Some Notes on the Stele of Ben-Hadad," *BASOR* 90 (1943): 30–31.

38 André Lemaire and Jean-Marie Durand, *Les inscriptions araméennes de Sfiré et l'Assyrie de Shamshi-ilu*, Hautes études orientales 20 (Genève – Paris: Droz, 1984); Joseph A. Fitzmyer, *The Aramaic Inscriptions of Sefire*, BibOr 19/A (Roma: Editrice Pontificio Instituto Biblico, 1995 [second revised edition]). Sefire I can be dated to 754 BCE, and the other two inscriptions, Sefire II and Sefire III, are probably contemporary, because their script and style are the same as that of Sefire I. See Jan Dušek, "Dating the Aramaic Stele Sefire I," *Aramaic Studies* 17 (2019): 1–14.

approximately fifty years earlier. The style of the Sefire inscriptions is extremely similar to that of the Phoenician inscriptions from Karatepe.

Apparently, the scribal tradition reflected in the Sefire inscriptions continued to exist on the territory of the kingdom of Arpad/Bīt-Agūsi even after its destruction by the Assyrian army of Tiglath-pileser III in 740 BCE, and the Aramaic inscriptions on the two mortuary stelae from Nērab from the early 7th century BCE,[39] a site situated ca. 16 km northwest of Sefire, belong to this tradition. Both stelae from Nērab were inscribed in a political context very different from that of the Sefire inscriptions, in the Assyrian province of Arpadda, but very probably on the territory of the ancient kingdom of Arpad/Bīt-Agūsi. Both inscriptions are carved without dividers, as are the inscriptions from Sefire; in the inscription Nērab B, the separation of words in a line is in some cases indicated by a larger space. However, the *zayin* in the Nērab inscriptions is different from Sefire; in the Nērab inscriptions it has the form of a Z.

3.4. There are a number of Phoenician inscriptions from the mid-8th to late 8th century BCE, discovered northwest of the Amanus Mountains, which are engraved in *scriptio continua*, e.g. the inscription from Hassan-Beyli and the Phoenician text of the bilingual Luwian-Phoenician inscription from Çineköy.[40] The Phoenician inscriptions from Karatepe,[41] especially the three Phoenician versions of the inscriptions of King Azatiwada probably dated to the last quarter of the 8th century BCE,[42] represent an excellent comparandum for the Sefire and the Nērab inscriptions and share many elements with them. Three Phoenician and two Luwian inscriptions recording the same message (with variants) of King Azatiwada were discovered in the city, and were situated in the gates giving access to the citadel and in their vicinity. The Phoenician inscription in the North/Lower Gate was inscribed on orthostats and ended on a lion. In the South/Upper Gate, the Phoenician inscription was carved on the portal lion and continued on an orthostat, and its text seems to be a slightly reduced version of the North/Lower

---

39 *KAI* 225–226; Simo Parpola, "Si'gabbar of Nerab Resurrected," *OLP* 16 (1985): 273–75.

40 André Lemaire, "L'inscription phénicienne de Hassan-Beyli reconsidérée," *RSF* 11 (1983): 9–19; Recai Tekoglu, André Lemaire, Ismet Ipek and A. Kazim Tosun, "La bilingue royale louvito-phénicienne de Çineköy," *CRAI* 144/3 (2000): 961–1006.

41 Halet Çambel, *Corpus of Hieroglyphic Luwian Inscriptions*, vol. 2: *Karatepe-Aslantaş. The Inscriptions: Facsimile Edition*, Untersuchungen zur indogermanischen Sprach- und Kulturwissenschaft 8.2 (Berlin – New York: De Gruyter, 1999).

42 François Bron, *Recherches sur les inscriptions phéniciennes de Karatepe*, Hautes études orientales 11 (Genève: Librairie Droz, 1979), 163–69.

Gate inscription.[43] The third version of the Phoenician inscription was carved on the statue of the Storm-God near the South/Upper Gate, and its text is slightly different from the other two Phoenician versions.[44]

These are the elements which allow us to compare the Karatepe inscriptions with those from Sefire and Nērab:

- The style of the inscriptions from Sefire and that of the Karatepe inscription in the North/Lower Gate are extremely similar. The inscriptions from Sefire are written in *scriptio continua*, with no dividers or spaces between words. The Karatepe inscription in the North/Lower Gate contains no dividers, only spaces are occasionally used to separate some words.
- The spacing between words, with no dividers, can be detected in some cases in inscription Nērab B and, more clearly, in the Karatepe inscriptions on the statue of the Storm-God and on some inscribed fragments from the South/Upper Gate.
- The script of the Phoenician inscriptions of Azatiwada is later than that of the Sefire inscriptions, but both the Sefire and Karatepe inscriptions contain the *zayin* in the form of a lying H. The Z-form is also attested at Karatepe. It appears in only one of the separate inscriptions, but the lying H-form is used in all the other Karatepe inscriptions.[45]
- Most part of the Phoenician inscription from the North/Lower Gate is carved on orthostats that follow each other from right to left.[46] It is very likely that Sefire III, also carved on an orthostat, originally belonged to a very similar set of orthostats, perhaps also situated in the gate of Sefire.

These common elements in the inscriptions from Sefire, Nērab, and Karatepe point to the same scribal school, with the same or a similar concept of creating inscriptions and their disposition in a public space. Apparently, this scribal concept crossed political and linguistic borders. It was used in two different lan-

---

43 See Albrecht Alt, "Ergänzungen zu den phönikischen Inschriften von Karatepe," *WO* 2 (1955): 172–83, especially 173–78. The reconstruction of the South/Upper Gate inscription by Wolfgang Röllig confirms that this text was indeed a slightly reduced version of the North/Lower Gate inscription; see Çambel, *Corpus*, 50–57.

44 Alt, "Ergänzungen," 178–182; Bron, *Recherches*, 18–22.

45 See the palaeographical table in Çambel, *Corpus*, 80–81, and the comments on *zayin*, pp. 75–76. The Z-form is used in the inscription Pho/S.I.a; see Çambel, *Corpus*, 35, 68–72, Plates 106–07.

46 See Çambel, *Corpus*, Plates 5–13.

guages (Aramaic and Phoenician), in two different kingdoms and different regions, and for completely different types of texts (*adê*-treaties at Sefire, commemorative inscriptions at Karatepe).

Last but not least, the style of the Aramaic inscription with Bar-Rākib's name on a silver ingot from Zincirli, which is on display in the British Museum in London (ME 134918),[47] is very similar to that of the Nērab inscriptions: the words are not separated by dividers, a space separates the words בר and פנמו, and the *kaf* used in the inscription is very similar to that which is used in the inscriptions from Nērab. The inscriptions of Bar-Rākib on other two silver ingots from Zincirli reflect a different style (the presence of dividers in the form of vertical strokes, and the *kaf* is different).[48]

3.5. I conclude the section on inscriptions from the vicinity of Aleppo. The available epigraphic evidence indicates that both phases of scribal styles, the early one (late 9th/early 8th century BCE) and the later as well (mid-8th century–early 7th century BCE), were somehow connected to the Phoenician scribal culture. The early tradition seems connected with Byblos; the later phase has a very interesting parallel in the Phoenician inscriptions from Karatepe. In the later phase, it is not easy to determine which scribal tradition was original and which was influenced: the Sefire inscriptions are older than those from Karatepe, but it does not mean that the Aramaean tradition influenced the Phoenician one. As I am not sure whether something like a typically Aramaean scribal culture really existed in the Iron Age, I would say that the Phoenician scribal culture represented the source of influence for Aramaean scribes in both phases, early and late. Yet the character of the Phoenician influence in the first phase was different from that in the later phase, and it is manifested in the change of style of the Aramaic inscriptions produced in the vicinity of Aleppo between the beginning and the end of the 8th century BCE.

---

47 *Sendschirli V*, 120, Tafel 58 *t*. Tropper, *Inschriften von Zincirli*, inscription Barrākib no. 8, pp. 152 and 164.
48 *Sendschirli V*, 119–20, Tafel 58 *u–v*. Tropper, *Inschriften von Zincirli*, inscription Barrākib nos. 9 and 10, pp. 152 and 164.

4 Damascus and Hamath

4.1. Thus far, no Aramaic inscriptions have been discovered in the city of Damascus; the epigraphic material associated with this Aramaean kingdom comes from elsewhere. I use for my analysis the Aramaic stelae fragments from Tel Dan and a set of Aramaic inscriptions mentioning Haza'el, probably King of Damascus in the second half of the 9th century BCE (small inscriptions from Arslan Tash, Euboia, Samos, and Nimrud). These inscriptions can be dated to the late 9th century BCE. Unfortunately, no monumental inscriptions with clearly attested scribal practices are associated with the later phase of the existence of the kingdom of Damascus, in the second third of the 8th century, before its destruction by the Assyrians in 732 BCE. This lack of Damascus inscriptions from the mid-8th century BCE can be partially supplemented by some of the inscriptions discovered in the city of Hama, dated to the 8th century BCE.

4.2. The stelae fragments from Tel Dan were probably inscribed in the late 9th century BCE.[49] The dividers used in the text have the form of dots. Dots are also used as dividers in the Aramaic inscription on an ivory plate mentioning Haza'el, discovered at Arslah Tash (ancient Ḥadattu).[50] I consider the ivory plate from Arslan Tash to have been inscribed before the stelae fragments from Tel Dan: the Arslan Tash inscription was probably carved under Haza'el in the second half of the 9th century BCE, whereas the Tel Dan fragments were probably issued later, under Bar-Hadad, son of Haza'el, around the end of the 9th century BCE.[51]

A set of nearly fifty Aramaic graffiti was discovered in the city of Hama. These inscriptions are dated to the 8th century BCE, most of them probably before 720

---

49 Avraham Biran and Joseph Naveh, "An Aramaic Stele Fragment from Tel Dan," *IEJ* 43 (1993): 81–98; Avraham Biran and Joseph Naveh, "The Tel Dan Inscription: A New Fragment," *IEJ* 45 (1995): 1–18. The dating to the late 9th century is based on my own analysis of the inscription: Jan Dušek, *Old Aramaic Inscriptions and Their Contexts. An Epigraphic, Archaeological, and Historical Synthesis*, vol. 1, Ancient Near Eastern Studies Supplement Series (Leuven: Peeters, forthcoming), chapter 3.
50 François Thureau-Dangin et al., *Arslan Tash*, vol. 1: *Texte*; vol. 2: *Atlas* (Paris: Librairie orientaliste Paul Geuthner, 1931), vol. 1: 135–38; vol. 2: Pl. XLVIII.
51 Thus, "my father" in Tel Dan, frg. A, lines 2 and 3, probably refers to Bar-Hadad's father, Haza'el. See e.g. Gershon Galil, "A Re-Arrangement of the Fragments of the Tel Dan Inscription and the Relations between Israel and Aram," *PEQ* 133 (2001): 16–21.

BCE.[52] Many of these inscriptions consist of a single word, or of two words separated by a gap.[53] Only two of these graffiti consist of more than two words separated by dividers, which have the form of dots.[54] Even if this evidence is extremely scanty, it seems to confirm the use of dividers of this type in the cultural perimeter of Damascus and modern Hama not only in the late 9th century BCE, but also during the 8th century BCE.[55]

4.3. Three small inscriptions mentioning Haza'el have no dividers. They are the inscription on a bronze horse's blinker from Eretria on Euboia, the inscription on a face-piece from Heraion on Samos,[56] and the fragment of an inscription with the name of Haza'el on an ivory plate, found at Fort Shalmaneser in Nimrud.

Concerning the ivory from Nimrud,[57] the inscription is fragmentary; the one and a half words of the inscription are not separated by a divider, and we do not know in which part of the Levant it originated. The two pieces of a horse's harness bearing inscriptions with Haza'el's name were equally found out of the Levantine context (on Greek islands Euboia and Samos), but their inscriptions may indicate their origin: they were given by "Hadad to our lord Haza'el from Umq," which means from the kingdom of Unqi in the northern Levant. It is not clear where the inscriptions were carved, whether it was in Unqi or in Damascus. The inscriptions can be compared with the inscription on the golden case from Zincirli bearing an

---

52 Benedikt Otzen, "Appendix 2: The Aramaic Inscriptions," in *Hama. Fouilles et recherches de la Fondation Carlsberg 1931–1938*, vol. II 2: *Les objets de la période dite syro-hittite (âge du Fer)*, ed. Poul J. Riis and Marie-Louise Buhl, Nationalmuseets skrifter, Større Beretninger XII (København: Nationalmuseet, 1990), 266–318 (on the date of the inscriptions, see pp. 272–74).

53 This concerns especially the inscriptions containing the term צבה combined with another word.

54 Otzen, "Aramaic Inscriptions," 275.

55 The inscription of Zakkur, king of Hamath and Lu'aš, is politically associated with the kingdom of Hamath, but it was discovered and probably also engraved in the vicinity of Aleppo, and this is the reason why I deal with it in the Aleppo group. Thus far, there is no evidence concerning Zakkur coming from the city of Hama or its close vicinity. The situation is different for Urhilina, king of Hamath; see Poul J. Riis and Marie-Louise Buhl, *Hama. Fouilles et recherches de la Fondation Carlsberg 1931–1938*, vol. II 2: *Les objets de la période dite syro-hittite (âge du Fer)*, Nationalmuseets skrifter, Større Beretninger XII (København: Nationalmuseet, 1990), 10.

56 François Bron and André Lemaire, "Les inscriptions araméennes de Hazaël," *RA* 83 (1989): 35–44.

57 Georgina Herrmann and Stuart Laidlaw, *Ivories from Rooms SW11/12 and T10, Fort Shalmaneser. Commentary and Catalogue*, vol. 1: *Commentary and Catalogue*; vol. 2: *Colour and Black & White Plates*, Ivories from Nimrud (1949–1963) VII, 1–2 (London: British Institute for Study of Iraq, 2013), 292, no. T310, Plate 243.

inscription of Kulamuwa, dated to the last third of the 9th century BCE,[58] similarly to the inscriptions of Haza'el. This small inscription of Kulamuwa, like the two inscriptions of Haza'el on the pieces of a harness and the Haza'el inscription on ivory from Nimrud, contains no dividers. However, it does not mean that *scriptio continua* would be a scribal practice typical only for the northern Syria. The presence or absence of dividers in such small inscriptions rather depended on the choice of individual scribes in various centers of the Levant and not on their geographical origin. The graphical constraints of small and short inscriptions engraved in a hard material such as bronze or ivory may have been different from those of large inscriptions engraved in stone. It is not difficult to understand the message of short and small inscriptions, which were often formulated in simple and stereotyped phrases. This may be the reason why dividers were sometimes omitted in small inscriptions. The situation is different in the case of large inscriptions engraved in stone, where the graphical separation of words may assist a reader to understand a complex text.

4.4. I conclude the section on the Aramaic inscriptions associated with the kingdom of Damascus, its king, or found in Hama. These inscriptions reflect two different scribal practices: using dividers in form of dots, and using no dividers. The attribution of the production of two of the three small inscriptions of Haza'el with no dividers to Damascene scribes is uncertain. The fact that they contain no dividers does not allow us to determine the geographical origin of their scribes (either southern or northern Syria).

The Aramaic fragments from Tel Dan, the inscribed ivory plate from Arslan Tash, and the two above mentioned graffiti from Hama indicate that the dividers in form of dots were used by the scribes in the perimeter of Damascus and Hama. Among the inscriptions that I analyze in this article, dots are used as dividers in some of the inscriptions from Zincirli, beginning with the inscription of Kulamuwa (ca. 825 BCE).[59] The dots are one of the few elements that the Tel Dan, Hama, and Zincirli inscriptions have in common: this said, the technique used for engraving a stone inscription in Tel Dan was completely different from that of Zincirli.

Dividers in the form of dots are well attested in other inscriptions from the southern Levant. For example, they are used in the Moabite inscription on the

---

58 Tropper, *Inschriften von Zincirli*, 50–53.
59 The practice current in the Zincirli inscriptions from the second half of the 8th century BCE seems to have been the use of vertical strokes, but dots are also used, perhaps as an imitation of the older style.

stela of Mesha from the second half of the 9th century BCE, where the dots separate words, and vertical lines mark larger textual units.[60] Dots are also used in a royal Moabite inscription on a broken octagonal basalt column, dated to the 8th century BCE,[61] as well as in a Hebrew inscription on ivory from Nimrud, perhaps written in the mid-8th century BCE.[62] Among later inscriptions, dots are also used as dividers in the Hebrew inscription of the "steward of the palace" from the burial cave in the Kidron Valley,[63] in the Hebrew inscription from the Siloam tunnel (early 7th century BCE?), and in the dedicatory inscription of Akayus, son of Padi, from Ekron (early 7th century BCE), which used ruling lines, as did most of the inscriptions associated with Zincirli. Apparently, dot dividers were commonly used in the southern Levant during the Iron Age, so the style of the Tel Dan fragments, of the Haza'el inscription from Arslan Tash, and of the two Hama inscriptions fits the practice in the southern Levant very well. On the other hand, dot dividers were not used exclusively in the southern Levant inscriptions. Vertical lines were also used; see, for example, the Gezer calendar, the stela fragment from Samaria, the inscription of [Ke]moshyat, probably Mesha's father,[64] or the plaster inscription from Deir 'Alla.[65]

5 Conclusion

I began the paper with a reference to Gzella's hypothesis, based on the analysis of the language, of the existence of one scribal school that would have formed the scribes who produced the Aramaic inscriptions in central Syria. What is true for the language is not for the scribal practices. From this point of view, the analysis of the scribal practices does not confirm the existence of such a single school. The central Syrian group, as defined by Gzella, contains a variety of scribal practices that preclude the existence of only one scribal school. Moreover, the inscriptions of Gzella's northwest Syrian group share some features with some of the central Syrian group.

---

60 Cf. Ashton, "The Persistence," 137.
61 Shmuel Aḥituv, *Echoes from the Past. Hebrew and Cognate Inscriptions from the Biblical Period* (Jerusalem: Carta, 2008), 419–23.
62 Aḥituv, *Echoes*, 329–30.
63 Aḥituv, *Echoes*, 44–47.
64 Aḥituv, *Echoes*, 253, 257, 387.
65 Jakob Hoftijzer and Gerrit van der Kooij, *Aramaic Texts from Deir 'Alla*, Documenta et Monumenta Orientis Antiqui 19 (Leiden: Brill, 1976), Combination I–II.

My analysis is focused on the inscriptions of Gzella's central Syrian and northwest Syrian groups. I proposed regrouping the inscriptions into three geographically defined nests: Sam'al/Ya'udi, the environs of Aleppo, and the inscriptions of Damascus and Hamath. The nests of Sam'al/Ya'udi and of the environs of Aleppo seem to belong to the same area of interconnected scribal cultures situated in the *northern Levant*. The scanty evidence of Damascus and Hama rather refers to the practices of the *southern Levant*, even if connections with the Aleppo and Sam'al/Ya'udi nests exist.

5.1. The scribal nests around Aleppo and in Sam'al/Ya'udi belong to the area of the northern Levant. The nest of Sam'al/Ya'udi is characterized by the existence of a single royal dynasty whose members commissioned the inscriptions. Here, we may speak of a scribal and engraving tradition that lasted for approximately a century. This nest is the only one among the three analyzed in this article where the use of ruling lines is attested. The scribal tradition of Sam'al/Ya'udi is characterized by a conservative and in the West Semitic culture not very common way of engraving inscriptions in raised relief, practiced in the stone inscriptions from the beginning to the end of the existence of this scribal nest. It is difficult to ascertain where the origin of this practice among the West Semitic scribes was. Was it in the vicinity of Byblos? Or rather in Zincirli? Or was the engraving in raised relief a result of influence coming from the Luwian scribes? We are unable to answer these questions. In any case, the engraving tradition in raised relief was apparently not lost among the Aramaean scribes with the end of the kingdom of Sam'al/Ya'udi (late 8th century BCE), and later reappeared in the oasis of Tayma in Arabia.

In the scribal tradition of the large stone inscriptions, we can observe a change from dividers in the form of dots to those in the form of vertical lines, as well as a change in the *zayin* from the form of a lying H to the form of a Z. It is not clear whether these changes were due to the natural development of the scribal practice in Zincirli, or rather to an influence coming from other scribal nests (cf. the practice attested in the vicinity of Aleppo in the late 9th/early 8th century BCE). Nevertheless, the evolution of the dividers in Sam'al/Ya'udi seems to invalidate Joseph Naveh's hypothesis that the dividers in the West Semitic inscriptions of the early first millennium developed from vertical strokes to dots.[66]

The character of the nest of scribal activities that I have defined around Aleppo is different from that of Sam'al/Ya'udi, because it was not defined by a

---

66 Joseph Naveh, "Word Division in West Semitic Writing," *IEJ* 23 (1973): 206–07.

single political authority. The inscriptions belonging to this nest were produced in three different political contexts (Bīt-Agūsi, Hamath/Luʿaš, Assyria), and none of these political powers had its center in Aleppo. In spite of this political diversity, the inscriptions belonging to this nest have some common denominators in each of the two phases, the late 9th/early 8th century BCE and the mid-8th to early 7th century BCE. In this scribal nest, we can observe a switch from one style in the first phase with dividers in the form of vertical lines to another scribal style in the second phase with no dividers.

I cannot exclude the possibility that this switch was due to a natural development in the region. But I am rather inclined to see in the cessation of the use of dividers a new scribal practice imported from elsewhere. Both forms of the *zayin* (the lying H and the form of a Z) are attested in both phases; in the first phase, nevertheless, the Z form predominates in the available evidence.[67] All these facts make it clear that the development of the style of engraving West-Semitic inscriptions in stone around Aleppo was different from that in Samʾal/Yaʾudi.

The scribal nests of the northern Levant, those of Samʾal/Yaʾudi and the vicinity of Aleppo, share some common elements and may have belonged, together with some regions northwest of the Amanus Mountains, to a network of scribal nests in the northern Levant whose members apparently communicated with one another. This geographical area consists of two parts: the regions southeast of the Amanus Mountains and the region northwest of them. It is mainly the similarity of scribal culture reflected in the inscriptions from Sefire, Nērab, and Karatepe, and also in the inscriptions from Çineköy and Hassan-Beyli, that indicates that the scribal centers on both sides of the Amanus Mountains were interconnected (at least in the 8th century BCE). The Phoenician language seems to have been used originally as an international language on both sides of the Amanus range, but in the regions southeast of Amanus Aramaic subsequently became dominant and stopped on the eastern slopes of Amanus.[68] This development can be observed in Zincirli, at the eastern foot of the Amanus Mountains, where, in the inscriptions of the royal palace, in the 8th century Aramaic replaced Phoenician, which was still being used in the late 9th century BCE. The site of Hassan-Beyli, a site situated only ca. 13 km west of Zincirli, but already on the western

---

67 The inscriptions from Tell Afis contain the *zayin* in the form of a Z; the inscription on the Melqart stela contains both forms of the *zayin*. The Sefire inscriptions contain the *zayin* in the form of a lying H, whereas the scribes of the Nērab inscriptions used the Z-form.
68 See Bron, *Recherches*, 180–81.

slopes of Amanus, yielded a Phoenician inscription that can be dated to the second half of the 8th century BCE[69] (thus written later than the Sefire inscriptions). This indicates where the linguistic border could have been situated in the second half of the 8th century BCE: between Zincirli at the eastern foot of the Amanus Mountains, and Hassan-Beyli on their western slopes.

Even if Aramaic was used in the regions southeast of Amanus, the scribes writing in Aramaic continued to produce their texts under the influence of the Phoenician scribes. We saw the Phoenician influence, especially dividers in the form of vertical lines, in the inscriptions from the vicinity of Aleppo in the late 9th/early 8th century BCE, probably coming from Byblos. Dividers of this type were later adopted in most of the Aramaic inscriptions in Zincirli in the second half of the 8th century BCE. We equally saw, in the mid-8th–early 7th century BCE, the inscriptions from Sefire and Nērab, as well as the inscription Bar-Rākib 8 from Zincirli, sharing elements with the Phoenician scribes at Karatepe, Hassan-Beyli, and Cineköy (no dividers, *scriptio continua*, spacing between words). Writing without dividers is already attested in the late 9th century BCE in a small inscription of Kulamuwa on a golden case, and in the Haza'el inscriptions from Euboia and Samos. *Scriptio continua* is also already attested in Greek inscriptions in the 8th century BCE,[70] during the same period of time as when the inscriptions from Karatepe, Sefire, etc. were engraved. June Ashton connected this style of writing with the scribes of Tyre.[71]

I do not believe that *scriptio continua* in the inscriptions from Sefire, Nērab, Karatepe, Hassan-Beyli, and Cineköy was due to the work of provincial or inexperienced scribes.[72] More probably, it was a specific and fully-fledged style of writing an inscription. Nevertheless, marking the division between words was more practical for understanding West Semitic texts, and this was perhaps the reason why spacing between words, perhaps replacing the older use of dividers,

69 Lemaire, "L'inscription phénicienne de Hassan-Beyli," 16–17.
70 Ashton, "The Persistence," 129. See the inscriptions in Joseph Naveh, *Early History of the Alphabet. An Introduction to West Semitic Epigraphy and Palaeography* (Jerusalem: The Magnes Press, The Hebrew University, 1997; reprint of the second revised edition 1987), 179, Figs. 159 and 161.
71 Ashton, "The Persistence," 129.
72 Millard considered the Aramaic inscriptions in *scriptio continua* to be a result of the work of provincial or inexperienced scribes; Alan R. Millard, "'Scriptio continua' in early Hebrew: Ancient practice or modern surmise?," *JSS* 15 (1970): 2–15, especially 13–14.

began to develop very quickly in the nests using *scriptio continua* in the second half of the 8th century BCE.[73]

5.2. Damascus and Hama seem to have been attached to the southern Levantine practices. The inscriptions hitherto associated with Damascus were produced in only one phase, the late 9th century BCE. The inscriptions from Tel Dan and Arslan Tash use dots as dividers. The inscription on the ivory fragment from Nimrud contains no divider in the text. Two later inscriptions from Hama, probably dated to the 8th century BCE (before 720 BCE), contain dot dividers. The inscriptions on the pieces of harness found on Greek islands (Euboia and Samos) and bearing the name of Haza'el could have been produced in Unqi (northern Syria) or in Damascus (southern Syria), and this is why it is difficult to consider them in the context of the scribal practices of Damascus. Their words are not separated by dividers.

It is interesting that, in the late 9th century BCE, inscriptions with dots as dividers are associated with Damascus, Hamath, and Sam'al/Ya'udi. This may point to a common origin of these scribal practices, whose source was probably situated elsewhere than in Damascus and Sam'al/Ya'udi. These scribal features are certainly not of local origin in Sam'al and Damascus. In Sam'al/Ya'udi, dots as dividers were replaced in the 8th century by vertical lines. We have seen above that the dot dividers are a scribal habit typical of the southern Levant, even if their use was not exclusive in this region. Ashton concluded that even if dividers of this type appear in some of the Phoenician inscriptions, their use was not customary among the Phoenician scribes.[74]

5.3. Concerning the form of the *zayin*, it becomes clear that, in the inscriptions analyzed in this study, the alternation between the lying H-form and the Z-form was different in each nest. In Sam'al/Ya'udi, we observe a change from the lying H-form to the Z-form. In the inscriptions from the vicinity of Aleppo, both forms of the *zayin* are attested in both phases, in the late 9th/early 8th century BCE as well as in the mid-8th to the early 7th century BCE. The Damascus evidence, which is extremely scanty, attests to the use of the lying H-form in the small inscriptions from Arslan Tash and Nimrud, whereas the Tel Dan fragment B, line 1, contains a *zayin* whose form is between the lying H- and the Z-forms.

The distribution of the forms of the *zayin* in various Aramaic inscriptions does not allow us to use it for the study of various scribal traditions.

---

73 The Phoenician inscriptions from Karatepe on the statue of the Storm-God and in the South/Upper Gate, and the Aramaic inscription Nērab B.
74 Ashton, "The Persistence," 125–26.

5.4. It is true that the number of inscriptions that I deal with in this article is extremely limited with regard to the relatively long period between the late 9th century and the early 7th century BCE. And it is also true that it is difficult to draw solid conclusions on this basis. Nevertheless, if we do not resign ourselves to abandoning any systematic analysis of the scribal practices as reflected in the Old Aramaic inscriptions, we must work with the evidence that is available.

Even if the available evidence is scanty, it proves that the scribal practices reflected in the Aramaic inscriptions of the late 9th to the early 7th century BCE were not uniform in all scribal nests. In the Levant, similar scribal practices were used across the linguistic and political borders. In the inscriptions analyzed in this paper, I am not able to isolate any specifically Aramaean scribal practice. The Iron Age Aramaic scribal practice can be defined as a kind of "hub" that adopted and adapted various scribal influences and techniques of engraving. As yet, I have no answer to the questions related to the causes of the changes in scribal practices in the nests of production of Aramaic inscriptions analyzed above. But it is clear that the scribal nests were not isolated, and their practices developed and were modified in accordance with other nests. The nature of the cultural or political streams that determined these changes are as yet obscure, but the existence of these streams, interconnecting the scribal traditions of various states and languages, is beyond doubt. The existence of one of these streams was probably manifested in the spread of *scriptio continua* in some scribal nests, Aramaic, Phoenician, but also Greek. Another stream can be connected with the use of dot dividers in Sam'al/Ya'udi and in the southern Levant, and yet another with the use of vertical line dividers in the vicinity of the late 9th-/early 8th-century Aleppo and its predominance in the late 8th-century BCE inscriptions of Sam'al/Ya'udi.

A similar case, which I did not include in my analysis, is the use of dividers in the form of two or three vertically aligned dots in the Aramaic inscription from Tell Fekheriye, in the inscription on the ostracon from Khirbet Qeiyafa, in an inscription on the Lachish Ewer,[75] in some inscriptions from Phrygia and Lycia, and also in Greek inscriptions of the classical and Hellenistic periods.[76] But these aspects must be left for another occasion.

---

75 Cf. for example Ruth Hestrin, "The Lachish Ewer and the 'Asherah," *IEJ* 37: 212–223.
76 Cf. Ashton, "The Persistence," 125. For the Greek inscriptions, see Bradley Hudson McLean, *An Introduction to Greek Epigraphy of the Hellenistic and Roman Periods from Alexander the Great down to the Reign of Constantine (323 B.C. – A.D. 337)* (Ann Arbor: The University of Michigan Press, 2002), 48.

6 Abbreviations

CIS   *Corpus inscriptionum semiticarum*, Paris 1881–.
COS   William W. Hallo and K. Lawson Younger, Jr., eds. *The Context of Scripture.*
                    Vol. 1: *Canonical Compositions from the Biblical World*; Vol. 2: *Monumental
                    Inscriptions from the Biblical World*; Vol. 3: *Archival Documents from the
                    Biblical World*, Leiden and Boston: Brill, 2003.
KAI I–III   Herbert Donner and Wolfgang Röllig. *Kanaanäische und Aramäische In-
                    schriften.* Band I: *Texte*, Wiesbaden: Harrassowitz, 1966 (2nd edition); Band
                    II: *Kommentar*, Wiesbaden: Harrassowitz, 1968 (2nd edition); Band III: *Glos-
                    sare und Indizes, Tafeln*, Wiesbaden: Harrassowitz, 1969 (2nd edition).
Sendschirli I   *Ausgrabungen in Sendschirli, ausgeführt und herausgegeben im Auftrage
                    des Orient-Comités zu Berlin I: Einleitung und Inschriften*, Königliche Mu-
                    seen zu Berlin, Mittheilungen aus den orientalischen Sammlungen 11. Ber-
                    lin: W. Spemann, 1893.
Sendschirli IV   *Ausgrabungen in Sendschirli, ausgeführt und herausgegeben im Auftrage
                    des Orient-Comités zu Berlin IV*, Mittheilungen aus den orientalischen
                    Sammlungen 14. Berlin: Georg Reimer, 1911.
Sendschirli V   Felix von Luschan. *Ausgrabungen in Sendschirli V: Die Kleinfunde von Send-
                    schirli*, Herausgabe und Ergänzung besorgt von Walter Andrae, Staatliche
                    Museen zu Berlin, Mitteilungen aus den Orientalischen Sammlungen 15.
                    Berlin: Walter de Gruyter, 1943.

7 Bibliography

Abou-Assaf, Ali, Pierre Bordreuil, and Alan R. Millard. *La statue de Tell Fekheriye et son inscrip-
    tion bilingue assyro-araméenne*, Etudes assyriologiques 7. Paris: Editions Recher-
    ches sur les civilisations, 1982.
Aḥituv, Shmuel, *Echoes from the Past. Hebrew and Cognate Inscriptions from the Biblical Pe-
    riod.* Jerusalem: Carta, 2008.
Alt, Albrecht. "Ergänzungen zu den phönikischen Inschriften von Karatepe." *WO* 2 (1955): 172–
    83.
Amadasi Guzzo, Maria Giulia. "Un fragment de stèle araméenne de Tell Afis." *Or* 78 (2008):
    336–47.
Ashton, June. "The Persistence, Diffusion and Interchangeability of Scribal Habits in the An-
    cient Near East Before the Codex." Ph.D. diss. The University of Sydney, 1999.
Biran, Avraham, and Joseph Naveh. "An Aramaic Stele Fragment from Tel Dan." *IEJ* 43 (1993):
    81–98.
Biran, Avraham, and Joseph Naveh. "The Tel Dan Inscription: A New Fragment." *IEJ* 45 (1995):
    1–18.
Bordreuil, Pierre. "Une inscription phénicienne champlevée des environs de Byblos." *Semitica*
    27 (1977): 23–27.

Bron, François. *Recherches sur les inscriptions phéniciennes de Karatepe*, Hautes études orientales 11. Genève: Librairie Droz, 1979.
Bron, François, and André Lemaire. "Les inscriptions araméennes de Hazaël." *RA* 83 (1989):
35–44.
Bryce, Trevor. *The Routledge Handbook of the Peoples and Places of Ancient Western Asia:
From the Early Bronze Age to the Fall of the Persian Empire*. London and New York:
Routledge, 2009.
Çambel, Halet. *Corpus of Hieroglyphic Luwian Inscriptions*. Vol. II: *Karatepe-Aslantaş. The
Inscriptions: Facsimile Edition*, Untersuchungen zur indogermanischen Sprach- und
Kulturwissenschaft 8.2. Berlin and New York: De Gruyter, 1999.
Dušek, Jan. "Dating the Aramaic Stele Sefire I." *Aramaic Studies* 17 (2019): 1–14.
Dušek, Jan. *Old Aramaic Inscriptions and Their Contexts. An Epigraphic, Archaeological, and
Historical Synthesis*, 2 vols., Ancient Near Eastern Studies Supplement Series. Leuven: Peeters, forthcoming.
Fales, Frederick Mario, and Giulia Francesca Grassi. *L'aramaico antico: Storia, grammatica,
testi commentati*. Udine: Forum, 2016.
Fitzmyer, Joseph A. *The Aramaic Inscriptions of Sefire*, Biblica et Orientalia 19/A. Roma:
Editrice Pontificio Instituto Biblico, 1995 (second revised edition).
Galil, Gershon. "A Re-Arrangement of the Fragments of the Tel Dan Inscription and the Relations between Israel and Aram." *PEQ* 133 (2001): 16–21.
Gilibert, Alessandra. *Syro-Hittite Monumental Art and the Archaeology of Performance*, Topoi:
Berlin Studies of the Ancient World 2. Berlin and New York: De Gruyter, 2011.
Gzella, Holger. *A Cultural History of Aramaic. From the Beginnings to the Advent of Islam*, HdO
111. Leiden and Boston: Brill, 2015.
Hawkins, John David. "The inscriptions of the Aleppo temple." *Anatolian Studies* 61 (2011): 35–
54.
Herrmann, Georgina, and Stuart Laidlaw. *Ivories from Rooms SW11/12 and T10, Fort Shalmaneser: Commentary and Catalogue*. Vol. 1: *Commentary and Catalogue*; Vol. 2:
Colour and Black & White Plates, Ivories from Nimrud [1949–1963] VII, 1–2. London:
British Institute for Study of Iraq, 2013.
Hestrin, Ruth. "The Lachish Ewer and the ʾAsherah," *IEJ* 37: 212–223.
Hoftijzer, Jakob, and Gerrit van der Kooij. *Aramaic Texts from Deir ʿAlla*, Documenta et Monumenta Orientis Antiqui 19. Leiden: Brill, 1976.
Klengel, Horst. "Die historische Rolle der Stadt Aleppo im vorantiken Syrien," in *Die Orientalische Stadt: Kontinuität, Wandel, Bruch*, ed. Gernot Wilhelm (Colloquien der Deutschen Orient-Gesellschaft [CDOG] 1, Berlin: Deutsche Orient-Gesellschaft, in Kommission bei SDV Saarbrücker Druckerei und Verlag, Saarbrücken, 1997), 359–74.
Lemaire, André. "L'inscription phénicienne de Hassan-Beyli reconsidérée." *Rivista di studi fenici* 11 (1983): 9–19.
Lemaire, André. "Les langues du royaume de Samʾal aux IXe – VIIIe s. av. J.-C. et leurs relations
avec le royaume de Qué," in *La Cilicie: espaces et pouvoirs locaux (IIe millénaire av.
J.-C. – IVe siècle ap. J.-C.). Actes de la Table Ronde d'Istanbul, 2–5 novembre 1999*,
ed. Eric Jean, Ali M. Dinçol, and Serra Durugönül (Varia Anatolica 13, Istanbul: Institut
Français d'Études Anatoliennes – Georges Dumézil, 2001), 185–93.
Lemaire, André, "West Semitic Epigraphy and the History of the Levant during the 12th–10th
Centuries BCE," in *The Ancient Near East in the 12th–10th Centuries BCE: Culture and
History. Proceedings of the International Conference held at the University of Haifa,*

2–5 May, 2010, ed. Gershon Galil, Ayelet Gilboa, Aren M. Maeir, and Dan'el Kahn (AOAT 392, Münster: Ugarit-Verlag, 2012), 291–307.

Lemaire, André, and Jean-Marie Durand. *Les inscriptions araméennes de Sfiré et l'Assyrie de Shamshi-ilu*, Hautes études orientales 20. Genève and Paris: Droz, 1984.

Lemaire, André, and Benjamin Sass. "The Mortuary stele with Sam'alian Inscription from Ördekburnu near Zincirli." *BASOR* 369 (2013): 57–136.

Levi Della Vida, Giorgio, and William F. Albright. "Some Notes on the Stele of Ben-Hadad." *BASOR* 90 (1943): 30–34.

Livingstone, Alasdair, et al. "Taimā': Recent Soundings and New Inscribed Material." *Atlal* 7, Part III (1983): 102–118.

Matthers, John, ed. *The River Qoueiq, Northern Syria, and its Catchment. Studies arising from the Tell Rifa'at Survey 1977–1979*, Parts i–ii, BAR International Series 98 (i–ii). Oxford: B.A.R., 1981.

McLean, Bradley Hudson. *An Introduction to Greek Epigraphy of the Hellenistic and Roman Periods from Alexander the Great down to the Reign of Constantine (323 B.C. – A.D. 337)*. Ann Arbor: The University of Michigan Press, 2002.

Michelini Tocci, Franco. "Un frammento di stele aramaica da Tell Sifr." *Oriens antiquus* 1 (1962): 21–22.

Millard, Alan R. 1970: "'Scriptio continua' in early Hebrew: Ancient practice or modern surmise?" *JSS* 15 (1970): 2–15.

Naveh, Joseph. "Word Division in West Semitic Writing." *IEJ* 23 (1973): 206–08. Reprinted in Joseph Naveh. *Studies in West-Semitic Epigraphy. Selected Papers* (Jerusalem: The Hebrew University Magnes Press, 2009), 402–04.

Naveh, Joseph. *Early History of the Alphabet. An Introduction to West Semitic Epigraphy and Palaeography*. Jerusalem: The Magnes Press, The Hebrew University, 1997 (reprint of the second revised edition 1987).

Orthmann, Winfried. *Untersuchungen zur späthethitischen Kunst*, Saarbrücker Beiträge zur Altertumskunde 8. Bonn: Rudolf Habelt Verlag, 1971.

Otzen, B. "Appendix 2: The Aramaic Inscriptions," in *Hama. Fouilles et recherches de la Fondation Carlsberg 1931–1938*. Vol. II 2: *Les objets de la période dite syro-hittite (âge du Fer)*, ed. Poul J. Riis and Marie-Louise Buhl (Nationalmuseets skrifter, Større Beretninger XII, København: Nationalmuseet, 1990), 266–318.

Pardee, Dennis. "A New Inscription from Zincirli." *BASOR* 356 (2009): 51–71.

Parpola, Simo. "Si'gabbar of Nerab Resurrected." *OLA* 16 (1985): 273–75.

Pitard, Wayne T. "The Identity of the Bir-Hadad of the Melqart Stela." *BASOR* 272 (1988): 3–21.

Puech, Émile. "La stèle de Bar-Hadad à Melqart et les rois d'Arpad." *RB* 99 (1992): 311–34.

Richelle, Matthieu. "The Fluctuating Borders of Hamath (10th–8th Centuries B.C.E.)," in *Aramaean Borders: Defining Aramaean Territories in the 10th–8th Centuries B.C.E.*, ed. Jan Dušek and Jana Mynářová (CHANE 101, Leiden and Boston: Brill, 2019), 203–228.

Riis, Poul J., and Marie-Louise Buhl. *Hama. Fouilles et recherches de la Fondation Carlsberg 1931–1938*. Vol. II 2: *Les objets de la période dite syro-hittite (âge du Fer)*, Nationalmuseets skrifter, Større Beretninger XII. København: Nationalmuseet, 1990.

Sass, Benjamin. *The Alphabet at the turn of the Millennium. The West Semitic Alphabet ca. 1150–850 BCE. The Antiquity of the Arabian, Greek and Phrygian Alphabets*, Tel Aviv, Journal of the Institute of Archaeology of Tel Aviv University Occasional Publications 4. Tel Aviv: Tel Aviv University Press, 2005.

Simon, Zsolt. "Aramaean Borders: the Hieroglyphic Luwian Evidence," in *Aramaean Borders: Defining Aramaean Territories in the 10th–8th Centuries B.C.E.*, ed. Jan Dušek and Jana Mynářová (CHANE 101, Leiden and Boston: Brill, 2019), 127–48.

Tekoglu, Recai, André Lemaire, Ismet Ipek, and A. Kazim Tosun. "La bilingue royale louvito-phénicienne de Çineköy." *CRAI* 144/3 (2000): 961–1006.

Thureau-Dangin, François, et al. *Arslan Tash*. Vol. 1: *Texte*; Vol. 2: *Atlas*, Paris: Librairie orientaliste Paul Geuthner, 1931.

Tropper, Josef. *Die Inschriften von Zincirli*, Abhandlungen zur Literatur Alt-Syrien-Palästinas 6. Münster: Ugarit-Verlag, 1993.

Anat Mendel-Geberovich

Judaean Glyptic Finds: An Updated Corpus and a Revision of Their Palaeography

This paper focuses on the question of the dating of Judaean seals and bullae from the 8th to the early 6th centuries BCE.[1] These were the focus of quite a few dissertations (Herr 1978; van der Veen 2014), articles (Herr 1998; Vaughn 1999) and one central corpus (Avigad and Sass 1997, commonly abbreviated WSS), most of which were written until the late 1990s. Many of these works have attempted to use these finds in order to build a paradigm of ancient Hebrew seal script typology and to offer pegs for their palaeographic dating. However, ever since the late 1990s, there has been an enormous increase in the yield of provenanced finds, their number now nearing 300 (!).

For several reasons, works focused on Hebrew glyptic finds from Judah: first, because there were many of them (in terms of excavations unearthing them, more so than in modern Jordan and other middle eastern countries, including northern Israel); and secondly, because of their purported pertinence to biblical figures and biblical studies in general (*e.g.*, Herr 1980; Hallo 1983; Avigad 1988; to name only a few; cf. Vaughn 1999: 43–44; Stanhope 2019). The search for connections between biblical figures and names appearing on finds from Judah/Jerusalem is common practice, and often leads to interesting interconnections between the biblical text and archaeological remains. That said, Christoph Uehlinger (2007) has rightly noted that such "name dropping" has limited the understandings that can be reached regarding Judahite administration, as other important aspects of

* The Hebrew University of Jerusalem and the Center for the Study of Ancient Jerusalem.
1 Research for this paper was supported by the Jack, Joseph and Morton Mandel Institute of Jewish Studies at the Hebrew University of Jerusalem and the Center for the Study of Ancient Jerusalem. The kind assistance of Mr. Michael Baruchi, Dr. Yuval Baruch, Ms. Efrat Bocher and Ms. Rebecca Cohen-Amin is gratefully appreciated. I would also like to thank the excavators who kindly shared information on new glyptic findings from their excavations and especially to those who offered me the opportunity to conduct research and eventually publish the material from their excavations: Dr. Joe Uziel and Mr. Ortal Chalaf, Prof. Yuval Gadot and Dr. Yiftah Shalev, Prof. Ronny Reich, Mr. Eli Shukron, Dr. Shlomit Weksler-Bdolah, Dr. Eilat Mazar, and Ms. Tehillah Lieberman. Special thanks go to Dr. Eythan Levy.
Versions of this paper were read by Prof. Christoph Uehlinger, Ms. Gemma Hayes and Dr. Prof. Peter G. van der Veen, all three of whom I am indebted to for their valuable comments and remarks.

the study of the seals have been neglected, and has urged us to take a greater step away from this "biblicizing-historicist" approach to Hebrew glyptic finds.

As said above, the corpus of Judaean seals and sealings has immensely grown over the past two decades, since the publication of the major works on the subject. Within WSS, only 7.3% of the seals and 25% of the bullae are provenanced (however, 91% of impressed jar handles in that corpus are provenanced; see Golub 2016: 371–372). Avigad's palaeographic conclusions were based, then – especially as regards stamp seals – on a very small statistical sample of provenanced finds.[2] Twenty years later, the percentage of provenanced seals and bullae taken together reaches 40% of the known finds.

This article includes an up-to-date list of the additional provenanced glyptic finds – stamp seals and bullae, including tax bullae ("fiscal bullae") but excluding stamped jar handles (see below) – discovered since the publication of WSS and therefore not included in it. The list (below) is a compilation of the Judaean seals and bullae brought to public attention, *i.e.* either published in the scholarly literature, announced in communications media or brought to my knowledge through personal communication until the writing of the present lines in September of 2019.

The enlarged corpus of Judaean provenanced glyptic finds now allows for the question of their dating as based mainly on their palaeography to be reopened and revisited. Moreover, since the number of provenanced finds – many of them coming from well-datable stratigraphic contexts – has so impressively grown, this new enlarged corpus now allows for the question of their dating to be analyzed in a much more secure, well-based manner than could have been done twenty years ago. Namely, I will address the question whether it is possible today to narrow the ranges and to date a given find more precisely – either to the late 8th century BCE, to around 650 BCE, or to the late 7th century BCE.

---

2 The importance of provenanced finds cannot be overstated. Using exclusively provenanced finds enhances the strength and quality of the dataset as we can now assure the purity of the corpus from possible forgeries, faded or abraded letters, and finds haling from unsecure stratigraphic contexts. See Rollston 2004, 2014. For the specific problem of unprovenanced glyptic finds, see Vaughn and Dobler 2006 and cf. Millard 2012 and Golub 2016.

1 A Short History of Hebrew Seal Script Research and Several Methodological Affirmations

In 1978, Larry G. Herr published his dissertation titled "the Scripts of Ancient Northwest Semitic Seals." The dissertation was severely criticized by Joseph Naveh (1980) for being "incomplete, immodest" and especially "overconfident" in the palaeographic dating of seals, suggesting very narrow dates for them. Later, Herr (1998) would reply to this criticism in a long palaeographic article on Hebrew and other northwest Semitic seals and bullae, which was in fact a review article of WSS. Essentially, Herr agrees with his critics that a larger time span than he had presented is appropriate for dating northwest Semitic glyptic finds (Herr 1998: 47).

Nahman Avigad was one of the leading voices on northwest Semitic seals and bullae, and his lifetime of work on them came to fruition in WSS, revised and completed after his passing by Benjamin Sass. In that corpus, Avigad and Sass compiled all the then-known northwest Semitic seals and their impressions (on bullae and jar handles). That volume is the basic corpus for epigraphic northwest Semitic glyptic finds, and the introduction chapter includes a palaeographic discussion by Avigad. An update to that corpus was never published besides the list included in the present paper.

In 1999, an article by Andrew Vaughn titled "Paleographic Dating of Judaean Seals" is based mainly on the provenanced material available until the late 1990s. This has been, until today, the "go-to," basic tool for the palaeographic dating of Hebrew seals and their impressions. However, Vaughn had to compare seals and bullae of the late 7th century to seal impressions on jar handles of the late 8th century, because that was the corpus available to him, even before the "House of the Bullae" at the City of David was fully published (Shoham 2000a), and prior to many other important seal-script discoveries. The connection of stamped jar handles to their archaeological context is stronger than that for seals and bullae, as the former are usually found together with the remaining sherds of the same jar as well as other datable pottery, while seals and bullae are less strongly associated with pottery. In addition, the change of pottery types is connected to different apparatuses of manufacture and its rate more easily traceable than that for seals, which are connected to persons' lives and their holding various bureaucratic positions (cf. Millard 2012: 186; Golub 2016: 379–380, n. 2). For these reasons, seals and bullae can rarely be used to date a stratum, as opposed to pottery.[3] Therefore, the chronology of stamped handles is relatively well established,[4] while for seals and bullae one usually has to base a dating mainly on their palaeography.[5]

More recently, Peter van der Veen (2014) published his "Study of Provenanced Official Seals and Bullae as Chronological Markers" with a good palaeographic analysis of Hebrew seal script, where he contends with both Herr 1998 and Vaughn 1999 (cf. van der Veen 2020). However, for the Judaean findings van der Veen chose to bring only those stratified seals and bullae which refer to historically known figures (*i.e.* from biblical narratives and/or extra-biblical sources), and those with official titles. Since the vast majority of the known Hebrew finds are not identifiable in the Hebrew Bible or extra-biblical sources, however, the purpose of the present study is to compile and address the broadest[6] possible corpus – again, after confirming that that corpus is based solely on a clean and securely dated dataset.[7]

---

3 In addition, seals and bullae "suffer" from their own special depositional situations (see below, n. 7).

4 Further affecting Vaughn's conclusions is his comparison between sealings and the so-called private stamped handles, which he dated to the late 8th century BCE. However, geomagnetic intensity analysis of these stamped handles suggests that they were produced over a longer period of time, ranging from the mid-8th to the late 7th century BCE (Ben-Yosef *et al.* 2017).

5 The chronology of the LMLK stamp impressions is based on the work of A. Lemaire (1981), who classified them between the 8th and the 7th centuries BCE (cf. Lipschits, Sergi and Koch 2010); as for the so-called private stamp impressions, their chronology seems to be delimited to the 8th century and no later than Sennacherib's campaign against Judah (Lipschits 2018: 66–75).

6 See Rollston 2014: 1: "Paleographic analyses made on the basis of a larger number of letters will be more secure than those made on the basis of a lesser number of letters." Cf. Parker 2013: 14–16, 22–23.

7 With respect to controlled archaeological contexts, it should be remembered that sometimes inscriptions are found in secondary contexts, especially in areas where human occupation has continued uninterruptedly for several generations, as is especially the case with Jerusalem (Parker 2013: 16). While such contexts do not necessarily raise doubts as to the authenticity of a seal or a bulla, it is not always an easy task to assign the find a clear archaeological date. Seals are different from bullae (and from impressed jar handles) in that sense: a seal, being an object of prestige, could have been passed down through generations as heirloom, while the administrative functionality of bullae was more ephemeral; consequently, time spans for bullae are generally shorter. In addition, seals or bullae belonging to a position rather than to a specific position holder, such as the Governor of the City docket (Ornan, Sass, and Weksler-Bdolah 2017), can have a longer lifespan. Eventually, an archaeological context of seals and bullae dates their *use* and occasionally *afterlife*, but a somewhat earlier *manufacture*, even by a few decades, cannot

Still in 2014, Herr contributed an article to the Frank Moore Cross memorial volume titled "An Eye for Form," a volume that seems to be the new "Bible" of northwest Semitic palaeography (Mendel-Geberovich 2018). Lamentably, his paleographic tables and conclusions are mainly based on unprovenanced finds (Herr 2014; cf. van der Veen 2014: 33, n. 57). It seems that this article was based on his previous publications from 1978 and 1998, and it is regrettable that these were not updated when included in such an important volume.

2 The Growing Corpus of Judeaen Glyptic Finds

Intense excavations being conducted in the area of Judah for the last two decades and the increased use of wet and dry sifting resulted in a dramatic growth in the number of seals and bullae unearthed:

In Judaean sites:
1. A seal from Beit Shemesh (Sass 2008);
2. A seal from Ramat Raḥel (Lipschits 2011);
3. A bulla from Tel 'Eton (Figure 1; Faust and Eshel 2012; cf. Mendel-Geberovich and Golub 2019);

Figure 1: A bulla from Tel 'Eton (Faust and Eshel 2012).

4. A seal from Hebron (Vainstub and Ben-Shlomo 2016);
5. Four bullae from Lachish (Figure 2; Klingbeil *et al.* 2019).

---

be ruled out. We should also bear in mind that a bulla or a seal are miniature objects that travel well across time and space, that is, they can easily be removed after their deposition by rodents or during man-inflicted removal of soil, and consequently they are rarely found in their real place of use.

Figure 2: A bulla from Lachish (Klingbeil et al. 2019).

In Jerusalem, excavations to the south and west of the Temple Mount have unearthed a total of more than 270 (!) glyptic finds. These include:

1. 45 bullae and a seal from Area G – the so-called House of the Bullae (Shoham 2000a; 2000b; Brandl 2012);
2. 107 bullae from the Summit of the City of David, some of them found in a Babylonian context but which may still be dated to the Iron Age II (Mazar and Livyatan Ben-Arie 2015). In addition, a seal published by Eilat Mazar as reading תמח and later understood to read שלמת was found during the same excavation (Mazar 2009: 78–79; Winderbaum 2015: 366–368);[8]
3. 34 bullae and bullae fragments from the Ophel excavations (Mazar and Livyatan Ben-Arie 2018), one of them is the bulla of Hezeqiah King of Judah, לחזקיהו אחז מלך יהד[ה] (Figure 3);

Figure 3: The bulla of חזקיהו א[ח]ז מלך יהד[ה] from the Ophel (Mazar and Livyatan Ben-Arie 2018. Photo by Uriah Tadmor; courtesy of Eilat Mazar ז"ל).

4. 13 bullae and a seal from Area U (Figure 4; Mendel-Geberovich, Chalaf and Uziel 2020). The seal reads למאסיהו אליקם; one of the bullae bears a clear impression reading לאחיאב בן מנחם. In addition, 2 bullae discovered in the same area in 2019 were published by Vukosavović and Chalaf (2020);

---

8 My thanks go to Ronny Reich who reminded me of this stamp-seal.

Figure 4: a. The bulla of אחיאב בן מנחם; b. The seal of מאסיהו אליקם from Jerusalem's Area U (Mendel-Geberovich, Chalaf and Uziel 2020. Photo by Clara Amit; Courtesy of the Israel Antiquities Authority).

5. 6 seals and 2 bullae from the Western Wall Plaza (Figure 5; Ornan *et al.* 2008; 2012; Ornan, Weksler-Bdolah, and Sass 2017); and an additional bulla fragment found in 2017 (Shlomit Weksler-Bdolah, personal communication);

Figure 5: Seals from the Western Wall Plaza. Top: לנתניהו בן יאש; bottom: לידעיהו אושא (Ornan et al. 2008).

6. Three seals from Iron Age tombs at Mamillah (Reich and Sass 2006);
7. Two seals and three bullae from the "Rock-Cut Pool" (Figure 6; Reich and Shukron 2009) in addition to 180 anepigraphic, earlier bullae (Reich, Shukron and Lernau 2007);

Figure 6: Finds from the rock-cut pool at the City of David: a. The seal of שלם [ו]רפאיהו, recto; b. The bullae of ריהו נחם[...; c. The bulla of ...]ירח (Reich and Shukron 2009; Photo by Vladimir Naikhin, courtesy of Ronny Reich and the Israel Antiquities Authority).

8. Two seals, a bulla and bulla fragments unearthed at the Giv'ati parking lot during Ben-Ami and Tchekhanovets's excavations (Figure 7: a-c; Ben-Ami and Tchekhanovets 2010; Ben-Ami and Misgav 2016);

9. The seal of אכר בן מתניהו and the bulla of נתנמלך עבד המלך found at the Giv'ati parking lot during Gadot and Shalev's excavations (Figure 7: d-e; Mendel-Geberovich *et al.* 2019), plus some 10 yet unpublished fragmentary bullae (Y. Shalev, personal communication).

10. A seal from the Western Wall foundations (Shukron 2012), and additional 5–10 bullae, yet to be published, one of them a so-called "fiscal bulla" with the letters למלך [remaining (see Wimmer, this volume); a second bulla belonging to אדניהו אשר על הב]ית[? (Eli Shukron, personal communication).

11. Temple Mount, several restorable Hebrew bullae from the sifting project (Barkay and Zweig 2006, 2007). One of the bullae mentions [ ] ליהו [בן] אמר (Barkay and Dvira 2016). Additional bullae were collected from a refuse aggregate to the foot of the Temple Mount (Barkay 2011; Dvira, Zigdon and Shilov 2011). One of them reads ג]בען למלך and is probably a fiscal bulla (see below; Figure 10);

12. Five bullae from Wilson's Arch (from Uziel, Solomon and Liebermann's excavations).

Figure 7: Finds from the Givʻati Parking Lot: a. The seal of עליהנה בת גאל; b. The seal of סעריהו בן שבניהו; c. The bulla of שאלה בן משלם; d. The seal of אכר בן מתניהו; e. The Bulla of נתנמלך עבד המלך (Ben-Ami and Tchekhanovets 2010; Ben-Ami and Misgav 2016; Mendel-Geberovich et al. 2019).

Figure 8: The bulla of קם[] ל[]לך (Gadot, Goren, and Lipschits 2013).

Figure 9: A bulla from the foot of the Temple Mount: [בעז למלך[(Barkay 2011).

There are many more bullae, some illegible (Steiner 2001: 122; Barkay and Zweig 2007, 2012: 71), others too fragmentary, which are more important for their accumulative value than for palaeographical analysis.

In addition, some yet-to-be-published finds that I am currently preparing for publication include:

1. 14 Hebrew and anepigraphic bullae from the City of David's Area C, near the Gihon Spring (Reich and Shukron's excavations).
2. 13 seals and bullae from the Western Wall's foundations (excavations by Eli Shukron).
3. Several bullae fragments from the Western Wall Plaza (Weksler-Bdolah's excavations).

Fiscal bullae were until recently known only from the antiquities market; three or four[9] fiscal bullae are now known from excavations or sifting (Barkay 2011, 2015 and Figure 9; Reich 2012; Gadot, Goren and Lipschits 2013 and Figure 8; cf.

---

9 The *editio princeps* (Gadot, Goren and Lipschits 2013) presents the bulla as the sealing of a private seal with the letters [lk (or [mlk, see Barkay and Deutsch 2017: 116) belonging to either a personal name (such as נתנמלך, אחמלך or the like) or a title such as עבד המלך or בן המלך (Gadot, Goren, and Lipschits 2013: 7–8). Barkay and Deutsch claim that the find is in fact a fiscal bulla that had three registers, as most known fiscal bullae (currently numbering, besides this bulla, 67 – only three of which are provenanced) have (Wimmer, this volume; Barkay and Deutsch 2017: 116). *Pace* Barkay and Deutsch, the published photograph of the bulla clearly shows that there is no reason to believe that it contained three written registers – on the contrary, the photograph clearly shows that the two extant registers were the only registers, as is evidenced by the remains of the oval frame and their current angle. In conclusion, this bulla is, unfortunately, to be taken off the list of provenanced fiscal bullae but fortunately added to the list of provenanced private bullae from Jerusalem. The reading and reconstruction of the seal legend as offered by Gadot, Goren and Lipschits, or a similar reconstruction, should be maintained.

Deutsch and Barkay 2017; Eli Shukron, personal communication). This fact is remarkable since fiscal bullae constitute an entire object genre of glyptic finds that was known until very recently (*ca.* 2010) only from the antiquities market.

As we can clearly see, there is a significant lack of balance in favor of Jerusalem. The reasons are, first and foremost, the introduction of wet sifting as well as current Israeli politics that are not relevant for this research. Nonetheless, for the sake of this study I shall examine all Judaean finds, including those found outside of Jerusalem.

3 Palaeographic Remarks Based on Some Test Cases of Judaean Seal Script

I have chosen only those findings that are securely dated by their archaeological context, that is, no items that come from later fills, or found in contexts of larger time-spans such as refuse dumps accumulated over several centuries (*e.g.*, Mazar and Livyatan Ben-Arie 2018: 247) or contexts damaged in later periods (Reich and Sass 2006: 313). However, even with multiple findings found in secure primary contexts in sequential strata of the same site, establishing chronological benchmarks for a script typology is not obvious (see, for example, Mendel-Geberovich, Chalaf and Uziel 2020).

In his article, and based on the dataset that he had gathered, Vaughn (1999: 60) concluded that Naveh was correct when urging caution in assigning dates purely on palaeography and stating that "the range of dates in most cases should be wider" than expected. More precisely, as glyptic finds from both the late 8th century and from the late 7th century BCE exhibit a wide variation in letter forms, and as the variation seems to be more pronounced in some letters than in others (due to the fact that each of the Hebrew letters evolves at a different rate) – this variation makes it "almost impossible to distinguish an isolated seal as belonging to either the eighth century group or the late seventh century group except in the case of a few letters" (Vaughn 1999: 60). Secondly, even in the case of these few diagnostic letters, there exist intermediate forms that are not chronologically diagnostic. Therefore, the dataset gathered by Vaughn does not enable us to assign a date between these two pegs – the late 8th and the late 7th centuries BCE. If what seems to be an intermediate form between these two pegs is encountered, at best one can date only certain letters to the general time period of the late 8th century or the general time period of the late 7th century—not even 650 BCE (Ibid.).

Vaughn also cautions against using the Hebrew script of the Siloam Tunnel In-scription as a starting point for the dating of Hebrew seals. Rather, he posits, He-brew seals themselves should serve to guide the dating of other Hebrew seals. The dates assigned (*i.e.* in works published until the late 1990s) based on palae-ography should be subject to revision "as more secure data become available" – preferably in large assemblages (Vaughn 1999: 60).[10] The aim of the present work is therefore to employ the abundant new data that have accumulated over the last 20 years to revise the palaeographic dating of Hebrew seals and bullae. By observing a few test cases of securely dated finds I will ask if it is now possible to narrow the ranges to the late 8th century BCE, *versus* to around 650 BCE, *versus* to the late 7th century BCE.

Below are some examples of the newer findings scrutinized based on Vaughn and others' palaeographic premises. However, their descriptions are to be read in light of my notes on "developed vs. non-developed letter forms" below.

Letter forms that are considered (by Vaughn and others) to be developed appear in early seals or bullae (see Table 1):

A developed *waw* in the Tel ʿEton bulla (pre-701 BCE) – comparable to late 7th century לנתניהו בן יאש and שבניהו בן סעריהו and to the House of the Bullae nos. B2, B9, B10, B27, B31 from the mid- to late 7th century BCE.

In the City of David's Area U, bullae that are said – according to stratigraphy and pottery dating – to be dated to the 8th or early 7th centuries, exhibit developed forms: the *aleph* on ע[ז]א / [ו]ה[י]לעש[י], the *mem* and the *waw* on ל[--]רֹיהו / חֹמֹ[ ], and the *nun* and the *he* on ב[בנה (see Table 1).

In the same site, a late 7th/early 6th seal exhibits both developed forms (*waw*, *qop*) and non-developed forms such as the *aleph, he, and samek.*

Mem has a developed occurrence in the pre-586 context bulla of נחם בן ענניהו (found in Lachish by Y. Aharoni), as well as in the House of the Bullae nos. B1, B2, B3, B5, B7, B8, and B16; but compare an earlier form on no. B8 from the same assemblage, and on the bulla of לשאלה בן משלם from the Givʿati parking lot. All of the above are dated by archaeology to the late 7th century.

---

10 See Vaughn's fourth conclusion on p. 60. This has been the case with the House of the Bullae assemblage from the City of David (Shoham 2000a), where the overall palaeographic (and strat-igraphic) character of the assemblage seems to be homogenous. However, with other large as-semblages of bullae, such as the ones unearthed in the City of David and in the Ophel by E. Mazar (Mazar and Livyatan Ben-Arie 2015, 2018), unfortunately, their numbers are large but their strat-igraphic context is either too broad (10th century – 586 BCE, see Mazar and Lang 2018) or simply not clear-cut enough (Mazar and Livyatan Ben-Arie 2015: 299), thus not allowing for a precise dating.

A similar situation occurs with *nun*: developed forms appear on the bullae of
יהוכל בן יהו[ח]י (Lachish - Aharoni), לנתניהו בן יאש from the Western Wall plaza,
גדליהו בן פשחור and סלוא בן אלירמ[] (Summit of the City of David, nos. 4 and 15
respectively, as well as nos. 3, 5, 7, 17, and 23 from the same assemblage), and
לירמיהו בן צפניהו בן נבי from Lachish (Mendel Geberovich, Arie and Maggen 2016).
However, the bullae לשאלה בן משלם ,לעליהנה בת גאל ,לסעריהו בן שבניהו – all
coming from the same assemblages and contexts as the ones mentioned before
them, exhibit Vaughn's so-called non-developed *nun*s.

Table 1: Letter Attestations on Select Seals and Bullae

	aleph	he	waw	mem	nun	samek	qop
8th cent.							
לשבניהוֹ / [י]הוֹאָב Tel 'Eton[11]							
לחזקיהו אחֹ/ז מלך יהד[ה] Jerusalem, the Ophel[12]							
לאליקם יהוזרח Lachish[13]							
לאחמלך / סמך Lachish[14]							
Late 8th – early 7th cent.							
לעשֹׁ[י]ה[ו] / ע[ז]א[Jerusalem, Area U[15]							

---

11 Faust and Eshel 2012.
12 Mazar and Livyatan Ben-Arie 2018.
13 Klingbeil et al. 2019.
14 WSS: no. 59, p. 70.
15 Mendel-Geberovich, Chalaf and Uziel 2020.

	aleph	he	waw	mem	nun	samek	qop
ל--[רֹיהֹו] / [חֹמֹ]] Jerusalem, Area U[15]							
בנה ב[ז]/[ ] Jerusalem, Area U[15]							

First half to middle of 7th cent.

	aleph	he	waw	mem	nun	samek	qop
לשאל[ן] / [ר]יהו Jerusalem, the Rock-Cut Pool[16]							

Late 7th – early 6th cent.

	aleph	he	waw	mem	nun	samek	qop
לאלישב / בן אשיהו Arad[17]							
לירמיהו בן צפניהו בן נבי Lachish[18]							
נחם בן ענניהו Lachish[18]							
יהוכל בן יהו[ח]י Lachish[18]							
לידעיהו / אושא Jerusalem, Western Wall plaza[19]							

16 Reich and Shukron 2009.
17 WSS: nos. 70–71, p. 73.
18 Mendel-Geberovich, Arie and Maggen 2016.
19 Ornan et al. 2008.

	aleph	he	waw	mem	nun	samek	qop
לנתניהו / בן יאש Jerusalem, Wes- tern Wall plaza[19]							
לשאלה ב/ן משלם Jerusalem, Giv'ati parking lot[20]							
לסעריהו בן שבניהו Jerusalem, Giv'ati parking lot[21]							
לעליהנה בת גאל Jerusalem, Giv'ati parking lot[21]							
לבלגי בן דליה[ו] House of the Bullae B1[22]							
לגמריהו [ב]ן שפן House of the Bullae B2[22]							
לחנמלך ישמעאל House of the Bullae B3[22]							
לטבשלם בן בנזכר House of the Bullae B5[22]							
לאלשמע בן סמכיה[ו] House of the Bullae B7[22]							

20 Ben-Ami and Tchekhanovets 2010.
21 Ben-Ami and Misgav 2016.
22 Shoham 2000a.

	aleph	he	waw	mem	nun	samek	qop
למכי[הו] בן חצי House of the Bullae B8[22]							
לאפרח אחיהו House of the Bullae B9, B10[22]							
לנתני[יהו] [ב]ן רח[ם] House of the Bullae B16[22]							
לעזריהו בן חלקיהו House of the Bullae B27[22]							
לבניהו בן הושעיהו House of the Bullae B31[22]							
לאחיאב בן מנחם Jerusalem, Area U[15]							
א(?)/לישע/יאוש Summit of the City of David B3[23]							
לגדליהו בן פשחור Summit of the City of David B4[23]							
ל(?)דליהו [ב]ן גדליהו Summit of the City of David B5[23]							

---

23 Mazar and Livyatan Ben-Arie 2015.

	aleph	he	waw	mem	nun	samek	qop
לסלוא(?)[ב]זן [ ]אלירמ Summit of the City of David B15[23]							
[ ]פניהו[Summit of the City of David B17[23]							
לשמעיה(?) נחמ] [Summit of the City of David B20[23]							
בן י] [Summit of the City of David B23[23]							

4 Developed vs. Non-developed Letter Forms: Principles of Palaeography

Before drawing palaeographic conclusions, a short pause is needed to reopen the question of what actually distinguishes a developed letter form from a non-developed letter form. Many innovations in letter forms involve improved function and are often practical, and can be explained by the need of scribes to write more rapidly and effortlessly than their usual or older practice. Such changes can be either deliberate or unintentional. For example, forming a letter in a more efficient way is done by eliminating the number of strokes and decreasing the times when the writing instrument is lifted from the writing surface. Determining if such a change was intentional or accidental is not always possible, but noting the presence of the change is the trade of the palaeographer (Parker 2013: 11–12). At the same time, palaeographers should be very careful not to employ overly-stringent analyses of the features of a script series by not recognizing the acceptable range of variance in a letter's form and thus overestimate the typological significance of a minor letter feature. Different features may appear side-by-side and constitute synchronic and recognizable variants of the same form (Parker 2013: 26).

The script used in informal texts such as lists and administrative texts is the cursive script, and the more often it was used, the more it developed. By contrast, the script of formal texts that are monumental and intended to be permanent, from personal seals to large stone inscriptions, developed more slowly and retained its graphic arrangement, graphemic clarity, uniformity of letter form and size, and general conservativeness (Parker 2013: 29; Rollston 2014: 3).

The form of *nun* and *mem* considered by Vaughn to be developed is the one with the head formed with two or three parallel short strokes intersected by a horizontal stroke. This form, according to him, is the more developed form as it becomes more widespread toward the end of the 7th century BCE. The older form, predominant in the late 8th century "private" seal impressions according to Vaughn's survey, has a head formed with two connected bars in the shape of a "V," which is connected to the vertical shaft at the very top of the right bar of the head (Vaughn 1999: 54). The case is similar with *aleph*: the form considered by Vaughn to be non-developed is the form where the vertical shaft is intersected by two crossbars that form a horizontal "V." The form considered developed has a head made with two separate, parallel strokes intersecting the vertical shaft (with an intermediate form where the two crossbars are separate but not parallel, see Vaughn 1999: 55–56).

Prima facie, these two changes seem to represent a transition from a more efficient, streamlined form, where the letter is formed with one continuous stroke without the need to lift the writing instrument, to a more laborious form where each stroke is executed separately and carefully. However, we should bear in mind that the script appearing on seals is engraved into hard stone, slowly and carefully done in any case; this fact is discernible not only in the care given to the design of individual letters but by the overall mindful graphic arrangement and graceful appearance of many of the seals. In addition, it is a necessarily formal and conservative script, and it was retained by seal-cutters for reasons of tradition and professional convenience over an extended period of time (Avigad 1997: 43). Hence, it should not bother us that seemingly demanding letter forms developed later than more simple ones.

Secondly, as mentioned above, Vaughn expressed the wish that Hebrew seals themselves serve to guide the dating of other Hebrew seals, and that the dates assigned based on palaeography be subject to revision as more secure data become available. While for the late 8th century, Vaughn looked at the script of the so-called "private" seal impressions, not a single seal corresponding to a private impression has been found until today. Moreover, there has not even been a correlation in the *names* of the persons attested on the seals and bullae and those attested on the private seal impressions. It is therefore generally agreed that these two groups represent two separately functioning administrative systems in the 8th century BCE, each run by different bureaucrats (Lipschits 2018: 68). Thus, the differences seen by Vaughn between letter forms of the late 8th century and those of the late 7th century may be at least partially explained as representing two separate systems, possibly hailing from two separate spheres of seal-engravers. Fortunately, with the new, enlarged corpus, there are today a few securely dated examplars of 8th century Judaean seals and bullae which may serve for the palaeographic analysis:

The Tel 'Eton bulla (Faust and Eshel 2012), as mentioned above, has an *aleph* with parallel strokes as well as a *waw* with a long lifespan (8th through early 6th centuries). Bulla A from Lachish (Klingbeil *et al.* 2019) has and *aleph* with the head a horizontal "V," but a *mem* with parallel short strokes. The bulla of חזקיהו [ה]יהד מלך אחז exhibits an *aleph*'s head with parallel strokes side by side with a *mem* whose head is formed with two connected bars in the shape of a "V." A similar *mem* is attested on the fiscal bulla [למלך בעֹן, dated by historical considerations to the first half of the 7th century (Barkay 2011, 2015).

As can be seen, then, from the enlarged corpus of provenanced Judaean glyptic finds, different styles (to avoid the usage of the terms "developed" vs. "non-developed") of letter forms exist side-by-side, sometimes on the very same seal; there is variation in letter forms within both the late-8th century and the late-7th to early 6th centuries, as already observed by Vaughn (1999: *passim*). There is a tendency (Herr 1998: 48) for some letter forms to become more widespread as we approach the second half of the 7th century BCE and up to 586, but some of them do appear earlier. In any case, a more refined dating, in a resolution of 30 or even 50 years, is still impossible today. Moreover, I expect such a refined resolution in the dating of Hebrew seal script to still be impossible in the future, since the burden we load on the archaeological context, in the case of seals and bullae, is too heavy for it to bear. As mentioned above, even in the cases where multiple seals and bullae are found in secure contexts in sequential strata of the same site, their association and link with a stratum's lifespan is inherently weaker than that for other small finds, and thus their stratigraphic dating is very difficult (Mendel-Geberovich, Chalaf and Uziel 2020).

5 Conclusions

One of the dominant features of a lapidary script is its conservativeness and slow pace of development, due, among other reasons, to the tradition and professional pride of generations of seal-cutters. The golden era of the Judaean personal seals and bullae lasted 150 years or less, a period which is simply too short for us to trace their chronology in a well-informed manner.

My short survey of the provenanced finds has shown that their palaeography cannot determine a date in a finer resolution than the general "peg" of the late 8th century as opposed to the "peg" of the late 7th to early 6th centuries BCE. Moreover, the survey asserts that variant forms of some letters are found in both timeframes. It seems that a more flexible view of the reality behind seals and bullae, their makers and their consumers/commissioners has to be brought to the forefront, and that the question of dating is not the only stance from which to look at things.

The corpus of Judaean glyptic finds provides fascinating opportunities to study not only its palaeography and dating, but also to probe other questions. The very presence of so many individuals, some of them holding official titles, some of them women, opens the door to new insights on onomasticon, officialdom, state administration, sealing practices, workshops and seal cutters, seal clientele, and other aspects of Judaean society in the first millennium BCE.

6 Bibliography

Avigad, Nahman. "Hebrew Seals and Sealings and Their Significance for Biblical Research." Pages 7–16 in *Congress Volume: Jerusalem, 1986*. Edited by J. A. Emerton. Supplements to Vetus Testamentum 40. Leiden: Brill, 1988.

Avigad, Nahman and Sass, Benjamin. *Corpus of West Semitic Stamp Seals*. Jerusalem: Israel Academy of Sciences, 1997 (abbrev. WSS).

Barkay, Gabriel. "A Fiscal Bulla from the Slopes of the Temple Mount – Evidence for the Taxation System of the Judean Kingdom." Pages 151–178 in *New Studies on Jerusalem* 17. Edited by E. Baruch, A. Levy-Reifer, and A. Faust. Ramat-Gan: Bar-Ilan University Press, 2011 (Hebrew).

Barkay, Gabriel. "Evidence of the Taxation System of the Judean Kingdom – A Fiscal Bulla from the Slopes of the Temple Mount and the Phenomenon of the Fiscal Bullae." Pages 17–50 in *Recording New Epigraphic Evidence: Essays in Honor of Robert Deutsch*. Edited by M. Lubetski and E. Lubetski. Jerusalem: Leshon Limudim, 2015.

Barkay, Gabriel, and Deutsch, Robert. "Another Fiscal Bulla from the City of David." Pages 115–121 in: *New Studies on Jerusalem* 22. Edited by E. Baruch and A. Faust. Ramat-Gan: Bar-Ilan University Press, 2017 (Hebrew with English abstract).

Barkay, Gabriel, and Dvira, Zachi. "The Temple Mount Sifting Project – Third Preliminary Report." Pages 47–95 in *New Studies on Jerusalem* 7. Edited by E. Meron. Ramat-Gan: Bar Ilan University Press, 2012 (Hebrew).

Barkay, Gabriel, and Dvira, Zachi. "Relics in Rubble: The Temple Mount Sifting Project," *BAR* nov/dec 2016: 44–55, 64.

Barkay, Gabriel, and Zweig, Zachi. "The Temple Mount Sifting Project – A Preliminary Report." Pages 213–237 in *New Studies on Jerusalem* 11. Edited by E. Baruch, Z. Greenhut and A. Faust. Ramat-Gan: Bar Ilan University Press, 2006 (Hebrew).

Ben-Ami, Doron, and Misgav, Hagai. "A Late Iron Age II Administrative Building Excavated in the City of David." Pages 103*-110* in *From Sha'ar Hagolan to Shaaraim: Essays in Honor of Prof. Yosef Garfinkel*. Edited by S. Ganor, I. Kreimerman, K. Streit and M. Mumcuoglu. Jerusalem: Israel Exploration Society, 2016 (Hebrew).

Barkay, Gabriel, and Zweig, Zachi. "New Data in the Sifting Project of Soil from the Temple Mount: Second Preliminary Report." Pages 27-68 in *City of David Studies of Ancient Jerusalem* 2. Edited by E. Meiron. Jerusalem: Megalim, 2007 (Hebrew).

Ben-Ami, Doron, and Tchekhanovets, Yana. "The Extent of Jerusalem during the Iron Age IIA." Pages 67–73 in *New Studies in the Archaeology of Jerusalem and its Region* IV. Edited by D. Amit, O. Peleg-Barkat, and G. D. Stiebel. Jerusalem: Israel Antiquities Authority, 2010 (Hebrew).

Ben-Yosef, Erez, Millman, Michael, Shaar, Ron, Tauxe, Lisa, and Lipschits, Oded. "Six Centuries of Geomagnetic Intensity Variations Recorded by Royal Judean Stamped Jar Handles." Pages 2160–2165 in *Proceedings of the National Academy of Sciences of the United States of America* 114/9, 2017. https://doi.org/10.1073/pnas.1615797114.

Brandl, Baruch. "Scarabs, Scaraboids, Other Stamp Seals, and Seal Impressions." Pages 377–396 in *Excavations in the City of David 1978–1985 Directed by Yigal Shiloh*, Vol. VIIB: *Area E: The Finds*. Edited by A. De Groot and H. Bernick-Greenberg. Qedem 54. Jerusalem: Institute of Archaeology, Hebrew University of Jerusalem, 2012.

Dvira, Zachi, Zigdon, Gal, and Shilov, Lara. "Secondary Refuse Aggregates from the First and Second Temple Periods on the Eastern Slope of the Temple Mount." Pages 63–106 in *New Studies on Jerusalem* 17. Edited by E. Baruch, A. Levy-Reifer, and A. Faust. Ramat-Gan: Bar-Ilan University, 2011. (Hebrew with English abstract, unnumbered pages).

Faust, Avraham, and Eshel, Esther. "An Inscribed Bulla with Grazing Doe from Tel 'Eton." Pages 62–70 in *Puzzling Out the Past: Studies in Northwest Semitic Languages and Literatures in Honor of Bruce Zuckerman*. Edited by M. J. Lundberg, S. Fine and W. T. Pitard. Leiden: Brill, 2012.

Gadot, Yuval, Goren, Yuval and Lipschits, Oded. "A 7th Century Bulla Fragment from Area D3 in the 'City of David'/Silwan." *Journal of Hebrew Scriptures* XIII, Article 8. 2013. http://jhsonline.org/Articles/article_190.pdf

Golub, Mitka R. "Revisiting Vaughn and Dobler's Provenance Study of Hebrew Seals and Seal Impressions." Pages 371–382 in *From Sha'ar Hagolan to Shaaraim: Essays in Honor of Prof. Yosef Garfinkel*. Edited by S. Ganor, I. Kreimerman, K. Streit and M. Mumcuoglu. Jerusalem: Israel Exploration Society, 2016.

Hallo, William W. "'As the Seal Upon Thine Arm': Glyptic Metaphors in the Biblical World." Pages 7–17 in *Ancient Seals and the Bible*. Edited by L. Gorelick and E. Williams-Forte. Occasional Papers on the Near East, vol. 2, no. 1. Malibu: Undena, 1983.

Herr, Larry G. *The Scripts of Ancient Northwest Semitic Seals*. Harvard Semitic Monographs 18. Missoula, MT: Scholars Press, 1978.

Herr, Larry G. "Paleography and the Identification of Seal Owners." *BASOR* 239 (1980): 67–70.

Herr, Larry G. "The Palaeography of West Semitic Stamp Seals (review of WSS)." *BASOR* 312 (1998): 45–77.

Herr, Larry G. "Hebrew, Moabite, and Edomite Seal Scripts." Pages 187–201 in *"An Eye for Form": Epigraphic Essays in Honor of Frank Moore Cross*. Edited by J.A. Hackett and W. Aufrecht. Winona Lake, Indiana: Eisenbrauns, 2014.

Klingbeil, Martin G., Hasel, Michael G., Garfinkel, Yosef, and Petruk, Néstor H. "Four Judean Bullae from the 2014 Season at Tel Lachish." *BASOR* 381 (2019): 41–56.

Lemaire, André. "Classification des estampilles royales judéennes." *Eretz-Israel* 15 (1981): 54–60.

Lipschits, Oded. "The Ivory Seal of šlm (Son of) klkl, Discovered at Ramat Raḥel." *IEJ* 61 (2011): 162–170.

Lipschits, Oded. *The Age of Empires: History and Administration in Judah in Light of the Stamped Jar Handles*. Jerusalem: Yad Ben Zvi, 2018 (Hebrew).

Lipschits, Oded, Sergi, Omer, and Koch, Ido. "Royal Judahite Jar Handles: Reconsidering the Chronology of the *lmlk* Stamp Impressions." *Tel Aviv* 37 (2010): 3–32.

Mazar, Eilat. *The Palace of King David. Excavations at the Summit of the City of David. Preliminary Report of Seasons 2005–2007*. Jerusalem and New York: Shoham, 2009.

Mazar, Eilat, and Lang, Tzachi. "Chapter II.2. Area A2009: Architecture and Stratigraphy." Pages 187–224 in *The Ophel Excavations to the South of the Temple Mount 2009–2013, Final Reports*. Volume II. Edited by E. Mazar. Jerusalem: Shoham, 2018.

Mazar, Eilat, and Livyatan Ben-Arie, Reut. "Chapter Six: Hebrew and Non-Indicative Bullae." Pages 299–362 in *The Summit of the City of David Excavations 2005–2008, Final Reports*. Volume I: *Area G*. Edited by E. Mazar. Jerusalem: Shoham, 2015.

Mazar, Eilat, and Livyatan Ben-Arie, Reut. "Chapter II.3: Hebrew Seal Impressions (Bullae) from the Ophel, Area A2009." Pages 247–279 in *The Ophel Excavations to the South of the Temple Mount 2009–2013, Final Reports*. Volume II. Edited by E. Mazar. Jerusalem: Shoham, 2018.

Mendel-Geberovich, Anat. "Review of 'An Eye for Form': Epigraphic Essays in Honor of Frank Moore Cross." *BASOR* 379 (2018): 231–234.

Mendel-Geberovich, Anat, Arie, Eran, and Maggen, Michael. "The Lachish Inscriptions from Yohanan Aharoni's Excavations Reread." Pages 119*–143* in *From Sha'ar Hagolan to Shaaraim: Essays in Honor of Prof. Yosef Garfinkel*. Edited by S. Ganor, I. Kreimerman, K. Streit and M. Mumcuoglu. Jerusalem: Israel Exploration Society, 2016 (Hebrew).

Mendel-Geberovich, Anat, and Golub, Mitka R. "The Tel 'Eton Bullae: A Revised Reading and Some Onomastic Remarks." *Semitica* 61 (2019): 49–58.

Mendel-Geberovich, Anat, Shalev, Yiftah, Bocher, Efrat, Shalom, Nitsan and Gadot, Yuval. "A Newly Discovered Personal Seal and a Bulla from the Excavations of the Giv'ati Parking Lot, Jerusalem." *IEJ* 69 (2019): 154–174.

Mendel-Geberovich, Anat, Chalaf, Ortal, and Uziel, Joseph. "The People Behind the Stamps: A Newly-Found Group of Bullae and a Seal from the City of David, Jerusalem." *BASOR* 384 (2020): 159–182.

Millard, Alan. "Hebrew Seals, Stamps and Statistics: How Can Fakes Be Found?" Pages 183–191 in *New Inscriptions and Seals Relating to the Biblical World*. Edited by M. Lubetski and E. Lubetski. Archaeology and Biblical Studies 19. Atlanta: SBL, 2012.

Naveh, Joseph. "Review of The Scripts of Ancient Northwest Semitic Seals by Larry G. Herr." *BASOR* 239 (1980): 75–76.

Ornan, Tallay, Sass, Benjamin, and Weksler-Bdolah, Shlomit. "A 'Governor of the City' Seal Impression from the Western Wall Plaza Excavations in Jerusalem." *Qadmoniyot* 154 (2017): 100–103 (Hebrew).

Ornan, Tallay, Weksler-Bdolah, Shlomit, Greenhut, Zvi, Sass, Benjamin, and Goren, Yuval. "Four Hebrew Seals, One Depicting an Assyrian-Like Archer, from the Western Wall Plaza Excavations, Jerusalem." *'Atiqot* 60 (2008): 115–129.

Ornan, Tallay, Weksler-Bdolah, Shlomit, Kisilevitz, Shua, and Sass, Benjamin. "'The Lord Will Roar from Zion' (Amos 1:2): The Lion as a Divine Attribute on a Jerusalem Seal and Other Hebrew Glyptic Finds from the Western Wall Plaza Excavations." *'Atiqot* 72 (2012): 1*–13*.

Reich, Ronny. "A Fiscal Bulla from the City of David, Jerusalem." *IEJ* 62 (2012): 200–205.

Reich, Ronny, and Sass, Benjamin. "Three Hebrew Seals from the Iron Age Tombs at Mamillah, Jerusalem." Pages 313–20 in *Essays on Ancient Israel in its Near Eastern Context: A Tribute to Nadav Na'aman*. Edited by Y. Amit, E. Ben Zvi, I. Finkelstein and O. Lipschits. Winona Lake: Eisenbrauns, 2006.

Reich, Ronny, and Shukron, Eli. "Two Hebrew Seals and Three Hebrew Bullae from the City of David in Jerusalem." *Eretz-Israel* 29 (2009): 358–362 (Hebrew with English abstract).

Reich, Ronny, Shukron, Eli, and Lernau, Omri. "Recent Discoveries in the City of David, Jerusalem." *IEJ* 57 (2007): 153–169.

Rollston, Christopher A. "Non-Provenanced Epigraphs I: Pillaged Antiquities, Northwest Semitic Forgeries, and Protocols for Laboratory Tests." *Maarav* 10 (2003): 135–193.

Rollston, Christopher A. "Non-Provenanced Epigraphs II: The Status of Non-Provenanced Epigraphs within the Broader Corpus of Northwest Semitic." *Maarav* 11 (2004): 57–79.

Rollston, Christopher A. "Prolegomenon to the Study of Northwest Semitic Paleography and Epigraphy." Pages 1–4 in *'An Eye for Form': Epigraphic Essays in Honor of Frank Moore Cross*. Edited by J. A. Hackett and W. E. Aufrecht. Winona Lake: Eisenbrauns, 2014.

Sass, Benjamin. "A Hebrew Seal from Bet Shemesh and Another of Unknown Provenance in the Israel Antiquities Authority Collection." *'Atiqot* 59 (2008): 1–4.

Shoham, Yair. "Hebrew Bullae." Pages 29–57 in *Excavations at the City of David 1978–1985 Directed by Yigal Shiloh*. Vol. VI: *Inscriptions*. Edited by D. T. Ariel. Qedem 41. Jerusalem: Institute of Archaeology, Hebrew University of Jerusalem, 2000a.

Shoham, Yair. "A Hebrew Seal and Seal Impressions." Pages 81–84 in *Excavations at the City of David 1978–1985 Directed by Yigal Shiloh*. Vol. VI: *Inscriptions*. Edited by D. T. Ariel. Qedem 41. Jerusalem: Institute of Archaeology, Hebrew University of Jerusalem, 2000b.

Shukron, Eli. "The Western Wall Foundations – Did Herod Build Them?" Pages 13*–27* in *City of David: Studies of Ancient Jerusalem 7*. Edited by E. Meron. Jerusalem: Megalim, 2012 (Hebrew).

Stanhope, Benjamin. *First Temple Hebrew Seals and Bullae Identifying Biblical Persons: A Study of Their Iconographic and Historical Significance*. MA Thesis, Faculty of the Asien-Afrika-Institut.

Steiner, Margreet L. *Excavations by Kathleen M. Kenyon in Jerusalem 1961–1967*, Vol. III: The Settlement in the Bronze and Iron Age. Sheffield: Sheffiel Academic Press, 2001.

Parker, Heather D.D. *The Levant Comes of Age: The Ninth Century BCE through Script Traditions*. PhD dissertation. Baltimore: Johns Hopkins University, 2013.

Uehlinger, Christoph. "Spurensicherung: alte und neue Siegel und Bullen und das Problem ihrer historischen Kontextualisierung." Pages 89–137 in *Behutsames Lesen: Alttestamentliche Exegese im interdisziplinären Methodendiskurs. Christof Hardmeier zum 65. Geburtstag*. Edited by S. Lubs. Arbeiten zur Bibel und ihrer Geshichte 28. Leipzig: Evangelische Verlagsanstalt, 2007.

van der Veen, Peter G. *The Final Phase of Iron Age II in Judah, Ammon, and Edom: A Study of Provenanced Official Seals and Bullae as Chronological Markers*. Alter Orient und Altes Testament 415. Münster: Ugarit Verlag, 2014.

van der Veen, Peter G. *Dating the Iron Age IIB Archaeological Horizon in Israel and Judah. A Reinvestigation of 'Neo-Assyrian (Period)' Sigillographic and Ceramic Chronological Markers from the 8th and 7th Centuries B.C.* (Ägypten und Altes Testament 98). Münster: Zaphon, 2020.

Vainstub, Daniel, and Ben-Shlomo, David. "A Hebrew Seal and an Ostracon from Tel Hebron." *IEJ* 66 (2016): 151–60.

Vaughn, Andrew G. "Paleographic Dating of Judaean Seals and its Significance for Biblical Research." *BASOR* 313 (1999): 43–64.

Vaughn, Andrew G. and Dobler, Carolyn P. "A Provenance Study of Hebrew Seals and Seal Impressions: A Statistical Analysis." Pages 757–771 in *'I Will Speak the Riddles of Ancient Times': Archaeological and Historical Studies in Honor of Amihai Mazar on the Occasion of His Sixtieth Birthday*. Edited by A. M. Maeir and P. de Miroschedji. Winona Lake: Eisenbrauns, 2006.

Vukosavović, Filip, and Chalaf, Ortal. "Raphayahu, Between Jerusalem and Babylon." Pages 31*-41* in *Studies of Ancient Jerusalem* 15. Edited by E. Meiron. Jerusalem: Megalim, 2020.

Winderbaum, Ariel. "Chapter Seven: The Iconic Seals and Bullae of the Iron Age." Pages 363–419 in *The Summit of the City of David. Excavations 2005–2008. Final Reports Volume I: Area G*. Edited by E. Mazar. Jerusalem: Shoham, 2015.

Stefan Jakob Wimmer
Hieratic Numerals on Iron Age Hebrew Tax Bullae

1 The context: "Palestinian Hieratic"[1]

The phenomenon of Egyptian numerals in West Semitic alphabetic inscriptions of the Iron Age has long been known. When in 1910 an archive of inscribed sherds was discovered in Israelite Samaria (Sebastya), its excavator George Reisner – who was a renowned Egyptologist, Assyriologist and archaeologist – immediately identified some non-alphabetic signs as numerals written in Egyptian Hieratic (Reisner et al. 1924: 227–238). The Biblical scholar Martin Noth commented: "Es ist sehr bedeutsam, daß da, wo wir zum ersten Male Zahlzeichen in Israel antreffen, es ägyptische Zeichen sind, die gebraucht werden." (Noth 1927: 243). In the 1960s, the famous ostraca from Judean Arad provided important new evidence (Aharoni 1975, 1981), as did the small corpus of ostraca discovered in the 1970s at the Judean border fortress of Qadesh Barnea (Tell el-Qudeirat; Lemaire/Vernus 1980, 1983; Cohen/Bernick-Greenberg 2007: 245–253; Wimmer 2008: 92–113). More sporadic material is spread over more than a hundred other inscriptions. In addition to inscribed vessels and ostraca, the object genre of inscribed weight stones (Kletter 1998; Wimmer 2008: 160–189) is of special importance, as even the sheqel based measuring system itself appears to be linked to the Egyptian *dbn*- and *qdt*-standard (Aharoni 1966; Wimmer 2008: 160). More and more so-called tax bullae or fiscal bullae, which are, unlike other bullae, mostly tokens and not seals, have been shown to contain numerals for year dates.[2] I attempted to collect and analyse all available evidence in my study Palästinisches Hieratisch. Die Zahl- und Sonderzeichen in der althebräischen Schrift (= Wimmer 2008). Since then, only few but meaningful new sources haven been published[3] or newly discovered.[4]

---

* I am most grateful to Anat Mendel-Geberovich, the respondent to my paper, who alerted me to a paper I had overlooked (Barkay/Deutsch 2017), raised relevant questions and gave valuable suggestions, which I incorporated in this article, with her kind approval.
1 The following is adopted from Wimmer 2018: 709–711.
2 Cf. this article.
3 Cf. Wimmer 2015: 146–149 for the material from Kuntillet Ajrud, and see below.
4 Cf. Wimmer 2018 and Bean et al. 2019 for the important Khirbet Ataruz inscription from Jordan.

Not surprisingly, these notations are all in the Hieratic ductus[5], since all available sources are either ink inscriptions or informal engravings, of administrative or private nature. The Hieroglyphic ductus was in Egypt applied, as a rule, for religious (and that includes political) inscriptions, in either cultic or funerary context, which were intended for the divine realm and for eternity. For all other texts, as a rule Hieratic (and from the 7th century on Demotic) was used. We have very few monumental inscriptions from the Iron Age Levant, and where these do mention numbers they are spelled in words, not written in numerals.[6] It is futile to speculate whether numerals had been written in Hieroglyphic style rather than Hieratic, when they were contained in monumental Hebrew temple or tomb inscriptions, as long as we have no such evidence.

In addition to the Hieratic style numerals, which are all attested from "1" to "9,000," several special signs appear as abbreviations for units of measure. Most of them apparently correspond with the familiar measures of capacity homer, kor, epha and se'a. Also the Egyptian ẖ3r (khar, "sack") and ḥq3t (heqat, "bushel") are attested, the latter in its full monogram version (S.38+U.9) as well as an abbreviated dot, and also udjat-eye-fractions for the heqat (Wimmer 2008: 260–266). Both the symbols for khar and heqat are not plainly identical with the Egyptian archetypes. They can easily be deduced from these, but display characteristic variant shapes with a tendency to reduce or fractionize the Egyptian standard shapes (Wimmer 2008: 262–264). The symbol for epha, too, is best explained as an intentional deduction from and reduction of the Egyptian sign U.9 for jpt (Greek oipe, the same lexem as the Hebrew epha; Wimmer 2008: 257–258). In contrast, other symbols appear to be independent creations by alphabetic scribes, without Egyptian inspirations. These denote the measures homer and kor, for which no Egyptian correlations were at hand. Both are simple graphic shapes, one in a curved (probably for homer) and one in a straight version (probably for kor; Wimmer 2008: 254–256). The symbol for se'a, finally, may be explained as a graphic deduction from the epha symbol (Wimmer 2008: 259–260).

In addition, there is the well-known loop symbol for sheqel (Wimmer 2008: 247–250)[7], and perhaps an alternative small cross-like sign for the same value,

---

5 But cf. the possible derivation of the sheqel symbol 𐎧 from the hieroglyph V.6 (Wimmer 2008: 250); cf. also below n. 8.

6 Cf. the Siloam Tunnel Inscription (Ahituv 2008: 19–25) and the stela fragment from Silwan (Ahituv 2008: 25–26); from non-Hebrew context the Mesha Stela (Ahituv 2008: 389–418), the Tel Dan Stela fragments (Ahituv 2008: 467–473), and more numerous Phoenician and Aramaic inscriptions.

7 Recently Vainstub 2016 suggested that the symbol might be derived from an early alphabetic ("Canaanite") letter for t(ql).

derived from an Abnormal Hieratic (i.e. Late Period cursive Hieratic) reduction of the term *dbn* (Wimmer 2008: 251).

The varying degrees of adoption of the Egyptian shapes and their adaption in alphabetic inscriptions, plus supplementing independently created, new symbols, provide sufficient justification to describe this hybrid, Egyptian and West Semitic writing practice as "Palestinian Hieratic." I introduced this term in Wimmer 2008, while commenting: "Alternativ käme freilich auch konkreter auf die Schrift bezogen die Qualifizierung hebräisches Hieratisch in Frage, oder, weniger präzise, da jeweils auf Nord- oder Südreich eingeschränkt, israelitisches, bzw. judaitisches Hieratisch. Mit diesen Bezeichnungen soll aber kein vom ägyptischen (also: eigentlichen) Hieratisch vollkommen losgelöstes Phänomen impliziert werden." (Wimmer 2008: 273).

In Wimmer 2008: 279, I claimed: "Von nicht zu unterschätzender Bedeutung bleibt die Beobachtung, dass ausschließlich in Juda und Israel hieratische Schreibungen übernommen wurden." Indeed, until recently, Hieratic numerals were exclusively attested in either Judahite or Israelite inscriptions. For the Kingdom of Judah, the Ramesside heritage, which is best attested in the south of former Canaan, may play a role here, as may later periods of political rapprochement towards Egypt. For Israel, this record is more surprising, in view of the close cultural orientation of the Northern Kingdom towards Phoenicia.

Phoenician and Aramaic inscriptions employ a different system for numerals, which must not be confused with Hieratic (Wimmer 2008: 195–196).[8] A few numerals, like the simple strokes for 1, 2, 3 and 4, and variants for 10, may appear similar to Hieratic, but they are not identical, and all other numerals are distinctly different. More than that, the system combines additive and multiplicative factors in writing numbers from the hundreds on, and therefore cannot be cognate with Egyptian. Its origins may instead be searched for in cuneiform numeric patterns. The Phoenician/Aramaic numeric system is best attested in the 5th-century Aramaic Elephantine papyri and in later Aramaic ostraca. The earliest evidence we have so far comes from the 8th-century Zincirli stela. This and a few other texts attest that the system was in use during the Iron Age, contemporaneous with Palestinian Hieratic. Yet, it is never used in Hebrew inscriptions. Vice versa, it seemed until recently that Palestinian Hieratic was never employed outside Judah or Israel, but the discovery of a Moabite inscription with impressive Hieratic numerals from Khirbet Ataruz in Jordan has changed this picture.[9]

---

8 Cf. Wimmer 2008: 195–196 for an overview of the Phoenician/Aramaic system, with literature. Such confusion does, however, occur, see e.g. Aufrecht 1989, Hamilton 2006: 337 n.6.
9 Wimmer 2018 and Bean et al. 2019.

As to the origin of this particular practice, my palaeographical analysis suggests that two factors were demonstrably of importance. In the Late Bronze Age, the Egyptian administration of the Ramesside pharaohs introduced Hieratic scribal practice in Canaan. Substantial evidence comes mainly in form of bowls inscribed with harvest tax registrations from administrative and agricultural centers in the southern Shephela, northern Negev and southern coastal areas.[10] Orly Goldwasser (1991 and again 2016: n.13) suggested that this scribal tradition may have survived the political and cultural shifts that separate these 13th- and early 12th-century inscriptions from the first attestations of Palestinian Hieratic. Their date depends on the much-debated stratigraphy of Arad, but none of the relevant ostraca can safely be dated before the 9th century. With only few exceptions, all other sources start to appear in the 8th century and have a climax in the 7th and early 6th centuries (Wimmer 2008: 276). There are indeed indications for Ramesside traits in the palaeography of some Palestinian Hieratic (or: Hebrew Hieratic) signs (Wimmer 2008: 273), which account for that scenario. Ramesside heritage may indeed have been a trigger for the later, Iron Age Hieratic scribal practice. The fact that these traces are few and by no means predominant, is not surprising, since they have been superimposed by strong, cultural and partly political orientations of the Hebrew kingdoms towards Egypt from the 8th century on (Wimmer 2008: 276–279). This impetus is easily substantiated with sign shapes that follow the development of Egyptian Hieratic during the Late Period, into so-called Abnormal Hieratic of the 25th and 26th dynasties. Even early Demotic shapes are tangible (Wimmer 2008: 273–274). The abrupt end of Palestinian/Hebrew Hieratic comes with the destruction of the Judean Kingdom. The very few later, archaic Hebrew inscriptions, on coins or at Qumran, contain no Hieratic numerals or special signs.

2 The tax bullae

In Wimmer 2008 I treated 18 bullae with Hieratic numerals – all those that had been published by then (in: Avigad 1990, Avigad/Sass 1997, Deutsch/Heltzer 1999, Deutsch 1999, 2003a, 2003b; all except one belong to the collections of Joseph Chaim Kaufman and Shlomo Moussaieff).

Since then, the amount of published fiscal bullae, with and without Hieratic numerals, has significantly increased. Robert Deutsch, to whom we owe, with

---

[10] Wimmer 2008: 11–12; for an updated list and map of all relevant inscriptions cf. Wimmer 2019.

few exceptions, all the editorial work in the related field, published another twelve of them in Deutsch 2011: 81–91, six in Deutsch 2012, plus ten in Deutsch 2015.

In the festschrift edited in honor of Robert Deutsch by Meir and Edith Lubetski (2015), two seminal articles treated the topic of fiscal bullae.[11] Martin Heide (2015) compared epigraphical features of the Phoenician and Hebrew fiscal bullae, and Gaby Barkay (2015) embedded his publication of the first fiscal bulla that was found in a controlled archaeological ambience in an extensive investigation of the phenomenon of fiscal bullae and the taxation system of the Judean Kingdom.

Barkay very conveniently lists all published tax bullae, with illustrations for all of them, dividing them into two groups (as others have done before): those that mention the name of a city (a toponym; "type 1" in Barkay 2015; "group A" in Deutsch 2011; I suggest to call them "toponymical tax bullae," in the following: TTB), and those which name an official instead (a personal name; "type 2" in Barkay 2015; "group B" in Deutsch 2011; I suggest to call them "personal tax bullae," in the following: PTB). He arrives at 29 toponymical plus 25 personal tax bullae; to be added are 2 toponymical tax bullae treated by Barkay in "additional new data" (2015: 42–44; one, mentioning Betlehem, having been published by Ronny Reich 2012; the second, mentioning Makkeda, not published previously)[12], as well as five personal and two out of five toponymical tax bullae from Deutsch 2015 (3 of the latter having been included in Barkay's list).

Altogether we now arrive at the impressive amount of 64 fiscal bullae: 34 TTB and 30 PTB. Among these, 36 display Hieratic numerals: 17 TTB and 19 PTB.

The intention of this paper is to catch up from the 18 bullae I discussed in 2008, with the 36 of relevance known today.

In Wimmer 2008 I chose to flag all unprovenanced objects with the sign "ⵁ."[13] This is the case for almost all tax bullae (except 2 or 3 newly published ones, see

---

11 Plus the above-mentioned Deutsch 2015, where a footnote conclusively accounts for the circumstance that this article by himself appeared in his own festschrift.

12 A fragmentary bulla from the City of David was published as another fiscal bulla from controlled excavations by Barkay and Deutsch 2017. It contains no numeral and its reconstruction as a tax bulla must remain doubtful. Another tax bulla was reported by Eli Shukron, but has not been published so far. I owe these pieces of information to Anat Mendel-Geberovich. Cf. also her paper in this volume with an overview of seals and bullae from controlled excavations at Judean sites, Mendel-Geberovitch 2022.

13 Following suggestions by Rollston 2004: 73 and 2005. See my more extensive statement Wimmer 2008: 7.

above). That circumstance shows that it should not only be legitimate, but considered compulsory to publish unprovenanced objects, instead of excluding them from the academic discussion. For many fields, such as the study of glyptics, and tax bullae among them, the serious treatment of unprovenanced objects is vital. This requires that we remain aware of the questions that unprovenanced objects raise (among them, in many cases, their authenticity), therefore some kind of flagging should be applied not only when editing such objects, but whenever they are referred to.[14]

3 Tax bullae treated in Wimmer 2008 revisited

In the earlier Hebrew version of his extensive treatment of fiscal bullae, Barkay (2012) did not mention my Wimmer 2008. In the English version, published in 2015, Wimmer 2008 is not found in the bibliography either, although Barkay did refer to it several times in the text. He explained: "13 fiscal bullae[15] appear in the study of Stefan Wimmer in a book dedicated to the use of Egyptian Hieratic numerals and signs used by the ancient Hebrew scribes (Wimmer 2008, 149–159). Many of his readings of the Hieratic numerals are correct, and the present author also arrives at them independently. In other cases his readings are problematic (e.g. MP 79b, on p. 155). The most important contribution of Wimmer is the identification of the 34th regnal year on two of the bullae (ibid. 150, 158), which marks the latest year in the corpus of the fiscal bullae. Wimmer discussed only 18 of the fiscal bullae[16]." (Barkay 2015: 20). He then refers to Wimmer 2008 sporadically in the discussion of some of the writings of Hieratic numerals; in most cases my readings, whether his readings concur with them or differ, are not referred to.

---

14 Anat Mendel-Geberovich, in her response, devoted much thought on the disputed topic of dealing with unprovenanced objects. She concluded: "Now that we have shown that tax bullae are an authentic genre in Hebrew epigraphy, I think it gives us the fortunate opportunity to study them as a fascinating group of objects, looking at their physical and technical features as well as at their wider implications for issues and questions in the history of Israel's and Judah's administration and taxation system."
15 *sic*; in fact 18; see also the end of this quote.
16 How does this relate to the figure "13" above? At the time of publication of Wimmer 2008, these 18 bullae were the complete material that had been published and was available to me.

B. Moussaieff MP 97b⁰

(= Barkay 2015: #1/3[17]; Heide 2015 #14; Wimmer 2008: 155)

This very badly preserved impression was published by Deutsch 1999: 166–168, together with B. Moussaieff MP 97a⁰ (= Barkay 2015: #1/2; Heide 2015: #13; Avigad/Sass 1997: #422). The latter is a well-preserved impression of a TTB mentioning the city of Lachish and the regnal year date 14 (10+1+1+1+1). The single strokes do not appear uniform. The first two are placed close together and parallel (even though the second stroke has an awkward shape), after a small space follows the third stroke, and the fourth is smaller and appears squeezed into the remaining space at the end of the line (cf. my facsimile Wimmer 2008: 155). It appears that the seal was inscribed for year "12," and reused in years 13 and 14, when an additional stroke each was added.[18] According to the published photograph (Deutsch 1999: 167), what follows on 97b⁰, the badly preserved impression, after the numeral 10, differs markedly from the same spot on 97a⁰. Two horizontal lines can quite clearly be seen, instead of any traces of small vertical strokes. If this is so, the numeral would obviously be read "18" (10+8) and the impression cannot be from the same seal as 97a⁰. Even though the rest of the impression, as far as the minute traces on 97b⁰ suggest, seems to be identical with 97a⁰, the exact layout is not. Line 2 on 97a⁰ is higher on its right edge than on the left edge, and for line 3 the opposite is the case. This is because the line divider between lines 2 and 3 is oblique, descending from left to right. On 97b⁰ this is not the case. Barkay 2015: 20 calls this reading "problematic," without any further reference or reasoning.[19]

A final verdict should be achieved by a thorough investigation of the originals. This pending, I suggest again that B. Moussaieff MP 97a⁰ and 97b⁰ must be impressions of two different seals, the first from year 14, the second from year 18.

---

17 In Barkay 2015 TTB ("type 1") are counted from no. 1 to no. 29, and PTB ("type 2") again from no. 1 to no. 25. To avoid confusion, I prefix 1/ and 2/ to the numbers.

18 This phenomenon of extending the use of the seals for TTB or PTB during several years, with the numerals subsequently amended, has been observed on several occasions. A very obvious example is B. Mousaieff MP 98⁰; see also B. Kaufmann 51⁰, B. Moussaieff MP 97a⁰, B. Moussaieff MP 101⁰.

19 Cf. also Heide 2015: 67: "... a barely readable bulla which seems to have been impressed by the same seal," without referring to my alternative reading.

97a: Barkay 2015: 21   97a: Barkay 2015: 21   97b: Barkay 2015: 21   97b: Wimmer 2008:155

B. Kaufman 51[0]
(= Barkay 2015: #2/8; Wimmer 2008: 151f.)

The numeral on this PTB is read "14" (10+1+1+1+1) in the edition by Deutsch 2003: 80f., followed by Barkay 2015: 24. On the published photograph, up to six very thin strokes can be discerned, rather than four, cf. my facsimile in Wimmer 2018: 152. As Hieratic has a proper numeral for "6," more than four strokes point again to the practise of extending the year date by the subsequent addition of strokes (s. above n. 19).

Barkay 2015: 25   Barkay 2015: 25   Wimmer 2008: 152

B. Kaufman 49a[0]
(= Barkay 2015: #2/5; Wimmer 2008: 151)

The numeral following "10" on this PTB was not identified in the edition Deutsch 2003: 78f. Barkay 2015: 29 is right in reading it "6," so that the year date is "16" (10+6). My facsimile in Wimmer 2008: 151, based on the published photograph, makes this clear.

Barkay 2015: 25   Barkay 2015: 25   Wimmer 2008: 151

B. Kaufman 54⁰
(= Barkay 2015: #1/8; Wimmer 2008: 153)

In the edition Deutsch 2003a: 84f. the numeral following "10" was misread as "probably 7," but should be read "6." Obviously inadvertently, it was not engraved in mirror writing into the seal so that it does appear in mirror writing on the impression. The same point was correctly made by Barkay 2015: 27. It will be meaningful for the discussion of other bullae below to note that such errors did occur to the engravers.

Barkay 2015: 22   Barkay 2015: 22   Wimmer 2008: 153

B. Kaufman 48⁰ and B. Moussaieff Fs 11⁰
(= Barkay 2015: #2/4, #2/23; Wimmer 2008: 150, 158)

In this case, two impressions from the same seal depict a locust in the top register and have a very peculiar shape for the numeral. It was read "24" in the edition Deutsch 2003a: 77 and Deutsch 2003b: 60f. (20+1+1+1+1), but the shape of the decade, which is well preserved, is clearly seen on the photographs and rendered well on the published facsimiles: it is not Hieratic "20." It is identical with a shape for "30" that was newly introduced in Demotic, and I suggested that this is one of a few examples for the adoption of contemporary, early Demotic sign shapes in "Palestinian Hieratic" (Wimmer 2008: 150, 274). Without referring to the point that this form is Demotic rather than Hieratic, Barkay 2015 accepts my reading (rendering it erroneously as "38" on p. 29, but correctly "34" on pp. 20, 24) as the basis for his thorough discussion of the date the tax bullae should be assigned to. We will return to this point below.

Barkay 2015: 25   Barkay 2015: 26

B. Moussaieff MP 100⁰
(= Barkay 2015: #1/5; Wimmer 2008: 156f.)

The inscription on this bulla, which mentions both a town and an official (so it is a hybrid TTB/PTB) is intriguing. The first line starts with a sign similar to the letter *taw*, an upright cross, but with a very short horizontal bar. In the edition Deutsch 1999: 171f. this is rendered by "+," without any comment. What follows is the date "In the tenth (year)," spelled in Hebrew as a word, not as a Hieratic numeral. Barkay 2015: 27 states that "the word עשרת (in the tenth [year]) appears in the uppermost register, and on each side of the word a sign similar to a *taw* or an X mark, fills the vacant space." This is puzzling, as the last sign to the left can only be the final *taw* of the word ꜥśrt, not at the same time a space filler. It differs from the first sign to the right of b-ꜥśrt, with its horizontal bar of equal length as the vertical stroke, in full accordance with the standard shape for the letter *taw*. Barkay 2015: 27 continues: "Deutsch read the second register as הארבת, but here, as in the upper register, the same *taw*-like sign appear (sic) to fill the empty space, and the actual city-name is ꞌrb (ארב), as on bulla no. 6; rather than reading ꞌrbt (ארובות), this should be read as ꞌrb." His attempt to read here the toponym Arab in Judah, which does appear on B. Kaufman 52⁰ (Deutsch 2003a: 81f.), instead of the northern Arubbot, is comprehensible. Yet, the final sign does, again, not differ in any way from a normal letter *taw*; moreover, empty space remains at the end of the line – so what sense would a space filler make, when it fails to fill the empty space? Occasionally space fillers do indeed occur on fiscal bullae, in the shape of small vertical strokes, dots, or even circles. But a sign identical with an alphabetic letter (in this case *taw*) functioning as a space filler, would be unexpected.

Moreover, the beginning of line 2 is damaged, and traces of a letter preceding *'rbt* are preserved. Barkay does not refer to this first letter. It could not be explained as yet another "*taw* like space filler," as all that is preserved is a horizontal top stroke. Deutsch suggests -ה as an article to the toponym, "The (city of) 'Arubboth." The horizontal bar could, in theory, be also part of a י, ס or perhaps even פ (but not ת), but I cannot offer an alternative explanation.

I did, though, suggest an explanation for the initial sign of the inscription, in line 1 (Wimmer 2008: 156f.). The hieroglyph ⌐, for Egyptian *rnpt*, "year," is in late Hieratic and early Demotic a vertical stroke with a small oblique or horizontal stroke attached or crossing. I cautiously suggested that the scribe chose to begin with the Egyptian sign for "year." The observation that this seems to be the only tax bulla, where the Hebrew word *šnh* for "year" is missing, would further support this idea. It remains a suggestion, though, as long as no other evidence for the use of the Egyptian logogram for "year" in Hebrew epigraphy is attested.

Barkay 2015: 21	Barkay 2015: 21	Wimmer 2008: 157

4 Tax bullae published after 2008

From among the six TTB and twelve PTB that were published after Wimmer 2008 was compiled, I would like to comment on a few. For those I do not mention here, I concur with the readings in the publications (Deutsch 2011, 2012, 2015, and adopted in Barkay 2015), but I include all in the palaeographic chart below.

Deutsch 2012: 60f.[020]
  (= Barkay 2015: #1/22; Heide 2015: 7)

This TTB, published under the heading "A Dated Brown-Clay Bulla," has the year date "16" (10+6), the numeral "6" being clear enough on the published photograph. Deutsch ignored in his facsimile the lower horizontal stroke and mistakenly read "13" (10+1+1+1), followed by Barkay 2015: 21.

Barkay 2015: 23   Barkay 2015: 23   SJW

Deutsch 2012: 61f.[021]
  (= Barkay 2015: #1/23: Heide 2015: #16)

This TTB from Lachish, published under the heading "A Dated Fragmentary and Damaged Black-Clay Bulla" is another good example of the reuse of a seal in a consecutive year. Following the decade digit, and above the line, a "1" was added. The decade should be read "20," so the seal was produced for regnal year "20," and reused in year "21" (20+1). This concurs with the reading by Deutsch, followed also by Barkay 2015: 28. I include this bulla, because the facsimile in Deutsch 2012: 62 appears misleading. According to this facsimile one is tempted to read the decade "10," followed by two single strokes (10+1+1). The photograph shows clear enough that the decade is indeed "20," which I try to show in my facsimile.

---

20 In Wimmer 2008 I chose to identify the bullae by their collections and adopting the numbers from the editions. In Deutsch 2012, the name of the collector is not given ("the owner prefers to remain anonymous," p. 60 n. 5), and no numbers are given either. Therefore, the bibliographic reference must suffice here for the nomenclature.
21 Cf. n. 21.

Barkay 2015: 23   Barkay 2015: 23   SJW

B. Kaufman 524[ø]
    (= Barkay 2015: #2/22)

The numeral on this PTB, read "22" (1+1+20) in the edition Deutsch 2011: 90f., followed by Barkay 2015: 30, is peculiar for two reasons. As was noted by Barkay, the single digits precede the decade instead of following it. Perhaps this is another case of inadvertently disregarding the mirror writing by the engraver of the seal. This, perhaps, may explain, too, why the decade has a very awkward looking shape. Barkay offers a small drawing, stating that its form "is deviant and poorly-executed." His drawing has a horizontal stroke on top of the sign, which does not appear on the published photograph (nor on the facsimile by Deutsch). Without this horizontal top stroke, however, the shape does not resemble the Hieratic numeral "20" at all. Barkay's drawing and the facsimile by Deutsch both show an X-like shape. Based on the photograph, I arrive at a somewhat different facsimile. The sign is blurred above its middle, but its very top is clearly forked. This shape can best be identified as the Hieratic numeral "30" (Wimmer 2008: 221f.). Strictly speaking, the same Hieratic shape for "30" continues also in early Demotic, alongside a newly introduced shape that was observed above on B. Kaufman 48[ø] and B. Moussaieff Fs 11[ø]. The year date is "32" (1+1+30), providing another high regnal year, with ramifications for dating the corpus of tax bullae, as will be discussed below.

Below the second line some enigmatic traces can be seen, which can best be explained by Barkay's suggestion that the seal "appears to have been a palimpsest" (2015: 30).

Barkay 2015: 26   Barkay 2015: 26   SJW

B. Chaya 5⁰
(= Barkay 2015: #1/28)

In the edition Deutsch 2015: 55f. the year is read "12" (10+1+1). Barkay 2015: 21 has "22." The top of the decade is missing, so that "22" and even "32" might be possible. Since the left oblique stroke of the sign is positioned very high, it does not appear plausible that the sign could have a loop higher on top for "20," or a forked top for "30" either, so the option "10" should indeed be preferred.

Deutsch 2015: 55   Deutsch 2015: 55   SJW

B. Chaya 9⁰
(Deutsch 2015: 59f., #9)

This PTB has a circular shape and its inscription is exceptional: The seal as a whole was engraved in normal script, not mirror writing, so that the bulla is completely in mirror writing. The year is correctly read "13" (10+1+1+1) by Deutsch.

Deutsch 2015: 58	Deutsch 2015: 59	SJW

B. Moussaieff 2003:8⁰
(Deutsch 2015: 58f., #8)

Exceptionally, the year date follows the official's name on this PTB, instead of preceding it. The numeral looks very strange on the facsimile by Deutsch (cf. his n. 15), but based on the photograph his reading "20" can be confirmed and the facsimile improved. His remark "Following the numeral, there are two slim and one thick strokes..." (Deutsch 2015: 59 n. 15) is incomprehensible to me. His own facsimile does not show any of these strokes, and on the photograph, only one thin stroke can perhaps be discerned at the very edge.

Deutsch 2015: 58	Deutsch 2015: 58	SJW

B. Kaufman 623⁰
(= Barkay 2015: #2/14)

Finally, the most enigmatic caption is singled out by Barkay 2015: 29 on this bulla, which was not identified as a fiscal bulla at all in the edition by Deutsch 2011: 161f. It has three registers, with a personal name with filiation in lines 1 and 2, extending over the first two signs of line 3. Its reading is clear: *l-Yšmᶜᵓl ᶜšyhw*. The letters appear awkward, e.g. the square *ᶜayin*. In line 3, after perhaps a small word divider, several strange small signs follow. Deutsch read them "ṣmt," commenting that the *ṣade* was "written in reverse" and the mem "uncertain." The *taw* would be written below the line and turned by 90°. Deutsch does not comment on its meaning.

Barkay 2015: 29 suggests: "But the identification of these signs as Hebrew letters is unlikely, and they are in fact Egyptian hieratic signs." He identifies the lower, x-like sign as "a cursive schematisation of the shekel sign, well known from the weights and ostraca of the Iron IIB" (without referring to Wimmer 2008: 251, where this sign is discussed). I cannot follow his interpretation that "The two other signs probably represent a large hieratic number, i.e. a large amount of shekels of silver; the left sign ⌐ appears to represent the one hundred (Wimmer 2008, 228), although it could also represent the volume unit *'ph* (Winner [*sic*] 2008, 257), while the right one is probably 20. Thus the three signs could mean 120 shekels (of silver)." "20" in Hieratic (and Demotic) is always characterised by a loop on top, open to the right. The traces that were identified as *ṣade* by Deutsch, are not compatible with "20," or with any other numeral or special sign in Palestinian Hieratic. The sign to the left does indeed look identical with the Palestinian Hieratic special sign for the epha-unit (Wimmer 2008: 259f.), but this provides no meaningful reading here. Barkay's preferred interpretation as the numeral "100" may be based on a misunderstanding of my sign table Wimmer 2008: 228. Hieratic (and Demotic) "100" starts with a small hook to the right and is then a long horizontal or descending line extending widely to the left. Some examples in my table (P1, 1.1, 2.2, 3.1) are incomplete, with the broken edge of the ostracon being marked by a fragmentary line. In these cases, the preserved part of the sign is short, and when the line marking the break is misinterpreted as part of the sign, the composition has some similarity to the enigmatic sign on the bulla (in mirror writing). I must confess that I have no solution to offer. I cannot see how the sign would have any resemblance with the letter *mem*, but it is not the numeral "100" either.

It does not seem plausible that a name seal would specify a given amount. A logical interpretation could be a papponym, which might be what Deutsch had in mind. However, the signs are very unfamiliar. Perhaps one should even look for an iconic, not epigraphic, motif, such as a winged scarab or the like (cf. e.g. Avigad/Sass 1997: nos. 86, 267, 343, 349, 867), with a schematized underlying ankh (turned by 90°, cf. e.g. Avigad/Sass 1997: no. 46). This would here be executed in a graphically much reduced manner, virtually beyond recognition.

Barkay 2015: 26   Barkay 2015: 26   SJW

5 Implications for the date of tax bullae

The tax bullae were dated to the reigns of Josiah (Avigad 1990) or Hezekiah (Deutsch 2012), but Barkay 2015: 39ff. has argued that the reign of the less prominent Manasseh, who reigned between the two for 55 years (698–643 BCE), was in fact the only possible candidate. He discusses in detail an impressive list of reasons why this should be so, the first being the fact that neither Josiah nor Hezekiah reached a regnal year 34. This is, according to my reading, attested on B. Kaufman $48^{\emptyset}$ and B. Moussaieff Fs $11^{\emptyset}$. Other regnal years on tax bullae range from year 3 to year 26.[22] One might therefore insinuate, should the reading "34" (30+1+1+1+1) be erroneous, that the decade is better read as "20," as in Deutsch 2003a and 2003b. The hiatus of 8 years that were unattested would indeed be odd. However, among the new bullae published in Deutsch 2015 is a new PTB from year 26 (p. 57f., no. $7^{\emptyset}$; the numeral is clear and the reading beyond doubt). We have shown above that B. Kaufman $524^{\emptyset}$ should be dated to year 32 (not 22). So the gap is narrowing (to currently 6 years), and Barkay's assessment for dating the tax bullae corpus to the reign of Manasseh is strengthened.

6 Further thoughts

Barkay 2015: 31ff. evaluates similarities and differences between the system of tax bullae (from the early 7th century), the LMLK stamped jar handles (from the

---

22 Barkay 2015: 30 writes erroneously year "24," when enumerating the attested regnal years, even though he has the year correct in his table (#1/1), insinuating a hiatus of 10 years between "24 and 34." In fact attested are regnal years 3, 4, 7, 10, 12, 13, 14, 16, 18, 19, 20, 21, 22, 23, 26, 32, 34.

late 8th century), and the Samaria ostraca (from the early 8th century).[23] I wonder whether a much earlier tradition of tax registration can be compared, namely the Hieratic inscribed bowls from Egyptian administered southern Canaan (13th century).[24] They list a specific term for the function of the deliveries ("The *b-r-t* which is in it"), the date, commodity, quantity, origin, destination, and sometimes the registering scribe.[25] It may be meaningful that these tax deliveries on bowls document the Hieratic tradition of Ramesside Canaan, which may have triggered the later practise of Palestinian Hieratic[26], which in turn is again attested so well for the systems of tax registration in the Hebrew Kingdoms.

7 Palestinian Hieratic on tax bullae

The following chart includes all Hieratic numerals on bullae published at present. All facsimiles are by SJW based on the published photographs, except where I perceive zero discrepancy from the editions; in these cases the facsimiles are rendered in outline. For better comparison, the facsimiles are reproduced in roughly equal size, disregarding scale. Bold numbers translate the numerals, while numbers in brackets refer to the key below for identifying sources.

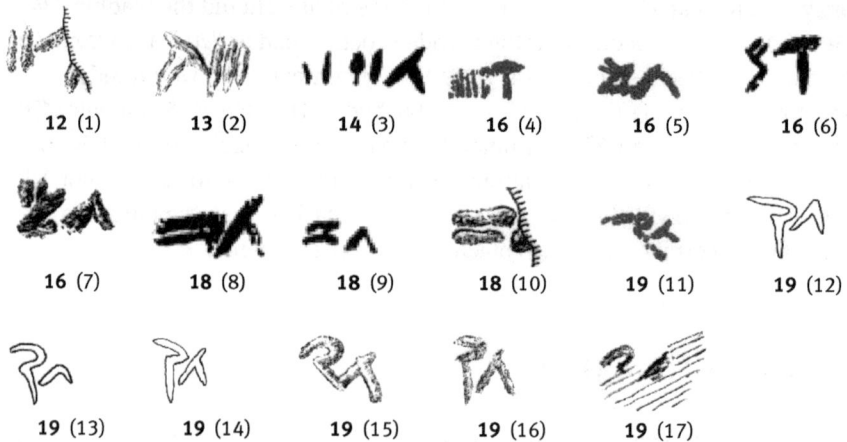

12 (1)	**13** (2)	**14** (3)	**16** (4)	**16** (5)	**16** (6)
16 (7)	**18** (8)	**18** (9)	**18** (10)	**19** (11)	**19** (12)
19 (13)	**19** (14)	**19** (15)	**19** (16)	**19** (17)	

---

23 Anat Mendel-Geberovich in her response, too, raised the question, whether the systems of bullae and impressed jar handles could complement each other.
24 Cf. above n. 11.
25 Cf. Wimmer 2019.
26 Cf. above n. 11.

20 (18)   20? (19)   **20** (20)   **21** (21)   **21** (22)

21 (23)   **21** (24)   **21** (25)   **22** (26)   **23** (27)

23 (28)   **23** (29)   **23** (30)   **26** (31)   **26** (32)

32 (33)   **34** (34)   **34** (35)   *rnpt* („regnal year")

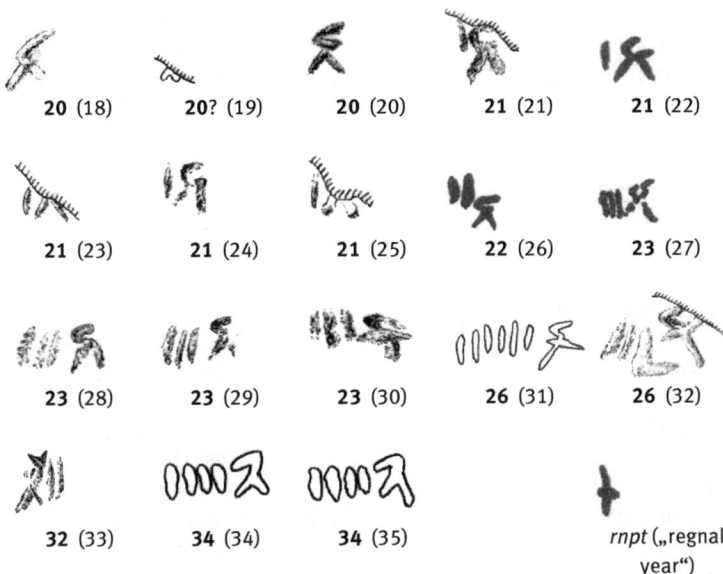

#	Bulla	Barkay 2015	Heide 2015	Wimmer 2008	Publication
1	**B. Chaya 5**$^{\emptyset}$	#1/28	#24		Deutsch 2015: #5
2	**B. Chaya 9**$^{\emptyset}$				Deutsch 2015: #9
3	B. Moussaieff MP 97a$^{\emptyset}$	#1/2	#13	154f.	Deutsch 1999: #97a
4	**B. Kaufman 51**$^{\emptyset}$	#2/8		151f.	Deutsch 2003a: #51
5	**B. Kaufman 49a**$^{\emptyset}$	#2/5		151	Deutsch 2003a: #49a
6	**B. Kaufman 54**$^{\emptyset}$	#1/8	#20	153	Deutsch 2003a: 54
7	**B. Deutsch 2012: 60f.**$^{\emptyset}$	#1/22	#7		Deutsch 2012: 60f.
8	**B. Moussaieff MP 97b**$^{\emptyset}$	#1/3	#14	155	Deutsch 1999: #97b
9	B. Kaufman 56$^{\emptyset}$	#1/14	#29	154	Deutsch 2003a: 56
10	B. Deutsch 2013$^{\emptyset}$				Barkay 2015: 43f.
11	B. Kaufman 55$^{\emptyset}$	#1/9	#25	153f.	Deutsch 2003a: 55
12	B. Saeedi DH 150$^{\emptyset}$	#1/10	#6	159	Deutsch/Heltzer 1999: #150a
13	B. Kaufman 52$^{\emptyset}$	#1/6	#2	152	Deutsch 2003a: 52
14	B. Kaufman 53$^{\emptyset}$	#1/7	#15	152f.	Deutsch 2003a: 53
15	B. Jeselsohn: Deutsch 2015: #6$^{\emptyset}$				Deutsch 2015: #6
16	B. Kaufman 518$^{\emptyset}$	#1/19	#26		Deutsch 2011: #518
17	B. Kaufman 522$^{\emptyset}$	#2/18			Deutsch 2011: #522
18	**B. Moussaieff 2003:8**$^{\emptyset}$				Deutsch 2015: #8

19	B. Kaufman 47ᵒ	#2/3		149f.	Deutsch 2003a: 47
20	**B. Deutsch 2012: 62f.ᵒ**	#1/24	#21		Deutsch 2012: 62f.
21	**B. Deutsch 2012: 61f.ᵒ**	#1/23	#16		Deutsch 2012: 61f.
22	B. Moussaieff MP 149ᵒ	#2/1		158	Deutsch/Heltzer 1999: #149
23	B. Kaufman 523aᵒ	#2/19			Deutsch 2011: #523a
24	B. Kaufman 523bᵒ	#2/20			Deutsch 2011: #523b
25	B. Kaufman 523cᵒ	#2/21			Deutsch 2011: #523c
26	B. Moussaieff MP 98ᵒ	#1/4	#19	156	Deutsch 1999: #98
27	B. Kaufman 50ᵒ	#2/7		151	Deutsch 2003a: 50
28	B. Kaufman 521aᵒ	#2/16			Deutsch 2011: #521a
29	B. Kaufman 521bᵒ	#2/17			Deutsch 2011: #521b
30	B. Kaufman 520ᵒ	#2/15			Deutsch 2011: #520
31	B. Moussaieff MP 101ᵒ	#1/1	#1	157f.	Deutsch 1999: #101
32	B. Chaya 7ᵒ				Deutsch 2015: #7
33	**B. Kaufman 524ᵒ**	#2/22			Deutsch 2011: #524
34	**B. Kaufman 48ᵒ**	#2/4		150	Deutsch 2003a: #48
35	**B. Moussaieff Fs 11ᵒ**	#2/23		158	Deutsch 2003b: #11
36	**B. Moussaieff MP 100ᵒ**	#1/5		156f.	Deutsch 1999: #100

Bullae in bold are discussed in this paper.

8 Bibliography

Aharoni, Yohanan
1966 The Use of Hieratic Numerals in Hebrew Ostraca and the Shekel Weights. *Bulletin of the American Schools of Oriental Research* 184, 13–19.
1975 כתובות ערד, ירושלים: מוסד ביאליק (Arad Inscriptions, Hebrew).
1981 *Arad Inscriptions*, Jerusalem: Israel Exploration Society.
Ahituv, Shmuel
2008 *Echoes from the Past. Hebrew and Cognate Inscriptions from the Biblical Period.* Carta: Jerusalem.
Aufrecht, Walter E.
1989 *A Corpus of Ammonite Inscriptions*, Lewiston/Queenston/Lampeter: Edwin Mellen Press.
Avigad, Nahman
1990 Two Hebrew 'Fiscal' Bullae. *Israel Exploration Journal* 40, 262–266.
Avigad, Nahman and Benjamin Sass
1997 *Corpus of West Semitic Stamp Seals.* Israel Academy of Sciences and Humanities: Jerusalem.

Barkay, Gabriel

2012   A Fiscal Bulla from the Slopes of the Temple Mount. Evidence for the Taxation System
        of the Judean Kingdom. *New Studies of Jerusalem* 17, 2012, 154–178 (Hebrew) –
        בולה פיסקאלית ממדרונות הר הבית – עדות למערכת המיסוי בממלכת יהודה. *חידושים*
        בחקר ירושלים י"ז, תשע"ב, 154–178.

2015   Evidence of the Taxation System of the Judean Kingdom. A Fiscal Bulla from the
        Slopes of the Temple Mount and the Phenomenon of Fiscal Bullae. In:
        Lubetski/Lubetski 2015. Pp. 17–49.

Barkay, Gabriel and Robert Deutsch

2017   Another Fiscal Bulla from the City of David, *New Studies of Jerusalem* 22, 2017, 115–
        121 (Hebrew) – בולה פיסקאלית נוספת מעיר דוד, *חידושים בחקר ירושלים* כ"ב, תשע"ז,
        115–121.

Bean, Adam L., Christopher A. Rollston, P. Kyle McCarter, and Stefan J. Wimmer

2019   An Inscribed Altar from the Khirbat Ataruz Moabite Sanctuary, *Levant* 2019, 1–27.

Cohen, Rudolf and Hannah Bernick-Greenberg

2007   *Excavations at Kadesh-Barnea (Tell el-Qudeirat) 1976–1982*, Israel Antiquity Authority
        Reports 34, Jerusalem: IAA.

Deutsch, Robert

1999   *Messages from the Past. Hebrew Bullae from the Time of Isaiah Through the Destruc-*
        tion of the First Temple. Shlomo Moussaieff Collection and an Up to Date Corpus. Ar-
        chaeological Center Publication: Tel Aviv-Jaffa.

2003a   *Biblical Period Hebrew Bullae. The Josef Chaim Kaufman Collection.* Archaeological
        Center Publication: Tel Aviv-Jaffa.

2003b   A Hoard of Fifty Hebrew Clay Bullae from the Time of Hezekiah. In: R. Deutsch (ed.),
        Shlomo (Festschrift Shlomo Moussaieff). Archaeological Center Publication: Tel Aviv-
        Jaffa. Pp. 45–98.

2011   *Biblical Period Epigraphy. The Joseph Kaufman Collection. Seals, Bullae, Handles.*
        Archaeological Center: Jaffa.

2012   Six Hebrew Fiscal Bullae from the Time of Hezekiah. In: Meir Lubetski, Edith Lubetski
        (eds.), *New Inscriptions and Seals Relating to the Biblical World.* Society of Biblical
        Literature: Atlanta. Pp. 59–67.

2015   Ten Unrecorded Hebrew Fiscal Bullae. In: Lubetski/Lubetski 2015. Pp. 51–61.

Deutsch, Robert and Michael Heltzer

1999   *West Semitic Epigraphic News of the 1st Millennium BCE.* Archaeological Center Publi-
        cation: Tel Aviv-Jaffa.

Goldwasser, Orly

1991   An Egyptian Scribe from Lachish and the Hieratic Tradition of the Hebrew Kingdoms,
        Tel Aviv 18, 248–253.

2016   האם "נעם רב נקבנ" היה ממציאי האלף-בית? ניתוח פלאוגרפי משווה של הכתובת על
        פסלו וכתובות במכרות הטורקיז, בתוך: ה. גבע, א. פריס (עורכים), *ספר יוסף נוה*, ארץ-
        ישראל 32, החברה לחקירת ארץ-ישראל, ירושלים 2016, ע' 21–32.
        A paleographic comparison of the alphabetic inscription on block-statuette 346 from
        Serabit el-Khadem to the alphabetic inscriptions of the mines, In: Hillel Geva, Alan
        Paris (eds.), *Joseph Naveh Volume*, Eretz-Israel 32, Jerusalem: Israel Exploration So-
        ciety 2016, 21–32 (Hebrew).

Hamilton, Gordon J.

2006   *The Origins of the West Semitic Alphabet in Egyptian Scripts*, The Catholic Biblical Quarterly Monograph Series 40, Washington D.C.: The Catholic Biblical Association of America.

Heide, Martin

2015   Some Notes on the Epigraphical Features of the Phoenician and Hebrew Fiscal Bullae. In: Lubetski/Lubetski 2015. Pp. 63–77.

Kletter, Raz

1998   *Economic Keystones. The Weight System of the Kingdom of Judah,* Journal for the Study of the Old Testament Supplement Series 276, Sheffield: Sheffield Academic Press.

Lemaire, André and Pascal Vernus

1980   Les ostraca paléo-hébreux de Qadesh-Barnéa. *Orientalia* 49, 341–345.

1983   L'ostracon paléo-hébreu n° 6 de Tell Qudeirat (Qadesh-Barnéa). In: M. Görg (ed.), *Fontes atque Pontes (Festschrift Hellmut Brunner)*, ÄAT 5, Wiesbaden: Harrassowitz, Pp. 302–326.

Lubetski, Meir and Edith Lubetski (eds.)

2015   *Recording New Epigraphic Evidence (Festschrift Robert Deutsch)*. Jerusalem.

Mendel-Geberovich, Anat

2022   Judaean Glyptic Finds: An Updated Corpus and a Revision of Their Palaeography. In: E. Eshel and M. Langlois (ed.), *The Scribe in the Biblical World*, BZAW, Berlin: De Gruyter.

Noth, Martin

1927   Das Krongut der israelitischen Könige und seine Verwaltung, *Zeitschrift des Deutschen Palästina-Vereins* 50, 211–244.

Reisner, George A., Fisher, Clarance S. and David G. Lyon

1924   *Harvard Excavations at Samaria 1908–1910*. Cambridge, MA.: Harvard University Press.

Rollston, Christopher A.

2004   Non-Provenanced Epigraphs II: The Status of Non-Provenanced Epigraphs within the Broader Corpus of Northwest Semitic. *Maarav* 11, 57–79.

2005   Navigating the Epigraphic Strom. *Near Eastern Archaeology* 68, 69–72.

Vainstub, Daniel

2016   האותיות הכנעניות š ו-t ומקוקו של סימן השקל, הטורקיז, בתוך: ה. גבע, א. פריס (עורכים), *ספר יוסף נוה*, ארץ-ישראל 32, החברה לחקירת ארץ-ישראל, ירושלים 2016, ע' 55–65. The Canaanite letters Š and T and the origin of the Shekel symbol, In: Hillel Geva, Alan Paris (eds.), *Joseph Naveh Volume,* Eretz-Israel 32, Jerusalem: Israel Exploration Society 2016, 21–32 (Hebrew).

Wimmer, Stefan

2008   *Palästinisches Hieratisch. Die Zahl- und Sonderzeichen in der althebräischen Schrift.* ÄAT 75. Harrassowitz: Wiesbaden.

2015   Hieratisch mit Migrationshintergrund. Neue Quellen zu den hieratischen Elementen in der hebräischen Alphabetschrift. In: Ursula Verhoeven (ed.), *Ägyptologische „Binsen"-Weisheiten I-II. Neue Forschungen und Methoden der Hieratistik.* Akademie der Wissenschaften und der Literatur: Mainz. Pp. 143–153.

2018   Palestinian Hieratic in Non-Hebrew Context: Egyptian Numerals and Special Signs in Regions Neighboring Israel. In: Itzaq Shai et al. (eds.), *Tell it in Gath. Studies in the*

History and Archaeology of Israel (Festschrift Aren M. Maeir). ÄAT 90, Zaphon: Münster. Pp. 709–721.

2019   Lachish is Lachish on the Lachish Bowl: an object lesson for reading Hieratic, with little surprising results. The Lachish Bowl in the context of Hieratic inscriptions from southern Canaan. In: Aren M. Maeir, Itzaq Shai, Chris McKinny (eds.), *The Late Bronze and Early Iron Ages of Southern Canaan,* Archaeology of the Biblical World 2, De Gruyter: Berlin/Boston 2019. Pp. 136–147.

Aren M. Wilson-Wright

Out of Egypt: Lexicographic Evidence for Egyptian Influence on West Semitic and Israelite Administrative and Scribal Practice

Of the 39 secure Egyptian loanwords in Hebrew, nine relate to scribal practice in some way:[1] *dəyô* 'ink', *gōme²* 'manufacturable papyrus', and *qeset* 'scribal palette' refer to the tools of the Israelite scribe; *zeret, qab, hîn,* and *²êpâ* belong to the set of metrograms employed by scribes in administrative work; and *ḥôtām* 'seal' and *ṭabbaʿat* 'signet ring' indicate the tools used for sealing written documents.[2] At first glance, this set of loanwords appears to offer impressive evidence for Egyptian influence on Israelite scribal practice. Yet it is unclear when and how these loanwords entered the Hebrew lexicon. Most scholars date the introduction of these terms to the Late Bronze Age since the pharaohs of the Eighteenth, Nineteenth, and Twentieth Dynasties exercised direct control over the Levant at this time.[3] Such a dating proves problematic, however, because many of these words appear in other Semitic languages that were not in contact with Egyptian during the Late Bronze Age. In this paper, therefore, I will use a combination of linguistic and material evidence to establish a timeline of borrowing for the Egyptian scribal terms found in Hebrew that begins 1500 years before the Late Bronze Age.

---

* I would like to thank André Lemaire, Michael Langlois, Tania Notarius, and the other conference participants for their comments and suggestions for improvement. I would also like to thank John Huehnergard and Na'ama Pat-El for reading an earlier draft of this paper. Any remaining errors are my own.

1 For a list of all of the Egyptian loanwords into Hebrew, see Aren M. Wilson-Wright, "Linguistic Contact between Hebrew and Egyptian," in *Oxford Handbook on Ancient Egypt and the Hebrew Bible*, ed. Susan Tower Hollis (Oxford: Oxford University Press, forthcoming).

2 I omit *²aḥû* 'sedge', *ʿarâ* 'reed', or *sûp* 'reed' from the discussion since these terms are only tangentially related to scribal practice. As Philip Zhakevich has shown in his study of Hebrew scribal terminology, only *gōme²* refers to the papyrus used in the manufacture of paper (*Scribal Tools in Ancient Israel: A Study of Biblical Hebrew Terms for Writing Materials and Implements* [HACL 9; University Park, PA: Eisenbrauns, 2020], 49). *²aḥû, ʿarâ,* and *sûp,* by contrast, each refer to different species of reed growing along the banks of the Nile.

3 Nili Sacher Fox, *In the Service of the King: Officialdom in Ancient Israel and Judah* (MHUC 23; Cincinnati: Hebrew Union College Press, 2000), 266; William M. Schniedewind, *A Social History of Hebrew: Its Origins through the Rabbinic Period* (AYBRL; New Haven: Yale University Press, 2013), 36–37, 59; idem, *The Finger of the Scribe: How Scribes Learned to Write the Bible* (Oxford: Oxford University Press, 2019), 6; Francis Breyer, *Ägyptische Namen und Wörter im Alten Testament* (ÄAT 93; Münster: Zaphon, 2019), 114; Zhakevich, Scribal Tools in Ancient Israel, 166–67.

In particular, I will argue that *ḥôtām*, *ṭabbaʿat*, *zeret*, *qab*, *hîn*, and *ʾêpâ* were borrowed into some of Hebrew's linguistic ancestors—hundreds of years before the emergence of Hebrew as a distinct linguistic entity—and reflect sporadic Egyptian influence on West Semitic administrative traditions. *qeset*, *dəyô*, and *gōmeʾ*, on the other hand, reflect direct Egyptian influence on Israelite scribal practice between the twelfth to eighth centuries BCE.

1 The Emergence of Hebrew as a Distinct Linguistic Entity

In order to distinguish between Egyptian loanwords that were borrowed into Hebrew and those that were adopted by one of Hebrew's linguistic ancestors, we must first establish a date for the emergence of Hebrew as distinct linguistic entity. This is easier said than done. Fortunately, the word *yəʾôr* 'river, the Nile' suggests that Hebrew emerged as a distinct language no earlier than the fourteenth century BCE. *yəʾôr* comes from Egyptian *jtrw* 'river, the Nile', which underwent an *ad hoc* sound change of *t* > *ʾ* during the Eighteenth Dynasty (1550–1295 BCE).[4] Both Coptic (Sahidic *eioor*, Bohairic *ior*, Fayyumic *iaar*) and transcriptional evidence (^(ld)*ia-ru-ʾu-ú* < *jʾrw* ʿ3) indicate that the resulting form was vocalized *yáʾru*.[5] This form, however, proves difficult to reconcile with the Hebrew vocalization of the word. If *yárʾu* were borrowed directly into Hebrew, we would expect the Hebrew form to be vocalized **ʾyeʾer* or **ʾyaʾar* (compare Hebrew *qeset* 'scribal palette' < Egyptian *gástv*). This difficulty goes away if *yáʾru* was borrowed into Pre-Proto-Canaanite, since *yaʾru* would eventually yield the attested Hebrew form through the application of regular sound rules: Pre-Proto-Canaanite *yaʾr* becomes *yā(ʾ)r* as in other II-ʾ *qatl* nouns such as *rô(ʾ)š* 'head' (< *raʾs*); *yā(ʾ)r* becomes *yō(ʾ)r* with the operation of the Canaanite shift; and *yō(ʾ)r* becomes *yəʾôr* via hypercorrection as in other II-ʾ *qvtl* nouns like *bəʾēr* 'well' (< *biʾr*) and *bəʾōš*

---

4 Allen, *The Ancient Egyptian Language*, 27, 42; idem, *Ancient Egyptian Phonology*, 92; Wb I 146:10–12. Because we do not possess full linguistic data for Egyptian or any of the ancient Semitic languages, the conclusions of this article are subject to revision if and when more information becomes available. To avoid analytical paralysis, however, I have treated the available data as if they were complete.
5 Hermann Ranke, *Keilschriftliches Material zur altägyptischen Vokalisation* (Berlin: Königl. Akademie der Wissenschaft, 1910), 29.

'stench' (< *buʔs).[6] Because yəʔôr reflects the shift of jtrw > jʔrw, which is first attested in the Eighteenth Dynasty, it is unlikely that its Egyptian antecedent entered Pre-Proto-Canaanite before 1550 BCE. The vocalization of yəʔôr thus establishes a *terminus post quem* of 1550 BCE for the transition from Pre-Proto-Canaanite to Proto-Canaanite.[7] This date is consistent with the earliest evidence for the Canaanite shift—the unconditioned shift of *ā > ō that triggered several morphological changes in the Canaanite languages—which appears in a sixteenth-century BCE contract from Hazor.[8]

As a Canaanite language, Hebrew cannot predate the emergence of Proto-Canaanite around 1550 BCE. But we cannot simply trace the origins of Hebrew to the sixteenth century BCE, since we must allow sufficient time for Proto-Canaanite to split into individual speech communities. The presence of Canaanite glosses in the Amarna letters suggests that this process began sometime before 1360 BCE. Thus, the mid-fourteenth century represents a reasonable estimate of the earliest possible date for the existence of Hebrew as a distinct linguistic entity. Any Egyptian words borrowed before this period must have entered one of Hebrew's linguistic ancestors rather than Hebrew itself. With this criterion in mind, we can now analyze the Egyptian scribal terminology found in Hebrew.

---

6 John Huehnergard, "Biblical Hebrew Nominal Patterns," in *Epigraphy, Philology, and the Hebrew Bible: Methodological Perspectives on Philological and Comparative Study of the Hebrew Bible in Honor of Jo Ann Hackett*, eds. Jeremy M. Hutton and Aaron D. Rubin (SBLANEM 12; Atlanta: SBL, 2015), 37, 40. For the subgrouping of the Semitic languages, see John Huehnergard and Na'ama Pat-El, "Introduction to the Semitic Languages and Their History," in *The Semitic Languages*, 2nd ed., eds. John Huehnergard and Na'ama Pat-El (London: Routledge, 2019), 3–13.

7 Hebrew ʔaḥû 'plants' and Old Aramaic ʔḥwh 'vegetation' (< Egyptian ȝḥj 'plants') provide further support for this date. The Egyptian phoneme conventionally transcribed as ȝ originally represented the lateral approximant /l/ but shifted to /ʔ/ at the beginning of the New Kingdom. The representation of Egyptian ȝ with Semitic ʔ in a word that is reconstructible to Proto-Aramaeo-Canaanite suggests that Proto-Aramaeo-Canaanite and hence Pre-Proto-Canaanite was still intact at the beginning of the New Kingdom.

8 William W. Hallo and Hayim Tadmor, "A Lawsuit from Hazor," *IEJ* 27 (1977): 5, 11.

2 Inherited Egyptian Loanwords in Hebrew Dealing with Scribal Practice

Hebrew *ḥôtām* ultimately comes from Egyptian *ḫtm* and represents the oldest Egyptian term found in Hebrew. Cognates of *ḥôtām* appear in many West Semitic languages and language families, including Classical Arabic (*ḫātam* 'signet ring'), Syriac (*ḥātmā* 'seal, signet ring'), Jewish Babylonian Aramaic (*ḥātmā* 'seal, sealing'), Mandaic (*hatma* 'seal, sign'), and Phoenician (*ḥtm* 'seal').[9] Denominative verbal forms related to *ḥôtām* also enjoy a widespread distribution in West Semitic, appearing in Ethiopic (*ḫatama* 'to seal'), Sabaic (*ḫtm* 'to seal'), Classical Arabic (*ḫatama* 'to seal'), and Syriac (*ḥtam* 'to seal').[10] Theoretically, this distribution could reflect a series of borrowings from Egyptian into individual West Semitic languages, coupled with inner-Semitic borrowing. But both

9 Edward William Lane, *Maddu-l-Kamoos: An Arabic-English Dictionary* (8 vols.; London: Williams & Norgate, 1863–1893), 2.703; Georg Wilhelm Freytag, *Lexicon Arabico-Latinum* (4 vols.; Halle: Schwetschke, 1830–1837), 1.460; Albert de Biberstein Kazimirski, *Dictionnaire arabe-français* (2 vols.; Paris: Maisonneuve, 1860), 1.540; Robert Payne Smith, *Thesaurus Syriacus* (3 vols.; GHD 7; Piscataway, NJ: Gorgias, 2007), 1.1405–6; Michael Sokoloff, *A Dictionary of Jewish Babylonian Aramaic of the Talmudic and Geonic Periods* (Publications of the Comprehensive Aramaic Lexicon Project; Ramat-Gan: Bar Ilan University Press, 2002), 490; E. Drower and R. Macuch, *A Mandaic Dictionary* (Oxford: Clarendon, 1963), 128; DNWSI, 1.413–14. See also Edward M. Cook, *Dictionary of Qumran Aramaic* (Winona Lake, IN: Eisenbrauns, 2015), 93. Cognates of *ḥôtām* also appear in several Modern South Arabian languages (e.g., Mehri *ḥôtem* 'ring'), but these forms may be Arabic loanwords: T. M. Johnstone, *Mehri Lexicon and English-Mehri Word-List* (London: SOAS, University of London, 1987), 451; idem, *Jibbāli Lexicon* (Oxford: Oxford University Press, 1981), 308; idem, *Ḥarsūsi Lexicon and English-Ḥarsūsi Word-List* (London: Oxford University Press, 1977), 143.
10 Wolf Leslau, *Comparative Dictionary of Ge'ez (Classical Ethiopic): Ge'ez-English / English-Ge'ez with an Index of the Semitic Roots* (Wiesbaden: Harrassowitz, 1991), 267–68; "Ghul A," in *Digital Archive for the Study of pre-Islamic Arabian Inscriptions* (Università degli studi di Pisa; online: http://dasi.cnr.it/index.php?id=37&recId=4149), line 9; Lane, Maddu-l-Kamoos, 2.702; Freytag, *Lexicon Arabico-Latinum*, 1.461; Kazimirski, *Dictionnaire arabe-français*, 1.539; Payne Smith, *Thesaurus Syriacus*, 1.1405–6. See also Cook, *Dictionary of Qumran Aramaic*, 93; Marcus Jastrow, *Dictionary of the Targumim, the Talmud Babli, and Yerushalmi, and the Midrashic Literature* (Peabody: Hendrickson, 2006), 514; Michael Sokoloff, *A Dictionary of Christian Palestinian Aramaic* (OLA 234; Leuven: Peeters, 2014), 142–43; idem, *A Dictionary of Jewish Babylonian Aramaic*, 489; idem, *A Dictionary of Jewish Palestinian Aramaic of the Byzantine Period* (3rd ed.; Ramat Gan: Bar Ilan University Press, 2017), 226; idem, *A Dictionary of Judean Aramaic* (Ramat Gan: Bar Ilan University Press, 2003), 51; Drower and Macuch, *A Mandaic Dictionary*, 154–55; Abraham Tal, *A Dictionary of Samaritan Aramaic* (2 vols.; HdO 50; Leiden: Brill, 2000), 1.300.

Ockham's razor and linguistic evidence militate against this possibility. It is more parsimonious, after all, to posit a single loan into Proto-West Semitic than a series of borrowings into individual West Semitic languages. Furthermore, the Hebrew and Aramaic forms exhibit sound changes that only affected inherited lexemes. The Hebrew form reflects the operation of the Canaanite shift, while the Syriac, Mandaic, and Jewish Babylonian Aramaic forms reflect the reduction of short unstressed vowels.[11] Thus, it is likely that Egyptian *ḥtm* was borrowed into Proto-West Semitic as **ḫātam* and inherited by Hebrew.[12]

Material evidence allows us to establish a tentative date for this borrowing. Because early West Semitic speakers most likely borrowed the Egyptian word for 'seal' at the same time that they adopted Egyptian sealing technology, we can use the first appearance of Egyptian-style seals in the Levant—the likely homeland of Proto-West Semitic[13]—to approximate the date of borrowing. The earliest evidence for Egyptian seals in the Levant comes from the EB I strata at En Besor, Nahal Tillah, and Gezer, which date to the end of Dynasty 0 and the beginning of Dynasty 1 (3100–3000 BCE).[14] All three of these sites have yielded administrative bullae bearing the impressions of Egyptian-style cylinder seals, some of which

---

11 In theory, the Hebrew form could represent a later, independent borrowing from Egyptian after the Egyptian shift of **á > ō* / _CV sometime between the thirteenth and eighth centuries BCE. But it would be quite a coincidence for the later Egyptian form to appear exclusively in a language that underwent a similar sound change.

12 Benjamin J. Noonan, *Non-Semitic Loanwords in the Hebrew Bible: A Lexicon of Language Contact* (LSAWS 14; Winona Lake, IN: Eisenbrauns, 2019), 17, 109. The presence of an alternative word for 'seal' in the East Semitic languages, *kunukku*, suggests that *ḥtm* was borrowed into Proto-West Semitic rather than Proto-Semitic, while the vocalic pattern of **ḫātam* distinguishes it as an Egyptian loanword into Proto-West Semitic rather than an indigenous Semitic coinage. As Joshua Fox notes, the *qātal* pattern is not reconstructible for Proto-Semitic or Proto-West Semitic (*Semitic Noun Patterns* [HSS 52; Winona Lake, IN: Eisenbrauns, 2003], 287).

13 Huehnergard and Pat-El, "Introduction to the Semitic Languages," 1.

14 Edwin C. M. van den Brink, "The 'En Besor Cylinder Seal Impressions in Retrospect," in *Excavations at 'En Besor*, ed. Ram Gophna (Tel Aviv: Ramot, 1995), 201; Baruch Brandl, "Evidence for Egyptian Colonization in the Southern Coastal Plain and Lowlands of Canaan During the EB I Period," in *The Nile Delta in Transition 4ᵗʰ – 3ʳᵈ Millennium B.C.: Proceedings of the Seminar Held in Cairo, 21. – 24. October 1990, at the Netherlands Institute of Archaeology and Arabic Studies*, ed. Edwin C. M. van den Brink (Tel Aviv: Edwin C. M. van den Brink, 1992), 446, 451, 456; Thomas E. Levy, et al., "Egyptian-Canaanite Interaction at Nahal Tillah, Israel (ca. 4500–3000 B. C. E.): An Interim Report on the 1994–1995 Excavations," *BASOR* 307 (1997): 8; Jane A. Hill, *Cylinder Seal Glyptic in Predynastic Egypt and Neighboring Regions* (BAR International Series 1223; Oxford: Archaeopress, 2004), 7.

preserve traces of hieroglyphic writing—a sure sign of their Egyptian origin.[15] Some of these bullae even feature the title *wr ḫ3st* 'chief of a foreign land'. They thus reflect the integration of the local populace into the Egyptian trade network centered at Tell es-Sakan. According to Peter Kaplony, these local chiefs

> sealed their names on the bags and sacks containing their tribute and brought it to collecting points like En Besor and Naḥal Tillah, where the bags were opened by Egyptian officials who checked their contents, threw the sealings of the foreign chiefs away, and sealed the bags and sacks with their proper Egyptian cylinders (or even repacked their contents) before sending them to Egypt.[16]

The presence of these bullae in EB I strata allows us to establish a rough date for the adoption of **ḫātam* into Proto-West Semitic and for the existence of Proto-West Semitic itself.[17]

After *ḥôtām*, *zeret* 'span' represents the second oldest Egyptian term inherited by Hebrew. This term ultimately comes from Egyptian *ḏr.t* 'hand', which survives into Coptic as *tōre* in the absolute form and *toot⸗* before possessive suffixes. The correspondence between Hebrew *z* and Egyptian *ḏ* suggests that *zeret* was borrowed into one of Hebrew's linguistic ancestors sometime before the end of

---

15 Thomas E. Levy et al., "The Protodynastic/Dynasty 1 Egyptian Presence in Southern Canaan: A Preliminary Report on the 1994 Excavations at Naḥal Tillah, Israel," in *Studies in the Archaeology of Israel and Neighboring Lands in Memory of Douglas L. Esse*, ed. Samuel R. Wolff (SAOC 59; Chicago: The Oriental Institute of the University of Chicago, 2001), 438; Peter Kaplony, "The 'En Besor Seal Impressions—Revised," in *Egypt and the Levant: Interrelations from the 4th through Early 3rd Millennium B.C.E.*, eds. Edwin C. M. van den Brink and Thomas E. Levy (London: Leicester University Press, 2002), 487–98; Hill, *Cylinder Seal Glyptic*, 79.
16 Kaplony, "The 'En Besor Seal Impressions," 494.
17 A late fourth millennium date for Proto-West Semitic is consistent with the earliest evidence for the existence of East Semitic, which appears in Sumerian texts from the first half of the third millennium. If Proto-Semitic split into Proto-West Semitic and Proto-East Semitic sometime in the late fourth millennium, then we would expect individual East Semitic languages to emerge in the early third millennium BCE. Walter Sommerfeld, "Prä-Akkadisch: Die Vorläufer der 'Sprache von Akkade' in der frühdynastischen Zeit," in *Language in the Ancient Near East: Proceedings of the 53e Rencontre Assyriologique Internationale*, vol. 1, ed. L. Kogan et al. (Winona Lake, IN: Eisenbrauns, 2010), 77–163; Huehnergard and Pat-El 2019, "Introduction to the Semitic Languages," 1.

the Old Kingdom in 2160 BCE. Phonologically, d represents the palatalized unaspirated voiceless dental stop /tʲ/.[18] This phoneme does not have an exact equivalent in the Semitic languages, but it resembles the Semitic affricate /ᵈz/—one of the two Proto-Semitic phonemes represented by Hebrew z[19]—in terms of its complex articulation and lack of aspiration. As James Hoch notes, Egyptian d frequently renders /ᵈz/ in Semitic loans into Egyptian from the New Kingdom (e.g., ᵈzêt 'olive' > djₛ=tu).[20] d, however, was phonologically unstable. Toward the end of the Old Kingdom, it underwent fronting in certain phonetic environments and merged with its non-palatalized counterpart d (= /t/).[21] But this phoneme is consistently rendered with t in Egyptian loanwords in Hebrew (e.g., bndw > ʾabnēṭ 'sash', dnj.t > ṭeneʾ 'basket').[22] The use of z to represent d in zeret indicates that d had not yet merged with d at the time of borrowing and that dr.t entered one of Hebrew's linguistic ancestors prior to 2160 BCE. This conclusion receives support from inner-Semitic evidence. Cognates of zeret occur in Imperial Aramaic (zrt 'span'), Targumic Aramaic (zartā 'span, hand'), Syriac (zartā 'span'), Christian Palestinian Aramaic (zrt 'span'), Jewish Palestinian Aramaic (zrt 'span'), Jewish Babylonian Aramaic (zartā 'span'), Samaritan Aramaic (zrt 'span'), and Mandaic (zirta 'span'); and if these forms are not loanwords from Hebrew, then there is a

---

18 Carsten Peust, *Egyptian Phonology: An Introduction to the Phonology of a Dead Language* (MzÄS 2; Göttingen: Peust & Gutschmidt, 1999), 119; James P. Allen, *The Ancient Egyptian Language: An Historical Study* (Cambridge: Cambridge University Press, 2013), 48; idem, *Ancient Egyptian Phonology* (Cambridge: Cambridge University Press, 2020), 75.

19 Huehnergard, "Proto-Semitic," in *The Semitic Languages*, 2nd ed., eds. John Huehnergard and Na'ama Pat-El (London: Routledge, 2019), 51.

20 James E. Hoch, *Semitic Words in Egyptian Texts of the New Kingdom and Third Intermediate Period* (Princeton: Princeton University Press, 2004), 395, 408.

21 Antonio Loprieno, *Ancient Egyptian: A Linguistic Introduction* (Cambridge: Cambridge University Press, 1995), 38; Peust, *Egyptian Phonology*, 124; Allen, *The Ancient Egyptian Language*, 49; idem, *Ancient Egyptian Phonology*, 75. The exact conditioning factors behind this shift are unclear (see Marwan Kilani, "Phonological Change and Interdialectal Differences between Egyptian and Coptic: ḏ, ṯ → c=ϫ, ḏ, ṯ → t=ⲧ," *Diachronica* [2021]: 1–27, for a recent discussion and proposal). As Coptic evidence demonstrates, however, dr.t did eventually undergo this sound change.

22 Egyptian d and Hebrew $ṭ$ were not exact equivalents, however: Egyptian d represented the unaspirated dental stop /t/, while $ṭ$ originally represented the ejective dental stop /tʼ/. Huehnergard, "Proto-Semitic," 50–51; Allen, *The Ancient Egyptian Language*, 49; idem, *Ancient Egyptian Phonology*, 75.

good chance that *ḏr.t* was loaned into Proto-Aramaeo-Canaanite or one of its ancestors.[23]

ṭabbaʕat 'signet ring' ultimately comes from Egyptian *ḏbʕ.t*, which entered the Semitic languages sometime after the borrowing of *ḏr.t* into Proto-Aramaeo-Cannanite. The rendering of Egyptian *ḏ* with *ṭêt* reflects the depalatalization of *ḏ* in Egyptian, which took place around 2160 BCE as noted above. At the same time, the final *-t* indicates that *ḏbʕ.t* was borrowed prior to the loss of the final feminine */-(a)tʰ/ in Egyptian sometime before 1360 BCE.[24] Taken together, these two criteria indicate that *ḏbʕ.t* entered Hebrew or one of its linguistic ancestors sometime between 2160 and 1360 BCE. The presence of similar-looking forms in other Semitic languages such as Phoenician (*ṭbʕt* 'seal'), Syriac (*ṭabʕā* 'seal'), and Classical Arabic (*ṭābiʕ*, *ṭābaʕ* 'signet, seal') suggests that *ḏbʕ.t* was borrowed into one of Hebrew's linguistic ancestors rather than Hebrew itself.[25] The Syriac and Classical Arabic forms, however, do not feature a final *-t* and as such, may represent later, independent borrowings after the final loss of the feminine */-(a)tʰ/ in Egyptian.[26] If this is the case, then *ḏbʕ.t* was most likely borrowed into Proto-Canaanite and inherited by Hebrew and Phoenician.

The metrological terms *qab* and *hîn* prove harder to date precisely since their Egyptian antecedents occur for large swathes of Egyptian history and do not participate in any datable Egyptian sound changes. *hnw* first appears in the Old Kingdom (2686–2160 BCE), while *qbj* makes its debut in the Middle Kingdom (2055–1650 BCE). Inner-Semitic evidence, however, suggests that these terms

---

23 DNWSI, 1.342; Jastrow, *Dictionary of the Targumim*, 415; Payne Smith, *Thesaurus Syriacus*, 1.1162–63; Sokoloff, *A Dictionary of Christian Palestinian Aramaic*, 115; idem, *A Dictionary of Jewish Babylonian Aramaic*, 422; idem, *A Dictionary of Jewish Palestinian Aramaic*, 184; Drower and Macuch, *A Mandaic Dictionary*, 168; Tal, *A Dictionary of Samaritan Aramaic*, 1.241.
24 The Egyptian feminine morpheme */-(a)tʰ/ was notoriously unstable. It began to disappear in word-final position (i.e., when not followed by a possessive suffix) already in the Sixth Dynasty (2345–2181 BCE) and vanished entirely sometime before 1360 BCE, as indicated by the Akkadian transcriptions of Egyptian words found in the Amarna letters. Loprieno, *Ancient Egyptian*, 60; Peust, *Egyptian Phonology*, 152; Allen, *The Ancient Egyptian Language*, 49, 61; idem, *Ancient Egyptian Phonology*, 92.
25 Siegmund Fraenkel, A. Jeffery, and Benjamin J. Noonan suggest that *ṭābaʕ* is an Aramaic loanword into Classical Arabic since the *qātal* pattern is otherwise unattested in Arabic (*Die aramäischen Fremdwörter im Arabischen* [Leiden: Brill, 1886], 192–94; *The Foreign Vocabulary of the Qurʾân* [Gaekwad's Oriental Series 79; Leiden: Brill, 1938], 204–5; *Non-Semitic Loanwords*, 109). Such a derivational pathway seems unlikely, however, because the Aramaic forms of this word do not conform to the *qātal* pattern (e.g., Syriac *ṭabʕā*). Instead, I would argue that the strange vocalization of *ṭābaʕ* reflects its Egyptian origin.
26 Noonan, *Non-Semitic Loanwords*, 110.

were borrowed into one of Hebrew's linguistic ancestors rather than Hebrew itself. Cognates of *hîn* appear in Imperial Aramaic (*hn*), Targumic Aramaic (*hîn*), Jewish Palestinian Aramaic (*hyn*), and Samaritan Aramaic (*hn*), while cognates of *qab* occur in Classical Arabic (*qibb*) as well as Imperial Aramaic (*qb*), Targumic Aramaic (*qabbā*), Syriac (*qabbā*), Jewish Palestinian Aramaic (*qb*), Jewish Babylonian Aramaic (*qabbā*), Samaritan Aramaic (*qb*), Judean Aramaic (*qb*), and Mandaic (*qaba*).[27] The distribution of these terms suggests that *hnw* was borrowed into Proto-Aramaeo-Canaanite and *qbj* was borrowed into Proto-Central Semitic, where its Arabic reflex underwent an *ad hoc* shift of *qabb* > *qibb*.[28] This sound change provides strong evidence that *qbj* was borrowed into Proto-Central Semitic since *qatl-qitl* variation only affects inherited words (e.g., Hebrew *melek* 'king' < **malk* vs. Phoenician *milk*).[29]

ʾêpâ is also difficult to date precisely. Its Egyptian antecedent first occurs in the Middle Kingdom (2055–1650 BCE) and thus cannot have entered one of Hebrew's linguistic ancestors prior to this point. At the same time, the presence of the feminine ending -*â* in the Hebrew form suggests that its Egyptian antecedent retained the feminine */-(*a*)*tʰ*/ since *â* in Hebrew normally comes from -*at*: Egyptian *áypatʰ > Pre-Hebrew *ʾaypat > Hebrew *ʾêpâ*.[30] Thus, *ʾêpâ* most likely entered one of Hebrew's linguistic ancestors before 1360 BCE.

---

27 Lane 7.2478; *DNWSI* 1.285, 977; Jastrow, *Dictionary of the Targumim*, 348, 1307; Payne Smith, *Thesaurus Syriacus*, 2.3465; Sokoloff, *A Dictionary of Jewish Babylonian Aramaic*, 977; idem, *A Dictionary of Jewish Palestinian Aramaic*, 160, 538; idem, *A Dictionary of Judean Aramaic*, 76; Drower and Macuch, *A Mandaic Dictionary*, 398; Tal, *A Dictionary of Samaritan Aramaic*, 205, 747. A cognate of *hîn* also appears in one of the Amarna letters (EA 14 iii:62). But as Noonan rightly notes, this form occurs in a letter sent from Egypt to Babylon and may not, therefore, reflect the adoption of this term into Amarna Canaanite (*Non-Semitic Loanwords*, 306n19).

28 As in the case of *ḥōtām*, it is more parsimonious to posit a single borrowing from Egyptian into a Semitic proto-language than multiple instances of borrowing into individual Semitic languages.

29 Huehnergard, "Biblical Hebrew Nominal Patterns," 39; Wilfred H. van Soldt, "The Vocalization of the Word *mlk* 'King' in Late Bronze Age Syllabic Texts from Syria and Palestine," in *Hamlet on a Hill: Semitic and Greek Studies Presented to Prof. T. Muraoka on the Occasion of His Sixty-Fifth Birthday*, eds. M. F. J. Baasten and W. Th. van Peursen (OLA 118; Leuven: Peeters, 2003), 470–71.

30 Noonan, by contrast, argues that *ʾêpâ* entered the Hebrew lexicon sometime between 1300 and 700 BCE since it reflects an intermediate stage in the development of the Egyptian feminine morpheme ("Egyptian Loanwords as Evidence for the Authenticity of the Exodus Tradition," in *"Did I Not Bring Israel Out of Egypt?": Biblical, Archaeological, and Egyptological Perspectives on the Exodus Narratives*, eds. James K. Hofffmeier, Alan R. Millard, and Gary A. Rendsburg [Winona Lake, IN: Eisenbrauns, 2016], 62–63; *Non-Semitic Loanwords*, 304). He argues on the basis of cuneiform transcriptions and later Egyptian loanwords into Aramaic that the Egyptian feminine

3 Direct Egyptian Loanwords into Hebrew Dealing with Scribal Practice

dəyô 'ink' (< Egyptian *rj.t*)[31] is the first Egyptian word related to scribal practice to be borrowed directly into Hebrew.[32] Epigraphic evidence suggests that this word entered the Hebrew lexicon sometime in or after the twelfth century BCE. Because Hebrew speakers most likely borrowed the Egyptian word for 'ink' along with the practice of writing in ink, we can use the first post-14th century BCE appearance of Semitic writing in ink from the Levant to approximate the date of borrowing.[33] The earliest securely datable such text is the Lachish bowl fragment, which hails

---

morpheme shifted from */-(a)t^h/ > -a > -i. According to his analysis, the final *â* of *ʾêpâ* reflects the intermediate stage between -at and -i, and so the borrowing of *ʾêpâ* must postdate the final loss of the feminine -t in Egyptian around 1360 BCE. Noonan's argument suffers from two problems, however. First, the final *a* of the feminine morpheme is only retained in Egyptian when it bears the stress (e.g., **bvyât^h* 'honey' > Sahidic, Bohairic, Fayyumic *ebyō*; Akhmimic *ebyū*), and Coptic evidence shows that the feminine morpheme was unstressed in *jp.t* (**áypat^h* > Sahidic *oipe*, Akhmimic *aeipe*, Bohairic *ōipi*, Fayyumic *aipi*). Second, Egyptian loanwords into Hebrew do not preserve their short final vowels: e.g., Egyptian *gástv > Hebrew *qeset* 'scribal palette'.

31 The correspondence between Egyptian *r* and Hebrew *d* reflects the pronunciation of Egyptian *r* as a flap /ɾ/. Hoch, *Semitic Words in Egyptian Texts*, 406–7, 430; Loprieno, *Ancient Egyptian*, 33; Peust, *Egyptian Phonology*, 127–29; Allen, *The Ancient Egyptian Language*, 40; idem, *Ancient Egyptian Phonology*, 53.

32 Although similar forms appear in Targumic Aramaic (*dyûtā*), Jewish Babylonian Aramaic (*dyôtā*), Syriac (*dyûtā*), and Mandaic (*diuta*), these words exhibit morphological and phonological differences from Hebrew *dəyô*. These discrepancies have led Noonan (*Non-Semitic Loanwords*, 87) to suggest that the Hebrew and Aramaic forms represent separate borrowings from Egyptian, with the Aramaic from presumably predating the loss of the Egyptian feminine ending. Jastrow, *Dictionary of the Targumim*, 298; Payne Smith, *Thesaurus Syriacus*, 1.880; Sokoloff, *A Dictionary of Jewish Babylonian Aramaic*, 328; Drower and Macuch, *A Mandaic Dictionary*, 107.

33 Of course, Hebrew speakers could have coined or borrowed another word for 'ink' when they first acquired the technology of writing with ink, and only later borrowed an Egyptian word for 'ink' due to the prestige of Egyptian scribal culture. There is, however, no internal Hebrew or comparative Semitic evidence that *dəyô* displaced another word for 'ink'. Hebrew does not preserve any other words for 'ink', and there is no word for 'ink' that is reconstructible to any of Hebrew's linguistic ancestors. Indeed, many of the Semitic words for 'ink' seem to be loanwords from non-Semitic languages (e.g., Syriac *srīqōn* < Greek σηρικόν 'red ink'; Payne Smith, *Thesaurus Syriacus*, 2.2740).

from the beginning of Lachish Stratum VI (1200–1130 BCE) and originally appeared on the exterior of an intact bowl.[34] The presence of this inscription in Lachish Stratum VI suggests that *rj.t* may have been borrowed into Hebrew in the twelfth century BCE. And while it is impossible to be sure, Lachish itself represents the most plausible site for the location of this borrowing. To date, excavators have uncovered fragments of ten hieratic inscriptions from Lachish, which span the Late Bronze Age.[35] These inscriptions appear on the exterior of votive bowls and record the delivery of harvest taxes to the Egyptian temple at Lachish. One of these fragments even contains the word 'scribe' (*zẖȝw*) followed by the beginning of a word or personal name written in syllabic orthography, the standard Egyptian method for representing non-Egyptian words. If this inscription contains a personal name, then it attests to the use of hieratic among local scribes at Lachish, who could have adopted ink as a medium for writing the Semitic alphabet.[36] Whatever the case, it is striking that the Lachish bowl fragment employs the same medium and writing surface as the hieratic inscriptions from Lachish. Perhaps the writer of the Lachish bowl fragment consciously imitated Egyptian models while producing this epigraph.[37]

---

34 Israel Finkelstein and Benjamin Sass, "The West Semitic Alphabetic Inscriptions, Late Bronze II to Iron IIA: Archaeological Context, Distribution and Chronology," *HBAI* 2 (2013): 153. The recently discovered Lachish ostracon from Lachish stratum S3-b (mid-15th century BCE) represents an even early example of Semitic writing in ink from the Levant, but it most likely predates the emergence of Hebrew as a distinct linguistic entity (Felix Höflmayer, et al., "Early Alphabetic Writing in the Ancient Near East: The 'Missing Link' from Tel Lachish," *Antiquity* 95 [2021]: 9).

35 Deborah Sweeney, "The Hieratic Inscriptions," in *The Renewed Archaeological Excavations at Lachish (1973–1994)*, vol. 3, ed. David Ussishkin (Tel Aviv: Emery and Claire Yass Publications in Archaeology, 2004), 1601. Archaeologists have also recovered similar hieratic inscriptions from Tell Sera', Tell Haror, Tell el-Far'ah South, Deir el-Balah, Qubur el-Walayda, and Tell es-Safi, but these sites have yet to yield any Semitic inscriptions written in ink (Stefan Wimmer, "Lachish is Lachish on the Lachish Bowl: An Object Lesson for Reading Hieratic, with Little Surprising Results," in *The Late Bronze and Early Iron Ages in Canaan*, eds. Aren M. Maier, Itzhaq Shai, and Chris McKinny [Berlin: De Gruyter, 2019], 144–45).

36 Orly Goldwasser, "An Egyptian Scribe from Lachish and the Hieratic Tradition of the Hebrew Kingdoms," *TA* 18 (1991): 248–49; Sweeney, "The Hieratic Inscriptions," 1610. Two of the hieratic sherds from Tell el-Far'ah South also mention scribes, as does the recently discovered Lachish Jar sherd (Orly Goldwasser and Stefan Wimmer, "Hieratic Fragments from Tell el-Far'ah (South)," *BASOR* 313 [1999]: 40; Benjamin Sass, et al., "The Lachish Jar Sherd: An Early Alphabetic Inscription Discovered in 2014," *BASOR* 374 [2015]: 236).

37 Orly Goldwasser, "From the Iconic to the Linear—The Egyptian Scribes of Lachish and the Modification of the Early Alphabet in the Late Bronze Age," in *Alphabets, Texts, and Artifacts in the Ancient Near East: Studies Presented to Benjamin* Sass, ed. Israel Finkelstein, Christian Robin, and Thomas Römer (Paris: Van Dieren, 2016), 156.

Hebrew *gōmeʾ* comes from Egyptian *qmꜣ*, which survives into Coptic as *kam* in the Sahidic and Bohairic dialects and *kēm* in Sahidic.[38] Because *qmꜣ* is first attested in Egyptian during the Nineteenth Dynasty (1295–1186 BCE), it most likely did not enter Hebrew prior to the thirteenth century BCE. The vocalization of the Hebrew form, on the other hand, suggests that *gōmeʾ* was borrowed before the eighth century BCE. *gōmeʾ* comes from earlier **gumʾ*, which matches the earliest vocalization of *qmꜣ* as **qúmʾv* as reconstructed from Coptic. But the Coptic reflexes of *qmꜣ* also show that *qmꜣ* was subject to the Egyptian shifts of *ú > a* in closed syllables and *ú > ē* in open syllables, which are first attested in Neo-Assyrian transcriptions of Egyptian from the eighth century BCE. Thus, *gōmeʾ* must have entered Hebrew before the operation of these sound changes.[39] Taken together, these two factors suggest that *gōmeʾ* entered the Hebrew lexicon between the thirteenth and eighth centuries BCE.

Material evidence helps narrow this date range by a century. Although papyrus rarely survives in the humid environment of the Israelite highlands, papyrus impressions on several ninth century BCE bullae from Jerusalem suggest that Israelite scribes had adopted papyrus as a writing medium by this time.[40] And if Israelite scribes borrowed the word *gōmeʾ* at the same time they began writing on papyrus, then the borrowing of *gōmeʾ* must predate the ninth century BCE.[41] Thus, *gōmeʾ* most likely entered the Hebrew lexicon sometime between the thirteenth and the ninth centuries BCE. This period overlaps with two of the four phases of Egyptian-Levantine contact that Shirly Ben-Dor Evian has identified in the material record: the end of the New Kingdom and the "Sheshonq Horizon," the period from the mid-tenth to the mid-ninth centuries BCE when imported and locally manufactured Egyptian objects appear in the Shephelah, the Beer Sheba

---

38 Similar forms appear in Imperial Aramaic (*gmʾ* 'reed'), Jewish Palestinian Aramaic (*gmy* 'papyrus'), Jewish Babylonian Aramaic (*gmy* 'plant fiber'), and Samaritan Aramaic (*gmʾ* 'reed'), which most likely represent independent borrowings from Egyptian or Hebrew rather than survivals from Aramaeo-Canaanite, since the Egyptian antecedent of these forms is not attested until the eleventh century BCE. DNWSI, 1.225; Sokoloff, *A Dictionary of Jewish Babylonian Aramaic*, 289; idem, *A Dictionary of Jewish Palestinian Aramaic*, 121; Tal, *A Dictionary of Samaritan Aramaic*, 149.

39 Peust, *Egyptian Phonology*, 222–23; Allen, *The Ancient Egyptian Language*, 25; idem, *Ancient Egyptian Phonology*, 73–4.

40 Ronny Reich, Eli Shukron, and Omri Lernau, "Recent Discoveries in the City of David, Jerusalem," *IEJ* 57 (2007): 156.

41 As in the case of *dǝyô*, Israelite scribes could have borrowed or coined a different word for 'papyrus' and only later borrowed the word *gōmeʾ*. But there is no evidence that *gōmeʾ* replaced an earlier word for 'manufacturable papyrus'.

valley, and the western Negev. [42] Both periods represent a plausible time for the adoption of scribal technology.

qeset 'scribal palette' comes from Egyptian *gstj* and is one of the last Egyptian loanwords to be borrowed into Hebrew. This word reflects a pair of Hebrew sound changes that help date its entry into the Hebrew lexicon more precisely: the palatalization of original **s* and the subsequent deaffrication of **'s*. Analysis of Egyptian loanwords into Hebrew proves crucial for understanding and dating these sound changes. In most Egyptian loanwords into Hebrew, Hebrew *šîn* represents Egyptian *s* (e.g., *ḥašman* 'libation vessel' < *ḥsmn*) and *sāmek* represents Egyptian *ṯ* (*sûp* 'reed' < *ṯwf*), reflecting the fact that Hebrew *šîn* was originally an alveolar fricative *s* and *sāmek* was originally an alveolar sibilant affricate *'s*.[43] At some point, however, *s* underwent palatalization to *š* and then *'s* deaffricated to *s*, which made *sāmek* a better proxy for Egyptian *s*.

The use of *sāmek* to represent Egyptian *s* in *sô?*—an abbreviation of Osorkon IV's personal name *wꜣ-sꜣ-r-kn* that appears in 2 Kings 17:4—indicates that these sound changes took place prior to Osorkon IV's ascension to the Lower Egyptian throne in 730 BCE.[44] Interestingly, Osorkon IV's ascension coincides almost exactly with the date of Zincirli 66, the only piece of material evidence for the use of Egyptian-style scribal palettes among Levantine scribes during the Iron Age. This relief dates to 730 BCE and depicts a scribe doing obeisance before the Samalian king, Barrakib (732–713 BCE) (Fig. 1). In his left hand, the scribe holds an Egyptian-style scribal palette, complete with a compartment for holding reed pens and a square depression for ink.[45] This palette closely resembles a Twenty-First Dynasty scribal palette on display in the Metropolitan Museum (Fig. 2). When combined with the data from 1 Kings 17:4, this material evidence suggests that *qeset* entered the Hebrew lexicon sometime after the mid-eighth century BCE. Plausible contexts for the borrowing of this word include the late-eighth

---

42 Shirly Ben-Dor Evian, "The Past and Future of 'Biblical Egyptology'," *JAEI* 18 (2018): 4.

43 Huehnergard, "Proto-Semitic," 50–51. The Egyptian phoneme *ṯ*—the voiceless aspirated palatalized stop *tʰ*—did not have an exact equivalent in Hebrew, but it resembled *'s* in terms of its complex articulation and perhaps aspiration. Allen, *The Ancient Egyptian Language*, 49; idem, *Ancient Egyptian Phonology*, 75.

44 Seung Il Kang, "A Philological Approach to the Problem of King So (2 Kgs 17:4)," *VT* 60 (2010): 241–48; Heath D. Dewrell, "Yareb, Shalman, and the Date of the Book of Hosea," *CBQ* 78 (2016): 417n14.

45 June Ashton, *Scribal Habits in the Ancient Near East: c. 3000 BCE to the Emergence of the Codex* (MSJ 13; Sydney: Mandelbaum, 2008), 55; Alessandra Gilibert, *Syro-Hittite Monumental Art and the Archaeology of Performance: The Stone Reliefs of Carchemish and Zinçirli in the Earlier First Millennium BCE* (TBSAW 2; New York: De Gruyter, 2011), 85–86.

century BCE, when the Judahite court maintained diplomatic contacts with the Nubian pharaohs of the Twenty-Fifth Dynasty, or the Saite period, when some Israelite scribes received training in Egyptian scribal techniques.[46]

At first glance, it may seem strange that *dǝyô* 'ink', *gōme²* 'papyrus', and *qeset* 'scribal palette' entered the Hebrew lexicon at different times. Because these three items formed a set within Egyptian scribal practice—Egyptian scribes wrote with ink on papyrus and stored their tools in a specially designed palette—we might expect these objects and the words designating them to have been borrowed at the same time. To explain this discrepancy, I suggest that the different dates of borrowing might reflect differences in the availability of these scribal tools. While Israelite scribes could easily produce ink using locally available materials (i.e., water, lamp black, and gum arabic) once they had learned the recipe, they most likely had to import papyrus from Egypt since there is no evidence for the production of papyrus outside of the Nile valley.[47] The use of papyrus as a writing medium thus depended on the strength of the Levant's economic and diplomatic ties with Egypt. When such ties were weak, as in the early Iron Age, Israelite scribes presumably used other writing surfaces, such as ostraca. Thus, even if Israelite scribes did use papyrus during the Late Bronze Age at sites like Lachish, the withdrawal of Egyptian hegemony in the mid-eleventh century BCE may have forced them to abandon this practice as well as any Egyptian word for 'papyrus' they may have borrowed. Only when Sheshonq reestablished contact between Egypt and the Levant in the mid-tenth century BCE could Israelite scribes (re)acquire the use of papyrus as a writing medium.[48] Availability also helps explain the relatively late adoption of Egyptian-style palettes into the Israelite scribal repertoire. Such items, after all, were not a necessary component of scribal practice. Presumably, Israelite scribes did not adopt Egyptian-style scribal palettes until sometime after the mid-eighth century BCE because they had other means of storing their writing implements (e.g., in jars or pots). The prestige of Egyptian scribal practice, rather than the functionality of Egyptian-style palettes, was most likely the primary motivation for this change.

---

46 Evian, "The Past and Future," 4–5; Bernd Schipper, "Egypt and the Kingdom of Judah under Josiah and Jehoiakim," *TA* 37 (2010): 211; Stefan Wimmer, *Palästinisches Hieratisch: Die Zahl- und Sonderzeichen in der althebräischen Schrift* (ÄAT 75; Wiesebaden: Harrassowitz, 2008), 279.
47 Ashton, *Scribal Habits in the Ancient Near East*, 51; Zhakevich, *Scribal Tools in Ancient Israel*, 10; Naphtali Lewis, *Papyrus in Classical Antiquity* (Oxford: Clarendon, 1974), 4, 116.
48 Evian, "The Past and Future," 4.

Figure 1: Zinçirli 66[49]

49 "Orthostat relief showing prince Barrakib and a writer; Zincirli, c. 730 BC"; photograph by Interfase (Pergamon Museum, Berlin, 2013; online: http://commons.wiki-media.org/wiki/File:Orthostat_relief_of_King_Barrakib_from_Zincirli.jpg).

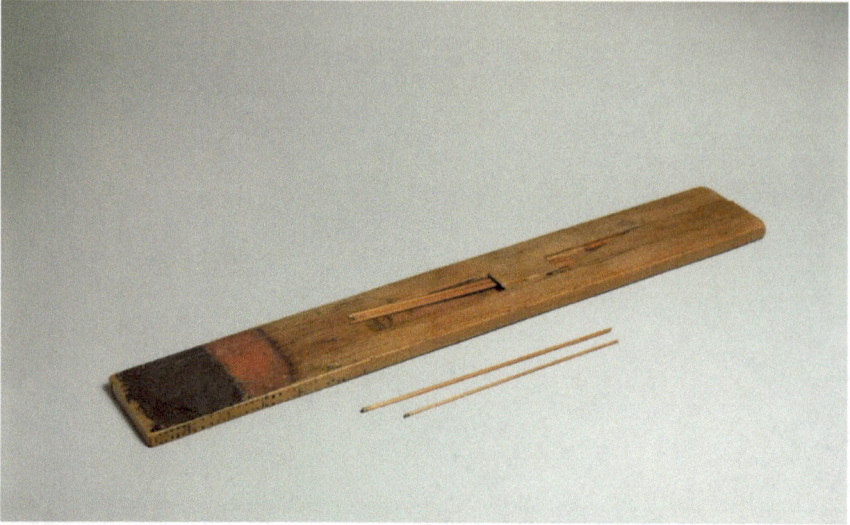

Figure 2: A Twenty-First Dynasty Egyptian scribal palette from the Metropolitan Museum[50]

4 Conclusion

By combining linguistic and material evidence, we can establish a timeline of borrowing for the Egyptian scribal terms found in Hebrew (Table 1). According to my analysis, Egyptian scribal terminology did not enter the Hebrew language in a single period of cultural contact as often suggested. In fact, most of the Egyptian scribal terminology found in the Hebrew lexicon was most likely borrowed into one of Hebrew's ancestors and merely inherited by Hebrew. The three words most directly connected with scribal practice, however—*dəyô* 'ink', *gōmeʾ* 'manufacturable papyrus', and *qeset* 'scribal palette'—were borrowed into Hebrew itself. This smaller set of scribal terms hints at direct Egyptian influence on Israelite scribal practice over a span of several centuries. *dəyô* may reflect the adoption of ink as a medium for writing around the twelfth century BCE, while *gōmeʾ* and *qeset* refer to new materials and tools for writing and likely entered the Hebrew lexicon between the eleventh and eighth centuries BCE. When considered from

---

50 "Palette inscribed for Smendes, High Priest of Amun, ca. 1045–992 B.C." (Harris Brisbane Dick Fund, 1947; online: http://www.metmuseum.org/art/collection/search/545113).

the point of view of lexicography, Egyptian influence on West Semitic and Israelite administrative and scribal practice was sporadic.

Table 1: Chronology of the Egyptian Words in Hebrew Related to Scribal Practice

Inherited Egyptian Loanwords in Hebrew

Word	Approximate Date of Borrowing
ḥôtām 'seal'	3100–3000 BCE
zeret 'hand(span)'	Before 2160 BCE
qab 'a dry measure'	Before 1550 BCE
hîn 'vessel, liquid measure'	Before 1550 BCE
ʔêpâ 'measure for corn and fruit'	Before 1360 BCE
ṭabbaʕat 'signet ring'	2160–1360 BCE

Direct Egyptian Loanwords into Hebrew

Word	Approximate Date of Borrowing
dəyô 'ink'	1200 BCE
gōmeʔ 'manufacturable papyrus'	1295–800 BCE
qeset 'scribal palette'	After 750 BCE

5 Bibliography

Allen, James P. *The Ancient Egyptian Language: An Historical Study.* Cambridge: Cambridge University Press, 2013.

Allen, James P. *Ancient Egyptian Phonology.* Cambridge: Cambridge University Press, 2020.

Ashton, June. *Scribal Habits in the Ancient Near East: c. 3000 BCE to the Emergence of the Codex.* MSJ 13. Sydney: Mandelbaum, 2008.

Brandl, Baruch. "Evidence for Egyptian Colonization in the Southern Coastal Plain and Lowlands of Canaan During the EB I Period." In *The Nile Delta in Transition 4th – 3rd Millennium B.C.: Proceedings of the Seminar Held in Cairo, 21. – 24. October 1990, at the Netherlands Institute of Archaeology and Arabic Studies,* edited by Edwin C. M. van den Brink, 441–77. Tel Aviv: Edwin C. M. van den Brink, 1992.

Breyer, Francis. *Ägyptische Namen und Wörter im Alten Testament.* ÄAT 93. Münster: Zaphon, 2019.

Cook, Edward M. *Dictionary of Qumran Aramaic.* Winona Lake, IN: Eisenbrauns, 2015.

Dewrell, Heath D. "Yareb, Shalman, and the Date of the Book of Hosea." *CBQ* 78 (2016): 413–29.

Drower, E., and R. Macuch. *A Mandaic Dictionary.* Oxford: Clarendon, 1963.

Evian, Shirly Ben-Dor. "The Past and Future of 'Biblical Egyptology'." *JAEI* 18 (2018): 1–11.

Finkelstein, Israel, and Benjamin Sass. "The West Semitic Alphabetic Inscriptions, Late Bronze II to Iron IIA: Archaeological Context, Distribution and Chronology." *HBAI* 2 (2013): 149–220.

Fox, Joshua. *Semitic Noun Patterns.* HSS 52. Winona Lake, IN: Eisenbrauns, 2003.

Fox, Nili Sacher. *In the Service of the King: Officialdom in Ancient Israel and Judah*. MHUC 23. Cincinnati: Hebrew Union College Press, 2000.

Fränkel, Siegmund. *Die aramäischen Fremdwörter im Arabischen*. Leiden: Brill, 1886.

Freytag, Georg Wilhelm. *Lexicon Arabico-Latinum*. 4 vols. Halle: Schwetschke, 1830–1837.

Gilibert, Alessandra. *Syro-Hittite Monumental Art and the Archaeology of Performance: The Stone Reliefs of Carchemish and Zincirli in the Earlier First Millennium BCE*. TBSAW 2. New York: De Gruyter, 2011.

Goldwasser, Orly. "An Egyptian Scribe from Lachish and the Hieratic Tradition of the Hebrew Kingdoms." *TA* 18 (1991): 248–53.

Goldwasser, Orly. "From the Iconic to the Linear—The Egyptian Scribes of Lachish and the Modification of the Early Alphabet in the Late Bronze Age." In *Alphabets, Texts, and Artifacts in the Ancient Near East: Studies Presented to Benjamin* Sass, edited by Israel Finkelstein, Christian Robin, and Thomas Römer, 118–60. Paris: Van Dieren, 2016.

Goldwasser, Orly, and Stefan Wimmer. "Hieratic Fragments from Tell el-Far'ah (South)." *BASOR* 313 (1999): 39–42.

Hallo, William W., and Hayim Tadmor. "A Lawsuit from Hazor." *IEJ* 27 (1977): 1–11.

Hill, Jane A. *Cylinder Seal Glyptic in Predynastic Egypt and Neighboring Regions*. BAR International Series 1223. Oxford: Archaeopress, 2004.

Hoch, James E. *Semitic Words in Egyptian Texts of the New Kingdom and Third Intermediate Period*. Princeton: Princeton University Press, 2004.

Höflmayer, Felix, et al. "Early Alphabetic Writing in the Ancient Near East: The 'Missing Link' from Tel Lachish." *Antiquity* 95 (2021): 705–719.

Hoftijzer, J., and K. Jongeling. *Dictionary of the Northwest Semitic Inscriptions*. 2 vols. HdO 21. Leiden: Brill, 1995.

Huehnergard, John. "Biblical Hebrew Nominal Patterns." In *Epigraphy, Philology, and the Hebrew Bible: Methodological Perspectives on Philological and Comparative Study of the Hebrew Bible in Honor of Jo Ann Hackett*, edited by Jeremy M. Hutton and Aaron D. Rubin, 25–64. SBLANEM 12. Atlanta: SBL, 2015.

Huehnergard, John. "Proto-Semitic." In *The Semitic Languages*, 2nd ed., edited by John Huehnergard and Na'ama Pat-El, 49–79. London: Routledge, 2019.

Huehnergard, John, and Na'ama Pat-El. "Introduction to the Semitic Languages and Their History." In *The Semitic Languages*, 2nd ed., edited by John Huehnergard and Na'ama Pat-El, 1–21. London: Routledge, 2019.

Jastrow, Marcus. *Dictionary of the Targumim, the Talmud Babli, and Yerushalmi, and the Midrashic Literature*. Peabody: Hendrickson, 2006.

Jeffery, A. *The Foreign Vocabulary of the Qur'ân*. Gaekwad's Oriental Series 79. Leiden: Brill, 1938.

Johnstone, T. M. *Ḥarsūsi Lexicon and English-Ḥarsūsi Word-List*. London: Oxford University Press, 1977.

Johnstone, T. M. *Jibbāli Lexicon*. Oxford: Oxford University Press, 1981.

Johnstone, T. M. *Mehri Lexicon and English-Mehri Word-List*. London: SOAS, University of London, 1987.

Kang, Seung Il. "A Philological Approach to the Problem of King So (2 Kgs 17:4)." *VT* 60 (2010): 241–48.

Kaplony, Peter. "The ʿEn Besor Seal Impressions—Revised." In *Egypt and the Levant: Interrelations from the 4th through Early 3rd Millennium B.C.E.*, edited by Edwin C. M. van den Brink and Thomas E. Levy, 487–98. London: Leicester University Press, 2002.

Kazimirski, Albert de Biberstein. *Dictionnaire arabe-français*. 2 vols. Paris: Maison-neuve, 1860.

Kilani, Marwan. "Phonological Change and Interdialectal Differences between Egyptian and Coptic: ḏ, ṯ → c=ϫ, ḏ, ṯ → t=ⲧ." *Diachronica* (2021): 1–27.

Lane, Edward William. *Maddu-l-Kamoos: An Arabic-English Dictionary*. 8 vols. London: Williams & Norgate, 1863–1893.

Lemaire, André. "An Alphabetic Canaanite Inscription." In *The Renewed Archaeological Excavations at Lachish (1973–1994)*, vol. 3, edited by David Ussishkin, 1597–1600. Tel Aviv: Emery and Claire Yass Publications in Archaeology, 2004.

Leslau, Wolf. *Comparative Dictionary of Geʿez (Classical Ethiopic): Geʿez-English / English-Geʿez with an Index of the Semitic Roots*. Wiesbaden: Harrassowitz, 1991.

Levy, Thomas E., et al. "Egyptian-Canaanite Interaction at Nahal Tillah, Israel (ca. 4500–3000 B. C. E.): An Interim Report on the 1994–1995 Excavations." *BASOR* 307 (1997): 1–51.

Levy, Thomas E., et al. "The Protodynastic/Dynasty 1 Egyptian Presence in Southern Canaan: A Preliminary Report on the 1994 Excavations at Naḥal Tillah, Israel." In *Studies in the Archaeology of Israel and Neighboring Lands in Memory of Douglas L. Esse*, edited by Samuel R. Wolff, 411–35. SAOC 59. Chicago: The Oriental Institute of the University of Chicago, 2001.

Lewis, Naphtali. *Papyrus in Classical Antiquity*. Oxford: Clarendon, 1974.

Loprieno, Antonio. *Ancient Egyptian: A Linguistic Introduction*. Cambridge: Cambridge University Press, 1995.

Noonan, Benjamin J. "Egyptian Loanwords as Evidence for the Authenticity of the Exodus Tradition." In *"Did I Not Bring Israel Out of Egypt?": Biblical, Archaeological, and Egyptological Perspectives on the Exodus Narratives*, edited by James K. Hofffmeier, Alan R. Millard, and Gary A. Rendsburg, 49–67. Winona Lake, IN: Eisenbrauns, 2016.

Noonan, Benjamin J. *Non-Semitic Loanwords in the Hebrew Bible: A Lexicon of Language Contact*. LSAWS 14. Winona Lake, IN: Eisenbrauns, 2019.

Payne Smith, Robert. *Thesaurus Syriacus*. 3 vols. GHD 7. Piscataway, NJ: Gorgias, 2007.

Peust, Carsten. *Egyptian Phonology: An Introduction to the Phonology of a Dead Language*. MzÄS 2. Göttingen: Peust & Gutschmidt, 1999.

Ranke, Hermann. *Keilschriftliches Material zur altägyptischen Vokalisation*. Berlin: Königl. Akademie der Wissenschaft, 1910.

Reich, Ronny, Eli Shukron, and Omri Lernau. "Recent Discoveries in the City of David, Jerusalem." *IEJ* 57 (2007): 153–69.

Sass, Benjamin, et al. "The Lachish Jar Sherd: An Early Alphabetic Inscription Discovered in 2014." *BASOR* 374 (2015): 233–45.

Schipper, Bernd. "Egypt and the Kingdom of Judah under Josiah and Jehoiakim." *TA* 37 (2010): 200–226.

Schniedewind, William M. *A Social History of Hebrew: Its Origins through the Rabbinic Period*. Anchor Yale Biblical Reference Library. New Haven: Yale University Press, 2013.

Schniedewind, William M. *The Finger of the Scribe: How Scribes Learned to Write the Bible*. Oxford: Oxford University Press, 2019.

Sokoloff, Michael. *A Dictionary of Christian Palestinian Aramaic*. OLA 234. Leuven: Peeters, 2014.

Sokoloff, Michael. *A Dictionary of Jewish Babylonian Aramaic of the Talmudic and Geonic Periods*. Publications of the Comprehensive Aramaic Lexicon Project. Ramat-Gan: Bar Ilan University Press, 2002.

Sokoloff, Michael. *A Dictionary of Jewish Palestinian Aramaic of the Byzantine Period*. 3rd ed. Ramat Gan: Bar Ilan University Press, 2017.

Sokoloff, Michael. *A Dictionary of Judean Aramaic*. Ramat Gan: Bar Ilan University Press, 2003.

Sommerfeld, Walter. "Prä-Akkadisch: Die Vorläufer der 'Sprache von Akkade' in der frühdynastischen Zeit." In *Language in the Ancient Near East: Proceedings of the 53e Rencontre Assyriologique Internationale*, edited by L. Kogan et al., vol. 1, 77–163. Winona Lake, IN: Eisenbrauns, 2010.

Sweeney, Deborah. "The Hieratic Inscriptions." In *The Renewed Archaeological Excavations at Lachish (1973–1994)*, vol. 3, edited by David Ussishkin, 1601–17. Tel Aviv: Emery and Claire Yass Publications in Archaeology, 2004.

Tal, Abraham. *A Dictionary of Samaritan Aramaic*. 2 vols. HdO 50. Leiden: Brill, 2000.

Ussishkin, David. "A Synopsis of the Stratigraphical, Chronological and Historical Issues." In *The Renewed Archaeological Excavations at Lachish (1973–1994)*, vol. 1, edited by David Ussishkin, 50–119. Tel Aviv: Emery and Claire Yass Publications in Archaeology, 2004.

Ussishkin, David. "Excavations at Tel Lachish 1978–1983: Second Preliminary report." *TA* 10 (1983): 97–175.

van den Brink, Edwin C. M. "The 'En Besor Cylinder Seal Impressions in Retrospect." In *Excavations at 'En Besor*, edited by Ram Gophna, 201–14. Tel Aviv: Ramot, 1995.

van Soldt, Wilfred H. "The Vocalization of the Word *mlk* 'King' in Late Bronze Age Syllabic Texts from Syria and Palestine." In *Hamlet on a Hill: Semitic and Greek Studies Presented to Prof. T. Muraoka on the Occasion of His Sixty-Fifth Birthday*, edited by M. F. J. Baasten and W. Th. van Peursen, 449–71. OLA 118. Leuven: Peeters, 2003.

Wilson-Wright, Aren M. "Linguistic Contact between Hebrew and Egyptian." In *Oxford Handbook on Ancient Egypt and the Hebrew Bible*, edited by Susan Tower Hollis. Oxford: Oxford University Press, forthcoming.

Wimmer, Stefan. "Lachish is Lachish on the Lachish Bowl: An Object Lesson for Reading Hieratic, with Little Surprising Results." In *The Late Bronze and Early Iron Ages in Canaan*, edited by Aren M. Maier, Itzhaq Shai, and Chris McKinny, 136–47. Berlin: De Gruyter, 2019.

Wimmer, Stefan. *Palästinisches Hieratisch: Die Zahl- und Sonderzeichen in der althebräischen Schrift*. ÄAT 75. Wiesebaden: Harrassowitz, 2008.

Zhakevich, Philip. *Scribal Tools in Ancient Israel: A Study of Biblical Hebrew Terms for Writing Materials and Implements*. HACL 9. University Park, PA: Eisenbrauns, 2020.

Tania Notarius

Northwest Semitic – Akkadian Linguistic Convergence: *sipr- and Other Terms for 'Writing' as a Case Study

1 Introduction

This paper is an attempt to investigate the origin and functional development of select ancient Northwest Semitic (NWS) terms for writing. "Ancient NWS" refers to the West Semitic (WS) languages and dialects extending from Northern Meso-potamia through Syria to Canaan,[1] starting ca 18th–17th cent. BCE, climaxing in the 14th–13th cent. BCE, and ending at the beginning of the 12th cent. BCE — the age the late Bronze Age civilizations "collapsed."[2] At that time Akkadian (Assyro-

* The Hebrew University; The University of the Free State. I want to thank Esti Eshel and Michael Langlois for inviting me to take part in the conference "The Scribe in the Biblical World"; I have enormously benefited from the comments of participants, conversations and discussions. Special thanks go to Esti Eshel who was the respondent at my talk and made very insightful observations and suggestions. The draft of the paper was read by Steven Fassberg and Aaron Hornkohl; I am indebted to their comments, all possible mistakes remain mine. The research was accomplished during my stay at the Martin-Luther University, Halle-Wittenberg with the generous support of the Humboldt Foundation.

1 On the NWS group of languages see Josef Tropper, "Kanaanäische Lehnwörter Im Ugaritischen," *UF* 35 (2003), 663–71; John Huehnergard, "Features of Central Semitic," in *Biblical and Oriental Essays in Memory of William L. Moran*, ed. Augustus Gianto (Roma: Editrice Pontificio Istituto Biblico, 2005), 155–203. The status of NWS as a separate, genetically reliable group is debated by some scholars; see Leonid Kogan, *Genealogical Classification of Semitic. The Lexical Isoglosses* (Berlin & Boston: De Gruyter, 2015), 227–241, who claimed that there is just one certain grammatical shared innovation (*w- > *y-), and a very low number of "exclusive lexical features," cf. also Leonid Kogan, "Genealogical Position of Ugaritic: The Lexical Dimension: Lexical Isoglosses between Ugaritic and Canaanite," *Sefarad* 70.1 (2010), 7–50; Leonid Kogan, "Genealogical Position of Ugaritic: The Lexical Dimension. Lexical Isoglosses between Ugaritic and Other Semitic Languages. Conclusions," *Sefarad* 70.2 (2010), 279–328. This topic is beyond the scope of this paper.

2 See Eric Clines, *1177 B.C. The Year Civilization Collapsed* (Princeton & Oxford: Princeton University Press, 2014) and the bibliography there.

Babylonian) East Semitic (ES) played the role of a major language of administration, economy, and culture in the region.[3] The importance of this period for the history of Semitic literacy is hard to overemphasize. It was the setting of intensive linguistic contact between these two branches of Semitic, and of an encounter between the long-entrenched cuneiform learning tradition and then-nascent alphabetic writing.[4] This interaction was anything but superficial: in Ugaritic, e.g., Akkadian cuneiform and Ugaritic alphabetic texts were produced in the same scribal schools by the same individuals; the cuneiform literary curriculum was

---

3 For Akkadian as a *koine* in Late Bronze Age Syria and Canaan, see Wilfred H. van Soldt, "Babylonian Lexical, Religious and Literary Texts and Scribal Education at Ugarit," in *UGARIT – Ein ostmediterranes Kulturzentrum im Alten Orient. Ergebnisse und Perspektiven der Forschung*, ed. Manfred Dietrich, and Oswald Loretz (Münster: Ugarit-Verlag, 1995), 171–212; Wilfred H. van Soldt, "The Akkadain of Ugarit: Lexicographic Aspects," *SEL* 12 (1995), 205–15; Juan-Pablo Vita, "Language Contact between Akkadian and Northwest Semitic Languages in Syria-Palestine in the Late Bronze Age," in *Semitic Languages in Contact* (Leiden & Boston: Brill, 2015), 375–404; cf. also John Huehnergard, *The Akkadian of Ugarit* (Atlanta: Scholars Press, 1989); Wilfred H. van Soldt, *Studies in the Akkadian of Ugarit: Dating and Grammar* (Neukirchen-Vluyn: Neukirchener Verlag, 1991); Anson Rainey, *The El-Amarna Correspondence: A New Edition of the Cuneiform Letters from the Site of El-Amarna Based on Collations of All Extant Tablets*, ed. William Schniedewind and Zipora Cochavi-Rainey (Leiden & Boston: Brill, 2015); Krzysztof Baranowski, *The Verb in the Amarna Letters from Canaan* (Winona Lake: Eisenbrauns, 2016); Wayne Horowitz, Takayoshi Oshima, and Seth Sanders, *Cuneiform in Canaan* (Jerusalem: The Hebrew University of Jerusalem, 2006).
4 Alphabetic writing, which originated in Egypt (see J.C. Darnell et al., "Two Early Alphabetic Inscriptions from the Wadi El-Ḥôl: New Evidence for the Origin of the Alphabet from the Western Desert of Egypt," *AASOR* 59 (2005): 65–124, Benjamin Sass and Carole Roche, "Wadi El-Hol and the Alphabet," in *D'Ougarit à Jérusalem* (Paris: De Boccard, 2008), 193–203), reached Mesopotamia and Syro-Canaan in the Bronze Age (see the review in Yigal Bloch, *Alphabet Scribes in the Land of Cuneiform: Sēpiru Professionals in Mesopotamia in the Neo-Babylonian and Achaemenid Period* (Piscataway: Gorgias, 2018), 1–20). According to some recent publications (based on data from a private collection) sporadic combinations of cuneiform and alphabetic writing predates Ugarit by some centuries; see Stephanie Dalley, *Babylonian Tablets from the First Sealand Dynasty in the Schøyen Collection* (Bethesda, Md.: CDL Press, 2009).

adopted by alphabetic scribes.[5] The foundations of Iron Age literacy in Syria-Canaan (10th–8th cent. BCE) were laid in the same time-period.[6]

For centuries, generations of scribes from the WS linguistic milieu were fluent in Akkadian and trained in cuneiform writing, operating in a situation of practical multilingualism that resulted in phenomena of linguistic *convergence*. Linguistic convergence implies that mutual interference between contact languages results in linguistic patterns that have no clear source, resembling both

---

5 Cuneiform literacy in the region and its impact on the alphabetic scribal curriculum is broadly overviewed in the research; see Jean Nougayrol, "L'influence babylonienne à Ugarit, d'après les textes en cunéiforms classiques," *Syria* 39 (1962): 28–35. See also Aaron Demsky, "The Education of Canaanite Scribes in the Mesopotamian Cuneiform Tradition," in *Bar-Ilan Studies in Assyriology Dedicated to Pinhas Artzi*, ed. J. Klein and A. Skaist (Ramat Gan: Bar-Ilan University, 1990), 157–70; Soldt, "Babylonian Lexical, Religious and Literary Texts and Scribal Education at Ugarit"; Robert Hawley, "On the Alphabetic Scribal Curriculum at Ugarit," in *Proceedings of the 51st Rencontre Assyriologique Internationale*, ed. R.D. Biggs, J. Meyers, and M. Roth (Chicago: Oriental Institute, 2008), 57–68; Yoram Cohen, "Cuneiform Writing in Bronze Age Canaan," in *The Social Archaeology of the Levant: From Prehistory to Present* (Cambridge: Cambridge University Press, 2019), 245–64.

6 The question of continuity between the Late Bronze and Early Iron Age cultural milieus has many aspects, not just the literacy practices; see Gershon Galil et al., eds., *The Ancient Near East in the 12th–10th Centuries BCE: Culture and History. Proceedings of the International Conference Held at the University of Haifa, 2–5 May, 2010* (Münster: Ugarit-Verlag, 2012). The main argument is the dispersion of inscriptions in the "short" Canaanite cuneiform alphabet outside Ugarit (see Dietrich and Loretz 1988), which, together with the evidence from other centers of alphabetic writing in the Late Bronze–Early Iron Age, particularly in Southern Canaan – Philistia and Lachish (see Jose-Ángel Zamora, "Les utilisations de l'alphabet lors du IIe millénaire av. J.-C. et le développement de l'épigraphie alphabétique : Une approche à travers la documentation ougaritique en dehors des tablettes (I)," in *Le Royaume d'Ougarit de la Crète à l'Euphrate : Nouveaux axes de recherche. Actes du congrès international de Sherbrooke, 2005*, ed. J.-M. Michaud (Québec: GGC, 2007), Israel Finkelstein and Benjamin Sass, "The West Semitic Alphabetic Inscriptions, Late Bronze II to Iron IIA: Archeological Context, Distribution and Chronology," *HeBAI* 2 (2013): 149–220) suggests a much smoother transition through the "dark ages"; cf. also André Lemaire, "West Semitic Epigraphy and the History of the Levant during the 12th–10th Centuries BCE," in *The Ancient Near East in the 12th–10th Centuries BCE: Culture and History. Proceedings of the International Conference Held at the University of Haifa, 2–5 May, 2010*, ed. Gershon Galil et al. (Münster: Ugarit-Verlag, 2012), 291–307; A. Millard, "Scripts and Their Uses in the 12th–10th Centuries BCE," in *The Ancient Near East in the 12th–10th Centuries BCE: Culture and History. Proceedings of the International Conference Held at the University of Haifa, 2–5 May, 2010*, ed. Gershon Galil et al. (Münster: Ugarit-Verlag, 2012), 405–12.

the 'source' and 'receiving' languages; in other words, a linguistic change is triggered by both internal development and external triggers.[7] The convergence between genetically cognate languages can become particularly tricky for historical linguistics: formally and functionally matching items merge to an extent that the analysis of specific isoglosses become highly delicate.[8] The contact between NWS and ES occurred not only on the level of linguistic structures, but also on the level of cultural notions; this process potentially involved the borrowing of certain words and notions, while the concrete path of such borrowings may remain obscure due to the situation of mutual interference.[9]

---

7 See the discussion in Sarah G. Thomason, *Language Contact* (Edinburgh: University Press, 2001), 89–90, 262; Raymond Hickey, ed., *The Handbook of Language Contact* (Malden, MA: Wiley-Blackwell, 2010). The phenomenon of linguistic convergence is studied by contact linguistics and comprises both separate developments by which languages in contact become structurally similar and *Sprachbund* situations (see Donald Winford, *An Introduction to Contact Linguistics* (Malden, MA: Blackwell, 2003); Carol Myers-Scotton, *Multiple Voices: An Introduction to Bilingualism* (Oxford: Blackwell, 2006), Yaron Matras, "Contact, Convergence, and Typology," in *The Handbook of Language Contact*, ed. Raymond Hickey (Malden, MA: Wiley-Blackwell, 2010), 66–85; and in particular Yaron Matras, "Contact, Convergence, and Typology," in *The Handbook of Language Contact*, ed. Raymond Hickey (Malden, MA: Wiley-Blackwell, 2010), 66–85.

8 An example of grammatical convergence between NWS languages and peripheral Akkadian of Syria and Canaan is the prevailing usage of -*t*- infixed forms in the Canaano-Akkadian of El-Amarna — does it represent the WS Gt or Akkadian perfect? (see Baranowski, *The Verb in the Amarna Letters from Canaan*: 36–60); for the phonological and lexicographic aspect cf. Soldt, "The Akkadian of Ugarit: Lexicographic Aspects." See also the discussion in Eva von Dassow, "Canaanite in Cuneiform," *JAOS* 124 (2004), 641–75; Eva von Dassow, "Peripheral Akkadian Dialects, or Akkadography of Local Languages?," in *Language in the Ancient Near East: Proceedings of the 53e Rencontre Assyriologique Internationale* , ed. Leonid Kogan, Sergey Loesov, and Sergey Tishchenko (Babel und Bibel 4/2; Winona Lake, Ind.: Eisenbrauns, 2010), 895–924.

9 The borrowing mechanism can be quite complicated, involving diverse contact phenomena. On the problems of borrowing in general see Martin Haspelmath, "Lexical Borrowing: Concepts and Issues," in *Loanwords in the World's Languages: A Comparative Handbook*, ed. Martin Haspelmath and Uri Tadmor (Berlin: De Gruyter; Mouton, 2009), 35–54. Select problems of lexical borrowing in Semitic languages are discussed in James Barr, *Comparative Philology and the Text of the Old Testament* (Oxford: Clarendon, 1968), 101–114; Steven Kaufman, "Languages in Contact: The Ancient Near East," *Israel Oriental Society* 20 (2002), 297–306. On borrowings between cognate, particularly Semitic, languages see Na'ama Pat-El, "Contact or Inheritance? Criteria for Distinguishing Internal and External Change in Genetically Related Languages," *Journal of Language Contact* 6 (2013), 313–28; Aaron Butts, *Semitic Languages in Contact* (Leiden & Boston: Brill, 2015); Lutz Edzard, "Zum Verhaltnis von Lehnbildung und Genetischer Verwandtschaft im Semitischen," in *Neue Beiträge zur Semitistik. Fünftes Treffen der Arbeitsgemeinschaft Semitistik in der Deutschen Morgenländischen Gesellschaft vom 15.–17. Februar 2012 an der Universität Basel*, ed. Viktor Golinetz et al. (Münster: Ugarit-Verlag, 2015). See also Lutz Edzard,

The main corpus for this research is the alphabetic texts from Ugarit — the site that provides most of the data for Late Bronze alphabetic writing and attests to extensive interaction between cuneiform and alphabetic writing traditions. I will concentrate on the etymology and functional scope of the term *sipr-* 'written document', and investigate its distribution with other nouns for 'messaging', such as *mal'akat-* 'message', *lūḥ(at)-* 'tablet', and some cognate items.[10] It will be claimed that the verbal noun spr 'counting, listing' was derived from the genuine NWS root spr 'count'; under the influence of the Akkadian šipru 'message, report, envoy, service' it developed the meanings 'message, written document', or, rather, merged with a corresponding loan-word from Akkadian that was reanalyzed as a derivative of the root spr 'count'; it gradually obtained many functions previously associated with the lexemes mlảk(t) 'message, missile' and lḥt 'tablet', eventually becoming the prototypical term for 'letter, message, written document'.

2 Ugaritic *spr*: an external borrowing or an inner lexical development?

Most dictionaries derive the NWS item *sipr-* (Hebrew סֵפֶר, Aramaic and Phoenician spr), as well as *sāpir-* 'scribe', from the root spr 'count; tell', but likewise emphasize a connection to the Akkadian lexemes šipru 'message, envoy' and correspondingly šāpiru 'overseer, ruler', derived from the Akkadian root šapāru 'send; write'.[11] The problem is that these two roots — the NWS spr 'count' and the

---

"Inner-Semitic Loans and Lexical Doublets vs. Genetically Related Cognates," in *Semitic Languages in Contact*, ed. Aaron Butts (Leiden & Boston: Brill, 2015), 181–97. On Akkadian borrowings in Ugaritic see Wilfred Watson, "Akkadian Loan-Words in Ugaritic: The Hippiatric Texts," in *Biblical and Near Eastern Essays*, ed. Carmel McCarthy and John F. Healey (London: Clark, 2004), 240–57; Wilfred Watson, *Lexical Studies in Ugaritic* (Sabadell: Editorial Ausa, 2007), 63–118 (but compare the discussion in Kogan, *Genealogical Classification of Semitic. The Lexical Isoglosses*, 365–369); Wilfred Watson, "Akkadian Cognates to Some Ugaritic Words," *SEL* 25 (2008), 57–62.

10 "An elephant in the room" is Ugaritic tḥm "message, decree" — a lexeme with an obscure etymology, but very wide distribution in both Ugaritic poetry and prose. This term is outside the scope of the paper.

11 See Ludwig Koehler and Walter Baumgartner, *The Hebrew and Aramaic Lexicon of the Old Testament*, 5 vols. (Leiden: Brill, 1994): 767; Wilhelm Gesenius, *Hebräisches und Aramäisches Handwörterbuch über das Alte Testament*, ed. Rudolf Meyer and Herbert Donner, 18th ed., 6 vols. (Berlin: Springer, 1987): 898–900; Gregorio del Olmo Lete and Joaquín Sanmartín, *A Dictionary*

ES *šapāru* 'send' — are not cognate, as regular phonetic correspondences indicate: Proto-Semitic s_3 (as in *spr* 'count', cognate to Ethiopic *safara* 'measure') and s_1 (as in *šapāru* 'send', cognate to Arabic *sfr* 'travel, send away' and Sabaic $s_1fr(t)$ 'arrive; extent') are separate phonemes in both NWS (Ugaritic and Hebrew) and Akkadian:[12]

Ex. 1

a. *s_3: NWS *spr* 'count', Ethiopic *safara* 'measure'; cf. *ʔsr 'to tie' > Akk. *esēru*, Ugr./Hbr. ʔsr;

b. *s_1: Akk. *šapāru* 'send', Arabic *sfr* 'travel, send away', Sabaic $s_1fr(t)$ 'arrive; extent'; cf. *šim- 'name' > Akk. *šumu*; Ugr./Heb. *šm*, Arab. ʔism.

Since the roots are not cognate, while NWS *sipr-* 'written document, letter' and the Akkadian *šipru* 'message, letter' correlate semantically, it was claimed that

---

of the Ugaritic Language in the Alphabetic Tradition, 2nd ed. (Leiden & Boston: Brill, 2015): 755; J. Hoftijzer and K. Jongeling, *Dictionary of the North-West Semitic Inscriptions*, 2 vols. (Leiden: Brill, 1995), 798; Wolfram von Soden, *Akkadisches Handwörterbuch* (Wiesbaden: Harrassowitz, 1965): 1170.

12 Cf. Leonid Kogan, "Proto-Semitic Phonetics and Phonology," in *The Semitic Languages: An International Handbook*, ed. Stefan Weninger (Berlin & Boston: De Gruyter, 2011), 54–151; for Arabic *sfr* cf. Edward W. Lane, *An Arabic-English Lexicon*, 8 vols. (London: Williams & Norgate Leslau, 1863), IV, 1370-1371; Ethiopic *safara* Wolf Leslau, *Comparative Dictionary of Geʿez (Classical Ethiopic)* (Wiesbaden: Harrassowitz, 1987): 488-489; Sabaic s_1prt (al-Ṣilwī 3:5 'arrived' and CIH 570:5–6 'extent') cf. in A.F.L. Beeston et al., *Sabaic Dictionary (English-French-Arabic)* (Louvain-La-Neuve: Editions Peeters, 1982): 125 s_1frt 'extent, area'.

the NWS term is an ancient borrowing from Akkadian, evidently through the Assyrian dialect.[13] However, some scholars remained skeptical about such a borrowing,[14] supposing a default option of genuine genetic and semantic links between the verbal root *spr 'to count, measure' and the noun *sipr- 'written document'.

2.1 *spr* 'number'; *mspr* 'recitation'

The Ugaritic lexicon distinguishes between several lexemes connected to the root *spr* 'count; tell': the verbal nouns *spr* III 'counting, number' and *mspr* 'recitation':[15]

Ex. 2

  a. *ḫpt d bl spr ṯnn d bl hg* "mercenaries without number, archers without count" 1.14 II 37–38, and parallels.

  b. *b py sprhn b špty mnthm* "in my mouth (I have) their inventory, on my lips (is) their list" 1.24:45–46.

  c. *ṯb l mspr* "return to the recitation" 1.40:35; cf. 1.4 V 42 (scribal gloss), 1.19 IV 62, 1.107:14; cf. also 1.179:41 (in a colophon, broken context).

---

13 Cf. Kogan, *Genealogical Classification of Semitic. The Lexical Isoglosses*: 306: "Contra HALOT 765–766, P[roto-] C[entral Semitic] *spr* 'to count' is to be strictly separated from the widely attested lexemes with the prototypes *sipr-* 'writing, inscription, document' and *sāpir-* 'scribe,' which are not autochthonous West Semitic, but ultimately go back to Akk. *šipru* and *šāpiru*." See also Heinrich Zimmern, *Akkadische Fremdwörter als Beweis für Babylonischen Kultureinfluss* (Leipzig: Hinrichs, 1917): 19; (1974, ספר קריית :ירושלים) ותולדותיה מילים ,קוטשר יחזקאל: 76; Ephraim A. Speiser, *Oriental and Biblical Studies: Collected Writings of E. A. Speiser*, ed. J.J. Finkelstein and Moshe Greenberg (Philadelphia: University of Pennsylvania Press, 1967): 439 (note 16); Hayim Tawil, *An Akkadian Lexical Companion for Biblical Hebrew* (Jersey City: Ktav, 2009): 266. For the Assyrian sibilant shift *š* > *s*, as reflected in the NWS loans, cf. Steven Kaufman, *The Akkadian Influences on Aramaic* (Chicago: University of Chicago Press, 1974): 140-142; Paul V. Mankowski, *Akkadian Loanwords in Biblical Hebrew* (Winona Lake, Ind.: Eisenbrauns, 2000): 155–157.
14 See the discussion in J. Muffs, *Studies in the Aramaic Legal Papyri from Elephantine* (Leiden: Brill, 1969): 207 and Kaufman, *The Akkadian Influences on Aramaic*: 29.
15 See Olmo Lete and Sanmartín, *DULAT*: 575, 757. All the Ugaritic quotations, unless marked differently, are from KTU: Manfred Dietrich, Oswald Loretz, and Joaquín Sanmartín, *The Cuneiform Alphabetic Texts from Ugarit, Ras Ibn Hani and Other Places*, 3rd ed. (Münster: Ugarit-Verlag, 2013).

There are not so many examples for *spr* 'number, counting', and all of them are in poetic language (ex. 2ab),[16] while in BH, Phoenician, and Aramaic the verbal noun *sipr-* is not used for 'number, counting'.[17] In ex. 2b *spr* is parallel to *mnt* 'portion, list'; the meaning 'incantation, pronouncement' is consistent with these terms due to the speech-act phrases *b py* 'in my mouth' and *b špty* 'on my lips'. *Mspr* 'recitation', in most of its usages (ex. 2c), is phrased with the verb *ṯb* 'do something again';[18] it is a part of instructions on ritual recitation of lists or other formulaic texts; the numeric connotation is present.

2.2 *sprt* 'instruction'

The feminine noun *sprt* has the meaning 'instruction, prescription' and is used twice in procedural discourse:[19]

Ex. 3

    a. *dbḥ kl kl ykly dbḥ k sprt* "sacrifice that is completely consumed, sacrifice according to prescript" 1.127:7–9.

    b. *mlḥm sprt* "(sorts of) salt (according to) prescription" 4.863:20.

Although the lexeme can be interpreted as a 'numeric prescription' and connected to the NWS verbal root *spr* 'count, tell', it also parallels perfectly with Akkadian *šipirtu*, particularly in its meaning 'order, legal document; work to be done': cf. *kî ši-pir-ti* PN "according to the order of PN"; the noun *šipirtu* is broadly distributed in the Akkadian corpus and is attested also in El-Amarna Akkadian (see EA 143:12, 14; 246:8).[20] The context in KTU 4.863:20 (ex. 2b) is particularly

---

16 Ugarit has other lexemes belonging to the semantic field of 'counting': *ḥṯb* 'bill' and *ḥṯbn* 'balance, account', *kbd* 'total, exact number; plus', *kl* 'totality, total number', distributed in different corpus parts, particularly in prose; see Olmo Lete and Sanmartín, *DULAT*: 373; 421, 432.

17 Hebrew and Phoenician use the derivative *mspr*, while Aramaic has another root for counting and its derivative, *ḥšb*.

18 Olmo Lete and Sanmartín, *DULAT*: 575; for a biblical attestation cf. Ju 7:15 (see Koehler and Baumgartner, *HALOT*: 607).

19 Olmo Lete and Sanmartín, *DULAT*: 758.

20 See von Soden, *AHw*: 1244–1245; see also Ignate Gelb et al., eds., *Chicago Assyrian Dictionary (The Assyrian Dictionary of the Oriental Institute of the University of Chicago)*, 26 vols. (Chicago: Oriental Institute, 1956), vol. Š/3: 65–68.

suggestive in this sense: part of this text is written in Akkadian, in syllabic cunei-form, and there are several other loan terms in it.[21] Interestingly, this lexeme did not continue into later NWS languages: Phoenician, Aramaic, and Hebrew do not have a feminine word cognate to *sprt 'instruction'.[22]

2.3 mlåk(t) 'mission, message'

The Ugaritic lexeme spr II 'written document' concurs semantically with two non-cognate lexemes: lḥt 'tablet(s); missive, message, letter' and mlåk(t) 'message, mission; embassy; messenger'.[23]

The noun mlåkt is derived from the WS root l'k 'send' — an exact semantic equivalent of Akkadian šapāru 'send'.[24] The feminine form mlåkt has two mean-ings: it denotes 'message, missive', namely the mission itself, the content of a message to be delivered (cf. 4a), or 'mission, embassy, envoy', namely the people who had a mission / message to transmit (ex. 4b). Although the distinction be-tween these two usages is tricky in some cases, this lexicographic attitude is more consistent with the nuances in the data.

Ex. 4

a. mlåkt špš the message of the "Sun" 2.23:7 (cf. also line 3: mlåkt ʕbdh "the mission of your servant" 2.23:3; line 5: mlåkty ʕmh 'my missive to him'); [w]mlå[k]tk ʕmy l lĭkt "and you did not send your missive to me" 2.36:11; w ånnå îlåk b mlåkt ʕmk "and I shall send you PN with the missive" 2.75:10.

b. bnš bnny ʕmn mlåkty hnd ylåk "may he send some intermediary with this my embassy" 2.33:35; cf. also 2.17:4. 7, 2.87:33. 2.90:17. 23.

---

21 Cf. kzy 'groom, squire' (cf. Akk. kizû; Hurr. */kuz=/), prś/s dry measure (cf. Akk. parīsu), tyt 'a plant' (Akk. tīyatu).
22 The Late BH ספרה 'writing' (Ps 56:9, Sir 44:4) — a feminine form of ספר 'book' — seems less relevant.
23 Olmo Lete and Sanmartín, DULAT: 490–491, 540.
24 Although Arab. laʔaka IV 'send a message, serve a messenger' is rather a denominative deri-vation (Hans Wehr, Dictionary of Modern Written Arabic: Arabic-English Dictionary, ed. J.M. Cowan, 4th ed. (Urbana IL: Spoken Language Services, 1994): 1000), Eth. laʔaka, "to send" (Leslau, CDG: 303) and Sabaic l'k 'schicken' (Peter Stein, Die Altsudarabischen Minuskelin-schriften Auf Holzstabchen Aus Der Bayerischen Staatsbibliothek in Munchen (Tübingen & Berlin: Warmuth, 2010): 726) point at a Proto-WS root; see Kogan, Genealogical Classification of Semitic. The Lexical Isoglosses: 120.

All the cases of the feminine form *mlåkt* are attested in prose, particularly in letters; there is no *mlåkt* in poetic language. The masculine form *mlåk* 'messenger' is, contrary to its feminine counterpart, primarily attested in poetry:[25]

Ex. 5

a. *mlåkm ylåk ym* "DN sent messengers" 1.2 I 11. 41–42 1.13:25, 1.124:11, 1.14 III 20. 35, 1.14 VI 35; (broken) 1,62:6, 2.76:3.

b. *tphn mlåk ym tˤdt ṯpṭ[nhr]* "(gods) saw the envoys of DN, the embassy of Judge DN" 1.2 I 22; cf. parallels in the same tablet 1.2 I 28. 30

c. *lḥt mlåk ym tˤdt ṯpṭ nhr* "the letter-tablet with the message of DN, accreditation of Judge DN" 1.2 I 26.

Its main meaning is 'messenger', ex. 5a. In ex. 5b the form *mlåk*, routinely translated as a dual construct of the agent-noun "messengers (of DN)," is parallel to the abstract noun *tˤdt* 'embassy, accreditation', and can be interpreted as a collective 'envoy, delegation' (one must admit that several messengers form a delegation, therefore plural / dual and abstract collective nouns overlap semantically). Moreover, the poetic expression *lḥt mlåk* in ex. 5c is a precise parallel to the prose expression *lḥt spr* "the letter-tablet concerning the message" (2.14:6–7, see the discussion below). The impression is that the poetic *mlåk* means not just 'messenger', but also 'embassy' and even 'message', partly overlapping semantically with the prose feminine *mlåkt*.[26]

---

25 There is just one case of *mlåk* in prose – 2.76:3. For other lexemes for 'messenger' in Ugaritic poetry, cf. *ʕnn* 'herald, messenger' (Olmo Lete and Sanmartín, *DULAT*: 166-167); *dll* 'messenger' (Olmo Lete and Sanmartín, *DULAT*: 268); *ʕdd* 'herald, messenger' (Olmo Lete and Sanmartín, *DULAT*: 145-146); also in Ugaritic prose there is a wide range of nouns for 'messenger': *ql* 'swift (courier, messenger)' (Olmo Lete and Sanmartín, *DULAT*: 689); *bn qlt* 'courier' (Olmo Lete and Sanmartín, *DULAT*: 691); *bn ḫrn* 'messenger' (Olmo Lete and Sanmartín, *DULAT*: 400); *blblm* 'messengers (?)' (Olmo Lete and Sanmartín, *DULAT*: 9); *ủdr* 'courier' (Olmo Lete and Sanmartín, *DULAT*: 24); *hlk* '(active participle) messenger' (Olmo Lete and Sanmartín, *DULAT*: 333 (?)).
26 The tendency to differentiate between the feminine *mlåkt* for 'message, embassy' and masculine *mlåk* for 'messenger' (cf. Hebrew מלאך 'messenger, angel' and מלאכה 'mission, work' for later attestation) seems to be a result of the semantic split, otherwise the pattern *maqtal* for an agent-noun is difficult to explain (cf. Carl Brockelmann, *Grundriss Der Vergleichenden Grammatik Der Semitischen Sprachen*, 2 vols. (Berlin: Reuther & Reichard, 1908), 1:376; and the discussion in John Huehnegard, *Ugaritic Vocabular in Syllabic Transcription* (Atlanta, GA: Scholars Press, 2008): 82). Similar processes are attested in Akkadian: *šipirtu* and *šipru* both mean 'message, mission; work', but *šipru* (together with *mār šipri*) can also denote 'messenger' (cf. Gelb et al., *CAD* Š/3, 74–76); cf. also Akk. *našpāru*, (von Soden, *AHw*, 761a), and see Wilhelm Eilers, "Zur Funktion von Nominalformen: Ein Grenzgang zwischen Morphologie und Semasiologie," *WO*

Ugaritic *mlåk(t)* is a full functional equivalent to the Akkadian *šipru* / *šipirtu* 'mission, message, work; messenger', although the technical meaning 'trade mission, work' (eventually characteristic in Hebrew)[27] is not attested in Ugaritic.

2.4 *lḥt* 'tablet(s); missive, message, letter'

The lexeme that most intersects with *spr* II 'written document' is *lḥt* 'missive, message; letter-tablet'.[28] It is well attested in Ugaritic, particularly in prose correspondence, referring to the content of a letter, 'message from / about' (ex. 6a) or to the 'tablet-letter' itself, 'letter concerning' (ex. 6b). There is just one usage in poetry: *lḥt* 'tablet(s)' is phrased with *mlåk* 'message' (cf. ex. 5c above), while its exact parallel in prose language is *lḥt spr* "letter-message" (ex. 6c). In these usages it overlaps with its functional equivalent in Akkadian – *ṭuppu*.[29]

Ex. 6

a. *lḥt šlm d likt* "message of greeting that (she) sent" 2.34:5–6; cf. also 2.39:17; 2.45:22–23; 2.46:10; 2.73:7, 2.73:12.

b. *w lḥt bt mlk åmr* "and the letter (about) the daughter of the king of TN" 2.72:17; see also 2.72:23; 2.90:4; 2.87:18; 2.103:17; 2.104:11; 2.31:43; 2.98:31; 2.100:16; 2.103:11; 2.100:14; 2.103:12.

c. *lḥt mlåk ym* "the letter-message of DN" 1.2 I 26; cf. 2.14:6 *lḥt spr d likt* "the letter-message that I sent."

2.5 *spr* II 'register, writing, letter'

The most common Ugaritic term that refers to a written document is *spr* II; it also manifests the broadest semantic scope: DULAT distinguishes between four main

---

3.1/2 (1964), 80–145, 133, who already suggested that the verbal noun 'mission' evolved into agent noun 'messenger'; the Ugaritic data presented here textually supports that assumption. It is hard to say whether this development in ancient NWS was calqued from Akkadian. The Aramaic, Ethiopic (see Leslau, *CDG*, 303), and Arabian (J.G. Hava, *Al-Faraid Arabic-English Dictionary* (Beirut: Catholic Press, 1964), 673) *malʔāk* "messenger, angel" seem to be later loans.

27 See Koehler and Baumgartner, *HALOT*: 586.

28 See Olmo Lete and Sanmartín, *DULAT*: 490. According to Joshua Fox, *Semitic Nouns Patterns* (Harvard Semitic Studies 59; Winona Lake, Ind.: Eisenbrauns, 2003): 76 this is a Proto-Semitic isolated nominal lexeme.

29 Cf. von Soden, *AHw*: 1394-1395; Gelb et al., *CAD* Ṭ: 129-148.

functions: 1) "tablet / register, list, inventory; in accounting, record of tribute; of instructions"; 2) "writing, document, warrant"; 3) "letter, missive"; 4) archival note of "reference, matter."[30] With hundreds of cases in the corpus, it is never used in poetry.

On the surface *lḥt* and *spr* demonstrate different distributions: if the former is attested in correspondence (see ex. 6), the latter is used primarily in administrative and procedural texts. It refers to 'record' and 'list, inventory' (ex. 7ab), commonly for the sake of 'accounting' (ex. 7c). In these usages the lexeme looks like a derivative of the root *spr* 'count'; I am not convinced that these usages can be strictly separated from the lexeme *spr* III 'counting, number' (see ex. 3 above):

Ex. 7

a. *spr npš d ʿrb bt mlk w b spr l št yrmʿl 3 ṣry 2 ...* "record of the individuals who entered the house of the king, but who had not been put in a record: PN – 3, PN – 2 ..." 4.338:1–6; see also 4.33:1; 4.322:1; 4.561:1; 4.320:1; 4.714:1; 4.288:1.

b. *spr bnš mlk d tåršn ʿmsn bṣr åbn špšyn* "register of the personnel of the king who claim the cargo: PN, PN, PN" 4.370:1–3; cf. 4.141 I 1; 4.144:1; 4.609:1; 4.367:1; + many.

c. *spr ḫtbn sbrdnm ḥmš[[x]] kkrm ålp[[x]] kbd ṯlṯ* "account book of the bronze-smiths: 5 talents, 1000 (shekels) of copper" 4.337:1–3; see also 4.610 I 1; 4.181:1; 4.369:1 etc.

The lexeme *spr* II has very broad semantics. It also means 'document, instruction' (cf. ex. 8ab), explicitly overlapping with the Akkadian *šipru / šipirtu* 'commission, report, message, task'[31] and Ugaritic *sprt* 'instruction, prescription' (ex. 3, discussed above), denoting 'matter, document' in general (cf. ex. 8c) or acquiring a nuance of 'warrant, license' in particular (ex. 8d):

Ex. 8

a. *spr nʿm śśwm* "(book of) instructions about the health of horses" 1.85:1.

---

30 See Olmo Lete and Sanmartín, *DULAT*: 756-757. Robert Hawley, Dennis Pardee, and Carole Roche-Hawley, "The Scribal Culture of Ugarit," *Journal of the Ancient Near Eastern Society* 2 (2015), 229–67: 252 derive this noun from the root s-p-r 'count' and notice (note 64): "Its morphological structure was probably /sipru/. The word /sipru/ appears in various literary genres in reference to the inscribed tablet itself, e. g., *spr ḫpr* 'document of rations' (RS 17.106), or *spr dbḥ ẓlm* 'document of sacrifices of the shades' (RS 34.126, a funerary ritual). It is clear that, as *spr* + X defines the type of document, *spr* + PN defines who put the document into writing."
31 Cf. Gelb et al., *CAD* Š 3: 73-84: the Akkadian lexeme *šipru* has very wide distribution in the cuneiform corpus, including the Akkadian of Ugarit and in El-Amarna.

b. *spr dbḥ ẓlm* "(record of) instructions for the sacrifice of the spirits" 1.161:1.

c. *spr šåb mq[dšt]* "document concerning the water carriers of the sanctuary" 6.25:1; see also 4.120:1, 6.24:1; 6.29:1; etc.

d. *spr mlk* 'royal warrant' 3.12:13; see also 3.12:9.

All these usages are attested in procedural, economic, and administrative texts. Seldom does *spr* II occur in correspondence in the meaning 'letter / writing; message, content of a letter' (ex. 9a), matching the lexeme *lḥt* in these functions (cf. ex. 6 above). Moreover, in the meaning 'message, missive' *spr* II overlaps with the prose *mlåkt* (ex. 4a above): *spr hnd ʿmk* "this message to you" matches *mlåktk ʿmy* "your message to me" (ex. 9b); and with the poetic *mlåk* (ex. 5b above): *lḥt spr* "the tablet-letter of message" is reminiscent of *lḥt mlåk* "the letter of the message" (ex. 9c):

Ex. 9

a. *b spr štnn* "put it in a letter" 2.108:14; see also 2.10:19, 1.179:43 (in a colophon, but broken).

b. *k ytnt spr hnd ʿmk* "when I gave this message (to be delivered) to you" 2.88:5; cf. *[w] mlåktk ʿmy l likt* "and your message to me you did not send" 2.36:11.

c. *îky lḥt spr d lîkt* "what about the letter of message that I sent?" 2.14:6–7; cf. *lḥt mlåk ym* "the letter-tablet with the message of DN" 1.2 I 26.

Both in the meaning 'register, record' (ex. 7) and in the meaning 'letter, message' (ex. 9) the Ugaritic *spr* II matches the Akkadian *ṭuppu* 'tablet, written document'; cf. the parallel examples in Ugaritic and in the Akkadian of Ugarit:

Ex. 10

a. KTU 4.610 I 1 *spr årgmn špš* "record book of the tribute(s) to the 'Sun'" // PRU 4 47 (RS 11.732):1 *[ṭup-pu an-nu-ú] ša ma-an-da[-at DINGIR.]UTU-ši*.

b. KTU 2.10:19 *št b spr ʿmy* "put into writing for me" // PRU 6 18 (RS 19:53):12 *i-na ṭup-pí šu-uk-un-ni*.

3 *spr* and related terms for correspondence and writing in Ugaritic: summary

This investigation started with a question about the origin of the NWS *spr* 'letter, written document' — whether it is a genuine derivative of the verbal root *spr* 'count' or a borrowing of Akkadian *šipru* 'message', while the Ugaritic corpus suggests the richest ancient alphabetic data for the analysis. The conclusion reached is that there is no unambiguous answer to this question. The interference of two languages, particularly involving the semantic field of 'writing' in the circles of the Syro-Canaanite scribes of the Bronze Age, resulted in convergence by which inner NWS development and foreign Akkadian influence cannot be easily separated. My conclusion is that both mechanisms were at work. On the way, some related lexemes were sorted out.

In the poetic register the noun *spr* is used twice: once for 'counting', another time for 'list, inventory', while the context suggests that the inventory was pronounced in ritual practice; it is a derivative of the verbal root *spr* 'count'. In the lexicographical approach of DULAT this is a separate lexeme *spr* III, distinguished from *spr* II, apparently because for *spr* II 'written document' DULAT implies the influence of Akkadian *šipru*. But in view of the solidly attested *spr* II 'list, record, inventory', referring to numbers and accounting, mainly in administrative and economic texts, this approach seems hardly justified. There is just one verbal noun *spr* in the Ugaritic lexicon — it is used twice in poetry and continues into prose language with a much broader scope of functions. In view of this, it is not justified to claim an unconditional discrepancy between the noun **sipr-* 'written document' and the WS root *spr* 'count'; on the contrary, the data from Ugaritic shows an operative connection between counting, listing, numeration, on the one hand, and writing documents, on the other, in the ancient NWS scribal milieu. However, the growing functional scope of this lexeme points to interference with the Akkadian terms.

In procedural and administrative discourse, one finds *sprt* 'instruction, prescript' twice in the corpus, and *spr* 'document, instruction, matter' dozens of times; this functional scope is not trivially derived from the root 'count' and is an exact match to the Akkadian lexemes *šipru* / *šipirtu*. It is plausible that these are old loans from Akkadian into WS, fully adopted by the recipient language; practically, such a full adoption means that these lexemes were borrowed by means of phono-semantic match and reanalyzed as derivatives of the root *spr* 'count', especially since this root already had usages connected to producing documents.

An additional argument that the NWS *spr* interfered with the ES *šipru* is its encroaching into the sphere of 'messaging'. In poetic language its partial equivalent was *mlåk* and in prose language it interchanges several times with *mlåkt*, both in the sense of 'mission, message'. This pair *mlåkt* / *mlåk* is an interesting topic of itself: an unequal distributing of these two items in the Ugaritic corpus

— *mlåkt* is in prose and *mlåk* is in poetry, partly overlapping semantically — suggests that they started as free variants but went through a semantic split at a certain stage.

Spr turned out to be an aggressive player. With almost no attestations in poetic language, it became one of the most frequently recurring lexemes in the language of prose. Massively concentrated in administrative and procedural discourse, it shows signs of penetrating into prose correspondence.[32] The notion of 'message' and 'document', led to strong intersection with another old NWS lexeme, *lḥt* 'tablet, message', which in Ugaritic has restricted referentiality to 'letter' or 'content of a letter' in the language of correspondence. In the latter function *spr* and *lḥt* became true linguistic variables, namely contrasting expressions in the same function: the lexical innovation *spr* gradually acquired the usages of the older lexeme *lḥt*, referring to 'letter, message' in the language of correspondence.[33] As expected in the process of convergence of matching phenomena, the origin and developmental path of some traits are hard to account for: *spr* in the meaning 'list, record, account' might be motivated by the verbal root *spr* 'count', as is claimed here, but it also overlaps with the Akkadian *ṭuppu* 'tablet, written document; record' — a functional parallel to the NWS *lḥt*, for which the innovative term *spr* was to become a replacement.

---

32 Cf. Wilfred Watson, "From List to Letter: Notes on Letter-Writing Techniques," in *Society and Administration in Ancient Ugarit. Papers Read at a Symposium in Leiden, 13-14 December 2007*, ed. Wilfred H. van Soldt (Leiden & Boston: Brill, 2010), 164–78, who claims for an intrinsic meaningful relation between writing lists and letters: according to his view, lists, inventories, and accounts were in the stock of the scribal documentation to be used in the body of a letter, when necessary.

33 This tendency continues into Biblical Hebrew; the unit לוּחַ has very limited usage: it is used dozens of times, but only in set phrases like לוּחֹת הַבְּרִית and לוּ(וֹ)חַ הָעֵדוּת, and a few times metaphorically in a poetic phrase לוּחַ לִבָּם. Just twice the lexeme לוּחַ is used with reference to a written text, both times in poetry: כְּתוֹב חָזוֹן וּבָאֵר עַל־הַלֻּחוֹת (Habakkuk 2:2) and עַתָּה בּוֹא כָתְבָהּ עַל־לוּחַ אִתָּם וְעַל־סֵפֶר חֻקָּהּ (Isaiah 30:8; cf. parallelism to סֵפֶר). The full survey on this development is outside the scope of the present research, and see Tania Notarius, "From *lūaḥ* to *sēp̄er* and Back: An Episode in the Historical Linguistics of Biblical Hebrew," *New Perspectives in Biblical and Rabbinic Hebrew*, eds. Aaron D. Hornkohl and Geoffrey Khan (Cambridge: University of Cambridge, 2021), 697-716.

4 Bibliography

Baranowski, Krzysztof J. *The Verb in the Amarna Letters from Canaan*. Winona Lake: Ei-senbrauns, 2016.

Barr, James. *Comparative Philology and the Text of the Old Testament*. Oxford: Clarendon, 1968.

Beeston, Alfred F.L., M.A. Ghul, W.W. Müller, and J. Ryckmans. *Sabaic Dictionary (English-French-Arabic)*. Louvain-La-Neuve: Editions Peeters, 1982.

Bloch, Yigal. *Alphabet Scribes in the Land of Cuneiform: Sēpiru Professionals in Mesopotamia in the Neo-Babylonian and Achaemenid Period*. Piscataway: Gorgias, 2018.

Brockelmann, Carl. *Grundriss Der Vergleichenden Grammatik Der Semitischen Sprachen*. 2 vols. Berlin: Reuther & Reichard, 1908.

Butts, Aaron. *Semitic Languages in Contact*. Leiden & Boston: Brill, 2015.

Clines, Eric. *1177 B.C. The Year Civilization Collapsed*. Princeton & Oxford: Princeton University Press, 2014.

Cohen, Yoram. "Cuneiform Writing in Bronze Age Canaan." Pages 245–64 in *The Social Archaeology of the Levant: From Prehistory to Present*. Cambridge: Cambridge University Press, 2019.

Dalley, Stephanie. *Babylonian Tablets from the First Sealand Dynasty in the Schøyen Collection*. Bethesda, Md.: CDL Press, 2009.

Darnell, J.C., F.M. Dobbs-Allsopp, M.J. Lundberg, P.K. McCarter, B. Zuckerman, and C. Manassa. "Two Early Alphabetic Inscriptions from the Wadi El-Ḥôl: New Evidence for the Origin of the Alphabet from the Western Desert of Egypt." *AASOR* 59 (2005): 65–124.

Dassow, Eva von. "Canaanite in Cuneiform." *JAOS* 124 (2004): 641–75.

Dassow, Eva von. "Peripheral Akkadian Dialects, or Akkadography of Local Languages?" Pages 895–924 in *Language in the Ancient Near East: Proceedings of the 53e Rencontre Assyriologique Internationale / Babel Und Bibel 4/2*. Edited by Leonid Kogan, Sergey Loesov, and Sergey Tishchenko. Winona Lake, Ind.: Eisenbrauns, 2010.

Demsky, Aaron. "The Education of Canaanite Scribes in the Mesopotamian Cuneiform Tradition." Pages 157–70 in *Bar-Ilan Studies in Assyriology Dedicated to Pinhas Artzi*. Edited by J. Klein and A. Skaist. Ramat Gan: Bar-Ilan University, 1990.

Dietrich, Manfred, Oswald Loretz, and Joaquín Sanmartín. *The Cuneiform Alphabetic Texts from Ugarit, Ras Ibn Hani and Other Places*. 3rd ed. Münster: Ugarit-Verlag, 2013.

Edzard, Lutz. "Inner-Semitic Loans and Lexical Doublets vs. Genetically Related Cognates." Pages 181–97 in *Semitic Languages in Contact*. Edited by Aaron Butts. Leiden & Boston: Brill, 2015.

Edzard, Lutz. "Zum Verhaltnis von Lehnbildung und genetischer Verwandtschaft im Semitischen." *Neue Beiträge zur Semitistik. Fünftes Treffen der Arbeitsgemeinschaft Semitistik in der Deutschen Morgenländischen Gesellschaft vom 15.–17. Februar 2012 an der Universität Basel*. Edited by Viktor Golinetz, Hans-Peter Mathys, Hanna Jenni, and S. Sarasin. Münster: Ugarit-Verlag, 2015.

Eilers, Wilhelm. "Zur Funktion von Nominalformen: Ein Grenzgang zwischen Morphologie und Semasiologie." *WO* 3.1/2 (1964): 80–145.

Finkelstein, Israel, and Benjamin Sass. "The West Semitic Alphabetic Inscriptions, Late Bronze II to Iron IIA: Archeological Context, Distribution and Chronology." *HeBAI* 2 (2013): 149–220.

Fox, Joshua. *Semitic Nouns Patterns*. Harvard Semitic Studies 59. Winona Lake, Ind.: Eisenbrauns, 2003.

Galil, Gershon, Ayelet Gilboa, Aren Maeir, and Dan'el Kahn, eds. *The Ancient Near East in the 12th–10th Centuries BCE: Culture and History. Proceedings of the International Conference Held at the University of Haifa, 2–5 May, 2010*. Münster: Ugarit-Verlag, 2012.

Gelb, Ignace J., Benno Landsberger, A. Leo Oppenheim, and Erica Reiner, eds. *Chicago Assyrian Dictionary (The Assyrian Dictionary of the Oriental Institute of the University of Chicago)*. 26 vols. Chicago: Oriental Institute, 1956.

Gesenius, Wilhelm. *Hebräisches und Aramäisches Handwörterbuch über das Alte Testament*. Edited by Rudolf Meyer and Herbert Donner. 18th ed. 6 vols. Berlin: Springer, 1987.

Haspelmath, Martin. "Lexical Borrowing: Concepts and Issues." Pages 35–54 in *Loanwords in the World's Languages: A Comparative Handbook*. Edited by Martin Haspelmath and Uri Tadmor. Berlin: De Gruyter; Mouton, 2009.

Hava, J.G. *Al-Faraid Arabic-English Dictionary*. Beirut: Catholic Press, 1964.

Hawley, Robert. "On the Alphabetic Scribal Curriculum at Ugarit." Pages 57–68 in *Proceedings of the 51st Rencontre Assyriologique Internationale*. Edited by R.D. Biggs, J. Meyers, and M. Roth. Chicago: Oriental Institute, 2008.

Hawley, Robert, Dennis Pardee, and Carole Roche-Hawley. "The Scribal Culture of Ugarit." *JANES* 2 (2015): 229–67.

Hickey, Raymond, ed. *The Handbook of Language Contact*. Malden, MA: Wiley-Blackwell, 2010.

Hoftijzer, Jacob, and Karel Jongeling. *Dictionary of the North-West Semitic Inscriptions*. 2 vols. Leiden: Brill, 1995.

Horowitz, Wayne, Takayoshi Oshima, and Seth Sanders. *Cuneiform in Canaan*. Jerusalem: The Hebrew University of Jerusalem, 2006.

Huehnergard, John. "Features of Central Semitic." Pages 155–203 in *Biblical and Oriental Essays in Memory of William L. Moran*. Edited by Augustus Gianto. Roma: Editrice Pontificio Istituto Biblico, 2005.

Huehnergard, John. *The Akkadian of Ugarit*. Atlanta: Scholars Press, 1989.

Huehnergard, John. *Ugaritic Vocabular in Syllabic Transcription*. Atlanta, GA: Scholars Press, 2008.

Kaufman, Steven. "Languages in Contact: The Ancient Near East." *Israel Oriental Society* 20 (2002): 297–306.

Kaufman, Steven. *The Akkadian Influences on Aramaic*. Chicago: University of Chicago Press, 1974.

Koehler, Ludwig, and Walter Baumgartner. *The Hebrew and Aramaic Lexicon of the Old Testament*. 5 vols. Leiden: Brill, 1994.

Kogan, Leonid. *Genealogical Classification of Semitic. The Lexical Isoglosses*. Berlin & Boston: De Gruyter, 2015.

Kogan, Leonid. "Genealogical Position of Ugaritic: The Lexical Dimension: Lexical Isoglosses between Ugaritic and Canaanite." *Sefarad* 70.1 (2010): 7–50.

Kogan, Leonid "Genealogical Position of Ugaritic: The Lexical Dimension. Lexical Isoglosses between Ugaritic and Other Semitic Languages. Conclusions." *Sefarad* 70.2 (2010): 279–328.

Kogan, Leonid. "Proto-Semitic Phonetics and Phonology." Pages 54–151 in *The Semitic Languages: An International Handbook*. Edited by Stefan Weninger. Berlin & Boston: De Gruyter, 2011.

Lane, Edward W. *An Arabic-English Lexicon*. 8 vols. London: Williams & Norgate Leslau, 1863.

Lemaire, André. "West Semitic Epigraphy and the History of the Levant during the 12th–10th Centuries BCE." Pages 291–307 in *The Ancient Near East in the 12th–10th Centuries BCE: Culture and History. Proceedings of the International Conference Held at the University of Haifa, 2–5 May, 2010*. Edited by Gershon Galil, Ayelet Gilboa, Aren Maeir, and Dan'el Kahn. Münster: Ugarit-Verlag, 2012.

Leslau, Wolf. *Comparative Dictionary of Geᶜez (Classical Ethiopic)*. Wiesbaden: Harrassowitz, 1987.

Mankowski, Paul V. *Akkadian Loanwords in Biblical Hebrew*. Winona Lake, Ind.: Eisenbrauns, 2000.

Matras, Yaron. "Contact, Convergence, and Typology." Pages 66–85 in *The Handbook of Language Contact*. Edited by Raymond Hickey. Malden, MA: Wiley-Blackwell, 2010.

Millard, A. "Scripts and Their Uses in the 12th–10th Centuries BCE." Pages 405–12 in *The Ancient Near East in the 12th–10th Centuries BCE: Culture and History. Proceedings of the International Conference Held at the University of Haifa, 2–5 May, 2010*. Edited by Gershon Galil, Ayelet Gilboa, Aren Maeir, and Dan'el Kahn. Münster: Ugarit-Verlag, 2012.

Muffs, Jochanan. *Studies in the Aramaic Legal Papyri from Elephantine*. Leiden: Brill, 1969.

Myers-Scotton, Carol. *Multiple Voices: An Introduction to Bilingualism*. Oxford: Blackwell, 2006.

Notarius, Tania. "From *lūaḥ* to *sēp̄er* and Back: An Episode in the Historical Linguistics of Biblical Hebrew." Pp. 697–716 in *New Perspectives in Biblical and Rabbinic Hebrew*. Edited by Aaron D. Hornkohl and Geoffrey Khan. Cambridge: University of Cambridge, 2021.

Nougayrol, Jean. "L'influence babylonienne à Ugarit, d'après les textes en cunéiformes classiques." *Syria* 39 (1962): 28–35.

Olmo Lete, Gregorio del, and Joaquín Sanmartín. *A Dictionary of the Ugaritic Language in the Alphabetic Tradition*. Translated by Wilfred Watson. 2nd ed. Leiden & Boston: Brill, 2015.

Pat-El, Na'ama. "Contact or Inheritance? Criteria for Distinguishing Internal and External Change in Genetically Related Languages." *J. Lang. Contact* 6 (2013): 313–28.

Rainey, Anson F. *The El-Amarna Correspondence: A New Edition of the Cuneiform Letters from the Site of El-Amarna Based on Collations of All Extant Tablets*. Edited by William Schniedewind and Zipora Cochavi-Rainey. 2 vols. Leiden & Boston: Brill, 2015.

Sass, Benjamin. "Wadi El-Hol and the Alphabet." Pages 193–203 in *D'Ougarit à Jérusalem*. Edited by Carole Roche. Paris: De Boccard, 2008.

von Soden, Wolfram. *Akkadisches Handwörterbuch*. Wiesbaden: Harrassowitz, 1965.

Soldt, Wilfred H. van. "Babylonian Lexical, Religious and Literary Texts and Scribal Education at Ugarit." Pages 171–212 in *UGARIT - Ein Ostmediterranes Kulturzentrum im Alten Orient. Ergebnisse und Perspektiven der Forschung*. Edited by Manfred Dietrich and Oswald Loretz. Münster: Ugarit-Verlag, 1995.

Soldt, Wilfred H. van. *Studies in the Akkadian of Ugarit: Dating and Grammar*. Neukirchen-Vluyn: Neukirchener Verlag, 1991.

Soldt, Wilfred H. van. "The Akkadian of Ugarit: Lexicographic Aspects." *SEL* 12 (1995): 205–15.

Speiser, Ephraim A. *Oriental and Biblical Studies: Collected Writings of E. A. Speiser*. Edited by Jacob J. Finkelstein and Moshe Greenberg. Philadelphia: University of Pennsylvania Press, 1967.

Stein, Peter. *Die Altsudarabischen Minuskelinschriften auf Holzstabchen aus der Bayerischen Staatsbibliothek in Munchen.* Tübingen & Berlin: Warmuth, 2010.

Tawil, Hayim. *An Akkadian Lexical Companion for Biblical Hebrew.* Jersey City: Ktav, 2009.

Thomason, Sarah G. *Language Contact.* Edinburgh: University Press, 2001.

Tropper, Josef. "Kanaanäische Lehnwörter Im Ugaritischen." *UF* 35 (2003): 663–71.

Vita, Juan-Pablo. "Language Contact between Akkadian and Northwest Semitic Languages in Syria-Palestine in the Late Bronze Age." Pages 375–404 in *Semitic Languages in Contact.* Leiden & Boston: Brill, 2015.

Watson, Wilfred. "Akkadian Cognates to Some Ugaritic Words." *SEL* 25 (2008): 57–62.

Watson, Wilfred. "Akkadian Loan-Words in Ugaritic: The Hippiatric Texts." Pages 240–57 in *Biblical and Near Eastern Essays.* Edited by Carmel McCarthy and John F. Healey. London: Clark, 2004.

Watson, Wilfred. "From List to Letter: Notes on Letter-Writing Techniques." Pages 164–78 in *Society and Administration in Ancient Ugarit. Papers Read at a Symposium in Leiden, 13–14 December 2007.* Edited by Wilfred H. van Soldt. Leiden & Boston: Brill, 2010.

Watson, Wilfred. *Lexical Studies in Ugaritic.* Sabadell: Editorial Ausa, 2007.

Wehr, Hans. *Dictionary of Modern Written Arabic: Arabic-English Dictionary.* Edited by J.M. Cowan. 4th ed. Urbana IL: Spoken Language Services, 1994.

Zamora, Jose-Ángel. "Les utilisations de l'alphabet lors du IIe millénaire av. J.-C. et le développement de l'épigraphie alphabétique : Une approche à travers la documentation ougaritique en dehors des tablettes (I)." *Le royaume d'Ougarit de la Crète à l'Euphrate : Nouveaux axes de recherche. Actes du congrès international de Sherbrooke, 2005.* Edited by J.-M. Michaud. Québec: GGC, 2007.

Zimmern, Heinrich. *Akkadische Fremdwörter als Beweis für Babylonischen Kultureinfluss.* Leipzig: Hinrichs, 1917.

קוטשר, יחזקאל. *מילים ותולדותיהן.* ירושלים: קריית ספר, 1974.

William M. Schniedewind

Adaptation in Scribal Curriculum: Examples from the Letter Writing Genre

Letters have a long history as part of the ancient near eastern scribal curriculum.[1] They were already used as part of the Mesopotamian school curriculum dating back centuries before the earliest Hebrew writing. These letter exercises from the Mesopotamian curriculum were adopted, adapted, and used in the alphabetic cuneiform of the ancient city-state of Ugarit. This common ancient near eastern letter writing tradition also influenced the early Israelite scribal curriculum, where letters likely served as one of the primary school exercises. It is hardly surprising then that we have three actual examples of this scribal exercise in the inscriptions from Kuntillet 'Ajrud. These examples illustrate aspects of adaptation that were critical to scribal training.

1 Letter Writing in the Ancient Near East

Letter writing was a basic part of near eastern scribal curriculum, and its significance is illustrated by the Ugaritic, Egyptian, and Mesopotamian letters that include narrated scenes of letters being sent and received. For example, *Enmerkar and the Lord of Aratta* explains the invention of writing as resulting from the need to write letters accurately.[2] At the end of the story, Enmerkar's message became too long for his messenger's memory, and the priest-king invented writing so that his messenger could take a written response—a letter—with him to Aratta. This etiological story illustrates the transition of messenger scene and its formulae from oral to written.

---

1 I wish to thank Sara Milstein for her comments at the conference, which were helpful in sharpening my arguments for this paper. This paper brings together and further develops a variety of discussions from my book, *The Finger of the Scribe: How Scribes Learned to Write the Bible* (New York: Oxford University Press, 2019).
2 See *Context of Scripture: Canonical Composition from the Biblical World*, eds. William W. Hallo and K. Lawson Younger (Leiden: Brill, 2003), 1.170. This text also has interesting parallels to Genesis 11 and the idea of "one language"; see Thorkild Jacobsen, *The Harps That Once* (New Haven: Yale University Press, 1987), 275–319.

Letter writing was also part of the literary canon in Egypt.[3] For example, the well-known story of "The Report of Wenamun" (ca. 1100 BCE) recounts the journey of an Egyptian emissary traveling up the eastern Mediterranean coast in order to acquire Lebanese timber.[4] Wenamun arrived in the Nile delta at Tanis bringing "*dispatches* of Amun-Re, King of the Gods. They had them read out before them and they said: 'I will do, I will do as Amun-Re, King of the Gods, our lord has said.'" Wenamun travels to Byblos where he gets stranded. There, he communicates daily with the prince of Byblos using traditional messenger formulas: "Then the prince of Byblos sent to me: 'Leave my harbor!' I sent to him, saying: 'Where shall I go? If you have a ship to carry me, let me be taken back to Egypt!'" Letters were explicitly mentioned as being sent back and forth to Egypt: "(The prince of Byblos) placed my letter in the hand of his messenger, ... and sent them to Egypt." These passages illustrate how messenger scenes using the traditional formulations of letters carry the narrative thread of the story.

Likewise, Ugaritic literature uses letters to frame its literary narratives. For example, in *The Baal Cycle* (see *KTU* 1.1–6) when Yamm's messengers arrive at the Great Assembly, they employ standard letter formulae: "speak to the Bull, his Father, El: the message of Yamm ..." (l. 33).[5] Messengers, messages, and messenger formulae carry the narrative thread as illustrated in *KTU* 1.2:i:11–17:

Yamm *sends messengers*, Ruler Naharu sends an embassy.
They rejoice, ...
Go, young servants, don't delay,
head for the Great Assembly, to Mount Lalu.
Do not bow down at El's feet,
Do not prostrate yourself before the Great Assembly.

---

3 The contact between Egyptian scribes and early alphabetic scribes is also suggested by other texts like the recently published bilingual hieroglyphic-alphabetic abecedary from Theban Tomb 99, an Egyptian medical text that uses Northwest Semitic incantations, or an eleventh century Northwest Semitic instructional letter written using hieratic script; see Ben Haring, "Halaḥam on an Ostracon of the Early New Kingdom?" *Journal of Near Eastern Studies* 74 (2015), 189–95; Richard Steiner, "Northwest Semitic Incantations in an Egyptian Medical Papyrus of the Fourteenth Century B.C.E.," *Journal of Near Eastern Studies* 51 (1992), 191–200; and, Ariel Shisha-Halevy, "An Early Northwest-Semitic Text in the Egyptian Hieratic Script," *Orientalia* n.s. 47 (1978), 145–62.
4 For a convenient translation, see Miriam Lichtheim, "The Report of Wenamun," in *Context of Scripture*, 1.41.
5 For an exhaustive treatment, see Mark Smith, The Ugaritic Baal Cycle, Volume I. Introduction with Text, Translation and Commentary of KTU/CAT 1.1-1.2 (VTSup, 105; Leiden/Boston: Brill, 1994); and, Mark Smith and Wayne Pitard, The Ugaritic Baal Cycle, Volume II. Introduction with Text, Translation and Commentary of KTU/CAT 1.3–1.4 (SVT, 114; Leiden/Boston: Brill, 2009).

Standing, make your speech, repeat your information.
Speak (*rgm*) to the Bull, my father, El, repeat to the Great Assembly.
Message (*thm*) of Yammu, your master, of your lord River [Naharu]: ...

The technical terminology used is known from both actual letters and practice letters—namely, "message (*thm*) of Sender" and "speak (*rgm*) to Recipient." This again illustrates how the letter genre influences other types of literature.

The influence can also be seen in biblical narrative.[6] For example, in the story of Jacob's confrontation with Esau on his return to the land, we read as follows in Gen 32:4–14:

> *Jacob sent messengers* ahead to his brother Esau in the land of Seir, the country of Edom, *and instructed them as follows*, "Thus shall you say, 'To my lord Esau, *thus says your servant Jacob*: I stayed with Laban and remained until now; I have acquired cattle, asses, sheep, and male and female slaves; and I send this message to my lord in the hope of gaining your favor.'" *The messengers returned to Jacob, saying,* "We came to your brother Esau; he himself is coming to meet you, and there are four hundred men with him." ... Then after spending the night there, Jacob took from what was at hand and sent presents for his brother Esau...

In this narrative, this story illustrates the oral *Sitz im Leben* from which the written genre of letters arises. Although these could have originally been oral performances (without the aid of letters), the oral conventions of messengers and messenger performances become encoded in the letter genre itself, and in turn they are studied as part of scribal curriculum. In this way, the orality is textualized. In this respect, "thus says your servant Jacob" is an oral convention that ceases to be "oral" when it becomes part of learned scribal curriculum and practice.

2 A Model Letter from Ugarit

Examples of model letters in the alphabetic curriculum from ancient Ugarit are especially instructive of creative adaptation. These Ugaritic letters draw upon the

---

6 See John Greene, The Role of the Messenger and Message in the Ancient Near East (Atlanta: Scholars Press, 1989), 77–136; Dirk Schwiderski, Handbuch des nordwestsemitischen Briefformulars: Ein Beitrag zur Echtheitsfrage des aramäischen Briefe des Esrabuches (BZAW, 295; Berlin: de Gruyter, 2000), 323–27. Also see examples in 2Sam 11; 2Kgs 5:5-7, 10:1-7, 19:14, 20:12; Jer 29:1-30; Esth 9:26-29; Ezra 4-7; Neh 2:8, 6:5; 2Chr 21:12.

formal elements of the Near Eastern letter genre that have been isolated in a variety of studies.[7] A full Near Eastern introductory formula might include an Address Formula, a Prostration Formula (when appropriate), a Greeting Formula, and a request for Divine Blessing. All these elements are not present in actual letters where an economy of expression was often preferred. There are at least four examples of model letters from the archives at Ugarit (*KTU* 5.9, 5.10, 5.11, 5.33), but one example in particular can shed some light on aspects of the training of alphabetic scribes and their creative reuse of the letter model.

The model letter published as *KTU* 5.9 (=*RS* 16.265) was written on a tablet containing scribal exercises both the front and back as well as its sides.[8] The recto has a complete model letter:

KTU 5.9: Recto to Lower Edge

(1) [t]ḥm iṭtl	Message of ʾIṭtēlu
(2) l mnn.ʾlm	to whomever. May the gods
(3) tġrk.tšlmk	guard you, keep you well,
(4) tʿzzk.ʾalp ym	strengthen you, for a thousand days
(5) w rbt šnt	and ten thousand years
(6) bʿd ʿlm	through eternity.
(7) iršt.aršt	A request, I request,
(8) l aḫy.l rʿy	to my brother, to my friend.
(9) w ytnnn	And may he grant it [impf/energ]
(10) l aḫh.l rʿh	to his brother, to his friend,
(11) rʿ ʿlm.	an eternal friend.
(12) ttn.w tn	May you give [juss], and give [impv]!
(13) w l ttn	and may you indeed give [asseverative l],
(14) w al ttn	and would you not give [rhetorical]?
(15) tn ks yn	Give a cup of wine [impv],
(16) w ištn	and I shall drink it [impf/energic].

While the front is a complete model letter (transcribed above), this whole tablet actually reflects six different types of scribal exercises: a practice letter (recto),

---

7 See Pardee, *Handbook of Hebrew Letters* (Chico, CA: SBL Press, 1982), 145–49; Robert Hawley, "Studies in Ugaritic Epistolography," (PhD dissertation, University of Chicago, 2003).

8 First published in *PRU* 2, no. 19. Recent discussions include Jonathan Yogev and Shamir Yona, "A Poetic Letter: The Ugaritic Tablet RS 16.265," *Studi Epigrafici e Linguistici* 31 (2014), 51–58; Juan-Pablo Vita, "The Scribal Exercise RS 16.265 from Ugarit in its Near-Eastern Context," in *The Ancient Near East, A Life! Festschrift Karel Van Lerberghe* (*Orientalia Lovaniensia Analecta*, 220; Leuven: Peeters, 2012), 645–52.

grammatical exercises (recto), sayings (recto), abecedaries (sides), lexical items (verso), and practice signs (verso). Here, I concentrate on the front, where we find a practice letter using a formulaic saying and playful grammatical exercises.[9]

Several aspects indicate that this is no ordinary letter, but rather an embellished scribal exercise. To begin, in line 2 the letter is addressed to *mnn*, which should be understood as deriving from the Ugaritic indefinite particle *mn* "whomever."[10] The scribe intentionally uses the indefinite, "whomever," and the second part of the letter will wax eloquent as a request to an unnamed person: "his brother, his friend, his eternal friend." Of course, as scribal practice, there is no need to have a specific addressee. The letter also heaps up parallelism. In lines 3–4, we find three possible blessing words—*nǵr*, *šlm*, and *'zz* ("to guard," "to be well," and "to strengthen") that all have cognates in Hebrew (שלם, נער, and עזז). This full blessing triad can be found in a just one Ugaritic letter (*KTU* 2.4); typically, Ugaritic letters would use just one or two of these terms, whereas this practice exercise used the entire array of terms. Students learned the full variety of

---

9 Scribal exercises continue on the edges of the tablet with partial abecedaries. On the right and left edges (lines 29, 31), there is preserved the first eleven letters of the Ugaritic alphabet. On the upper edge (l. 30), there is a partial abecedary with just five letters preserved written by a less accomplished student. The reverse of the tablet has different exercises. They include lexical items, practice writing different graphemes, and a conclusion (ll. 21-23) that transpose the names from lines 1-2 (Figure 1). The verso lines are numbered slightly differently in the original publication in *PRU* 2 (no. 19), *KTU*, and by Pardee; see Pardee, "The Ugaritic Alphabetic Cuneiform Writing System in the Context of Other Alphabetic Systems," in *Studies in Semitic and Afroasiatic Linguistics Presented to Gene B. Gragg*, ed. Cynthia Miller (Chicago: Oriental Institute, 2007), figure 12.5 (p. 192). Using Pardee's numbering, the verso may be transcribed as follows:

(17) *'bd*	"servant"
(18) *qrq*	QRQ "sounds"?
(*Column II*)	
(24) *qnṣṣ.bṣṣṣpn*[ ]	random letter shapes?
(25) *ddn.dḥld*[ ]	random letter shapes?
(26) *ddwaṭd*[ ]	random letter shapes?
(*Column III*)	
(19) *prṭ*	PRṬ (PN?)
(20) *pṭ*	PṬ (PN?)
(*Column IV*)	
(21) *tḥm* +palimpsest	"Message
(22) *ḏ mn* +palimpsest	of whomever
(23) *l iṭtl*	to 'Iṭtēlu"

10 See another example of use of *mn* in a practice legal text from Ugarit; Alice Mandell, "When Form is Function: A Reassessment of the *Marziḥu* Contract (*KTU* 3.9) as a Scribal Exercise," *MAARAV* 23 (2019), 39–67.

formulae and terminology in practice exercises, but the actual letters usually reflect an economy of expression.

Most practice letters ended with the introductory section of a message as only
the formal introduction of a letter could be practiced and repeated. The body of a
letter obviously varied. Therefore, in the Ugaritic example cited above, the exercise continued with grammatical, lexical, and semantic practice. In lines 8 and
10, we have the alternative terms *aḥ* "brother" and *r'* "friend," which are never
used together in an actual Ugaritic letter—indeed, they are not really a logical
parallel, even though they are part of the larger semantic field of relationships
that are typically found in letters. Using relational terms like "mother,"
"brother," "son," or "servant" is quite typical in letters, but "my brother, my
friend" is purely a scribal flourish in this student exercise. Line 11 further embel-
lishes by adding, "an *eternal* friend." Apparently, an eternal friend is anyone who
gets you a glass of wine. Such flourishes reflect the freedom of the scribe to adapt
and be creative even within the confines of a written exercise. This creativity
would become even more important as scribes used and adapted their learning
in a variety of real-world situations.

The body of the letter also embeds adapted grammatical exercises. In line 7,
there is a reciprocal formula using a cognate accusative structure, "a request I
request," with a nominal and verbal formulation of the root *'rš* "to request." In
lines 9–15, five different verbal formulations of the Ugaritic verbal root *ytn* "to
give" appear. The last of these instances creates the jocular request, "give me a
cup of wine so that I may drink!" In the end, this letter is not a letter at all because
it is missing one of the most standard features of a letter, namely the word *rgm*
"speak!," which is a critical part of the performative aspect of the ancient missive.[11] This is not a letter to be performed, but rather a scribal exercise framed by
adapting traditional message conventions.

3 Model Letters from Kuntillet ʿAjrud

Ugaritic practice letters have several parallels in the scribal practice letters from
Kuntillet ʿAjrud. I contend that there are three practice letters (3.1, 3.6, and 3.9)
from Kuntillet ʿAjrud.[12] They illustrate aspects of the three formulaic parts of the

---

11 This is noted by Hawley, "Studies in Ugaritic Epistolography," 214–15.
12 These are now published in the official version by Ahituv, Eshel, and Meshel, "The Inscriptions," in *Kuntillet ʿAjrud: a Religious Centre from the Time of the Judaean Monarchy on the Border*

letter genre in Hebrew—the Address, the Greeting, and the Blessing. Two letters have different versions of an introductory formula, representing the two types of letters reflecting the different relationships between sender and addressee. A third practice letter is fragmentary and includes only the Blessing as well as a formulaic saying.

The introductory formula in the first example (KA 3.1 on Pithos A) can be reconstructed as follows:

KA 3.1: Superior to Inferior
1) 'mr.'[šyw.]hm[l]k.'mr.lyhl῾y'.wlyw῾šh.wl[...]brkt.'tkm.
2) lyhwh.šmrn.w'šrth

"Message of A[šyaw,] the k[in]g: "Say to Yaheli and to Yoʿasah and to [PN]. I have blessed you by Yahweh of Samaria and to his 'asherah.""

This is a shorter practice exercise that is more typical of actual letters. Letters from those of superior or equal status did not require all the embellishments of a letter sent from an inferior to a superior. To be sure, the most important part of a practice letter was the introductory formula since this is the only part of the formula that was invariably utilized, but there was still quite a bit of flexibility in the formulas that were used. For example, "Yahweh of Samaria" (in KA 3.1) might have been more appropriate in a letter from an Israelite king, whereas "Yawheh of Teman" (in KA 3.6) would be appropriate for a letter emanating from the military outpost at Kuntillet ῾Ajrud. In general, however, introductions show an economy of expression, and most actual letters known from the epigraphic corpus are quite mundane with abbreviated introductions. KA 3.1 has a concise formula used from a superior to an inferior. The personal name in this letter seems to be modeled after Joash, who was the contemporary Israelite king, hence "Ashyaw, the king"; the orthographic difference between 'šyw, "'Ashyaw," and biblical yw'š, "Joash" simply reflects the difference of the divine theophoric Yahweh (in this case, "-yaw" or "Jo-") as either a prefix or suffix that we see with other names

of Sinai, ed. Zeev Meshel (Jerusalem: Israel Exploration Society, 2012), 87, 95–97. For inscription 3.1, I follow K. McCarter, "Kuntillet ῾Ajrud: Inscribed Pithos 1 (2.47A)," in *Context of Scripture* 2:171. McCarter points out that the reign of Joash in Israel (ca. 802–787 BCE) corresponds with the dating of the Kuntillet ῾Ajrud inscriptions. Aḥituv, Eshel, and Meshel are more reserved in the official publication and do not offer a reconstruction (pp. 89-90). McCarter's reconstruction is hypothetical, but it fits with the content of the practice introduction that suggests it is from a superior to an inferior. Early on, Lemaire recognized these were student exercises, *Les écoles et la formation de la Bible dans l'ancien Israël* (OBO, 39; Fribourg, 1981).

(e.g., Ahaziah [2 Kgs 8:24] or Jehoahaz [2 Chr 21:17]; Jehoiachin [2 Kgs 24:6] or Jeconiah [Jer 24:1]).[13]

The second example is KA 3.6 (on Pithos B), which uses a fuller presentation of a possible introductory formula because it was addressed to a superior as indicated by "my lord." This example should be placed in its larger context on a pithos, which includes other scribal exercises including four abecedaries (KA 3.11–14):

Transcription KA 3.6
1) *'mr*
2) *'mryw '*
3) *mr l.'dn'y'*
4) *hšlm.'t*
5) *brktk.ly*
6) *hwh tmn*
7) *wl'šrth.yb*
8) *rk wyšmrk*
9) *wyhy 'm.'dn*
10) *y*

"Message of Amaryaw, say to my lord: 'Are you well? I have blessed you by Yahweh of Teman and his *'asherah*. May he bless you and may he keep you, and may he be with my lord."

The formal language of KA 3.6 finds close parallels in biblical literature. For example, the use of the root *'mr* "to say, speak" found in 2Kgs 22:15, the words of the prophetess Huldah, are couched in letter format: "And (Huldah) said to them: 'Thus said [*'mr*] Yahweh, the God of Israel: Say to [*'mr l-*] the man who sent you to me: ..." Here, we see both the sender and the addressee identified as we have in the practice letters. And, the identification is made with the repeated of *'mr* to reference both the speaker and the addressee—which we may generalize as, "Thus *said* Sender" and "*Say* to Addressee." The prominence of the root *'mr* "to speak" in this practice letter should remind us of the well-known prophetic introductory phrase, "Thus said YHWH (*kh 'mr YHWH*)." The phrase has its specific origins in the letter genre that begins, *'mr* PN, "Message of the Sender." In this

---

13 The reconstruction of a fictive king as an addressee in a practice letter is further supported by examples from the Amarna Scholarly tablets where three fragmentary practice letters, EA 333-344, have the expression *ana* LUGAL "to the king"; see Shlomo Izre'el, *The Amarna Scholarly Tablets* (Groningen: Styx, 1997).

respect, the prophetic speech formula, "Thus said YHWH," is directly related to the textualization of the writing prophets.[14]

There is a third example of a practice letter in KA 3.9 (on Pithos B), but the opening part of the address is missing. KA 3.9 consists of three lines written on the very top of Pithos B.[15]

KA 3.9 Transcription and Translation
1) [*'mr* PN[1] *'mr l*PN[2] *brktk*]*lyhwh.ht'm'n wl'šrth.*
2) [*w't*]*kl 'šr yš'l m'š ḥnn h' w'm pth wntn lh yhw~*
3) *klbbh*

1) [Message of PN[1], say to PN[2]: I bless you]by Yahweh of the Teman and by his *Asherah*.[16]
2) [And now,] whatever he asks from a man, he will give generously. And if he petitions, then Yahwe(h) will give to him
3) according to his heart.

Without the formal opening, scholars have not generally recognized that this is a practice letter and usually interpret it as a dedicatory inscription based on the

---

14 See my development of this observation in "Scripturalization in Ancient Judah," in *Contextualizing Israel's Sacred Writings: Ancient Literacy, Orality, and Literary Production*, ed. Brian Schmidt (Atlanta: SBL, 2015), 314–18.

15 The reconstruction is developed on the basis of the official publication and photos by Aḥituv, Eshel, and Meshel, "The Inscriptions." A more elaborate reconstruction is offered by Émile Puech, but he offers no evidence of different or better photographs upon which he bases his readings so it is difficult to have any confidence in his readings, see Puech, "Les inscriptions hébraïques de Kuntillet 'Ajrud (Sinaï)," *RB* 121-2 (2014), 172.

16 The interpretation of the Hebrew *'šrh*, which is here translated as a proper noun, is debated. See, for example, Benjamin Sass, "On epigraphic Hebrew *'ŠR* and **'ŠRH*, and on Biblical Asherah*," *Transeuphratène* 46 (2014), 50–60. Many scholars point out that a proper noun in Hebrew normally does not take a pronominal suffix as in "his Asherah." This is true in biblical Hebrew, but a proper noun also does not take a definite article as in "the Teman," which we also have here. Some scholars would therefore argue that these are not proper nouns. However, I do not think the grammar of vernacular Israelian Hebrew of the early Iron Age should be completely defined by the grammar of biblical Hebrew or even Judean Hebrew of the late Iron Age. Note the discussion by Aḥituv, *Echoes from the Past*, 221-24, 319; Mark Smith, *The Early History of God: Yahweh and the Other Deities in Ancient Israel* (2d ed; Grand Rapids: Eerdmans, 2002), 108–147; Paolo Xella, "Le dieu et 'sa' déesse: l'utilisation des suffixes pronominaux avec des théonymes d'Ebla à Ugarit et à Kuntillet 'Ajrud," *UF* 27 (1995), 599–610; Steve Wiggins, *A Reassessment of Asherah: With Further Considerations of the Goddess* (Piscataway: Gorgias Press, 2007), 197–208; Puech reads line 1 as *hmlk.'šyw.'mr.brkt.'tkm.lyhwh.htmn.w'šrth*, "Les inscriptions hébraïques de Kuntillet 'Ajrud (Sinaï)," 172–74, but he does not give any substantive evidence for these readings nor does he see this as a practice letter (even though his reading might fit such an interpretation).

fragmentary part that can be transcribed with some certainty in line 1.[17] The obscured space in line 1 is about 17–20 letters, which gives room for the reconstruction for a letter introduction according to the pattern that we have in 3.1 and 3.6. The "dedication" itself is typical of that used in letters. Given the overall context of other scribal exercises on this pithos, the introductory formulae of a letter is a straightforward and contextually supported reconstruction. The use of "dedicatory formulae" (i.e., the blessing) in letters illustrates how scribal learning involves adaption and reuse in a variety of contexts.

The second part (lines 2–3) utilizes a reciprocal saying akin to *KTU* 5.9:7 as the body of the letter. More generally, the combination of the letter genre with other student exercises is paralleled in *KTU* 5.9. This parallel text was discussed above, but it is worth recalling it here since it also incorporates a different type of student exercise into a practice letter. Indeed, the tablet as a whole continues with lexical and writing exercises, so it actually mixes a variety of types of student practice into one tablet. The main point to this parallel is simply that the body of a practice letter can provide the opportunity for a student to practice other traditional parts of student exercises. Many exercises in writing letters may just include the first part, that is, the formal introductory elements. These are rigid and repeatable. The content of a letter, however, must be completely flexible. This opens up the possibility for a playful student exercise in *KTU* 5.9 as well as the pious proverbial saying in the Kuntillet ʿAjrud example. Indeed, in the playful and practical adaptations of student exercises, we begin to witness scribal creativity that would be a foundation for authoring literature.

The introductions to such model letters tend to be more complete than actual letters. In our Hebrew exemplars, the most complete practice letter is exemplified by Inscription 3.6 on Pithos B. A good parallel to this is found in the Ugaritic tablet, which is a relatively complete student exercise. Two aspects of the Ugaritic practice letter are especially notable. First, the triple invocation of the gods' protection is unusual; in actual Ugaritic letters, there is never more than one or two of these phrases used. Typically, "may the gods of Ugarit keep you well (Ugaritic, *šlm*; cp. Hebrew, שלם)." Actual letters evince more economy, whereas practice exercises can reflect nice scribal flourishes as well as the combination of different

17 This is partially recognized in the treatment by Dobbs-Allsop et al., where they call it a "blessing formula" but not a practice letter (see *Hebrew Inscriptions from the Biblical Period* [New Haven: Yale University Press, 2005], 296). It is not observed in the official publication by Aḥituv, Eshel, and Meshel, "The Inscriptions," 98–100 nor in the inscription handbook by Aḥituv, *Echoes of the Past: Hebrew and Cognate Inscriptions from the Biblical Period* (Jerusalem: Carta, 2008), 318–19.

types of school texts. For example, many of the Arad letters skip most of the elements of the introduction except an abbreviated Address Formula (e.g., *'l 'lšb* "To Eliashib," see Arad letters 1–11; or, *'l 'dny 'lšb* "To my lord, Eliashib," Arad 18:1–2).[18] A more complete Address formula with a Greeting is found in Arad 16: *'ḥk ḥnnyhw šlḥ lšlm 'lšb wlšlm bytk* "Your brother, Hananiah, sends greetings to Eliashib and greetings to your house." The Divine Blessing is one of the standard parts of a form letter that is preserved in several letters (e.g., *brktk lyhwh* "I bless you to Yahweh," Arad 16:2–3, 21:2, 40:3). An alternative type of divine blessing is found in most of the Lachish letters but not in the Arad correspondence: "May Yahweh cause you to hear a report of peace (or, a good report)" (see Lachish 2:1–2, 3:2–3; 4:1–2; 5:1–2; 8:1–2; 9:1–2).[19] In general, the letters found at the major Judean city of Lachish have more complete, formal introductions than the abbreviated introductions found in the remote fortress of Arad.

Student exercises indicate that there was no rigid form to actual letters, even though there are a number of typical elements. Students needed to learn the various permutations of the introduction as well as the transition. In Hebrew letters, typical elements begin with an introduction (*praescriptio*) that includes an address formula. The introduction sometimes includes a greeting formula or a divine benediction.[20] The introduction is then followed by a formal transition to the body of the letter, "and now" (written *w't* in inscriptions and *plene, w'th,* in biblical texts). The body of the letter, of course, was entirely variable. There was apparently no rigid form to the model letter that students practiced. In this respect, we should not be surprised by the differences between the three practice letters from Kuntillet ʿAjrud.

---

18 This pattern actually follows the large corpus of the Mari letters, which also have just the abbreviated address without all the additional formalities; see Wolfgang Heimpel, *Letters to the King of Mari: A New Translation, with Historical Introduction, Notes, and Commentary* (Winona Lake: Eisenbrauns, 2003).

19 Alternatively, the sender may wish that "Yahweh cause you to see peace" (e.g., Lachish 6:1-2).

20 See Juan-Luis Cunchillos, "The Correspondence of Ugarit," in *Handbook of Ugaritic Studies*, eds. Wilfred Watson and Nicolas Wyatt (Leiden: Brill, 1999), 359–74; Hawley, "Studies in Ugaritic Epistolography," and Pardee, *Handbook of Ancient Hebrew Letters.*

4 Letter Writing Exercises and Biblical Literature

The content within ancient Hebrew letters also alludes to the central role of letters and messengers in ancient Israel. Several mention letters and messengers as a subject matter discussed within the letter (see Arad 16, 24, 40; Lachish 3, 5, 6, 7, 16, 18). Lachish Letter 3 nicely illustrates an interaction with multiple letters.

> [Introduction] Your servant Hoshaiah sends (*šlḥ*) to report (*ngd*) to my lord Yaush: May Yahweh cause my lord to hear a good report.
>
> [Body] And now (*wʿth*), please explain to your servant the meaning of the letter (*spr*) that you sent (*šlḥ*) to your servant yesterday. For your servant has been sick at heart ever since you sent (*šlḥ*) it to your servant. And, because my lord said, "Don't you know how to read a letter (*spr*)?" As Yahweh lives, no one has ever tried to read me a letter (*spr*)! And also, any letter (*spr*) comes to me, I can read it. And moreover, I can recount everything in it.
>
> And, as for your servant, it has been reported (*ngd*), saying (*l'mr*), "General Koniah son of Elnatan has moved south in order to enter Egypt." He has sent (*šlḥ*) (messengers) to fetch Hodaviah son of Aḥiah and his men from here.
>
> And, as for the letter (*spr*) of Tobiah, servant of the king, which came to Shallum son of Yadaʿ, from the prophet saying (*l'mr*), "Beware," your servant has sent (*šlḥ*) it to my lord.

The body of the letter begins with a direct response by a junior officer to a superior officer questioning whether he was able to read or needed a scribe to help with the letter. The scribe's claim to be able to recite the content of the letter also recalls the etiological origins of letter writing—that is, as an aid to memory in the oral delivery of messages. In the next paragraph, the junior officer then relates a communiqué about the commander of the army traveling to Egypt. He apparently is sending letters (*šlḥ*) to fetch some other personnel to his location. Finally, in the last paragraph, he relays a message from an unnamed prophet written in a letter from a royal servant named Tobiah to Shallum. Thus, in addition to his own correspondence, he is relaying the contents of two other separate correspondences. This is not unusual. Another letter, Lachish 6, mentions other letters passed along to him from the king and military officers that apparently contained some disconcerting news, although the exact content is not relayed. These examples serve to underscore how significant the writing of letters had become in Judean bureaucracy at all levels.

The terminology utilized in ancient Hebrew letters would also be used in biblical narratives. These terms include *l'mr* "saying," *spr* "letter," *ngd* "to report,"[21]

---

21 Always in the *Hiphil* conjugation, for example, *lhgd* */lehaggīd/* "to report," in Lachish 3:1-2.

šlḥ "to send," and *šlm* "welfare" (as illustrated in Lachish Letter 3 above). These are some of the most common terms and expressions in the Hebrew Bible. Especially note the use of *l'mr* "saying" as part of the reporting of previous letters. This stylistic letter writing feature would become a standard part of biblical narrative where it is used to introduce direct quotes. The phrase occurs about 900 times in the Hebrew Bible. Two of the more interesting examples of this expression in biblical literature underscore its close association with the letter genre. In 2Kgs 5:6, a messenger from the king of Aram "brought the letter from the king of Israel, saying (*l'mr*): 'And now (*w'th*), ...'." And, according to 2Kgs 10:1–2, "Jehu wrote letters and sent them to Samaria, to the rulers of Jezreel, to the elders, and to the guardians of the sons of Ahab, saying (*l'mr*): 'And now (*w'th*), ...'." Both of these examples are striking because they incorporate—without adaptation—the standard transitional expression that is found in the Hebrew epigraphic corpus, "and now" (*w'th*); this directly connects the use of *l'mr* "saying" with the letter genre (see further discussion below).[22] In other words, although *l'mr* often seems to just repeat the idea of the speech act already expressed in the narrative framing, it is actually the formal introduction to direct speech drawn out of the *Sitz im Leben* of messenger formulas and the letter genre.

The background of *l'mr* "saying" in the letter genre is further underscored by the two practice letters from Kuntillet ʿAjrud. These letters use with the same verbal root as *l'mr* "saying" in the prefatory introduction, "Speech (*'mr*) of PN." The introduction to the letter is not direct speech, but rather it introduces the direct "speech" /*'ōmer*/ by the sender of the letter. And, the connection is further developed in the use of the expression, "thus *says* PN" (*kh 'mr* PN), in the messenger formula. This is well-known in the expression, "thus says Yahweh," but it can be used more generally as in "thus says Pharaoh" (Exod 5:10), "thus says Balak" (Num 22:16), or "thus says Ben-Hadad" (1Kgs 20:5). Indeed, the latter examples are the origin of what becomes the more frequently used expression in the Bible, "Thus said YHWH." The sending of messages with messengers did not require actual written letters. But with the advent and spread of writing, the letter becomes a physical witness in the oral performance by a messenger.

The letter genre finds a variety of expressions in biblical literature. Perhaps the most well-known of these is prophetic speech—"Thus said YHWH"—which

---

22 Formally, the expression *l'mr* "saying" parallels the use of the imperative verb *rgm* "speak thus," which introduces direct speech in Ugaritic letters. For example, *KTU* 2.16 begins, "Message of Talmiyanu: To Ṭarriyell, my mother, *speak* (*rgm*): 'May it be well ...'." Other parallels may be found in Mesopotamian letters such as the Mari corpus where we find *qibima umma* "speak, thus."

borrows directly from the genre and *Sitz im Leben* of letter writing. The role of the messenger and written letters is also a trope in biblical storytelling. But the influence of practicing to write letters can also be quite prosaic.

The expression, *w ʿt(h)*[23] "and now," was an important device that functioned as a new paragraph marker and was learned by ancient scribes when practicing the writing of model letters.[24] The use of *w ʿt(h)* is especially important in ancient Hebrew because the writing system did not have many auxiliary markers to mark semantic functions in the way we have in modern languages (e.g., commas, periods, spaces, line breaks, tabs, paragraphs, etc). The only regularly used auxiliary marker in epigraphic Hebrew was a dot "•" that was often used as a word divider. By the time of the Dead Sea Scrolls, the "•" was replaced by the space.[25] In addition, paragraphing and larger breaks using empty space were beginning to be seen in the Scroll manuscripts. However, there is little evidence that such conventions were used in epigraphic Hebrew. For this reason, the use of *w ʿt(h)* as a paragraph marker is especially critical in the early development of Hebrew writing.

Paragraph dividers in letter writing serve a universal semantic function. In the Amarna Letters and Ugarit, auxiliary scribal markers served as a functional equivalent to the lexical *w ʿt(h)* "and now." Both the Amarna Letters and Ugaritic regularly employed a horizontal line in a variety of ways to distinguish logical

---

23 The typical spelling in Epigraphic Hebrew is the shorted form *w ʿt*, while the longer (*plene*) spelling *w ʿth* is found in Standard Biblical Hebrew. The orthography has been the subject of some discussion. Dennis Pardee rightly rejected Freedman's suggestion that the defective spelling in inscriptions "indicates a pronunciation of *ʿat* or *ʿēt*" (David Noel Freedman, "The Orthography of the Arad Ostraca," *IEJ* 19 [1969], 52; cited by Dennis Pardee, "Letters from Tel Arad," *UF* 10 [1978], 292). Pardee favors Aharoni's vocalization, *ʿattā*, which was based on the variation in the spelling of 2ms verbal forms (e.g., *yd ʿth*, Arad 40:9; see Aharoni, *Arad Inscriptions* [Jerusalem: IES, 1981], 12). Freedman's suggestion makes it is difficult to account for the Standard Biblical Hebrew orthography. As Pardee had noted, the vocalization of *w ʿt* is uncertain, and it is difficult to know whether its status in Epigraphic Hebrew as a homograph with *ʿēt* "time" might have influenced the biblical orthography or whether its orthography was simply the reflection of a phonological development.

24 The transitional particle *w ʿt* was identified by Pardee in an article ("Letters from Tel Arad," *UF* 10 [1978], 289–336) as well as his co-authored *Handbook of Ancient Hebrew Letters* (1982). He notes that although he translates *w ʿt* literally, "it corresponds more nearly to a paragraph division in English usage" (1978: 292). For a more complete discussion of this marker in NWS texts, see my forthcoming contribution to the Pardee *Festschrift*, "'And now': The Transition Particle in Epigraphic Hebrew and Biblical Hebrew."

25 For a general overview of the history and function of the space in writing, see Paul Saenger, *Space Between Words: The Origins of Silent Reading* (Figurae: Reading Medieval Culture; Palo Alto: Stanford University Press, 1997).

semantic units in texts, and this included marking off sections (or "paragraphs") within letters.[26] Alphabetic Ugaritic letters often utilized a single horizontal line to separate the *praescriptio* (that is, the address and the greeting) from the body of a letter. Frequently, Ugaritic letters separated both elements of the *praescriptio* with a line. Occasionally, they omitted the line, so it is not entirely consistent (e.g., KTU 2:10).

The use of *w't* as a sectional divider in Epigraphic Hebrew letters is consistent and impressive. It either occurs or can be restored from context in seventeen of the Arad letters (1:2, 2:1, 3:1, 5:1–2, 6:1, 7:1–2, 8:1, 9:1, 10:1, 11:2, 14:1, 16:3, 17:1, 18:3, 21:3, 40:4); it appears five times in the Lachish Letters (2:3, 3:4, 4:1–2, 5:2–3; 9:3); and, it also appears once in a Wadi Murabba'at papyrus.[27] Other Iron Age Canaanite letters use *w't* as well; for example, it is found in an Edomite letter from Horvat 'Uza and an Ammonite letter from Tell El-Mazār.[28] In all of these cases, *w't* served as a transitional particle denoting the shift from the *praescriptio* (that is, the formal address and greeting) to the body of the letter. From a formal point of view, *w't* marks the progression from the scribe announcing the sender (and sometimes a formal stereotyped greeting) to the actual content of the message. This makes explicit the shift in speaker from the scribe himself to the scribe as mouthpiece of the sender. The paragraph marker *w't* realigns the focus from the metapragmatic structure of the letter to the actual letter itself.[29] A few examples illustrate both the variety and consistency of its usage in inscriptions:

---

26 See Fred Mabie, "Ancient Near Eastern Scribes and the Mark(s) They Left: A Catalog and Analysis of Scribal Auxiliary Marks in the Amarna Corpus and in the Cuneiform Alphabetic Texts of Ugarit and Ras Ibn Hani" (PhD dissertation, UCLA, 2004).

27 Some of the unprovenanced texts like the Moussaieff Ostracon or the "Silver, Pistachio and Grain" Ostracon must be treated with some skepticism (see Dobbs-Allsopp et al., *Hebrew Inscriptions*, 570–71, and Aḥituv, *Echoes from the Past*, 199–202). The latter, for example, has the incorrect epigraphic spelling *w'th* (as in SBH, but not Epigraphic Hebrew), which makes it even more suspect as a forgery.

28 On Horvat 'Uza, see Itzhaq Beit-Arieh and Bruce Cresson, "An Edomite Ostracon from Ḥorvat 'Uza," *Tel Aviv* 12 (1985), 97–98; and, on Tell el-Mazār letter, see Khair Yassine and Javier Teixidor, "Ammonite and Aramaic Inscriptions from Tell el-Mazār in Jordan," *BASOR* 264 (1986), 47. Also see Schwiderski, *Handbuch des nordwestsemitischen Briefformulars*, 55–61.

29 Metapragmatics is the linguistic anthropology category that studies how language characterizes speech awareness, functions, and reference. In the present case, metapragmatics seems like a useful theoretical category for *w't* inasmuch as it marks an awareness in the shift of the function of language and speakers. On metapragmatics, see Michael Silverstein, "The Limits of Awareness," in *Linguistic Anthropology: A Reader*, Alessandro Duranti, ed. (Malden: Blackwell, 2001), 382–401.

1) Arad 1
1:1 ʾl.ʾlyšb.w
1:2 ʿt.ntn. lktym
"To Elyashib: And now, give to the Kittim ..."

2) Arad 16
16:1 ʾḥk.ḥnnyhw.šlḥ lšl
16:2 m.ʾlyšb.wlšlm bytk br
16:3 ktk lyhwh.wʿt kṣʾty
"Your brother, Hananiah, sends for the welfare of Elyashib and for the welfare of your house. I bless you by Yahweh. And now, when I left ..."

3) Lachish 3
3:1 ʿbdk.hwšʿyhw šlḥ.l
3:2 hgd lʾdny yʾwš.yšmʿ
3:3 yhwh ʾt ʾdny šmʿt šlm
3:4 wšmʿt ṭb[.]wʿt.hpqḥ
"Your servant, Hoshayahu, sends to tell my lord Yaush: May Yahweh cause my lord to hear a report of peace and a good report. And now, please open..."

The use of *wʿt* is as a transition marker so consistent in Iron Age inscriptions that one must assume that it was a device that scribes learned to use in writing letters.[30]

So, how did this rudimentary element of letters impact biblical literature? The expression *wʿth* (always with the full spelling) is remarkably common in biblical Hebrew, appearing 273 times. In other words, more than half of the 435 occurrences in biblical literature of the word *ʿth* (עתה, "now") are with the conjunctive particle *waw* underscoring its predominant usage as a transitional expression.[31] This is unusual. The word *ʿth* "now" should be a common enough word, but the even more frequent use of *wʿth* is noteworthy. This frequent construction

---

30 The paragraph marker was also used in Aramaic dialects as well. Beginning with biblical Aramaic, the Book of Ezra uses *wkʿnt*, *wkʿt*, and *wkʿn*—which all may be translated "and now"—as opening transitional particles in its letters (4:11, 17; 5:17; 7:12). The Aramaic Hermopolis Papyri frequently employ *wkʿt* (e.g., 1:3, 2:4, 4:4, 5:2, 6:3, 10:2), and we also find *wkʿn*, *kʿn*, *kʿnt*, and *wkʿt* in the Elephantine papyri. See James Lindenberger, *Ancient Aramaic and Hebrew Letters* (Atlanta: Scholars Press, 1994). Also see Schwiderski, *Handbuch des nordwestsemitischen Briefformulars*, 164–73.

31 The standard Hebrew Dictionary of Koehler and Baumgartner suggests that 241 out of 273 occurrences introduce a new section, while 24 times it may be translated "but now." A few of these adversarial examples are actually suspect (e.g., Gen 32:11; Deut 10:22), while the remainder are concentrated in later Biblical Hebrew (e.g., Isa 43:1, 44:1, 47:8, 48:16, 49:5, 64:7; Hag 2:4; Ezr 9:8).

reflects the basic scribal education where the expression *w'th* was taught to all young scribes as part of the rubrics of letter writing. The usefulness of *w'th* as a transition particle in letters was then adapted in a variety of contexts in biblical literature.

The use of the expression *w'th* within oral discourse is complicated by its role in the scribal rubric. The oral aspects of the expression are evident in biblical literature. For example, *w'th* is sometimes followed by an imperative of *šm'* "hear, listen" (e.g., Gen 27:8, 43; Deut 4:1; 1Sam 8:9, 15:1, 26:19, 28:22), and the Dead Sea Scrolls also feature this construction (e.g., CD 1:1, 2:2, 2:14, 4Q185, 4Q525). This use of *w'th* with an imperative of *šm'* "hear, listen" can be taken as evidence of its use as a marker in oral discourse. For example, Pardee suggests, "Such a usage arose from standard speech wherein *w't* marks the point of transition between a preamble of any kind (historical, circumstantial, causal) and the point of a given statement."[32] This suggestion is substantiated by a survey of its use in biblical literature. Indeed, all 26 occurrences of *w'th* in the Book of Genesis appear within direct speech. For example, in Gen 3:22 we read (using the NRSV translation for illustrative purposes),

> Then the LORD God said, "See, the man has become like one of us, knowing good and evil; *and now (w'th)*, he might reach out his hand and take also from the tree of life."

At the same time, direct speech is textualized in letter writing, and learned as part of scribal practice. Indeed, these examples precisely represent the use of *w'th* in the context of a letter. It transitions the introduction to the body of the model letter as follows: "Message/Speech of the Sender to the Recipient: May you be blessed by YHWH. How is your well-being? *And now*, [Body of the Message]." Thus, *w't(h)* was formally embedded in direct speech, and it was also learned as a textual formula. Since the origin of the expression was as a regular feature of oral discourse, we might have expected it to continue in vernacular Hebrew, especially Rabbinic Hebrew. But it did not. It disappears in Rabbinic Hebrew. On the other hand, if a primary role of *w't(h)* was as a scribal marker for a semantic transition, that is, as a formal scribal device taught to scribes as a marker of a new section within a messenger's speech, then the disappearance in later Hebrew can be explained with a change in scribal education.

The relationship between the use of *w't(h)* in Epigraphic Hebrew and in SBH warrants some reflection. To wit, how is its regular usage as a transitional parti-

---

32 Pardee, "Arad Letters," 292.

cle, essentially a paragraph divider, reflected in biblical literature? It is quite regularly used in biblical speeches as a transitional marker in the speech. In addition to marking transitions in oral discourse, there are instances that recall its more formal use in letter writing. For example, we read in 1Sam 15:1, "Samuel said to Saul, "YHWH sent me to anoint you king over his people Israel; and now (w'th), listen to the words of YHWH. ..." Here the function of w'th is both transitional and metapragmatic as in Epigraphic Hebrew. Likewise, the use of w'th followed by the imperative šm' "hear" seems to harken back to the messenger formula utilized in letters.[33] For example, the narrator subtly employs features of a formal messenger scene in 1Sam 28:21–22, "The woman came to Saul, and when she saw that he was terrified, she said to him, 'Your maidservant has listened to you; I have taken my life in my hand, and have listened to what you have said to me. And now, you also listen (w'th šm'-n') to your maidservant: let me set a morsel of bread before you.'" The role of w'th in letters is most explicit in 2Kgs 5:6, "He brought the letter (hspr) to the king of Israel, which read (l'mr): 'And now (w'th), when this letter reaches you, know that I have sent to you my servant Na'aman that you may cure him of his leprosy.'" Similarly, we read in 2Kgs 10:1–2, "So Jehu wrote letters and sent them to Samaria, to the rulers of Jezreel, to the elders, and to the guardians of the sons of Ahab, which read (l'mr): 'And now (w'th), your master's sons are with you...'" In these last two examples, the use of w'th most closely reminds us of Epigraphic Hebrew with regard to their context of written letters; it is worth noting that w'th actually follows l'mr which is traditionally translated "saying" but is functionally a metapragmatic marker of a direct quotation translated in these contexts as "which read." These examples indicate an awareness and probably the influence of the metapragmatic use of w't known from Epigraphic Hebrew letters. Since writing lacks many of the semiotic cues of speech, developing semiotic markers like the dot (•) as a word divider (i.e., a "space"), l'mr as a quotation mark, and w'th as a paragraph marker gave biblical authors the pragmatic tools needed to help readers understand the written word.

While the origins of w't(h) was probably as a marker in oral discourse, it was borrowed for formal use in the practice of writing letters—one of the main tasks of the scribal enterprise and one of the foundations of early scribal education. It was this formal use that in turn explains why w't(h) came to be used so commonly in biblical texts. It certainly was a textual device of great familiarity to the scribes of biblical literature just as it was a regular feature in letters written in Epigraphic Hebrew.

---

33 Examples of the expression w'th šm' (or variations thereof) include Gen 27:8, 42; Ex 19:5; Deut 4:1; 1Sam 8:9, 15:1, 25:7, 26:19; Isa 44:1, 47:8; Jer 37:20, 42:18; Amos 7:16; Prov 5:7.

5 From Letters and Messengers to Prophetic Speech

The most striking adaption of the letter genre in biblical literature is prophetic speech, although most scholars emphasize its roots in the *Sitz im Leben* of the messenger and messenger speech (e.g., Gen 32:4–14).[34] The messenger scene involved a sender, a messenger, a message, and an audience. These elements were all part of prophetic speech. God sent (*šlḥ*) the prophet, his messenger, with the "word of God" (the message), to an audience—usually, the Judean people as a group. One of the titles that became associated with prophet is *mal'āḵ* "messenger." In post-exilic biblical literature, the term developed into a synonym for a prophet. The last book of the Hebrew canon is, in fact, the prophetic book of Malachi, literally "my messenger." The prophet Haggai was given the title, "the messenger of God" (1:13); the book of Chronicles concludes by referring to the prophets as divine messengers (2Chr 36:15); and deutero-Isaiah refers to the prophets as "my messengers" (Isa 44:26). This adoption of the term *mal'āḵ* "messenger" for the prophets reflected the fact that they were sent (*šlḥ*) by God; for example, in 2Sam 12:25, "YHWH sent (a message) by the hand of the prophet Nathan" (also see Judg 6:8; 2Kgs 17:13; Jer 14:14–15, 23:21, 25:4; etc).

The prophetic message was the "word of YHWH"—a technical term in the Hebrew Bible that refers to a divine speech.[35] Thus, we find the formal expression, "the word of YHWH came to the prophet," repeated frequently (more than 40x) within the Hebrew Bible.[36] The meaning and form of the "word of YHWH" was transformed in the post-exilic period. Specifically, prophetic speech—"the word of YHWH"—was textualized and broadened. For example, it came to be equated with *Torah* as a written text (e.g., 2Chr 34:21; 35:6). The genre of the letter itself

---

34 See already Ludwig Köhler, *Deuterojesaja (Jesaja 40–55) stilkritisch untersucht* (BZAW, 37; Giessen: Töpelmann, 1923). Also see Claus Westermann, *Basic Forms of Prophetic Speech* (translated from German; Louisville: Westminster/John Knox, 1991), 98–128; and James Ross, "The Prophet as Yahweh's Messenger," in *Israel's Prophetic Heritage: Essays in Honor of James Muilenberg*, eds. Benedict Anderson and Walter Harrelson (New York: Harper, 1962), 98–107.

35 This point is made in a classic article by Sigmund Mowinckel, "'The Sprit' and the 'Word' in the Pre-exilic Reforming Prophets," *JBL* 53 (1934), 199–227.

36 Occasionally, this expression will be used for someone not normally considered a prophet; e.g., Abram in a vision (Gen 15:1), Solomon (1Kgs 6:11). These are exceptions.

facilitated this shift from the oral message ("word of YHWH") to a physical manuscript ("scroll of the Torah").[37] But the shift from oral to written was easily facilitated by the shift in the messenger *Sitz im Leben* from an oral message to a messenger carrying written texts. In this respect, the transition from the early (oral)
prophets like Nathan and Samuel to the so-called writing prophets of the Hebrew
Bible was shaped by the development of the scribal curriculum itself—particularly in the development of letter writing. That is, the development of the letter
genre and its linguistic formalities paved the path for the writing prophets.

Royal bureaucracy may have also played a role in the adaptation of the messenger formula. As the writing prophets became royal counselors in a bureaucracy that increasingly utilized writing, so also the prophets adapted the tools of
that bureaucracy—in this case, letter writing. Some of the most famous prophets
of Hebrew Bible are portrayed as members of the royal administration. Of course,
it was not necessary to be a part of the royal administration for prophets to be
acquainted with the protocols of sending messengers or writing letters. Prophets
like Jeremiah were clearly outside of the official bureaucracy, yet the Book of Jeremiah shows evidence of adapting the protocols of letter writing in its presentation of the "word of YHWH." This observation accords well with John Holladay's
classic essay on "Statecraft and the Prophets of Israel," where he argued that
royal letters were one of the categories of Assyrian statecraft that had a particular
influence on the rise of the writing prophets. Holladay argues that the royal messenger was a figure and a form that transcended boundaries, and he describes
"the spectacular rise to prominence of the royal herald as an essential instrument
of imperial government."[38] But Holladay probably overstates the immediate impact of Assyrian statecraft. We should notice instead how the writing prophets
borrow and adapt elements of their own scribal curriculum.

The introductory language of the message is reflected in prophetic speech.
The expression, "Thus said YHWH (*kh 'mr yhwh*)," is adapted from "the typical
letter form."[39] Almost a century ago, Jack Lundblom pointed out that this formula
had strong parallels in Near Eastern letter writing, and new discoveries have only
further confirmed his observation.[40] The formula occurs 293 times in the Hebrew

---

37 See my comments in "Scripturalization in Ancient Judah," 314–15.

38 John Holladay, "Assyrian Statecraft and the Prophets of Israel," in *Prophecy in Israel: Search for Identity*, ed. David Petersen (Philadelphia: Fortress; London: SPCK, 1987), 130.

39 Holladay, "Assyrian Statecraft and the Prophets of Israel," 123.

40 Jack Lindblom, "Die prophetische Orakelformel," in *Die literarische Gattung der pro-phetischen Literatur* (Uppsala: A-B Lundequistska Bokhandeln, 1924), appendix; see further Westermann, *Forms of Prophetic Speech*, 35–36., and especially for the Mari Letters, Wolfgang

Bible, and the formula lent authority to the prophetic word. As pointed out above, there are two formal forms to a letter: one from a superior to an inferior and one from an inferior/equal to a superior/equal. The prophetic messenger formula naturally followed the form of a letter from a superior to an inferior. The most common Ancient Near Eastern example for this were letters written from a king. Indeed, in Marc Brettler's study, *God is King: Understanding an Israelite Metaphor*, he discusses the many parallels wherein divine kingship draws directly upon human kingship. [41] His study could have been extended further to include the use of messengers and the adaptation of the letter genre for prophetic speech. In the Hebrew Bible God is like a human king in his use of messengers, and prophetic speech is essentially an adaptation of the royal letter genre.

One of the more striking examples of prophecy by letter is in Jeremiah 29. The chapter begins, "These are the words of a letter that the prophet Jeremiah sent." It also mentions the scribe who served as the messenger (v. 3), "The letter was sent through Elasah, son of Shaphan and Gemariah, son of Hilkiah." A second letter is then mentioned in Jer 29:24–32:[42]

> To Shemaiah the Nehelamite you shall say: Thus said YHWH of Hosts, the God of Israel: Because you sent letters in your own name to all the people in Jerusalem, to Zephaniah son of Maaseiah, the priest, and to the rest of the priests, saying, "YHWH appointed you priest instead of Jehoiada, the priest, to exercise authority in the House of YHWH over every madman who plays a prophet, to put him into the stocks and into the pillory. Now why have you not rebuked Jeremiah of Anathoth, who plays a prophet among you? For he has actually sent a message [in a letter] to us in Babylon, saying: 'It will be a long time. Build houses and live in them, plant gardens and enjoy their fruit.'" The priest Zephaniah read this letter in the hearing of Jeremiah, the prophet. And, the word of YHWH came to Jeremiah: Send a message [in the form of a letter] to all the exiles, saying: "Thus said YHWH concerning Shemaiah the Nehelamite: Because Shemaiah prophesied to you, though I did not send him, and has led you to trust a lie, assuredly, thus said YHWH: 'I am going to punish Shemaiah the Nehelamite and his offspring. There shall be no man of his line dwelling among this people or seeing the good things I am going to do for My people'—declares YHWH —for he has urged disloyalty toward YHWH."

Heimpel, *Letters to the King of Mari: A New Translation with Historical Introduction, Notes, and Commentary* (Winona Lake: Eisenbrauns, 2003).

41 Marc Brettler, *God is King: Understanding an Israelite Metaphor* (JSOTSS, 76; Sheffield: Sheffield Academic Press, 1989).

42 See Meindert Dijkstra, "Prophecy by Letter (Jeremiah XXIX 24-32)," *VT* 33 (1983), 319–22.

In these letters, the textualization of the prophetic word is actualized in the form of letters. Of course, the letter genre more generally became the genre of prophetic speech, but these examples give this textualization an explicit narrative framing. One might even suggest that the word of YHWH was commissioned as a text in the form of letters. In a sense, these examples offer justification for the textualization of the divine word, that is, for the genre of the writing prophets.

6 Wisdom Sayings in Letter Writing

The practice letter KA 3.9 also includes a fragment from the proverbial sayings genre (lines 2–3), "whatever he asks from a man, he will give generously. And if he petitions, then Yahwe(h) will give to him according to his desire," as part of a student exercise that begins with a practice letter. Indirect parallels can be found in a variety of places. For example, in an Aramaic Inscription from eastern Turkey, the Sam'alian king Panamu wrote, *wmz 'š'l mn 'lhy ytn ly* "And whatever I shall ask from my god, may he give to me" (*KAI* 214:4), and also in the same inscription, *wmh 'š'l mn 'lhy mt ytnw ly* "and whatever I shall ask from my god, surely he shall give me" (ll. 12–13). There are close linguistic parallels here with the terms *š'l* "to ask" and *ntn* "to give" as well as with the syntactic structure. Scholars have also suggested a number of biblical correlates including the following:

> Ps 20:5 *ytn lk klbbk* "He shall give to you according to your desire"
> Ps 37:21 *ṣdyq ḥwnn wnwtn* "the righteous is generous and gives"
> Ps 37:26 *kl hywm ḥwnn wmlwh* "he is always generous and lends"
> Ps 112:5 *ṭwb 'yš ḥwnn wmlwh* "all goes well with the man who lends generously"

We may imagine that such language would have been learned and memorized from school exercises, then applied in a variety of literary contexts. Indeed, the example from Psalm 112, which is an acrostic psalm, might itself have its origins as an adapted school exercise.

Arguably, the most striking parallel to the Kuntillet 'Ajrud wisdom saying is Psalm 20:5. The appeal to the "God of Jacob" suggests that Psalm 20 may have originally been a northern psalm, and this would add another connection to the northern traits of the site of Kuntillet 'Ajrud and its inscriptions.[43] The psalm also

---

43 But the language of the psalm as a whole is not demonstrably northern; see Gary Rendsburg, *Linguistic Evidence for the Northern Origin of Selected Psalms* (*SBLMS* 43; Atlanta: Scholars,

has some salient motifs that point to its use in royal liturgy. For example, the psalm ends with the enjoinder, "O Yahweh, give victory to the king!" (v. 10a [English, 9a]). This is significant given the royal motifs in the iconography of the Kuntillet ʿAjrud drawings,[44] as well as the apparent mention of a king in one of the letter templates (KA 3.1).

The combination of the letter genre with a different scribal exercise is paralleled in one school tablet from Ugarit, *KTU* 5.9. After the introduction, the body of the letter (ll. 7–16) is used for a humorous grammatical exercise (e.g., using the verbal forms of the word *ytn* "to give"): "And may he give it to his brother … and I shall drink it." The content of a letter, of course, must be completely flexible. This opens up the possibility of attaching a playful student exercise as we find in *KTU* 5.9, or adding a pious proverbial saying as we find in the Kuntillet ʿAjrud example. What is relevant here is the way the genre of a letter allows the student to adapt the body of the letter to various types of practice.

The proverbial saying in KA 3.9 is more significant than first meets the eye. In this particular case, such sayings were learned by scribes and employed especially in diplomatic correspondence (although they could be adapted and used for various purposes). Once we recognize the pattern, we can adduce further parallels. For example, scholars have long noted certain correlations between the biblical Psalms and the Amarna diplomatic corpus.[45] One example is Psalm 21:3 [Eng. v. 2], תַּאֲוַת לִבּוֹ נָתַתָּה לּוֹ וַאֲרֶשֶׁת שְׂפָתָיו בַּל־מָנַעְתָּ "You give him the desire of his heart, and you do not withhold any request." This also has a certain general resonance with KA 3.9, but has an even more impressive parallel with a Babylonian letter to Pharaoh (EA 9:7–10):

> ul-tu ab-bu-ú-a-a ù ab-bu-ka it-ti a-ḫa-mi[-iš] ṭa-bu-ta id-bu-bu šu-ul-ma-na ba-na-a a-na a-ḫa-mi-iš ul-te-bi-i-lu ù me-re-el-ta ba-ni-ta a-na a-ḫa-mi-iš ul ik-ʾlu-ʾù
>
> "From the time my fathers and your fathers mutually spoke in friendship, they sent good gifts to one another, and they did not withhold any request."[46]

1990). If it were originally northern, then we must hypothesize that it was redacted and adapted in Jerusalem leaving only "the God of Jacob" as a trace of its origins.

44 See Tally Ornan, "Sketches and Final Works of Art: The Drawings and Wall Paintings of Kuntillet ʿAjrud," *TA* 43 (2015), 3–26.

45 See already Anton Jirku, "Kanaʿanäische Psalmenfragmente in der vorisraelitischen Zeit Palästinas und Syriens," *JBL* 52 (1933), 108–20. More recently, these are developed by Richard Hess, "Hebrew Psalms and Amarna Correspondence from Jerusalem," *ZAW* 101 (1989), 249–65, and Avi Shveka, "A Trace of the Tradition of Diplomatic Correspondence," *JSS* 100 (2005), 297–320.

46 The translation is my own, and I use the transcription from the new edition by A. F. Rainey, *The El-Amarna Correspondence*, volume 1, 92–93.

As Avi Shveka points out, this Babylonian letter uses diplomatic language typical of requests. It was stock terminology evoking a mutual relationship or "brotherhood." This particular parallel is notable because of the unusual word אֲרֶשֶׁת in Ps 21:3. The lexeme is a clear cognate to the Amarna term mēreltu "request" (< Akkadian, mērestu) from the root erēšu "to desire, request."[47] However, while Ps 21:3 employs this Akkadian term, it is a *hapax legomenon* in Biblical Hebrew, and it never appears in later Hebrew.[48] The word appears to be an older loanword from Akkadian. Shveda latches onto the last part of the expression, "they did not withhold any request," as a "common idiom" deriving from diplomatic correspondence. The reciprocity results in requests and desires being mutually fulfilled by the diplomatic "brothers." And, this is not the only example. Shevda notes a variety of other occurrences such as a letter from Ebla: "You are a brother, and I am a brother. Brother, whatever desire from your mouth I will fulfill, and you, my desires fulfill" (TM.75.G.2342).[49] Moshe Weinfeld explains this fulfilling of desires as a part of diplomatic exchange intended to create good relationships. Within the biblical narrative, this dynamic is especially clear in the messages between Israel and Phoenicia.[50] The example of Solomon and Hiram illustrates this well. In fact, Hiram's letter to Solomon encodes the general paradigm in 1Kgs 5:22: "Hiram sent word to Solomon: 'I have heard that you have sent to me, and I will do all that which you desired (אֲנִי אֶעֱשֶׂה אֶת־כָּל־חֶפְצֶךָ)'." Or, to paraphrase in the language from the Amarna letters or Ps 21:3, Hiram received Solomon's request, and he will not withhold any request.

Diplomatic terminology also creates the backdrop to the playful phrasing in *KTU* 5.9, the Ugaritic school text referenced above, *iršt.aršt/l aḫy.l rʿy* "A request, I request, to my brother, to my friend." The language and lexemes of requesting (ʾrš) appear in this context both as grammatical exercise and scribal practice. The exact same term is also known from Ps 21:3 and the Amarna correspondence. In the case of *KTU* 5.9, the grammatical exercise plays with diplomatic terminology, and it appropriates it within a specific concrete example in a scribal curricular exercise. The Ugaritic school text goes on to utilize comically the diplomatic language in its extended grammatical exercise on the forms of the verb "to give"

---

47 Shveka, "A Trace of the Tradition of Diplomatic Correspondence," 298-99.

48 The word may also appear in Ps 61:6, but there it is spelled יְרֻשַּׁת, which seems to be a corrupted form of the original root ʾrš, see *HALOT, ad loc.*

49 Cited from Avi Shveka, "A Trace of the Tradition of Diplomatic Correspondence," *JSS* 50 (2005), 301.

50 See Moshe Weinfeld, "The Significance of the Political 'Brotherhood Covenant' in Israel and in the Ancient Near East," in *Homage to Shmuel: Studies in the World of the Bible*, eds. Zipora Talshir, Shamir Yona, Daniel Sivan (Jerusalem: Bialik, 2001), 178-83 [Hebrew].

(cited above). It looks like just a playful little grammatical exercise, and it is. But this playful scribal exercise has its roots in diplomatic terminology and relationships. This Ugaritic school text illustrates the general connection that we see between diplomatic language and its practice in school curriculum.

What these examples seemingly lack is the invocation of a deity, which Psalm 21:3 implies. There are, however, ancient Near Eastern monumental inscriptions that supply such parallels. In two separate places in the Aramaic inscription of Panamuwa, we read as follows: *wmz 's['l m]n 'lhy ytn ly* "And whatever I shall ask from my god, he shall grant me" (*KAI* 214:4) and *wmh 'š'l mn 'lh[y] mt ytnw ly* "And whatever I shall ask from my gods, surely they will grant me" (*KAI* 214:12–13). These phrases echo quite strikingly the example from inscription 3.9. Here, however, the diplomatic language of request and receipt was adapted for a monumental Aramaic inscription. Like in 3.9, the inscription writes of reciprocity between deities and their subjects, but the roots still must be traced back to common school sayings of Near Eastern scribes.

A much later parallel in Papyrus Amherst 63 (or, PapAm 63) reflects the long and conservative reach of scribal curriculum.[51] Psalm 20 seems to have been translated, adapted, and incorporated into PapAm 63 column XII. As Raik Heckl has suggested, it seems likely that "the text served for instruction in the Aramaic language."[52] This is one way to account for the use of Demotic script to write Aramaic. An educational scribal context helps explain the transmission of the Psalm (as well as some of the other parallels discussed by Steiner, van der Toorn, and others). Steiner understands the Papyrus as related to the military camp of Jews at Elephantine; and, van der Toorn connects the liturgical composition with

---

51 Now published in a new edition by Karel van der Toorn, *Papyrus Amherst 63* (AOAT, 448; Münster: Ugarit-Verlag, 2018). Van der Toorn's work relies upon the groundbreaking work of Richard Steiner and Charles Nims, which is published in an online preliminary edition, "The Aramaic Text in Demotic Script: Text, Translation, and Notes" (available on Steiner's academia.edu page with a copyright of 2017).

52 Raik Heckl, "Inside the Canon and Out: The Relationship Between Psalm 20 and Papyrus Amherst 63," *Semitica* 56 (2014), 362.

refugees from the northern kingdom of Israel.[53] The specific parallel relevant for KA 3.9 is found in lines 14–16, but a more general context will be instructive:[54]

PapAm 63, Column XII, 11–16	Psalm 20:2–5
[11] May Yaho answer us in our troubles,	[2] May YHWH answer you in the day of trouble, may the name of the God of Jacob protect you.
[12] May Adonai answer us in our troubles.	
O bow in heaven [13] crescent moon, shine forth.	
(and) send your emissary from the temple of Arash, and from Zaphon [14] may Yaho help us.	[3] May he send you help from the sanctuary and may he support you from Zion.
	[4] May he remember all your offerings and may he favor your burnt offerings.
May Yaho give us the desire of our hearts. May [15] *Mar* [i.e., the Lord] give us according to our hearts. All plans, Yaho should fulfill. May Yaho fulfill—may Adonai not be deficient [16] in satisfying—every request of our hearts.	[5] May he give you the desire of your heart, and may he fulfill all your plans.

The parallels between PapAm 63 and Psalm 20 are convincing, but they are blurred by layers of transmission and translation. As is evident in the parallel columns above, PapAm 63 is not a simple translation of Psalm 20, but a reworking of it. We now can add KA 3:9 to the scholarly discussion of Psalm 20 and PapAm 63.

Given the parallel between KA 3:9 and Ps 20:5, it seems more than coincidental that Psalm 20 is also echoed in PapAm 63. The saying in KA 3:9 seems to have been copied and transmitted in scribal circles and then adapted in a variety of ways in different contexts. It was not scripture, but rather was a school saying that could be used and adapted to serve a variety of different functions. We see a glimpse of its origins as a school text in Kuntillet ʿAjrud. The text was then adapted into the psalter as we see in Psalm 20, where it retains some of its vestiges as a northern text of the "God of Jacob" but has been thoroughly tailored as

---

53 See Karel van der Toorn, "Celebrating the New Year with the Israelites: Three Extrabiblical Psalms from Papyrus Amherst 63," *JBL* 136 (2017), 633-49; and "Psalm 20 and Amherst Papyrus 63, XII, 11–19: A Case Study of a Text in Transit," in *Le-maʿan Ziony: Essays in Honor of Ziony Zevit*, eds. Frederick Greenspahn and Gary Rendsburg (Eugene: Cascade Books, 2017), 244–62.
54 This parallel follows the layout by Karel van der Toorn, "Egyptian Papyrus Shed New Light on Jewish History," *BAR* 44/4 (2018), 37; also see his critical edition, *Papyrus Amherst 63*, 165–69.

Judean liturgy in the psalter.[55] We finally see another guise of this school text as it is repurposed in PapAm 63 where it becomes part of a liturgy composed in Aramaic and dressed up in the Egyptian garment of the Demotic script. And, line 16 of PapAm, which refers to the "request" which should be satisfied, also brings us back to the Amarna letters and the Ugaritic letter that were discussed earlier. To be sure, PapAm 63 is quite distant from KA 3.9, *KTU* 5.9, and the Amarna letters, but its triangulation through Psalm 20 suggests an original curricular setting that was adapted and used in a variety of contexts.

7 Conclusion

In sum, the student exercise of learning to write letters shaped literature in a number of ways. First of all, the sending of messages formed one of the backbones of literary narratives. And, the technical terminology of letter writing also influenced the framing of biblical literature. To begin with, the very structuring of texts using the expression, "and now," as a paragraphing device depended on the school lessons in letter writing. Other devices, such as the use of "saying" (*lēmôr*) as a marker of direct speech, was dependent on the sending and delivering of letters through messengers. The form of biblical prophecy was directly adapted from the *Sitz im Leben* of the sending and receiving of letters. Finally, the reciprocity saying, which is so critical for diplomatic correspondence, illustrates how scribal curriculum was learned, used, and adapted into a variety of contexts.

8 Bibliography

Aḥituv, Shmuel, Esti Eshel, and Ze'ev Meshel. "The Inscriptions." Pages 73–142 in *Kuntillet 'Ajrud: a Religious Centre from the Time of the Judaean Monarchy on the Border of Sinai*, ed. Zeev Meshel. Jerusalem: Israel Exploration Society, 2012.

Aḥituv, Shmuel. *Echoes of the Past: Hebrew and Cognate Inscriptions from the Biblical Period.* Jerusalem: Carta, 2008.

Beit-Arieh, Itzhaq and Bruce Cresson. "An Edomite Ostracon from Ḥorvat 'Uza." *Tel Aviv* 12 (1985): 96–101.

---

55 See Moshe Weinfeld, "The Pagan Version of Psalm 20:2-6: Vicissitudes of a Psalmodic Creation in Israel and its Neighbors," *EI* 18 (1985), 130-140 [Hebrew], 70*.

Brettler, Marc. *God is King: Understanding an Israelite Metaphor*, JSOTSS, 76. Sheffield: Sheffield Academic Press, 1989.

Cunchillos, Juan-Luis. "The Correspondence of Ugarit." Pages 359–74 in *Handbook of Ugaritic Studies*, eds. Wilfred Watson and Nicolas Wyatt. Leiden: Brill, 1999.

Dijkstra, Meindert. "Prophecy by Letter (Jeremiah XXIX 24–32)." *VT* 33 (1983): 319–22.

Dobbs-Allsopp, Frederick et al., eds. *Hebrew Inscriptions: Texts from the Biblical Period of the Monarchy with Concordance*. New Haven: Yale University Press, 2005.

Freedman, David Noel. "The Orthography of the Arad Ostraca." *IEJ* 19 (1969): 52–56.

Greene, John. *The Role of the Messenger and Message in the Ancient Near East*. Atlanta: Scholars Press, 1989.

Haring, Ben. "*Halaḥam* on an Ostracon of the Early New Kingdom?" *Journal of Near Eastern Studies* 74 (2015): 189–96.

Hawley, Robert. "Studies in Ugaritic Epistolography." PhD dissertation, University of Chicago, 2003.

Heckl, Raik. "Inside the Canon and Out: The Relationship Between Psalm 20 and Papyrus Amherst 63." *Semitica* 56 (2014): 359–79.

Heimpel, Wolfgang. *Letters to the King of Mari: A New Translation, with Historical Introduction, Notes, and Commentary*. Winona Lake: Eisenbrauns, 2003.

Hess, Richard. "Hebrew Psalms and Amarna Correspondence from Jerusalem." *ZAW* 101 (1989): 249–65.

Holladay, John. "Assyrian Statecraft and the Prophets of Israel." Pages 29–51 in *Prophecy in Israel: Search for Identity*, ed. David Petersen. Philadelphia: Fortress; London: SPCK, 1987.

Izre'el, Shlomo. *The Amarna Scholarly Tablets*. Groningen: Styx, 1997.

Jacobsen, Thorkild. *The Harps That Once.* New Haven: Yale University Press, 1987.

Jirku, Anton. "Kana'anäische Psalmenfragmente in der vorisraelitischen Zeit Palästinas und Syriens." *JBL* 52 (1933): 108–20.

Köhler, Ludwig. *Deuterojesaja (Jesaja 40–55) stilkritisch untersucht*. BZAW, 37; Giessen: Töpelmann, 1923.

Lemaire, André. *Les écoles et la formation de la Bible dans l'ancien Israël*. Fribourg, 1981.

Lindblom, Jack. *Die literarische Gattung der prophetischen Literatur*. Uppsala: A-B Lundequistska Bokhandeln, 1924.

Lindenberger, James. *Ancient Aramaic and Hebrew Letters*. Atlanta: Scholars Press, 1994.

Mabie, Fred. "Ancient Near Eastern Scribes and the Mark(s) They Left: A Catalog and Analysis of Scribal Auxiliary Marks in the Amarna Corpus and in the Cuneiform Alphabetic Texts of Ugarit and Ras Ibn Hani." PhD dissertation, UCLA, 2004.

Mandell, Alice. "When Form is Function: A Reassessment of the *Marziḥu* Contract (*KTU* 3.9) as a Scribal Exercise." *MAARAV* 23 (2019): 39–67.

Mowinckel, Sigmund. "'The Sprit' and the 'Word' in the Pre-exilic Reforming Prophets." *JBL* 53 (1934): 199–227.

Ornan, Tally. "Sketches and Final Works of Art: The Drawings and Wall Paintings of Kuntillet ʿAjrud." *TA* 43 (2015): 3–26.

Pardee, Dennis. "Letters from Tel Arad." *UF* 10 (1978): 289–336.

Pardee, Dennis. "The Ugaritic Alphabetic Cuneiform Writing System in the Context of Other Alphabetic Systems." Pages 181–200 in *Studies in Semitic and Afroasiatic Linguistics Presented to Gene B. Gragg*, ed. Cynthia Miller. Chicago: Oriental Institute, 2007.

Pardee, Dennis. *Handbook of Hebrew Letters*. Chico, CA: SBL Press, 1982.

Puech, Emile. "Les inscriptions hébraïques de Kuntillet ʿAjrud (Sinaï)." *RB* 121–2 (2014): 161–94.

Rendsburg, Gary. *Linguistic Evidence for the Northern Origin of Selected Psalms*. SBLMS 43. Atlanta: Scholars, 1990.

Ross, James. "The Prophet as Yahweh's Messenger." Pages 98–107 in *Israel's Prophetic Heritage: Essays in Honor of James Muilenberg*, eds. Benedict Anderson and Walter Harrelson. New York: Harper, 1962.

Saenger, Paul. *Space Between Words: The Origins of Silent Reading*. Palo Alto: Stanford University Press, 1997.

Sass, Benjamin. "On epigraphic Hebrew ʾŠR and *ʾŠRH, and on Biblical Asherah*." *Transeuphratène* 46 (2014): 50–60.

Schniedewind, William. "Scripturalization in Ancient Judah." Pages 305–21 in *Contextualizing Israel's Sacred Writings: Ancient Literacy, Orality, and Literary Production*, ed. Brian Schmidt. Atlanta: SBL, 2015.

Schniedewind, William. *The Finger of the Scribe: How Scribes Learned to Write the Bible*. New York: Oxford University Press, 2019.

Schwiderski, Dirk. *Handbuch des nordwestsemitischen Briefformulars: Ein Beitrag zur Echtheitsfrage des aramäischen Briefe des Esrabuches*, BZAW, 295. Berlin: de Gruyter, 2000.

Shisha-Halevy, Ariel. "An Early Northwest-Semitic Text in the Egyptian Hieratic Script." *Orientalia* n.s. 47 (1978): 145–62.

Shveka, Avi. "A Trace of the Tradition of Diplomatic Correspondence." *JSS* 100 (2005): 297–320.

Silverstein, Michael. "The Limits of Awareness." Pages 382–401 in *Linguistic Anthropology: A Reader*, ed. Alessandro Duranti. Malden: Blackwell, 2001.

Smith, Mark. *The Ugaritic Baal Cycle, Volume I. Introduction with Text, Translation and Commentary of KTU/CAT 1.1–1.2*. VTSup, 105; Leiden/Boston: Brill, 1994.

Smith, Mark. *The Early History of God: Yahweh and the Other Deities in Ancient Israel*. 2d ed. Grand Rapids: Eerdmans, 2002.

Smith, Mark and Wayne Pitard. *The Ugaritic Baal Cycle, Volume II. Introduction with Text, Translation and Commentary of KTU/CAT 1.3–1.4*, VTSup, 114. Leiden/Boston: Brill, 2009.

Steiner, Richard. "Northwest Semitic Incantations in an Egyptian Medical Papyrus of the Fourteenth Century B.C.E." *Journal of Near Eastern Studies* 51 (1992): 191–200.

Toorn, Karel van der. "Psalm 20 and Amherst Papyrus 63, XII, 11–19: A Case Study of a Text in Transit." Pages 244–62 in *Le-maʿan Ziony: Essays in Honor of Ziony Zevit*, eds. Frederick Greenspahn and Gary Rendsburg. Eugene: Cascade Books, 2017.

Toorn, Karel van der. "Celebrating the New Year with the Israelites: Three Extrabiblical Psalms from Papyrus Amherst 63." *JBL* 136 (2017): 633–49.

Toorn, Karel van der. "Egyptian Papyrus Shed New Light on Jewish History." *BAR* 44/4 (2018): 32–39.

Toorn, Karel van der. *Papyrus Amherst 63*. AOAT, 448; Münster: Ugarit-Verlag, 2018.

Vita, Juan-Pablo. "The Scribal Exercise RS 16.265 from Ugarit in its Near-Eastern Context." Pages 645–52 in *The Ancient Near East, A Life! Festschrift Karel Van Lerberghe*, eds. Tom Boiy et al. *Orientalia Lovaniensia Analecta*, 220. Leuven: Peeters, 2012.

Weinfeld, Moshe. "The Pagan Version of Psalm 20:2–6: Vicissitudes of a Psalmodic Creation in Israel and its Neighbors." *EI* 18 (1985): 130–40 [Hebrew].

Weinfeld, Moshe. "The Significance of the Political 'Brotherhood Covenant' in Israel and in the Ancient Near East." Pages 178–83 in *Homage to Shmuel: Studies in the World of the Bible*, eds. Zipora Talshir, Shamir Yona, Daniel Sivan. Jerusalem: Bialik, 2001 [Hebrew].

Westermann, Claus. *Basic Forms of Prophetic Speech*. Louisville: Westminster/John Knox, 1991.

Wiggins, Steve. *A Reassessment of Asherah: With Further Considerations of the Goddess*. Piscataway: Gorgias Press, 2007.

Xella, Paolo. "Le dieu et 'sa' déesse: l'utilisation des suffixes pronominaux avec des théonymes d'Ebla à Ugarit et à Kuntillet 'Ajrud." *UF* 27 (1995): 599–610.

Yassine, Khair and Javier Teixidor. "Ammonite and Aramaic Inscriptions from Tell el-Mazār in Jordan." *BASOR* 264 (1986): 45–50.

Yogev, Jonathan and Shamir Yona. "A Poetic Letter: The Ugaritic Tablet RS 16.265." *Studi Epigrafici e Linguistici* 31 (2014): 51–58.

Esther Eshel

Combining Different Types of Scripts in the Aramaic Texts

1 General Introduction

In his detailed pioneering study on "The Development of the Aramaic Script,"
Joseph Naveh wrote: "Paleography, as an auxiliary to history, should aim to establish the date of undated documents through a methodological study of the
development of the script." Immediately after, he noted:

> The process of development was evolutionary. A new form would first appear sporadically
> in the writing of a few individuals, usually alongside the older form. Even after the new
> form had become thoroughly entrenched, the older one remained in use for several dec-
> ades... Not all letters followed parallel paths of development... There were also parallel de-
> velopments among groups of letters...[1]

Naveh's main concern in his study was establishing the dating of the various Aramaic inscriptions. To his comment about variability in rate and patterns of
scribal development, one should add the factors of content and archaeological
context, to recognize that deciphering and dating an inscription is a complex and
multi-faceted process.

In my paper I would like to focus on some inscriptions that fit Naveh's description of "A new form ... alongside the older form," written in the Aramaic lapidary script, which was used for Aramaic inscriptions in a region extending from
Asia Minor and Egypt to Afghanistan, during the Persian and Hellenistic periods.
These inscriptions use the Aramaic script, but it is defined as a special type of
script by its preservation of older forms of the letters *alef, zayin* and *yod*.

We shall start with a short survey of the research done on the inscriptions
written in Aramaic lapidary script during the last half century. We then continue

---

* Thanks are due to Boaz Zissu, with whom I prepared and presented the lecture in the Strasbourg conference, parts of which this paper is based upon. I would also like to thank André Lemaire for his helpful remarks and bibliography, as well as Jan Dušek for his response during the
conference and written remarks, some of which I included in the article.
1 J. Naveh, "The Development of the Aramaic Script," *Proceeding of the Israel Academy of Sciences and Hummanities* 5 (1976), 4.

and introduce two new unpublished inscriptions written in the Aramaic lapidary script.

2 The Aramaic Lapidary Script

2.1 An Introduction

Here it would be helpful to note that originally, the adjective 'lapidary', as we learn from the Merriam-Webster Dictionary, comes from the Latin word *lapis* meaning 'stone', and "Since the 1700s, *lapidary* has also been used as an adjective describing things having the elegance and precision of inscriptions carved on stone monuments or things relating to the art of gem cutting."[2] Therefore, the term "lapidary script" was initially applied only with reference to stone inscriptions, used for official purposes, but later it was used to describe non-stone inscriptions as well, as in the case of the inscriptions discussed below, some of which were on non-lapidary material.

Let us now take a closer look at the history of research of the Aramaic lapidary script, starting with the concept suggested by Naveh (with some adaptations he made in his own research), followed by his successors, and by new finds that emerged after the publication of his study.

In his study of the development of the lapidary script, Naveh noted that:[3]

> It is only in the 5th and the 4th centuries BCE that a true stable Aramaic lapidary script is found. But even in the 5th and 4th centuries BCE the lapidary script tends to imitate the cursive: most of the letters are cursive forms adapted to stone, and only *alef, zayin* and *yod* preserved their older forms. Other letters occasionally lag behind in assuming the new, cursive form... If an inscription is short and lacks the key-letters (*alef, zayin* and *yod*), it is difficult, and sometime even impossible, to determine whether the scribe intended to use the cursive forms of the lapidary.

As part of the history of research one should note a development that already occurred during the first detailed study of Naveh. His Hebrew study was written in 1966, while his English version was published in 1976. In 1971 a new Aramaic

---

2 See https://www.merriam-webster.com/dictionary/lapidary#learn-more.
3 Naveh, "The Development," 52.

inscription was published by André Caquot which he dated to the Assyrian period,[4] while Naveh preferred the dating to the Neo-Babylonian period.[5] This publication had an impact on the study of the Aramaic lapidary script, since Naveh amended his conclusions as an addendum of the Hebrew version, and there is a shift in the English one as follows: While at first he thought that no lapidary script was known prior to the Persian period, now he wrote that already in the 7th century there was a lapidary Aramaic script that started slowly to develop in the Persian period.

In 2014, André Lemaire made a survey of the scripts of post-Iron Age Aramaic inscriptions and ostraca. He updated earlier studies and suggested distinguishing between two periods: the Neo-Babylonian period (ca. 587–539 B.C.E. and the Persian and Hellenistic periods (ca. 539–305 B.C.E).[6] Lemaire updated the list of Naveh (2014: 235, 237),[7] including some new Aramaic inscriptions, mostly short ones on seals, sherds, bricks and dockets on cuneiform tablets, and two long inscriptions. To that one should add the funerary stele from Saqqara, dated to the 5th century BCE.[8]

In his updated list of Aramaic lapidary inscriptions found in the western part of the Achaemenid Empire, that is, from Egypt, Arabia, Israel, and Asia Minor (Lemaire 2014: 240, Table 1), the following are included:[9]

2.2 The Inscriptions

Inscriptions from Egypt

No.	Inscription	Date
1	Saqqara funerary stele	Ca. 482 BCE
2	Aswan commemorative stele	Ca. 458 or 398 BCE
3	Memphis funerary stele	Ca. 400 BCE

---

4 André Caquot, "Une inscription araméenne d'époque assyrienne," *Hommages à André Dupont-Sommer*, 1971, 9–16.

5 Naveh, "The Development of the Aramaic Script," *Proceedings of the Israel Academy of Sciences and Humanities* 5/1. Jerusalem: Israel Academy of Sciences and Humanities [Hebrew], 57.

6 André Lemaire, "Scripts of Post-Iron Age Aramaic Inscriptions and Ostraca," in *"An Eye for Form": Epigraphic Essays in Honor of Frank Moore Cross* (Winona Lake, Indiana: Eisenbrauns, 2014), 235–52.

7 Lemaire, "Scripts," 235, 237.

8 H. Lozachmeur and V. Dobrev, "Nouvelle inscription araméenne à Saqqara," in *Comptes rendus de l'Académie des Inscriptions et Belles-Lettres (CRAI)* 2008, 911-925.

9 For detailed bibliography of each inscription, see Lemaire, "Scripts," Table 1.

| 4 | Carpentras funerary stele | Ca. 400 BCE |
| 5 | Tell el-Maskhuta Bowls 1–4 | Ca. 400 BCE |

Inscriptions from Arabia

| 6 | Taima stele | Ca. 5th century BCE |
| 7 | Taima votive | Ca. 4th century BCE |

Inscription from Israel

| 8 | The Lachish incense altar | Ca. 475 BCE |

Inscriptions from Asia Minor

9	Saraïdin	Ca. 500 BCE
10	Hemite marble	Ca. 4th century BCE
11	Gözneh boundary stone	Ca. 400–350 BCE
12	Meydancikkale 1	Ca. 5th century BCE
13	Meydancikkale 2	Ca. 5th century BCE
14	Kesecek Köyü votive	Ca. 4th century BCE
15	Bahadrili boundary stone	Ca. 4th century BCE
16	Cilician funerary stelae 1–4	Ca. 5th or 4th centuries BCE
17	Abydos lion weight	Ca. 500 BCE
18	Daskyleion funerary stele 1	Ca. 450–400 BCE
19	Daskyleion funerary stele 2	Ca. 450–400 BCE
20	Sultaniye Köy funerary stele	Ca. 5th century BCE
21	Sardis bilingual funerary stele	Ca. 349 BCE
22	Xanthos trilingual	Ca. 337 BCE

A table of the script of these inscriptions is also presented,[10] as well as a detailed description of each letter and its development.[11]

As noted by Lemaire:

> One of the main difficulties of the paleographical study of these lapidary inscriptions comes from the fact that very few of them are dated. And, even when the inscription contains a date, there may be some uncertainty about its correlation to absolute dates, since several Persian kings bore the same name ..."

An important note regarding our study here follows: "In addition, more-or-less formal style may be contemporary, so the paleographical dating of most of these inscriptions remains approximate."[12]

---

10 Lemaire, "Scripts," 242-243, Figs. 2-3.
11 Lemaire, "Scripts," 241, 244.
12 Lemaire, "Scripts," 239.

A new era in the study of the Aramaic lapidary script started when the Mount Gerizim inscriptions were discovered. Before that discovery, as mentioned above, most inscriptions came from Asia Minor, and only one from Lachish, Israel. This situation was irrevocably changed when more that 50 new inscriptions were discovered on Mt. Gerizim.

3 The Inscriptions Written in the Aramaic Lapidary Script from Mount Gerizim, Israel

3.1 Introduction

Mount Gerizim is located on the south side of Shechem. The excavator, Yitzhak Magen, describes the temple built there as follows:

> During the Persian period, a sacred precinct and temple were built on Mt. Gerizim, as it was sacred to the Israelite population, the surviving remnants of the Kingdom of Israel. ... Two main construction phases have been identified at the sacred precinct: The first dates from the Persian period until the reign of Antiochus III (ca. 200 BCE); the second dates from the reign of Antiochus III until the conquest of Mt. Gerizim by John Hyrcanus I (111–110 BCE)."[13]

3.2 The Inscriptions

During the excavation there, hundreds of inscriptions were discovered. With regard to the corpus of inscriptions, Magen wrote:

> The excavations of Mt. Gerizim brought to light some four hundred inscription fragments in Neo-Hebrew and Aramaic (Lapidary and Proto-Jewish) scripts, inscribed on building and paving stones, that were found inside the city's Hellenistic period's sacred precinct....[14]

---

13 Yitzhak Magen, Haggai Misgav and Levana Tsfania, *Mount Gerizim Excavations*, Jerusalem: Staff Officer of Archaeology, Civil Administration for Judea and Samaria, Israel Antiquities Authority Judea and Samaria Publications; vol. 2. *A Temple city.* Jerusalem: 2008, 98.
14 Yitzhak Magen, Haggai Misgav and Levana Tsfania, *Mount Gerizim Excavations*, Jerusalem: Staff Officer of Archaeology, Civil Administration for Judea and Samaria, Israel Antiquities Authority Judea and Samaria Publications; Vol. 1: *The Aramaic, Hebrew and Samaritan Inscriptions*, Jerusalem: 2004, 13.

The inscriptions were first published by Magen and Naveh in 1997,[15] followed by a detailed study by Haggai Misgav in 2004. In this last and detailed publication, the corpus was divided according to two formulae: (1) *that which offered*, and (2) *for good remembrance*, to which some "Miscellaneous" were added. A short discussion of the Aramaic lapidary script, made by Haggai Misgav was also added.[16]

These inscriptions were generally dated to the Hellenistic Period, 3rd-2nd centuries BCE, since they were not found *in situ*, and thus, as noted by Misgav: "the extant parallels to these inscriptions have not enabled us to fix the chronology of the lapidary style."[17] He also observed that "the Mt. Gerizim inscriptions in the lapidary style do not differ from similar inscriptions dating from the Persian and early Hellenistic period uncovered elsewhere." In addition to the known distinguishing feature of this script, including the 'old form' of the letters *alef, zayin* and *yod*, he noted that "the other letters are cursive, although they, too, exhibit some conservative features," adding that "all the inscriptions date from the Hellenistic period (third-second centuries BCE) a time in which, with a few exceptions, the lapidary style is not known to have been in use."[18]

Out of the 381 Aramaic inscriptions, 56 were written in the lapidary Aramaic script. Eight years later, this corpus received new attention. In 2012 this corpus was further studied in depth by Jan Dušek,[19] where 48 lapidary inscriptions were included. He argued that the title Lapidary Script for the Mt. Gerizim corpus should be changed to Monumental Script, comparing them to other such inscriptions.

Based on his detailed study of the Aramaic inscriptions from Mt. Gerizim, and taking into account their historical background, Dušek argued that the monumental Aramaic script should be dated to the Hellenistic period, summarizing: "More generally, we propose dating the inscriptions to the time of Antiochus III (223–187 BCE) and to the period after his death... it seems probable to consider the *terminus post quem* the Seleucid conquest of Palestine during the 5th Syriac

---

15 Joseph Naveh and Yitzhak Magen, "Aramaic and Hebrew Inscriptions of the Second-Century BCE at Mount Gerizim," *'Atiqot* 32 (1997): 9–17.

16 Magen et al., *Mount Gerizim Excavations*, vol. 1, 2004, 13-41, esp. 36-41.

17 Magen et al., *Mount Gerizim Excavation*, vol. 1, 2004, 37.

18 Magen et al, Mount Gerizim Excavations, 37.

19 Jan Dušek, *Aramaic and Hebrew Inscriptions from Mt. Gerizim and Samaria between Antiochus III and Antiochus IV Epiphanes* (Culture and History of the Ancient Near East 54), Leiden and Boston: Brill 2012.

war, in 200 BCE."[20] Accepting Naveh's definition, Dušek showed that the Monumental Aramaic script style is characterized by the independent lapidary older form of *alef, zayin* and *yod*. He admitted that dating the Aramaic monumental script is more difficult than the cursive script, and "the monumental style archaizes and its development is slower than cursive."[21]

To sum up – looking at the examples discussed by Dušek we can see that the dating suggested by scholars for the major Aramaic lapidary inscriptions is quite wide in its time range,[22] we therefore need to wait for future finds with clear dates, which hopefully will enable us to establish a firm chronology and dating for the Aramaic lapidary inscriptions.

Next, I would like to add two new inscriptions that have not yet been published, written in Aramaic lapidary script, with one twist: one of them has the old form of *alef* and *zayin*, but with the regular Aramaic form of a *yod*.

4 New Lapidary Inscriptions

One of the two unpublished inscriptions we will now discuss was found in Jerusalem, and the other was confiscated from an antiquities dealer by the Thefts Prevention Unit of the Israel Antiquities Authority.

The earlier inscription can be dated to the Persian period, while the later one is from the Hellenistic period. Both are problematic in terms of dating, as the site of origin of the earlier one is unknown, while the one that was found in a legal excavation nevertheless has no archeological support from accompanying finds.

---

20 Dušek, Aramaic and Hebrew Inscriptions, 37.
21 Dušek, Aramaic and Hebrew Inscriptions, 37.
22 See the different dating by scholars of the lapidary Aramaic inscriptions, and their re-dating by Jan Dušek, *Aramaic and Hebrew Inscriptions from Mt. Gerizim and Samaria between Antiochus III and Antiochus IV Epiphanes* (Culture and History of the Ancient Near East 54; Leiden and Boston: Brill, 2012), 29-33.

4.1 Inscription No. 1

4.1.1 Introduction

This inscription is written on the shoulder of a storage jar. Unfortunately, we do not have the neck and rim – the indicative parts of this vessel – therefore we cannot date it by comparison to similar vessels found in dated contexts.[23]

In his study of the script post Iron Age, Lemaire discussed ostraca, including the alphabets and detailed descriptions of each letter.[24] As noted by Lemaire, they are written in "various styles: from more-or-less formal hand to the extreme cursive."[25] Among these inscriptions, Lemaire noted an exceptional group of inscriptions written on jars, on which Lemaire noted: "Inscriptions on jars must be distinguished from ostraca because they were written on a larger surface and could be read by anyone who could read. Their script, therefore, generally tends to be formal, often similar to the lapidary script (e.g., *zayin* and *yod*)."[26] Such an example can be found in his inscription No. 254, reading [ף]למלך כס "belonging to the king, silv(er?)" with the old forms of *kaph* and *samek*.[27]

In what follows we will look at some issues regarding the new inscription. Based on its script, this inscription is close in form to the known inscription from the Persian period discussed above, that is, the Taima stele (No. 6 in the table above), dated to ca. 400 BCE. We can tentatively date the new inscription to the 4th century BCE, which makes it an important addition to the list of the Persian Period Aramaic lapidary inscriptions.

---

23 The storage jar was acquired through enforcement of Israeli antiquities law. It originates from a circle of West Bank looters active in the area of the ancient Hellenistic city of Maresha. It was transferred for further study by Amir Ganor, head of the IAA Unit of Prevention of Antiquities Looting. A full publication of the find, co-authored by Ganor, Boaz Zissu and the author, will appear in the near future.
24 Lemaire, "Scripts," 244-248, and Fig. 4.
25 Lemaire, "Scripts," 244.
26 Lemaire, "Scripts," 244.
27 103, Pl. XLIII.

Some notes on the content of the inscription

In what follows, I will look at two issues concerning the content of this inscription: the question of where does it start, and the ethnicity of the people it refers to.

a. Starting with our first enigma: the inscription is written around the jar with no clear indication of where the inscription begins and ends. So – where does it start?

We were able to identify the beginning of two sentences. One start with זי ישתכח, "which will be found," and the other כאן הא זנה "Now behold! this..." The *vacat* before the first sentence זי ישתכח is a little larger than that of the second one, כען הא זנה.

Both options look like a continuation of a sentence: כען (like כענת, or Hebrew עתה), a relative pronoun, is "a link into what is to follow, and marks the transition to the real point of concern in a letter,"[28] or "introducing the subject of a message,"[29] while זי (or later form די) either refers back to something mentioned before or is used at the beginning of many Aramaic inscriptions on objects without mentioning the object donated. See e.g. the inscriptions written on a silver bowl from Tel Maskhuṭa in Egypt, dated to the first half of the 5ᵗʰ century BCE and reading זי הקרב צחא בר עבדעמרו להנאלת "That which Seha son of Abdamru offered to Hanilat."[30] A group of such formulas was found on the dedicatory inscriptions found on Mt. Gerizim, where many are from the same time period as our inscription. They start with זי הקרב.[31]

b. Another clue might be found in the names mentioned in the inscription: one of them is בניה. In the כען sentence he is mentioned in full: בניה עבד עדק, while in the זי ישתכח sentence he is named בניה (see below). We might therefore prefer the כען sentence as the beginning of the inscription: כען הא זנה... "Now behold, this..."

---

28 Köhler, Ludwig, *The Hebrew and Aramaic Lexicon of the Old Testament*, vol. 5: Aramaic (Leiden and Boston: Brill, 2000), 1901.

29 Comprehensive Aramaic Lexicon, http://cal.huc.edu.

30 William J Dumbrell, "The Tell El-Maskhuta Bowls and the "kingdom of Qedar in the Persian Period." *BASOR* 203 (1971): 33-44, esp. 35.

31 Magen et al., *Mount Gerizim Excavation*, vol. 1, 2004, 16-18.

c. Having no clear context, what can this inscription tell us about the ethnicity of the people it names? The following proper names are mentioned:

The first proper name is בניה עבד עדק, later referred in short as בניה. This Jewish name בניה is mentioned in the Bible, in the Elephantine Papyri,[32] and in some Masada Ostraca.[33]

עבד עדק can either be interpreted "Benaiah, the slave of 'DQ"; or "Benaiah (son of) 'BD'DQ." עדק is a rare Safaitic name, an Arabic name coming from 'Adiq "self-reliant."

4.2 Inscription No. 2

4.2.1 Introduction

The second new inscription was revealed during a well-organized excavation, directed by Joe Uziel of the Israel Antiquities Authority, together with Avraham Solomon, Tehillah Lieberman and Anat Cohen-Weinberger.[34]

The excavations beneath Wilson's Arch, located at the foot of the Western Wall of the Temple Mount, yielded monumental remains spanning from the 1st century BCE to the late Islamic period. Among the outstanding finds are the remains of a small theater-like structure, the pier of Wilson's Arch and another segment of the western wall of the Temple Mount.

4.2.2 The Inscription

Alongside the significant architectural remains, many small finds were discovered within the fills beneath the arch reflecting various cultural aspects of a wide time range. Amongst the finds, a sherd from the body of a small storage jar was

---

32 Bezalel Porten and Ada Yardeni, *Textbook of Aramaic Documents from Ancient Egypt. Vol. 4: Ostraca & Assorted Inscriptions*, vol. 4: *Ostraca & Assorted Inscriptions* (Jerusalem, 1999), 96, D3.17:4.
33 Yigael Yadin and Joseph Naveh, "The Aramaic and Hebrew Ostraca and Jar inscriptions from Masada," in *Masada I: The Yigael Yadin Excavations 1963-1965: Final Reports*. Masada Reports, Jerusalem: Israel Exploration Society 1989, 61, No. 609:3.
34 E. Eshel, A. Solomon, T. Lieberman, J. Uziel and A. Cohen-Weinberger, "An Aramaic Inscription from beneath Wilson's Arch" *'Atiqot* 106 (2022), pp. 75-88.

found, bearing an Aramaic inscription of two broken lines. The sherd could not be identified chronologically, as it is very small and not indicative.

The inscription reads as follows:

[...]לֹֿאשיהו בר תא[...]   .1

[...]לֹֿמשלמת ברת מ∘[...]   .2

Translation:

1.   [...] to/for 'ŠYHW son of T'[...]
2.   [...] to/for MŠLMT daughter of M[...]

Two names are included in our inscription, one of a man and the other of a woman, with the name of their father, both of which only the beginning had survived. There is no way to know what was before and after the names. The names: אשיהו[י, Josiayahu, is known as the biblical name of a king of Judah (1Kgs 13:2; 2Kgs 21:24 etc.); in the short form יאשיה (Zeph 6:10); while the name משלמת – known from the Bible as the name of the mother of King Amon: משלמת בת חרוץ מן יטבה, "Meshullemeth daughter of Haruz of Jotbah" (2Kgs 21:19). This Jewish name of a woman is mentioned a few times in the Elephantine documents, for example:

- In a fragmentary letter about gold, dated to the last quarter of the 5th Century BCE, as part of a list of names whom the writer Hosea is greeting, we read: משלמת שלם, "Greeting (to) Meshullemeth."[35]
- A collection account of the Jewish garrison that "gave silver to YHW the God, each person silver [2] shekels," on June 1st, 400 BCE includes many names of men and women, among them four women by the name משלמת.[36] The first person in the list is: משל[מ]ת ברת גמר[י]ה בר מחסיה "Meshull[em]eth daughter of Gemar[ia]h son of Mehaseiah" (Col. A:2); and see משלמת ברת צפליא "Meshullemeth daughter of Zepelia" (Col. A:96). Finally, משלמת is mentioned twice on an ostracon including instructions regarding legumes and barley, reading:[37]... אל תתכלי על משלמת ועל שמעיה "Do not rely on Meshullemeth and on Shemaiah...," who is later being rebuked: הן משלמת לא יצפה לי אנתי מה תאמרן "I Meshullemeth is not concerned about me, you, what will you say?!" (ll. 11–12).

---

35 Bezalel Porten and Ada Yardeni, *Textbook of Aramaic Documents from Ancient Egypt*, vol. 1: *Letters, Texts and Studies for Students* (Jerusalem: The Hebrew University Department of the History of the Jewish People Texts and Studies for Students, 1986), 40-41, A3.7:3.

36 Bezalel Porten and Ada Yardeni, *Textbook of Aramaic Documents from Ancient Egypt*, vol. 3: *Literature, Accounts, Lists, Texts and Studies for Students* (Jerusalem: The Hebrew University Department of the History of the Jewish People Texts and Studies for Students, 1993), 226-228, C3.15.

37 Porten and Yardeni, *Textbook*, Vol. 4, 168-169; D7.16:4-5.

The third, partly preserved name is: [...]תא, the father of אשיהו; it can be reconstructed in various ways:

a. The name [ע]רתא, biblical תַּאְרֵעַ, Taarea (1 Chron. 8:35), with the variant
תַּחְרֵעַ Taharea (1 Chron 9:41), who was a Benjaminite from the descendants of
Saul, one of the great-grandsons of Jonathan.[38]

b. The name לתאשר "belonging to Teshur" on a stone burial marker found in
South Saqqara, now lost.[39] This name might be connected to the tree name
תְּאַשּׁוּר, usually translated as a box tree or a type of a cedar.

c. Another possibility is one of the following Greek names: [תא]ודוטוס,
[תא]ודוסיוס, or תא]ופילוס.[40]

This last suggestion brings us to the next point: Our inscription is written left to
right in mirror writing, to which we can suggest some possible interpretations.

The mirror writing, to my knowledge, is known in ancient times only from
seals. A possible interpretation, suggested to us by Jan Dušek in his response to
our lecture, follows:[41]

> The inscription consists of two lines, each with a proper name and a patronymic. This kind
> of text usually appears on personal seals. In order to produce the impressions with a text
> written correctly from right to left, the text on epigraphic seals must be carved in a reversed
> "mirror" position. Perhaps the inscription is a copy of a text carved on two seals? This would
> explain the reversed character of the text. In the Persian period, the angular Aramaic script
> was used for inscribing small objects like seals and coins. It can be compared with some
> Aramaic seals of various dates.[42] Of special interest is a votive seal, *WSS* 575.

I would like to add here two more possible interpretation of the "mirror writing":
- A variant of this interpretation is a draft of at least two seals made on clay,
  done before carving them on an expensive material.
- Another possible explanation is that the writer might be accustomed to Greek
  writing of left to right. Such early knowledge of Greek might be compared to
  a contemporaneous bilingual inscription, written in Aramaic and Greek from

---

38 No etymology has been suggested, just a change of the gutturals א/ח.

39 Porten and Yardeni, *Textbook of Aramaic Documents, Vol. 4*, 260; D 21:3 .

40 Tal Ilan, *Lexicon of Jewish Names in Late Antiquity*, Texte und Studien zum antiken Judentum
(Tübingen: Mohr Siebeck 2002), 285, 287.

41 Quoted from his e-mail to me.

42 Nahman Avigad and Benjamin Sass, *Corpus of West Semitic Stamp Seals*, Publications of the
Israel Academy of Sciences and Humanities. Section of Humanities (Jerusalem: Israel Academy
of Sciences and Humanities, Israel Exploration Society: Institute of Archaeology, Hebrew University of Jerusalem, 1997), 284ff, Nos. 575ff.

Telloh, which Naveh dates to the end of the 4th century BCE.[43] Some support might be found on a Greek ossuary, taking into consideration the time gap between our inscription and those of the 1st century BCE to 1st century CE. This inscription reads: ΝΑΔΥΟΙ, Ἰουδαν, Ioudan. If we accept the editor noted on it as being: "imitation of Semitic practice," in our case we might have the reverse order, where the writer, who was accustomed with left-to-right writing of Greek, mistakenly wrote his Aramaic inscription in this direction. This may be taken as a tentative explanation, as we await more parallels that will bring this enigma to its solution.

4.2.3 The Script

We have *alef and zayin* written in the independent lapidary form paralleled with other such inscriptions mentioned earlier, dated to the 4th–3rd centuries BCE. What is unique here, is that the *yod* is not written in the independent lapidary form, but is rather the early type of Aramaic *yod*, made with two strokes. The upper right stroke slants down to the right and the lower left stroke is almost horizontal. Another early form is that of a *lamed*, without a "tail," dated to the end of the 4th century BCE.

Based on the shapes of the letters, especially the usage of their earlier forms and the type of the *yod*, we would tentatively suggest dating it between the 4th and the 3rd centuries BCE. The combination of the independent lapidary form of *alef* with the early Aramaic form of *lamed* and *mem*, together with a possible development of the *yod* from the independent lapidary form to the early Aramaic one, could point to the later period of the 3rd century BCE.

Unfortunately, we have no external evidence for this dating, since no archeological remains of the suggested time period were found. Nevertheless, since it was found in a layer of fill with finds dated to the Iron Age II-III and the early Roman Period and the 2nd–3rd centuries CE, our inscription might be from the time in between which did not leave other remains.

This script finds its parallels with two other inscriptions, both mentioned above: the stone burial marker found in South Saqqara, Egypt mentioned above, reading לתאשר "belonging to Teshur,"[44] and an Aramaic inscription on the boundary stone from Bahadrili (No. 15 in the table above), dated to the 5th or 4th century BCE.

---

43 CIS II, No. 72; Naveh, Development, 53.
44 Porten and Yardeni, *Textbook of Aramaic Documents, Vol. 4*, 260; D 21:3 .

4.3 Conclusion

The two new inscriptions discussed here are a welcome addition to the group of inscriptions written in the Aramaic lapidary script. The first was dated, based on its script, to the 4th century BCE, while the second was dated to the 3rd century BCE. The second one is important since it includes a combination of independent lapidary form of *alef* with the early Aramaic form of the *lamed,* and *mem*, together with a possible development of the *yod* from the independent lapidary form to the early Aramaic one, which adds to the subject of our conference of combining different types of scripts. We have also discussed some issues concerning the content of both inscriptions.

5 General Summary

This study on the relatively small corpus of Aramaic lapidary inscriptions serves as a good example of the complicated situation in which epigraphers might find themselves, with a lot of missing parts of the puzzle and requiring some imagination and a lot of patience.

We surveyed the extant inscriptions in Aramaic lapidary script, focusing on some of the problems characterizing the study of this corpus, especially the diverse dating suggested by scholars, which ranges across decades in some instances, but which sometimes also includes suggestions of very precise dating.

We would like to suggest that this specific type of script might be misleading, as it includes some old forms of the letters *alef, zayin* and *yod* in most groups of inscriptions discussed here, alongside a new inscription coming from Wilson's Arch in Jerusalem, which features a developed Aramaic *yod*.

We might tentatively suggest that, following Naveh, we should allow for different lines of development of this script, such that in some roots some letters were written in the old form, while others were developed. It is thus difficult to give a firm dating to the Aramaic lapidary script.

One should also take into consideration other aspects of the script that have not been addressed, such as the place of origin, type of inscription and the material used.

It is possible that this special script was developed slowly in different places, where the old form changed at a different pace in different places and types of script.

Finally, two short notes:

1. A discovery of a single inscription might influence our understanding and dating of a script – like the one published by Caquot that changed Naveh's conclusions.

2. Small inscriptions, which are the majority of our finds, sometimes can shed light on our study of the development of a script, such is the case of the new inscription from Jerusalem dealt with above – where we can see the old form of *alef* and *zain*, alongside a developed *yod*.

Being aware of our limited information – with a lot of optimism and patience – we hope, with the addition of other inscriptions to be found in the future, to learn more on this fascinating subject.

6 Bibliography

Avigad, Nahman. *Corpus of West Semitic Stamp Seals / by Nahman Avigad ; Revised and Completed by Benjamin Sass.* Publications of the Israel Academy of Sciences and Humanities. Section of Humanities Y. Jerusalem: Israel Academy of Sciences and Humanities : Israel Exploration Society : Institute of Archaeology, Hebrew University of Jerusalem, 1997.

Caquot, André. "Une inscription araméenne d'époque assyrienne." *Hommages à André Dupont-Sommer*, 1971, 9–16.

Dušek, Jan. *Aramaic and Hebrew Inscriptions from Mt. Gerizim and Samaria between Antiochus III and Antiochus IV Epiphanes / by Jan Dusek.* Culture and History of the Ancient Near East ; v. 54, 2012.

Ilan, Tal. *Lexicon of Jewish Names in Late Antiquity / Tal Ilan.* Texte Und Studien Zum Antiken Judentum ; 91,126,141 Y, 2002.

Lemaire, André. *Nouvelles inscriptions araméennes d'Idumée / A. Lemaire.* Transeuphratène. Supplément à Transeuphratène ; no. 3, 9, 1996.

Lemaire, André. "Scripts of Post-Iron Age Aramaic Inscriptions and Ostraca." In *"An Eye for Form": Epigraphic Essays in Honor of Frank Moore Cross*, 235–52. Winona Lake, Indiana, 2014.

Magen, Izchak. *Mount Gerizim Excavations / Yitzhak Magen, Haggai Misgav and Levana Tsfania ; [English Translations, Edward Levin and Michael Guggenheimer ...].* Judea and Samaria Publications ; 2, 8 Y, 2004.

Masada : The Yigael Yadin Excavations 1963–1965 : Final Reports. Masada Reports, 1989.

Naveh, Joseph. "The Development of the Aramaic Script." *Proceeding of the Israel Academy of Sciences and Hummanities* 5 (1976): 1–69.

Naveh, Joseph, and Magen, Y. "Aramaic and Hebrew Inscriptions of the Second-Century BCE AT Mount Gerizim." *ATIQOT* 32, no. 1997 (1997): 9–17.

Bezalel Porten, and Yardeni, A. *Textbook of Aramaic Documents from Ancient Egypt.* Vol. 1: *Letters. Texts and Studies for Students.* Jerusalem: The Hebrew University Department of the History of the Jewish People Texts and Studies for Students, 1986.

Porten, Bezalel, and Yardeni, A. *Textbook of Aramaic Documents from Ancient Egypt.* Vol. 4: *Ostraca & Assorted Inscriptions.* Jerusalem: The Hebrew University Department of the History of the Jewish People Texts and Studies for Students, 1999.

Yadin, Yigael and Naveh, J. The Aramaic and Hebrew ostraca and jar inscriptions from Masada, in *Masada I: The Yigael Yadin Excavations 1963–1965: Final Reports.* Vol. 1, Masada Reports, 1989, pp. 1–68.

Michael Langlois
Theonyms in Palaeo-Hebrew and Other Alternate Scripts on Dead Sea Scrolls

This paper is a follow-up to my palaeographical study of the Dead Sea Scrolls copied with the (Palaeo-)Hebrew script.[1] In my earlier study, I limited myself to scrolls that were integrally copied with this script. I outlined an evolution of the Hebrew script in the Second Temple period and would now like to confront this new typology against Palaeo-Hebrew graphemes attested in scrolls that otherwise use the Aramaic script. In this study, I will limit myself to the use of that script for theonyms. Other uses (such as scribal notations or the so-called cryptic scripts) will be dealt with in another study.

I will now discuss individually, in the order of their inventory number, the palaeography of the Dead Sea scrolls that use the Palaeo-Hebrew script for divine names and titles.

1 1Q11 (1QPs[b])[2]

This manuscript is not dated by the editor; a detailed palaeographical analysis of the Aramaic script attested on this manuscript—as well as the other manuscripts studied here—is beyond the scope of the present essay, so I will limit myself to general observations. Suffice here to say that 1Q11 was probably copied during the first century BCE.

It features a single occurrence of a Palaeo-Hebrew 𐤀 (frag. 4 l. 1), which corresponds to the end of the tetragrammaton. Its ductus is common and does not allow for a precise dating. There is no other attestation of a divine name or title on this fragmentary scroll.

---

1 Michael Langlois, "Dead Sea Scrolls Palaeography and the Samaritan Pentateuch," in *The Samaritan Pentateuch and the Dead Sea Scrolls*, ed. by Michael Langlois, Contributions to Biblical Exegesis and Theology 94, Leuven, Peeters, 2019, p. 255–285.
2 Dominique Barthélemy, "11. Psautier (second exemplaire)," in *Qumran Cave I*, ed. by Dominique Barthélemy and Józef Tadeusz Milik, Discoveries in the Judaean Desert I, Oxford, Clarendon Press, 1955, p. 71, pl. XIII.

2 1Q14 (1QpMic)³

This manuscript is not dated by the editor but was probably copied around the turn of the era. Frag. 3 features two partial occurrences of the tetragrammaton.[4] The first is broken and its reading is unclear: Milik reads יהו[ה but the י seems wide and the angle too open; as for the following ה, its upper stroke does not seem to protrude to the right, contrary to the ה on the following line. Another option would be to read ה]יהו, but the ו would be quite high (unless the trace does not correspond to the base), and the י would feature a thick, striated diagonal. Finally, one could also try and read וי]יהו, but the problem with the י remains (notwithstanding the unusual use of a *mater lectionis* here). In any case, this occurrence is too damaged to serve as evidence for the evolution of the script.

The second occurrence, by contrast, exhibits two well-preserved letters: הו. Both use a common ductus that prevents any specific dating. The thickness and beveling of some of the strokes may however indicate that another calamus was used; this does not mean that the tetragrammaton was penned by another scribe, but it is a possibility.

Finally, an occurrence of Palaeo-Hebrew אל is partially preserved on frag. 12 l. 2.[5] א is partially erased, but ל is well preserved. It features a straight, slanted ascender that does not seem to have been penned together with the base. The base is narrow and features a tick at its right end. A similar tick is nascent in 11Q1 and developed and 4Q22 (where it is sometimes more rounded, as in 1Q35, 3Q14). Its use here could be indicative of a typological development around the first century BCE; such conclusion remains hypothetical, however, as there is but a single occurrence on this scroll, and it is in a degraded context.

---

3 Józef Tadeusz Milik, "14. Commentaire de Michée," in *Qumran Cave I*, ed. by Dominique Barthélemy and Józef Tadeusz Milik, Discoveries in the Judaean Desert I, Oxford, Clarendon Press, 1955, p. 77–80, pl. XV.

4 See especially PAM 40.545 available at https://www.deadseascrolls.org.il/explore-the-archive/image/B-278281.

5 See especially PAM 40.445 available at https://www.deadseascrolls.org.il/explore-the-archive/image/B-278226. See also PAM 40.548, available at https://www.deadseascrolls.org.il/explore-the-archive/image/B-278284.

3 1Q15 (1QpZeph)[6]

This manuscript is attested by a single fragment for which Milik gives no date in his *editio princeps*. The few letters that are preserved may have been penned around the first half of the first century BCE, but a slightly earlier or later date is possible, as the lack of samples for each letter of the alphabet prevents a more accurate dating.

The fragment features an almost complete occurrence of the tetragrammaton in Palaeo-Hebrew (l. 4), notwithstanding a trace of ink at the previous line which Milik believes to be the beginning of another occurrence. ⌐ is drawn in a common fashion, whereas ꓩ seems to feature a large zigzag-shaped head with a particularly wide upper stroke. This ductus is well attested on coins from both the Hasmonaean period[7] and the Judaean revolt,[8] but it is only nascent on Palaeo-Hebrew Dead Sea scrolls (compare 1QpHab and 4Q171 below). ⌐ is incomplete but seems to feature a slanted backward stroke well attested at the time.

4 1Q27 (1QMyst)[9]

This manuscript is not dated by its editor but may have been copied in the first century BCE, perhaps around the middle of the century. A single occurrence of a Palaeo-Hebrew ⌐ꓩ is preserved on a small fragment[10] that was later joined at the bottom of frag. 1 col. ii.[11] ꓩ is incomplete but seems to feature a long left stroke, which may be indicative of a late development. ⌐ follows a common ductus, without any additional ornamentation or development.

---

6 Józef Tadeusz Milik, "15. Commentaire de Sophonie," in *Qumran Cave I*, ed. by Dominique Barthélemy and Józef Tadeusz Milik, Discoveries in the Judaean Desert I, Oxford, Clarendon Press, 1955, p. 80, pl. XV.

7 Ya'akov Meshorer, *A Treasury of Jewish Coins: From the Persian Period to Bar Kokhba*, Jerusalem, Yad Ben-Zvi, 2001, p. 43ff.

8 Meshorer, *Treasury of Jewish Coins*, p. 132.

9 Józef Tadeusz Milik, "27. 'Livre des Mystères,'" in *Qumran Cave I*, ed. by Dominique Barthélemy and Józef Tadeusz Milik, Discoveries in the Judaean Desert I, Oxford, Clarendon Press, 1955, p. 102–107, pl. XXI–XXII.

10 See PAM 40.446, available at https://www.deadseascrolls.org.il/explore-the-archive/image/B-277262.

11 See PAM 40.523, available at https://www.deadseascrolls.org.il/explore-the-archive/image/B-278259.

5 1Q35 (1QHᵇ)¹²

In his edition of this manuscript, Milik does not offer any date, but the script is a typical Herodian formal hand. 1Q35 was thus probably copied around the first century CE, preferably around the first half of the century, as none of the so-called "late" Herodian features are observed. (And even those features might already be attested in the first century BCE.¹³)

A single occurrence of a Palaeo-Hebrew 𐤋𐤀 is preserved on this manuscript (frag. 1 l. 5).¹⁴ 𐤀 follows a common ductus; the lower parallel stroke protrudes to the right so as to reach the guideline, a phenomenon sometimes (but not always) observed on 4Q11, when the Palaeo-Hebrew letters start hanging from the ceiling line;¹⁵ see further 4Q183 below. 𐤋 features a straight ascender, which contrasts with the concave base ending in a small curve or tick. The same phenomenon is observed in 3Q14 and 4Q22, where it is sometimes more angular, as in 1Q14. See further below 4Q57, 4Q183, 4Q258 and 6Q18.

6 1QHᵃ (1QHodayotᵃ)¹⁶

The Hodayot scroll was subjected to radiocarbon dating by Bonani *et alii*. Five fragments were tested, three gelatinized and two non-gelatinized. The results

12 Józef Tadeusz Milik, "35. Recueil de cantiques d'action de grâces (1QH)," in *Qumran Cave I*, ed. by Dominique Barthélemy and Józef Tadeusz Milik, Discoveries in the Judaean Desert I, Oxford, Clarendon Press, 1955, p. 136–138, pl. XXXI.
13 Compare *e.g.* the palaeographical and radiocarbon dating of MS 2861 in Torleif Elgvin, Kipp Davis, and Michael Langlois, eds., *Gleanings from the Caves. Dead Sea Scrolls and Artefacts from The Schøyen Collection*, Library of Second Temple Studies 71, London, Bloomsbury T&T Clark, 2016, p. 120.193. My "blind" palaeographical analysis led me to conclude that it was penned by a late or post-Herodian hand, hence a date "during or slightly after the second half of the first century AD" (p. 120). Yet, radiocarbon dating (p. 193) favors the first century BCE, though the first half of the first century CE is not excluded. See further 1QpHab and 4Q267 below.
14 See esp. PAM 40.451, available at https://www.deadseascrolls.org.il/explore-the-archive/image/B-278227.
15 Langlois, "Dead Sea Scrolls Palaeography and the Samaritan Pentateuch," p. 271.
16 Hartmut Stegemann, Eileen M. Schuller, and Carol A. Newsom, *Qumran Cave 1. III. 1QHodayotᵃ with Incorporation of 1QHodayotᵇ and 4QHodayotᵃ⁻ᶠ*, Discoveries in the Judaean Desert XL, Oxford, Clarendon Press, 2009.

were not aberrant, with uncalibrated dates of 2006±52 BP and 1943±36 BP.[17] I used the intCal 20.14c calibration dataset to produce calibrated dates:

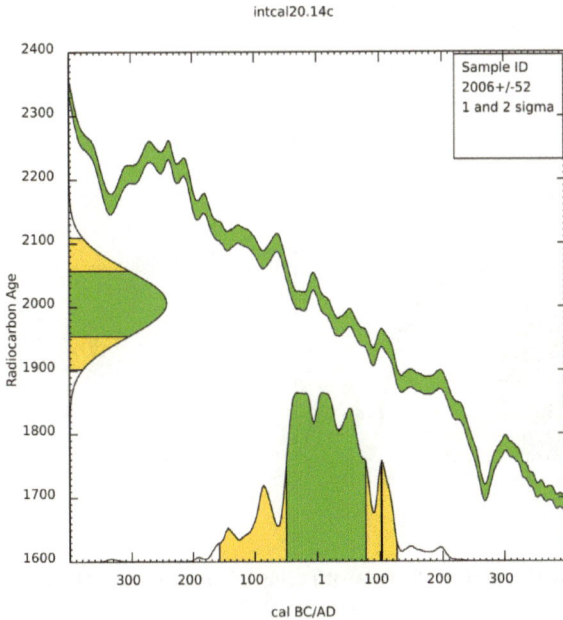

Figure 1: Calibrated radiocarbon dating of 1QHᵃ (1QHodayotᵃ) using intCal 20.14c (uncalibrated date: 2006±52 BP)

---

17 Georges Bonani, Susan Ivy, Willy Wolfli, Magen Broshi, Israel Carmi, and John Strugnell, "Radiocarbon Dating of Fourteen Dead Sea Scrolls," *Radiocarbon* 34/3, 1992, p. 848.

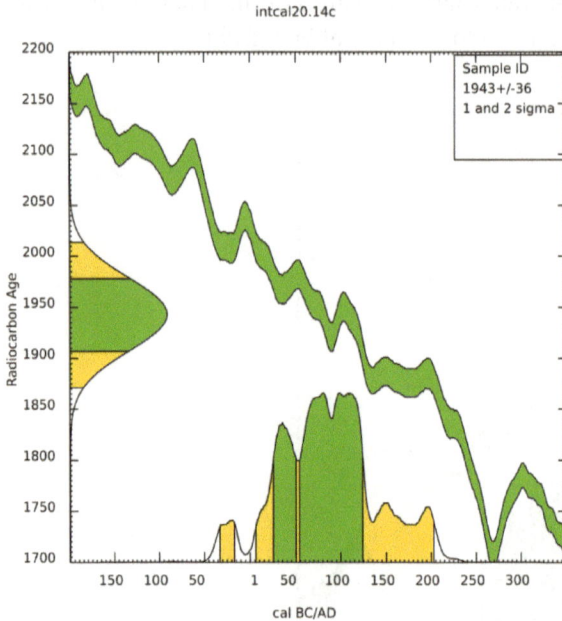

Figure 2: Calibrated radiocarbon dating of 1QHᵃ (1QHodayotᵃ) using intCal 20.14c (uncalibrated date: 1943±36 BP)

For the gelatinized fragments, the 1σ-calibrated ranges are 49 BCE–78 AD and 102–104 CE, while the 2σ-calibrated range is 158 BCE–127 CE. For the non-gelati-nized fragments, the 1σ-calibrated ranges are 25–51 CE and 54–124 CE, while the 2σ-calibrated ranges are 32–16 BCE, and 7–204 CE. These results show that the degradation of fragments complicates their dating; yet, they also suggest that the manuscript was probably copied around the first century CE. From a palaeo-graphical standpoint, the columns that occasionally use the Palaeo-Hebrew script (see below) were copied by a formal and developed Herodian hand at home in the first century CE.

Three occurrences of Palaeo-Hebrew 𐤀𐤋 have been preserved: VII 38, IX 28 and X 36, the latter with a pronominal suffix 𐤉. There is no occurrence of יהוה or אלהים in any script, but there are multiple occurrences of אדוני, none of which are in Palaeo-Hebrew. Furthermore, there are other occurrences of אל that have not been copied with the Palaeo-Hebrew script (see *e.g.* XI 35; XII 13.19.32; etc.). This could be attributed to a change of scribe; there is indeed a clear change of hands at col. XIX,[18] but the problem is that occurrences of אל in the Palaeo-Hebrew and Jewish scripts are found in columns that seem to have been penned by the same scribe (compare cols. X and XI for instance). Unless two scribes with an almost identical hand are responsible for these columns, it is better to suppose that a single scribe stopped using the Palaeo-Hebrew script for the divine name. This may be of his own will, but one may also hypothesize that the source(s) he was copying already featured such a change. He may for instance have copied a manuscript that was itself penned by several scribes with differing scribal practices, notably regarding the copy of the divine name using the Palaeo-Hebrew script. This may also be due to the compilation, by himself or by his predecessors, of multiple literary sources, some of which—but not all—were copied using a Palaeo-Hebrew divine name. For instance, the occurrence of אל in the Jewish script in XI 35 is part of a complete psalm (in ll. 20–37)[19] different from the one that features the Palaeo-Hebrew 𐤀𐤋 in X 36.[20] Such a hypothesis is challenged by a possible occurrence of אל in the Jewish script in XI 4 which, according to some, is part of the same psalm as X 36.[21] The reading of אל is, however, uncertain, and the degraded state of the manuscript complicates the division of the text into literary units. Last but not least, an apparent lack of consistency or generalization in the use of the Palaeo-Hebrew script for theonyms may also be observed in 4Q57 (4QIsaᶜ); this additional documentation may help weigh various explanations.

Let us now have a closer look at the Palaeo-Hebrew script used in 1QHᵃ. The shaft of 𐤀 is vertical, sometimes almost slanted forward (see IX 28). Vertical shafts are sometimes observed on Iron age seals, as well as on coins from the Hasmonaean period and the two Judaean revolts.[22] Forward-slanting shafts are more unusual but attested in 11Q1. The two diagonal strokes are drawn independently; the upper parallel seems to cross the shaft so as to produce a left stroke, according to a common ductus attested as early as the Iron age.

The single occurrence of 𐤃 likewise follows a common ductus and features a highly slanted right stroke that does not protrude to the left of the shaft. 𐤋 is

---

18 "Scribe A" stops at the middle of l. 25, and is replaced by "Scribe B" and "Scribe C" (or "Scribe A-two" and "Scribe B") according to Stegemann, Schuller, and Newsom, *1QHodayotᵃ*, pp. 241–242.

19 Stegemann, Schuller, and Newsom, *1QHodayotᵃ*, p. 146.

20 This psalm starts at X 33 according to Stegemann, Schuller, and Newsom, *1QHodayotᵃ*, p. 134.

21 Stegemann, Schuller, and Newsom, *1QHodayotᵃ*, p. 146.

22 See e.g. Meshorer, *Treasury of Jewish Coins*, p. 32.132.163.

more or less concave, sometimes thickened at the top, but with little or no bevel-ing. The calamus used for Palaeo-Hebrew letters does not appear to be different from the one used to copy the rest of the text. There is, however, a large gap in IX 28 which may suggest that ✚ was added later. Yet, such gaps may be observed on the same column, even in the middle of a sentence (e.g. מה אדבר l. 25). It is therefore not necessary to suppose that the Palaeo-Hebrew letters were added at a later stage.

7 1QpHab[23]

This manuscript's parchment was subjected to radiocarbon dating, which yielded an absolute date of 2054±22 BP.[24] I used the intCal 20.14c calibration da-taset to produce calibrated dates:

---

23 Millar Burrows, ed., *The Dead Sea Scrolls of St. Mark's Monastery. Volume I, The Isaiah Manu-script and the Habakkuk Commentary*, New Haven, American Schools of Oriental Research, 1950. Color photographs are available at http://dss.collections.imj.org.il/habakkuk.
24 Timothy A. J. Jull, Douglas J. Donahue, Magen Broshi, and Emanuel Toy, "Radiocarbon Da-ting of Scrolls and Linen Fragments from the Judean Desert," *Radiocarbon* 37/1, 1995, p. 14.

intcal20.14c

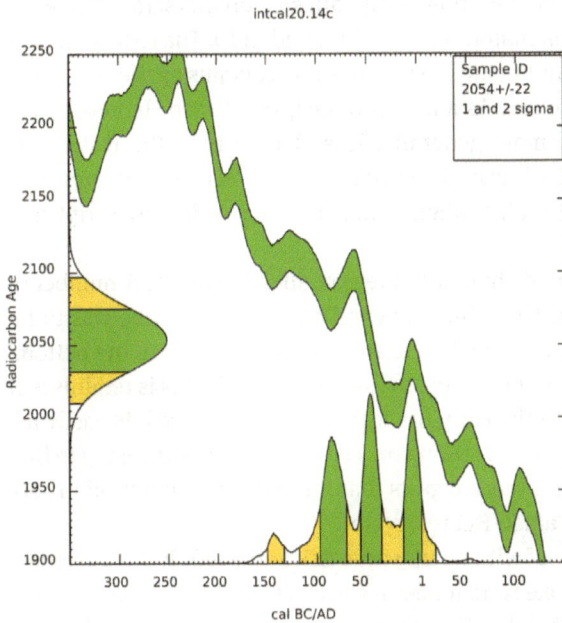

Figure 3: Calibrated radiocarbon dating of 1QpHab using intCal 20.14c (uncalibrated date: 2054±22 BP)

The 1σ-calibrated ranges are 97–71 BCE, 57–36 BCE, and 14 BCE–5 CE. The 2σ-calibrated ranges are 150–133 BCE and 117 BCE–18 CE. From a palaeographical standpoint, the script is Herodian and would usually be dated to the turn of the era or even the early first century CE.[25] The difference between the two methods of dating is not big enough to invoke a contamination of the samples that were radiocarbon-dated. One could argue that the calibration curve should be adjusted a little, or that the copy of the manuscript took place sometime after the animal was killed. But the likeliest explanation is that what are traditionally called "Herodian" features arose slightly earlier than previously thought,[26] and that this manuscript was indeed copied in the first century BCE, preferably in the second half of the century.

---

25 It is classified as "Mid- to Late Herodian," *i.e.* 1–68 CE, in Emanuel Tov, ed., *The Texts from the Judaean Desert. Indices and an Introduction to the Discoveries in the Judaean Desert Series*, Discoveries in the Judaean Desert XXXIX, Oxford, Clarendon Press, 2002, p. 374.
26 See already n. 13 above.

Let us now look at the Palaeo-Hebrew script attested on this scroll. There are four instances of the tetragrammaton: VI 14, X 7.14, and XI 10. The letters are suspended from the guideline and penned with the same calamus as the rest of the text, without additional beveling. As a matter of fact, the Palaeo-Hebrew letters are often less beveled and, more generally, less elegant than the rest of the script;[27] they are reminiscent of incised inscriptions rather than inked documents. The scribe seems less comfortable when using the Palaeo-Hebrew script and makes more mistakes.

⩍ features a barely slanted shaft and three parallel diagonals. A number of occurrences have been corrected, which may indicate that the scribe was unfamiliar with the Palaeo-Hebrew script. The shaft does not protrude to the bottom, and the upper diagonal does not protrude to the right. This ductus is reminiscent of some Hasmonaean coins in the early first century BCE,[28] where it is easily accounted for by the constraints of inscribing on a coin. It is more surprising to find such a ductus on a parchment; this suggests that the scribe was not used to copying parchments using the Palaeo-Hebrew script.

ﬞ features a horizontal roof with an upwards tick at the left. It is followed by a long diagonal. The last stroke is no longer a vertical shaft but a short diagonal that joins the body at mid-height. This development is quite remarkable and without exact parallels: coins of the Judaean revolt do exhibit an angular "zig-zag" head followed by a short shaft[29] and are not unlike the ﬞ attested here after rotation; but the first stroke is not as short as what may be observed here.

⩯ features a very short shaft followed by a long backward stroke. Some occurrences may give the impression that the second diagonal and the backward stroke are penned together, but this is due to the fact that the shaft barely protrudes at the bottom; a closer examination reveals that the two strokes are actually independent (see esp. VI 14 and XI 10). This phenomenon is reminiscent of some Hasmonaean coins, perhaps minted by Hyrcanus II, in which the two strokes are indeed penned together.[30] This ductus follows a development that is diametrically opposed to the one which will give rise to the Samaritan ⩯, where

27 Which is quite the opposite of what Stegemann states according to Emanuel Tov, *Scribal Practices and Approaches Reflected in the Texts Found in the Judean Desert*, Studies on the Texts of the Desert of Judah 54, Leiden, Brill, 2004, p. 240.

28 See e.g. group E in Meshorer, *Treasury of Jewish Coins*, p. 44. See also Mark David McLean, "The Use and Development of Palaeo-Hebrew in the Hellenistic and Roman Periods," Harvard University, 1982, pl. 14.

29 Meshorer, *Treasury of Jewish Coins*, p. 132.

30 See goup S in Meshorer, *Treasury of Jewish Coins*, p. 46.

the backwards stroke protrudes to the left and gives rise to a third diagonal stroke.[31]

8 2Q3 (2QExod^b)[32]

This manuscript was published by Baillet, who identifies the hand as Herodian. The script, however, is semi-formal and the few letters that are preserved do not exhibit typical Herodian features. 2Q3 may therefore have been copied around the first century BCE.

At least two occurrences of the Palaeo-Hebrew tetragrammaton have been preserved. At the beginning of frag. 2 l. 2, a Palaeo-Hebrew 𐤉 is followed by what may be read as a Palaeo-Hebrew 𐤄. At the end of frag. 7 l. 1, Baillet reads the beginning of a Palaeo-Hebrew tetragrammaton, but his identification of the fragment must be abandoned: l. 2, the third letter features an angular elbow and cannot therefore be a 𐤅.[33] This leaves us with only one other instance of the tetragrammaton: frag. 8 l. 3, where the initial 𐤉 has disappeared in the lacuna and the first 𐤄 is broken. From a palaeographical standpoint, the ductus attested by 𐤄 is quite common. 𐤉 features a large angular head, with a diagonal horn reminiscent of the scribe's (Aramaic) ר. The same scribe probably copied the Palaeo-Hebrew tetragrammaton. A similar ductus for 𐤉 may be observed in 11Q1, albeit less beveled.

Besides the tetragrammaton, a possible occurrence of אלהים might be found in frag. 5 l. 5, where there might be the end of a final ם at the beginning of the line, followed by a trace of the following word. This reconstruction is uncertain, however, so that no conclusion may be drawn as to the use of Palaeo-Hebrew for other theonyms.

---

31 Langlois, "Dead Sea Scrolls Palaeography and the Samaritan Pentateuch," pp. 278–279.
32 Maurice Baillet, "3. Exode (deuxième exemplaire)," in *Les 'petites grottes' de Qumrân*, ed. by Maurice Baillet, Józef Tadeusz Milik, and Roland de Vaux, Discoveries in the Judaean Desert of Jordan III, Oxford, Clarendon Press, 1962, p. 52–55, pl. XI.
33 See especially PAM 42.958, available at https://www.deadseascrolls.org.il/explore-the-archive/image/B-284856. See also PAM 40.556, available at https://www.deadseascrolls.org.il/explore-the-archive/image/B-278362.

9 3Q3 (3QLam)[34]

In his *editio princeps*, Baillet qualifies the script as a "small Herodian calligraphy." The reduced size of both the fragments and the script makes it quite difficult to offer a palaeographical dating, but the manuscript may indeed have been copied around the turn of the era. A single occurrence of ⟨Hebrew⟩ in the Palaeo-Hebrew script is preserved on frag. 1 l. 2.[35] The second and third parallel strokes of ⟨letter⟩ tend to join at their left end, and the shaft might be slightly curved at the bottom. The head of ⟨letter⟩ seems to follow a zigzag ductus. ⟨letter⟩ has a long diagonal tail. All of these features are quite common.

10 3Q14 frag. 18[36]

Twenty-one unidentified Hebrew and Aramaic fragments from Qumran cave 3Q have been grouped together and labeled 3Q14. One of them, frag. 18, has preserved but a few letters, including a Palaeo-Hebrew ⟨letters⟩.[37] The ductus is quite common. ⟨letter⟩ has a concave ascender and a rounded base that seems to produce a tick. An even more rounded base is found in 1Q35 and sometimes in 4Q22, but in those manuscripts the ascender is straighter.

---

34 Maurice Baillet, "3. Lamentations," in *Les 'petites grottes' de Qumrân*, ed. by Maurice Baillet, Józef Tadeusz Milik, and Roland de Vaux, Discoveries in the Judaean Desert of Jordan III, Oxford, Clarendon Press, 1962, p. 95, pl. XVIII.

35 See especially the new photograph, B-482068, available at https://www.deadseascrolls. org.il/explore-the-archive/image/B-482068. See also PAM 42.955, available at https:// www.deadseascrolls.org.il/explore-the-archive/image/B-284853.

36 Maurice Baillet, "14. Fragments isolés," in *Les 'petites grottes' de Qumrân*, ed. by Maurice Baillet, Józef Tadeusz Milik, and Roland de Vaux, Discoveries in the Judaean Desert of Jordan III, Oxford, Clarendon Press, 1962, p. 102–104, pl. XIX.

37 See PAM 42.956, available at https://www.deadseascrolls.org.il/explore-the-archive/image/B-284854. See also PAM 41.564, available at https://www.deadseascrolls.org.il/explore-the-archive/image/B-299014.

11 4Q20 (4QExodʲ)³⁸

This manuscript is attested by two identified and five tiny unidentified fragments. Their editor, Judith Sanderson, dates its copy to "approximately the early first century CE." The few letters preserved on frag. 1³⁹ indeed seem to exhibit Herodian features and Sanderson's dating may thus be adopted. The end of a Palaeo-Hebrew ◄ is visible at the beginning of l. 3 and attests to the use of that script to write the tetragrammaton. Not much can be said from a palaeographical standpoint, except that the three strokes are parallel and that the Palaeo-Hebrew script seems a bit larger than the rest of the text.

12 4Q26b (4QLevᵍ)⁴⁰

This single fragment is not dated in the *editio princeps*. It is in bad condition⁴¹ but seems to have been penned by a formal Herodian hand, perhaps around the turn of the era. It features two occurrences of the tetragrammaton, both preceded by the preposition ל. The second occurrence, including the preposition,⁴² is penned with the Palaeo-Hebrew script. Such an inconsistency is attested elsewhere for other theonyms (e.g. 4Q57, see **Table 1**), but not for the tetragrammaton.

In terms of palaeography, the fragment is badly damaged, so that it is difficult to give a meaningful description of ◄ and ◄, except that they seem to adopt a common ductus with little beveling. ↗ is less slanted than ◄ and features a long upper stroke, followed at an angle by an almost equally long diagonal. This

38 Judith E. Sanderson, "20. 4QExodʲ," in *Qumran Cave 4. VII. Genesis to Numbers*, Discoveries in the Judaean Desert XII, Oxford, Clarendon Press, 1994, p. 149–150, pl. XXI.
39 See PAM 42.603, available at https://www.deadseascrolls.org.il/explore-the-archive/image/B-284014. The condition of the fragment has since degraded, compare B-472350 available at https://www.deadseascrolls.org.il/explore-the-archive/image/B-472350.
40 Emanuel Tov, "26b. 4QLevᵍ," in *Qumran Cave 4. VII: Genesis to Numbers*, ed. by Eugene C. Ulrich, Frank Moore Cross, James R. Davila, Nathan Jastram, Judith E. Sanderson, Emanuel Tov, and John Strugnell, Discoveries in the Judaean Desert XII, Oxford, Clarendon Press, 1994, p. 203–204, pl. XXXVII.
41 See B-359506, available at https://www.deadseascrolls.org.il/explore-the-archive/image/B-359506. See also PAM 43.036, available at https://www.deadseascrolls.org.il/explore-the-archive/image/B-284277.
42 Contrary to what may be seen *e.g.* in the "Dead Sea Scrolls Biblical Corpus" software module by Martin G. Abegg *et alii* (v. 3.3). But the *editio princeps* correctly notes it.

leaves little room for the middle stroke, unless it protruded beyond the upper stroke, which is unlikely; it was probably short, as in 11Q1 and sometimes 4Q22 or 4Q45. The ascender of l seems straight, rather than concave, and its base quite long, slightly slanted, following a common ductus.

13 4Q38a (4QDeut[k2])[43]

According to the *editio princeps*, this manuscript was copied by "an Early Herodian formal hand (*c.* 30–1 BCE)." This dating is possible but a bit narrow, as the hand is actually semiformal and sometimes exhibits further development (see *e.g.* ʋ). The influence of cursive forms precludes such a specific dating, and I would not exclude a date in the early first century CE. It might thus be safer to suggest that 4Q38a was copied around the turn of the era.

A single occurrence of the tetragrammaton is preserved in 4Q38a, and it is written in the Palaeo-Hebrew script (frag. 5 l. 6).[44] ᚱ features a thick shaft and thin horizontals; the upper parallel protrudes to the right, and the lower is slightly curved upwards on the left so as to join the middle horizontal. The overall ductus is quite common, and the scribe seems confident. ᚤ features a zigzagged head followed by a thick shaft, which is even more thickened at the bottom. ᚦ does not exhibit beveling; its tail is short, does not protrude to the left, and is penned slightly above the bottom of the shaft (see 4Q171 below).

But is this really the only occurrence of the tetragrammaton? Duncan initially thought that these fragments belonged to 4Q38, since they were "copied by the same scribe," but the slightly smaller letter size and, more importantly, the use of Palaeo-Hebrew for the tetragrammaton led her to treat them separately, as "no other manuscript exhibits a discrepancy like this in the writing of the divine name."[45] This artificial separation into two manuscripts could be problematic for

---

43 Julie Ann Duncan, "38a. 4QDeut[k2]," in *Qumran Cave 4. IX. Deuteronomy, Joshua, Judges, Kings*, ed. by Eugene C. Ulrich, Frank Moore Cross, Sidnie White Crawford, Julie Ann Duncan, Patrick W. Skehan, Emanuel Tov, and Julio Trebolle Barrera, Discoveries in the Judaean Desert XIV, Oxford, Clarendon Press, 1995, p. 99–103, pl. XXV.
44 See especially B-368501, available at https://www.deadseascrolls.org.il/explore-the-archive/image/B-368501.
45 Julie Ann Duncan, "38. 4QDeut[k1]," in *Qumran Cave 4. IX. Deuteronomy, Joshua, Judges, Kings*, ed. by Eugene C. Ulrich, Frank Moore Cross, Sidnie White Crawford, Julie Ann Duncan, Patrick W. Skehan, Emanuel Tov, and Julio Trebolle Barrera, Discoveries in the Judaean Desert XIV, Oxford, Clarendon Press, 1995, p. 93.

the present study, as 4Q38 could actually document an inconsistent use of the Palaeo-Hebrew script in the same manuscript. Such inconsistency is attested for other theonyms (see 1QHª above and 4Q57 etc. below), and it is of paramount importance not to be trapped in circular reasoning.

Fortunately, it was actually wrong to believe that all fragments had been copied by the same scribe: a closer examination (see esp. ט) reveals that there are indeed two hands, which correspond to 4Q38 and 4Q38a. The former is slightly less developed, which explains why its palaeographical date range is a bit earlier.[46] But the two ranges overlap, of course, so that 4Q38 and 4Q38a may have been copied at the same time. As a matter of fact, they might even be part of the same scroll: evidence from the few well-preserved Dead Sea scrolls suggests that they may have been copied by several scribes (*e.g.* 11QTª). Since both 4Q38 and 4Q38a preserve the Book of Deuteronomy, since their fragments do not overlap, and since they were penned around the same time, it is possible that they actually belonged to the same manuscript. If so, the inconsistent use of Palaeo-Hebrew for the tetragrammaton may simply be due to different scribal practices (see further 4Q171 below).

14 4Q57 (4QIsaᶜ)[47]

4Q57 was copied by a skilled, formal Herodian hand. Such developed scripts are traditionally dated to the mid-first century CE,[48] but radiocarbon dating could reveal that they appeared in the first century BCE.[49] I would thus not exclude a date at the turn of the era. In this manuscript, divine names and titles are regularly, but not systematically, written using the Palaeo-Hebrew script, as shown on **Table 1** below.

---

46 The semicursive features and the absence of further development led me to suggest that 4Q38 was copied around the second half of the first century BCE; see Langlois, "Dead Sea Scrolls Palaeography and the Samaritan Pentateuch," pp. 258–259.
47 Patrick W. Skehan and Eugene C. Ulrich, "57. 4QIsaᶜ," in *Qumran Cave 4, X. The Prophets*, ed. by Frank Moore Cross, Russell E. Fuller, Judith E. Sanderson, Patrick W. Skehan, and Emanuel Tov, Discoveries in the Judaean Desert XV, Oxford, Clarendon Press, 1997, p. 45–74, pl. VII–XII.
48 It is thus dated "from about the middle third of the first century CE" by Skehan and Ulrich, "4QIsaᶜ," p. 46.
49 See 1Q35 above (esp. n. 13); see also 1QpHab.

Table 1: Theonyms in 4Q57 and their script

Theonym	Palaeo-Hebrew script	Aramaic script	Total
אדוני	3× (9 i 25; 18–20 11; 63 2)	2× (3–5 + 50 2; 9 ii + 11 + 12 i + 52 27)	5×
אל		1× (27 35)	1×
אלוהים	3× (24 39; 33–35 + 55–57 10; 36–38 3)	1× (44–47 16)	4×
יהוה	26× (1–2 + 49 11; 6 6; 8 2.6; 9 i 25; 9 ii + 11 + 12 i + 52 15.24.25.26.30.40; 13 8; 12 ii + 14–15 + 53 30.34; 21–22 1.4; 23 9; 24 36.38; 25–26 35.40; 36–38 2; 44–47 5.9; 62 1.2)		26×
צבאות	2× (24 38; 62 1)	1× (40 3)	3×

The table only lists occurrences that are sufficiently preserved for a relatively confident identification. The most common theonym is, by far, יהוה; all occurrences are written with the Palaeo-Hebrew script. The same cannot be said of other theonyms: not only are they less frequent, but they are usually attested in both scripts. What are the circumstances that may account for such phenomenon? One may think that the Palaeo-Hebrew script was used for other titles only when they immediately followed the tetragrammaton, but צבאות is attested in both scripts after יהוה. Moreover, אלוהים is found in Palaeo-Hebrew both with and without a preceding tetragrammaton. One may also wonder whether the Palaeo-Hebrew script indicates that the theonym is not to be pronounced, but this raises a similar issue; for instance, the syntagm [כו]ֹה אמר א[דוני יהוה] "[thu]s says the L[ord Yhwh]" (3–5 50 2 = Isa 10:24) uses the Aramaic script for אדוני, but the same syntagm [כוה [אֹמר אדונ]י יהוה] "[thus]says the Lor[d Yhwh]" (18–20 11 = Isa 30:15) uses the Palaeo-Hebrew script. It is difficult to explain why אדוני would be pronounced in the first case and not in the second—and if so, what would it be substituted by?

Another explanation would be to distinguish between various passages in the book of Isaiah, or between different scribes, or between multiple sources, as was already suggested above for 1QHᵃ. The first two options are unlikely here, unless two or more scribes with very similar hands were responsible for the copy of the scroll, which is possible but cannot be demonstrated. As for the existence of various sources, such an explanation is possible but would only confirm that the scribe did not feel the need to harmonize the use of the Palaeo-Hebrew script, except perhaps for the tetragrammaton.

In the end, the simplest explanation is that such use of the Palaeo-Hebrew script began with the tetragrammaton and was later expanded to other theonyms. This expansion was perhaps only nascent when this manuscript was copied, or at least not sufficiently rooted in the scribal practices surrounding its copy to be generalized. As **Table 1** shows, other theonyms are much less common than יהוה, which may have slowed down a possible process of generalization. But such process remains uncertain: in two cases, אדוני or אלוהים may have immediately followed a Palaeo-Hebrew tetragrammaton (40 3; 44–47 16). If so (and this remains conjectural, since the tetragrammaton is lost in both cases), the scribe was already using the Palaeo-Hebrew script and could have been inclined to keep using it.

Overall, this manuscript documents both the tendency to expand the use of the Palaeo-Hebrew script to other theonyms, and the lack of generalization of this practice. It is thus an important witness in the evolution of this phenomenon.

A corollary to the use of the Palaeo-Hebrew script for common names is the occasional presence of a suffix, which is then written with the same script, as was already observed above in 1QHᵃ (see further 4Q243). Prefixes—such as conjunctions or prepositions—are likewise copied using the same script, as already seen on 4Q26b (4QLevᵍ), and unlike 4Q171 (see below). This increases the repertoire of Palaeo-Hebrew letters, as we will see now.

𐤉 is rather small. The diagonal is straight, and the upper parallel is almost as long. The lower parallel is short, does not protrude to the right, and sometimes slightly less slanted.[50] 𐤐 follows an angular ductus, with marked triangular head. The upper stroke protrudes to the right, which might indicate a further development, unless it is an occasional phenomenon (since this is the only head of 𐤐 preserved on this scroll). Such a protrusion seems to develop during the Hasmonaean period,[51] but the best parallels are found in coins from the first Judaean revolt.[52] The shaft is long, slightly slanted, and features an angular elbow followed by a long horizontal base.[53] 𐤁 likewise follows an angular ductus, with a narrow triangular head that's as long as the shaft.

𐤎 features three parallel strokes of equal length. The two lower strokes do not join at the end; on the contrary, they are sometimes curved downwards on

---

50 See frag. 18-20 l. 11 on PAM 43.022, available at https://www.deadseascrolls.org.il/explore-the-archive/image/B-284263.
51 See *e.g.* Meshorer, *Treasury of Jewish Coins*, p. 45. For a more developed form at the turn of the Herodian period, see *e.g.* McLean, "Palaeo-Hebrew in the Hellenistic and Roman Periods" pl. 24 n° 3.
52 Meshorer, *Treasury of Jewish Coins*, p. 132.
53 See frag. 12 ii + 14-15 + 53 l. 30 on the same photograph.

the left. This phenomenon probably develops the ductus attested *e.g.* on 6Q2 l. 2, where the lower strokes are more slanted than the upper.

The head of 𐤀 is usually quite angular, but sometimes a bit thicker and more rounded. The shaft is much thicker and slanted. 𐤃 is more slanted and, on some occurrences at least, each stroke seems penned separately. The tail is raised, so that it is usually not parallel to the left strokes, though on occasion these are quite slanted. 𐤋 features a tall and concave ascender, sometimes thickened at the top. The base is raised and thickened at its end, or even rounded, a phenomenon already observed in 1Q35 (see also 4Q258) and that will be much more developed in 4Q183 and 6Q18.

The descender of 𐤌 is slanted and angled, to the extent that it is raised at the end and protrudes to the left. The same phenomenon occurs with 𐤍, whose head is narrower and features a small horn. The ductus of 𐤔 differs from the usual accordion shape adopted by the scribes of the Dead Sea scrolls: the strokes are stacked on top of each other, like those of 𐤕. The closest parallels are 4Q124 and 11Q1, but the ductus is much more pronounced here; elbows are more rounded, and the lower stroke barely protrudes to the right. This is not a new ductus, though, as it is already found on ostraca from the late Iron Age; its presence here confirms that it was not lost during the second half of the first millennium BCE, and that the use of the Palaeo-Hebrew script retained its diversity.

The scribe used a dot to separate two words in frag. 9 col. i l. 25, but not in frag. 24 l. 38. This absence may be due to the fact that the scribe rarely has an opportunity to use such a dot, since his use of the Palaeo-Hebrew script is limited to theonyms. In such scrolls as 4Q45 and 4Q124, which are entirely copied in Palaeo-Hebrew, the use of separating dots has been abandoned.[54] In the case of 4Q57, the limited number of attestations precludes any firm conclusions but seems consistent with the evolution of scribal practices.

15 4Q161 (4QpIsaᵃ)[55]

The *editio princeps* does not discuss the script of this manuscript, but a quick look suffices to conclude that it was penned by a semi-formal Herodian hand, with a few developed features. It is very similar to that of 4Q171 (see below), but a few

54 Langlois, "Dead Sea Scrolls Palaeography and the Samaritan Pentateuch," p. 267.
55 John Marco Allegro, *Qumrân Cave 4. I (4Q158–4Q186)*, Discoveries in the Judaean Desert of Jordan V, Oxford, Clarendon Press, 1968, pp. 11–15, pl. IV–V.

differences suggest that the manuscripts were copied by different scribes (compare *e.g.* ט). By comparison, the ductus of 4Q38a (see above) is more rounded and slightly less developed. In all likelihood, 4Q161 and 4Q171 were copied around the same time, after 4Q38a. On the basis of radiocarbon dating carried out on 4Q171 (see below), we may conclude that 4Q161 was probably copied around the mid-first century CE.

A single occurrence of יהוה, in frag. 8–10 l. 13, is written in the Palaeo-Hebrew script. A few lines below (l. 18), the theonym אל does not receive the same treatment. This was already the case for a possible fragmentary אדוני on frag. 2–4 l. 6. The few Palaeo-Hebrew letters preserved on the fragment[56] are much more angular than the Aramaic script, and they also differ from 4Q38a. Yet, the two scrolls exhibit similar hands with semi-cursive influences. This raises the question of scribal training: the scribes of 4Q38a and 4Q161 seem to have received a similar training when it comes to the Aramaic script, but not for the Palaeo-Hebrew one. The latter script may thus have been taught separately. On the other hand, there are affinities in the Palaeo-Hebrew script between 4Q161 and 4Q171, as well as between 4Q38a and 4Q171. It is thus possible that more samples of the script would document a better typological continuum.

The shaft of ⟨glyph⟩ does not protrude at the bottom, but it is quite short and it is possible that other occurrences were taller. The upper stroke of ⟨glyph⟩ protrudes to the right, which is seldom attested among Dead Sea Scrolls (see *e.g.* 4Q45 frag. 5–6 l. 8) and may be accidental, unless it documents a typological development.

16 4Q165 (4QpIsaᵉ)?[57]

In his *editio princeps*, John Allegro does not ascribe a palaeographical dating to this manuscript, but suffice to say that it was penned by a formal hand traditionally ascribed to the Herodian period, with few developments.[58] 4Q165 may thus have been copied around the second half of the first century BCE or at the turn of the era.

---

56 See esp. B-478051, available at https://www.deadseascrolls.org.il/explore-the-archive/image/B-478051.

57 Allegro, *Qumrân Cave 4. I (4Q158–4Q186)*, pp. 28–30, pl. IX.

58 My assessment is in line with that of Strugnell, who ascribed the manuscript to an "early Herodian" hand; see John Strugnell, "Notes en marge du volume V des « Discoveries in the Judaean Desert of Jordan »," *Revue de Qumrân* 7/2 (26), 1970, p. 197.

The case of this manuscript is particular in this study, as there is no attestation of a Palaeo-Hebrew theonym. But it features a *vacat* in frag. 6 1. 4,[59] where one would expect the tetragrammaton according to Isa 32:6. John Allegro notes this omission, which, according to Tov,[60] may indicate that the tetragrammaton was supposed to be penned by another scribe. That the tetragrammaton was written by another scribe is so far unattested in this study (see further 11Q5), and it is quite unlikely that such an omission was not corrected. As evidenced by other Dead Sea Scrolls, the tetragrammaton was sometimes substituted by mere dots, which raises the issue of what, if anything, was actually pronounced in its stead; a *vacat* here may indicate that, at least in this case, nothing was actually pronounced.

17 4Q171 (4QpPsª)

This manuscript was tested for radiocarbon dating; its uncalibrated age is 1944±23 BP.[61] I used the intCal 20.14c calibration dataset to produce calibrated dates:

---

59 See esp. B-364600, available at https://www.deadseascrolls.org.il/explore-the-archive/image/B-364600.

60 Tov, *Scribal Practices*, p. 240.

61 Jull, Donahue, Broshi, and Toy, "Radiocarbon Dating of Scrolls and Linen Fragments from the Judean Desert," p. 14.

intcal20.14c

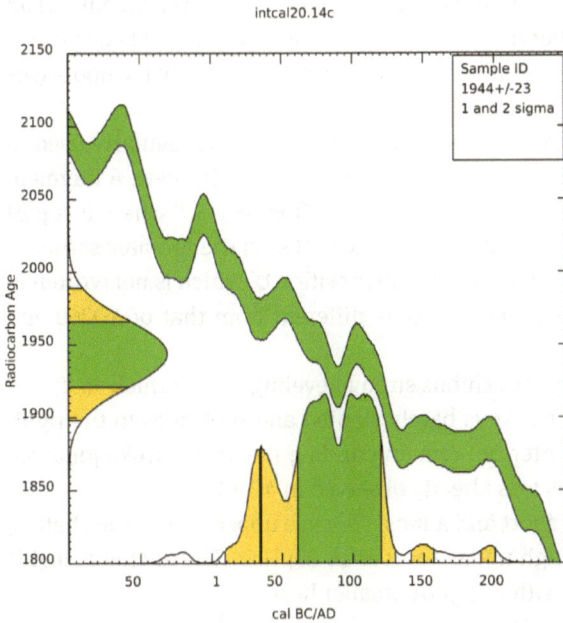

Figure 4: Calibrated radiocarbon dating of 4Q171 (4QpPsᵃ) using intCal 20.14c (uncalibrated date: 1944±23 BP)

The 1σ-calibrated ranges (68.3% confidence) are 34–36 CE and 61–121 CE, while the 2σ-calibrated ranges (95.4% confidence) are 9–131 CE, 141–158 CE, and 190–201 CE. In other words, 4Q171 was probably copied in the second half of the first century CE or early second century CE.

Up to seven occurrences of the Palaeo-Hebrew script may be observed, and they all preserve the tetragrammaton:[62] col. ii l. 4; l. 12;[63] l. 24; col. iii l. 14; l. 15;[64]

---

62 See esp. PAM 42.628, available at https://www.deadseascrolls.org.il/explore-the-archive/image/B-284039.

63 This occurrence appears on a small fragment initially published as 4Q183 frag. 3, but later joined to 4Q171 col. ii l. 12; see esp. PAM 44.189, available at https://www.deadseascrolls.org.il/explore-the-archive/image/B-285029. See discussion on 4Q180 below.

64 For col. iii, see also B-513046, available at https://www.deadseascrolls.org.il/explore-the-archive/image/B-513046.

perhaps col. iv l. 7;[65] l. 10.[66] יהוה is attested once in the Aramaic script, but it is an interlinear addition by another hand (col. iii l. 5a). This confirms that such use of the Palaeo-Hebrew script was limited to certain scribes or scribal schools (see 4Q38a above).

Other theonyms do not receive the same treatment. אל is regularly used in the *pesher* (col. ii l. 14.18 etc.) and is never written in Palaeo-Hebrew. A fragmentary occurrence of אלוהים seems to be preserved in frag. 13 l. 3,[67] where it is part of a biblical quotation (Ps 60:8 or Ps 108:8); it is written in the Aramaic script.

In col. iii l. 14, 𐤉𐤄𐤅𐤄 is preceded by a preposition מ, which is not written in Palaeo-Hebrew. The scribe's practice is thus different from that of 4Q26b and 4Q57.

In terms of palaeography, 𐤄 exhibits strong beveling, with a thick shaft and thin horizontals. The upper stroke is barely slanted and protrudes to the right; the second and third are shorter but remain parallel; the lower stroke joins the shaft almost at the bottom, as was already observed in 4Q161.

𐤅 has a tall head, with a short and almost concave upper stroke; the shaft is, by contrast, quite short, though not as short as in 1QpHab. The ductus of 4Q161 is similar but more angular, with a slightly smaller head.

𐤉 is not beveled; the shaft is almost vertical; the tail is short, almost parallel to the left strokes, and usually joins the shaft above its lower end. This is perhaps the main difference with 4Q161, though the paucity of evidence precludes a precise comparison, especially since a similar tail may be observed on 4Q38a, whose Aramaic script is close to 4Q171. Despite their differences, these three scrolls may perhaps form a typological cluster.

18 4Q173a

This fragment was initially published by Allegro as 4Q173 (4QpPs[b]) frag. 5.[68] In his review, Strugnell noted that the hand was different (and, according to him,

---

65 See esp. B-506747, available at https://www.deadseascrolls.org.il/explore-the-archive/image/B-506747.

66 See esp. B-506739, available at https://www.deadseascrolls.org.il/explore-the-archive/image/B-506739.

67 See esp. PAM 43.421, available at https://www.deadseascrolls.org.il/explore-the-archive/image/B-284454.

68 Allegro, *Qumrân Cave 4. I (4Q158–4Q186)*, pp. 51–53, pl. XVIII.

later), and that this fragment was not necessarily a *pesher*.[69] Subsequent editions thus renamed this fragment 4Q173a,[70] though it often remains listed as 4Q173 frag. 5. From a palaeographical standpoint, the ductus is indeed quite different from that of the other four fragments.[71] 4Q173a was penned by a more developed formal hand at home in the first century CE, though radiocarbon dating suggests that such formal scripts may have existed in the first century BCE.[72]

Line 4 seems to quote Ps 118:20, but instead of ליהוה 𝔐, one finds לאל. This particular variant reading seems so far unattested in other textual witnesses (including 𝔊, 𝔖, 𝔏 and 𝔗), but such substitutions are well known. For instance, Ps 53:3 has אלהים 𝔐 for יהוה 𝔐 in Ps 14:2. At Qumran, יהוה was corrected to אדוני in 1QIsᵃ III 25 (Is 3:18), after אדוני was corrected to יהוה in the previous line (l. 24, Is 3:17). It is thus not surprising that a redactor substituted אל for יהוה, perhaps in a milieu where אל had become the most common theonym. This is for instance the case of Qumran *pesharim* such as 4Q171 above, where the commentary uses אל in reference to verses that use יהוה. In the case of 4Q173a, it is unclear whether l. 4 is a quotation of Ps 118:20 or a mere reference; nor do we know whether the tetragrammaton appeared elsewhere on the manuscript or was systematically substituted by אל (or another term).

Beyond this variant reading, the reason why this manuscript is included in the present study is its use of an alternate script for אל, as is the case *e.g.* for 4Q57 (see **Table 1**). Here, as well as in 4Q57 and 4Q26b, the prefixed preposition is also written in the alternate script. But the nature of the alternate script is different: it is not Palaeo-Hebrew, as elsewhere, and is so far unique. א looks like a slightly rotated looped א (or a fully rotated α) and resembles the א of the Cryptic A script. But ל is radically different from Cryptic A.[73] Its ascender is identical to others in the fragment (see especially two lines below), but its base lacks the usual hook, which is instead represented by a leftward horizontal stroke. Similar cases are

---

69 Strugnell, "Notes en marge du volume V des « Discoveries in the Judaean Desert of Jordan »," pp. 219–220.

70 See *e.g.* Florentino García Martínez and Eibert J. C. Tigchelaar, eds., *The Dead Sea Scrolls Study Edition*, 2nd ed., Leiden, Brill, 1999, pp. 350–351.

71 See esp. PAM 41.817, where the five fragments are side by side. The photograph is available at https://www.deadseascrolls.org.il/explore-the-archive/image/B-280235. For 4Q173a, see also B-359948, available at https://www.deadseascrolls.org.il/explore-the-archive/image/B-359948.

72 See n. 13 above.

73 See recently Émile Puech, "4Q173a : Note épigraphique," *Revue de Qumrân* 24/2 (94), 2009, p. 289. Puech talks about "Cryptic A letters" in plural, but acknowledges that ל exhibits "another form," which he does not attempt to explain.

documented in the Aramaic script, drawn without lifting the pen in a right-left, back-and-forth movement. The ductus attested here is more formal and symmetrical, with the left stroke perhaps penned after lifting the pen (see the first ל).

Overall, this script is unfamiliar to us but I would not consider it "cryptic" since the shapes of the letters do match the expected graphemes. It may simply be an unknown variant or evolution of the Aramaic script. In any case, I doubt that ancient readers would have trouble deciphering it. Its use here is not meant to puzzle readers, but to highlight the theonym's otherness.

19 4Q180 (4QAgesCreat A)[74]

The *editio princeps* does not date this manuscript, but a quick look suggests that it was penned by a skilled formal hand around the turn of the era. Strugnell ascribes it to the late Herodian period,[75] but I do not see typically late Herodian developments; there is therefore no need to push the copy far into the first century CE, though such a date is always possible of course.

A single occurrence of a divine name appears in this manuscript: אל in frag. 1 l. 1.[76] It is written in Palaeo-Hebrew, and does not occur in a biblical quotation; on the contrary, it is preceded by פשר. The same scribe wrote both the Aramaic and Palaeo-Hebrew graphemes, with the same pen, at the same time. ꓭ has a straight and very short diagonal; the left stroke protrudes to the right and forms the upper parallel. The lower parallel does not reach the ceiling line. ⏌ has a tall, straight, thin ascender, barely thicker at the top. The base is very narrow, reduced to a simple elbow.

20 4Q183 (4Q Historical Work)[77]

In his *editio princeps*, John Allegro does not discuss the palaeography of this scroll. Strugnell qualifies the script as rustic semiformal, close to (but different

---

74 Allegro, *Qumrân Cave 4. I (4Q158–4Q186)*, pp. 77–79, pl. XXVII.

75 Strugnell, "Notes en marge du volume V des « Discoveries in the Judaean Desert of Jordan »," p. 252.

76 See esp. B-295794, available at https://www.deadseascrolls.org.il/explore-the-archive/image/B-295794.

77 Allegro, *Qumrân Cave 4. I (4Q158–4Q186)*, pp. 81–82, pl. XXVI.

from) 4QpHos^b (4Q167).[78] 4Q183 was indeed penned by a skilled semiformal hand with few Herodian features, and would thus be at home around the second half of the first century BCE.

The main fragment exhibits a single occurrence of a divine name, אל (frag. 1 col. ii l. 3); it is written in Palaeo-Hebrew.[79] Two additional fragments have been associated to it, but the script seems quite different; Skehan and Strugnell already suggested that frag. 3 be joined to 4Q171 ii 12.[80] But frag. 2 should also be removed, as the final ם exhibits another ductus, and ש exhibits further development; furthermore, the fragment does not feature any dry ceiling line, as opposed to frag. 1. I will thus treat frag. 2 separately below.

Back to frag. 1: א features a short diagonal; the left stroke protrudes to the right and creates the upper parallel, while the lower parallel extends to the ceiling line, as in 1Q35 (1QH^b) discussed above. The shaft does not protrude at the bottom, for which see 6Q15 and perhaps 4Q413. ל is very tall and highly slanted; it features a wide base highly curled at the end, a phenomenon already observed in 1Q35 and 4Q57 but much more developed here.

21 4Q183 frag. 2

As explained above, palaeographical and codicological features suggest that this fragment might not belong to 4Q183. The few letters preserved on this fragment preclude a precise date, but the script is a bit later, perhaps around the turn of the era or in the first century CE. The tetragrammaton appears in l. 1, and it is written in Palaeo-Hebrew.[81] ה is broken at the margin; ה exhibits an interesting ductus: the shaft is short, but prolonged at the bottom by the lower parallel stroke, which is angled at the right. The middle parallel stroke is slightly curved downward at the end, though not like 4Q57. The upper stroke protrudes to the right and reaches above the previous letter, for which see 11Q2. ו is quite unusual, with a very wide head composed of a simple slanted stroke; the shaft is then

---

78 Strugnell, "Notes en marge du volume V des « Discoveries in the Judaean Desert of Jordan »," p. 256.

79 See esp. B-358519, available at https://www.deadseascrolls.org.il/explore-the-archive/image/B-358519.

80 Strugnell, "Notes en marge du volume V des « Discoveries in the Judaean Desert of Jordan »," pp. 259, 263. See discussion on 4Q180 above.

81 See esp. B-358521, available at https://www.deadseascrolls.org.il/explore-the-archive/image/B-358521.

crossed by a small parallel stroke. The ductus itself is not new, as it is already attested in the late Iron age,[82] but it is less common among Palaeo-Hebrew Dead Sea Scrolls (see *e.g.* 11Q1). It is on the contrary quite common at Mount Gerizim (see *e.g.* inscriptions no. 385, 386, 388)[83] as well as coins from the first Judaean revolt;[84] by the time of Bar-Kokhva, the ductus has undergone further development.[85] But the form attested here, with such a wide head, is so far unparalleled. If not accidental, it may be indicative of a hitherto unknown typological development around the turn of the era or during the first century CE.

22 4Q243 (4QpsDan^a ar)[86]

According to the *editio princeps*, this manuscript was copied in the early first century CE. This date is possible, but too narrow, as the script is semiformal and exhibits few Herodian developments. It could as well have been penned in the latter part of the first century BCE. For this reason, I suggest a broader ranger around the turn of the era.

This is the only Aramaic scroll evidencing the use of the Palaeo-Hebrew script for a theonym. In frag. 1 l. 2, אלה is written in Palaeo-Hebrew;[87] this is the only occurrence of a divine name or title in that manuscript. It is followed by a pronominal suffix, which is also written in Palaeo-Hebrew, as in 1QH^a and 4Q57.

ϟ follows a common ductus. The shaft is short, straight, and slanted. The two right strokes are straight and parallel; the upper stroke is thicker at the end because of the movement of the hand towards the left as the scribe lifts the pen.

82 See *e.g.* Gordon J. Hamilton, "Paleo-Hebrew Texts and Scripts of the Persian Period," in *"An Eye for Form": Epigraphic Essays in Honor of Frank Moore Cross*, ed. by Jo Ann Hackett and Walter Emanuel Aufrecht, Winona Lake, Eisenbrauns, 2014, p. 256.
83 Yitzhak Magen, Haggai Misgav, and Levana Tsfania, *Mount Gerizim Excavations Volume I: The Aramaic, Hebrew and Samaritan Inscriptions*, Judea and Samaria Publications 2, Jerusalem, Staff Officer of Archaeology, Civil Administration for Judea and Samaria, 2004, pp. 255–258.
84 See *e.g.* Meshorer, *Treasury of Jewish Coins*, p. 132.
85 See *e.g.* Meshorer, *Treasury of Jewish Coins*, p. 163.
86 John J. Collins and Peter W. Flint, "243. 4Qpseudo-Daniel^a Ar," in *Qumran Cave 4. XVII Parabiblical Texts, Part 3*, ed. by George Brooke et al., Discoveries in the Judaean Desert XXII, Oxford, Clarendon Press, 1996, p. 97–121, pl. VII–VIII.
87 See esp. B-366133, available at https://www.deadseascrolls.org.il/explore-the-archive/image/B-366133.

⤙ has a slightly slanted shaft which, in the first occurrence, is curved backwards at the bottom. The upper parallel protrudes to the right; the lower two parallels are shorter, of equal length, and tend to join.

⤛ features a chevron-shaped head, thus following a cursive ductus that evolved from the traditional two-step head.[88] The *editio princeps* refers to Milik's comment that the shape is Samaritan.[89] But this is usually not the case of the later Samaritan script, to which Milik must have been alluding, since the Mount Gerizim inscriptions had not yet been published; as a matter of fact, even these inscriptions do not feature such ductus for ⤛.[90] What is even more puzzling is Emanuel Tov's statement that the כ is not written in the Palaeo-Hebrew script, "which may point to the scribe's ignorance of some paleo-Hebrew letters." This is simply not the case: not only is this scribe's Aramaic כ markedly different (cp. *e.g.* frag. 31. 2),[91] but the cursive ductus of this ⤛ is attested elsewhere at Qumran, especially in 11Q1 (see also, to a lesser extent, 1Q3).

ⅼ has a straight ascender, slightly curved at the top; the base is short and rounded at the end, for which see 1Q35, 4Q57, 4Q183, 4Q258 and 6Q18.

23 4Q258 (4QS^d)[92]

4Q258 has been tested for radiocarbon dating. The uncalibrated age was 1823±24 BP,[93] that is, second or third century CE, which was deemed anomalous and probably due to a contaminated sample. A second, cleaner sample was thus tested and yielded an uncalibrated age of 1964±45 BP. Here are the calibrated dates using the intCal 20.14c calibration dataset:

---

88 Langlois, "Dead Sea Scrolls Palaeography and the Samaritan Pentateuch," p. 268.
89 Collins and Flint, "4Q243," p. 98.
90 Magen, Misgav, and Tsfania, *Mount Gerizim Excavations Vol. I*, pp. 254–259.
91 See esp. B-366127, available at https://www.deadseascrolls.org.il/explore-the-archive/image/B-366127.
92 Philip S. Alexander and Geza Vermes, "258. 4QSerekh Ha-Yaḥad^d," in *Qumran Cave 4. XIX Serekh h-Yaḥad and Two Related Texts*, Discoveries in the Judaean Desert XXVI, Oxford, Clarendon Press, 1998, p. 83–128, pl. X–XIII.
93 Jull, Donahue, Broshi, and Toy, "Radiocarbon Dating of Scrolls and Linen Fragments from the Judean Desert," pp. 13–14.

intcal20.14c

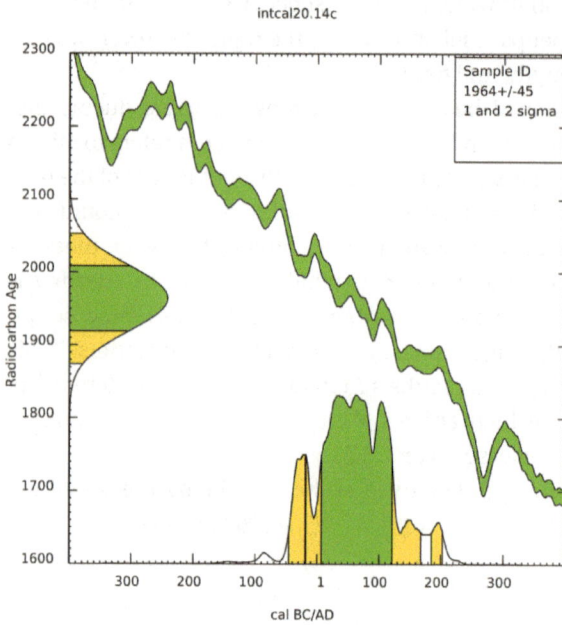

Figure 5: Calibrated radiocarbon dating of 4Q258 (4QS^d) using intCal 20.14c (uncalibrated date: 1964±45 BP)

The 1σ-calibrated ranges (68.3% confidence) are 19–18 BCE and 7–121 CE. The 2σ-calibrated ranges (95.4% confidence) are 46 BCE–169 CE and 185–203 CE. In other words, 4Q258 was probably copied between the late first century BCE and the early second century CE. From a palaeographical perspective, the script features few Herodian developments and would traditionally be ascribed to the late first century BCE.[94] This date fits the 1σ-calibrated range but, as the curve suggests, a later date is possible.

The only theonym used in this manuscript is אל; it occurs twice (col. VIII l. 9[95] and col. IX l. 8[96]), and is written in Palaeo-Hebrew, which is not the case *e.g.* in 1QS. The script is confident and elegant, with strong beveling. אל has a thick,

---

[94] The *DJD* editors thus follow Cross's dating "ca. 30–1 BCE"; see Alexander and Vermes, "4Q258," p. 89.

[95] See esp. B-499632, available at https://www.deadseascrolls.org.il/explore-the-archive/image/B-499632.

[96] See esp. B-511753, available at https://www.deadseascrolls.org.il/explore-the-archive/image/B-511753.

slightly slanted shaft, crossed by a (sometimes very) thin diagonal. The lower parallel does not protrude to the right in order to reach the visible dry ceiling line. l is slightly concave, barely thickened at the top, and has a slanted base curved at the end (compare 1Q35, 4Q57, 4Q183, 4Q243 and 6Q18).

24 4Q267 (4QD[b])[97]

This manuscript was radiocarbon dated to 2094±29 BP.[98] Here are the calibrated dates using the intCal 20.14c calibration dataset:

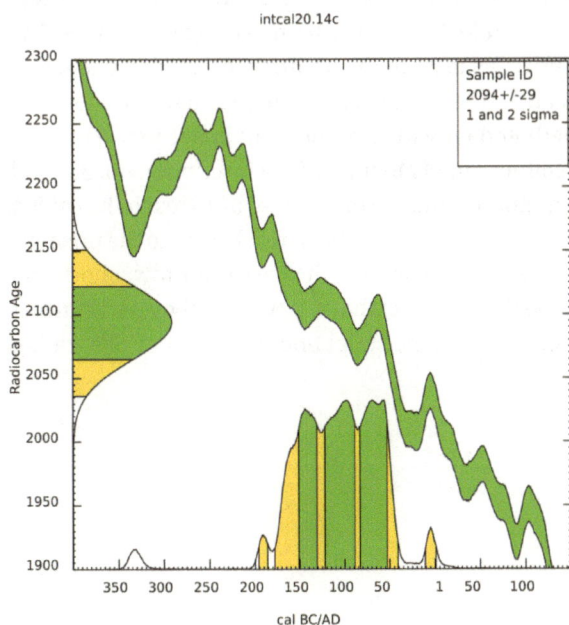

Figure 6: Calibrated radiocarbon dating of 4Q267 (4QD[b]) using intCal 20.14c (uncalibrated date: 2094±29 BP)

---

97 Joseph M. Baumgarten, "267. 4QDamascus Document[b]," in *Qumran Cave 4. XIII The Damascus Document (4Q266–273)*, Discoveries in the Judaean Desert XVIII, Oxford, Clarendon Press, 1996, p. 95–113, pl. XVIII–XXI.
98 Jull, Donahue, Broshi, and Toy, "Radiocarbon Dating of Scrolls and Linen Fragments from the Judean Desert," p. 14.

The 1σ-calibrated ranges (68.3% confidence) are 151–130 BCE, 122–88 BCE, and 83–52 BCE. The 2σ-calibrated range (95.4% confidence) are 196–185 BCE, 177–40 BCE, and 10 BCE–1 CE. In other words, this manuscript was probably copied between the second century BCE and the mid-first century BCE. From a palaeographical perspective, 4Q267 was copied by a skilled semiformal hand traditionally ascribed to the early Herodian period.[99] Unless there was a problem with the sample, or unless the calibration curve needs to be adjusted, it seems that features traditionally deemed Herodian were in fact attested earlier,[100] for instance in the first half of the first century BCE.

Palaeo-Hebrew אל is attested four times: in frag. 3 l. 7;[101] frag. 9 col. i l. 2.;[102] col. iv l. 4;[103] col. v l. 4.[104] But the same theonym is written six times in the Aramaic script: in frag. 2 l. 5.7.13; frag. 7 l. 6; frag. 9 col. iv l. 11. Such inconsistency was already observed in 4Q57 (see **Table 1**) and will be noted again in 6Q15. The ductus is difficult to characterize, as most of the occurrences are damaged. ᚨ is best preserved in frag. 9 col. i l. 2, where it features a curved shaft that does not protrude to the top. The length and curvature of the shaft is not new (compare *e.g.* 1Q3), but its position is reminiscent of Mount Gerizim inscription no. 387 and 11Q1.[105] The lower parallel does not protrude to the right so as to reach the ceiling line. ⟋ is highly slanted yet very tall, to the point that it reaches up to the previous line. It is markedly thicker at the top. By contrast, the base is narrow, short, and barely (if at all) thickened at the end. The fact that ⟋ is written above ᚨ is further evidence that the scribe is familiar with the script and its use on scrolls, rather than borrowing it from coins or seals.

---

99 Baumgarten, "4Q267," p. 96.

100 See n. 13.

101 See esp. B-358107, available at https://www.deadseascrolls.org.il/explore-the-archive/image/B-358107.

102 See esp. B-358135, available at https://www.deadseascrolls.org.il/explore-the-archive/image/B-358135.

103 See esp. B-358131, available at https://www.deadseascrolls.org.il/explore-the-archive/image/B-358131.

104 See esp. B-358139, available at https://www.deadseascrolls.org.il/explore-the-archive/image/B-358139.

105 See discussion in Langlois, "Dead Sea Scrolls Palaeography and the Samaritan Pentateuch," p. 273.

25 4Q268 (4QDᶜ)[106]

The *editio princeps* features a detailed palaeographical discussion concluding that "the handwriting should be dated to the early first century CE."[107] The characterization and dating offered for this skilled book hand are correct, though I would be more careful and date it around the turn of the era.

A single occurrence of a divine name or title occurs: אל, in frag. 1 l. 9; it is written in Palaeo-Hebrew. The paucity of evidence precludes any conclusion as to the script used for other occurrences of this and other theonyms in the same scroll. As a matter of fact, this unique attestation of אל is preserved on a small unnumbered fragment that the editor located towards the end of the column, without physical joint to the main fragment.[108]

א features a short, straight diagonal, joined at mid-height by the left stroke. This stroke is long and does not protrude to the right, or at least not in a straight way: the upper right parallel is located higher, and it is possible that the two strokes were drawn in one stage, without lifting the pen, through a double bend.

ל has a straight ascender of moderate inclination and length. It is gradually thickened at the top in the same way as the Aramaic ל (see *e.g.* the following line), which suggests that the same scribe was familiar with both scripts. The base is narrow and rounded, as in 4Q22 and other scrolls from the first century BCE onwards.

26 4Q406 (4QShirShabbᵍ)[109]

The *editio princeps* does not discuss the palaeography of this manuscript due to its fragmentary and damaged condition. It was penned by a skilled formal hand

---

106 Joseph M. Baumgarten, "268. 4QDamascus Documentᶜ," in *Qumran Cave 4. XIII The Damascus Document (4Q266–273)*, Discoveries in the Judaean Desert XVIII, Oxford, Clarendon Press, 1996, p. 115–121, pl. XXII.

107 Baumgarten, "4Q268," p. 118.

108 See esp. B-361423, available at https://www.deadseascrolls.org.il/explore-the-archive/image/B-361423.

109 Carol A. Newsom, "406. 4QShirot ʿOlat HaShabbatᵍ," in *Qumran Cave 4. VI Poetical and Liturgical Texts, Part 1*, ed. by Esther Eshel, Hanan Eshel, Carol A. Newsom, Bilhah Nitzan, Eileen M. Schuller, and Ada Yardeni, Discoveries in the Judaean Desert XI, Oxford, Clarendon Press, 1998, p. 395–398, pl. XXXI.

but, beyond these global observations, it is difficult to identify typological markers. The scroll was certainly copied in the first centuries BCE and CE, and there may be Herodian features favoring the turn of the era or the first century CE. Unfortunately, the lack of evidence precludes a more specific dating. For now, suffice to say that 4Q406 was probably copied around the turn of the era.

Two occurrences of the Palaeo-Hebrew script have been preserved: אלוהים in frag. 1 l. 2,[110] and, in a broken context, ל in frag. 3 l. 2.[111] There is no other occurrence of a theonym on this very fragmentary manuscript; it is thus not possible to make any statement as to the extent of this practice. Other copies of Shirot ʿOlat HaShabbat do not feature Palaeo-Hebrew.

א seems to follow a common ductus; the shaft slightly protrudes at the bottom, and perhaps also at the top, whereas the upper parallel does not appear to protrude to the right. ו features a long upper stroke heading a vertical shaft. The shaft is off-center, located beneath the right end of the upper stroke, as in 11Q1 or Mount Gerizim inscriptions except that the upper stroke is here much longer. ה features a thick shaft and two short left parallel strokes; on the right, a trace of ink seems to prolong the lower parallel stroke, but there does not seem to be a tail. Such cursive ductus is well known from Hebrew ostraca, but it is quite uncommon among Dead Sea scrolls. Another explanation is that what appears to be the protrusion of the lower stroke would actually be the end of an almost vertical tail; but I am not sure that this ductus would be more likely.

ל has a straight, slanted ascender, perhaps a bit thicker at the top. The base is either short or written above the ו that precedes, whose traces are visible. מ features a vertical descender angled at the bottom and followed by a wide, almost horizontal base. The best parallel for such a descender is 4Q124 and, to a lesser extent, 4Q22. It becomes standard in coins from the first and second Judaean revolts[112] as well as the Samaritan script.[113]

---

110 See esp. PAM 42.748, available at https://www.deadseascrolls.org.il/explore-the-archive/image/B-284161. The fragment has since degraded, cp. B-358697, available at https://www.deadseascrolls.org.il/explore-the-archive/image/B-358697.

111 See esp. B-358701, available at https://www.deadseascrolls.org.il/explore-the-archive/image/B-358701.

112 See *e.g.* Meshorer, *Treasury of Jewish Coins*, pp. 132, 163.

113 See *e.g.* McLean, "Palaeo-Hebrew in the Hellenistic and Roman Periods," pl. 8.

27 4Q413 (4Q Composition concerning Divine Providence)[114]

According to the *editio princeps*, the two fragments that preserve 4Q413 have been copied by a Herodian hand. The smaller fragment exhibits material and palaeographical features that differ from the larger one[115] and may actually belong to another scroll, but this is without consequence for our study, as the two occurrences of a divine name are preserved on the larger fragment. The scribe struggled to write on the rough surface and produced an inelegant script in spite of a rather consistent ductus.[116] Several Herodian features may be observed and point to a copy around the turn of the era, preferably in the first century CE, though a date in the first century BCE cannot be excluded.

As mentioned above, two occurrences of a theonym are preserved on this scroll: אל in ll. 2 and 4. Both use the Palaeo-Hebrew script, but it is uncertain whether this practice extended to the entire scroll or to other divine names or titles.

The shaft of 𐤀 does not seem to protrude at the top or at the bottom, but it is damaged and may have been a bit longer; the best parallel is 4Q183. 𐤋 has a narrow base and, more importantly, is barely slanted, which is quite unusual among Dead Sea scrolls but paralleled on coins from the first and second Judaean revolts;[117] this might be indicative of a late development, for which see further 6Q15 below.

---

114 Elisha Qimron, "413. 4QComposition Concerning Divine Providence," in *Qumran Cave 4. XV Sapiential Texts, Part 1*, ed. by Torleif Elgvin, Menahem Kister, Timothy H. Lim, Bilhah Nitzan, Stephen J. Pfann, Elisha Qimron, Lawrence H. Schiffman, and Annette Steudel, Discoveries in the Judaean Desert XX, Oxford, Clarendon Press, 1997, p. 169–171, pl. XIV.

115 Compare *e.g.* B-294960 and B-294961, respectively available at https://www.deadseascrolls. org.il/explore-the-archive/image/B-294960 and https://www.deadseascrolls.org.il/explore-the-archive/image/B-294961.

116 See esp. B-295504, available at https://www.deadseascrolls.org.il/explore-the-archive/image/B-295504.

117 See *e.g.* Meshorer, *Treasury of Jewish Coins*, pp. 132, 163.

28 6Q15 (6QD)[118]

In his *editio princeps*, Maurice Baillet indicates that this manuscript was copied during the first century CE. There are, indeed, Herodian features at home in the first century CE, but the script is semiformal and could therefore go back to the first century BCE. I would thus advise caution and simply state that 6Q15 was copied around the turn of the era.

Three occurrences of a theonym are preserved on this manuscript: אל in frag. 3 ll. 4–5, and in frag. 5 l. 5. The first two occurrences use the Palaeo-Hebrew script, but not the third. Such inconsistency was already observed in 1QHᵃ, 4Q57 and 4Q267, the latter being another copy of the Damascus Document.

א has a short shaft that barely protrudes at the bottom,[119] which is reminiscent of 4Q183 and 4Q413. Unlike 4Q183, however, the lower parallel does not extend to the ceiling line. ל exhibits a very unusual ductus: the ascender is straight, vertical, or even slightly slanted leftward at the top. The phenomenon observed on 4Q413 is even more pronounced here, and finds good parallels on Bar-Kokhva coins.[120] The base is straight, raised, and long; since the ascender is quite short, the base is almost as long, which is quite unusual and once again reminiscent of coins.

29 6Q18 (6Q papHymn)[121]

According to the *editio princeps*, this manuscript exhibits a very stylized Herodian calligraphy. Cursive influence may indeed be observed throughout the script, which complicates dating; but since there are few typically "late Herodian" features, the manuscript fits the early Herodian period. 6Q18 may thus have been copied around the turn of the era.

---

118 Maurice Baillet, "15. Document de Damas," in *Les 'petites grottes' de Qumrân*, ed. by Maurice Baillet, Józef Tadeusz Milik, and Roland de Vaux, Discoveries in the Judaean Desert of Jordan III, Oxford, Clarendon Press, 1962, p. 128–131, pl. XXVI.

119 See esp. B-482262, available at https://www.deadseascrolls.org.il/explore-the-archive/image/B-482262.

120 Meshorer, *Treasury of Jewish Coins*, p. 163.

121 Maurice Baillet, "18. Composition hymnique," in *Les 'petites grottes' de Qumrân*, ed. by Maurice Baillet, Józef Tadeusz Milik, and Roland de Vaux, Discoveries in the Judaean Desert of Jordan III, Oxford, Clarendon Press, 1962, p. 133–136, pl. XXVII.

Up to three occurrences of a theonym are preserved on these fragments: אל,
in frag. 6 l. 5; frag. 8 l. 1; and probably frag. 10 l. 3. All of them use the Palaeo-
Hebrew script.[122] 𐤀 features two long parallel strokes curved at the top; the lower
parallel may extend to reach the ceiling line, though the upper parallel seems to
cross it. The lower parallel crosses the shaft so as to create the left stroke, which
is quite unusual and without close parallels; it might be an idiosyncratic feature
or indicative of a typological development.

𐤋 is tall, moderately slanted, and features a curved base, for which see 4Q183,
though the latter features a wide base; see also 4Q57 for a narrower but less
rounded base.

30 11Q2 (11QLev[b])[123]

According to the *editio princeps*, the manuscript was copied by a "late Herodian
formal bookhand (*c.* 50 CE)."[124] The hand indeed exhibits features traditionally
associated with the late Herodian period but, as signaled above (see n. 13), these
features may have appeared earlier than previously thought. Bearing this uncertainty in mind, I suggest that 11Q2 was copied around the first half of the first
century CE, with an emphasis on "around."

Three occurrences of a theonym are preserved on this manuscript: יהוה in
frag. 2 ll. 2.6.7, all written in Palaeo-Hebrew.[125] Compared to the Aramaic script,
letters have the same size and strokes have the same thickness, but they lack ornamentation; the same scribe wrote both scripts but Palaeo-Hebrew had apparently not undergone the same evolution as the Aramaic script, and the elegant
beveling attested in ostraca and some of the Dead Sea scrolls has disappeared.

𐤉 features three long parallel strokes with little room between them; the upper stroke protrudes to the right to the point of covering the previous letter. This
is reminiscent of 4Q183 frag. 2, though in the latter the parallel strokes are
shorter, and the third one prolongs the shaft.

---

122 See esp. PAM 42.947, available at https://www.deadseascrolls.org.il/explore-the-ar-
chive/image/B-284845.

123 Florentino García Martínez, Eibert J. C. Tigchelaar, and Adam Simon van der Woude, "2.
11QLeviticus[b]," in *Qumran Cave 11. II 11Q2–18, 11Q20–31*, Discoveries in the Judaean Desert XXIII,
Oxford, Clarendon Press, 1998, p. 1–9, pl. I.

124 García Martínez, Tigchelaar, and van der Woude, "11Q2," p. 2.

125 See esp. B-364446, available at https://www.deadseascrolls.org.il/explore-the-archive/im-
age/B-364446.

ꓕ is different from 4Q183 frag. 2 and follows a common ductus; the head is slanted and probably followed by the shaft without lifting the pen, the diagonal stroke being added later. Compared to 11Q1, the diagonal starts here before the shaft, whereas there it does not protrude to the right. Another interesting feature of the present script is the small tick at the bottom of the shaft: while 4Q184 frag. 2 and other hands tend to curve the shaft at the bottom towards the next letter, in 11Q2 this phenomenon has developed into a short foot. The second occurrence (at the end of l. 6) is almost completely erased but may have featured an even larger foot.

ꓶ has, like ꓳ, long parallel strokes of equal length with little room between them. The tail is a bit shorter and almost parallel. The shaft does not protrude and is thus quite short; it is slightly slanted leftward at the bottom.

31 11Q5 (11QPsᵃ)¹²⁶

In his *editio princeps*, James Sanders concludes that the manuscript may be assigned to "the first half of the first century AD."¹²⁷ I agree with him, albeit with the same reservations I expressed above (see n. 13).

This long manuscript preserves numerous occurrences of אל, אלוהים, יהוה, and אדוני. The pattern is consistent: יהוה is always written in Palaeo-Hebrew, and is the only theonym to receive this treatment. Prefixes are not written in Palaeo-Hebrew: ב in col. IV l. 3; col. XVI ll. 4–5; כ in col. XIV l. 13; ל in frag. E col. i l. 5, col. iii l. 8, col. XV l. 6, col. XVI l. 1.6, מ in col. II l. 2.

Palaeo-Hebrew letters are sometimes larger and thicker than the Aramaic script, and they may exhibit wider letter spacing. This could suggest the use of another calamus. Another piece of evidence may be added: in the middle of col. III l. 4, the scroll has a *vacat* where 𝔐 has יהוה (see also 𝔊, 𝔗, 𝔖, 𝔏), and it is difficult to interpret this *vacat* as the end of a sentence. It could be an omission on the part of the scribe who was supposed to copy the tetragrammaton in Palaeo-Hebrew (see already 4Q165). On the other hand, other *vacat*s appear elsewhere in the same scroll (*e.g.* col. VIII l. 3) that do not seem to indicate the end of

126 James A. Sanders, *The Psalms Scroll of Qumrân Cave 11 (11Psᵃ)*, Discoveries in the Judaean Desert of Jordan IV, Oxford, Clarendon Press, 1965; Florentino García Martínez, Eibert J. C. Tigchelaar, and Adam Simon van der Woude, "5. 11QPsalmsᵃ, Fragments E, F," in *Qumran Cave 11. II 11Q2–18, 11Q20–31*, Discoveries in the Judaean Desert XXIII, Oxford, Clarendon Press, 1998, p. 29–36, pl. IV–V.
127 Sanders, *11QPsᵃ*, p. 9.

a sentence or the omission of the tetragrammaton. They might, however, be explained by a defect in the parchment that the scribe wanted to avoid (*e.g.* col. XX ll. 3.8); this complicates the assessment of the present issue. In any case, it is possible that another calamus was used for Palaeo-Hebrew; if so, there is no need to suppose that someone else wrote the tetragrammaton (though this is possible of course), as the scribe probably did not want to switch too often between calami. He may have copied a few lines, or an entire column, or perhaps even the entire scroll, before switching to another calamus and writing the tetragrammaton.

In terms of palaeography, the ductus is quite common. ⊀ features a thick slanted shaft and three thin parallel strokes, of equal length, parallel and straight. The upper parallel crosses the shaft slightly below its top and protrudes to the right so as to reach the ceiling line. ⅄ has a zigzagged angular head with two parallel strokes of equal length; the shaft is penned in the middle and extends slightly below adjacent letters. ⁊ is very thin; the two parallel strokes are of varying distance and length, as is the tail, which is usually straight but sometimes slightly convex at the end. Overall, the hand is skilled, formal and elegant, as is the Aramaic script.

32 Analysis

After having individually studied all of the Dead Sea scrolls that document the use of an alternate script for divine names and titles, let us analyze this phenomenon.

32.1 Chronological Distribution

The first approach is chronological: When is this phenomenon attested? The dates ascribed to the *ca.* 30 Dead Sea scrolls are indicated in **Table 2**.

Table 2: Chronological list of Dead Sea scrolls that use an alternate script for theonyms

Timeline	Manuscripts
ca. 1st c. BCE	4Q267 (4QD^b)
	1Q15 (1QpZeph)
	1QpHab
	1Q11 (1QPs^b)
	2Q3 (2QExod^b)
ca. mid-1st c. BCE	1Q27 (1QMyst)
	4Q165 (4QpIsa^e)

	4Q183 (4Q Historical Work)
ca. turn of era	4Q258 (4QS^d)
	1Q14 (1QpMic)
	3Q3 (3QLam)
	4Q26b (4QLev^g)
	4Q38a (4QDeut^{k2})
	4Q180 (4QAgesCreat A)
	4Q243 (4QpsDan^a ar)
	4Q268 (4QD^c)
	4Q406 (4QShirShabb^g)
	6Q15 (6QD)
	6Q18 (6Q papHymn)
ca. 1st c. CE	1Q35 (1QH^b)
	4Q20 (4QExod^j)
	4Q57 (4QIsa^c)
	4Q183 frag. 2
	4Q413 (4Q Composition concerning Divine Providence)
	11Q2 (11QLev^b)
	11Q5 (11QPs^a)
	4Q161 (4QpIsa^a)
	4Q173a
	1QH^a
	4Q171 (4QpPs^a)
Unknown	3Q14 frag. 18

The earliest manuscript to document this practice is 4Q267 (4QD^b), which was radiocarbon-dated between the second century BCE and the mid-first century BCE. The script strongly favors the latter part of that range, that is, the first century BCE. At that time, the use of the Palaeo-Hebrew script to copy entire scrolls is very limited.[128] Around the second century BCE, the scribes of the Dead Sea scrolls have progressively adopted the Aramaic script for Hebrew texts, so that by the first century BCE the Palaeo-Hebrew script could be viewed as an unusual script on such manuscripts—at least in the milieus that produced the Dead Sea scrolls.

This does not mean, however, that they—or other Judaean readers—were unfamiliar with that script, as it is well attested in Judaea and continues to evolve, which is a sign of vitality. The fact that one scroll (4Q173a) uses another alternate script does not imply that the Palaeo-Hebrew script was no longer known at that time; the use of the Palaeo-Hebrew script for theonyms is attested throughout the

---

128 Langlois, "Dead Sea Scrolls Palaeography and the Samaritan Pentateuch," p. 277.

Herodian period, until such scrolls as 1QHᵃ and 4Q171 (4QpPsᵃ), which have been radiocarbon-dated to the first century CE or the early second century CE.

32.2 Geographical Distribution

In terms of geographical distribution, this practice is documented only at Qumran. I should emphasize that the present study does not include Greek scrolls, which do document a similar practice, both among Dead Sea scrolls—with 8Hev1 (8HevXII gr)—and in Egypt. But as far as Hebrew scrolls are concerned, there is no evidence that this practice was attested at Masada or Wadi Murabbaʿat for instance. The lack of evidence does not necessarily imply that this phenomenon was limited to Qumran: it is attested by *ca.* 30 scrolls only, which represents quite a small proportion of all Qumran scrolls from that period. As a matter of fact, if the same proportion is applied to literary Hebrew scrolls of the same period from other find sites, we should not expect any scroll to exhibit the same practice. I do not believe, therefore, that this practice was limited to Qumran. As mentioned above, it is evidenced by Egyptian Greek manuscripts and was thus a widespread phenomenon.

If we focus on the Qumran caves, it is noteworthy that the practice is not only attested in cave 4Q, but in 1Q, 2Q, 3Q, 6Q and 11Q as well. That is, in all of the caves where one could reasonably expect some kind of evidence. The proportion seems actually quite high in cave 1Q, which contained only a few dozen scrolls (the exact figure being difficult to determine given the number of unidentified fragments) and yet contained seven scrolls with Palaeo-Hebrew script for a theonym.

32.3 Scribal Training

Palaeographical analysis suggests that Palaeo-Hebrew letters were penned by the same scribe, with the same calamus and ink, at the same time as the rest of the text. In 1QpHab, the scribe seems less skilled when writing Palaeo-Hebrew, but there is no evidence that Palaeo-Hebrew letters were added at a later stage. The two possible exceptions are 4Q165 and 11Q5, where the tetragrammaton may have been added later. But this does not mean that the scribe did not know how to write Palaeo-Hebrew, contrary to what Tov suggested on the basis of what he thought was an Aramaic כ (instead of a Palaeo-Hebrew 𐤊) in 4Q243. In 11Q5, there is no evidence that another scribe wrote the Palaeo-Hebrew letters, but rather that he used another calamus. This may also account for the *vacat* in 4Q165, though it may have been left blank on purpose.

32.4 Theonyms

This raises the question of the pronunciation of the Palaeo-Hebrew letters. Since the script was well known, the purpose was not to puzzle readers and keep them from understanding the text. It was not a cryptic script—even in the case of 4Q173a, which uses another alternate script. Readers knew what the text said and could easily read it. Was the text supposed to be substituted by another title? This could be the case in scrolls that restrict this practice to the tetragrammaton, which could then be pronounced אדוני as in 1QIs². But what about scrolls that extend this practice to other theonyms? In later rabbinical Judaism, even אדוני becomes ineffable and is replaced by השם or שמא. But what about אלוהים, אל, and צבאות? Were they all replaced by some title? In which case, was it the same for all of them, or did each divine name receive its own substitute? What about pronominal suffixes: Were they added to the substitute, or simply ignored? To answer this question, let us look at the extent of this practice. The various theonyms written with an alternate script are listed, together with the manuscripts that attest this practice, in **Table 3**.

Table 3: Occurrences of theonyms written with an alternate script[129]

Manuscript	אדוני	אל	אלה	אלוהים	יהוה	צבאות
1Q11 (1QPsᵇ)	?	?	?	?	1	?
1Q14 (1QpMic)	?	1	?	?	2	?
1Q15 (1QpZeph)	?	?	?	?	1	?
1Q27 (1QMyst)	?	1	?	?	?	?
1Q35 (1QHᵇ)	?	1	?	?	?	?
1QHª	0	3/N	?	?	?	?
1QpHab	?	0	?	?	4	0
2Q3 (2QExodᵇ)	?	?	?	?	2	?

---

129 In this table, "?" indicates lack of evidence for the theonym in the manuscript, whereas "/" precedes the total occurrences of the theonym in the manuscript; "N" stands for "numerous" occurrences.

Manuscript	אדוני	אל	אלה	אלוהים	יהוה	צבאות
3Q3 (3QLam)	?	?	?	?	1	?
3Q14 frag. 18	?	1	?	?	?	?
4Q20 (4QExod^j)	?	?	?	?	1	?
4Q26b (4QLev^g)	?	?	?	?	1/2	?
4Q38a (4QDeut^k2)	?	?	?	0	1	?
4Q57 (4QIsa^c)	3/5	0/1	?	3/4	26	2/3
4Q161 (4QpIsa^a)	0	0	?	?	1	?
4Q165 (4QpIsa^e)	?	?	?	?	*vacat*	?
4Q171 (4QpPs^a)	?	0	?	0	7	?
4Q173a	?	1	?	?	?	?
4Q180 (4QAgesCreat A)	?	1	?	?	?	?
4Q183 (4Q Historical Work)	?	1	?	?	?	?
4Q183 frag. 2	?	?	?	?	1	?
4Q243 (4QpsDan^a ar)	?	?	1	?	?	?
4Q258 (4QS^d)	?	2	?	?	?	?
4Q267 (4QD^b)	?	4/6	?	?	?	?
4Q268 (4QD^c)	?	1	?	?	?	?
4Q406 (4QShirShabb^g)	?	?	?	2	?	?
4Q413 (4Q Composition concerning Divine Providence)	?	2	?	?	?	?
6Q15 (6QD)	?	2/3	?	?	?	?
6Q18 (6Q papHymn)	?	3	?	?	?	?
11Q2 (11QLev^b)	?	?	?	?	3	?
11Q5 (11QPs^a)	0	0	?	0	N	?
Number of manuscripts that:						
a. Always use alt. script	0	11	1	1	14	0
b. Sometimes use alt. script	1	3	0	1	1	1
c. Never use alt. script	3	5	0	3	0	1
d. May or may not use alt. script	27	12	30	26	16	29

As the table indicates, the most "popular" theonym is יהוה (15 mss), followed closely by אל (14 mss). However, no scroll seems to use the Palaeo-Hebrew script for other theonyms while not already using it for יהוה, which is not the case for אל. In other words, if a scribe is going to use an alternate script for theonyms, he will first of all use it for יהוה and, possibly, for other divine names or titles, in which case אל is the most likely candidate. This is also confirmed by the number of scrolls in which the practice is mixed: 1 out of 15 for יהוה and 3 out of 14 for אל. The proportion is very low for the tetragrammaton, and quite low for אל. The only theonym that exhibits a lower proportion is Aramaic אלה, with 0 out of 1; but this Palaeo-Hebrew theonym is attested in a single, very fragmentary scroll (4Q243), so that the statistics might not reflect the actual practice.

Other theonyms are far behind יהוה and אל. The use of Palaeo-Hebrew is rare, often mixed, and often countered by the number of scrolls that verifiably do not share this practice. It is also possible that the practice extended to these other theonyms at a later stage: 4Q406 is difficult to date, given its damaged state, but 4Q57 would be more at home in the first century CE. However, the limited number of scrolls that document this extended practice precludes any firm conclusion; without the testimony of 4Q406, one might actually think that this phenomenon was idiosyncratic to 4Q57. On the other hand, a vast majority of scrolls simply have no attestation of these theonyms, in any script. It is thus possible that this practice was actually more popular than what one may believe based on the few occurrences preserved on these fragments.

When the practice extends to theonyms other than יהוה, which are common nouns susceptible of receiving pronominal suffixes, these suffixes are always written in Palaeo-Hebrew (see 1QHᵃ, 4Q57 and 4Q243). The situation is a bit more complex with prefixes: they are written in Palaeo-Hebrew in three manuscripts (4Q26b, 4Q57, 4Q173a) but the opposite is true in two manuscripts (4Q171 and 11Q5). The other 26 manuscripts simply have no occurrence of such prefix. This practice is thus largely uncertain, but it is at least documented in the Herodian period. The presence of a Palaeo-Hebrew prefix suggests that the alternate script is not meant to indicate a substitution, for there is no reason to replace a preposition by another one. Likewise, if a theonym is not to be pronounced at all, the text is easily understood with a gap in pronunciation, but less so if the preceding preposition is not pronounced either. Alternatively, Palaeo-Hebrew letters may have indicated another accent, but evidence is again lacking. In the end, the most probable explanation is that the alternate script was simply meant to visually distinguish the theonym (and the letters that are in contact with it) from the rest of the text.

32.5 Biblical vs. Non-Biblical Scrolls

Contrary to what is sometimes said, such distinction is not limited to "biblical" scrolls, that is, books that were later included in the Hebrew Bible. Only 9 scrolls out of 31 are biblical, that is, less than a third. The proportion is thus not markedly higher than elsewhere among Dead Sea Scrolls. Other categories of texts are well represented here: *pesharim*, hymns, pseudepigraphs, narratives, etc. Aramaic compositions are almost absent, however, except for a Daniel-like manuscript (4Q243). But let us keep in mind that the Palaeo-Hebrew script is, first and foremost, the script of the Hebrew language; its use, albeit limited to theonyms, is thus more natural in a Hebrew composition. When used in a Greek manuscript, such as 8Ḥev1 (8ḤevXII gr), it writes a Hebrew word—the tetragrammaton—and not a Greek theonym. It is thus quite surprising to find Palaeo-Hebrew in an Aramaic composition for an Aramaic word such as אלה. Furthermore, even in Hebrew scrolls the use of Palaeo-Hebrew for the (almost) equivalent term אלוהים is limited to a couple of witnesses. One would thus not expect a higher proportion in Aramaic scrolls.

33 Conclusion

In conclusion, the use of Palaeo-Hebrew letters for theonyms began after the Palaeo-Hebrew script was abandoned by scribes of the Dead Sea scrolls to copy literary compositions. At the turn of the first century BCE, a few scribes began to use it for יהוה and אל, probably to indicate the sacredness of these theonyms. Such practice was usually neither consistent throughout the scroll nor shared by other scribes—as can be seen in scribal corrections and, more generally, in the vast majority of Dead Sea scrolls. This is not due to a lack of knowledge of the script, which was commonly used in Judaea—including in secular contexts—and evolved throughout the Hasmonaean and Herodian periods. The use of Palaeo-Hebrew did not prevent or complicate the pronunciation of the theonym, nor did it even encourage a substitution, as can be seen by its use for prefixes.

The Palaeo-Hebrew script was probably simply used to distinguish the theonym and highlight its sacredness. This, after all, is the very definition of sacred—separated, distinguished—and turns out to be the basic meaning of the Hebrew participle מפורש before it came to be translated "ineffable."

34 Bibliography

Alexander, Philip S., and Geza Vermes. "258. 4QSerekh Ha-Yaḥad[d]." Pages 83–128, pl. X–XIII in *Qumran Cave 4. XIX Serekh h-Yaḥad and Two Related Texts*. Discoveries in the Judaean Desert XXVI. Oxford: Clarendon Press, 1998.

Allegro, John Marco. *Qumrân Cave 4. I (4Q158–4Q186)*. Discoveries in the Judaean Desert of Jordan V. Oxford: Clarendon Press, 1968.

Baillet, Maurice. "3. Exode (deuxième exemplaire)." Pages 52–55, pl. XI in *Les 'petites grottes' de Qumrân*. Edited by Maurice Baillet, Józef Tadeusz Milik, and Roland de Vaux. Discoveries in the Judaean Desert of Jordan III. Oxford: Clarendon Press, 1962.

Baillet, Maurice. "3. Lamentations." Page 95, pl. XVIII in *Les 'petites grottes' de Qumrân*. Edited by Maurice Baillet, Józef Tadeusz Milik, and Roland de Vaux. Discoveries in the Judaean Desert of Jordan III. Oxford: Clarendon Press, 1962.

Baillet, Maurice. "14. Fragments isolés." Pages 102–4, pl. XIX in *Les 'petites grottes' de Qumrân*. Edited by Maurice Baillet, Józef Tadeusz Milik, and Roland de Vaux. Discoveries in the Judaean Desert of Jordan III. Oxford: Clarendon Press, 1962.

Baillet, Maurice. "15. Document de Damas." Pages 128–31, pl. XXVI in *Les 'petites grottes' de Qumrân*. Edited by Maurice Baillet, Józef Tadeusz Milik, and Roland de Vaux. Discoveries in the Judaean Desert of Jordan III. Oxford: Clarendon Press, 1962.

Baillet, Maurice. "18. Composition hymnique." Pages 133–36, pl. XXVII in *Les 'petites grottes' de Qumrân*. Edited by Maurice Baillet, Józef Tadeusz Milik, and Roland de Vaux. Discoveries in the Judaean Desert of Jordan III. Oxford: Clarendon Press, 1962.

Barthélemy, Dominique. "11. Psautier (second exemplaire)." Page 71, pl. XIII in *Qumran Cave I*. Edited by Dominique Barthélemy and Józef Tadeusz Milik. Discoveries in the Judaean Desert I. Oxford: Clarendon Press, 1955.

Baumgarten, Joseph M. "267. 4QDamascus Document[b]." Pages 95–113, pl. XVIII–XXI in *Qumran Cave 4. XIII The Damascus Document (4Q266–273)*. Discoveries in the Judaean Desert XVIII. Oxford: Clarendon Press, 1996.

Baumgarten, Joseph M. "268. 4QDamascus Document[c]." Pages 115–21, pl. XXII in *Qumran Cave 4. XIII The Damascus Document (4Q266–273)*. Discoveries in the Judaean Desert XVIII. Oxford: Clarendon Press, 1996.

Bonani, Georges, Susan Ivy, Willy Wolfli, Magen Broshi, Israel Carmi, and John Strugnell. "Radiocarbon Dating of Fourteen Dead Sea Scrolls." *Radiocarbon* 34.3 (1992): 843–49.

Burrows, Millar, ed. *The Dead Sea Scrolls of St. Mark's Monastery. Volume I, The Isaiah Manuscript and the Habakkuk Commentary*. New Haven: American Schools of Oriental Research, 1950.

Collins, John J., and Peter W. Flint. "243. 4Qpseudo-Daniel[a] Ar." Pages 97–121, pl. VII–VIII in *Qumran Cave 4. XVII Parabiblical Texts, Part 3*. Edited by George Brooke, John J. Collins, Torleif Elgvin, Peter W. Flint, Jonas C. Greenfield, Erik Larson, Carol A. Newsom, Émile Puech, Lawrence H. Schiffman, et al. Discoveries in the Judaean Desert XXII. Oxford: Clarendon Press, 1996.

Duncan, Julie Ann. "38. 4QDeut[k1]." Pages 93–98 in *Qumran Cave 4. IX. Deuteronomy, Joshua, Judges, Kings*. Edited by Eugene C. Ulrich, Frank Moore Cross, Sidnie White Crawford, Julie Ann Duncan, Patrick W. Skehan, Emanuel Tov, and Julio Trebolle Barrera. Discoveries in the Judaean Desert XIV. Oxford: Clarendon Press, 1995.

Duncan, Julie Ann. "38a. 4QDeut[k2]." Pages 99–103, pl. XXV in *Qumran Cave 4. IX. Deuteronomy, Joshua, Judges, Kings*. Edited by Eugene C. Ulrich, Frank Moore Cross, Sidnie White Crawford, Julie Ann Duncan, Patrick W. Skehan, Emanuel Tov, and Julio Trebolle Barrera. Discoveries in the Judaean Desert XIV. Oxford: Clarendon Press, 1995.

Elgvin, Torleif, Kipp Davis, and Michael Langlois, eds. *Gleanings from the Caves. Dead Sea Scrolls and Artefacts from The Schøyen Collection*. Library of Second Temple Studies 71. London: Bloomsbury T&T Clark, 2016.

García Martínez, Florentino, and Eibert J. C. Tigchelaar, eds. *The Dead Sea Scrolls Study Edition*. 2nd ed. Leiden: Brill, 1999.

García Martínez, Florentino, Eibert J. C. Tigchelaar, and Adam Simon van der Woude. "2. 11QLeviticus[b]." Pages 1–9, pl. I in *Qumran Cave 11. II 11Q2–18, 11Q20–31*. Discoveries in the Judaean Desert XXIII. Oxford: Clarendon Press, 1998.

García Martínez, Florentino, Eibert J. C. Tigchelaar, and Adam Simon van der Woude. "5. 11QPsalms[a], Fragments E, F." Pages 29–36, pl. IV–V in *Qumran Cave 11. II 11Q2–18, 11Q20–31*. Discoveries in the Judaean Desert XXIII. Oxford: Clarendon Press, 1998.

Hamilton, Gordon J. "Paleo-Hebrew Texts and Scripts of the Persian Period." Pages 253–90 in *"An Eye for Form": Epigraphic Essays in Honor of Frank Moore Cross*. Edited by Jo Ann Hackett and Walter Emanuel Aufrecht. Winona Lake: Eisenbrauns, 2014.

Jull, Timothy A. J., Douglas J. Donahue, Magen Broshi, and Emanuel Toy. "Radiocarbon Dating of Scrolls and Linen Fragments from the Judean Desert." *Radiocarbon* 37.1 (1995): 11–19.

Langlois, Michael. "Dead Sea Scrolls Palaeography and the Samaritan Pentateuch." Pages 255–85 in *The Samaritan Pentateuch and the Dead Sea Scrolls*. Edited by Michael Langlois. Contributions to Biblical Exegesis and Theology 94. Leuven: Peeters, 2019.

Magen, Yitzhak, Haggai Misgav, and Levana Tsfania. *Mount Gerizim Excavations Volume I: The Aramaic, Hebrew and Samaritan Inscriptions*. Judea and Samaria Publications 2. Jerusalem: Staff Officer of Archaeology, Civil Administration for Judea and Samaria, 2004.

McLean, Mark David. "The Use and Development of Palaeo-Hebrew in the Hellenistic and Roman Periods." Harvard University, 1982.

Meshorer, Ya'akov. *A Treasury of Jewish Coins: From the Persian Period to Bar Kokhba*. Jerusalem: Yad Ben-Zvi, 2001.

Milik, Józef Tadeusz. "14. Commentaire de Michée." Pages 77–80, pl. XV in *Qumran Cave I*. Edited by Dominique Barthélemy and Józef Tadeusz Milik. Discoveries in the Judaean Desert I. Oxford: Clarendon Press, 1955.

Milik, Józef Tadeusz. "15. Commentaire de Sophonie." Page 80, pl. XV in *Qumran Cave I*. Edited by Dominique Barthélemy and Józef Tadeusz Milik. Discoveries in the Judaean Desert I. Oxford: Clarendon Press, 1955.

Milik, Józef Tadeusz. "27. 'Livre des Mystères.'" Pages 102–7, pl. XXI–XXII in *Qumran Cave I*. Edited by Dominique Barthélemy and Józef Tadeusz Milik. Discoveries in the Judaean Desert I. Oxford: Clarendon Press, 1955.

Milik, Józef Tadeusz. "35. Recueil de cantiques d'action de grâces (1QH)." Pages 136–38, pl. XXXI in *Qumran Cave I*. Edited by Dominique Barthélemy and Józef Tadeusz Milik. Discoveries in the Judaean Desert I. Oxford: Clarendon Press, 1955.

Newsom, Carol A. "406. 4QShirot 'Olat HaShabbat[g]." Pages 395–98, pl. XXXI in *Qumran Cave 4. VI Poetical and Liturgical Texts, Part 1*. Edited by Esther Eshel, Hanan Eshel, Carol

A. Newsom, Bilhah Nitzan, Eileen M. Schuller, and Ada Yardeni. Discoveries in the Judaean Desert XI. Oxford: Clarendon Press, 1998.

Puech, Émile. "4Q173a : Note épigraphique." *Revue de Qumrân* 24.2 (94) (2009): 287–90.

Qimron, Elisha. "413. 4QComposition Concerning Divine Providence." Pages 169–71, pl. XIV in *Qumran Cave 4. XV Sapiential Texts, Part 1*. Edited by Torleif Elgvin, Menahem Kister, Timothy H. Lim, Bilhah Nitzan, Stephen J. Pfann, Elisha Qimron, Lawrence H. Schiffman, and Annette Steudel. Discoveries in the Judaean Desert XX. Oxford: Clarendon Press, 1997.

Sanders, James A. *The Psalms Scroll of Qumrân Cave 11 (11Ps^a)*. Discoveries in the Judaean Desert of Jordan IV. Oxford: Clarendon Press, 1965.

Sanderson, Judith E. "20. 4QExod^j." Pages 149–50, pl. XXI in *Qumran Cave 4. VII. Genesis to Numbers*. Discoveries in the Judaean Desert XII. Oxford: Clarendon Press, 1994.

Skehan, Patrick W., and Eugene C. Ulrich. "57. 4QIsa^c." Pages 45–74, pl. VII–XII in *Qumran Cave 4, X. The Prophets*. Edited by Frank Moore Cross, Russell E. Fuller, Judith E. Sanderson, Patrick W. Skehan, and Emanuel Tov. Discoveries in the Judaean Desert XV. Oxford: Clarendon Press, 1997.

Stegemann, Hartmut, Eileen M. Schuller, and Carol A. Newsom. *Qumran Cave 1. III. 1QHodayot^a with Incorporation of 1QHodayot^b and 4QHodayot^{a–f}*. Discoveries in the Judaean Desert XL. Oxford: Clarendon Press, 2009.

Strugnell, John. "Notes en marge du volume V des « Discoveries in the Judaean Desert of Jordan »." *Revue de Qumrân* 7.2 (26) (1970): 163–276.

Tov, Emanuel. "26b. 4QLev^g." Pages 203–4, pl. XXXVII in *Qumran Cave 4. VII: Genesis to Numbers*. Edited by Eugene C. Ulrich, Frank Moore Cross, James R. Davila, Nathan Jastram, Judith E. Sanderson, Emanuel Tov, and John Strugnell. Discoveries in the Judaean Desert XII. Oxford: Clarendon Press, 1994.

Tov, Emanuel. *Scribal Practices and Approaches Reflected in the Texts Found in the Judean Desert*. Studies on the Texts of the Desert of Judah 54. Leiden: Brill, 2004.

Tov, Emanuel, ed. *The Texts from the Judaean Desert. Indices and an Introduction to the Discoveries in the Judaean Desert Series*. Discoveries in the Judaean Desert XXXIX. Oxford: Clarendon Press, 2002.

Paul Mandel
Between סֹפֵר and סָפַר: The Evolution of the Second Temple Period 'Scribe'

1 Introduction

The focus of the present conference, in studying the nature and function of writing professionals during the period of Ancient Israel, is no doubt motivated to a large extent by the immense importance of the material which these professionals bequeathed to subsequent generations, as formulated in the literary and judicial matter of the books of the Hebrew Bible. Such a study requires research into the physical and material aspects of recording, the historical and physical contexts of the documents produced, questions of genre and canon and the relationships between form and content, studies of literacy, comparative studies of similar collections of the period, cross-cultural influences, the impact of alternate modes of transmission (epigraphic remains as well as putative modes of oral and aural transmission), and, finally, descriptions of the occupation, function and societal role of the writing professional in biblical society (Hebrew and Aramaic) and in parallel societies, in particular those in the neighboring cultures of Egypt and Mesopotamia. Most of these areas are covered by the numerous papers presented at this conference. The aim of the present paper is to summarize my investigation of the name commonly applied to these writing professionals: primarily, the use of *sofer* (Hebrew) and *safar* (Aramaic) in biblical texts and in other literary documents in these languages throughout the first millennium BCE (and during the first centuries thereafter), and the related terms *grammateus* and *scriba*, which appear as Greek and Latin equivalents, respectively, for these words in the early biblical translations and in related works (2 Maccabees and the synoptic gospels of the New Testament).[1] The Latin term, of course, is the source for the widespread use of "scribe" in English and in Latinate languages to denote writing professionals of all periods, as evidenced in the title of the present conference. In stating my conclusions at the beginning of this paper I wish to delineate the boundaries of my discussion and its implications—and the limitation of these implications—for related studies such as those presented at this conference.

---

[1] The detailed investigation is found in chapter 2 of my recently published book, *The Origins of Midrash: From Teaching to Text* (Leiden: Brill, 2017), 23–86.

The conclusion may be stated simply, if a bit starkly: the Hebrew term *sofer* and its Aramaic cognate, *safar*, as found in biblical texts and in all relevant documents of the period of the first millennium BCE (in Hebrew and in Aramaic), **do not refer to the writing professional associated with the production and transmission of biblical and associated texts** (or any other 'text' of a literary or judicial genre, for that matter). This conclusion also applies to the use of *grammateus* and *scriba*, both in more general texts in Greek and Latin and, in particular, in documents such as those in the synoptic gospels where Jewish groups with this name are mentioned. I will explain below what I believe are the most accurate descriptions of the individuals named by these terms. The sense of the word *sofer* **underwent a major change** from pre-exilic usage (in Hebrew) to post-exilic terminology; the change is associated with the development of a new sense of the cognate term in Aramaic (*safar*) which transpired within the Mesopotamian linguistic and cultural *milieu*. Thus, we must differentiate between the pre-exilic *sofer* and the Hebrew term given to Ezra (primarily in Ezra 7); the latter is the one associated with this semantic change, which is also reflected in many, but not all, instances of the use of Aramaic *safar* during the latter half of the first millennium BCE.

Two points are in order at this time:

1. It is clear that this study must take into account similar terms for writing professionals found in associated cultures and languages; in particular, the Akkadian *ṭupšarru* (lit., inscriber on tablet), and Egyptian *sš* (*sesh*). In the course of the comparison, however, care must be applied to discriminate between historical periods and cultural backgrounds which may not be similar. In particular, it is important to note that the heyday of the Egyptian and Mesopotamian 'scribes' (or, more accurately, writing professionals), from which much of the understanding of the occupations of ancient 'scribes' has been deduced, occurred during the mid- and late-3rd and early-2nd millennia BCE (with centers of 'scribal' activity in the Mesopotamian *bit ṭuppi* and the 'House of Life' in Egypt)—more than one thousand years before the appearance of the biblical *sofer* and the Aramaic *safar*. Thus, while these ancient writing professionals often occupied central and authoritative roles in their respective societies, coalescing into what has been called a "scribal class" with manifold duties in the transmission and interpretation of culture and the creation and propagation of literary epics and judicial texts, it has been demonstrated that this elevated status declined drastically by the end of the second millennium BCE even in these centers, as literacy became more

widespread among the higher classes.[2] If at this time the *ṭupšarru* himself became no more than an inscriber/recorder employed mostly for the drawing up of legal documents, it will come as no surprise that the biblical-era writing professional—whatever his name—did not occupy the type of role, as envisioned by many current scholars, of those responsible for the creation and transmission of the ancient biblical literary genres.

2. Secondly, in divorcing the sense of the terms *sofer* and *safar* from that of the writing professional and literary creator who are the focus of the present conference, I do not doubt the relevance of these studies. The very existence of the Hebrew Bible bears eloquent witness to a long and complex period of compilation and transmission of a written text (with connections to the oral transmission of associated material), while the centrality of the biblical and associated texts insured continued and varied modes of textual commentary, themselves becoming objects of transmission by writing professionals. The importance of the study of the function of these professionals in the society, their relationship to legal texts and the formation and creation of various legal and literary genres, and their roles as creators, transmitters and teachers of these texts is not to be doubted. The importance of the conclusions of my study is limited to emphasizing the care which must be taken to separate out from our discussion those texts which might have been used (incorrectly, in my opinion) as data for the understanding of the

---

2 The earliest functions of both the Mesopotamian and Egyptian writing professionals were not in the literary realm (which was mostly still in an oral stage of creation and transmission), but were specifically concentrated in the commercial and military realms, where the relatively new "invention" of writing was used to record royal inventories, battle data and commercial transactions: "Contrary to commonly held expectations, these activities [of cuneiform writing in Mesopotamia] had nothing to do with the recording of mental ideas, or the transmission of verbal 'messages.' The early scribes were mere accountants, and [...] there is no trace of 'literary' texts in the earliest periods" (Bendt Alster, 'Scribes, Sages and Seers in Ancient Mesopotamia,' in *Scribes, Sages and Seers: The Sage in the Eastern Mediterranean World*, ed. Leo G. Perdue [Gottingen, 2008], 47). Regarding the later period: "After the second Old Babylonian period [mid-second millennium BCE], the tablet-house disappeared, and scribal education [...] fell into the hands of individual families" (Benno Landsberger, 'Babylonian Scribal Craft and its Terminology,' in *Proceedings of the 23rd Congress of Orientalists* [London, 1954], 123–6, and see 97–9). See also Victor A. Hurowitz, 'Tales of Two Sages: Towards an Image of the "Wise Man" in Akkadian Writings,' in *Scribes, Sages and Seers*, 70, n. 16: "[C]ontrary to popular misconception, basic skills in reading and writing cuneiform were readily acquirable and widespread in the second and first millennia BCE, meaning that mere literacy would not have marked a person as particularly wise or skilled." The situation of the Egyptian *sesh* is somewhat different, but here, too, the so-called "scribal class" of the ancient period was vastly different, and greatly declined, during the first millennium BCE.

writing professional occupied in the literary and judicial realms during this period.[3]

2 First Temple period *sofer*: Recorder, Tally-man

In passages describing the courts of David, Solomon, Yoash, Hezekiah and Yo-
shiah, the *sofer* functions as **accountant, enumerator** and **tallyman**. Thus, the
סופר המלך **counts** monetary contributions to the Temple (2 Kings 12:11), a heavenly *sofer* (bearing a scribal 'kit') takes a population census (Ezekiel 9:2–6), and
the סופר שר הצבא is given the responsibility to muster the army (2 Kings 25:19).
The *sofer* writes on parchment (or papyrus), and therefore we find reference to
his tools: a stylus or "pen" (עט סופר [Ps 45:2]), a knife (תער הסופר [Jer 36:23]) to
cut the parchment, and a 'kit' (קסת הסופר [Ezek 9:3]) in which to hold these utensils (or the ink). While these tools are necessary for a **recorder**, they do not necessarily designate their bearers as **scholars** or *literati*, just as owning a computer
today does not imply that one computes or is involved with algorithms, or writes
novels. The evidence shows that writing took place for **military, governmental**

---

3 It may be pertinent to mention here the various *later* uses of the word *sofer*, which are often
confused, mostly in non-scholarly circles, with the ancient *sofer*. Thus, the use of the Hebrew
sofer to designate both ritual "scribe" of Torah scrolls and ritual parchments (*tefillin, mezuzot*)
and a copyist of manuscripts is a development of the late Byzantine period, deriving from the
mishnaic-talmudic usage of *sofer* as a designation of a clerk/notary responsible for the compos-
ing of legal documents. (Concerning the use of *sofer* in rabbinic sources for a clerk/notary, see
below, note 22.) The collection of laws concerning the writing of Torah scrolls and the ritual
reading from them in tractate *Soferim* is not attested before the Geonic period (see Michael Higger, *Seven Minor Treatises* [New York, 1930]; idem, *Massekhet Soferim* [New York: *Debé Rabbanan*, 1937], Introduction); the work's original title was most likely *Sefarim*, that is, concerning
the reading of Scriptures (see Myron Bialik Lerner, "The External Tractates," in *The Literature of
the Sages*, First Part: Oral Tora, Halakha, Mishna, Tosefta, Talmud, External Tractates, ed.
Shmuel Safrai [Philadelphia and Assen/Maastricht, 1987], 397–8). Besides the sense of no-
tary/law clerk for *sofer* in early rabbinic (tannaitic) sources, the sense of *sofer* as a teacher of
elementary studies, in contrast to *mashneh*, a teacher of the oral literature, is attested mostly in
amoraic sources; for the few tannaitic sources, see t. Sukkah 2:6; t. Meg. 3:28. This later designation is related to the word *sefer* as designating the object of elementary education, *viz.*, the Bible.
Nowhere in the rabbinic material does the word refer to "copyists"; these are named *kotev(im)*,
"writers" (Tosefta *Bikkurim* 2:15). On the other hand, the term דברי סופרים found in rabbinic
sources to designate earlier law decisors is directly related to the post-exilic development of the
term discussed here; see section 4.2 below. Obviously, the current Hebrew use of *sofer* as "writer,
author" has no relevance to our study.

and **commercial** operations: the *sofer* provided necessary legal documentation and, most importantly, was responsible for the **archival storing of documents** (stored in the *lishkat ha-sofer*).

In all Hebrew and Aramaic documents from the first half of the first millennium BCE the *sofer/safar* denotes a **formulator of deeds** or a **notary**, that is, a specialist in **recording** and **preserving** documents in the legal, economic and military realms. The *spr* is not to be identified with officials putatively considered as "letter readers" and "letter writers": Regarding a passage in the early sixth-century BCE Lachish Letter 3 (ostraca), "קרא ספר," Frank Cross reads, "Call a scribe [...] any scribe who may have come to me" ('A Literate Soldier: Lachish Letter III,' *Biblical and Related Studies Presented to Samuel Iwry*, ed. Ann Kort and Scott Morschausen [Winona Lake, Ind., 1985], 43, 46–7). However, William F. Albright correctly translates *spr* there as "letter" or "document": "Read [my] letter" (*BASOR* 61 [1936], 12–13; idem, 'The Oldest Hebrew Letters: The Lachish Ostraca,' *BASOR* 70 [1938], 13; idem, 'A Re-Examination of the Lachish Letters,' *BASOR* 71 [1938], 26). It has been demonstrated (conclusively, in my opinion) that the root of the substantive *sofer* derives from the West Semitic verb *spr*, "to count," and is not to be confused with the Hebrew word *sefer*, "book," which derives from the Akkadian noun *šipru* and the verb *šapāru*, related to the senses of "sending an **envoy**," a "(delivered) report" or a "(conveyed) **message**."[4] Deeds from Ugarit (14th to 12th cent. BCE) mention the Akkadian *ṭupšarru* and the *spr* who are responsible for the authorization and deposition of transactions and their associated documents, and who should not be understood as 'copyists' of the documents. The root *spr* in the Ugaritic documents is attested exclusively in the verb "to count" and the nouns "list," "number," and "record"—all derived principally from the basic sense of "count."[5] Similarly, Baruch ben Neriah was not Jeremiah's amanuensis, but a notary whose responsibility lay in the actualization and retention (storing) of legal transactions. Thus, Baruch is called in by Jeremiah to be the **repositor** for the deed of purchase of Hanamel's field. While Baruch may have been instrumental in the drafting of the deed, there is no evidence for any writing on his part: "Take these deeds ... store them in an earthen vessel that they may last many days" [Jer 32:14]. Presumably Jeremiah could have written the deed

---

4 See Yochanan Muffs, *Studies in the Aramaic Legal Papyri from Elephantine* (Leiden, 2003), 207, and note to p. 188: "Aramaic/Hebrew *spr/sofer* 'scribe' is not to be derived from Akkadian *sapiru*, as so commonly assumed. [...] On the contrary, it was Akkadian that borrowed the term *sipirru* 'scribe' from West-Semitic." On *sepīru*, see below, note 18. The contrary view was proposed by Edward Yehezkel Kutscher (*Milim ve-Toledotehen* [Jerusalem, 1965], 67–8).
5 See Mandel, *The Origins of* Midrash, 31–3 and notes there.

himself; Baruch was instrumental for his role in *preserving* the document (which Jeremiah was not in a position to do in captivity). In no biblical passage can *sofer* be related to an official whose principal responsibilities were literary-epistolary. While the biblical First Temple period *soferim* were at times asked to read from a document (*sefer*; cf. Jer 36:15–18, 2 Kgs 22:8), this does not define their occupation; note, for example, that Shafan "the *sofer*," who reads from the *sefer Torah*, is called in by King Josiah primarily in order to count the Temple money (cf. ספרי המלך in 2 Kgs 12:11), while Yehudi, who reads out Jeremiah's written prophecies to King Yehoyakim, does not bear the title *sofer* (Jer 36:21–23; cf. 36:14). In Jer 36:17–18, the royal ministers do not question Baruch's prowess as stenographer but rather his role in *authenticating* Jeremiah's prophecies: in his response, Baruch emphasizes that these are indeed the *ipsissima verba* of Jeremiah ("מפיו" – note that it is with this word that Baruch begins his answer).[6]

The Greek translators of the biblical texts in the Septuagint knew this to be the sense of *sofer* and correctly translated the word into the Greek *grammateus*, which never denotes a 'writer' or 'copyist,' but rather a **clerk** and **registrar** with civil and communal duties:

> Die *grammateis* sind in der griechischen Welt … **Sekretäre** … In Athens hieß der Hauptsekretär des Staates "Ratssekretär" … Er war für die Veröffentlichung von Dokumenten aus der Tätigkeit des Rats oder der Volksversammlung zuständig.[7]

This, in turn, was properly translated into Latin *scriba*, an official who similarly has no connection with the production or copying of texts or writing *per se* (those functions are indicated by the Latin *scriptor* and *librarius*), but serves as one of the Roman *apparitores*, civil servants acting as paid auxiliaries to the Roman magistrate:

---

6 See Chaim Cohen, "The Hapax Legomenon דיו (Ink) in the Context of 'ואני כותב על הספר בדיו' (Jer 36:18): A 'False Friend' in Modern Hebrew Due to the Masoretes' Misunderstanding of the Preposition בד Meaning 'To' or 'For'," *Shnaton: An Annual for Biblical and Ancient Near Eastern Studies* 24 [2015], 77–102 [Hebrew].) The *reading out* of prophecies from a written document was unusual, as prophetic utterances were normally recited orally; in this case, the secondary reading of Jeremiah's prophecy was necessitated due to Jeremiah's incarceration, as Jeremiah himself explains (Jer 36:5–6). The additional reference to Baruch's writing down of Jeremiah's prophecies in Jer 45:1 should be seen in the context of his activity in chap. 36. Similar functions apply to Shemayah ben Netanel *ha-sofer* mentioned in 1 Chr 24:6 (a registrar), and can be assumed for those mentioned in 2 Sam 8:17, 20:25, and 1 Kgs 4:3.
7 *Der Neue Pauly: Enzyklopädie der Antike* (Stuttgart, 1996–2003), Altertum, 4:1197.

Scribae hiessen in Rom professionelle Schreibkundige mit höhere Qualifikation, also **nicht einfache Abschreiber** (*librarii*), **sondern Sekretäre und Rechnungsführer.**[8]

The Latin word *scriba* was borrowed in the medieval period by Old French and English as the loanword 'scribe,' but even then it did not denote **writing professionals;** its use as 'copyist' is of late Medieval origin, and is therefore misleading for understanding the ancient world.[9]

3 *sofer* and *safar* in Mesopotamian Aramaic (1st millennium BCE)

An anomalous use of *sofer* in biblical texts, where the title has no relation to the (relatively low-level) function of notary and recorder, is attested in the title of Ezra, introduced in Ezra chapter 7:

וְהוּא סֹפֵר מָהִיר בְּתוֹרַת מֹשֶׁה אֲשֶׁר נָתַן י"י אֱלֹהֵי יִשְׂרָאֵל (7:6)

עֶזְרָא הַכֹּהֵן הַסֹּפֵר, סֹפֵר דִּבְרֵי מִצְוֹת י"י וְחֻקָּיו עַל יִשְׂרָאֵל (7:11)

In both cases the author takes pains to *explain* the term in relation to the divinely-given **law** and **commandments.** This anomaly led Martin Luther to coin a new term for the title 'scribe' of Ezra, *Schriftgelehrte*, in contrast with *Schreiber* used in the other biblical passages containing *sofer*. Luther no doubt understood *torat Moshe* as referring to the Scriptural text. However, **nowhere in post-exilic literature does תורת משה refer to the *text* of 'Moses' law'** (this is referred to exclusively as ספר משה), but denotes, rather, the **legal content** of the divine Law in its entirety.[10] Thus, Ezra's title is related by the author to a set of laws, not to a text containing these laws.

---

8 *ibid.*, Altertum, 11:299.

9 Note the definitions of "scribe" as listed in *Webster's Third New International Dictionary* (1966), where the order of the definitions is historical: "1 : one of a class of men devoted to the study and exposition of the law during the Persian and early Greek periods of Jewish history ... 2 a : an official or public writer acting usually as a clerk or keeper of accounts ... d. a copier of manuscripts. 3 a : one who writes: author, writer." As I note below, the earliest definition of the English term (definition 1) is based on the later derivative sense of *scriba* < *grammateus* < סֹפֵר (Hebrew; late 1st mill. BCE) < סָפַר (Mesopotamian Aramaic, early 1st mill. BCE).

10 See Ezra 6:18; Neh 13:1; 2 Chr 25:4, 35:12. Cf. 2 Chr 25:4 (ככתוב בתורה בספר משה) with 2 Kgs 14:6 (ככתוב בספר תורת משה), which demonstrates the earlier method of reference to Moses's

The title is clearly intended to represent a higher level of responsibility, one that must be related to a *judicial* function. In his explanatory digressions, the author of Ezra 7 feels the necessity to further define the title because he uses the word here (already known in Hebrew as a title for a notary) **as a loanword from Aramaic**: the original Aramaic term is found in the Artaxerxes rescript in this chapter, where Ezra is called סָפַר דָּתָא דִּי אֱלָהּ שְׁמַיָּא (Ezra 7:12, 21). As this phrase originates in **Mesopotamian (Achaemenid) Aramaic**, and since *data* refers to a (royal) legal edict (cf. Ezra 7:25–26; Esther 3:8), the solution for the proper understanding of this term and its Hebrew loan may be found in Aramaic texts of this period (*Reichsaramäisch* and associated texts), where we shall find a close relation between a *safar* and the authorization (and propagation) of *legal edicts* from various sources.

3.1 Enoch

Although it has become commonplace among scholars to call attention to the title 'scribe' (*safar*) appended to the figure of Enoch in the eponymous pseudepigraphic works as evidence of his role in the transmission of some kind of literary matter or as representing him as a "sage,"[11] there are, in fact, few passages where this title occurs. In all passages in 1 Enoch where Enoch is referred to as *safar*, his function is that of a *deliverer of a celestial message* (to the fallen angels)—"'scribe" of righteousness' or 'of truth' (1 Enoch 12:3–4; 15:1–3);[12] ספר פרשא = 'discerning "scribe"' (*Book of Giants* [Qumran]: 4Q203 [EnGiantsᵃ] 8, 1–4)—or as an *interpreter of dreams* (4Q530 [EnGiantsᵇ] ii, 14).[13]

---

text as *sefer torat Moshe*; see Avi Hurvitz, "On the Borderline between Biblical Criticism and Hebrew Linguistics: The Emergence of the Term ספר-משה," in *Tehillah le-Moshe: Biblical and Judaic Studies in Honor of Moshe Greenberg*, ed. Mordechai Cogan, Barry L. Eichler, and Jeffrey H. Tigay (Winona Lake, Ind., 1997), 37*–43*. This is evidenced also in the Qumran literature, where כתוב *never* appears with the term *torat Adonai* or *torat Moshe* but only with *sefer Moshe*. See also Tobit 6:13 and 7:13 in *Codex Sinaiticus*, and cf. 4Q197 (*Tobitᵇ*) 4ii, 6.

11 See the description of Enoch by James Kugel: "Of a piece with 'Enoch the Heavenly Scribe' are the still more numerous references to him as a wise man and, in particular, an astronomer. *After all, any Jewish scribe of late antiquity was almost by definition also a sage*" (*Traditions of the Bible* [Cambridge, Mass., 1998], 177; emphasis added).

12 Both "righteousness" and "truth" in the Ethiopic text may translate Aramaic קושטא; see George W. E. Nickelsburg, *1 Enoch 1: A Commentary on the book of 1 Enoch, Chapters 1–36, 81–108* (Minneapolis, 2001), 270, 441–2.

13 In a number of passages Enoch is mentioned in the context of writing and books; he writes a petition for the angels ("Watchers") and recites it on high (13:4–7; 14:4); he is commanded to

3.2 Aḥiqar

The tale of Aḥiqar, the great counselor to the 7th century BCE Neo-Assyrian king Esarhaddon, is attested in a 5th century Aramaic text from papyri found at Elephantine; the tale has undoubtedly devolved from a more ancient Mesopotamian tradition. Aḥiqar's title is ספר חכים ומהיר, mirroring the title in Ezra chapter 7 (סֹפֵר מָהִיר בְּתוֹרַת מֹשֶׁה; *mahir* = expert). Aḥiqar functions as the main "counselor" of the king and of all Assyria; the fact that he is the "keeper of the (royal) ring seal" indicates his role as **chief promulgator of royal decrees.**[14]

3.3 *safar* in early Aramaic *targum*

It has been noticed that the early Aramaic *targumim* to the Pentateuch (Targum Onqelos and Targum Neofiti) and the Prophets (Targum Jonathan ben Uziel) contain an anomalous translation for the Hebrew word נביא. In contexts where the Hebrew denotes a divinely sanctioned prophet, whether true or false, the normal Aramaic cognate נביא is used (Genesis 20:7, Jeremiah 23:13). However, in certain instances the targumist chooses to translate the word נביא by Aramaic *safar*. A perusal of these passages shows that they refer to a *diviner* who, through "deductive divination," is able to *answer queries*: see 1 Samuel 19:24 (הגם שאול בנביאים <); 28:6 (וישאל שאול בי״י ולא ענהו י״י, גם בחלמות גם באורים גם בנביאם <); האף שאול בספריא

---

read from heavenly tablets (81:1–3) and write down for his son and posterity an account of the revelations granted to him (82:1–2, and cf. 83:2 and 10; 108:1). In none of these passages is he given the title of *safar*. Reading written material and writing epistles and petitions is a natural activity for the roles performed by Enoch, but this does not imply a special status nor should this activity be connected with the title *safar*. In 92:1, a superscription to the epistle of Enoch, the title "Enoch the scribe" is mentioned. However, compare the passage as found in 4Q212 (En[g] ar) II, 22–4, and discussed by Milik, *The Books of Enoch*, 260–62 (and cf. the small Greek fragment cited there, 261, containing the word *gra[mmateus]*); see especially Milik's discussion of the Ethiopic word *tě'měrt* as "sign" (261), and cf. Stuckenbruck, *1 Enoch 91–108*, 217–21; Helge S. Kvanvig, *Primeval History: Babylonian, Biblical and Enochic: An Intertextual Reading* (Leiden: Brill, 2011), 331–5. I suggest that the title *safar* in this passage, if original, should be rendered "*interpreter* of the sign[s] of wisdom"; see below.

14 On the title "keeper of the ring-seal of the king," see Jonas Greenfield, "Studies in Aramaic Lexicography I," *JAOS* 82 (1962), 292–3; idem, "The Wisdom of Aḥiqar," in *Wisdom in Ancient Israel: Essays in Honour of J. A. Emerton*, ed. John Day, Robert P. Gordon and Hugh G. M. Williamson (Cambridge, 1995), 43–52. See below, note 19 (end), concerning the identical role played by Haman (Esther 3:10) and Mordechai (8:2), initiated at precisely the moment when they are invested with the authority as **authoritative propagators of the king's edict.**

וישלח ... לחלות את פני י"י לאמר אל הכהנים (7:2–3 .Zach ;(גם בנביאים < אף בספריא
ולספריא < ואל הנביאים לאמר ...). In addition, the Hebrew word מחוקק, in contexts
which the targumist understood as *law-giver*, is translated *safar:* Gen. 49:10
כי שם חלקת (33:21 .Deut ;(ומחקק מבין רגליו < ואף לא ספרין מלפי אוריה מבני בנוי)
(מחקק ספון < תמן באחסנתה משה ספרא רבא דישראל קביר).[15]

We may conclude that in Aramaic texts from the Achaemenid period, some of
which reflect earlier traditions from the Neo-Assyrian period, *safar* denotes an
authoritative figure who serves as a *counselor,* disclosing to others *divine secrets*
or *royal decrees*. These functions accord with two roles that acquired central importance in Mesopotamian culture during the first millennium BCE: 1) the *diviner*,
who can interpret heavenly signs and predict according to his 'decoding' of these
signs the messages they portend, and who was of supreme importance to the Akkadian kings during the first half of this period; 2) the *law-decisor* and *counsel*
who perform a similarly authoritative function in the later Achaemenid empire
(when divination was not deemed as important as the institution and propagation of legal edicts; cf. Esther, chapter 1).

This empirical observation explains the particular use of *safar data* for Ezra
by Artaxerxes (ספר דתא די אלה שמיא), who viewed Ezra in his role as *legal counselor*. The Aramaic term was then loaned by the author of Ezra, where the older
Hebrew *sofer* now became the term for this legal decisor; the author explicitly
determines the renewed use of the old term by adding the modifying clauses,
both of which emphasize the legal body of decrees with which Ezra is entrusted
in his authoritative capacity as legal counselor.

Why and how did a term designating a common notary and accountant become the title for a high-level diviner and law counsel? The semantic shift is an
example of "linguistic specification," particularly common in *bilingual* societies
such as that of the Neo-Assyrian empire.[16] Current examples of such linguistic

15 See Robert Hayward, "Some Notes on Scribes and Priests in the Targum of the Prophets," *JJS*
36 (1985), 210–21; Anthony J. Saldarini, "'Is Saul Also Among the Scribes?': Scribes and Prophets
in Targum Jonathan," *"Open Thou Mine Eyes...": Essays on Aggadah and Judaica Presented to
Rabbi William G. Braude on His Eightieth Birthday and Dedicated to His Memory*, ed. Herman J.
Blumberg et al. (Hoboken, NJ, 1992), 239–53.
16 See Hayim Tadmor, "The Aramaization of Assyria: Aspects of Western Impact," in Mesopotamien und seine Nachbarn: Politische und kulturelle Wechselbeziehungen im alten Vorderasien
vom 4. bis 1. Jahrtausend v. Chr. vol 2., Proceedings of the XXVe RAI, ed. Hans J. Nissen and
Johannes Renger (Berlin, 1982), 449–70, and esp. 453–55 ("Bilingualism and Lexical Interference").

specification include the use of 'Filipino' in modern spoken Israeli Hebrew to denote *any* caregiver, especially of the elderly: because of the great influx of foreign workers from the Philippines, mostly women, who were employed almost exclusively as caregivers for the elderly, it has become the norm in modern Hebrew to use this term for any caregiver; thus, "my father's Filipino comes from Sri Lanka." An older example may be cited from the Spanish-American subculture of the 19th and 20th centuries, where *ministro*, originally denoting in Spanish a "communal officer" or "cabinet official," came to be used by Spanish speakers in the Southwest United States for "Protestant clergyman," influenced by English usage.[17] In these cases, the speakers of a local language appropriate a foreign title, or substitute a foreign sense for an already known title, *with a definition that is applicable to the perceived **function** of the 'official,' although the speakers may not be fully aware or conscious of the original meaning and semantic evolution of the title.*

As shown in the mural painting below (from *Til Barsib*, the palace of Tiglath Pileser III), the Aramaic *safar*-recorder writing on parchment (increasingly integrated into Akkadian society through military conquests) is seen employed side by side with the Akkadian *ṭupšarru*, inscribing a tablet in cuneiform, in official recording capacities (depicted here in a military context). To the Akkadian speaker of the first centuries of the first millennium BCE, this Aramaic official was perceived as one able to *decode* signs on papyrus that were totally illegible to the Akkadian speaker and to *translate* these signs for him. In this way, *safar* became for the Akkadian speaker a by-word for any *decoder* or *translator* of foreign signs.

---

17 The meaning of 'minister' to denote a Protestant clergyman arose during 16th century Reformation England, where, due to objections to the use of 'priest,' it became the preferred term for the Anglican clergyman. See Uriel Weinreich, *Languages in Contact: Findings and Problems* (The Hague, 1963), 47–63, and esp. 47–50; cf. Mario Pei, *The Story of Language* (Philadelphia, 1949), chap. 6, "Semantics and Semantic Change," 138–48; Avi Hurvitz, "Continuity and Innovation in Biblical Hebrew: The Case of 'Semantic Change' in Post-Exilic Writings," AbrNSup 4 (1995), 1–10. For an example of linguistic specification of a term from the same historical and linguistic context as the one under discussion here, consider Hebrew *saris*/Akkadian *ša rēš* ("one who stands at the head [of the king]"), which came to denote a "eunuch" (cf. Isa 56:3); see A. Leo Oppenheim, "A note on *ša rēši*," *JANUSCU* 5 (Gaster Festschrift, 1973), 325–34 (see esp. 331), and cf. Hayim Tadmor, "*Rab-saris* and *Rab-shakeh* in 2 Kings 18," in *The Word of the Lord Shall Go Forth: Essays in Honor of David Noel Freedman in Celebration of His Sixtieth Birthday*, ed. Carol L. Meyers and M. O'Connor (Winona Lake, Ind., 1983), 279–85 (see esp. n. 10, pp. 281–82). The word originally denoted high-placed officials in the king's retinue, but due to the socio-functional equivalence between such officials and their particular characteristic as being castrated, the word came to apply to one who possessed this characteristic even in contexts outside of the royal courts.

Figure 1: *safar / sepīru* (Aramaic) on the left; *ṭupšarru* (cuneiform) on the right. Two sorts of scribes, one practiced in the art of indenting cuneiform inscriptions [on clay tablets] and one skilled in the writing of Aramaic documents [on papyrus, parchment and leather], enjoyed equal prestige during the last two centuries of Assyrian history. (Raymond P. Dougherty, 'Writing upon Parchment and Papyrus among the Babylonians and the Assyrians,' Journal of the American Oriental Society 48 [1928], 130)

Thus, the foreign word *safar* (and its Akkadian loanword *sepīru*) acquired the meaning, especially for Akkadians who were required to understand Aramaic documents in their official duties, of 'translator' and 'decoder of foreign signs,' and as a *decisor/advisor* for the élite. Since precisely during this period (900–600 BCE) the (*royal*) *counselor-diviner* became a fixture of aristocratic life, it became the norm to use the foreign term *safar/sepīru* for the diviner who could 'read' and 'translate' the 'heavenly writing.'[18]

---

18 On the Neo-Assyrian diviner as one who decoded 'heavenly writing,' see Francesca Rochberg, *The Heavenly Writing: Divination, Horoscopy, and Astronomy in Mesopotamian Culture* (New York, 2004). The use of *safar* in this context influenced a parallel linguistic specification for the original Akkadian term for a notary/writing professional, *ṭupšarru* ("recorder"-notary), so that *ṭupšarru* became (although not exclusively) a name for the celestial diviner (especially in the term *ṭupšar Enūma-anu-enlil*; see Rochberg, *The Heavenly Writing*, 109–236), and *ṭupšarrutu* a term for 'celestial divination' (see Hermann Hunger, *Astrological Reports to Assyrian Kings*, SAA 8 [Helsinki, 1992], nos. 338 and 342, and Victor A. Hurowitz, "Tales of Two Sages: Towards an Image of the 'Wise Man' in Akkadian Writings," in *Scribes, Sages and Seers* [above. note 2], p. 69, n. 15: "It seems that the connotations of *ṭupšarrūtu* changed over time. The word with a primary meaning of inscribing a tablet [DUB.SAR] expanded to connote all the activities which involved

During the subsequent Persian period, when the members of the Achaemenid court had little belief in celestial divination or need thereof, there still existed a linguistic gap between the Aramaic *lingua franca* used throughout the empire and the spoken Persian language of the rulers (many of whom now relocated to the provinces which they governed). In this culture the *legal expert* and *advisor* in the promulgation of royal edicts (*data*) and law became paramount (such as in the depiction of Aḥiqar in the later Aramaic tale); these experts were consulted on all aspects of law, especially regarding the royal edicts (cf. Esther, chapter 1). And so the ancient-new term for 'decoder/decisor,' the Aramaic *safar*, acquired a new meaning denoting a function related to that of the earlier 'decoder/decisor': the advisor as law-consultant. This is precisely the role given to Ezra by Artaxerxes, as is made evident at the end of the rescript of Ezra chapter 7 where Ezra is entrusted with the establishment of a judicial system in the renewed province of Judea (Ezra 7:25–26).[19]

---

writing, but in later periods developed the specialized meaning of divinatory art, especially in astronomy and astrology"; see there, p. 76). It is noteworthy that the Akkadian *sepīru*, as a loanword in Akkadian from Aramaic *safar*, refers not only to the standard "accountant/notary," but also to a *translator*: see Julius Lewy, "The Problems Inherent in Section 70 of the Bisutun Inscription," *HUCA* 25 (1954), 188–199, and notes 105, 108; Muhammed A. Dandamaev, "The Social Position of Neo-Babylonian Scribes," in *Gesellschaft und Kultur im alten Vorderasien*, ed. Horst Klengel (Berlin, 1982), 35–9 (cf. Muhammed A. Dandamaev and Vladimir G. Lukonin, *The Culture and Social Institutions of Ancient Iran*, English ed., Philip L. Kohl [Cambridge, 1989], 363); and Pierre Briant, *From Cyrus to Alexander: A History of the Persian Empire*, trans. Peter T. Daniels (Winona Lake, Ind., 2002), p. 509 and note on p. 956.

19 Further evidence for the *sofer* as diviner and translator-interpreter is found in biblical texts: In 2 Kgs 20:12–13 (and parallel in Isa 39:1–2) the Babylonian king Merodach Bal'adan sends סְפָרִים וּמִנְחָה to Hezekiah, who then shows "them" (!?) the royal treasury. The account directly follows the celestial anomaly of the retraction of the sun given to Hezekiah by Isaiah as a sign that he will survive his mortal illness (2 Kgs 20:1–12); Hezekiah's acceptance of the envoy provokes great wrath on the part of Isaiah who prophecies dire consequences for his progeny. The offer of "books" to the recovered king Hezekiah is a conundrum and bears no particular significance in the present context; however, the word can easily be read as *soferim* = **diviners**, a particularly Babylonian occupation, reflecting an archival text (original *safraya*?) from the pre-exilic period. These diviners had come to offer Hezekiah their (idolatrous) services in **interpreting** the celestial wonder that had no doubt received international reknown. Hezekiah's gratitude to them was the reason, then, for the divine punishment and Isaiah's anger. In the rewritten account of 2 Chr 32:31, the ancient "Mesopotamian" term of *soferim* as diviner is replaced with *meliẓei sarei Bavel* (*meliẓ* = translator!), which, in Hebrew of the Second Temple period, refers to an "interpreter of divine messages" (cf. occurrences in the *Hodayot* texts: 1QHᵃ xiv, 16 and *passim*); their activity is described there are לדרוש המופת ("to interpret [decode] the sign"). (For a different explanation, see Alan D. Crown, "Messengers and Scribes: The ספר and מלאך in the Old Testament," *VT* 24 [1974], 366–70; cf. Joseph Blenkinsopp, "Hezekiah and the Babylonian

4 Corroboration in texts and inscriptions from the Second Temple period

The conclusions reached above are corroborated by, and, in turn, shed light on the following attestations of *sofer* and its Greek cognate, *grammateus*, during the Second Temple period, the proper function of which has puzzled scholars.

4.1 Inscriptions on Second Temple period ossuaries

Epigraphic remains from the Second Temple period provide evidence that the *sofer* was ubiquitous in Jewish society and recognized as an honored individual. *Sofer* is the most common official title, besides *kohen*, regularly appearing on ossuaries of the Second Temple period, and must therefore have been a title of respect.[20] Based on other writings reflecting honored individuals in Jewish society of the Second Temple period (1 and 2 Maccabees, Apocryphal works such as Tobit

---

Delegation: A Critical Reading of Isaiah 39:1–8," in *Essays on Ancient Israel in Its Near Eastern Context: A Tribute to Nadav Na'aman*, ed. Yairah Amit et al. [Winona Lake, Ind., 2006], 107–22.) In the book of Esther, the function of the המלך סופרי (Est 3:12, 8:9) should be understood in the context of the **authorization** and **propagation** of the royal edict (*data*), including perhaps the **translation** of the edict into the empire's many languages, as expressly mentioned (3:12, 8:9–10). See below, note 39.

20 See Rachel Hachlili, *Jewish Funerary Customs, Practices and Rites in the Second Temple Period* (Leiden, 2005), 213, 215–16, regarding the evidence for *sofer* on ossuaries of the Second Temple period. See also there, 216, on the Greek title *didaskalos* on Jewish ossuaries of the period. The Hebrew title [*h*]*a-sofer* is attested in Greek transliteration in deeds from the first century CE (Pierre Benoit and Józef T. Milik, *Les grottes de Murabba'at*, DJD II [Oxford, 1961], no. 103a, line 1, p. 232), and an Aramaicized form is similarly found in Greek transliteration (as a personal name? ibid., no. 94, line 15, p. 225, and see note on p. 227). The title continued as an honorary one in the later, rabbinic period: cf. the Susiya synagogue inscription in Hebrew (fourth century CE), noting a "Rabbi Yoḥanan, the *sofer*, the *kohen*, *bērebbi* [an honorary title]" (Joseph Naveh, *On Stone and Mosaic: The Aramaic and Hebrew Inscriptions from Ancient Synagogues* [Tel-Aviv, 1978], no. 75, 115–16); and also *safra'* as an Aramaic proper name in Palestine and Babylonia (cf. the fifth-sixth century CE Na'aran synagogue inscription [Naveh, *op. cit.*, no. 60], the Aramaic and Greek dedicatory inscriptions in the third century CE Dura Europos synagogue [Naveh, *op. cit.*, nos. 88, 127, 131], and the Babylonian sage of the fourth century CE, Rav Safra [b. Pesaḥ. 52b, b. Ḥul. 110b]).

and Susanna, New Testament passages and others), the most plausible occupation of an honored *sofer* is not that of teacher or interpreter of Scripture but rather
scholar and teacher of law.[21]

4.2 דברי סופרים – An archaism in rabbinic literature

Although the term *sofer* in rabbinic sources regularly refers to a notary who draws
up legal documents,[22] the plural term *soferim* designates a class of sages from a
previous age whose "words" (*divré soferim*) carry authority in the specification of
laws: the *soferim* were responsible for specifying the parameters of ordinances of
the oral law (thus, the *divré soferim* are distinct from *divré Torah*, ordinances deriving from the written law) and enacting new laws.[23] Even when these *soferim*
are mentioned in relation to a scriptural passage, their interpretation in relation
to the passage concerns a *legal* argument and not a literary-textual interpretation
of Scripture.[24]

---

21 It has been noted that the descriptions of Sabbath activity in the synagogues during the late
Second Temple period by Philo and Josephus do not emphasize reading and commentary of
Scripture as much as the **teaching of laws**; see Philo, *Hypothetica* 7.11–14, *Moses* 2.211 and
2.215–216, *De specialibus legibus* 156–7, *De opificio mundi* 128; *Against Apion* 2.175–8. See also
the Theodotus inscription, which lists the *reading* of the Law and the *instruction* in the commandments as the primary activities taking place in the synagogue.
22 The *sofer* in the Mishnah is almost always a notary, whose occupation was to write and document deeds, especially writs of marriage and divorce; see m. Git. 3:1; 8:8; m. Qidd. 4:13; m. B.
Meṣ. 5:11; and cf. m. Ned. 9:2. The tools of the trade of the *sofer* as notary are his writing implements and desk; see m. Šabb. 12:5; m. Pesaḥ. 3:1; m. Kelim 24:6. The term also applies to a public
law clerk (m. Sanh. 4:3). See below, section 5, regarding the vernacular/colloquial nature of this
usage.
23 See t. Miqw. 5:4 (and parallels in y. Sanh. 11:6, 30b; b. Sanh. 87a). For the enactment of new
(rabbinically ordained) laws see m. 'Or. 3:9; m. Yebam. 2:4; m. Kelim 13:7; and y. 'Erub. 5:1, 22c.
Many enactments of the *soferim* are in the realm of purities, a classic aspect of ritual law. It is
probable that the term *pleṭat safraya'*, the survivors of the *soferim*, mentioned in the enigmatic
incident in *Megillat Ta'anit* (17 Adar; see also y. Ta'an. 2:13, 66a) and possibly attested in the
original benediction *birkat ha-ẓadiqim* of the *Amidah* prayer, also refers to a teacher of traditional laws; the *scholion* to *Megillat Ta'anit* explains these *soferim* as *ḥakhamim* and connects
the incident to the time of Alexander Jannaeus.
24 See Sifré Num 5 (ed. Horovitz, 14), where Rabban Gamaliel objects to a legalistic explanation
of a verse (Num 5:15) propounded by the *soferim* ("Let me alone, *soferim*!"), and proposes in its
stead a literary, figurative explanation (*ke-min ḥomer* = "as a jewel," denoting a figurative explanation that 'beautifies' the text as opposed to the legal argument for the wording of the text propounded by the *soferim*).

4.3 *grammateus* in the Synoptic Gospels of the New Testament and in 2 Maccabees

The so-called "scribes" mentioned frequently in the synoptic gospels, who are mentioned with the Pharisees and who seem to refer to a well-defined group of Jewish leaders, have naturally drawn much interest among scholars who have offered numerous and varied explanations for the use of the term. As mentioned above, the Greek *grammateus* of ancient Athens was a clerk responsible for recording and propagation of a civil and legal nature, and this word was thus a proper translation in Septuagint texts for the First Temple period *sofer* who held similar duties as an official recorder. It is natural that Jewish speakers of *koiné* Greek would continue to use this term as a *literal* translation of Hebrew and Aramaic *sofer/safar* (a *calque*) even in contexts where it appears in its newer sense of "law deciders"; these are precisely the contexts in which the *grammateis* are found in the New Testament accounts.[25] Similarly, the use of *sofer* as a title for the elder Eliezer in 2 Macc. 6:18–31, who is described as "one of the foremost *grammateis*" and zealous for the particulars of the law, fits precisely the sense suggested above.[26] Proof that this was the sense of *grammateus/sofer* intended and understood by the gospel authors is the appearance of Greek *nomikos* in parallel

---

25 The *grammateis* claim to wield "authority" (ἐξουσία) in teaching (Mark 1:22), and in their teachings they claim access to the "tradition of the elders" (Mark 7:2, 8–9); they are particularly concerned with laws of purities (Mark 7:1–13), oaths and tithes (Matt 23:16–26), and the relative importance of the commandments (Mark 12:28–34); they command respect and honor (Mark 12:38–40, Matt 23:2–7), and, along with the Pharisees, "sit on the seat of Moses" (Matt 23:2), that is, they consider themselves—and presumably are considered by portions of the populace—to have inherited the right to teach the law to the people. The activity of providing personal guidance in questions of law is well attested in the passages in the New Testament, where questions in law are asked of Jesus by the *nomikoi/grammateis*/Pharisees (Mark 12:28–34 and Matt 22:34–40; Mark 12:35; Luke 10:25–28). On the importance of questions in law for the authors of the synoptic gospels, see Luke 2:46–47, where Jesus as a child asks and answers questions in the Temple; cf. Josephus, *Vita 9*, where Josephus relates a similar story of himself as a young man. See also the use of the word *grammateus* in the Greek translation of the Hebrew *meḥoqeq* in Sir 10:4, which demonstrates the semantic equivalence in the eyes of the translator of the terms *meḥoqeq* (Hebrew), *safar* (Aramaic) and *grammateus* (Greek), all denoting a "law-instructor/interpreter."
26 See also 1 Macc 7:12, where a "band of *grammateis*" are considered Jewish leaders. In 1 Macc 5:42 the phrase *grammateis tou laou*, translation for שוטרי העם, reflects the Septuagint translation of the phrase (cf. LXX to Josh 1:10 and Deut 20:5–9) and is not to be confused with the later sense of the term.

passages;[27] the *nomikos* was primarily a jurist who served as *legal advisor* and *interpreter of law* (similar to the Roman *jurisconsult*).[28] Thus, while *grammateus* was the *literal* translation of *sofer/safar*, the title was (properly) translated *idiomatically* by these authors as *nomikos*, law consultant.[29]

4.4 The *sofer* in *Sirach* and other Hebrew writings of the Second Temple period

Ben Sira, the author of *Ecclesiasticus*, is often identified with the putative Second Temple period "scribe," primarily on the basis of his "ode to the *sofer*" in Sir 38:24–39:11. However, **this *sofer* is never identified with texts**; rather, he is described as one who "studies the law of the Most High, seeks out wisdom of the ancients," and fulfills the functions of judge, counselor, and law-consultant, where "he serves among the great and appears before rulers; he travels in foreign lands" (Sir 39:4). These activities accord with the definition of the Second Temple period *sofer* as law-consultant.

Elsewhere in Hebrew works from the Second Temple period the *sofer* is similarly lauded for his wisdom and counsel: Jonathan, the uncle of David, is called *yo'eṣ*, *mavin* and *sofer* (1 Chr 27:32),[30] and David is described as *ḥakham*, *sofer*, and *navon* in the Qumran Psalms Scroll (11QPsᵃ).[31] These depictions accord with

---

27 Matt 22:34–40, Luke 10:25–28; Luke 11:45–54; 14:1–6; 4 Macc 5:4.

28 See Epictetus, *Diatr.* 2.13.6–8 (concerning "an anxious man"); and cf.: Gerhard Kittel, *TDNT* 4:1088; George D. Kilpatrick, "Scribes, Lawyers, and Lucan Origins," *Journal of Theological Studies* n.s. 1 (1950), 56–60; Alfred Robert C. Leaney, "ΝΟΜΙΚΟΣ in St. Luke's Gospel," *Journal of Theological Studies* n.s. 2 (1951), 166–7.

29 Not all Jewish uses of the term *grammateus* from this period should be understood in this light. The word appears on Greek tomb inscriptions in the Jewish catacombs of Rome, where it is most probably used in the usual senses of the Greek as a type of secretarial function (in some cases, a hereditary post); see: Harry J. Leon, *The Jews of Ancient Rome* (Philadelphia, 1960), 183–6, and David Noy, *Jewish Inscriptions of Western Europe*, vol. 2 (Cambridge, 1995), 91–2 (cf. the discussion by Christine Schams, *Jewish Scribes in the Second-Temple Period* [Sheffield, 1998], 234–38). On the other hand, Josephus uses the term *hierogrammateus* for advisor-diviners, those who can foretell the future and serve as interpreters of dreams (*Ant.* 2.205, 209, 234, 243, 255; *J.W.* 6.291; *Ag. Ap.* 1.289, 290), as opposed to *grammateus*, which he uses in the usual Greek sense of "clerk," "secretary."

30 Cf. Isa 3:3, where the *yo'eṣ* is included in a list of important individuals of a city.

31 11Q5 XXVII, 2; see James A. Sanders, *The Psalms Scroll of Qumran Cave 11 (11QPsᵃ)*, DJD IV (Oxford, 1965), 48, 92.

the understanding of *sofer* as an important advisor, but do not point to textual acumen, writing expertise or literary knowledge.[32]

It is only in the book of Jubilees, written in Hebrew during the second century BCE, that we find an emphasis on "book-learning" that may reflect a different understanding of the traditional function of *sofer*. In the description of Enoch, who, as we have seen, was given the title *safar* in the earlier, Aramaic texts, the author of the book of Jubilees places special emphasis on Enoch's skills in writing and books: "He was the first to learn writing, instruction and wisdom[33] and he wrote in a book the signs of the heaven [...] He was the first to write a testimony [...] He saw everything and wrote his testimony" (Jub. 4:16–24). The importance of written transmission and Enoch's role in writing down his "testimony," found already in passages in 1 Enoch unrelated to his title as *sofer*,[34] are central themes in the book of Jubilees and other Jewish literature of the period; these may have been influenced by an understanding of Enoch's title as related to the word *sefer* as "book."[35]

---

32 See above, note 19 (end), concerning the *soferei ha-melekh* in the book of Esther (3:12, 8:9).

33 See Cana Werman, The Book of Jubilees: Introduction, Translation, and Interpretation (Jerusalem, 2015), 195, 201–2.

34 See above, note 13.

35 Writing and books occupy a central role in the book of Jubilees; see: Jub. 10:13–14 (Noah), 12:27 (Abraham), 21:10 (books of Enoch and Noah), 45:16 (Jacob). The book of Jubilees itself, of course, is regarded by its author as the book written for Moses by the "angel of the Presence" on Mt. Sinai, containing "the laws of the seasons" (50:13). Note the phrase ספר ומוסר חכמה in the Aramaic Levi Document (88, 90), where ספר appears to refer to "book"; cf. Daniel 1:4 and 17, and see Jonas C. Greenfield and Michael E. Stone, "Remarks on the Aramaic Testament of Levi from the Geniza," *RB* 86 (1979), 226–7, who explain the phrase as "reading and writing." (Cf. Benjamin G. Wright III, "Jubilees, Sirach, and Sapiental Tradition," in *Enoch and the Mosaic Torah: The Evidence of Jubilees*, ed. Gabriele Boccaccini and Giovanni Ibba [Grand Rapids, 2009], 126–8.) See also the place of books and writing in the later pseudepigraphical works of 2 Baruch and 4 Ezra. Although the two biblical figures are depicted in these works as writing books and epistles (2 Bar. 77:11–26, and the "Epistle of Baruch," chapters 78–87; 4 Ezra 14:22–47), it is not this activity that informs their special character and function, and the title of *sofer* is nowhere applied to them. See, however, the concluding sentence in 4 Ezra (14:48 [50]), attested in several manuscripts, which declares, "He [Ezra] was called the scribe of the knowledge of the Most High forever" (in the Syriac version: ספרא דידעתה דמרימא; perhaps a play on the title of the biblical Ezra as *safar data*), which may be rendered as "revealer/instructor of (hidden) divine knowledge" (cf. יודע דעת עליון [Num 24:16]).

5 *safar* in *Reichsaramäisch* in contrast to vernacular Aramaic usages

The linguistic specification of the word *safar* as interpreter/law consultant in the official register of the Aramaic language during the Achaemenid period (*Reichsaramäisch*) superseded the more original sense of "recorder," which is notably absent in official Aramaic documents and deeds. Thus, the publisher of the *Wadi Daliyeh* Samaritan papyri notes that "one peculiarity of the Samaria papyri ... is the fact that **the scribe never names himself in the document**," even though the documents contain detailed subscriptions.[36] The title *safar* would seem to appear in subscriptions to the letters contained in the Aršam correspondence found at Elephantine, where ספרא is coupled with the title ידע טעמא ("transmitter [or cognizant] of the report") and was originally translated by G. R. Driver in his first edition of the letters as "scribe."[37] However, as Richard Frye astutely observed, the title *safra'* cannot here be identified as the 'writer' of the document, since various documents in this collection which mention the same *safar* display different styles of handwriting. In fact, as the subscriptions appear only in those letters which include *a direct order by a superior to a subordinate* (letters 4 and 6 through 10 in the Driver collection), Frye concluded that this *safar* was one who had "mastered the art of translation and style,"[38] and who can therefore be understood as the one responsible for the publication (and translation into Aramaic) of these orders.[39] Thus what might have served as a counter-example to the thesis presented here actually provides further corroboration for the special linguistic status of *safar* in the Aramaic of this period.

There are attestations of Aramaic *safar* in letters, inscriptions and documents of this period where the word undoubtedly refers to a notary/accountant, or to

---

36 Douglas M. Gropp, Wadi Daliyeh II: The Samaria Papyri from Wadi Daliyeh, DJD XXVIII (Oxford, 2001), 32.

37 See similar titles in the introduction to the letter included in Ezra 4 (vv. 8, 9, 17, 23): רְחוּם בְּעֵל טְעֵם וְשִׁמְשַׁי סָפְרָא.

38 Driver subsequently corrected his translation to "clerk," which, as I ascertain here, incorrectly applies the more archaic use for *safar*.

39 See above, note 19, on the *soferei ha-melekh* in Est 3:12 and 8:9, who may have performed a similar function. The absence of any mention of *safar* as notary in deeds originating in Jewish Aramaic circles (with the exception of those of Nabatean origin—see below) is remarkable and supports the claim for the particular use of Aramaic *safar* during this period as a special function.

one who "wrote" the document.⁴⁰ However, the provenance and nature of each one of these items show them to be the exceptions which prove the rule, for **all such instances are found in writings *outside* the literary contexts of "Official Aramaic," and reflect a *vernacular* Aramaic**; that is, an Aramaic vocabulary distant from that of the bureaucratic Aramaic of the Persian empire, and which developed continuously among local populations. Thus, it is only in letters originating in Egypt that we find the use of the word *safar*, in singular and plural form, denoting Egyptian officials involved in *accounting* and *financial* duties, as found in the earlier Hebrew uses of the word.⁴¹ Influence of Egyptian scribal culture, where the scribe (*sesh*) played a central role in many aspects of Egyptian administration and intellectual activities,⁴² explains these and other occurrences of *safar* in Aramaic inscriptions and deeds originating in Egypt where mention is made of the *safar* as one who "wrote" the document. These include *safar* mentioned as the "writer" of the Sheikh-Fadl wall inscription (fifth century BCE), and of two third-century BCE receipts written on ostraca.⁴³ A similar anomaly is found

---

40 The original deciphering of Aramaic deeds from the Bar Kokhba era found in the Naḥal Ḥever and Wadi Murabbaʻat caves exhibited the use of the title *safra* appended to names in witness-lists (see Józef T. Milik, "Deux documents inédit du désert de Juda," *Biblica* 38 [1957], 265 line 17; idem, "Un contrat juif de l'an 134 apres J.-C.," *RB* 61 [1954], 183, and see note on p. 188; Pierre Benoit and Józef T. Milik, *Les Grottes de Murabbaʻât*, DJD II [Oxford, 1961], no. 21, line 22, p. 115). However, these readings were subsequently proven to be incorrect, and were corrected in each case to *memreh* (ממרה; see Yadin et al., *The Documents from the Bar Kokhba Period*, papLease of Land [P.Yadin 44], lines 29 and 30, and the discussion there, pp. 52–53; the corrective note by Yigael Yadin, "Expedition D: The Cave of the Letters," *IEJ* 12 [1962], 253–5, and note 47 there; Émile Puech, "L'acte de vente d'une maison a Kafar-Bébayu en 135 de notre ère," *RQ* 9 [1977–78], 213–21, and 220; and cf. XḤev/Se padDeed of Sale C ar, line 15, in *Aramaic, Hebrew and Greek Documentary Texts from Nahal Hever and Other Sites*, The Seiyâl Collection II, ed. Hanah M. Cotton and Ada Yardeni, DJD XXVII [Oxford, 1997], 36).
41 See Arthur E. Cowley, *Aramaic Papyri of the Fifth Century B.C.* (Oxford, 1923), papyrus no. 17: *safré medinta* = notaries of the province; papyrus no. 2: *safré ʼoẓraʼ* = treasury clerks/accountants; cf. Bezalel Porten and Ada Yardeni, *Textbook of Aramaic Documents from Ancient Egypt. Newly copied, edited and translated into Hebrew and English: 1 Letters* (Jerusalem, 1986), document A3.3 (Padua 1), line 5: *safraya'* = accountants responsible for paying a salary. A named accountant ("Ḥananiah *safra'*") and anonymous *safraya'* are found in ostraca originating in Egypt from the third century BCE detailing silver and grain distributions, respectively (Porten and Yardeni, *Textbook, vol. IV: Ostraca and Assorted Inscriptions* [Jerusalem, 1999], D8.6 and D8.8), clearly also referring to a *safar* as accountant.
42 On the scribes of the Egyptian "House of Life," see Alan H. Gardiner, "*Per Ankh*: The House of Life," *Journal of Egyptian Archaeology* 24 (1938), 157–79.
43 At the conclusion of a long narrative inscribed on the wall of a burial cave near Sheikh Fadl in Egypt we find: "Peace be to the *safra* **who wrote** (זי כתב) this document"; see André Lemaire,

in Nabatean-Aramaic deeds from the end of the first century CE written by professional (Nabatean) scribes, where the concluding subscription reads: "X son of
Y *the safar* wrote this."[44] The Aramaic of the Nabatean scribes preserves a more
conservative dialect and reflects local legal norms.[45] It is therefore not surprising
to find here explicit mention that the *safar*/notary was the "writer" (or issuer) of
the document. The continual colloquial use of *sofer* from pre-exilic times as ac-
countant/notary similarly explains *sofer* in early rabbinic (tannaitic) texts as the
usual term for notary.[46]

"Les inscriptions araméennes de Cheikh-Fadl (Égypte)," *Studia Aramaica: New Sources and New
Approaches*, JSSSup 4, ed. Markham J. Geller, Jonas C. Greenfield and Michael P. Weitzman (Oxford, 1995), 77–132; Porten and Yardeni, *Textbook IV*, D23.1, panel 16C). The text represented in
the inscription may have originated in the seventh century BCE, perhaps as a translation from a
demotic original. See the recent study by Tawny L. Holm, "The Sheikh Fadl Inscription in its
Literary and Historical Context," *Aramaic Studies* 5 (2007), 193–224. On two ostraca from Luxor
of the third century BCE containing salt tax receipts, the receipts conclude with the statement,
"Yosef the *safar* wrote (this)"; see Mark Lidzbarski, *OLZ* 30 (1927), cols. 1043–4, and cf. Bezalel
Porten and Ada Yardeni, "Two Aramaic Salt-tax Receipts by the Scribe Joseph," in *Enchoria* 29
(2004–5), 55–9. The first text has been lost; the second text is bilingual, including also a demotic
text.
44 See Yigael Yadin, Jonas Greenfield, et al., *The Documents from the Bar Kokhba Period in the
Cave of Letters* (Jerusalem, 2002), papDowry Settlement? nab (P.Yadin 1), lines 59 and 66; pap-
Sale of Property nab (P.Yadin 2), line 49 and papSale of Property nab (P. Yadin 3), line 55 (pp.
212 and 240, respectively). See also the reconstructions in papFragmentary Deed nab (P.Yadin
4), line 26 (p. 250, and cf. 253), and papSale of Donkeys ar (P.Yadin 8), line 10 and above (p. 113;
cf. the discussion on p. 115 and note the name of this individual also as witness [and "scribe"?]
in papQuittance nab [P.Yadin 9], line 13 [p. 272], and see pp. 116-117). On the factitive usage of
ktb, from which it may be concluded that the *safar*, at least in some of these attestations, was
responsible for the *authorization*, or *issuance*, of the document but not for its manuscript, see
ibid., General Introduction, pp. 12-13.
45 See Matthew Morgenstern, "The History of the Aramaic Dialects in the Light of Discoveries
from the Judean Desert: The Case of Nabatean," *Eretz-Israel* 26 (1999), 134*–142*. On the differences between legal formulae in Jewish and Nabatean documents as evidenced in the Naḥal
Ḥever archive, see Baruch A. Levine, "The Various Workings of the Aramaic Legal Tradition:
Jews and Nabateans in the Nahal Hever Archive," in *The Dead Sea Scrolls: Fifty Years After Their
Discovery 1947–1997*, ed. Lawrence H. Schiffman, Emanuel Tov, and James C. VanderKam (Jerusalem, 2000), 836–51: "It thus becomes clear that Nabatean scribes used their vernacular
when formulating these legal documents."
46 See above, note 22.

6 Summary

Whereas the ancient West Semitic *sofer* of the first millennium BCE, like his eastern counterpart, the *ṭupšarru*, functioned primarily as **notary, enumerator** and **accountant**, the bearer of the Aramaic cognate title *safar* was perceived by Akkadian speakers of the Neo-Assyrian period as a "**decoder** of foreign signs" and "translator-interpreter." This led to the use of the title for **celestial diviners** who served the élite of the time as responders to queries, and, in the subsequent Persian period, for the royal-governmental **legal advisor** who authorized and promulgated edicts and decrees. In *Reichsaramäisch* the term for "decoder-responder" was then applied exclusively to the **law-interpreter** and **authorizer**. In this sense Ezra is called *safar data di elah shemaia* by Artaxerxes in appreciation of his role as **decisor/interpreter of the divine law.**

As a result of the introduction of the Jewish élite to Mesopotamian language and culture following the Babylonian exile in the sixth century BCE, the Aramaic term *safar* influenced Hebrew *sofer*, which now denoted, as in Aramaic, the **law responder-interpreter** and "teacher/interpreter of law" of the Second Temple period. Although the terms *safar* and *sofer* continued to be used in the vernacular for notary in local dialects, **nowhere does the title refer to those involved in the creation, transmission or interpretation of narrative "texts."** This is contrary to scholarly consensus which views Jewish *soferim* of the Second Temple period as explicators of the biblical text and, according to some, as those who wrote and preserved that text and produced "interpretations" later known as *midrash*.[47] The *sofer* did play a central role in Jewish society, not in the transmission of **text**, but in the teaching of **law** and **custom**. This title was superseded in the late Second Temple period by the rabbinic term *ḥakham* (cf. *sophistes* employed by Flavius Josephus), probably under Roman and Latin influence (as a *calque* of the Latin *jurisprudens*).

---

47 See Saul Lieberman, "Rabbinic Interpretation of Scripture," in *Hellenism in Jewish Palestine* (New York, 1950), 47–8: "Indeed the Soferim were grammarians, and they engaged in the same activity which was pursued by the Alexandrian scholars. They elaborated the so-called *Midrash* [interpretation] of the Bible"; and cf. E. E. Urbach, *The Halakhah: Its Sources and Development*, transl. Raphael Posner (Jerusalem, 1986), 96–7; *idem*, 'The *derasha* as Basis for the *halakha* and the Problem of the *soferim*' (Hebrew), *Tarbiẓ* 27 (1958), 166–82.

7 Bibliography

Alster, Bendt. "Scribes, Sages and Seers in Ancient Mesopotamia." Pages 47–63 in *Scribes, Sages and Seers: The Sage in the Eastern Mediterranean World*. Edited by Leo G. Perdue. Göttingen: Vandenhoeck & Ruprecht, 2008.

Benoit, Pierre and Józef T. Milik. *Les grottes de Murabba'at*. Discoveries in the Judean Desert II. Oxford: Clarendon Press, 1961.

Blenkinsopp, Joseph. "Hezekiah and the Babylonian Delegation: A Critical Reading of Isaiah 39:1–8." Pages 107–22 in *Essays on Ancient Israel in Its Near Eastern Context: A Tribute to Nadav Na'aman*. Edited by Yairah Amit et al. Winona Lake, IN: Eisenbrauns, 2006.

Briant, Pierre. *From Cyrus to Alexander: A History of the Persian Empire*. Translated by Peter T. Daniels. Winona Lake, IN: Eisenbrauns, 2002.

Cohen, Chaim. "The Hapax Legomenon דיו (Ink) in the Context of 'ואני כותב על הספר בדיו' (Jer 36:18): A 'False Friend' in Modern Hebrew Due to the Masoretes' Misunderstanding of the Preposition בדי Meaning 'To' or 'For'" (Hebrew). *Shnaton: An Annual for Biblical and Ancient Near Eastern Studies* 24 (2015): 77–102.

Cotton, Hanah M. and Ada Yardeni, eds. *Aramaic, Hebrew and Greek Documentary Texts from Naḥal Ḥever and Other Sites*. The Seiyâl Collection II, DJD 27. Oxford: Clarendon Press, 1997.

Cowley, Arthur E. *Aramaic Papyri of the Fifth Century B.C.* Oxford: Clarendon Press, 1923.

Crown, Alan D. "Messengers and Scribes: The ספר and מלאך in the Old Testament." *Vetus Testamentum* 24 (1974): 366–70.

Dandamaev, Muhammed A. "The Social Position of Neo-Babylonian Scribes." Pages 35–9 in *Gesellschaft und Kultur im alten Vorderasien*. Edited by Horst Klengel. Berlin: Akademie-Verlag, 1982.

Dandamaev, Muhammed A. and Vladimir G. Lukonin. *The Culture and Social Institutions of Ancient Iran*. Edited by Philip L. Kohl. Cambridge: Cambridge University Press, 1989.

Gardiner, Alan H. "*Per Ankh*: The House of Life." *Journal of Egyptian Archaeology* 24 (1938): 157–79

Greenfield, Jonas. "Studies in Aramaic Lexicography I." *Journal of the American Oriental Society* 82 (1962): 290–99.

Greenfield, Jonas C. and Michael E. Stone. "Remarks on the Aramaic Testament of Levi from the Geniza." *Revue Biblique* 86 (1979): 214–30.

Gropp, Douglas M. *Wadi Daliyeh II: The Samaria Papyri from Wadi Daliyeh*. Discoveries in the Judean Desert XXVIII. Oxford: Clarendon Press, 2001.

Hachlili, Rachel. *Jewish Funerary Customs, Practices and Rites in the Second Temple Period*. Leiden: Brill, 2005.

Hayward, Robert. "Some Notes on Scribes and Priests in the Targum of the Prophets." *Journal of Jewish Studies* 36 (1985): 210–21.

Higger, Michael. *Seven Minor Treatises*. New York: Bloch, 1930.

Higger, Michael. *Massekhet Soferim*. New York: Debé Rabbanan, 1937.

Holm, Tawny L. "The Sheikh Fadl Inscription in its Literary and Historical Context." *Aramaic Studies* 5 (2007): 193–224.

Horsley, Richard A. *Revolt of the Scribes: Resistance and Apocalyptic Origins*. Minneapolis: Fortress Press, 2010

Hunger, Hermann. *Astrological Reports to Assyrian Kings*. State Archives of Assyria VIII. Helsinki: Helsinki University Press, 1992.

Hurowitz, Victor A. "Tales of Two Sages: Towards an Image of the 'Wise Man' in Akkadian Writings." Pages 64–94 in *Scribes, Sages and Seers: The Sage in the Eastern Mediterranean World*. Edited by Leo G. Perdue. Göttingen: Vandenhoeck & Ruprecht, 2008.

Hurvitz, Avi. "Continuity and Innovation in Biblical Hebrew: The Case of 'Semantic Change' in Post-Exilic Writings." Pages 1–10 in *Studies in Ancient Hebrew Semantics*. Edited by Takimitsu Muraoka. Abr-Nahrain Supplement Series, vol. 4. Louvain: Peeters Press, 1995.

Hurvitz, Avi. "On the Borderline between Biblical Criticism and Hebrew Linguistics: The Emergence of the Term ספר-משה." Pages 37*–43* in *Tehillah le-Moshe: Biblical and Judaic Studies in Honor of Moshe Greenberg*. Edited by Mordechai Cogan, Barry L. Eichler, and Jeffrey H. Tigay. Winona Lake, IN: Eisenbrauns, 1997.

Kilpatrick, George D. "Scribes, Lawyers, and Lucan Origins." *Journal of Theological Studies* n.s. 1 (1950): 56–60.

Kugel, James L. *Traditions of the Bible: A Guide to the Bible As It Was at the Start of the Common Era*. Cambridge, MA: Harvard University Press, 1998.

Kutscher. Edward Yehezkel. *Milim ve-Toledotehen*. Jerusalem: Kiryat Sefer, 1965.

Kvanvig, Helge S. *Primeval History: Babylonian, Biblical and Enochic: An Intertextual Reading*. Leiden: Brill, 2011.

Landsberger, Benno. "Babylonian Scribal Craft and its Terminology." Pages 123–26 in *Proceedings of the 23rd Congress of Orientalists*. London: Royal Asiatic Society, 1954.

Leaney, Alfred Robert C. "ΝΟΜΙΚΟΣ in St. Luke's Gospel." *Journal of Theological Studies* n.s. 2 (1951): 166–7.

Lemaire, André. "Les inscriptions araméennes de Cheikh-Fadl (Égypte)." Pages 77–132 in *Studia Aramaica: New Sources and New Approaches. Journal of Semitic Studies* Supplements 4. Edited by Markham J. Geller, Jonas C. Greenfield and Michael P. Weitzman. Oxford: Oxford University Press, 1995.

Leon, Harry J. *The Jews of Ancient Rome*. Philadelphia: Jewish Publication Society, 1960.

Lerner, Myron Bialik. "The External Tractates." Pages 367–403 in *The Literature of the Sages, First Part: Oral Tora, Halakha, Mishna, Tosefta, Talmud, External Tractates*. Edited by Shmuel Safrai. Philadelphia: Fortress Press and Assen/Maastricht: Van Gorcum, 1987.

Levine, Baruch A. "The Various Workings of the Aramaic Legal Tradition: Jews and Nabateans in the Naḥal Ḥever Archive." Pages 836–51 in *The Dead Sea Scrolls: Fifty Years After Their Discovery 1947–1997*. Edited by Lawrence H. Schiffman, Emanuel Tov, and James C. VanderKam. Jerusalem: Israel Exploration Society, 2000.

Lewy, Julius. "The Problems Inherent in Section 70 of the Bisutun Inscription." *Hebrew Union College Annual* 25 (1954): 188–199.

Lidzbarski, Mark. *Orientalistische Literaturzeitung* 30 (1927), cols. 1043–4.

Lieberman, Saul. *Hellenism in Jewish Palestine*. New York: Jewish Theological Seminary of America, 1950.

Mandel, Paul. "Midrashic Exegesis and its Precedents in the Dead Sea Scrolls." *Dead Sea Discoveries* 8 (2001): 149–68.

Mandel, Paul. "The Origins of Midrash in the Second Temple Period." Pages 14–23 in *Current Trends in the Study of Midrash*. Edited by Carol Bakhos. Leiden: Brill, 2006.

Mandel, Paul. *The Origins of Midrash: From Teaching to Text*. Leiden: Brill, 2017.

Milik, Józef T. "Un contrat juif de l'an 134 après J.-C." *Revue Biblique* 61 (1954): 182–90.

Milik, Józef T. "Deux documents inédit du désert de Juda," *Biblica* 38 (1957): 245–68.

Milik, Józef T., and Matthew Black. *The Books of Enoch: Aramaic Fragments of Qumran Cave 4.* Oxford: Clarendon Press, 1976.

Morgenstern, Matthew. "The History of the Aramaic Dialects in the Light of Discoveries from the Judean Desert: The Case of Nabatean." *Eretz-Israel* 26 (1999): 134*–142*.

Muffs, Yochanan. *Studies in the Aramaic Legal Papyri from Elephantine.* Leiden: Brill, 2003.

Naveh, Joseph. *On Stone and Mosaic: The Aramaic and Hebrew Inscriptions from Ancient Synagogues.* Tel-Aviv: Israel Exploration Society, 1978.

Nickelsburg, George W. E. *1 Enoch 1: A Commentary on the Book of 1 Enoch, Chapters 1–36, 81–108.* Minneapolis: Fortress Press, 2001.

Noy, David. *Jewish Inscriptions of Western Europe.* 2 vols. Cambridge: Cambridge University Press, 1995.

Oppenheim, A. Leo. "A note on *ša rēši*." *Journal of the Ancient Near Eastern Society of Columbia University*, vol. 5: The Gaster Festschrift (1973): 325–34.

Pei, Mario. *The Story of Language.* Philadelphia: Lippincott Co., 1949.

Porten, Bezalel and Ada Yardeni, *Textbook of Aramaic Documents from Ancient Egypt. Newly copied, edited and translated into Hebrew and English: 1 Letters.* Jerusalem: Hebrew University of Jerusalem, 1986.

Porten, Bezalel and Ada Yardeni, "Two Aramaic Salt-tax Receipts by the Scribe Joseph." *Enchoria* 29 (2004–5): 55–9.

Puech, Émile. "L'acte de vente d'une maison a Kafar-Bébayu en 135 de notre ère." *Revue de Qumran* 9 (1977–78): 213–21.

Rochberg, Francesca. *The Heavenly Writing: Divination, Horoscopy, and Astronomy in Mesopotamian Culture.* New York: Cambridge University Press, 2004.

Saldarini, Anthony J. "'Is Saul Also Among the Scribes?': Scribes and Prophets in Targum Jonathan." Pages 239–53 in *"Open Thou Mine Eyes...": Essays on Aggadah and Judaica Presented to Rabbi William G. Braude on His Eightieth Birthday and Dedicated to His Memory.* Edited by Herman J. Blumberg et al. Hoboken, NJ: Ktav, 1992.

Sanders, James A. *The Psalms Scroll of Qumran Cave 11 (11QPsᵃ).* Discoveries in the Judean Desert IV. Oxford: Clarendon Press, 1965.

Schams, Christine. *Jewish Scribes in the Second-Temple Period.* Sheffield: Sheffield Academic Press, 1998.

Schniedewind, William M. *How the Bible Became a Book: The Textualization of Ancient Israel.* Camridge: Cambridge University Press, 2004.

Tadmor, Hayim. "The Aramaization of Assyria: Aspects of Western Impact." Pages 449–70 in vol. 2 of *Mesopotamien und seine Nachbarn: Politische und kulturelle Wechselbeziehungen im alten Vorderasien vom 4. bis 1. Jahrtausend v. Chr.* Proceedings of the XXVe RAI. Edited by Hans J. Nissen and Johannes Renger. X vols. Berlin: D. Reimer, 1982.

Tadmor, Hayim. "*Rab-saris* and *Rab-shakeh* in 2 Kings 18." Pages 279–85 in *The Word of the Lord Shall Go Forth: Essays in Honor of David Noel Freedman in Celebration of His Sixtieth Birthday.* Edited by Carol L. Meyers and M. O'Connor. Winona Lake, IN: Eisenbrauns, 1983.

Tadmor, Hayim. "Monarchy and the Elite in Assyria and Babylonia: The Question of Royal Accountability." Pages 203–24 in *The Origin and Diversity of Axial Age Civilizations.* Edited by Shmuel N. Eisenstadt, Albany: State University of New York Press, 1986.

Toorn, Karl van der. *Scribal Culture and the Making of the Hebrew Bible*. Cambridge, MA and
    London: Harvard University Press, 2007.

Urbach, E. E. *The Halakhah: Its Sources and Development*. Translated by Raphael Posner. Jeru-
    salem: Masada, 1986.

Urbach, E. E. "The *derasha* as Basis for the *halakha* and the Problem of the *soferim*" (Hebrew).
    Tarbiz 27 (1958): 166–182

Weinreich, Uriel. *Languages in Contact: Findings and Problems*. The Hague: Mouton, 1963.

Werman, Cana. *The Book of Jubilees: Introduction, Translation, and Interpretation*. Jerusalem:
    Yad Izhak Ben-Zvi Press, 2015.

Wright, Benjamin G., III. "Jubilees, Sirach, and Sapiental Tradition." Pages 116–30 in *Enoch
    and the Mosaic Torah: The Evidence of Jubilees*. Edited by Gabriele Boccaccini and
    Giovanni Ibba. Grand Rapids: Eerdmans, 2009.

Yadin, Yigael. "Expedition D: The Cave of the Letters." *Israel Exploration Journal* 12 (1962):
    253–55.

Yadin, Yigael, Jonas C. Greenfield, Ada Yardeni and Baruch A. Levine. *The Documents from the
    Bar Kokhba Period in the Cave of Letters: Hebrew, Aramaic and Nabatean-Aramaic
    Papyri*. Jerusalem: Israel Exploration Society, 2002.

Guy D. Stiebel
Text Case: Writing under Extreme Conditions at Masada

Yielding hundreds of *ostraca*, dozens of *tituli picti* and the largest collection of documents outside of Khirbet Qumran, most notably from the time of the First Jewish Revolt (66–73/4 CE), Masada presents an exceptional test case for students of the epigraphic evidence in context to an extent that one may refer to it as a unique "text case."[1]

The celebrated site has been known to modern scholarship for over 200 years. It was mentioned for the first time, as early as 1806, by the German orientalist Ulrich Jasper Seetzen. The ruins were then known by the local Bedouins as es-Sebbah – in Arabic: the "cursed one." In 1838 the site was identified for the first time by Eli Smith, with the arena of the dramatic events so vividly narrated by Josephus in his account, the *Bellum Judaicum*. The assistant of the American scholar Edward Robinson was observing the site from En-Gedi via a telescope. It was four years thereafter that westerns managed to ascend the mountain's top (Walcott and Tipping), an achievement that generated a long list of renown European and American scholars that were drawn to this remote and exotic site. Explorers such as Lynch, de Saulcy, Tristram, Warren, Conder and Kitchener, Brünnow and von Domaszewski and Schulten, to name only few, explored Masada and its environs, noting among others the fortified palatial complex and its advanced water system, the "serpent trail" as well as the Roman siege system. In 1955/6 an Israeli joint expedition, headed by Avi-Yona, Avigad, Aharoni, Dunayevski and Gutman, conducted two short seasons that demonstrated the great archaeological potential of the site, particularly from the era of King Herod the Great. However, it was no doubt the three years of long extensive work by the expedition headed by Yadin (1963–65), on behalf of the Hebrew University and the Israel Exploration Society, that with the labor of hundreds of volunteers from all over the world provided an intimate insight into the palaces of King Herod and the poor makeshift dwellings of the Jewish rebels, marking Masada as a key site in the understanding of the early Roman period in Judaea and beyond and not least shedding light on the phenomenon of the revolt. From the epigraphic point

---

1 The paper is based on an extended version of my lecture at the conference: *The Scribe in the Biblical World*, Strasbourg, 17–19 June 2019 and has retained the style of the oral presentation. I wish to express my thanks to Ester Eshel and Michael Langlois for the kind invitation to take part in the workshop and not least for the warm hospitality in Strasbourg.

of view, during the excavations of Yadin's expedition, 15 scrolls were found, one of which was written on a papyrus[2], 18 Latin papyri, 9 Greek papyri, 2 bi-lingual papyri, 150 Greek and Latin *ostraca* and *tituli picti*[3], as well as 701 Aramaic and Hebrew *ostraca*.[4] Scores of papers and books were devoted to the site and its findings. One should mention the eight final reports volumes that have been published to date and the work that is currently proceeding on two more volumes that amass the rich material culture remains still awaiting publication. In 1989 a short season was conducted by Netzer, who returned to the mountain more extensively together with the author from 1995 till 2001 and in 2007/8. One short season was conducted by Foerster, Goldfus, Arubas and Magness in 1995 in Camp F and in the Roman assault ramp.[5]

In light of the above and Yadin's assertion in his popular book that 97% of the site had been excavated, one may wonder about the actual motivation to return to Masada. To begin with, the vast amount of published archaeological data allows one to ask today questions that have never been dealt with before, such as identity, diversity, space, symbolism, economy, networks, site formation, water management and the like. Furthermore, the arsenal of technological tools that is currently available to archaeologists evolved dramatically in the past decades. Moreover, the excavation methodology that has much developed allows one to extract much more data than was possible before and in much smaller excavation areas. Thus, under the auspices of the Institute of Archaeology of Tel-Aviv University I have returned at the head of the Neustadter Masada Expedition to the field in 2017 that have since conducted four excavation seasons. One of our major goals was to examine the period of the First Revolt (66–73/4 CE) through a new methodological approach.[6]

2 Talmon and Yadin 1999.
3 Cotton and Geiger 1989.
4 Yadin and Naveh 1989.
5 To name only few recent publications: Stiebel 2006a, with bibliography; Arubas and Goldfus 2008; Davies 2006; Netzer and Stiebel 2008; Ben-Tor 2009; and recently Magness 2019 and Stiebel 2020.
6 Stiebel and Gross 2018.

1 Refugee Camp

It suffices to watch or read recent years' news reports to recognize that we are amidst an immigration period.[7] Be it due to security instability, global warming and deteriorating health conditions or the search for economic safety, millions of inhabitants from Africa, South-West Asia, the Middle East and South and Central America are on the move. Countless temporary and more permanent installations and camps had been established around the world. This human tragedy, nonetheless, provides us with a unique opportunity to examine in near lab conditions the ways refuges under stress and extreme conditions act; how one keeps his/her own identity, both as an individual and as part of a social or religious group. What is the "memory package" one takes along as a forced immigrant, and not least interesting from an archaeological point of view – how are these issues manifested in the material culture record, what one may call the "archaeology of refugees" or the "archaeology of forced migration."[8] Our quest in the footsteps of the rebels of Masada stems from the fundamental understanding that this community was *not* monolithic and far more complex in nature than perceived before. The notion that the community was far more heterogeneous in composition stands as a keystone for our current scholarly work at Masada, a perception that is further supported by the archaeological evidence.[9] Of great importance is the vast assemblage of *ostraca* and *tituli picti* (few of the 150 Greek and Latin *ostraca* and *tituli picti* and most of the 701 Aramaic and Hebrew *ostraca* and *tituli picti*), that not only provided the framework for the present paper but also further indicated that Masada forms a mirror or microcosm of the society of Early Roman Judaea during those turbulent times.[10] The epigraphic evidence appears to shed new light on the identity of the scribes and their social and ideological affiliations within the community of rebels at Masada.

---

[7] The paper was written pre COVID19 epidemic. Nonetheless, following the recent conflict in Ukraine, at least 12 million refugees have fled the country.

[8] Hamilakis 2016.

[9] Stiebel 2006a; *apud* 2013a and 2020. For the archaeological testimony for the presence of members of the Sect of Qumran at Masada, see: Stiebel 2013a, pp. 170–174, against Netzer 1991, p. 634.

[10] Since the focus of the present paper is the period of the First Revolt, the rich assemblage of epigraphic material from the time of Herod the Great and the small but growing assemblage from the Byzantine period (5th–7/8th century CE) that were executed under utterly different and clearly less strenuous circumstances were naturally excluded from the discussion (see: Stiebel 2013a; Stiebel and Gross 2018).

In light of the commonly shared notion that the Hebrew documents were not penned at the site and were probably brought to Masada by the rebels[11], the present paper will less cover the theme of the biblical and non-biblical texts and so will be devoted mainly to the corpus of inscriptions that were written at the site and during the time of the revolt, which aside of a sole example of a papyrus (Mur 19), comprises chiefly of *ostraca*, *tituli picti* and *graffiti*. The epigraphical material that was written at the site by the Roman side and is discussed further below comprised of *ostraca* (Mas 750–771) and a single wooden tablet (Mas 743), as well as papyri (Mas 721–738, 748–749) and *graffiti* (Mas 937, 938–941). The scribal practices related to the Hebrew documents from Masada were discussed at length by Emanuel Tov for which he devoted an entire chapter in his seminal book: *Scribal Practices and Approaches Reflected in the Texts Found in The Judean Desert*.[12] The writing materials of the Greek and Latin documents are discussed briefly by Cotton and Geiger in the opening of the volume *Masada* II.[13]

It should be firstly noted that the large epigraphic assemblage that had been penned at the site was uncovered in the living quarters and in the locations of public activities at Masada and stands out in comparison to all other sites in Judaea and the Judaean Desert alike. Few *ostraca* were found in the refuge caves of Murabba'at (Mur 72–87, 165–168), Naḥal Ḥever (8Hev 5–6) and Naḥal Mishmar (1Mish 4–8), apparently reflecting the size of the community that sought shelter there.[14] When it comes to the materials used for writing at the site, in addition to pottery shards, as aforesaid one should further note a single papyrus (Mur 19) that was evidently penned at Masada and a single wooden tablet (Mas 743). Other than ink, charcoal was used for *graffiti* writing, in addition to the employment of sharp tools.[15]

The manifestation of what may be described as a "writing obsession" of the rebels/refugees community at Masada sparks the question of what stood behind it and has the need, or the will, to write and to document oneself anything having to do with the extreme conditions of the revolt and the Roman siege? I would like to suggest that in addition to the rare preservation conditions, the fact that so many *ostraca* from the First Revolt were discovered at Masada is not coincidental.

---

11 The recently published research that harness the study of DNA may add another scholarly tool to approach this theme (Anava *et al.*, 2020).

12 Appendix 6 in: Tov 2004, pp. 317–322.

13 Cotton and Geiger 1989, pp. 1–2.

14 At Khirbet Qumran few ostraca were reported (KhQ Ostraca 1–3) and Qumran Cave 10 (10QOstracon).

15 For writing materials and implements see: Lemaire 1992 and Tov 2004, pp. 31–56.

I wish to further claim that at times during which a more orderly and a better controlled and regulated regime was in power would have generated an epigraphic evidence of a more formal nature, while the case of a refugee camp like that of Masada, which comprised a large number of individuals and several groups from varied backgrounds and ideologies, generates much more of the former. Moreover, the definable particular conditions of a settlement under siege were thoroughly illustrated by Israel Eph'al in his *The City Besieged: Siege and Its Manifestations in the Ancient Near East* (2013), demonstrating the distinctiveness of this environment that evidently had an impact and was reflected in many aspects of life. One such aspect is the economic uncertainty and instability if not the collapse of the economic system that commonly resulted in the emergence of alternative monetary and administrative systems, such as tags that may have functioned as currency replacements.[16] I would like to offer that those extreme conditions resulted in a certain state of mind that may be described as: "Eat, Drink, and Write, for Tomorrow We Die," one outcome of which is an intensive writing phenomenon, such as observed at Masada.[17] To a degree, it represents another dimension of the activity of societies and individuals living in times of crisis, during which great attempts were made to save documents and particularly the holy literature, for future generations, such as bringing along documents and storing them (see below).[18]

Few attempts to harness archaeological methodological tools in order to "read" or "decipher" the social implications of the epigraphic evidence were made over the years; such was Netzer's review of the inscriptions' spatial distribution at the site.[19] He followed a functional approach through which he suggested reconstructing certain foci of the rebels' activity at the site, most notably the tentative placing of the rebel's alleged archive in a room adjacent the "Water Gate" at the northern palace complex. It should be noted that Yadin's suggestions to associate the group of twelve *ostraca* from Locus 113 with the "Lots," has created over the years a bias amongst some of his students that marked the northern Palace complex as the main arena of the dramatic events of the end of the revolt;

---

16 See the letter Mas 554 found in the Lower Terrace of the Northern Palace, which requested the payment of a 5 denarii debt (rather than the preliminary "500" reading in Yadin 1965, p. 111) for X loaves of bread (Yadin and Naveh 1989, pp. 49–50).

17 For the Roman point of view and the mechanisms of pressure that prevailed in the lines of the Roman army during siege, *cf.* Goldsworthy 1999.

18 *Cf.* Popović 2012.

19 Netzer 2004.

whereas more and more evidence appears to signify the Western Palace as the main "headquarters" of the community, most notably from an administrative point of view. One however should note that for our purpose, in attempting to single out the scribes, a material culture approach has not proven to be of much help, mainly due to the fact that no inkwells or other facilities such as proper tables have been found to date at the site. Still, several copper-alloy *stylii* are attested at Masada in the revolt's context and their publication in the coming years will hopefully provide us with more indications concerning the possible location of scribal activity within the site. Several scribal exercises were noted by Yadin and Naveh at Masada under the category of "Writing Exercises and Scribbles" (Mas 606–641)[20], though at least two of which (Mas 606–607) were evidently abecedaries that may be linked to the spiritual sphere rather than penned exercises (and see below).[21]

It is commonly accepted that the numerous Hebrew, Aramaic and Greek *ostraca* and *tituli picti* uncovered in Yadin's and in Netzer and Stiebel's excavations and dated to the time of the revolt were inscribed at the site. Generally speaking, the *ostraca* may be divided into three major groups that represent the spheres of activity within the refugee camp of Masada in 66–73/4 CE: the ritual, administrative and personal circles.

A plethora of names and most notably nicknames appears on the *ostraca* assemblage from Masada, shedding much light on the onomasticon of names in Judaea.[22] The fact that so personal names are further attested on the surface of vessels indicates the identity of the owner of the vessels. Although it would be hard to be certain that the inscriptions were inscribed by the owner, the non-formal manner in which they were executed and the variety of handwritings (or hands) appear to suggest that this was indeed the case.[23] The fact that among these *ostraca* were several names of females raises the question of gender and literacy among women and perhaps serves as a testimony that writing was not an unknown practice, at least among high status females; such is the example of the daughter or a female member of the priestly house of Katros (בת קתרא) that was uncovered at the site.[24] Alternatively, the names may represent the ownership of

---

20 Yadin and Naveh 1989, pp. 61–64. As scribal exercises see the discussions by: Lemaire 1992, pp. 7–33 and Tov 2004, p. 13 and chapter 7a.

21 Hezser 2001, p. 220 and notes 198–204, with bibliography.

22 Yadin and Naveh 1989, pp. 1–68; Hachlili 1999; Ilan 2002 and Stiebel 2021.

23 *Cf.* an inscribed oil-lamp, exhibiting the name Johanan (יהוחנן): Yadin and Naveh 1989, p. 42, no. 485.

24 Yadin and Naveh 1989, p. 22, no. 405; see further Stiebel 2019, pp. 36–37, note 177, with bibliography.

goods by female members of the community of rebels.[25] The names of three women that had been identified as the "wife of PN," were documented in the excavations (Nos. 399, 400, 402): "wife of [Ze]bida" (אתת [ז]בידא), "wife of Jacob" (אתת יעקוב), "wife of *Tobi*" (אשת טובי).[26] In addition, we learn about the presence of the daughters of PN (Nos. 401, 403, 405): "daughter of N[...]"; "the daughter of Domli" (בת דמלי); the above noted "daughter of Qatra" (בת קתרא) and one "Shalom/Salome the Gali[lean]" (שלום הגלי[לית]) that is identified by her own name (Mas 404).[27]

Interestingly, part of the inscriptions radiate from storerooms, most notably near the Large Bathhouse (Loci 114 and 174) and the Western Palace. Much of the public activity, that is weapons as well as food storing and production, particularly bread baking and distribution, took place in the boundaries of the Western Palace.[28] This administration activity generated much epigraphic material that shed light on the central organization of the community of rebels and refugees. Amongst the examples one may note the instructions for bread supply that followed a formula, attested as early as the First Temple period: "at a certain date, give PN, xxx amount of loaves of bread." Thus, the plotting of these inscriptions may at least in part reflect foci of activities and even betray the identity of some of the scribes. For example, Locus 502 in the Western Palace is to date the only known storeroom from the time of the revolt in which lines of vessels were found *in situ*. Interestingly, in front of many of these clusters of vessels were *ostraca* noting their status of purity; the latter were clearly written by the religious authorities of this community.[29]

---

25 Salome Komaise Archive: Cotton and Yardeni 1997. For ownership of property by women as it emerges from the Babatha Archive: Cotton and Greenfield 1994.
26 Yadin and Naveh 1989, pp. 21–22.
27 Ibid.
28 For weapon production at the site Magness 1992 (about the weapons: Stiebel and Magness 2007). During the last excavation season at Masada, February 2020, clear archaeological indications for a smithy from the time of the revolt were uncovered in Area A, adjacent to the southwestern corner of the Western Palace. For bread production and distribution, see: Stiebel 2004 and *apud* 2011.
29 Yadin suggested to identify several single private names, written in the formal script as names of priests (Yadin 1965, p. 115; see further Stiebel 2019, pp. 36–37). For Locus 502, see Netzer 1991, pp. 306–307, plan 17, ills. 365, 491.

2 A Scribe in Proxy

An additional epigraphic aspect concerns the fact that several inscriptions documented at Masada were generated through the use of stamps or dies. This find reminds us of these items' rather common role in daily life, one that left its mark on products of varied industries and trades and not least as a result of ritually associated activity.[30] An intriguing such example is an intact *ostracon* with three lines noting "Yehoseph the [professional] baker" (יהוסף הנחתום). The *ostracon* was uncovered in a water cistern adjacent the synagogue of Masada (Locus 902). Its bi-lingual text, in Hebrew and Aramaic, notes that Yehoseph (=Josephus) vowed to grant a certain priest by the name of Bar Haggai, lit. son of Haggai (בר חגי), with a tithe of one *challah* each week.[31] Interestingly, several imprints of a Latin bread stamp[32] bearing the Jewish name IOSEPV(S) were documented in casemate Locus 1156 during Yadin's excavations and were further suggested by the author to be the imprint of the die of the same baker, noted in the above-mentioned *ostracon*. The re-interpretation of a large circular installation that was found in the Western Palace as a *furnus* indicated the existence of a central communal bakery during the time of the revolt from which the loaves of bread were distributed in the nearby courtyard (Locus 401) to at least ten groups. As attested by the bread supply instruction found there, all the recipients were men that represented groups of several dozens to several hundred members each. It is very likely that this *ostracon* that was meant to be used for a prolonged period of time by the priest, served as a receipt for both parties. It allowed Bar Haggai the priest (who wrote it?) to be provided with a tithe, in a time that the entire infrastructure on which the priesthood existed collapsed, as a result of the destruction of Temple and Jerusalem. It appears that towards the end of the Second Temple period tithes and offerings were given directly to the priests and without the mediation of the Temple (*Life* 12.63), a turn of events that generated much tension and even violence among the priesthood (*AJ* 20.181).[33] An *ostracon* with the legend "priest's tithe" (מעשר כוהן) was further unearthed in the synagogue of Masada.[34]

Priests are noted in *Hazal* literature to use stamps/dies (*cf.* חותם כהן גדול), while tags and stamps/dies noting degrees of quality (Alpha, Beta and Gamma) are noted in Mishnah Shekalim 3.2. Moreover, the discovery at Masada of a sort

30 Ferere, Roxen and Tomlin 1990, *RIB* 2409, pp. 73–81.
31 Stiebel 2011, pp. 298–299.
32 Cotton and Geiger 1989, p. 211, no. 936, pl. 44.
33 Stiebel 2011, pp. 296–302.
34 Yadin and Naveh 1989, pp. 32–33, no. 441.

of *kashrut* certification (הכשר בד"ץ) shed light on the identity of the scribe, one Akaviah – the son of the High Priest (ח]נני[ה כהנא רבה עקביא ברה = Akaviah the son of Hannania the High Priest).[35] The latter was suggested to be identified with the son of Ananias son of Nebedeus the High Priest and the brother of Eleazar, whose defying acts in the Temple in 66 CE were considered by the Romans as the *casus belli* for the *Bellum Judaicum*.[36]

A group of fifty-five stamped stoppers ("מגופות") were documented at the site, all but one was discovered in a revolt context.[37] However, they were all linked by Rachel Bar Nathan, who published the final report of the ceramics assemblage, with amphorae from Herod's time. New reading of the signs and letters produced by the stamps indicates that they should not be identified as Latin letters but rather as Hebrew letters executed in the Palaeo-Hebrew script that was still in use during the Early Roman period by the community of Qumran, noting the Tetragrammaton, as well as in the coinage of the First and Second Jewish Revolts (66–73/4 CE and 132–135/6 CE respectively), the usage of the "holy letters" in the numismatic material clearly aimed to manifest nationalistic propaganda.[38] The stamped stoppers that bear Hebrew inscriptions appear to be identical to the stamp of a high priest, published by Avigad, noting the name of Eliyahueyni (אליהועיני) that is attested in Josephus's account (*AJ* 19.342), as well as in several rabbinical sources (for example: Mishnah, Parah 3.5). This new interpretation of the inscribed stopper from Masada indicates an additional medium through which priests could leave their mark and practice and manifest their religious authority. It apparently had an even greater significance in light of the destruction of the Temple and the collapse of the entire social infrastructure of the Jewish population in Roman Judaea. The mobility of priests may be further reflected by the discovery of a possibly additional specimen of the [חנניה הכהן ע]קביה for-mula at Machaerus, Jordan on the eastern side of the Dead Sea.[39]

---

35 *Ibid.* pp. 37–39, no. 461.
36 Ibid.
37 Bar-Nathan 2007, pp. 214–215, 217–219, pl. 36.
38 Tov 2004, pp. 231–234.
39 Misgav 2013, p. 266, no. 15 and p. 277.

3 The Ritual and Spiritual Sphere

To the blurred space between the ritual and secular activities one may attribute a rare divorce bill – *get* (Mur 71) that was apparently written and signed by witnesses at Masada in 71 CE, a year following the destruction of the Temple in Jerusalem. The bill that was uncovered in Wadi Murabba'at bears witness to the complexity of the social, cultural and ritual activity that was taking place, presumably in a somewhat high intensity atmosphere at the rebellious site.[40]

Such times of crisis are known to invoke an increase of ritual activity. The scribal products had an important role in the expression of individual and collective anxiety. Inscribed expressions were charged with meaning, such as the use of Hebrew letters in the Paleo-Hebrew script, alongside the Tetragrammaton, that echoed and enforced nationalistic cohesion, as is further attested by the coinage of the First and Second Revolts. The vast and complex world of Jewish magic during the Roman period draws beyond the scope of this paper. Nevertheless, several *ostraca* (Nos. 606–607) that were in all likelihood written at Masada, seemingly manifest attempts to harness the assistance and gain the attention of the supernatural. Thus, like in Herodium and Murabba'at, these abecedary inscriptions were not necessarily scribal exercises but were rather perceived as amulets that had apotropaic meanings and forces.[41]

Curses present a more aggressive and active strategy against one's rivals or enemies. The "you (pl.) will/should die!" (תמותו) *ostracon* (Mas 643) may very well be interpreted according to this line of explanation. *Ostracon* Mas 611 notes twice the word אסרטין, which may be refer to "(Roman) soldiers" or "a band." If indeed this legend had a negative connotation than it might have been written twice in an attempt to express contempt.[42] Such an elucidation may reflect the sense and degree of despair, conditions that generated a desire to leave a message behind. Such was seemingly the case with the drawings and inscription that were found on the plastered wall of a cistern in the cliffs of Naḥal Michmash, in the northern Judaean Desert. In addition to a pentagram and a candelabrum that have evident symbolic and magical meaning, a most dramatic scenario was offered to the circumstance under which the inscription "יועזר אתעקר עלו מטרנ[א]" ("Yoezer was uprooted, the guards came in") was executed. Patrich suggested

---

40 Initial publication: de Vaux, Milik and Benoit 1961, no. 19, pp. 104–109. For "Year 6": Yadin 1965, p. 119, note 112; Yadin and Naveh 1989, pp. 9–11; also: Ilan 1996 and Friedman 2011.
41 See above note 20.
42 Cotton and Geiger 1989, no. 611, pp. 62–63.

that the inscription was written following the injury of the scribe and just before Roman soldiers stormed the refuge complex.[43]

Lastly, in light of the above noted combination of an inscription alongside a graphic motif, I wish to briefly dwell upon the artistic expression as an additional scribal medium. At Masada several such manifestations were documented, mostly as *graffiti*, such as boats (Locus 120),[44] and an architectural enclosure (palace?) with palm and cypress trees on the wall structures within the Herodian Northern Palace complex.[45] Nonetheless, to these one may further add drawings and sketches on ceramic body shards that appears to belong to the time of the revolt and as such may shed light on the state of mind of the community of rebels. Accordingly, a drawing of a structure that consists of two columns which support an architrave and an arch was uncovered in Locus 1054, just south of the synagogue in an occupation layer from the revolt.[46] The columns are crowned by Ionic capitols and rest on prominent plinths that are shaped in a like manner of inverted Ionic capitols. The columns, the shaft to the left of which was suggested to be decorated by a twining leafy vine, were penned standing on a latticework stylobate. This description bears much resemblance to the depiction of the Temple's façade on the later Bar-Kokhba *Sela* (tetradrachms) coins, though the latter has four columns rather than two.[47] Despite the claim of Bar-Nathan that the drawing appears to be incomplete[48], I find no support to it whatsoever, particularly in light of the rare half-*Sela* coin ("Shekel") that exhibits a Temple's façade with two column[49]; hence, the drawing under discussion may indeed presented a depiction of the recently destroyed Temple in Jerusalem.[50] The human tendency to document oneself and perhaps even to leave something behind, particularly during stressed and desperate circumstances (as emerges from the interpretation of the above noted inscription and drawing from Naḥal Michmash), may be further attributed to the somewhat naive charcoal drawing of a bust of a plaited girl

---

43 Patrich 1985.

44 Netzer 1991, p. 120. *Cf.* Zissu 2015.

45 Avi-Yona *et al.* 1957, p. 27, fig. 11A and pl. 5B. *Cf* the sketches and incisions carried out by the workers that dismantled the small theatre at Herodium during Herod's reign (Netzer *et al.* 2010, pp. 101–102).

46 Bar-Nathan 2007, p. 274, cat. no. 73, fig. 81, pl. 4 (bottom left).

47 Meshorer 1997, pp. 127–128, 134 and 138; For the golden vine: Patrich 1989 and Baratz 2017.

48 Bar-Nathan 2007, p. 274.

49 Meshorer 1997, pp. 139, 228: no. 271 and pl. 69.

50 We may regard this drawing as an early expression of the Jewish artistic trend that developed most notably following the suppressing of the Second Revolt and manifested the Jewish yearning for redemption.

that was uncovered in the excavation of the terrace adjacent the western case-mate wall and the Roman breach (Netzer and Stiebel's Area W1).

4 The Roman Side

MacMullen illustrated the evolution of the Romans' "obsession" for writing.[51] Thus, it is commonly held that the discovery of Latin inscriptions in early Roman Palestine should be primarily associated with either the Roman government or the Roman army. Not surprisingly, Jews in Judaea regarded over the years Latin as the language of war (רומי לקרב).[52] Amongst others, Latin inscriptions were found on milestones, dedication inscriptions and documents that are related directly to the Roman military administration (correspondences and diplomas), as well as on everyday utensils. To the initial category one may attribute the pay record from Masada which associates directly martial material culture with individual soldiers and units (Mas 722); it contains important details concerning military dress and equipment items and their costs. The latter category commonly comprises the names of the owner, his unit or the maker. Only a few inscriptions have been found on *militaria* in Roman Judaea. Three *tabulae ansatae* from Gamla bear the names of Roman soldiers and their unit affiliation. They were apparently used as ownership tags, which were fastened on both sides of the boss and appears to be written by the soldiers themselves.[53] A forth *nota* was recently uncovered at Motza/Moẓa (Roman Colonia), west of Jerusalem.[54] To this rare group one may add military bread-stamps/dies and the *AVCISSA* brooches.[55] Lastly, *militaria* was used as a platform for political and religious propaganda. An example for the former are inscribed leaden slingshots that functioned not only as ammunition in battlefields of the Late Republic and the Early Principate but also as a mean to convey support and blemish messages. One such leaden

---

51 MacMullen 1982.

52 Palestinian Talmud, Sotah 7b.

53 Stiebel 2014, pp. 84–86.

54 Bar-Nathan *et al.* 2020, pp. 364–366, fig. 10:2.

55 Bread stamps: Jerusalem (Stiebel 1999, pp. 72–74; Stiebel 2011c); Murabbaʿat (de Vaux, Milik and Benoit 1961, pp. 35–36, fig. 12.9, pl. IX.26; Stiebel 2010, pp. 328–329); Legio/Lajjun (Stiebel 2006b; Eck and Tepper 2019, pp. 122–123); Motza/Moẓa (Bar-Nathan *et al.* 2020, p. 364, fig. 10:1). For inscribed *AVCISSA* brooches see: Cypros (Stiebel 2013b, p. 295); Jerusalem (Iliffe 1936, p. 21, fig. 3; Weksler-Bdolah and Di Segni 2020); Motza/Moẓa (Bar-Nathan *et al.* 2020, pp. 366–367, fig. 10:3).

pellet from Judaea appears to carry the name of Mark Antony.[56] This function played an important role in the psychology of war and contributed to the morale of the individual soldier and the cohesion of the unit.

In general, it seems that any examination of military scribal activity should take into account the context and most notably the viewpoint of time and place; namely are we dealing with a scribal activity that was executed during the rage of a military campaign or amidst times of peace, and was the document written in a permanent or in a temporary camp in the field. The Roman military commanders' practise to produce field accounts and commentaries (*commentarii* or *hypomnemata*), as well as military memoirs, the most famous of all being the accounts of Julius Caesar regarding his Gallic campaign, places in our hands an invaluable plethora of scribal products. Suggestions were made that the military nature of Josephus's narrative of the siege of Masada may be attributed to his use of Roman military *commentarii* that were available to him in Rome.[57] Broshi postulated that sources for not a few of the details in Josephus's narration were the commentaries of Vespasian and Titus, the existence of which is mentioned by Josephus himself.[58]

Turning to the Roman epigraphic evidence from Masada, one may classify it under tactical considerations and administrative correspondence, not much different from the way we have analysed above the epigraphic material of the rebels. A military letter concerning a dangerous situation that necessitated the sending of a *centurion* to inspect it, was further reported from Masada (Mas 726). It was written "in a neat and clearly legible cursive hand," seemingly dictated by a rank higher than a centurion.[59] A letter concerning the Balsam trade (Mas 725), the most expensive product of the region, if not of the entire province of Judaea, appears to fall under the category of administrative as well as tactical correspondences (see also Mas 749 frag. (b) and possibly also Mas 732).[60] As noted above, a Roman salary document was uncovered at Masada (Mas 722).[61] The rare document provides us a glimpse into the immense bureaucracy and administration and as a result the scribal work the Roman army was involved in, providing each soldier three times a year with a salary. The fact two copies were produced every

56 Stiebel 1997.

57 Broshi 1982.

58 *Against Apion*, 1.56; *Life* 342 and 358; See also: Schanz 1935, pp. 432–433; Stern 1991, pp. 382–383, note 18.

59 Cotton and Geiger 1989, no. 726, pp. 70–72.

60 Ibid., no. 725, pp. 68–70, pl. 5; no. 749, pp. 98–99, pl. 10; no. 732 (?), p. 77, pl. 7.

61 Ibid., no. 722, pp. 35–56, pls. 2–3.

four months, for the soldier and the army's archive as well, suggests that the 300,000 strong body of the Roman army had produced *circa* 1.8 million salary documents *per annum*! Military operations were a good justification to award the soldiers with money and military decorations, most notably following a victory.[62] Moreover, the chance to increase the motivation of the fighters amidst the extreme conditions of the fighting was not overlooked or missed by the Roman commanders. Thus, Josephus notes in his account about the siege of Jerusalem (70 CE) that Titus:

> "decided to suspend the siege for a while and to afford the factions an interval for reflection, to see if the demolition of the second wall or haply dread of famine might lead to any surrender, as the fruits of their rapine could not long suffice them; and he turned the period of inaction to good account. For the appointed day having arrived for the distribution of the soldiers' pay, he ordered his officers to parade the forces and count out the money to each man in full view of the enemy. So the troops, as was their custom, drew forth their arms from the cases in which till now they had been covered and advanced clad in mail, the cavalry leading their horses which were richly caparisoned. The area in front of the city gleamed far and wide with silver and gold, and nothing was more gratifying to the Romans, or more awe-inspiring to the enemy, than that spectacle. For the whole of the old wall and the north side of the temple were thronged with spectators, the houses across the wall were to be seen packed with craning heads, and there was not a spot visible in the city which was not covered by the crowd. Even the hardiest were struck with dire dismay at the sight of this assemblage of all the forces, the beauty of their armour and the admirable order of the men; and I cannot but think that the rebels would have been converted by that vision, had not the enormity of their crimes against the people made them despair of obtaining pardon from the Romans. But, death being the punishment in store for them if they desisted, they thought it far better to die in battle. Fate, moreover, was prevailing to involve both innocent and guilty, city and sedition, in a common ruin."[63]

In addition to the evident Roman morale merits of this event, the extravagant ceremony that lasted four days, until all the Roman force received its pay (*BJ* 5.356), had a clear propagandistic impact on the rebels that were observing it from the walls of the besieged city. One may wonder whether the discovery of the pay record at Masada indicates an early pay event (namely *circa* April), given the attestation in Dura Europos that soldiers seemingly received their pay on the 1st day of January, May and September.[64]

62 *BJ* 7.14ff.
63 *BJ* 5.348–355.
64 Fink 1971, 72.7; Fink 66 fr. BI 230 and Fink 66 fr. BII 3.

Sick and particularly wounded soldiers in the lines of the army were to be expected during a campaign, a situation that would have required their hospitalization in the *valetudinarium*. A rare medical care document that was written in the field during the siege, seemingly by the *librarius* of the *ratio valetudinarii* or of the *praefectus castrorum* was found at Masada.[65] A Roman military physician of Greek origin, by the name of Nicostratus, is noted in the document. Instructions are there given to provide one sick Valerius with 1 ounce of a certain eating oil, while the bandages of an evidently wounded soldier are ordered to be replaced by clean ones – "laundered fine bandages," to be precise.

Yet, beyond the immediate physical danger, the military environment had also a severe mental cost. The danger and anxiety of the battle, in addition to the inevitable exposure to casualties and to the horrors that formed an integral part of the combative experience of so many soldiers, clearly left its mark.[66] A unique scrap of a papyrus comprising a quote from Virgil's *Aeneid* 4, 9: "Anna, my sister, what dreams thrill me with fears?" was uncovered at the site.[67] In the face of parallel Virgil graffiti from Pompeii, the editors noted that the quotation under discussion seems to relate to the feelings and circumstances of the writer. Hence it may reflect his longing for a certain Anna, thus being charged with an erotic undertone[68]; or alternatively it may have conveyed the feeling of the writer in face of the horrors he had witnessed on Masada, hinting to the episode of the collective mass suicide of the defenders.[69] Be that as it may, their concluding remarks are of particular interest for the sake of our discussion regarding the identity of the scribe: "the writer," note Cotton and Geiger, "must have belonged to the besieging Roman forces. Of course we do not know his rank; he may have been an officer. Nor do we know the rank of the writer of the line of Virgil from Vindolanda. Nevertheless, they illustrate one of the avenues through which the diffusion of classical education took place. If it could be proven that the writer belonged to the rank and file of the Tenth Legion, the papyrus would have important implications for the question of the literacy, indeed the education, of Roman soldiers."[70]

---

65 Cotton and Geiger 1989, pp. 56–61, no. 723.
66 For a discussion of the pressures during the siege of Jerusalem, see Goldsworthy 1999.
67 "Anna soror quae me suspensam insomnia terrent" (Ibid. no. 721, pp. 31–35).
68 *Cf.* with the *graffito* from Herodium (Testa 1972, no. 37, pp. 59–62).
69 Cotton and Geiger 1989, p. 34.
70 Ibid. and see note 22.

5 Kilroy Was Here

A more-earthly scribal habit has been the evident human desire to commemorate one's presence in a given place, and even more-so following dramatic events such as a battle or a war. Be it the name of an individual soldier, the name of his commander, or not less common that of his unit and even his army, soldiers of all ranks, statuses and cultural backgrounds left throughout history their mark on countless walls and makeshift monuments. Following his victory at the River Hydaspes, India, Alexander the Great left behind altars to mark the limits of his empire. The existence of a bronze tablet there with the legend "Alexander stopped here" was further noted. Despite Philostratus's affirmation that one should credit the Indians across the river for this dedication, it is difficult to avoid attributing the humble legend that was erected on the *eastern* bank of the river to Alexander himself.[71] The famous American military version of WWII: *Kilroy was here* evidently followed the earlier WWI British version of *Mr. Chad* or simply *Chad* and the Australian equivalent: *Foo was here*. Returning to Roman Judaea, during the excavations of Corbo at the site of Herodium in the 1960's, a graffito of a vulgar nature that was claimed to be accompanied by a phallic symbol was found engraved on the frescoed walls of the mountain palace. The editor of the inscriptions suggested that it was inscribed by a follower of Bar Kokhba and was directed against Christian belief.[72] At Masada, a charcoal graffito (Mas 937) noting "LEG X" was uncovered on the wall of the *caldarium* of the Large Bathhouse.[73] It was clearly executed by one of the soldiers of the unit (the Tenth Legion) that besieged and conquered Masada. The remains of a ceramic bowl on which was found the title of this legion "Leg(io)...AU [...] FRE(tensis)" was incised on the rim of a bowl after firing, possibly indicating ownership of the vessel (Mas 853).[74] An additional personal Greek graffito, featuring the Roman name of one ΓΑΙΟϹ ΑϹΚΛΑϹ (Gaius Asclas) was uncovered during the Israeli archaeological survey and excavation of 1955–56 at Masada.[75] The *graffito* that following its initial publication has oddly escaped the eyes of most scholars was engraved on the upper course of the inner corner pilaster of the hall in the Lower Terrace of the Northern Palace. I concur with the interpretation of the excavators that the inscription was

71 Philostratus, *Apollonius of Tyana*. II.43, Translated by Christopher P. Jones, 2005-6, Loeb Classical Library.
72 Testa 1972, pp. 39, 41, no. 24.
73 Cotton and Geiger 1989, p. 212, no. 937, pl. 44.
74 Ibid. pp. 176–177, no. 853, pl. 29.
75 Avi-Yona *et al.* 1957, p. 45, fig. 13, and fig. 22, *infra*, p. 60.

executed following the conquest of the site. It appears that the engraving was executed when the plastered pilaster was still standing in light of its height (*c.* 3.10 m) and one may indeed suggest that Gaius Asclas was standing on the collapse of the roof and part of the building while etching his name. The evident usage of Roman *praenomen* and *nomen* indicates the scribe was a Roman citizen. Interestingly, no *cognomen* is used, a phenomenon that is unusual for the period, however it is in fact attested in all the names noted in the pay record from Masada (Mas 722).[76] The *praenomen*, Gaius, is very common whereas his *nomen*, Asclas, suggests an eastern origin, either Egyptian[77] or Syrian.[78] This combination appears to indicate that scribe was a legionary. Moreover, given the fact that the citizen unit that conquered Masada was the Tenth Legion Fretensis, whose soldiers were recruited in Syria, as gleaned for example from Josephus's account (*BJ* 4.38), as well from the pay record uncovered at the site[79], it appears safe to assume that the scribe was affiliated with this unit as well. To this we may further add several other *graffiti*, and particularly the Greek and Latin abecedaries discussed above (Mas 938–941).

6 Conclusions

Summing up, the abundance of epigraphic evidence at Masada during the time of the First Revolt stands out and may not be elucidated merely by the extensive scope of excavation and/or the excellent conditions of preservation. The great number of written finds that shed invaluable light on the rebel community appears to be the result of the reality in which it operated, i.e. times of crisis. The diversity of the groups of rebels/refugees within the desert fortress necessitated the existence of an administrative body that seemingly produced many of the *ostraca* under discussion. Added to the products of tactical assignments, ritual activities flourished in the hope to gain divine attention and assistance. The observation that pressure and times of crisis may have acted as a catalyst, namely, that

---

76 For discussion and extended bibliography, see: Cotton and Geiger 1989, p. 49, and lines 3, 6a, 14a and 15a.

77 A high-priest of Gaius Caesar Augustus Germanicus, *exegetes* and *strategus* Gaius Julius Asclas is mentioned in a petition from 39 CE, Egypt (P. Ryl. 2.149 = HGV P. Ryl. 2 149 = Trismegistos 12935, lines 2–3).

78 The eastern origin of the name, among the Hellenised communities, is further attested in Panias: one Ascla is there noted (*CIL* X 1985).

79 Cotton and Geiger 1989, no. 722, line 3, pp. 49–51.

it contributed to the increase in writing activity on one hand and the attempt to save it on the other hand, may in fact be further applied to the community of Qumran that to a large extant acted, despite the different circumstances, as a community under extreme conditions. Using this perspective allows setting the Qumranic literary assemblage in a broader context of scribal activity, such as, for example, Popović's discussion of Qumran as scroll storehouse in times of crisis.[80]

Lastly, we should not overlook the notion that in addition to the focus on survival and endurance, many of the deeds of the rebels and refugees, regardless place and time, contain aspects that are symbolic in nature and in intention. In that respect, discussing Masada, one cannot avoid treating along these lines the act of suicide, which, according to Josephus, stood out as the bluntest example of all, both in the eyes of the rebels and the Romans alike.[81] Not less symbolic was the call of Eleazar ben Yair not to fully burn down the entire fortress. At the end of his first speech (*BJ* 7.336) he urged the men, according to Josephus, to spare only their provisions "for they will testify, when we are dead, that it was not want which subdued us, but that, in keeping with our initial resolve, we preferred death to slavery" – a final *unwritten* message from the vanquished to the conquering Roman side.

7 Bibliography

Anava Sarit *et al.*, "Illuminating Genetic Mysteries of the Dead Sea Scrolls," *Cell* 181 (2020), pp. 1218–1231.

Arubas Benjamin and Goldfus Haim, s.v. "Masada – The Roman Siege Works," in: Stern Ephraim (ed.), *The New Encyclopedia of Archaeological Excavations in the Holy Land 5 (Supplementary volume)*, Jerusalem and Washington, DC, Israel Exploration Society and Biblical Archaeology Society, 2008, pp. 1937–1939.

Avi-Yona Michael, Avigad Nahman, Aharonoi Yohanan, Dunayevski Immanuel and Shmarya Gutman, "The Archaeological Survey of Masada, 1955–1956," *Israel Exploration Journal* 7 (1957), pp. 1–60.

Baratz Daphne, "A Golden Vine/Garden in the Temple," in Ilan Tal and Noam Vered (eds.), *Josephus and the Rabbis, Vol. 1: The Lost Tales of the Second Temple Period*, Jerusalem, Yad Izhak Ben-Zvi, 2017, pp. 341–347 (Hebrew).

Bar-Nathan Rachel, The Pottery of Masada, *Masada VII, The Yigael Yadin Excavations 1963–1965, Final Reports*, Jerusalem, Israel Exploration Society, 2007.

Bar-Nathan Rachel, Zilberbod Irina, Landes-Nagar Annette, Di Segni Leah and Taxel Itamar, "Moẓa in the Early Centuries CE: On the Identification and Nature of Roman Colonia,"

---

80 Popović 2012.
81 *BJ* 7.405–406 and also *BJ* 7.388. Stiebel 2013a, pp. 175–177 and Stiebel 2020, pp. 180–181.

in Khalaily Hamoudi, Re'em Amit, Vardi Jacob and Milevski Ianir (eds.), *The Mega Project at Motza (Moẓa): The Neolithic and Later Occupations up to the 20ᵗʰ Century*, New Studies in the Archaeology and Its Region Supplementary Volume, Jerusalem, Israel Antiquities Authorities, 2020, pp. 351–379.

Beltrán Lloris Francisco, "The Epigraphic Habit in the Roman World," in Bruun Christer and Edmonson Jonathan (eds.), *The Oxford Handbook of Roman Epigraphy*, Oxford–New York, Oxford University Press, 2015, pp. 131–148.

Ben-Tor Amnon, *Back to Masada*, Jerusalem, Israel Exploration Society, 2009.

Broshi Magen, "The Credibility of Josephus," *Journal of Jewish Studies* 33 (1982), pp. 379–384.

Cotton Hannah M. and Geiger Joseph, *The Latin and Greek Documents, Masada II, The Yigael Yadin Excavations 1963–1965, Final Reports*, Jerusalem, Israel Exploration Society, 1989.

Cotton Hannah M. and Greenfield Jonas C., "Babatha's Property and the Law of Succession in the Babatha Archive," *Zeitschrift für Papyrologie und Epigraphik* 104 (1994), pp. 211–224.

Cotton Hannah M. and Yardeni Ada, *Aramaic, Hebrew and Greek Documentary Texts from Nahal Hever and Other Sites, with an Appendix Containing Alleged Qumran Texts* (The Seiyal Collection II), *DJD* XXVII, Oxford, Oxford University Press, 1997.

Davies Gwyn, *Roman Siege Works*, Stroud, Tempus 2006.

Di Segni Leah and Weksler-Bdolah Shlomit, "Three Military Bread Stamps from the Western Wall Plaza Excavations, Jerusalem," *'Atiqot* 70 (2012), pp. 21–31.

Eck Werner and Tepper Yotam, "Latin Inscriptions of the Legio VI Ferrata from Legio / Lajjun and its Vicinity," *Scripta Classica Israelica* 38 (2019), pp. 117–128.

Eph'al Israel, *The City Besieged: Siege and Its Manifestations in the Ancient Near East*, Jerusalem, Magnes Press, 2013.

Ferere Sheppard S., Roxen Margaret and Tomlin Roger S.O., *The Roman Inscriptions of Britain, Instrumentum Domesticum*, Vol. II, Fasc. 1, Gloucester, Alan Sutton Publishing, 1990.

Fink Robert O., *Roman Military Records on Papyrus*, An American Philological Association Book 26, Cleveland, Oh, 1971.

Friedman Shamma, "The Jewish Bill of Divorce – From Masada Onwards," in Baumgarten Albert I., Eshel Hanan, Katzoff Ranon and Tzoref Shani (eds.), *Halakhah in Light of Epigraphy*, Journal of Ancient Judaism Supplements 3, Göttingen, Vandenhoeck & Ruprecht, 2011, pp. 175–183.

Goldsworthy Adrian, "Community under Pressure: The Roman Army at the Siege of Jerusalem," in Goldsworthy Adrian and Haynes Ian (eds.), *The Roman Army as a Community*, Journal of Roman Archaeology Suppl. Ser. 34, Portmouth, RI, 1999, pp. 197–210.

Hachlili Rachel, "Names and Nicknames at Masada," *Eretz-Israel* 26, Frank Moore Cross Volume, Jerusalem, Israel Exploration Society, 1999, pp. 49–54.

Hamilakis Yannis, "Archaeologies of Forced and Undocumented Migration," *Journal of Contemporary Archaeology* 3:2 (2016), pp. 121–139.

Hezser Catherine, *Jewish Literacy in Roman Palestine* (Texts and Studies in Ancient Judaism 81), Tübingen, Mohr Siebeck, 2001.

Ilan Tal, "On a Newly Published Divorce Bill from the Judaean Desert," *The Harvard Theological Review* 89:2 (1996), pp. 195–202.

Ilan Tal, *Lexicon of Jewish Names in Late Antiquity*, Vol. I: Palestine 330 BCE – 200 CE, Tübingen, Mohr Siebeck, 2002.

Iliffe John H., "Sigilita Wares in the Near East, a List of Potters' Stamps," *Quarterly of the Department of Antiquities in Palestine* 6 (1936), pp. 4–53.

Jackson-Tal Ruth, "Miscellaneous Small Finds: Metal and Glass," In: Syon Danny, *Gamla* III, *The Shmarya Gutmann Excavations 1976–1989, Finds and Studies Part 2*, IAA Reports 59, Jerusalem, Israel Antiquities Authority 2016, pp. 191–212.

Lemaire André, "Writing and Writing Materials," *The Anchor Bible Dictionary* Vol. 6, New York, Doubleday, 1992, pp. 999–1008.

MacMullen Ramsay, "The Epigraphic Habit in the Roman Empire," The *American Journal of Philology* 103 (1982), 233–246.

Magness Jodi, "Masada – Arms and the Man," *Biblical Archaeology Review* 18:4 (1992), pp. 58–67.

Magness Jodi, *Masada: From Jewish Revolt to Modern Myth*, Princeton, Princeton University Press, 2019.

Mason Steve, *A History of the Jewish War: A.D. 66–74*, Cambridge, Cambridge University Press, 2016.

Meshorer Yaakov, *A Treasury of Jewish Coins, from the Persian Period to Bar-Kochba*, Jerusalem, Yad Izhak Ben-Zvi, 1997.

Misgav Hagai, "The Ostraca," in Győző Vörös, *Machaerus I, History, Archaeology and Architecture of the Fortified Herodian Royal Palace and City Overlooking the Dead Sea in Transjordan*, Milano, Studium Biblicum Franciscanum, 2013.

Netzer Ehud, "The Rebels' Archives at Masada," *Israel Exploration Journal* 54 (2004), pp. 218–229.

Netzer Ehud, Kalman Yakov, Porat Roi, Chachy-Laureys Rachel, "Preliminary Report on Herod's Mausoleum and Theatre with a Royal Box at Herodium," *Journal of Roman Archaeology* 23 (2010), pp. 84–108.

Netzer Ehud and Stiebel Guy D., s.v. "Masada," in: Ephraim Stern (ed.), *The New Encyclopedia of Archaeological Excavations in the Holy Land* 5 (Supplementary volume), Jerusalem and Washington, DC, Israel Exploration Society and Biblical Archaeology Society, 2008, pp. 1935–1937.

Patrich Joseph, "Caves of Refuge and Jewish Inscriptions on the Cliffs of Naḥal Michmas," *Eretz-Israel* 18, Nahman Avigad Volume, Jerusalem, Israel Exploration Society, 1985, pp. 153–166.

Patrich Joseph, "The Golden Vine, The Sanctuary Portal and its Depiction on the Bar Kokhba Coins," *Proceedings of the World Congress of Jewish Studies* 10, Division B, Volume I: The History of the Jewish People (1989), pp. 8–14 (Hebrew).

Popović Mladen, "Qumran as Scroll Storehouse in Times of Crisis? A Comparative Perspective on Judaean Desert Manuscript Collections," *Journal for the Study of Judaism* 43 (2012), pp. 551–594.

Schanz Martin, *Geschichte der römischen Literatur*, II (ed. Carl Hosius), Munich, C.H. Beck, 1935.

Stern Menahem, *Studies in the History of the People of Israel in the Period of the Second Temple*, Jerusalem, Yad Izhak Ben-Zvi, 1991 (Hebrew).

Stiebel Guy D. "'...You Were the Word of War': A Sling Shot Testimony from Israel," *Journal of Roman Military Equipment Studies* 8 (1997), pp. 301–307.

Stiebel Guy D., "Masada," s.v. in *Encyclopaedia Judaica* (2nd ed.), Detroit, Thomson Gale (Macmillan Reference), 2006a, Vol. 13, pp. 593–599.

Stiebel Guy D. "Roman Military Artifacts," in Tepper Yotam and Di Segni Leah, *A Christian Prayer Hall of the Third Century CE at Kefar 'Othnay (Legio) – Excavations at the Megiddo Prison 2005*, Jerusalem, Israel Antiquities Authority, 2006b, pp. 29–30.

Stiebel Guy D., "'Meager Bread and Scant Water' – Food for thought at Masada," in: Baumgarten Albert I., Eshel Hannan, Katzoff Ranon and Tzoref Shani (eds.), *Halakhah in Light of Epigraphy* (Journal of Ancient Judaism Supplements 3), Göttingen, Vandenhoeck & Ruprecht, 2011a, pp. 283–303.

Stiebel, Guy D., "A Military Die from the Bakery," In Mazar Eilat (ed.), *Temple Mount Excavations Volume IV: The Tenth Legion in Aelia Capitolina*, Qedem 52, Jerusalem, Institute of Archaeology, the Hebrew University of Jerusalem, 2011b, pp. 229–231.

Stiebel Guy D., "About Identity and Space at Masada of the Great Revolt," in: Schiller Eli and Barkai Gabriel (eds.), *Architecture and Art in Second Temple Jerusalem*, Ariel 200–201 (2013a), pp. 169–178 (Hebrew).

Stiebel Guy D., "Military Equipment From Jericho and Cypros," in Bar-Nathan R. and Gärtner J. (eds.), *Hasmonean and Herodian Palaces at Jericho, Volume V, Final Reports of the 1973–1987 Excavations, The Finds from Jericho and Cypros*, Jerusalem, 2013b, pp. 290–298.

Stiebel Guy D., "Military Equipment," in Syon Danny (ed.), *Gamla III. The Shmarya Gutmann Excavations 1976–1989, Finds and Studies Part 1*, IAA Reports 56, Jerusalem, Israel Antiquities Authority, 2014, pp. 57–107.

Stiebel Guy D., "'Burns Like Fire' – Mustard and Viniculture in Roman Palestine," *Tarbiẓ* 86 (2019), pp. 5–37 (Hebrew).

Stiebel Guy D., "What Have the Romans Ever Done for Us," *Scripta Classica Israelica* 39 (2020), pp. 175–182.

Stiebel Guy D., "What's in a Name? About an Ostracon from Masada, Names, Nicknames and Masqueraded Nicknames," in Binder Stéphanie E., Ratzon Eshbal, Shivtiel Yinon (eds.), *"A Work of Wisdom" (Exod. XXXII-XXXIII 35:33), Studies in Honor of Professor Bezalel Bar-Kochva*, Teudah: Studies of the Haim Rosenberg Schoold for Jewish Studies 33 (2021), pp. 423–450 (Hebrew).

Stiebel Guy D. and Gross Boaz, "Masada Shall Never Fail (to Surprise) Again," *Biblical Archaeology Review*, 44 (2018), pp. 30–40.

Stiebel Guy D. and Magness Jodi, "Military Equipment from Masada," *Masada VIII, The Yigael Yadin Excavations 1963–1965, Final Reports*, Jerusalem, Israel Exploration Society, 2007, pp. 1–94.

Talmon Shemaryhu and Yadin Yigael, "Hebrew Fragments from Masada" and "The Ben Sira Scroll from Masada," *Masada VI, The Yigael Yadin Excavations 1963–1965, Final Reports*, Jerusalem, Israel Exploration Society, 1999.

Testa Emmanuele, *I Graffiti E Gli Ostraka*, Herodium IV, Jerusalem 1972.

Tov Emmanuel, *Scribal Practices and Approaches Reflected in the Texts Found in The Judean Desert*, Studies on the Texts of the Desert of Judah 54, Leiden, Brill, 2004.

De Vaux, Roland, Milik Jozef T. and Benoit Pierre, *Les Grottes de Murabba'ât. Discoveries in the Judaean Desert II*, Oxford, Oxford University Press, 1961.

Weksler-Bdolah Shlomit and Di Segni Leah, "A Latin Epitaph of a soldier from Magen's Excavations in the Damscus Gate and the Burial Grounds of Jerusalem between 70 and 130 CE," *Israel Exploration Journal* 70 (2020), pp. 90–98.

Yadin Yigael, "The Excavation of Masada – 1963/64: Preliminary Report," *Israel Exploration Journal* 15 (1965), pp. 1–120.

Yadin Yigael and Naveh Joseph, "The Aramaic and Hebrew Ostraca and Jar Inscriptions," *Masada I, The Yigael Yadin Excavations 1963–1965, Final Reports*, Jerusalem, Israel Exploration Society, 1989, pp. 1–68 and pls. 1–60.

Zissu Boaz, "Graffito of a Ship and a Boat," in Porat Roi, Chachy Rachel and Kalman Yakov (eds.), *Herodium I: Herod's Tomb Precinct, Final Reports of the 1972–2010 Excavations Directed by Ehud Netzer*, Jerusalem, Israel Exploration Society, pp. 511–514.

Jeffrey Stackert
Scribal Fatigue in Ancient Revisionary Composition

Revisionary compositions exhibit a range of evidence for reconstructing their genesis, including evidence of the various *processes*—mental, material, and otherwise—undertaken by the scribes who produced them. Especially in instances where both literary patrimony and inheritor text are available to be compared, detailed identification and rich analysis of this evidence is possible. In this paper, I will consider the phenomenon variously termed "editorial fatigue" or "docile reproduction" that sometimes attends revisionary composition. In such cases, a revisionary author carries over material from a literary patrimony that conflicts with innovations otherwise introduced by that author in the new work created. The result is a lack of content consistency in the revisionary composition. I will begin by addressing the theory of editorial fatigue—or, as I will term it, *scribal fatigue*—as it has been developed especially in the study of New Testament gospel texts before turning to a number of additional examples, primarily from the Hebrew Bible. I hope to show that literary details ascribed to so-called "fatigue" are part of a larger constellation of related characteristics that together shed important light on the scribal processes involved in revisionary composition. I will then conclude with a brief consideration of the effects of fatigue-related discrepancies on readers, including why these features are relatively easily noticed yet oftentimes perceived as unproblematic and how they can help illuminate scribal practice in literary composition.

1 Fatigue Theory: Theoretical Considerations

Building upon observations of scholars such as G. M. Styler and Michael Goulder,[1] Mark Goodacre has developed the theory of fatigue in revisionary composition in his study of the New Testament synoptic gospels.[2] As part of their arguments for Markan priority, these scholars have shown that, in several instances, Matthew and Luke have innovated in relation to Mark only then to revert to a rote recitation of Markan details that contradict the innovations introduced. For example, in the corresponding accounts of the death of John the Baptist in Mark and Matthew (Mark 6:14–29//Matt 14:1–12), Herod is alternatively termed "king" or "tetrarch." Yet the distribution of these titles in the two accounts is telling: Mark repeatedly and consistently refers to Herod as "king" (6:14, 22, 25, 26, 27), but Matthew, apparently correcting this terminology to reflect Herod Antipas's actual position, refers to him as "tetrarch" at the beginning of his account (14:1). In line with this change, Matthew also excises the Markan reference to Herod's "kingdom," omitting the ruler's offer to give Herodias's daughter "up to half my kingdom" (ἕως ἡμίσους τῆς βασιλείας μου, Matt 14:7//Mark 6:23). Yet later in the passage, the Matthean author reproduces from Mark the title of "king" for Herod (14:9). And lest there be any question of the origin of this title in Matthew, the line in which it appears is a near verbatim reproduction of the Markan line (cf. Mark 6:26).[3]

A similar scenario obtains in the accounts of the leper's healing in Mark 1:40–45 and Matt 8:1–4. As scholars have noted, though each of these accounts includes an instruction from Jesus to the leper to tell no one of his healing, this instruction in Matt 8:4 is nonsensical in light of the unit's opening notice that Jesus performed the miracle in the presence of many crowds (8:1). Yet the corresponding secrecy instruction in Mark is easily comprehensible (Mark 1:44), for in the Markan account, Jesus performs the miracle in private. Cases such as these can be multiplied many times over in both Matthew and Luke.[4]

---

1 G. M. Styler, Excursus 4 in C. F. D. Moule, *The Birth of the New Testament*, 3rd ed. (London: Adam & Charles Black, 1981), 285–316; Michael Goulder, *Midrash and Lection in Matthew* (London: SPCK, 1974).

2 Mark Goodacre, "Fatigue in the Synoptics," *NTS* 44 (1998): 45–58. For recent interaction with Goodacre's treatment of fatigue and its relevance for study of the synoptic gospels, see Tobias Hägerland, "Editorial Fatigue and the Existence of Q," *NTS* 65 (2019): 190–206.

3 Goulder, *Midrash and Lection*, 35; Goodacre, "Fatigue," 46.

4 For a range of examples, see Goodacre, "Fatigue."

In his 1998 article, "Fatigue in the Synoptics," Goodacre makes a number of claims regarding fatigue that deserve further consideration and perhaps even some friendly amendment, especially as the data set is enlarged. The first relates to the literary context or level upon which scribal fatigue might be identified. Goodacre argues for fatigue at the level of the *pericope* or, perhaps better, the *episode*. He states,

> In most cases, Matthew and Luke differ from Mark at the beginning of the pericope, at the point where they are writing most characteristically, and they agree with Mark later in the pericope, where they are writing less characteristically.[5]

The examples from the synoptics that he adduces are compelling and do work in this way. Yet one might also ask to what extent the identification of fatigue should be understood *only* at the episodic level.

As I will highlight below, the revision in some derivative texts does not appear mainly or only at the level of the pericope or episode but instead extends across a larger literary work, where a single theme, motif, or plot element occurs repeatedly. In such instances, the phenomenon observable appears to be very similar to that identified as fatigue or docile reproduction: a revisionary author fails to fully integrate and update inherited material with the innovations introduced in the revisionary composition, even if these discrepancies range beyond the boundaries of the pericope or episode.

This possibility of transgressing the episodic boundary also raises the question of whether fatigue should be understood in strictly sequential terms, namely, as a phenomenon in which a revising author fails to carry through an innovation from beginning to end. The label "fatigue" itself presumes such a sequential cursus, and it might be retained when applied beyond the bounds of the episode, provided that it is accompanied by a broader conceptualization of ancient literary composition and its processes. As alluded to already, many ancient works, including many narrative works in the Bible, exhibit clear evidence of overall planning, with plot and character development, foreshadowing, and other internal cross-referencing. Might the issue of fatigue and the sequence that it implies be considered in relation to the larger and more complex planning processes that stand behind and inform a revisionary work?

In his recent study of the scribal processes involved in producing the Old Greek of Exodus 1–14, John Screnock has argued for the notion of a "mental text" to account for certain variants that appear in this Greek translation. He states,

---

5 Goodacre, "Fatigue," 52.

Whether the translator was conscious of it or not, there existed a version of the Hebrew text in the mind of the translator, based on the physical *Vorlage* but not necessarily identical to it. In other words, the translation process did not involve one single move from the physical *Vorlage* directly to the physical text of the translation; rather, in the translator's mind there were additional intermediary stages, appropriately conceived of as texts, through which this move was channeled.[6]

Screnock applies this notion of mental text to, among other things, the scribal practices of translation. Instead of moving word by word, translators oftentimes moved segment by segment, reading aloud and retaining a segment in short term memory, a process that necessarily required moving through the text multiple times. Screnock also acknowledges the complications introduced by a scribe's prior knowledge of the text/tradition,[7] which also have implications for the sequence in which the material is thought.

If the idea of a mental text is applied to the compositional process—and, in particular, to the process of revisionary composition, which is in many respects comparable to translation (and, more precisely, *intralingual* translation)[8]—it is possible to move beyond a strictly sequential assessment of scribal fatigue. In planning their works, I would suggest that revisionary authors necessarily created something like a mental text; indeed, it seems likely that they did so repeatedly, both at the global and the local levels. If this assessment is correct, the move from innovation to parroting need not be limited to a straightforward progression from beginning to end. Intermediate steps, and, in particular, the non-sequential nature and iterative procedure of planning, afford significant opportunity to introduce problematic elements into a revisionary work. Viewed in this manner, "before and after" in the compositional process becomes a more complex issue: while a written narrative will indeed have a beginning, middle, and end, as will the episodes within it, it will not necessarily be *thought* in that order in its production—or only in that order, or only once.

---

6 John Screnock, *Traductor Scriptor: The Old Greek Translation of Exodus 1–14 as Scribal Activity*, VTSup 176 (Leiden: Brill, 2017), 76.

7 Screnock, *Traductor Scriptor*, 80–82.

8 See esp. John Screnock, "Translation and Rewriting in the Genesis Apocryphon," in *Reading the Bible in Ancient Traditions and Modern Editions: Studies in Memory of Peter W. Flint*, ed. Andrew B. Perrin, Kyung S. Baek, and Daniel K. Falk (Atlanta: SBL Press, 2017), 453–81; idem, "Is Rewriting Translation?: Chronicles and Jubilees in Light of Intralingual Translation," *VT* 68 (2018): 475–504. Screnock seeks to distinguish between two types of rewriting—small scale ("editing/rewording") and large scale ("extending")—and sees correlations between the former and translation.

A final issue to raise here relates to Goodacre's general statement, "Editorial fatigue is a phenomenon that will inevitably occur when a writer is heavily dependent on another's work."[9] Yet one might ask, Is fatigue indeed inevitable? At least in the manner that Goodacre imagines it, my cautious answer is "no." For example, texts such as Deuteronomy or Chronicles—both texts that exhibit a high level of literary dependence upon source material and in this way are quite similar to the synoptic gospels—do exhibit fatigue, but only infrequently.[10] While an explanation for such occasional appearance is not necessarily forthcoming, it does suggest that scribal fatigue is not an inexorable feature of revisionary composition. This point is important because the non-systematic appearance of fatigue may offer some insight into both those instances when it does occur—or occur *in a particular way*—and those in which it does not.

2 An Expanded View of Fatigue

With these preliminary remarks in view, I will turn to a number of posited instances of scribal fatigue from the Hebrew Bible, some of which will capitalize on and exemplify the proposals for broadening the definition of fatigue that I have suggested. Yet before doing so, it is worth observing that fatigue can also be observed in non-biblical, ancient Near Eastern revisionary texts.

2.1 Atrahasis in Gilgamesh Tablet 11

One such instance is well-known from the eleventh tablet of the Epic of Gilgamesh, whose account of the Flood was derived from the earlier Atrahasis myth. The name of the character who survived the Flood in Gilgamesh tablet 11 is *Utanapishtim*, likely meaning "he found life." In the Atrahasis myth, by contrast, the survivor of the Flood is *Atrahasis*, meaning "exceedingly wise." The renaming of this character in the Gilgamesh Epic is unproblematic, of course; revision in ancient literary reuse is a commonplace. What is surprising and potentially difficult

9 Goodacre, "Fatigue," 46.
10 Note that Goulder explicitly compares the gospel of Matthew with texts such as Deuteronomy, Chronicles, and the pentateuchal Priestly source, grouping them all in a somewhat imprecisely defined category of midrash. See Goulder, *Midrash and Lection*, 28–46.

in this instance is the rare occurrence of the name *Atrahasis* in the Gilgamesh text to refer to the character otherwise known there as *Utanapishtim.*

Twice in Gilgamesh tablet 11 Utanapishtim is called Atrahasis. The first instance is in line 49, which appears as part of the preparation for building the boat that would preserve Utanapishtim through the Flood:[11]

> 48 *mimmû šēri ina namāri*
> 49 *ana bāb atarḫasīs ipaḫḫur mā[tum]*
> 50 *naggāru naši pas[su]*
> 51 *atkuppu naši ab[aššu]*
> 48 At the first shining of morning light,
> 49 At the gate of Atrahasis the land assembled,
> 50 The carpenter was carrying his hatchet,
> 51 The reed-craftsman was carrying his stone...

The second such instance is in line 197, which is part of the god Ea's speech to an enraged Enlil after Enlil learned of Utanapishtim's survival of the Flood:[12]

> 196 *anāku ul aptâ pirišti ilī rabûti*
> 197 *atraḫasīs šunāta ušabrīšum-ma pirišti ilī išme*
> 198 *eninnā-ma milikšu milku*
> 196 I did not reveal the secret of the great gods directly:
> 197 I made Atrahasis see dreams; thus he learned the gods' secret.
> 198 Now make a decision concerning him!

Apart from these two examples, the survivor of the Flood in Gilgamesh is consistently called Utanapishtim.

In the case of its second appearance (l. 197), it is possible to argue that Atrahasis ("exceedingly wise") is not properly a name but an epithet applied to Utanapishtim. Ea employs the appellation "Atrahasis" when describing the special knowledge of the Flood that he disclosed to Utanapishtim. In a sense, then, Utanapishtim became, in comparison with other humans, *exceedingly wise*, and it was this special wisdom (here called a divine secret) that allowed him to survive the Flood.

In the first appearance of Atrahasis in Gilgamesh tablet 11 (l. 49), the situation is different. There is no contextual explanation for its use and thus no reason to assume that it is a special epithet for Utanapishtim. Even more significantly,

---

11 For the text, see A. R. George, *The Babylonian Gilgamesh Epic: Introduction, Critial Edition and Cuneiform Texts*, 2 vols. (Oxford: Oxford University Press, 2003), 1: 706 (translation is my own).
12 For the text, see George, *Babylonian Gilgamesh Epic*, 1: 716.

literary factors in this case suggest that the appearance of Atrahasis is the result of scribal fatigue. As Andrew George has noted in his commentary,

> From a literary point of view Uta-napishti's self-reference in the third person does not sit well with the use of the first person in the rest of the narration; it is perhaps an indication that the adaptation of the story was not carried out as expertly as it might have been.[13]

What George has identified as inexpert adaptation in the Gilgamesh text, I would submit, is an example of fatigue. Gilgamesh tablet 11 contains a dialogue between Gilgamesh and Utanapishtim in which Utanapishtim recounts his experience in the first person. However, line 49 offers third person narration—a discourse that is at home in the Atrahasis myth but not in the Gilgamesh epic. Thus, while the author in Gilgamesh mostly succeeded in presenting an internally cohesive revision of the Atrahasis Flood account, the apparent challenge of juggling multiple, interrelated revisions (in this case the name change and the revoicing of the narration) lead to at least one fatigue-induced mistake—an inadvertent parroting of the third person narration of his literary patrimony. Conspicuous, however, is the fact that, if the reference to Atrahasis in line 49 is of a piece with the rest of the Gilgamesh Flood account, the revising author here quickly righted himself, resuming his use of Utanapishtim and first-person narration.

2.2 Forty Years in the Wilderness

There are a number of examples of scribal fatigue in the Hebrew Bible. I will begin with two from the pentateuchal Deuteronomic (D) composition. Owing to its highly learned, revisionary character, D is an ideal locus for examining compositional processes.[14] The first example, D's depiction of Israel's forty-year wilderness journey, points to a more complex process of composition and planning

---

13 George, *Babylonian Gilgamesh Epic*, 2: 880.
14 On the revisionary nature of D and especially its interaction with both legal and non-legal material in Exodus and Numbers, see, e.g., the chapter entitled "Deuteronomy as Interpretation" in Marc Z. Brettler, *The Creation of History in Ancient Israel* (London: Routledge, 1995), 62–78; Eckart Otto, "The Pre-exilic Deuteronomy as a Revision of the Covenant Code," in *Kontinuum und Proprium: Studien zur Sozial- und Rechtsgeschichte des Alten Orients und des Alten Testaments* (Wiesbaden: Harrassowitz, 1996), 112–22; Bernard M. Levinson, *Deuteronomy and the Hermeneutics of Legal Innovation* (New York: Oxford University Press, 1997); vol. 2 of Menahem Haran, *The Biblical Collection: Its Consolidation to the End of the Second Temple Times and Changes of Form to the End of the Middle Ages*, 4 vols. (Jerusalem: Magnes, 1996–2014); Joel S.

than do the gospel examples reviewed above; the second, Moses's exclusion from the land of Canaan, matches a narrower definition of fatigue.

The Deuteronomic presentation of Israel's desert experience exhibits marked correspondences with narratives in Exodus and Numbers that suggest a direct literary connection between them. Recent scholarship has sought to reverse earlier arguments for D's dependence upon the Exodus and Numbers materials and, in some cases, the assignment of those materials to the Yahwistic (J) and Elohistic (E) sources of the Documentary Hypothesis.[15] Even so, in my view the best explanation of the evidence remains that D employed and revised non-Priestly materials now found in Exodus and Numbers and accessed them in the form of long, literary works.

In the case of Israel's wilderness trek, D imagines a prolonged journey from Egypt to Canaan, a view also attested in both the J and P sources. The J account does not specify the precise length of this period; P and D enumerate it as 40 years (P: Num 14:33–34; Deut 1:3; D: Deut 2:7, 14*; 8:2, 4; 29:4).[16] In both J and P—as attested in originally independent accounts now interwoven in Num 13–14—the extension of Israel's wilderness journey is introduced in response to the

---

Baden, *J, E, and the Redaction of the Pentateuch*, FAT 68 (Tübingen: Mohr Siebeck, 2009), 99–195; Kevin Mattison, *Rewriting and Revision as Amendment in the Laws of Deuteronomy*, FAT//II 100 (Tübingen: Mohr Siebeck, 2018).

15 Particularly in the case of Numbers texts, recent scholarship has identified late, post-Priestly reworkings of D texts. For arguments favoring the lateness of the Exodus and Numbers materials in these instances, see, e.g., Reinhard Achenbach, *Die Vollendung der Tora: Studien zur Redaktionsgeschichte des Numeribuches im Kontext von Hexateuch und Pentateuch*, BZABR 3 (Wiesbaden: Harrassowitz, 2002); Christophe Nihan, "'Moses and the Prophets': Deuteronomy 18 and the Emergence of the Pentateuch as Torah," *SEÅ* 75 (2010): 21–55; Rainer Albertz, "Ex 33,7-11, ein Schlüsseltext für die Rekonstruktion der Redaktionsgeschichte des Pentateuch," *BN* 149 (nF) (2011): 13–43. For new argumentation in favor of the opposite direction of dependence, based in part on identifiable patterns of correspondences among the related materials, see, e.g., Joel S. Baden, "The Deuteronomic Evidence for the Documentary Theory," in *The Pentateuch: International Perspectives on Current Research*, ed. Thomas B. Dozeman, Konrad Schmid, and Baruch J. Schwartz, FAT 78 (Tübingen: Mohr Siebeck, 2011), 327–44; Jeffrey Stackert, *A Prophet Like Moses: Prophecy, Law, and Israelite Religion* (New York: Oxford University Press, 2014); Simeon Chavel, "A Kingdom of Priests and its Earthen Altars in Exodus 19–24," *VT* 65 (2015): 169–222.

16 Note that even as D and P both reflect the forty-year duration of Israel's wilderness wandering, the lack of extensive correspondence between their accounts of the spies suggests that there is no direct, literary relationship between these texts. D and P here apparently attest independently a common tradition. For detailed discussion of D's portrayal of Israel's forty years in the wilderness, see Jeffrey Stackert, "The Wilderness Period without Generation Change: The Deuteronomic Portrait of Israel's Forty-Year Journey," *VT* 70 (2020): 696–721.

same event, the spies' mission to Canaan, and serves a punitive purpose.[17] At the command of the deity, Moses sent spies to reconnoiter the land, and they returned to report what they found. This report emphasized the daunting task that they would face if they attempted to take the land as Yahweh had commanded them and their doubts about Israel's ability to accomplish that task. Though Caleb (or, in the case of the P account*, Joshua and Caleb) broke with his (their) fellow spies and advised moving forward, the Israelites were swayed by the majority and despaired that they had ever left Egypt.

Yahweh's response in both J and P is intense anger, with a specific focus on the faithlessness of the spies and the Israelites who heeded them. Yahweh judged the extent of Israel's disloyalty as so great that he decided that none of that generation would be permitted to enter the land that they had rejected. They would instead die in the wilderness, a punishment to be accomplished through their extended traverse (J: Num 14:21–25; P: Num 14:28–35). Once the entire adult population had died off, their children would be permitted to enter the land. The duration of the wilderness wandering was thus set to the length of a full generation—forty years (Num 14:33–34).[18]

For its part, D significantly recasts the wilderness period, even as it maintains elements of its literary inheritance. D's changes include substantial revision of J's spies account in its own rendition of this event (Deut 1:19–46),[19] but its most significant adjustment is to construe the wilderness era not as one of *punishment* for

---

17 The J account in Num 13–14 comprises 13:17b–20, 22–24, 26*–31, 33; 14:1b, 11–25, 39–45. The P account comprises 13:1–16, 17a, 21, 25–26*, 32; 14:1a, 2–10, 26–38. For this source division, see Baden, *J, E, and the Redaction*, 114–17. For recent treatments of posited complexity within these source divisions, see Gili Kugler, "The Threat of Annihilation of Israel in the Desert: An Independent Tradition within Two Stories," *CBQ* 78 (2016): 632–47; Itamar Kislev, "Joshua (and Caleb) in the Priestly Spies Story and Joshua's Initial Appearance in the Priestly Source: A Contribution to an Assessment of the Pentateuchal Priestly Material," *JBL* 136 (2017): 39–55.

18 Note that P correlates the forty years with the forty days of spying (Num 14:34). Even so, the forty years was meant to accomplish the full generation change that Yahweh sought (v. 35; cf. v. 29). For the age range of twenty to sixty as the span of adult vigor, see Lev 27:3, 7. Num 1:3 sets the minimum age for military service at twenty.

19 For treatments of D's spies account, see, e.g., Eckart Otto, *Das Deuteronomium im Pentateuch und Hexateuch: Studien zur Literaturgeschichte von Pentateuch und Hexateuch im Lichte des Deuteronomiumrahmens*, FAT 30 (Tübingen: Mohr Siebeck, 2000), 12–109; Baden, *J, E, and the Redaction*, 114–30. For a recent reevaluation of the relationship between the spies accounts in Num 13–14 and Deut 1:19–46 and reassertion of D's dependence upon the non-Priestly spies account in Num 13–14*, see Gili Kugler, *When God Wanted to Destroy the Chosen People: Biblical Traditions and Theology on the Move*, BZAW 515 (Berlin: deGruyter, 2019), 87–92.

the Israelites but instead as one of *pedagogy* and *preparation*. D treats the wilderness era's purpose explicitly in Deut 8:2–5, a text that also draws from J:[20]

² וזכרת את כל הדרך אשר הליכך יהוה אלהיך זה ארבעים שנה במדבר למען ענתך לנסתך לדעת
את אשר בלבבך התשמר מצותו אם לא ³ ויענך וירעבך ויאכלך את המן אשר לא ידעת ולא ידעון
אבתיך למען הודעך כי לא על הלחם לבדו יחיה האדם כי על כל מוצא פי יהוה יחיה האדם ⁴
שמלתך לא בלתה מעליך ורגלך לא בצקה זה ארבעים שנה ⁵ וידעת עם לבבך כי כאשר ייסר איש
את בנו יהוה אלהיך מיסרך

² You shall remember the entire journey upon which Yahweh, your god, led you these
forty years in the wilderness in order to try you with hardships, that he might know what
your will was—to keep his commands or not. ³ He afflicted you with hunger and then fed
you with the manna that you did not recognize and your ancestors had never known in
order to teach you that a human does not live by bread alone but by every issuance of Yahweh's command. ⁴ Your garments did not wear out, nor did your feet swell these forty years.
⁵ You are thus able to recognize by your own reflection that Yahweh your god has been
disciplining you as a man disciplines his son.[21]

As these verses make clear, the wilderness experience was meant to teach the
Israelites to obey—a preparation that would position them optimally to live in
and keep possession of the land that Yahweh would give them (cf. Deut 4:1; 5:33;
8:1; 16:20; 30:19). This innovation is part of D's larger reconceptualization of the
Horeb revelation of laws, the promulgation of which D postpones until the end
of the Israelites' wilderness journey. In the text that D revised, Israel received

---

20 Dependence upon the J manna account may be observed especially in Deut 8:2, which draws
specific language from Exod 16:4, including in their shared conceptualization of the manna as a
test. For discussion of the composition of Exod 16, see Simeon B. Chavel, "Numbers 15, 32–36: A
Microcosm of the Living Priesthood and Its Literary Production," in *The Strata of the Priestly
Writings: Contemporary Debate and Future Directions*, ed. Sarah Shectman and Joel S. Baden,
AThANT 95 (Zürich: Theologischer Verlag Zürich, 2009), 45–55 (at 48 n 13); Joel S. Baden, "The
Original Place of the Priestly Manna Story in Exodus 16," *ZAW* 122 (2010): 491–504. For an alter-
native view that nonetheless responds to many of the same issues, see Christoph Berner, "Der
Sabbat in der Mannaerzählung Ex 16 und in der priesterlichen Partien des Pentateuch," *ZAW* 128
(2016): 562–78. See additional discussion below.
21 Scholars have debated the composition of Deut 8, sometimes identifying multiple strata
within this text. For discussion of scholarly views and a new proposal, see Timo Veijola, "'Der
Mensch lebt nicht vom Brot allein': Zur literarischen Schichtung und theologischen Aussage von
Deuteronomium 8," in *Bundesdokument und Gesetz: Studien zum Deuteronomium*, ed. Georg
Braulik, HBS 4 (Freiburg: Herder, 1995), 143–58. Veijola identifies vv. 2–6 as the latest stratum
in this text (154–58). Yet these verses are well integrated into, and play an important role in, the
larger argument of D. Removing them creates significant problems for understanding earlier
posited forms of the work, which then casts doubt on the claim that they are late.

these laws while still at Horeb, immediately upon Moses's return from the mountain (Exod 24:3–8, 11bβ).[22] For D, recasting the wilderness era as a preparatory period and delaying the promulgation of the Horeb laws work together: since the Israelites were not yet ready to receive the laws, Moses did not announce them immediately after he received them. He instead waited, relaying the laws to Israel only once they were ready, namely, *after* they had undergone their wilderness training. All of these details point to an underappreciated innovation: in D, the Exodus generation *did not* die off in the desert but was instead miraculously preserved (Deut 2:7; 8:4; 29:4).[23] At the same time, D emphasizes that Israel was horribly rebellious against Yahweh (Deut 9:7, 24), and it is this recalcitrance that warrants an extended training period.

Yet in the midst of D's innovation, one may ask, why *forty* years? As noted already, the tradition of forty years is explicable specifically in relation to the claim of generation change. Once generation change is removed and the wilderness era is recast as a period of preparation, it is unclear why such preparation should last for forty years instead of a different number. For D's purposes, any substantial length of time would serve well. In the end, D offers no rationale for the specific length of time that it claims Israel spent in the wilderness.

This apparent oversight shares much in common with instances of scribal fatigue: the revising author made significant changes to his source's view of the wilderness era, but he did not carry those changes through to all elements of the tradition he was reworking. Indeed, inspired by the generation change tradition, D even specified the duration of Israel's extended sojourn as forty years, a duration left undefined in J (Num 14:22–25).[24] Yet as much as this instance looks like fatigue, it is not easily attributable to the "beginning to end" definition that

---

22 See esp. Chavel, "A Kingdom of Priests."

23 A number of D texts straightforwardly assume the persistence of the Exodus generation. See, e.g., Deut 1:30; 5:3; 6:20–24; 11:2–7; 29:15. Some scholars noticed this persistence of the Exodus generation in D but downplayed or dismissed it (e.g., August Dillmann, *Die Bücher Numeri, Deuteronomium und Josua*, KHAT, 2nd ed. [Leipzig: S. Hirzel, 1886], 239; A. D. H. Mayes, *Deuteronomy*, NCB [London: Marshall, Morgan, and Scott, 1979], 165, 212; Moshe Weinfeld, *Deuteronomy 1–11: A New Translation with Introduction and Commentary*, AB 5 [New York: Doubleday, 1991], 238). This is partially due to Deut 1:35, 39 and 2:14–16. However, these verses contain harmonizing interpolations that secondarily introduce generation change into D. For discussion, see Gili Kugler, "Moses died and the people moved on: A hidden narrative in Deuteronomy," *JSOT* 43 (2019): 191–204 (at 202); Stackert, "Wilderness Period," and bibliography there. See also below for discussion of 1:35.

24 As noted above, P too specifies the length of Israel's wilderness sojourn as forty years. Due to the absence of strong literary ties between the P and D accounts, is likely that they reflect a common tradition rather than a direct, literary connection.

Goodacre offers for this scribal phenomenon. References to the forty years appear several times in D (Deut 2:7; 8:2, 4; 29:4), and D's novel view of the wilderness is assumed in a number of texts that appear prior to its explanation of the period's preparatory function (e.g., Deut 1:19–46; 5:3; 6:21–24). One might consider whether this sequential problem is the result of the redactional history of the text, which is theoretically possible. Yet in this case, a redactional argument does not account well for the evidence. This instance appears rather more like the circus trick of spinning plates: the juggler moves back and forth among plates as they spin on the tops of sticks, seeking to keep them all aloft. Oftentimes a plate falls.

2.3 "On account of you" (Deut 1:37)

The second example from D is related to the first: it is D's explanation for why, even though the Exodus generation would survive their wilderness trek to enter Canaan, Moses would not. As part of his recollection of the spies incident, Moses states,

גם בי התאנף יהוה בגללכם לאמר גם אתה לא תבא שם

But Yahweh was enraged against me on your account and said, "Neither shall you enter there!" (Deut 1:37; cf. 3:26, 4:21)

This line is striking in several respects. Neither it specifically, nor its general sentiment, appears in D's source material—the spies account from J. Indeed, J never characterizes Moses's non-entry into the land as a punishment. P does, but it does so in relation to the water-from-the-rock incident in Num 20 (see v. 12), not the spies incident. Moreover, as noted already, in D the Israelites are not punished for their faithlessness in response to the spies. The Exodus generation instead persists through the wilderness period owing to Yahweh's consistent care. It is only the spies themselves who are punished, according to D[25]—a detail preserved in the LXX of Deut 1:35 but obscured by a late interpolation in the MT of this verse (with the relevant plus marked):

MT: אם יראה איש באנשים האלה <u>הדור הרע הזה</u> את הארץ הטובה אשר נשבעתי לתת לאבתיכם

---

[25] In P the entire Exodus generation of adults are punished (Num 14:29–35), as are the spies specifically (Num 14:36–38). Yet note that the spies die immediately by plague. D includes no such plague, suggesting that the spies will die slowly over time, as all of the Israelite adults do in J.

LXX: Εἰ ὄψεταί τις τῶν ἀνδρῶν τούτων τὴν γῆν τὴν ἀγαθὴν ταύτην, ἣν ὤμοσα τοῖς πατράσιν ὑμῶν

No one from among these men, this evil generation, shall see the good land that I swore to give to your ancestors.[26]

Given D's unique storyline, where the spies are punished while the Israelites are left unpunished, Deut 1:37 is difficult to explain. Why should Yahweh be so upset with Moses on account of the Israelites to bar him from entering Canaan—especially when Yahweh decided not to punish the Israelites?[27] Verse 37 would perhaps make more sense if Moses had reported that Yahweh's anger was on account of the spies' discouraging testimony, but among the Israelites listening to Moses's valedictory address in D, it is *only* the spies who are absent, having died off during the wilderness trek. The spies thus cannot be among Moses's addressees in Deut 1:37. Moreover, Deut 1:34 makes the same point: Yahweh was incensed when he heard *your words*—words that D attributes to the Israelites addressed by Moses and not to the spies (Deut 1:27–28).

For reasons such as these, some scholars have argued that Deut 1:37 is a late interpolation.[28] Yet this solution may not be necessary. The verse can also be explained in light of the J text that D here revises. According to Num 14:11–25, Yahweh despaired over the Israel's faithlessness and, had it not been for Moses's intervention, Yahweh would have totally destroyed the people (14:12, 15). Yet Moses was not entirely successful in his plea: though he agreed not to destroy the people immediately, Yahweh insisted that the Exodus generation should not enter the land (14:22–23). D's revisionary composition in Deut 1:35–36 tracks the J text of Num 14:22–23 very closely. The preceding J section (Num 14:11–21), however, is mostly omitted from D:

---

26 For discussion of this plus, see, e.g., Dillmann, *Numeri, Deuteronomium und Josua*, 239; Carl Steuernagel, *Übersetzung und Erklärung der Bücher Deuteronomium und Josua: und allgemeine Einleitung in den Hexateuch*, HAT 1.3 (Göttingen: Vandenhoeck & Ruprecht, 1900), 6; Stephen Germany, *The Exodus-Conquest Narrative: The Composition of the Non-Priestly Narratives in Exodus-Joshua*, FAT 115 (Tübingen: Mohr Siebeck, 2017), 217; Stackert, "Wilderness Period," 709–10.

27 Deut 3:25–26 take up this topic again, narrating the disagreement between Moses and Yahweh over Yahweh's decision. It is possible that 3:25–26 are the response to a perceived theological problem in 1:37: why should Moses be punished for Israel's faithlessness? The response in 3:26 is an appeal to the inscrutability of the deity. 4:21 offers no further insight on the issue.

28 For alternative treatments of this line, including the suggestion that it is an interpolation, see Mayes, *Deuteronomy*, 132, 147; Otto, *Das Deuteronomium im Pentateuch und Hexateuch*, esp. 22–24, 135; Kugler, "Moses died," 195–98.

Num 14:11	Deut 1:32, 34
Num 14:14	Deut 1:33
Num 14:12–13, 15–21	∅
Num 14:22–23	Deut 1:35
Num 14:24	Deut 1:36
∅	Deut 1:37

It nonetheless appears that D was influenced by the J material it did not reproduce. Specifically, D carried over Yahweh's intense anger with Israel, employing it as the basis for Moses's exclusion from entering Canaan. In so doing, D overlooked its earlier innovation, namely, its elimination of Israelite punishment. If this analysis is correct, D here exhibits fatigue much like that observable elsewhere: an innovation in the work (non-punishment of the Israelites) is followed by a docile reproduction of details from the literary patrimony ("on account of you") at odds with the earlier innovation. The result is a dubious claim to vicarious punishment—one that departs significantly from the theological perspectives expressed elsewhere in D and for which no alternative explanation is included.[29]

Ironically, this instance of fatigue may arise as part of an attempt to clarify a detail that D understood to be implicit in Num 14:24:

ועבדי כלב עקב היתה רוח אחרת עמו וימלא אחרי והביאתיו אל הארץ אשר בא שמה וזרעו יורשנה
> But as for my servant, Caleb, because he had a different spirit and was fully committed to me, I will bring him to the land that he entered, and his offspring will possess it.

If, among the Exodus generation, Caleb alone was to survive to enter into Canaan, where did this leave Moses? It appears that D finds in Num 14:24's exception for Caleb (and the larger expression of divine anger that attends it) a rationale for Moses's non-entry into the land: if Yahweh said that only Caleb would

---

29 For treatment of D's retributive theology and its various expressions, see, e.g., John G. Gammie, "The Theology of Retribution in the Book of Deuteronomy," *CBQ* 32 (1970): 1–12. It is important to note that in at least one instance, D does attest a type of vicarious punishment, viz., in the Decalogue's intergenerational punishment (Deut 5:9–10). Yet this is an instance of *partial* rather than complete vicarious punishment (as in D's spies story source; see Num 14:14–23) and thus unlike that required by Deut 1:37. It is also part of D's inheritance (Exod 20:5–6; cf. Num 14:18) that it apparently did not operationalize more broadly in its theological construction. For discussion of intergenerational punishment, see esp. Yochanan Muffs, *Love and Joy: Law, Language, and Religion in Ancient Israel* (New York: Jewish Theological Seminary of America, 1992), 16–22.

enter, Moses could not. This detail is especially important for D because of D's elimination of Israelite generation change. Without Num 14:24, why should Moses *not* enter the land? It seems that D knew the tradition of Moses's exclusion from the land (probably from J, Deut 34:4–5*);[30] through an interpretation of Num 14:24, D could also explain it—and in light of its elimination of generation change, D *needed* to explain it.

2.4 The Tithe in H

A third biblical example is found in the tithe law in Numbers 18, which belongs to the so-called Holiness (H) stratum of the pentateuchal Priestly source.[31] Like the forty years in the wilderness, this example is notable for its potential to contribute to an expanded notion of scribal fatigue. The tithe is conspicuously absent from the earlier, P stratum of the Priestly source: P contains no tithe law; nor does it ever refer to the tithe. In its expansion of P, H introduces the tithe and offers

---

30 For the ascription of parts of Deut 34:4–5 to J, see Joel S. Baden, *The Composition of the Pentateuch: Renewing the Documentary Hypothesis*, AYBRL (New Haven/London: Yale University Press, 2012), 56, 147–48.

31 On the identification of Num 18 as H, see esp. Israel Knohl, *The Sanctuary of Silence: The Priestly Torah and the Holiness School*, trans. Jackie Feldman and Peretz Rodman (Minneapolis: Fortress, 1995), 53–54, 72–73; Jeffrey Stackert, *Rewriting the Torah: Literary Revision in Deuteronomy and the Holiness Legislation*, FAT 52 (Tübingen: Mohr Siebeck, 2007), 191–98. In my view, H is a supplement, revision, and expansion of the earlier Priestly (P) source, and its boundaries are not limited to Lev 17–26, the "Holiness Code" (*Heiligkeitsgesetz*). H sought to create a combined P+H that, especially by drawing from and reformulating material from other law collections now found in the Torah, would supplant those alternative law collections and the narrative histories of which they are a part. See Stackert, *Rewriting the Torah*; idem, "The Holiness Legislation and its Pentateuchal Sources: Revision, Supplementation, and Replacement," in *The Strata of the Priestly Writings: Contemporary Debate and Future Directions*, ed. Sarah Shectman and Joel S. Baden, AThANT 95 (Zürich: Theologischer Verlag Zürich, 2009), 187–204; idem, "Distinguishing Innerbiblical Exegesis from Pentateuchal Redaction: Leviticus 26 as a Test Case," in *The Pentateuch: International Perspectives on Current Research*, ed. Thomas B. Dozeman, Konrad Schmid, and Baruch J. Schwartz, FAT 78 (Tübingen: Mohr Siebeck, 2011), 369–86. For alternative arguments that identify H as a/the pentateuchal redactor, see, e.g., Eckart Otto, "Das Heiligkeitsgesetz Leviticus 17–26 in der Pentateuchredaktion," in *Altes Testament, Forschung und Wirkung: Festschrift für Henning Graf Reventlow*, ed. Peter Mommer and Winfred Thiel (Frankfurt am Main/New York: P. Lang, 1994), 65–80; Knohl, *Sanctuary of Silence*, 101–103; Christophe Nihan, *From Priestly Torah to Pentateuch: A Study in the Composition of the Book of Leviticus*, FAT/II 25 (Tübingen: Mohr Siebeck, 2007), 548–59.

several instructions concerning its distribution and proper handling. I have argued elsewhere that it does so under the influence of the Deuteronomic tithe law in Deut 14:22–29. Indeed, this is one of several examples of apparent reuse of Deuteronomic legal material by H.[32] Significant for this discussion of the tithe is the consistent pattern in H's legal revisions of D. H frames its laws not as updates, revisions, or addendums to D's laws; in fact, H never acknowledges the existence of D's laws at all (which it could do, for example, through cross-references, explicit citation, and the like). H instead takes pains to frame its laws in exclusivist terms, using labels such as חקת עולם ("a perpetual statute") and its expanded formulation, חקת עולם לדרתיכם בכל משבתיכם ("a perpetual statute for your generations in all your habitations"), to characterize its legislation, thus presenting its laws as irrevocable and universally applicable among the Israelites. To the extent that H's laws contravene D's, then, D's must be set aside (at least in H's view).[33]

The case of H's tithe, then, is striking, for it omits the basic requirement that all Israelites present a tithe, skipping over this detail to focus instead on the rights of the Levites and priests to particular tithe portions. Yet H also clearly assumes that the requirement to tithe applies to all Israelites. For example, Num 18:26 states,

ואל הלוים תדבר ואמרת אלהם כי תקחו מאת בני ישראל את המעשר אשר נתתי לכם מאתם בנחלתכם והרמתם ממנו תרומת יהוה מעשר מן המעשר

Now to the Levites you shall speak, saying to them, "When you take from the Israelites the tithe that I have given to you as your inheritance, you shall offer up from it as an offering to Yahweh a tithe from the tithe."

This verse, and the surrounding section of laws to which it belongs, characterizes the tithe as Levitical wages—a necessity for survival—and requires of the Levites a tithe akin to the tithe offered by lay Israelites. It may thus be concluded that H really did intend all Israelites to offer a tithe—a statutory requirement like the many others that it offers explicitly. But in this case, H includes no such law.

---

[32] See, *inter alia*, Eckart Otto, "Innerbiblische Exegese im Heiligkeitsgesetz Levitikus 17–26," in *Levitikus als Buch*, ed. H.-J. Fabry and H.-W. Jüngling, BBB 119 (Berlin: Philo, 1999), 125–96; Christophe Nihan, "The Holiness Code between D and P: Some Comments on the Function and Significance of Leviticus 17–26 in the Composition of the Pentateuch," in *Das Deuteronomium zwischen Pentateuch und Deuteronomistischem Geschichtswerk*, ed. Eckart Otto and Reinhard Achenbach, FRLANT 206 (Göttingen: Vandenhoeck & Ruprecht, 2004), 81–122; Stackert, *Rewriting the Torah*.

[33] Stackert, "The Holiness Legislation and Its Pentateuchal Sources," 196.

What would such a law look like? The opening instruction in the Deuteronomic tithe unit is a good candidate. Deut 14:22 states,

עשר תעשר את כל תבואת זרעך היצא השדה שנה שנה

You shall set aside each year a tenth-part from all of the produce of your seed that comes from the field.

That H apparently knew and employed D's tithe law as a source for its own legislation on this topic makes H's omission especially striking. It might be concluded, then, that H carried through its revision of D across its tithe legislation *with the exception of its beginning*, where it omitted the basic requirement for all Israelites to tithe.[34]

In this instance, I would argue that the issues of compositional planning and mental text that I discussed earlier offer a way to explain this unit-initial omission and allow the categorization of this example as a kind of scribal fatigue. That is, even though the inconsistency introduced appears at the beginning of the unit rather than its end, it is an oversight of the revisionary author that creates the difficulty in the derivative composition.[35] Yet if this is the case, the error in this instance may also be characterized differently. That is, it might be diagnosed not as the result of fatigue but of *exuberance*: in his excitement to revise the procedures for the tithe, the author arguably moved too quickly to these details and overlooked the need for a basic tithe law.[36] Even so, depending on how the material was thought—and *for how long* it was thought—it might also be identified as a case of fatigue.

---

34 For the view that H's omission of a basic tithe law indicates the intent that it be included alongside D in a compiled Pentateuch, see Christophe Nihan, "The Priestly Laws of Numbers, the Holiness Legislation, and the Pentateuch," in *Torah and the Book of Numbers*, ed. Christian Frevel, Thomas Pola, and Aaron Schart, FAT/II 62 (Tübingen: Mohr Siebeck, 2013), 109–37 (esp. 120–32).

35 Note that Goodacre considers examples with omissions early in a unit that create inconcinnities in relation to material later reproduced from a source. Yet Goodacre vacillates between characterizing the initial omissions as intentional vs. unintentional ("Fatigue," 49–50). It is difficult to justify a description of these unintentional instances as fatigue in the terms that Goodacre offers.

36 Compare H's revision of P in Exod 31:12–17, where H introduces a command concerning Sabbath observance (v. 13) before the Sabbath itself is introduced and defined (v. 15). For discussion, see Jeffrey Stackert, "Compositional Strata in the Priestly Sabbath Law: Exodus 31:12–17 and 35:1–3," *Journal of Hebrew Scriptures* 11 (2011), article 15 (online: https://jhsonline.org/index.php/jhs/article/view/16438).

The tithe case also deviates from examples from the gospels in another respect: in the New Testament examples, problematic elements are carried over from the literary patrimony and included in the revisionary text but not fully integrated there. In the Holiness tithe, I am identifying an element of the parent text that was *not* carried over but should have been. Yet this difference is not so great: an omission from a revisionary work, such as H's failure to include a requirement to tithe, functions very similarly to infelicitous inclusions in a rewritten work and is profitably understood in relation to them.

2.5 The Pentateuchal Compiler's Repositioning of the Priestly Manna Account

A final example (or variation) of scribal fatigue is found in Exod 16 or, more precisely, part of Exod 16, and moves beyond the bounds of composition to another scribal activity—that of compilation. This chapter is an interwoven text that combines the J and P accounts of Yahweh's gift of manna in the wilderness. It is significant for this case to observe that the common practice of the pentateuchal compiler when combining texts was to maintain the sequence of the original source texts in his sequencing of their parts in the newly interwoven work.[37] This means that, even though J, E, P, and, to a lesser extent, D, have been broken apart and interspliced with each other, when one of these sources is separated from the rest of the Pentateuch, it needs no resequencing to be read coherently, which is to say, it is ordered as it was when it existed as an independent literary document. This is because the sequence of the compiled Pentateuch generally follows the sequence of its underlying sources—a sequence that is remarkably consistent across these different documents.

There are, however, occasional exceptions. That is, there are instances in which corresponding events in the pentateuchal sources are located at different points in an otherwise shared fabula. In such instances, the compiler breaks from his convention of maintaining the original sequence of a source. The Priestly manna account in Exod 16* is one such instance. There is good internal evidence from this account to suggest that its original position was not where it occurs presently in the larger pentateuchal timeline—in the wilderness prior to the Israelites arrival at Sinai—but instead after the account of the spies in Num 13–14*—

---

37 See Baruch J. Schwartz, "How the Compiler of the Pentateuch Worked: The Composition of Genesis 37," in *The Book of Genesis: Composition, Reception, and Interpretation*, ed. C. A. Evans et al., VTSup 152 (Leiden: Brill, 2012), 263–278.

in the wilderness, but *after* the departure from Sinai. For example, Exod 16:35 references the Israelites' forty years in the desert, even though it is only in Num 14:33–34, a moment in the plotline long after this one, that the people are sentenced to this period of wilderness wandering. Likewise, Exod 16:34 reports that Aaron placed a memorial jar of manna before the עדת, an object that, according to P, God gave the Israelites at Sinai (Exod 31:18)[38]—again, long after the moment narrated in Exod 16.[39]

What happened in this instance? The compiler prioritized the timeline of one source's manna account—here, J's account—and repositioned the Priestly account in order to create a single account—and thus a single event—out of the two manna narratives he had. Yet once he did so, he did not make additional changes to the Priestly description of Yahweh's gift of the עדת to the Israelites to address the anachronisms created by moving the manna account. He could have, for example, repositioned the gift of the עדת to a moment prior to the manna account in Exod 16 or made some other harmonizing change, but he did not. He instead maintained the original chronology of the עדת gift when he carried it over. This instance might thus be characterized as one of scribal fatigue: an innovation made earlier in the work is not carried through later in the work, where the original, (now) discrepant claims of the source text are maintained.

Yet this example also differs from those in the gospels in two important respects. First, it occurs in a case in which the revisionary work does not include newly penned material. The Pentateuch is instead a case of combining and reordering existing texts, not writing new material. The result, however, is definitely a new and substantially derivative literary work. Second, in all of the examples of scribal fatigue examined thus far, and in the New Testament examples, too,

---

38 For discussion of the gift of the עדת in P, see esp. Baruch J. Schwartz, "The Priestly Account of the Theophany and Lawgiving at Sinai," in *Texts, Temples, and Traditions: A Tribute to Menahem Haran*, ed. Michael V. Fox et al. (Winona Lake, Ind.: Eisenbrauns, 1996), 103–34 (esp. 115–16).

39 See Baden, "Original Place," 496–98. See also Simeon Chavel, *Oracular Law and Priestly Historiography in the Torah*, FAT/II (Tübingen: Mohr Siebeck, 2014), 20 n 51, which augments Baden's argument. In a subsequent article, Baden has suggested that the Priestly manna account was originally situated between Num 15:16 and 17. In this position, this story would introduce the law of the first-baked offering in Num 15:17–21 and serve as a focal point in the structure and logic of Num 15 as a whole (Joel S. Baden, "The Structure and Substance of Numbers 15," *VT* 63 [2013]: 351–67 [at 354–57]). On the relationship among the manna, the Sabbath, and Priestly compositional layers, see Jeffrey Stackert, "How the Priestly Sabbaths Work: Innovation in Pentateuchal Priestly Ritual," in *Ritual Innovation in the Hebrew Bible and Ancient Judaism*, ed. Nathan MacDonald, BZAW 468 (Berlin: Walter de Gruyter, 2016), 79–111 (esp. 100–104).

the assumption is that the revisionary author would have preferred to avoid the infelicity created by fatigue if he had been able to do so. Yet I would suggest that in this respect too the case of the pentateuchal compiler is different: the compiler was apparently not concerned to harmonize discrepancies in the work he was creating. This disregard is manifest in the compiler's combination of conflicting material originating from different sources; it can also be observed in the compiler's occasional reordering of material from a single source, as with the Priestly manna account.

3 The Effects of Scribal Fatigue upon Readers

Though there are more biblical examples that fit, at least in part, the definition of scribal fatigue, I will forego them and conclude with a consideration of the impact of fatigue on readers, the reading process, and, by extension, the compositional process. A striking characteristic of the examples that I have discussed as well as those identified in the synoptic gospels is their relatively modest effect upon readers. This is not to claim that the problems observed are not there, are not real, or are not important; it is instead to observe something about the reading process—and, insofar as revisionary composition includes a reading process as a fundamental part of it, the compositional process. To this end, I will examine some social scientific evidence that sheds light on why so many readers do not observe or are not bothered by fatigue-induced problems in biblical texts. I have previously applied this data to the duplications, contradictions, and discontinuities created by the compilation of the Torah,[40] but it is also relevant for understanding instances of fatigue in revisionary composition.

Social scientists have done extensive research on the process of reading and the ability of readers to recognize and process internal discrepancies within texts. Some of the example texts that these researchers present to their test subjects contain inconsistencies that are strongly reminiscent of those observable in biblical texts, including those attributable to scribal fatigue. What these experiments

---

[40] Jeffrey Stackert, "Pentateuchal Coherence and the Science of Reading," in *The Formation of the Pentateuch: Bridging the Academic Cultures of Europe, Israel, and North America*, ed. Jan C. Gertz et al., FAT 111 (Tübingen: Mohr Siebeck, 2016), 253–68. For further discussion of issues of coherence in ancient texts and partial response to this article, see now Andrew Teeter and William Tooman, "Standards of (In)coherence in Ancient Jewish Literature," *HBAI* 9 (2020): 94–129; Michael A. Lyons, "Local Incoherence, Global Coherence?: Allusion and the Readability of Ancient Israelite Literature," *OTE* 34 (2021): 141–64.

have shown is that, even when inconsistencies are separated from each other in a text by several sentences or paragraphs, readers can detect them. For example, when presented with a story that introduces its main character as a strict vegetarian who is very concerned about their health, but that later describes (with no attendant explanation) that same character as ordering a cheeseburger and fries in a restaurant, researchers find that readers are able to observe the discrepancy in characterization. This is determined by measuring the reading times of test subjects; readers slow by approximately 15% when they read the discrepant sentence.[41]

Yet psychologists have demonstrated that readers also overlook discrepancies and, in some cases, very blatant ones. The best demonstration of this phenomenon may be "The Moses Illusion" experiment. This experiment poses to participants the question, "How many animals of each kind did Moses take on the ark?" (as well as other, similarly problematic questions). The Moses question is only answerable if the test subject has prior knowledge of the biblical Flood story, but with that knowledge, the substitution of Moses for Noah should make the question nonsensical. Yet researchers consistently find that test subjects do not observe the discrepancy in this question. Even when various controls are introduced into the testing—for example, for participant compliance, incomplete encoding, mode of reception, phonological similarity between the correct and discrepant term, participant expectations, focus, and verbal articulation of the text with the discrepant term—test subjects regularly fail to detect the inconsistency.[42]

There are limits, however, to the distortion that test subjects will tolerate. These limits oftentimes (though not always) relate to word meanings. The semantic relationship between the discrepant and expected terms is an important predictor of the illusion. Thus, for example, in the Flood example, test subjects regularly fail to detect distortion when names of biblical characters are substituted

---

41 J. E. Albrecht and E. J. O'Brien, "Updating a Mental Model: Maintaining Both Local and Global Coherence," *Journal of Experimental Psychology: Learning, Memory, and Cognition* 19 (1993): 1061–70 (at 1064).

42 T. D. Erickson and M. E. Mattson, "From Words to Meaning: A Semantic Illusion," *Journal of Verbal Learning and Verbal Behavior* 20 (1981): 540–51; E. N. Kamas, L. M. Reder, and M. S. Ayers, "Partial Matching in the Moses Illusion: Response Bias Not Sensitivity," *Memory and Cognition* 24 (1996): 687–99; H. Park and L. M. Reder, "Moses Illusion: Implications for Human Cognition," in *Cognitive Illusions*, ed. R. F. Pohl (Hove: Psychology Press, 2004), 275–91. For discussion of the Moses Illusion in relation to the coherence of biblical texts (with special focus on the book of Judges), see Marc Zvi Brettler, "The 'Coherence' of Ancient Texts," in *Gazing on the Deep: Ancient Near Eastern and Other Studies in Honor of Tzvi Abusch*, ed. Jeffrey Stackert, Barbara Nevling Porter, and David P. Wright (Bethesda, Md.: CDL Press, 2010), 411–19.

for Noah (e.g., Adam, Abraham, Moses). By contrast, all test subjects recognize the distortion in the question, "How many animals of each kind did Nixon take on the ark?" Other points of relatedness between the distorted term and the larger context in which it appears similarly increase the occurrence of the illusion.[43]

One explanation for the Moses Illusion relates its occurrence to a general model of human cognition based on "partial matching." According to this model, new data—words, sentences, and ideas—are introduced into an existing network of information in a person's memory. A person makes matches between various aspects of the new data and the information in existing memory, and once a threshold of overlap is reached, even inconsistent data is perceived as coherent.[44] According to this model, it is human nature to "do a 'sloppy' job of matching"— probably because of the benefits that partial matching affords.[45] People regularly encounter incomplete information and must draw inferences on the basis of it. If they fail to do so, they may not respond adequately to that information, which may disadvantage them.[46] Moreover, research shows that complete information is usually unnecessary for successful communication. In spite of the ambiguities that attend them, both underspecified expression and underinformed interpretation operate very effectively in real communication situations.[47]

Underinformed cognition expresses a prior assumption about the meaningfulness of stimuli. In the context of reading, it suggests that readers exhibit a natural bias toward finding coherence in texts. It also suggests that *finding* coherence does not necessarily correlate with a text's *actual* internal consistency. Psychologists conducting Moses Illusion experiments do not determine whether details in their prompts are contradictory or noncontradictory based on their test subjects' ability to recognize discrepancy. They even have empirical evidence that recommends against doing so. When researchers have confronted their test subjects with unobserved discrepancies (e.g., the reference to Moses rather than Noah as the Flood story's protagonist), those subjects have immediately recognized the problematic element in the questions posed to them. Some have even expressed surprise at having failed to detect the discrepancy.[48]

---

43 Kamas, Reder, and Ayers, "Partial Matching in the Moses Illusion," 688, 697; Park and Reder, "Moses Illusion: Implications for Human Cognition," 282–84.
44 Park and Reder, "Moses Illusion," 285–86.
45 Park and Reder, "Moses Illusion," 281, 285.
46 Kamas, Reder, and Ayers, "Partial Matching in the Moses Illusion," 698.
47 A. J. Sanford and P. Sturt, "Depth of Processing in Language Comprehension: Not Noticing the Evidence," *TRENDS in Cognitive Sciences* 6 (2002): 382–86.
48 Erickson and Mattson, "From Words to Meaning," 541.

To apply these findings to scribal fatigue, I would suggest that even as fatigue-induced discrepancies in biblical texts function as a clue to their compositional history and, in particular, their use of source material, the damage they do to a text's internal cohesion does not significantly affect readers' ability to create coherence in the reading process—whether readers consciously observe inconsistencies or not. This is likely due to the more general phenomenon of partial matching in cognition, a phenomenon that extends to the reading process. Put differently, even texts that exhibit fatigue-induced infelicities display enough cohesion that their readers are able to make sense of them. Thus, the use of the title "king" instead of "tetrarch" in Matthew, or the use of the name "Atrahasis" rather than "Utanapishtim" in the Gilgamesh Epic, does little to lead a reader off course, especially given the high level of consistency otherwise attested in these works. Just as the Gilgamesh author quickly got back on track after his error, so too does this text's reader. In the case of "king" and "tetrarch," the fact that these titles can be associated under the umbrella category of "ruler" may make disregarding the discrepancy even easier.

As for D's failure to explain why Israel's wilderness sojourn was forty years and not some other length, this is arguably a problem only observable by a reader comparing the different wilderness traditions; there is really no need in D to explain the significance of this length of time as opposed to some other duration. A similar claim can be made for the tithe laws in Num 18: even if the larger pentateuchal Priestly composition has omitted a basic command requiring all Israelites to tithe, it is clear that Num 18 presumes such a requirement. It can thus be inferred from its laws with little difficulty.

At the same time, it is also clear that fatigue-induced discrepancies are not always simply overlooked. In fact, the reception history of biblical texts suggests that these discrepancies have sometimes become special loci for interpretation. The example of בגללכם in Deut 1:37 is one such instance. Interpreters have long puzzled over how to make sense of Moses's exclusion from the land in this verse, and they have in some instances offered solutions that amount to partial matches. In cases of anachronism such as that in Exod 16*, interpreters worked harder, developing extraordinary interpretive principles such as אין מוקדם ומאוחר בתורה, "There is no chronology in the Torah," which acknowledges the problem of chronological inconsistency precisely by asserting its nonexistence.[49]

---

49 See, e.g., *b. Pesaḥ.* 6b; *Mek. Besh.* 7; *Sipre Num.* 64; *Eccl. Rab.* 1:12. On the origin and various meanings and applications of this rabbinic dictum, see, e.g., Rimon Kasher, "The Interpretation of Scripture in Rabbinic Literature," in *Mikra: Text, Translation, Reading and Interpretation of the Hebrew Bible in Ancient Judaism and Early Christianity*, ed. Martin Jan Mulder (Van Gorcum:

The fact that readers have been able to satisfy themselves with interpretive solutions to problems of anachronism in pentateuchal narrative is what makes such a principle palatable.

Finally, in observing these details, it is possible to see ways that the reading process sheds light on the compositional process. Some instances of fatigue appear to emerge in the "mental text" created by the revisionary scribe when engaging a literary patrimony. In the scribe's act of reading that source it is also transformed: something different than *Vorlage* and derivative composition is created, and that creation, in turn, affects and even guides the revisionary process. This mental text is closely related to both literary patrimony and revisionary composition, yet it is also dissimilar from each. It is this dissimilarity—and the "losing track" that it entails—that produces instances of fatigue. To identify this aspect of the ancient compositional process is to retrieve an important element of scribal practice itself. Accordingly, fatigue stands alongside the many technical, mechanical, and material aspects of writing that individualize and humanize ancient scribes and their work.[50]

4 Bibliography

Achenbach, Reinhard. *Die Vollendung der Tora: Studien zur Redaktionsgeschichte des Numeri-buches im Kontext von Hexateuch und Pentateuch*. BZABR 3. Wiesbaden: Harrassowitz, 2002.

Albertz, Rainer. "Ex 33,7–11, ein Schlüsseltext für die Rekonstruktion der Redaktionsgeschichte des Pentateuch." *BN* 149 (nF) (2011): 13–43.

Albrecht, J. E., and E. J. O'Brien. "Updating a Mental Model: Maintaining Both Local and Global Coherence." *Journal of Experimental Psychology: Learning, Memory, and Cognition* 19 (1993): 1061–70.

Assen/Maastricht; Philadelphia: Fortress, 1988), 547–94 (at 558–60, 590–91). For the debates among the medieval Jewish commentators (e.g., Nahmanides and Abarbanel vs. Rashi and Ibn Ezra) concerning the issue of chronological presentation in the Torah, see Yaakov Elman, "Moses ben Nahman/Nahmanides (Ramban)," in *Hebrew Bible/Old Testament: The History of its Interpretation*, ed. Magne Sæbø; 3 vols. (Göttingen: Vandenhoeck & Ruprecht, 1996), I/2: 416–32 (at 423–27).

50 I wish to express my appreciation to the participants in the conference, "The Scribe in the Biblical World: A Bridge between Scripts, Languages and Cultures," who offered their constructive feedback on this paper. I would especially like to thank Paul Mandel, who served as my respondent at the conference. My Chicago colleague, Simeon Chavel, also offered helpful feedback on an earlier draft of this essay; I am very grateful to him. Any shortcomings that remain here are, of course, entirely my responsibility.

Baden, Joel S. *The Composition of the Pentateuch: Renewing the Documentary Hypothesis.* AYBRL. New Haven/London: Yale University Press, 2012.

Baden, Joel S. "The Deuteronomic Evidence for the Documentary Theory." Pages 327–44 in *The Pentateuch: International Perspectives on Current Research.* Edited by Thomas B. Dozeman, Konrad Schmid, and Baruch J. Schwartz. FAT 78. Tübingen: Mohr Siebeck, 2011.

Baden, Joel S. *J, E, and the Redaction of the Pentateuch.* FAT 68. Tübingen: Mohr Siebeck, 2009.

Baden, Joel S. "The Original Place of the Priestly Manna Story in Exodus 16." *ZAW* 122 (2010): 491–504.

Baden, Joel S. "The Structure and Substance of Numbers 15." *VT* 63 (2013): 351–67.

Berner, Christoph. "Der Sabbat in der Mannaerzählung Ex 16 und in der priesterlichen Partien des Pentateuch." *ZAW* 128 (2016): 562–78.

Brettler, Marc Zvi. "The 'Coherence' of Ancient Texts." Pages 411–19 in *Gazing on the Deep: Ancient Near Eastern and Other Studies in Honor of Tzvi Abusch.* Edited by Jeffrey Stackert, Barbara Nevling Porter, and David P. Wright. Bethesda, MD: CDL Press, 2010.

Brettler, Marc Zvi. *The Creation of History in Ancient Israel.* London: Routledge, 1995.

Chavel, Simeon. "A Kingdom of Priests and its Earthen Altars in Exodus 19–24." *VT* 65 (2015): 169–222.

Chavel, Simeon. *Oracular Law and Priestly Historiography in the Torah.* FAT/II. Tübingen: Mohr Siebeck, 2014.

Chavel, Simeon B. "Numbers 15, 32–36: A Microcosm of the Living Priesthood and Its Literary Production." Pages 45–55 in *The Strata of the Priestly Writings: Contemporary Debate and Future Directions.* Edited by Sarah Shectman and Joel S. Baden. AThANT 95. Zürich: Theologischer Verlag Zürich, 2009.

Dillmann, August. *Die Bücher Numeri, Deuteronomium und Josua.* KHAT. 2nd ed. Leipzig: S. Hirzel, 1886.

Elman, Yaakov. "Moses ben Nahman/Nahmanides (Ramban)." Pages 416–32 in vol. I/2 of *Hebrew Bible/Old Testament: The History of its Interpretation.* Edited by Magne Sæbø. 3 vols. Göttingen: Vandenhoeck & Ruprecht, 1996.

Erickson, T. D., and M. E. Mattson. "From Words to Meaning: A Semantic Illusion." *Journal of Verbal Learning and Verbal Behavior* 20 (1981): 540–51

Gammie, John G. "The Theology of Retribution in the Book of Deuteronomy." *CBQ* 32 (1970): 1–12.

George, A. R. *The Babylonian Gilgamesh Epic: Introduction, Critical Edition and Cuneiform Texts.* 2 vols. Oxford: Oxford University Press, 2003.

Germany, Stephen. *The Exodus-Conquest Narrative: The Composition of the Non-Priestly Narratives in Exodus–Joshua.* FAT 115. Tübingen: Mohr Siebeck, 2017.

Goodacre, Mark. "Fatigue in the Synoptics." *NTS* 44 (1998): 45–58.

Goulder, Michael. *Midrash and Lection in Matthew.* London: SPCK, 1974.

Hägerland, Tobias. "Editorial Fatigue and the Existence of Q." *NTS* 65 (2019): 190–206.

Haran, Menahem. *The Biblical Collection: Its Consolidation to the End of the Second Temple Times and Changes of Form to the End of the Middle Ages.* 4 vols. Jerusalem: Magnes, 1996–2014 (in Hebrew).

Kamas, E. N., L. M. Reder, and M. S. Ayers. "Partial Matching in the Moses Illusion: Response Bias Not Sensitivity." *Memory and Cognition* 24 (1996): 687–99.

Kasher, Rimon. "The Interpretation of Scripture in Rabbinic Literature." Pages 547–94 in *Mikra: Text, Translation, Reading and Interpretation of the Hebrew Bible in Ancient Judaism and Early Christianity*. Edited by Martin Jan Mulder. Van Gorcum: Assen/Maastricht; Philadelphia: Fortress, 1988.

Kislev, Itamar. "Joshua (and Caleb) in the Priestly Spies Story and Joshua's Initial Appearance in the Priestly Source: A Contribution to an Assessment of the Pentateuchal Priestly Material." *JBL* 136 (2017): 39–55.

Knohl, Israel. *The Sanctuary of Silence: The Priestly Torah and the Holiness School*. Translated by Jackie Feldman and Peretz Rodman. Minneapolis: Fortress, 1995.

Kugler, Gili. "The Threat of Annihilation of Israel in the Desert: An Independent Tradition within Two Stories." *CBQ* 78 (2016): 632–47.

Kugler, Gili. "Moses died and the people moved on: A hidden narrative in Deuteronomy." *JSOT* 43 (2019): 191–204.

Kugler, Gili. *When God Wanted to Destroy the Chosen People: Biblical Traditions and Theology on the Move*. BZAW 515. Berlin: de Gruyter, 2019.

Levinson, Bernard M. *Deuteronomy and the Hermeneutics of Legal Innovation*. New York: Oxford University Press, 1997.

Lyons, Michael A. "Local Incoherence, Global Coherence?: Allusion and the Readability of Ancient Israelite Literature." *OTE* 34 (2021): 141–64.

Mattison, Kevin. *Rewriting and Revision as Amendment in the Laws of Deuteronomy*. FAT/II 100. Tübingen: Mohr Siebeck, 2018.

Mayes, A. D. H. *Deuteronomy*. NCB. London: Marshall, Morgan, and Scott, 1979.

Muffs, Yochanan. *Love and Joy: Law, Language, and Religion in Ancient Israel*. New York: Jewish Theological Seminary of America, 1992.

Nihan, Christophe. *From Priestly Torah to Pentateuch: A Study in the Composition of the Book of Leviticus*. FAT/II 25. Tübingen: Mohr Siebeck, 2007.

Nihan, Christophe. "The Holiness Code between D and P: Some Comments on the Function and Significance of Leviticus 17–26 in the Composition of the Pentateuch." Pages 81–122 in *Das Deuteronomium zwischen Pentateuch und Deuteronomistischem Geschichtswerk*. Edited by Eckart Otto and Reinhard Achenbach. FRLANT 206. Göttingen: Vandenhoeck & Ruprecht, 2004.

Nihan, Christophe. "The Priestly Laws of Numbers, the Holiness Legislation, and the Pentateuch." Pages 109–37 in *Torah and the Book of Numbers*. Edited by Christian Frevel, Thomas Pola, and Aaron Schart. FAT/II 62. Tübingen: Mohr Siebeck, 2013.

Nihan, Christophe. "'Moses and the Prophets': Deuteronomy 18 and the Emergence of the Pentateuch as Torah." *SEÅ* 75 (2010): 21–55.

Otto, Eckart. "Das Heiligkeitsgesetz Leviticus 17–26 in der Pentateuchredaktion." Pages 65–80 in *Altes Testament, Forschung und Wirkung: Festschrift für Henning Graf Reventlow*. Edited by Peter Mommer and Winfred Thiel. Frankfurt am Main/New York: P. Lang, 1994.

Otto, Eckart. "The Pre-exilic Deuteronomy as a Revision of the Covenant Code." Pages 112–22 in *Kontinuum und Proprium: Studien zur Sozial- und Rechtsgeschichte des Alten Orients und des Alten Testaments*. Wiesbaden: Harrassowitz, 1996.

Otto, Eckart. *Das Deuteronomium im Pentateuch und Hexateuch: Studien zur Literaturgeschichte von Pentateuch und Hexateuch im Lichte des Deuteronomiumrahmens*. FAT 30. Tübingen: Mohr Siebeck, 2000.

Otto, Eckart. "Innerbiblische Exegese im Heiligkeitsgesetz Levitikus 17–26." Pages 125–96 in *Levitikus als Buch*. Edited by H.-J. Fabry and H.-W. Jüngling. BBB 119. Berlin: Philo, 1999.

Park, H., and L. M. Reder. "Moses Illusion: Implications for Human Cognition." Pages 275–91 in *Cognitive Illusions*. Edited by R. F. Pohl. Hove: Psychology Press, 2004.

Sanford, A. J., and P. Sturt. "Depth of Processing in Language Comprehension: Not Noticing the Evidence." *TRENDS in Cognitive Sciences* 6 (2002): 382–86.

Schwartz, Baruch J. "How the Compiler of the Pentateuch Worked: The Composition of Genesis 37." Pages 263–78 in *The Book of Genesis: Composition, Reception, and Interpretation*. Edited by C. A. Evans et al. VTSup 152. Leiden: Brill, 2012.

Schwartz, Baruch J. "The Priestly Account of the Theophany and Lawgiving at Sinai." Pages 103–34 in *Texts, Temples, and Traditions: A Tribute to Menahem Haran*. Edited by Michael V. Fox et al. Winona Lake, Ind.: Eisenbrauns, 1996.

Screnock, John. "Is Rewriting Translation?: Chronicles and Jubilees in Light of Intralingual Translation." *VT* 68 (2018): 475–504.

Screnock, John. *Traductor Scriptor: The Old Greek Translation of Exodus 1–14 as Scribal Activity*. VTSup 176. Leiden: Brill, 2017.

Screnock, John. "Translation and Rewriting in the Genesis Apocryphon." Pages 453–81 in *Reading the Bible in Ancient Traditions and Modern Editions: Studies in Memory of Peter W. Flint*. Edited by Andrew B. Perrin, Kyung S. Baek, and Daniel K. Falk. Atlanta: SBL Press, 2017.

Stackert, Jeffrey. "Compositional Strata in the Priestly Sabbath Law: Exodus 31:12–17 and 35:1–3." *Journal of Hebrew Scriptures* 11 (2011), article 15 (online: https://doi.org/10.5508/jhs.2011.v11.a15).

Stackert, Jeffrey. "Distinguishing Innerbiblical Exegesis from Pentateuchal Redaction: Leviticus 26 as a Test Case." Pages 369–86 in *The Pentateuch: International Perspectives on Current Research*. Edited by Thomas B. Dozeman, Konrad Schmid, and Baruch J. Schwartz. FAT 78. Tübingen: Mohr Siebeck, 2011.

Stackert, Jeffrey. "The Holiness Legislation and its Pentateuchal Sources: Revision, Supplementation, and Replacement." Pages 187–204 in *The Strata of the Priestly Writings: Contemporary Debate and Future Directions*. Edited by Sarah Shectman and Joel S. Baden. AThANT 95. Zürich: Theologischer Verlag Zürich, 2009.

Stackert, Jeffrey. "How the Priestly Sabbaths Work: Innovation in Pentateuchal Priestly Ritual." Pages 79–111 in *Ritual Innovation in the Hebrew Bible and Ancient Judaism*. Edited by Nathan MacDonald. BZAW 468. Berlin: Walter de Gruyter, 2016.

Stackert, Jeffrey. "Pentateuchal Coherence and the Science of Reading." Pages 253–68 in *The Formation of the Pentateuch: Bridging the Academic Cultures of Europe, Israel, and North America*. Edited by Jan C. Gertz et al. FAT 111. Tübingen: Mohr Siebeck, 2016.

Stackert, Jeffrey. *A Prophet Like Moses: Prophecy, Law, and Israelite Religion*. New York: Oxford University Press, 2014.

Stackert, Jeffrey. *Rewriting the Torah: Literary Revision in Deuteronomy and the Holiness Legislation*. FAT 52. Tübingen: Mohr Siebeck, 2007.

Stackert, Jeffrey. "The Wilderness Period without Generation Change: The Deuteronomic Portrait of Israel's Forty-Year Journey." *VT* 70 (2020): 696–721.

Steuernagel, Carl. *Übersetzung und Erklärung der Bücher Deuteronomium und Josua: und allgemeine Einleitung in den Hexateuch*. HAT 1.3. Göttingen: Vandenhoeck & Ruprecht, 1900.

Styler, G. M. "Excursus 4." Pages 285–316 in C. F. D. Moule, *The Birth of the New Testament*. 3rd ed. London: Adam & Charles Black, 1981.

Teeter, Andrew, and William Tooman. "Standards of (In)coherence in Ancient Jewish Literature." *HBAI* 9 (2020): 94–129.

Weinfeld, Moshe. *Deuteronomy 1–11: A New Translation with Introduction and Commentary*. AB 5. New York: Doubleday, 1991.

Esther Eshel and Michael Langlois
Conclusion

As we reach the end of these proceedings, let us summarize the main results presented at the conference and how they help us better understand the role, training, and practices of scribes in the Biblical world.

In his article entitled "Approaches of Scribes to the Biblical Text in Ancient Israel," Emanuel Tov delves into the possibility of illuminating the individuality of scribes. In the past, scholars (including Tov) focused on the technicalities of scribal craft. However, in this study Tov focuses on texts found at Qumran that reveal individual characteristics of certain scribes by carefully taking into account the distinction between inherited tradition and individuality. This is in clear contradistinction to the later transmitters of the Masoretic Text. One particular example Tov brings is with regards to tefillin found at Qumran, where phylacteries were separated into two groups: one which represents a proto-MT tradition, and one which is freer and where the individuality of the scribe can be seen. Similarly, with regards to biblical texts at Qumran, there are two groups of texts: a proto-MT group showcasing very careful transmission with minimal intervention, and a freer group of non-aligned texts. Tov also discusses examples of non-biblical texts where the same pattern emerges. Thus, he demonstrates that, at Qumran, there are two groups of scribes, one that intervened and one that didn't, in both biblical and non-biblical texts respectively.

André Lemaire, in "West Semitic Royal Scribes ca. 1250–600 BCE," examines the evidence of scribes from a number of different cities. He begins with evidence from Ugarit as an example of scribal transition where the logo-syllabic Akkadian tradition and the newly invented Ugaritic alphabetic script co-existed. Lemaire postulates that we may even have autographs from the inventor of the Ugaritic alphabet. He next turns to Lachish, which is also important as a scribal center where direct contact between Egyptian and Canaanite scribes may have occurred. Indeed, according to Lemaire, Lachish at this time represents an important counterexample to the widespread view of collapse during the Late Bronze to Iron Age transition. Lemaire also discusses a number of other sites including Byblos and Jerusalem. His study reveals the bilingual skills of many royal scribes during this period and the implications this has for the formation of Biblical and related literature.

Sara Milstein, in her contribution entitled "The Role of Legal Texts in Scribal Education: Implications for Biblical Law," highlights the fact that no previous study on Mesopotamian law has focused exclusively on model contracts and cases, and that such an investigation should be a priority for illuminating the world of scribal education in the ancient Near East. Thus, Milstein discusses the model contracts and model court cases from the Old Babylonian Period, arguing that particular characteristics of these texts reveals their pedagogical nature. She next discusses legal extracts, which can be interpreted as exercises. Indeed, she argues that the famous example of Hazor 18 is an instructor's exercise. Throughout her analysis, the relationship between these texts and the codes is central. Using this discussion of Mesopotamian law as a backdrop, Milstein then turns to the origins of Pentateuchal law collections and argues that they are not all based on an old family law, as often supposed, but on Israelite models used in scribal education. She closes by arguing against direct Israelite dependence on the Laws of Hammurabi and instead posits a tradition of scribal exercises based on laws of damages augmented by unique Israelite features. Indeed, according to Milstein, the integration of Israelite law with ethics and cult is unique within the context of Ancient Near Eastern law.

Aaron Demsky, in "Cursing an Authority: Scribal Tradition from Babylonia to Canaan and Back," discusses the transmission of curse formulae between Mesopotamia and Canaan. Through the course of this study, he begins with the Ahiram inscription, and ends with a story from the Talmud. In the course of his tracing of this tradition, he shows how H. L. Ginsburg first pointed out a connection between Ahiram and the Baal myth, and how the latter adapted the formula. Furthermore, Demsky then brings in the Azitawada inscription, and ultimately traces the formula there back to the epilogue of the Laws of Hammurabi. A fascinating aspect of his textual analysis of Ahiram and Azitawada involves the central role of the deity 'Il as the head of the pantheon, who is listed first in the former, and second in the latter. This argues for an earlier period for the Ahiram inscription prior to his demotion and replacement by Baal, an observation sure to play a role in future discussions of this text. With the previous discussion in place, Demsky then offers a new reading of the Ahiram inscription, before concluding with reflexes of the tradition in the Hebrew Bible and the Babylonian Talmud.

"The 'Nests' of the Aramaic Scribal Culture in the Late 9th – Early 7th Centuries BCE Levant: An Attempt at Identification" by Jan Dušek evaluates Holger Gzella's theory that a group of central and northwestern Syrian inscriptions from the 9th to 7th centuries BCE were produced by the same scribal school. Beginning with the region of Samal/Ya'udi, he discusses commonalities between the various groups in chronological stages, starting from Kulamuwa's inscription as the guiding exemplar, with a particular focus on the various inscriptions of Bar-Rakib. Among the distinctions between the inscriptions are dots as opposed to riling lines as well as language differences; nevertheless, they can still be mined for their historical relationship and commonalities in style. Moving to the Aleppo region, he ultimately concludes an ultimate source in the Phoenician inscriptions, with two chronological stages of influence from the late 9th to the early 7th centuries BCE. For Damascus, nothing survives from the city itself but only from its surroundings and thus he looks at the inscriptions from Tel Dan and Hama. Word dividers in the form of dots are an important distinguishing feature here. Dušek concludes that Gzella's theory of a unified scribal school behind the inscriptions cannot be maintained, and offers an alternate analysis dividing the inscriptions into three groups.

Using the most up-to-date provenanced finds, Anat Mendel-Geberovich, in "Judaean Glyptic Finds: An Updated Corpus and a Revision of Their Palaeography," attempts to date the corpus of Judean glyptic seals more accurately than ever before, while adhering to Uehlinger's advice to avoid knee-jerk linkages with biblical personages. An essential aspect of her argument is the incorporation of hundreds of new seals discovered since the late 1990s. Distinguishing between seals and bullae on the one hand and jar-handle impressions on the other, she argues that the latter are more useful for dating due to their stratigraphic context as pottery, and she also interrogates Vaughn's schema of developed vs. non-developed letter forms and its usefulness for paleographic analysis. The distinctions between lapidary Aramaic and the non-lapidary formats are also essential to her thesis. She concludes that Vaughn's postulated evolution of letter forms is ultimately unable to securely narrow down the dating of the forms to the chronology he suggests, as the varied forms can co-exist and can't be used for specific dates other than the wider range of 700–586 BCE.

In this study, "Hieratic Numerals on Iron Age Hebrew Tax Bullae," Stefan Jakob Wimmer brings together the latest evidence for Palestinian hieratic usage on tax bullae. He helpfully links the symbols used in this tradition to Egyptian hieratic. Wimmer also suggests that there may be a connection between Ramesside policy in Canaan and the rise of Palestinian hieratic and its ultimate adoption by the kingdoms of Israel and Judah. After the fall of the Hebrew kingdoms this scribal practice ceases. Throughout his study he engages in careful paleographic analysis, helpfully localizing the chronological and geographic scope of these inscriptions. Reviewing all the latest studies on this corpus, Wimmer provides the most up-to-date analysis on Palestinian hieratic, and follows it up with a chart collecting all the known published hieratic bullae.

Aren Wilson-Wright, in "Out of Egypt: Lexicographic Evidence for Egyptian Influence on West Semitic and Israelite Administrative and Scribal Practice," argues that a number of Egyptian loanwords related to scribal practice long predate the rise of Hebrew, since they are found in other Semitic languages that were not directly in contact with Egypt when such borrowing would have occurred. Thus, he distinguishes between two sets of loanwords: a group that was inherited by Hebrew from a linguistic ancestor, and a group that was directly imported into Hebrew from Egyptian. The two groups are situated in the later 4th and 3rd millennia BCE on the one hand, and between the 13th and 8th centuries BCE on the other. As an important locus, Wilson-Wright carefully considers the Lachish hieratic bowls from the 13th century BCE and posits that this city was an epicenter for the transmission of scribal techniques into Canaan. In the course of his discussion, he also provides an excellent overview of the linguistic relationships and transformations between Egyptian, Hebrew, and Aramaic, and provides a useful historical and linguistic synthesis which will help scholars working in this culturally diverse period.

Tania Notarius, in "Northwest Semitic – Akkadian Linguistic Convergence: *sipr-* and Other Terms for 'Writing' as a Case Study," shows that the northwest Semitic root *spr* is in fact not cognate with East Semitic *šapāru*. Utilizing a brilliant analysis based on contact linguistics, Notarius shows how these two independent phonemes influenced each other over time. Indeed, this study shows that although the roots of these terms may correlate semantically, and much scholarship has claimed that the former is a borrowing from the latter, Notarius focuses on the Ugaritic corpus where an excellent example of linguistic interference occurred. She shows that although there is no clear answer to the question, the bilingual Ugaritic scribes of the Bronze Age demonstrated the linguistic concept of convergence, where both inner development within Northwest Semitic occurred combined with Akkadian influence. Focusing further on distinctions between poetic and prose usage, Notarius demonstrates that there was a growing connection between these two semantic fields under Akkadian influence, eventually leading to a reanalysis of the East Semitic lexeme within Northwest Semitic. Included in the discussion are other terms within the semantic field relevant to the discussion such as the northwest Semitic lexeme *lḥt* and the Akkadian *ṭuppu*. Overall, this remains an excellent introduction to the development of some crucial terms used in scribal technology along the Mesopotamia-North Syria-Canaan geographic continuum.

In his study, "Adaptation in Scribal Curriculum: Examples from the Letter Writing Genre," William M. Schniedewind shows how the tradition of letter writing as student exercise in Mesopotamia, Ugarit, and Kuntillet ʿAjrud, played a decisive role in the process of scripturalization in Israel and Judah. Schniedewind gives a number of examples of this process, such as the use of messengers mentioned in a number of texts, showing how letter writing formed a crucial element of communication, and by implication the literary conventions used in such let-ter-writing would have been a bedrock of scribal education. He also shows how certain terms used in letters, such as the expression w'th, served as structural markers in letter writing and were eventually adapted by biblical writers as a transition particle with the introduction of direct speech signified by the use of the term lēmôr. This process would ultimately play a significant role in the devel-opment of the form of biblical prophecy.

Esther Eshel, in her contribution "Combining Different Types of Scripts in the Aramaic Texts," focuses on the development of the Aramaic Lapidary script and offers an excellent review of the scholarship on the script and its basic periodiza-tion. In this context, she discusses the monumental contribution of the Mt. Ger-izim inscriptions to our understanding of the Aramaic script. She then follows up this review with a detailed discussion of two new Aramaic inscriptions to add to the corpus. The first is from a storage jar, and aside from providing the correct starting point from which to begin reading the inscription (as it is written around the jar), Eshel provides a tentative dating, as well as a look into the ethnicity of the individuals referred to in the inscription. The second inscription, which men-tions two names, comes from a non-diagnostic shard which is intriguingly writ-ten in reverse or "mirror script," and various theories are discussed as to the rea-son for this. This second inscription is also significant since it seems to combine different stages in the development of the Aramaic script. Thus, Eshel concludes that there were two different lines of development for the script, with these lines either preserving or not preserving some old form letters. It is therefore difficult to assign a precise dating to the Lapidary Aramaic script, as it may have devel-oped at different rates in various places.

In "Theonyms in Palaeo-Hebrew and Other Alternate Scripts on Dead Sea Scrolls," Michael Langlois discusses the use of Palaeo-Hebrew for divine names and titles in Dead Sea Scrolls that are otherwise written using the Jewish Aramaic script. He proceeds through a series of 30 scrolls that exhibit such practice and studies them individually. Langlois helpfully lists the various paleo-Hebrew let-ters in each scroll and fragment, and provides a dating based on paleographical analysis and carbon dating. His analysis yields useful information on scribal technique, helping to illuminate the scribes themselves based on their handwrit-ing. Additionally, it is interesting to see how other divine names aside from the Tetragrammaton were also sometimes rendered in the palaeo-Hebrew script, and Langlois provides helpful tables demonstrating this inconsistent practice across the corpus of both biblical and non-biblical texts. He closes his study by empha-sizing the implications of such scribal practice on religious beliefs and traditions within Second Temple Judaism.

Paul Mandel, in "Between סֹפֵר and סָפַר: The Evolution of the Second Temple Period 'Scribe'," examines the use of the Hebrew word *sofer* and its Aramaic equivalent *sāfar* through the first millennium BCE and into the early centuries of the common era. This latter period also encompasses discussion of the related Greek and Latin terms *grammateus* and *scriba*. Mandel shows how the meaning of these terms is not the one usually associated with them, namely, that of a composer or transmitter of text (i.e. a "scribe" in the classical sense). Furthermore, he demonstrates how the sense of the Hebrew term shifted from the pre-exilic era to the post-exilic era under the influence of the Aramaic term, which was itself affected by its use within a Mesopotamian milieu. As a prime example of his argument, he discusses the figure of Ezra ha-Sofer at length, demonstrating that his title referred to his role as an interpreter or decisor of divine law. To further buttress his argument, he includes textual evidence from the later Second Temple period and the post-Second Temple period demonstrating the different semantic meaning that the terms *sofer* and *safar* possessed than has been usually assumed.

In his article, "Text Case: Writing under Extreme Conditions at Masada," Stiebel presents the epigraphic remains found at Masada as a test-case for examining the phenomenon of scribal activity under extreme duress. The Jewish war against the Romans provides such a backdrop, with the climactic events at Masada as a focal point. His research uncovers the unusually high rate of production of scribal material at the site and compares it to the similarly intense situation at Qumran, arguing that such volatile situations are an impetus for creative activity. Building on his thesis further, Stiebel also marshals evidence for an increase in ritual and magic activity and presents intriguing evidence for artistic expression as well. Lastly, Stiebel peers into the epigraphic remains left by the Roman side at Masada and illuminates for us their own world which was likewise under the extreme stress of battle. Included in his survey of the Roman camp is a graffito of a dramatic quote from the Aeneid on a scrap of papyrus.

In "Scribal Fatigue in Ancient Revisionary Composition," Jeffrey Stackert introduces to readers the concept of editorial fatigue. Bringing together the latest research on this psychological phenomenon from the relevant literature, Stackert applies it to biblical studies and terms it "scribal fatigue." It is essentially a type of literary revisionism, with the additional corollary of scribal failure to carry through the revision to its fullest and most consistent extent, ultimately revealing a strong reliance by the revising author on a patrimonial text. In the body of the article, Stackert brings examples of this scribal occurrence from the Synoptic Gospels, the Epic of Gilgamesh, and the Pentateuch. He demonstrates how, in each case, one can detect instances of the revising author experiencing scribal fatigue as well as the points at which the fatigue lifted, producing an ultimately inconsistent text in some places. However, as an upshot to this phenomenon, Stackert delves into the reading process, and how the readers of these texts attempt to smooth out the inconsistencies by cloaking the scribal fatigue underneath layers of later interpretation.

Overall, the fifteen studies collected in these proceedings shed new light on all aspects of scribal activity in the Biblical world. They demonstrate the significant progress that the scholarly community can achieve thanks to new archaeological findings and research methods that go beyond traditional boundaries of academic disciplines. We hope that this volume will inspire further research on this fascinating topic, as numerous questions on scribal curriculum, milieu and role are yet to be answered.

Index